A Bibliography of
the writings of
ROBERT GRAVES

To

OUR FRIENDS' CHILDREN

A Bibliography of
the writings of
ROBERT GRAVES

by

Fred H. Higginson

Second Edition
Revised by

William Proctor Williams

ST. PAUL'S BIBLIOGRAPHIES
1987

The first edition was published in 1966 by
Nicholas Vane (Publishers) Ltd.
The second edition is published by
St. Paul's Bibliographies
West End House, 1 Step Terrace,
Winchester, Hampshire, England
in 1987

British Library Cataloguing in Publication Data
Higginson, Fred H.
A bibliography of the writings of
Robert Graves – 2nd ed.
1. Graves, Robert – Bibliography
I. Title   II. Williams, William Proctor
016.821'912   Z8367.5

ISBN 0 906795 16 8

Prepared for press by Celliwic Maid/Ivory Head Press,
Sturminster Newton, Dorset,
and printed in England by
Henry Ling, Dorchester, Dorset

Contents

Illustrations

The title pages of *Treasure Box* and *Goliath and David*

Some covers of *I, Claudius*

Some covers of *Claudius the God*

Part of a page of the MS of *Sergeant Lamb of the Ninth*

Covers of the American issue of *Collected Short Stories,* fourth and fifth impressions.

Part of the MS from *Poems: Abridged for Dolls and Princes*

The dustjacket from the 1975 edition of *Collected Poems*

MS of 'A Country Mood'

Introduction

If the study of the writings of Robert Graves has not quite become a scholarly industry since the publication of the first edition of this bibliography by Fred H. Higginson in 1966, it has certainly become a significant craft guild. Furthermore, there have been many new publications by Graves, and subsequent editions of previously published works since this bibliography was first published. There have been several collections of addenda and corrigenda published in journal articles during the two decades which have elapsed since this bibliography first appeared (see citations at the end of the Introduction) and I hope not only that the second edition of this bibliography will serve to incorporate those additions into the original bibliography but that it will also provide a complete record of the publications by Graves to approximately the end of 1985.

Because Higginson's first edition of this bibliography has become a standard reference tool I have not renumbered new items which fall within the scope of the first edition. New entries are recorded using decimal points. Thus, a new work appearing between A30 and A31 of the first edition will be numbered A30.1. Of course, in the A, B and C sections all those new entries which occur after the latest numbers in the first edition have been numbered in sequence. In those few instances where an entry has been cancelled the old number is retained with the notation of cancellation and a cross-reference to the new number, if appropriate.

The arrangement of the works in this bibliography follows that of the first edition. Thus, Section A includes not only books and pamphlets written by Graves alone, but also those written in collaboration with others, works edited, largely rewritten or translated by him, and published collections of his writing edited by others. Translations of his works into other languages are recorded in the notes section of the entry for the first appearance of the work in question. However, translations which do not match any particular primary publication, i.e, Hungarian translations of his poems drawn from five or six different English language collections, have been recorded in Appendix I. A large proportion of the material included in Section A falls into one or more of these categories:

1   *Collaborations:* the books written with Laura Riding, Alan Hodge, Joshua Podro and Raphael Patai.

2   *'Editions':* the Skelton and nursery rhyme collections, both editions of the ballad books and the edition of letters from T. E. Lawrence.

3   *Rewritings: The Real David Copperfield*, the two books of Frank Richards and the Echard translantion of Terence.

4   *Translations:* Apuleius, Galvan, Alarcon, Sand, Lucan, Suetonius, Hesiod, Homer, Omar Khayaam and (with Laura Riding) Schwarz.

Section B consists of books and pamphlets containing contributions by Graves and is restricted to first book printings only, with occasional notes about significant subsequent printings. Section C includes contributions to the press and periodicals, including a few translations, and normally restricts itself to first periodical appearance in the United Kingdom and first periodical appearance elsewhere in the world only.

In both Sections B and C I have decided not to include printings, either whole or in part, of manuscripts by Graves which have appeared in auction or booksellers' catalogues. This was a matter over which I debated and I am sure that my decision to exclude them will not please some. An interesting debate on this point was carried out during 1984 in the *Times Literary Supplement* (Stanley Weintrab, "Evidence of Success" 18 May 1984, p.563; B.C. Bloomfield, "Slim Leavings" 18 May 1984, p.563; Ronald Ayling, "Bibliographical Practice" [a letter] 22 June 1984, p.697; B. C. Bloomfield, "Bibliographical Practice" [a letter] 13 July 1984, p.783) and although I cannot claim that this debate was crucial to my decision it may be of interest to those who wish to see some of the thinking behind the decision not to include catalogue material. Indeed, in those instances in which booksellers' catalogue material supplements information already found in the first edition of this bibliography I have included those items which appeared relevant as they came to hand.

'As they came to hand' also indicates the primary reason for my excluding such information from the bibliography. Unless I were fortunate, or unfortunate, enough to be on the mailing list of every bookseller and auction house in the world which might deal with Graves material I could not present such information with the degree of certainty and inclusiveness with which other information in the A, B and C Sections is presented. I would, in other words, mislead many readers into thinking that I had included all the catalogue information there was whereas I would really only have been recording that catalogue information that I had been fortunate enough to see. Since that is not the bibliographical principle upon which any of the sections of this bibliography are constructed it seemed, in the long run, better to confine my presentation to the proven rather than to mislead.

A second question, no less important than the first, but different in kind, is the matter of whether or not the publication of all, or part, of a Graves' writing in a sale catalogue constitutes any sort of 'true' first publication. Of course, one could argue in the case of an author no longer living that any publication of any piece of writing is 'true' publication. But in the case of a living author and with the purpose of the printing of his writing being advertising for sale a piece of hitherto unpublished material, one must seriously consider whether this set of conditions is any kind of real publication. In the end I concluded that it was not and have not included any such printings of manuscript material in any sections of this bibliography.

In the first edition of this bibliography there were sections D and E. The former section dealt with manuscript collections, phonograph records, music, ephemera and the like and the latter was a 'highly selective bibliography of works about Graves.' The D Section has become Appendix II, containing information about collections, but no attempt has been made to provide a discography or filmography of Graves' numerous recordings, television appearances, and the like. For example, the video history of the television series *I, Claudius*, or the film history of *The Shout*, or Graves' many interviews or readings on radio are material for another sort of scholarly record and this book has been restricted to print material only. In

Appendix Two I have tried to record all significant manuscript collections which have been reported publicly and to which something like free and open access is allowed to the serious scholar. In other words, private collectors who allow access only on very restricted terms, if any, are not included. The history of the passage of the manuscripts of Robert Graves from his possession to the possession of collectors and/or collections is not the subject of any part of this bibliography. In the case of the E Section the amount of work about Graves since the first edition of this bibliography; the fact that in all other respects this bibliography was complete but that the E Section was selective; and the fact that enumerative bibliographies are different in character and scope from descriptive bibliographies persuaded me that such a secondary bibliography would best be undertaken by other hands. However, I do recommend the annotated bibliography on Robert Graves published by David E. Pownall in *Focus*, 2 (1973), 17–23 and Hallman Bell Bryant, *Robert Graves: An Annotated Bibliography* (New York: Garland, 1986).

The published extensions of Higginson's first edition have been a great help to me and some references to them are included in the notes to various entries. They are, in order of publication:

A.S.G. Edwards and J. Pinsent, "Additions to F. Higginson's *Bibliography of Robert Graves*", *Papers of the Bibliographical Society of America (PBSA)*, 68 (1974), 67–68.

A.S.G. Edwards and Diane Tolomeo, "Robert Graves: A Checklist of His Publications, 1965–1974", *The Malahat Review*, 35 (1975), 168–179.

John Woodrow Presley, "Addenda to F. H. Higginson's *Bibliography of the Works of Robert Graves*", *PBSA*, 69 (1975), 568–569.

A.S.G. Edwards, "Further Addenda to Higginson: The Bibliography of Robert Graves", *PBSA*, 71 (1977), 374–378.

Ellsworth Mason, "Emendations and Extensions of the Bibliography of Robert Graves", *Analytical & Enumerative Bibliography (AEB)*, 2 (1978), 265–315.

A. S. G. Edwards, "Robert Graves Bibliography: Addenda and Corrigenda", *AEB*, 4 (1980), 37–39.

A.S.G. Edwards, "Further Addenda to Higginson: The Bibliography of Robert Graves", *PBSA*, 75 (1981), 210–211.

In the case of books published by the Hogarth Press I have made use of the information to be found in J. Howard Woolmer's *A Checklist of the Hogarth Press: 1917–1938*, Andes, New York: Woolmer/Brotherson, 1976, and references to Woolmer refer to entries from this book.

I wish to thank the publishers' archivists and publishers who have helped with this bibliography. They are far too great in number to thank individually. Suffice it to say that whenever the number of copies of an edition, state, issue, or impression are reported, and in many cases when 'unknown' or other information is reported, there lies behind this brief statement the work of the publisher or the publisher's archivist for that publishing firm. They have my undying thanks. I would also like to thank the staffs of the British Library (particularly the North Library), the Bodleian Library, the Cambridge University Library, the State Library of New South

Wales, the Baillieu Library of the University of Melbourne, the State Library of Victoria (particularly Trevor Mills, then Rare Books Librarian), the Flinders University Library, the Library of Congress, the Newberry Library, the Department of Special Collections at the Morris Library of Southern Illinois University, the Poetry/Rare Books Collection of the Libraries of the State University of New York at Buffalo, the University Libraries of Northern Illinois University, the Indiana University Library, and the Rare Books Department of the Kansas State University Libraries. I wish especially to thank John J. Vander Velde, Special Collections Librarian at Kansas State University, for assistance and advice well above and beyond the duty of a librarian working with a scholar; in several instances he was able to provide information which I had been unable to obtain during my researches on three continents.

I am indebted to several scholars and collectors for assistance with the preparation of the second edition of this bibliography. Chief among them is Professor A. S. G. Edwards of the University of Victoria who has been unstinting in his advice, encouragement, and the provision of information. I would also like to thank William Reese and Carl R. Hahn for their comments on a draft of this book and for the information they so willingly supplied, particularly Mr. Hahn for valuable information about dust-jackets and variant bindings. I would like to thank Elizabeth Williams, especially for her poetic sensitivity. Professor Antonia Forster has provided more in the way of research assistance than words can quite convey and "thanks" seems hardly the correct word to describe her assistance with this volume.

I am grateful to Mary Hill for compiling the index to the revised edition.

I must thank Professor Fred H. Higginson and his wife Jeanette for entrusting me with the task of preparing this second edition of Fred's bibliography of Graves. Before his illness Fred had kept a very up-to-date record of new editions and I have benefited immensely from his notes. All that is accurate and complete in this bibliography is directly or indirectly owing to Fred and his colleagues in the study of Graves; the errors and omissions are, alas, all mine. Fred taught me bibliography and textual criticism and I hope he taught me well.

WILLIAM PROCTOR WILLIAMS
DeKalb, Illinois,
April 1987

Technical Note

Graves issued several books in revised versions. Each edition of his collected poems is listed separately; but revisions or abridgements of other books are listed under the earlier book.

Collations
Occasionally a notation such as X/X*$^{8/8}$ is used; this signifies an octavo in sixteens, signed on X1 and X9 (/X*1). No notice has been taken of signings on second and/or third leaves of regular gatherings. Doubled and tripled signings (XX or XXX) are rendered as 2X or 3X as is current bibliographical practice.

Bulk
For cloth-bound books the notation 2.3/2.8 cm means that the sheets and endpapers bulk 2.3 cm and that with the binding included the bulk is 2.8 cm.

Number of copies
It has not always been possible to determine the number of copies. 'Unknown' means that the publisher no longer knows; 'undisclosed' means that the publisher has not revealed the number; 'undetermined' means that the publisher no longer exists or has not responded to letters.

Contents
When not given, the contents of subsequent volumes with the same number may be assumed to be that of the first edition.

Dust-jackets
These are described where seen; others certainly exist.

Editions
Interest, notoriety or descriptive detail have sometimes necessitated separate listings for different impressions of the same edition; but generally subdivisions represent separate editions. Second and later editions are described in some detail. A certain light is thus thrown on Graves as a popular author, on modern publishing practice (see the extraordinary collations of the Belle Sauvage editions, the accommodation of the type revision done in *The White Goddess* and the unusual succession of editions of *Old Soldiers Never Die*) and on the texts themselves. With the expansion of higher education in the United States, the United Kingdom, and the English-speaking world generally, there have sprung up a number of firms who have devoted themselves to the production of photographic reprints of earlier works. This is a most irregular and unregulated traffic and, of course, a photographic reprint

cannot constitute either a new edition or even a true issue or impression. Such photographic reprints are not normally described but some attempt has been made to record their existence in the description of the edition they reproduce.

A. Books and pamphlets by Robert Graves, alone or in collaboration, and works edited, translated or rewritten by him

A1 OVER THE BRAZIER 1916

a. First edition:

OVER THE BRAZIER | BY | ROBERT GRAVES | LONDON | THE POETRY BOOKSHOP | 35 DEVONSHIRE STREET., THEOBALDS ROAD., W.C. | 1916

Collation: [1]⁴ 2–4⁴, 16 leaves.

p.[1] title-page; p.[2] blank; p.[3] CONTENTS; p.[4] THE POET IN THE NURSERY; pp.[5] 6–17 [18] 19–32 text.

20.4 × 15.0 cm. Bulk: 0.5 cm. White wove paper; top edges unopened; fore and bottom edges untrimmed. Bound in grey paper covers; front cover: OVER THE BRAZIER | [cut in black with blue background and soldiers around a red brazier] | BY | ROBERT GRAVES | THE POETRY BOOKSHOP 8ᴰ· NET; inside front and back covers: publisher's advertisements; back cover blank.

Price: 8d. Number of copies unknown. Published 1 May 1916.

Contents: The Poet in the Nursery – [Charterhouse:] – The Dying Knight and the Fauns – Willaree – The Fate of the Heavens – Jolly Yellow Moon – Youth and Folly – Ghost Music – Free Verse – In the Wilderness – Oh, and Oh! – Cherry Time – [La Bassée:] – On Finding Myself a Soldier – The Shadow of Death – A Renascence – The Morning before the Battle – Limbo – The Trenches – The First Funeral – The Adventure – I Hate the Moon – Big Words – The Dead Fox Hunter – It's a Queer Time – 1915 – Over the Brazier

Notes: Impressions: 2nd, 1917.

The design of Menin Gate on the cover is by Claud Lovat Fraser.

A photographic facsimile of the British Library copy, including black and white facsimile of inside and outside of the front and back covers, was issued in 1975 by the St. James Press in London and the St. Martin's Press in New York as part of their Poetry Reprint Series. There is a preliminary series title-page and the book is bound in dark blue cloth.

Folcroft Press also issued a photocopy publication of this edition in 1977.

A1b. Second edition ([1920]):

OVER THE BRAZIER | BY ROBERT GRAVES | LONDON – THE POETRY |
BOOKSHOP, 35 DEVONSHIRE | ST., THEOBALDS RD. W.C.1

Collation: [1] – [2]^8, 16 leaves.
    p.[1] title-page; p.[2] list of books by Graves and edition notice; p.[3] FOREWORD
TO NEW EDITION; p.[4] THE POET IN THE NURSERY; p.[5] PART I. – Poems
Mostly Written | at Charterhouse – 1910–1914; pp.6–18 text; p.[19] PART II. – Poems
Written | Before La Bassée – 1915; p.[20] blank; pp.21 [22] 23–30 [31] 32 text.
    21.4 × 13.8 cm. Bulk: 0.3/0.6 cm. White wove paper; all edges trimmed. White laid
endpapers watermarked: [in double rule rectangular box enclosing also clubs and
balls;] Gold [and] J. R. Lockwood & Co. Bound in grey boards with narrow
medium-blue cloth spine; back and spine blank; front, in blue: OVER THE
BRAZIER | BY ROBERT GRAVES | [cut as cover of A1a, but blue only] | THE
POETRY BOOKSHOP

Price: 3s. Number of copies: 1,000. Published in May 1920 in light blue dust-jacket;
front of jacket: OVER THE BRAZIER | BY ROBERT GRAVES | [cut as in A1a but not
coloured as there] | THE POETRY BOOKSHOP

Contents: As A1a, but omitting 'On Finding Myself a Soldier' and 'A Renascence.'

A2   GOLIATH AND DAVID   [1916]

First edition:

GOLIATH AND DAVID | BY | ROBERT GRAVES

Collation: 10 leaves, unsigned, sewn at centre.
    p.[1] title-page; p.[2] blank; pp.3–17 text; p.[18] printer's notice; pp.[19]–[20]
blank.
    18.2 × 13.7 cm. Bulk: 0.2 cm. White laid paper; all edges untrimmed. Bound in
heavy dark red paper cover; all sides blank.

Price: Not for sale. Number of copies: 200. Printed late in 1916.

Contents: The Bough of Nonsense – Goliath and David – A Pinch of Salt –
Babylon – Careers – The Lady Visitor in the Pauper Ward – The Last Post – A
Dead Boche – Escape – Not Dead

Notes: Printer: Chiswick Press: Charles Whittingham & Co., Tooks Court, Chancery
Lane, London.
    H. S. Boutell ["Modern English First Editions: Robert (Von Ranke) Graves, 1895–."
Publishers Weekly 117 (1930), 2140–2142], who consulted Graves, assigns the date
1916 to this book and says there were 150 copies, possibly less. A letter from
Siegfried Sassoon, dated 27 February 1917, says that 118 copies of the book had by
that time been distributed by him according to Graves' instructions and that 82
copies remained at the printer's for his disposal. Graves himself now 'guesses' that
the book was published in December 1916. Both versions of *Good-Bye to All That*

speak of *Over the Brazier* as Graves' first book. The impression which exists in some quarters that *Goliath and David* is Graves' first book would therefore appear to be erroneous; and while the book is something of a rarity in catalogues, records of the Chiswick Press (British Library Add. MS. 50927, f.288b), dated 28 February 1917, state that 200 copies were printed.

A3   FAIRIES AND FUSILIERS   [1917]

a. First edition:

FAIRIES AND | FUSILIERS | BY | ROBERT GRAVES | [publisher's emblem] | LONDON | WILLIAM HEINEMANN

Collation: [A]^4 χ^2 B–L^4 M^2, 48 leaves.

2 pp. blank; p.[i] FAIRIES AND FUSILIERS; p.[ii] publisher's advertisements; p.[iii] title-page; p.[iv] publisher's notice; p. [v] TO THE ROYAL WELCH FUSILIERS; p.[vi] blank; p.[vii] acknowledgement; p.[viii] blank; pp.[ix–x] CONTENTS; pp.[1–83] text; p.[84] text and printer's notice.

18.0 × 11.9 cm. Bulk: 1.3/1.6 cm. Heavy white wove paper; all edges trimmed. Light white wove endpapers. Bound in wine-red cloth; front and back blank; spine stamped in gold: Fairies | and | Fusiliers | [leaf and curlicue design] | Robert | Graves | HEINEMANN

Price: 3s. 6d. Number of copies: 1,000. Published 8 November 1917 in green dust-jacket printed in black.

Contents: To an Ungentle Critic – The Legion – To Lucasta on Going to the Wars for the Fourth Time – Two Fusiliers – To Robert Nichols – Dead Cow Farm – Goliath and David – Babylon – Mr. Philosopher – The Cruel Moon – Finland – A Pinch of Salt – The Caterpillar – Surley's Weather – The Cottage – The Last Post – When I'm Killed – Letter to S.S. from Mametz Wood – A Dead Boche – Faun – The Spoilsport – The Shivering Beggar – Jonah – John Skelton – I Wonder What It Feels Like to be Drowned? – Double Red Daisies – Careers – I'd Love to Be a Fairy's Child – The Next War – Strong Beer – Marigolds – The Lady Visitor in the Pauper's Ward – Love and Black Magic – Smoke-Rings – A Child's Nightmare – Escape – The Bough of Nonsense – Not Dead – A Boy in Church – Corporal Stare – The Assault Heroic – The Poet in the Nursery – In the Wilderness – Cherry-Time – 1915 – Free Verse

Notes: Impressions: 2nd, January 1919; it collates [A]^4 B–L^4 [M]^4, 48 leaves; p.[iv] adds an edition notice; size: 18.0 × 12.0 cm.; bound in bright red cloth.

"Double Red Daisies" and "Dead Cow Farm" appeared in the same month (November 1917) in *Oxford Poetry 1917*, (Oxford: Blackwell, 1917), pp.24–25; "Finland" had an almost simultaneous appearance in the Poetry Bookshop's *New Broadside*, No. 14, 1917.

A3b. First American edition (1918):

Fairies | and Fusiliers | *By* | Robert Graves | [publisher's emblem] | *New York* | Alfred
A. Knopf | *MCMXVIII*

Collation: [1] – [5]⁸ [6]⁴ [7]⁸, 52 leaves.

    p.[i] [2 ll. at upper left:] Fairies | and Fusiliers | [at lower right:] [publisher's
emblem]; p.[ii] publisher's advertisement; p.[iii] title-page; p.[iv] copyright and
printing notices; p. [v] *TO* | *THE ROYAL WELCH FUSILIERS*; p.[vi] blank; p. [vii]
acknowledgement; p.[viii] blank; pp.[ix] – [x] CONTENTS; pp.1–94 text.

    15.5 × 10.3 cm. Bulk 1.0/1.4 cm. White wove paper watermarked with a D in a
diamond and a script Regal Antique; top and fore-edges trimmed; top edge stained
chartreuse. White wove endpapers. Bound in bright blue boards; chartreuse label
pasted from front to back across spine; on front and back: [rule] | *FAIRIES* | *AND*
FUSILIERS | *POEMS BY* | *ROBERT GRAVES* | [rule]; on spine: [rule] | *Fairies* | *and* |
Fusiliers | *by* | *Robert* | *Graves* | *1918* | [rule].

Price: $1.00. Number of copies undisclosed. Published in November 1918 in green
dust-jacket printed in violet.

Notes: Norwood Editions published a photographic reprint in 1977.

A3c. Second American edition (1919):

FAIRIES | AND FUSILIERS | BY | ROBERT GRAVES | [publisher's emblem] | NEW
YORK | ALFRED . A . KNOPF | MCMXIX

Collation: [1] – [6]⁸, 48 leaves.

    p.[3] [2 ll. at right:] FAIRIES | AND FUSILIERS; p.[4] publisher's advertisements;
p.[5] title-page; p.[6] copyright and printing notices; p.[7] *TO* | *THE ROYAL WELCH*
FUSILIERS; p.[8] acknowledgement; p.[9] – [10] CONTENTS; p.[11] [flush right:]
FAIRIES AND FUSILIERS; p.[12] blank; pp. 13–97 text; p.[98] blank.

    15.4 × 10.2 cm. Bulk: 0.9/1.1 cm. White wove paper watermarked OLDE STYLE;
all edges trimmed. White wove endpapers watermarked OLDE STYLE. Bound in
purple cloth embossed with fine diagonal crosshatching; chartreuse label as A3b,
printed in blue; *1918* becomes *1919*.

Price: $1.25. Number of copies undisclosed. Published in May 1919.

A4   TREASURE BOX [1919]

First edition:

TREASURE BOX | [rule] | [cut of girl looking into box] | BY | ROBERT GRAVES

Collation: 8 leaves, unsigned, stapled at centre.

    p.[1] title-page; p.[2] blank; pp.3–11 text; p.[12] illustration; pp.13–14 text; p.[15]
printer's notice; p.[16] blank.

    17.8 × 13.5 cm. Bulk: 0.1 cm. White laid paper watermarked ALDWYCH; all edges
trimmed. Bound in light blue paper covers; all sides blank.

Price: Not for sale. Number of copies: 200. Printed December 1919.

Contents: Morning Phoenix – Catherine Henry – The Kiss – Lost Love – Fox's Dingle – Four Rhymes from *The Penny Fiddle:* The Dream – The Fiddler – The Gifts – Mirror, Mirror

Notes: Printer: Chiswick Press, Tooks Court, Chancery Lane, London.
   Records of the Chiswick Press (British Library Add. MS. 50928, f. 72b), dated 20 January 1920, state that 200 copies were printed.
   Carl Hahn reports two variant bindings of this edition: one is in purple cloth embossed with five diagonal cross-hatchings and a chartreuse label printed in blue; the other is pebbled blue cloth with chartreuse label printed in blue with a yellow dust-jacket printed in blue.

A5 COUNTRY SENTIMENT [1920]

a. First edition:

COUNTRY SENTIMENT | BY ROBERT GRAVES | LONDON: MARTIN SECKER

Collation: [A]$^{8-1}$ B–D^8 E^{8+1}, 40 leaves.
   p.[3] COUNTRY SENTIMENT; p.[4] blank; p.[5] title-page; p.[6] edition and printer's notice; p.[7] TO | NANCY NICHOLSON; p.[8] NOTE; pp.9–10 CONTENTS; pp.11–63 text; p.[64] blank; p.[65] RETROSPECT; p.[66] blank; pp.67–81 text; p.[82] blank.
   18.7 × 12.6 cm. Bulk: 0.9/1.2 cm. White wove paper; top edges only trimmed. White wove endpapers. Bound in light blue boards with cobbled design; front and back blank; label pasted at top of spine: [rule] | *Country* | *Sentiment* | [diamond] | *Robert* | *Graves* | [rule].

Price: 5s. Number of copies· 1,000. Published in March 1920 in cream dust-jacket printed in purple.

Contents: A Frosty Night – Song for Two Children – Dicky – The Three Drinkers – The Boy out of Church – After the Play – One Hard Look – True Johnny – The Voice of Beauty Drowned – The God Called Poetry – Rocky Acres – Advice to Lovers – Nebuchadnezzar's Fall – Give Us Rain – Allie – Loving Henry – Brittle Bones – Apples and Water – Manticor in Arabia – Outlaws – Balloo Loo for Jenny – Hawk and Buckle – The *Alice Jean* – The Cupboard – The Beacon – Pot and Kettle – Ghost Raddled – Neglectful Edward – The Well-Dressed Children – Thunder at Night – To E.M.–A Ballad of Nursery Rhyme – Jane – Vain and Careless – Nine o'Clock – The Picture Book – The Promised Lullaby – [RETROSPECT:]Haunted – Retrospect: The Jests of the Clock – Here They Lie – Tom Taylor – Country at War – Sospan Fach – The Leveller – Hate Not, Fear Not – A Rhyme of Friends – A First Review

Note: A2 is tipped to A1; E9 is tipped to E8.

A5b. First American edition (1920):

COUNTRY | SENTIMENT | BY | ROBERT GRAVES | [publisher's emblem] | NEW YORK | ALFRED . A . KNOPF | 1920

Collation: [1] – [5]⁸ [6]⁴ [7]⁸, 52 leaves.

p.[1] [at top right:] COUNTRY SENTIMENT; p.[2] list of books by Graves; p.[3] title-page; p.[4] copyright and printing notices; p.[5] TO | NANCY NICHOLSON; p.[6] blank; p.[7] NOTE; p.[8] blank; pp. [9] – [10] CONTENTS; p.[11] [at top right:] COUNTRY SENTIMENT; p.[12] blank; pp.13–83 text; p.[84] blank; p.[85] [at top right:] RETROSPECT; p.[86] blank; pp.87–104 text.

15.5 × 10.5 cm. Bulk: 0.9/1.3 cm. White wove paper watermarked OLDE STYLE; top edges only trimmed and stained light green. White wove endpapers. Bound in blue boards with green label running from front to back across spine; on front and back of label in blue: [rule] | *COUNTRY SENTIMENT* | *POEMS BY* | *ROBERT GRAVES* | [rule]; on spine, in blue: [rule] | *Country* | *Senti-* | *ment* | *by* | *Robert* | *Graves* | *1920* | [rule].

Price: $1.25. Number of copies undisclosed. Published in March 1920.

A5.1   CHRISTMAS 1920   1920

First edition:

CHRISTMAS | 1920 | [short rule]

Collation: stiff card folded at centre, 2 leaves.

p.[1] title-page; p.[2] "Gifts"; p.[3] illustration; p.[4] colophon.

17.9 × 11.4 cm. White stiff card. Illustration printed in black, red, green, blue, and yellow on cream background. Colophon: *This is Number Four of a series* | *of six Christmas Cards by* | *modern artists and is* | *designed by Nancy Nicholson.* | *Published by Lund, Humphries* | *& Co., Limited at Three* | *Amen Corner, London,* | *E.C. 4, and printed at* | *the Country Press* | *Bradford*

Price: unknown; number of copies unknown; published in late 1920.

Note: Graves' contribution is "Gifts," or "Henry and Mary"; see A8.

A6   THE PIER-GLASS   [1921]

a. First edition:

THE PIER-GLASS | BY ROBERT GRAVES | LONDON: MARTIN SECKER

Collation: [A]⁸ B–D⁸, 32 leaves.

p.[1] THE PIER-GLASS; p.[2] blank; [plate, facing title-page: portrait of Graves by Ben Nicholson]; [protective tissue tipped to title-page]; p.[3] title-page; p.[4] quotation (2 ll.) from Skelton and printer's notice; p.[5] TO | NANCY NICHOLSON; p.[6] blank; p.[7] NOTE; p.[8] blank; p.9 CONTENTS; p.[10] blank;

pp.11–45 text; p.[46] blank; p.[47] THE CORONATION MURDER and epigraph of 2 ll.; p.[48] blank; pp.49–53 text; p.[54] blank; p.[55] author's advertisement; p.[56] blank; pp.[57] – [64] publisher's advertisements.

18.8 × 12.5 cm. Bulk: 1.0/1.4 cm. White wove paper; top edges only trimmed. White wove endpapers. Bound in yellowish buff boards with black cobbled design; front and back blank; white label at top of spine: [rule] | *The* | *Pierglass* | [diamond] | *Robert* | *Graves* | [rule].

Price: 5s. Number of copies: 500. Published in February 1921 in cream dust-jacket.

Contents: The Stake – The Troll's Nosegay – The Pier-Glass – The Finding of Love – Reproach – The Magical Picture – Distant Smoke – Morning Phoenix – Catherine Drury – Raising the Stone – The Treasure Box – The Kiss – Lost Love – Fox's Dingle – The Gnat – The Patchwork Bonnet – Kit Logan and Lady Helen – Down – Saul of Tarsus – Storm: At the Farm Window – Black Horse Lane – Return – Incubus – The Hills of May – The Coronation Murder

A6b. First American edition (1921):

THE PIER-GLASS | BY | ROBERT GRAVES | [publisher's emblem] | NEW YORK | ALFRED . A . KNOPF | 1921

Collation: [1] – [4]^8, 32 leaves.

p.[1] THE PIER-GLASS; p.[2] list of books by Graves; p.[3] title-page; p.[4] copyright and printing notices; p.[5] TO | NANCY NICHOLSON; p.[6] blank; p.[7] NOTE; p.[8] blank; p.[9] CONTENTS; p.[10] blank; pp.11–63 text; p.[64] blank.

15.1 × 11.3 cm. Bulk: 0.6/1.0 cm. White wove paper; top edges only trimmed and stained green. White wove endpapers. Bound in orange boards with green label running from front to back across spine; on front and back: [rule] | THE PIER-GLASS | POEMS BY |ROBERT GRAVES | [rule]; on spine: [rule] | *The* | *Pier-* | *Glass* | *by* | *Robert* | *Graves* | *1921* | [rule].

Price: $1.25. Number of copies undisclosed. Published in September 1921.

Note: Ellsworth Mason reports his copy, now at the University of Tulsa Library, as measuring 15.6 × 12.1 cm. In addition, Mason records a variant state which differs as follows: 15.3 × 11.8 cm. Bulk: 0.7/1.1 cm. All edges trimmed; cream wove endpapers. Bound in green cloth with chartreuse label running from front to back across spine, lettered as above. Published in a green dust-jacket printed in black.

J. Stephan Laurence (Catalogue No. 50, winter, 1980–81) lists a scarce, and perhaps discoloured binding in orange, printed in red with red paper spine printed in blue: [all within double box rules] ON | ENGLISH | POETRY | * | ROBERT GRAVES | 1922 [not seen].

A7 ON ENGLISH POETRY 1922

a. First edition:

ON ENGLISH POETRY | *Being an Irregular Approach to the Psychology* | *of this Art,* *from Evidence Mainly Subjective* | By ROBERT GRAVES | [publisher's emblem] | New York ALFRED . A . KNOPF Mcmxxii

Collation: [1] – [9]^8 [10]^4, 76 leaves.

p.[i] [at top right:] ON | ENGLISH POETRY; p.[ii] list of books by Graves; p.[iii] title-page; p.[iv] copyright, publishing, printer's, binder's and manufacturing notices; p.[v] *To T. E. Lawrence of Arabia and* | *All Soul's College, Oxford, and to* | *W.H.R. Rivers of the Solomon Is-* | *lands and St. John's College, Cam-* | *bridge, my gratitude for valuable* | *critical help, and the dedication of* | *this book.*; p. [vi] quotations from Skelton (2 ll.) and Shelley (2 ll.); pp. vii–viii NOTE; pp.ix–xi CONTENTS; p.[xii] blank; pp.13–149 text; pp.[150] – [152] blank.

19.3 × 13.3 cm. Bulk: 1.7/2.3 cm. White wove paper; all edges trimmed; top edges stained red. White wove endpapers. Bound in cream boards; back blank; front printed with cobbled design in red, with a rounded cream box near top, inside which, in red: *On* | ENGLISH POETRY | *Robert Graves*; near bottom is publisher's emblem; spine printed in red: ON | ENGLISH POETRY | [rule] | GRAVES

Price: $2.00. Number of copies undisclosed. Published in May 1922.

Contents: Note – I. Definitions – II. The Nine Muses – III. Poetry and Primitive Magic – IV. Conflict of Emotions – V. The Pattern Underneath – VI. Inspiration – VII. The Parable of Mr. Poeta and Mr. Lector – VIII. The Carpenter's Son – IX. The Gadding Vine – X. The Dead End and the Man of One Poem – XI. Spenser's Cuffs – XII. Connection of Poetry and Humour – XIII. Diction – XIV. The Daffodils – XV. Vers Libre – XVI. Moving Mountains – XVII. La Belle Dame Sans Merci – XVIII. The General Elliott – XIX. The God Called Poetry – XX. Logicalization – XXI. Limitations – XXII. The Naughty Boy – XXIII. The Classical and Romantic Ideas – XXIV. Colour – XXV. Putty – XXVI. Reading Aloud – XXVII. L'Arte della Pittura – XXVIII. On Writing Musically – XXIX. The Use of Poetry – XXX. Histories of Poetry – XXXI. The Bowl Marked Dog – XXXII. The Analytic Spirit – XXXIII. Rhyme and Alliteration – XXXIV. An Awkward Fellow Called Ariphrades – XXXV. Improvising New Conventions – XXXVI. When in Doubt. . . . – XXXVII. The Editor with the Muckrake – XXXVIII. The Moral Question – XXXIX. The Poet as Outsider – XL. A Polite Acknowledgement – XLI. Fake Poetry, Bad Poetry and Mere Verse – XLII. A Dialogue on Fake Poetry – XLIII. Asking Advice – XLIV. Surface Faults, An Illustration – XLV. Linked Sweetness Long Drawn Out – XLVI. The Fable of the Ideal Gadget – XLVII. Sequels Are Barred – XLVIII. Tom Fool – XLIX. Cross Rhythm and Resolution – L. My Name Is Legion, for We Are Many – LI. The Pig Baby – LII. Apology for Definitions – LIII. Time and Seasons – LIV. Two Heresies – LV. The Art of Expression – LVI. Ghosts in the Sheldonian – LVII. The Laying-On of Hands – LVIII. Ways and Means – LIX. Poetry as Labour – LX. The Necessity of Arrogance – LXI. In Procession – Appendix: The Dangers of Definition.

Notes: Both A7a and A7b have the misprints "that" for "than that" on p. 33, IX, l.2, and "have" for "how" on p. 145, l. 5.

Both A7a and A7b were printed in the U.S.

Photographic reprints were issued by Haskell House (1972) and Folcroft Press (1975).

A7b. English issue (1922):

ON ENGLISH POETRY | *Being an Irregular Approach to the Psychology* | *of This Art, from Evidence Mainly Subjective* | By | ROBERT GRAVES | 19 [publisher's emblem] 22 | LONDON: WILLIAM HEINEMANN

Collation: as A7a, except p.[iv] printing notice.

20.2 × 13.0 cm. Bulk: 1.7/2.1 cm. White wove paper; all edges trimmed. White wove endpapers. Bound in bright yellow cloth printed in black; back blank; front printed with cobbled design; rounded box near top as A7a and publisher's emblem in rounded box near bottom; spine: *On* | ENGLISH | POETRY | *Robert* | *Graves* | HEINEMANN

Price: 8s.6d. Number of copies: 1,560. Published 6 July 1922 in buff dust jacket printed in black cobbled design as front boards.

Notes: Impressions: 2nd, September 1922.

The first English issue exists in a variant binding. Neither William Nicholson (the designer) nor Graves liked the effect of the first state. The second state is buff boards with cobbled design in black; an off-white label on front reads: *On* | ENGLISH POETRY | *Robert Graves*; tan label on spine: [all flush left:] On | English | Poetry | Robert | Graves | Heinemann

The half-title of the first impression is a cancel.

J. Stephen Laurence (Catalogue 45, 1979, no. 856) lists a variant binding with orange boards printed in red, with red paper label printed in blue (not seen).

A8   WIIIPPERGINNY   [1923]

a. First edition:

WHIPPERGINNY | BY | ROBERT GRAVES | [publisher's emblem] | LONDON | WILLIAM HEINEMANN, LTD.

Collation: [A]⁴ B–E⁸ F⁴, 40 leaves.

p.[i] WHIPPERGINNY; p.[ii] blank; p.[iii] title-page; p.[iv] TO | EDWARD MARSH and printing notice; pp.v–vi AUTHOR'S NOTE; pp.[vii]–[viii] CONTENTS; pp.1–71 text; p.[72] text and printer's notice.

18.8 × 12.1 cm. Bulk: 0.9/1.4 cm. White wove paper; top and fore-edges trimmed. White wove endpapers. Bound in magenta boards printed with cobbled design; back blank; red label on front: *WHIPPER-GINNY* | *Robert Graves*; red label on spine: [all flush left:] Whipper- | ginny | Robert | Graves | Heinemann

Price: 5s. Number of copies: 1,000. Published 15 March 1923 in magenta dust-jacket printed in black.

Contents: Author's Note – Whipperginny – The Bedpost – A Lover Since Childhood – Song of Contrariety – The Ridge Top – Song in Winter – Unicorn and the White Doe – Sullen Moods – A False Report – Children of Darkness – Richard Roe and John Doe – The Dialecticians – The Lands of Whipperginny – 'The General Elliott' – A Fight to the Death – Old Wives' Tales – Christmas Eve – The Snake and the Bull – The Red Ribbon Dream – In Procession – Henry and Mary – An English Wood – Mirror, Mirror! – What Did I Dream? – Interlude: On Preserving a Poetic Formula – A History of Peace – The Rock Below – An Idyll of Old Age – The Lord Chamberlain Tells of a Famous Meeting – The Sewing Basket – Against Clock and Compasses – The Avengers – On the Poet's Birth – The Technique of Perfection – The Sibyl – A Crusader – A New Portrait of Judith of Bethulia – A Reversal – The Martyred Decadents: A Sympathetic Satire – Epigrams: On Christopher Marlowe; A Village Conflict; Dedicatory; To R. Graves, Senior; 'A Vehicle, to wit, a Bicycle'; Motto to a Book of Emblems – The Bowl and the Rim – A Forced Music – The Turn of a Page – The Manifestation in the Temple – To Any Saint – A Dewdrop – A Valentine.

Notes: Both A8a and A8b were printed in Great Britain.

Norwood Editions issued a photographic reprint of this edition in 1977.

A8b. American issue (1923):

WHIPPERGINNY | BY | ROBERT GRAVES | [publisher's emblem] | NEW YORK | ALFRED A. KNOPF: MCMXXIII

Collation as A8a, except A2 is a cancel, recto as above, verso as A8a.

   18.7 × 12.5 cm. Bulk: 0.9/1.4 cm. White wove paper; top edges only trimmed and stained pink. White wove endpapers. Bound in boards printed with flame-like design (13 × 11 designs) in blue, flesh, brown and green; pink label runs from front to back across spine with continuous decorative rule above and below legends; on front and back in green: [decorative rule] | *WHIPPERGINNY* | *POEMS BY* | *ROBERT GRAVES* | [decorative rule]; on spine: [decorative rule] | *Whip-* | *per-* | *ginny* | *by* | *Robert* | *Graves* | *1923* | [decorative rule].

Price: $2.00. Number of copies undisclosed. Published 29 June 1923.

A9   THE FEATHER BED   1923

First edition:

THE FEATHER BED | BY ROBERT GRAVES | *With a cover design by WILLIAM NICHOLSON* | PRINTED AND PUBLISHED BY | LEONARD & VIRGINIA WOOLF | AT THE HOGARTH PRESS | HOGARTH HOUSE RICHMOND | 1923

Collation: [1] – [4]⁴, 16 leaves.

   p.[1] title-page; p.[2] blank; p.[3] *INTRODUCTORY LETTER*; p.[4] blank; pp.5–8 text; p.[9] *THE FEATHER BED*; pp.[10] blank; pp.11–13 text; p.[14] blank; pp.15–28 text; pp. [29] – [30] blank; pp.[31] – [32] blank, pasted to back cover.

   21.9 × 17.0 cm. Bulk: 0.4/0.7 cm. White laid paper; all edges untrimmed;

watermarked HAND MADE C C & CO and a circle with a cross. Front endpaper white laid; free recto blank; free verso has label: *This edition of THE FEATHER | BED is limited to 250 signed copies | of which this is Number* [number written in] | [signature]. Bound in pink boards printed in black, showing black spine and on front a repeated pattern (6 × 4) of feathers with rounded box containing: *The* | Feather Bed | *Robert Graves*

Price: 5s. Number of copies: 254. Published 20 July 1923. Woolmer #33.

Contents: Introductory letter (to John Crowe Ransom) – The Feather Bed: Prologue – The Feather Bed – Epilogue.

A10   MOCK BEGGAR HALL   1924

First edition:

MOCK BEGGAR HALL | BY ROBERT GRAVES | *With a cover design by WILLIAM NICHOLSON* | PUBLISHED BY | LEONARD & VIRGINIA WOOLF | AT THE HOGARTH PRESS | 52 TAVISTOCK SQUARE | LONDON, W.C.1 | 1924

Collation: [A]⁴ B–F⁸, 44 leaves.
   p.[i] title-page; p.[ii] blank; p.[iii] CONTENTS; p.[iv] blank; pp.1–79 text; p.[80] blank; pp.[81]–[84] publisher's advertisements.
   25.1 × 18.7 cm. Bulk: 1.0/1.3 cm. Cream-white wove paper watermarked with crown and in Gothic: Abbey Mills | Greenfield; all edges untrimmed. White wove endpapers. Bound in grey boards; back and spine blank; front printed with design of hanging bat in upper foreground and house in lower background; at top left: Mockbeggar | Hall; at top right: by | Robert Graves

Price: 7s.6d. Number of copies unknown. Published in May 1924. Woolmer #46.

Contents: Diplomatic Relation – Hemlock – Full Moon – Myrrhina – Twin Souls – The North Window – Attercop: The All-Wise Spider – Antinomies – Northward from Oxford – Witches – Antigonus: An Eclogue – Essay on Continuity – Interchange of Selves, by Basanta Mallik. The Editing and Prologue by Robert Graves – Knowledge of God – Mock Beggar Hall: A Progression – The Rainbow and the Sceptic.

A11   THE MEANING OF DREAMS   [1924]

a. First edition:

THE MEANING OF DREAMS | BY | ROBERT GRAVES | [publisher's emblem] | CECIL PALMER | FORTY-NINE | CHANDOS | STREET | W.C.2 | [flush left, within square brackets:] *Printed in Great Britain*

Collation: [A]⁶ B–L⁸ [M]⁴, 90 leaves.
   p.[i] THE MEANING OF DREAMS; p.[ii] blank; p.[iii] title-page; p.[iv] copyright and printer's notices; p.[v] TO SUSAN | AND | JOHN BUCHAN; p.[vi] blank; pp.[vii] viii–xi TABLE OF CONTENTS; p.[xii] blank; p.[1] chapter title; p.[2] blank;

pp.3–167 text, with pp.[17, 31, 61, 77, 103, 113, 133] being chapter titles and pp.[18, 32, 60, 62, 76, 78, 102, 104, 112, 114, 134] blank; p.[168] blank.

18.7 × 12.3 cm. Bulk: 2.1/2.5 cm. White wove paper; top edges only trimmed. White wove endpapers. Bound in dark blue cloth; front and back blank; white label pasted on spine: [whole enclosed within rectangular decorative rule box:] THE | MEANING | OF | DREAMS | Robert | Graves | Cecil | Palmer

Price: 6s. Number of copies undetermined. Published in September 1924.

Contents: Past Theories as Far as Freud – Theory of Double-Self – Primitive Thought – Varieties of Dreams – Survival of the Past and Other Problems – Value of Dreams on Their Own Account – Practical Benefits of Interpretation – Dreams and Poetry.

Note: A11a and A11b were both printed in England.
Carl Hahn reports a variant binding in black cloth.

A11b. American issue (1925):

THE MEANING OF DREAMS | BY | ROBERT GRAVES | [publisher's emblem] | NEW YORK | GREENBERG, PUBLISHER, INC. | 1925

Collation: [A]⁶ B-K⁸ L¹², 90 leaves.
Remainder as A11a.
18.5 × 12.4 cm. Bulk: 2.1/2.7 cm. (sheets). Paper as A11a. Bound in coarse purple cloth; front and back blank; white label pasted on spine printed in blue:[all within a decorative rectangular border:] THE | MEANING | OF | DREAMS | Robert | Graves | GREENBERG

Price: $2.00. Number of copies unknown. Published in May 1925.

A12 POETIC UNREASON [1925]

First edition:

POETIC | UNREASON | AND OTHER | STUDIES | BY | ROBERT GRAVES| AUTHOR OF | 'THE MEANING OF DREAMS', 'ON ENGLISH POETRY' | 'MOCK BEGGAR HALL', ETC. | [publisher's emblem] | CECIL PALMER | FORTY-NINE | CHANDOS | STREET | W.C. | 2

Collation: [A]⁸ B–S⁸, 144 leaves.
pp.[i] – [ii] blank; p.[iii] POETIC UNREASON; p.[iv] blank; p. [v] title-page; p.[vi] edition, copyright and printing notices; p.[vii] TO | HENRY HEAD; p.[viii] quotation from Skelton; pp. [ix] – [x] AUTHOR'S NOTE; p.[xi] CONTENTS; p.[xii] blank; pp. 1–276 text, with printer's notice also at bottom of p.276.
18.2 × 12.4 cm. Bulk: 2.8/3.3 cm. White wove paper; top edge only trimmed. White wove endpapers. Bound in dark blue cloth; front and back blank; white label pasted on spine: [whole enclosed in rectangular decorative box rule:] POETIC | UNREASON | Robert | Graves | Cecil | Palmer

Price: 6s. Number of copies unknown. Published in February 1925 in grey-green dust-jacket printed in black.

Contents: Author's Note – What is Bad Poetry? (An Address given at Leeds University, December, 1922) – A Theory of Consciousness – Jekyll and Hyde – Defence of Poetic Analysis – Secondary Elaboration – The Illogical Element in Poetry – Classical and Romantic – Problems for Classification – Naturally – The Tempest: An Analysis – Control by Spirits – Poetic Genius – Succession – Sensory Vehicles of Poetic Thought.

Note: Biblio and Tannen, New York, issued a photo-offset reprinting of this edition on 14 March 1969 [dated 1968] (630 copies; price $10.00) which differ only in binding, bulk, and the removal of the printer's notice on p.276 and the alteration of the copyright and printing notices on p.[vi].

A13   JOHN KEMP'S WAGER   1925

a. First edition:

John Kemp's Wager | A Ballad Opera | By ROBERT GRAVES | *Therefore roome! you moral precepts.* | *Give my legs leave to ende my Mor-* | *rice, or that being ended, my hands* | *leave to perfect this worthlesse poore* | *tattered volume.* | William Kemp's *Nine Daies Wonder* | Oxford: Basil Blackwell | *Publisher to the* Shakespeare Head Press | *of* Stratford-upon-Avon | 1925

Collation: [a]⁸ b–f⁸, 48 leaves.
    p.[i] blank; p.[ii] British Drama League notice; p.[iii] [all flush left:] The British Drama | League Library | of Modern British | Drama No. 11 | John Kemp's | Wager | Robert Graves; p [iv] British Drama League and British acting rights notice; p. [v] John Kemp's Wager; p.[vi] blank; p.[vii] title-page; p [viii] printer's notice; p.[ix] To my friend | ERNEST NEALE | of Islip Post Office; p.[x] blank; pp. xi–xiii Author's Note; p. [xiv] Persons of the Play; p. xv Synopsis of Scenery; p.[xvi] blank; pp.1–75 text; p.[76] blank; p.[77] colophon; pp. [78] – [80] blank.
    18.5 × 12.4 cm. Bulk: 0.6/1.0 cm. White wove paper; all edges trimmed. No endpapers; pp [i] – [ii] and [79] – [80] pasted down to covers. Bound in white boards; front and back have green borders and overall interlocked ring design; back without legend; front has green-bordered box with: THE BRITISH DRAMA LEAGUE LIBRARY | OF MODERN BRITISH DRAMA. NO. 11 | JOHN KEMP'S WAGER | BY ROBERT GRAVES; at lower left, in green-bordered box, in green: OXFORD. BASIL BLACKWELL | AT THE SHAKESPEARE HEAD; spine, from bottom to top: BRITISH DRAMA LEAGUE LIBRARY. NO. 11 JOHN KEMP'S WAGER.

Price: 3s. 6d. Number of copies: 750. Published 12 May 1925.

Note: A13a–c were all printed in Great Britain.
    In 1973 Folcroft Press issued a photocopy reproduction of this edition.

A13b. Limited issue (1925):

Title-page as A13a.

Collation as A13a
    Remainder differs as follows: p.[iv] adds: ONE HUNDRED COPIES OF THIS

PLAY | HAVE BEEN PRINTED ON KELMSCOTT | HAND-MADE PAPER, OF WHICH THIS | IS NUMBER [number] | [signature of Graves].
19.3 × 12.3 cm. White laid paper; top edges unopened; all edges untrimmed. White laid endpapers. Bound in white boards with parchment spine; front and back have paper labels as A13a; spine stamped in gold, from top to bottom, same legend as A13a.

Price: 10s. 6d. Number of copies: 100. Published in June 1925.

A13c. American issue (1925):

John Kemp's Wager | A Ballad Opera | By ROBERT GRAVES | [6 ll. quotation as A13a] | COPYRIGHT 1925, BY ROBERT GRAVES | SAMUEL FRENCH (*Incorporated* 1898) | T. R. Edwards, *Managing Director* | 25 West 45th Street, NEW YORK CITY | 1925

Collation as A13a.
Remainder differs as follows: p.[iv] has a paper label pasted below the League notice assigning American and Canadian acting rights to French; pp.[vii] – [viii] is a cancel, pasted to the stub of a4.
18.5 × 12.4 cm. Bulk: 0.8/1.2 cm. Paper and binding as A13a.

Price: $1.25. Number of copies: 250. Published in 1925.

A14   MY HEAD! MY HEAD!   1925

a. First edition:

My Head! My Head! | Being the History of Elisha and the | Shunamite Woman; with the History | of Moses as Elisha related it, and | her Questions put to him. | *by* | Robert Graves | 1925 | [rule] | *London:* Martin Secker

Collation: [A]⁸ B–I⁸, 72 leaves.
p.[1] My Head! My Head!; p.[2] quotation (4 ll.) from Skelton; p.[3] title-page; p.[4] printing and publisher's notices; p. [5] *To* | *T.E LAWRENCE* [no point after initial E]; p.[6] blank; p.[7] *CONTENTS*; P.[8] blank; pp.9–27 ARGUMENT; p. [28] blank]; p.[29] MY HEAD! MY HEAD!; p.[30] blank; pp.31–141 text; p.[142] printer's notice; pp.[143] – [144] publisher's advertisements.
19.0 × 11.5 cm. Bulk: 1.6/2.1 cm. White laid paper; top and fore-edges trimmed. Bound in red cloth with black veining design; spine black cloth stamped in gold: MY | HEAD! | MY | HEAD! | [circle] | GRAVES | SECKER

Price: 5s. Number of copies: 1,000. Published in June 1925 in cream dust-jacket printed in red.

Notes: A second issue was made up from 500 sheets of the earlier edition in March 1928; it differs as follows: title-page: [whole enclosed within rectangular heavy-rule box:] My Head! My Head! | *by* | Robert Graves | 1928 | [rule] | *London:* Martin Secker; [A] 1,2 are cancels and I7 has been removed and the stub is followed by four pages listing series titles on slightly smaller paper; p.[2] series notice; p [4] publication and publisher's notices; pp.[143] – [144] publisher's advertisements; 17.2

× 11.0 cm.; bound in green cloth; spine stamped in gold: MY HEAD! | MY HEAD! | [star] | GRAVES | NEW | ADELPHI | LIBRARY; series device stamped in gold on front board and back board blank.

Both A14a and A14b were printed in Great Britain.

Haskell House issued a photographic facsimile of this edition in 1974.

A14b. American issue (1925):

My Head! My Head! | Being the History of Elisha and the | Shunamite Woman; with the History | of Moses as Elisha related it, and | her Questions put to him. | *by* | Robert Graves | [publisher's emblem] | 1925 | [rule] | *New York:* Alfred A. Knopf

Collation: [A]⁸ B–H⁸ I⁷, 71 leaves.

Remainder differs from A14a as follows: p.[4] printing notice; pp.[143]–[144] missing.

18.7 × 12.0 cm. Bulk: 1.8/2.2 cm. White laid paper; top edges only trimmed and stained yellow. White wove endpapers. Bound in cream boards printed with large angular design in black and irregular ink-blots of red, blue, yellow, orange and green; back blank; front has yellow label: [rectangular decorative box rule enclosing all:] My Head! My Head! | ROBERT GRAVES; spine has orange label: [rectangular decorative box rule enclosing all:] *My* | *Head!* | *My* | *Head!* | *ROBERT* | *GRAVES*

Price: $2.00. Number of copies: 500. Published 5 June 1925 in light purple dust-jacket printed in black.

A15 CONTEMPORARY TECHNIQUES OF POETRY 1925

a. First edition:

Contemporary Techniques | *of Poetry* | *A POLITICAL ANALOGY* | *By* | *Robert Graves* | [publisher's emblem] | *Published by* | *Leonard & Virginia Woolf at The Hogarth Press* | *52 Tavistock Square, London, W.C.1* | *1925*

Collation: [1]⁸ 2–3⁸, 24 leaves.

p.[1] *Contemporary Techniques* | *of Poetry*; p.[2] publisher's advertisements; p.[3] title-page; p.[4] TO | EDITH SITWELL | IN ALL FRIENDSHIP and printer's notice; pp.5–46 [47] text; p.[48] printer's notice.

21.7 × 13.8 cm. Bulk: 0.4 cm. White wove paper; all edges trimmed. White wove endpapers. Bound in light blue boards; back blank; front printed: THE HOGARTH PRESS | *Contemporary Techniques* | *of Poetry* | ROBERT GRAVES | [design of vase with columns at sides and grid beneath] | THE HOGARTH PRESS

Price: 3s.6d. Number of copies unknown. Published in July 1925. Woolmer #63.

Contents: The State of the Parties – Diction – Metre – Texture – Rhyme – Structure.

Note: Issued as Hogarth Essays, Series 1, No. VIII. The design is by Vanessa Bell.

A15b. Second impression (1929):

Contemporary Techniques | *of Poetry* | *A POLITICAL ANALOGY* | *Robert Graves* | *Second*

Impression | *Published by* | *Leonard & Virginia Woolf at the Hogarth Press* | *52 Tavistock Square, London, W.C.1* | *1929*

Collation as A15a.

p.[1] *Contemporary Techniques* | *of Poetry*; p.[2] publisher's advertisements for Hogarth Essays I–IX; p.[3] title-page; p.[4] *First published 1925* | *Second Impression 1929.* | TO | EDITH SITWELL | IN ALL FRIENDSHIP | Printed in Great Britain by | LOWE AND BRYDONE (PRINTERS) LTD., PARK STREET, LONDON, N.W.1; pp.5–46[47] text; p.[48] blank.

21.5 × 13.7 cm. Bulk: 0.45 cm. White wove paper; all edges trimmed. White wove endpapers. Bound in white boards; back blank; front printed as A15a.

Price: 3s. 6d. Number of copies unknown. Published in 1929.

A16   WELCHMAN'S HOSE   1925

First edition:

WELCHMAN'S HOSE | BY | ROBERT GRAVES | [engraving of bird on lectern] | WOOD ENGRAVINGS BY PAUL NASH | LONDON | THE FLEURON | 1925

Collation: [A]/A2⁴ᐟ⁴ B/B2–D/D2⁴ᐟ⁴ E⁴, 36 leaves.

p.[i] WELCHMAN'S HOSE; p.[ii] *This edition is limited to 525 copies* | *of which 500 copies are for sale*; p.[iii] title-page; p.[iv] printer's notice; p.[v] TO EDITH AND WILLIAM NICHOLSON; p.[vi] blank; p.vii CONTENTS; p.[viii] blank; p.ix quotations from Skelton (7 ll.) and Jewel (3 ll.); p.[x] illustration; pp.1–13 text; p.14 illustration; pp.15–61 text with engraving of head on pp.21 and 44 and engraving of form on pp.38 and 61; p.[62] blank.

20.6 × 15.0 cm. Bulk: 0.5/0.9 cm. White wove paper watermarked P.M.P.; top edges only trimmed. Bound in boards with repeated (6 × 4 designs) floral designs; black cloth spine stamped in gold from bottom to top in upper half: WELCHMAN'S HOSE : ROBERT GRAVES

Price: 12s.6d. Number of copies: 525. Published in September 1925 in transparent parchment wrapper.

Contents: Alice – Burrs and Brambles – From Our Ghostly Enemy – The Figure-Head – Ovid in Defeat – Diversions: I. To an Editor – II. The Kingfisher's Return – III. Love Without Hope – IV. The Traveller's Curse after Misdirection (from the Welsh) – V. Tilly Kettle – The College Debate – Sergeant-Major Money – A Letter from Wales – The Presence – The Clipped Stater – The Poetic State – Essay on Knowledge – At the Games

Note: A photocopy publication of this edition was issued by Folcroft Press in 1976.

A17 ROBERT GRAVES [1925]

First edition:

[rectangular heavy rule box enclosing all:] | [rectangular light rule box enclosing all:] | [rectangular broad decorative rule box enclosing all:] | [rectangular light rule box enclosing all:] | *THE AUGUSTAN BOOKS OF* | *MODERN POETRY* | [rule] | *ROBERT* | *GRAVES* | [rule] | *LONDON: ERNEST BENN LTD.* | *8, BOUVERIE STREET, E.C.4*

Collation: 16 leaves, unsigned, stapled twice at centre.

 p.[i] title-page; p.[ii] publisher's advertisement and printer's notice; p.iii ROBERT GRAVES; p.iv CONTENTS; pp.5–30 text; p.31 BIBLIOGRAPHY; p.[32] publisher's advertisements.

 22.1 × 14.0 cm. Bulk: 0.2 cm. White wove paper; top and fore-edges trimmed. Pp.[i]–[ii] and 31–[32] serve as covers.

Price: 6d. Number of copies unknown. Published in November 1925.

Contents: In the Wilderness – A Boy in Church – Escape – Vain and Careless – Pot and Kettle – Song: One Hard Look – Dicky – Ghost Raddled – Allie – A Frosty Night – Rocky Acres – A Lover Since Childhood – A Crusader – The Ridge-Top – Song of Contrariety – A Forced Music – I Am the Star of Morning – The North Window – The Rainbow and the Sceptic – Diplomatic Relations – Alice – The Presence – From Our Ghostly Enemy

Notes: Ellsworth Mason records a variant copy stitched twice at the centre with all edges trimmed.

 There was a second impression in 1933 printed from the same plates save for the cover leaves (pp.[i]–[ii] and 31–[32]) which are reset. The variants are as follows: title-page: [rectangular heavy rule box enclosing all:] | [rectangular light rule box enclosing all:] | [rectangular broad decorative border enclosing all:] | [rectangular light rule box enclosing all:] | THE AUGUSTAN BOOKS OF | MODERN POETRY | [in open type] ROBERT GRAVES | London: Ernest Benn Ltd. | BOUVERIE HOUSE, FLEET STREET

Collation: as in first impression.

 p.[i] title-page; p.[ii] publisher's advertisement [no printer's notice]; and p.[32] publisher's advertisements and printer's notice have all been re-set.

 22.0 × 14.0 cm. Bulk: 0.2 cm. White wove paper; top and fore-edges trimmed.

A18 THE MARMOSITE'S MISCELLANY 1925

a. First edition:

The Marmosite's | Miscellany. | JOHN DOYLE. | *Published by Leonard and Virginia Woolf at* | *The Hogarth Press, 52, Tavistock Square, W.C.1.* | 1925.

Collation: 1/2⁴/⁸, 12 leaves.

p.[1] THE | MARMOSITE'S MISCELLANY; p.[2] blank; p.[3] title-page; p.[4] NOTE; pp.5–23 text; p.[24] blank.

22.5 × 14.7 cm. Bulk: 0.5 cm. White wove paper; all edges trimmed. White wove endpapers. Bound in mauve and yellow floral boards; back and spine blank; front has label: [rectangular double box rule enclosing all:] THE | MARMOSITE'S MISCELLANY | JOHN DOYLE

Price: 3s. Number of copies unknown. Published in December 1925. Woolmer #59.

Contents: To M. in India; with the Poem that Follows – The Marmosite's Miscellany – Tail Piece – Notes – The Moment of Weakness

Note: Acknowledged by Graves by republication in A23, see also C217.

A18b. First Canadian edition (1975):

[in black and **red**] THE | *Robert Graves* **MARMOSITE'S** | **MISCELLANY** | **1975** | **THE PHAROS PRESS** | **Victoria, British Columbia**

Collation: [1] – [2]^8 [3]^4 [4]^8, 28 leaves.
    p.[1] THE MARMOSITE'S MISCELLANY; p[2] blank; p.[3] title-page; p.[4] copyright and printer's notices; p.[5] [all in red] *Preface*; p.[6] *incipit:* A sniff at every flask; pp.7–10 *To M. in India; with the Poem that Follows* [text of the poem in red]; pp.11–42 text [head-title in red and text black]; pp.43–47 NOTES; p.[48] blank; pp.49–52 [all in red:] *The Moment of Weakness* [text of poem in black]; p.[53] blank; p.[54] THIS EDITION OF | *The Marmosite's Miscellany* | IS PUBLISHED IN CELEBRATION OF | THE EIGHTIETH BIRTHDAY OF | *Robert Graves* | The edition consists of seven hundred and fifty numbered copies of | which six hundred and seventy are printed on Rolland's Zephyr Book | paper and numbers one to eighty specially bound and signed copies on | Strathmore's Grandee paper. The typeface is Intertype Baskerville with | Arrighi display italics and Centaur titles. | THIS IS COPY NUMBER [number written in over dots] | [Graves' signature] ; pp. [55] – [56] blank.
    22.6 × 15.1 cm. Bulk: 0.4/0.9 cm. White wove paper; all edges trimmed. Endpapers printed on outward facing side in a series of floral patterns. Copies 1–80 bound in olive cloth and copies 81–750 bound simulated olive cloth; front and back blank; spine stamped in gold, top to bottom: *Robert Graves* THE MARMOSITE'S MISCELLANY The Pharos Press

Price: $60.00 Canadian, copies 1–80 and $20.00 Canadian, for the remainder. Number of copies: 750. Published in 1975. Copies 1–80 without dust-jacket in slipcase; copies 81–750 without dust-jacket or slipcase.

A19   ANOTHER FUTURE OF POETRY   1926

First edition:

ANOTHER FUTURE | OF POETRY | BY | ROBERT GRAVES | [publisher's emblem] | Published by | Leonard & Virginia Woolf at the Hogarth Press | 52 Tavistock Square, London, W.C.1 | 1926

Collation: [A]^8 B^8 C^2, 18 leaves.
    p.[1] ANOTHER FUTURE OF POETRY; p.[2] publisher's advertisement; p.[3]

title-page; p.[4] TO | L. R. G. and printer's notice; pp.5–33 text; p.[34] printer's notice; pp. [35]–[36] blank.

21.7 × 13.8 cm. Bulk: 0.6 cm. White wove paper; all edges trimmed. White wove endpapers. Bound in light blue boards; back and spine blank; on front: THE HOGARTH ESSAYS | *Another Future of* | *Poetry* | ROBERT GRAVES | [design of vase and flowers, two line crook at left and right, hatching below] | THE HOGARTH PRESS

Price: 2s. 6d. Number of copies: 1,000. Published in July 1926. Woolmer #92.

Notes: Issued as Hogarth Essays, Series I, Number XVIII. Cover design by Vanessa Bell. Woolmer says 1,000 copies were printed of which 400 were pulped.

A20   THE ENGLISH BALLAD   1927

a. First edition:

[heavy-light-light rectangular rule box enclosing all:] The | English Ballad | [star] | *A Short Critical Survey* | *by* | ROBERT GRAVES | [star] | LONDON | *Ernest Benn Ltd.* | *Bouverie House, Fleet Street* | 1927

Collation: [A]⁸ B–H⁸ I⁶, 70 leaves.

p.[1] [at top right:] The | English Ballad; p.[2] blank; p.[3] title-page; p.[4] TO | MY FATHER and printing notice; p.5 INDEX OF BALLADS; p.6 completion of index and acknowledgements; pp. 7–36 INTRODUCTION; p.[37] [at top right:] BALLADS; p.[38] blank; pp.39–138 text; p.139 text and printer's notice; p. [140] blank.

18.8 × 12.7 cm. Bulk: 1.7/2.1 cm. White wove paper; top edges only trimmed. Bound in red cloth; front and back blank; white label on spine: THE | ENGLISH | BALLAD | [star] | GRAVES | [star]

Price: 6s. Number of copies unknown. Published in January 1927 in yellow dust-jacket printed in black.

Contents: Introduction – The Maid Freed from the Gallows: or, The Briary Bush – The Cleveland Lyke Wake Dirge – The False Knight on the Road – The Twa Corbies – Kemp Owyne – Sir Patrick Spens – The Wife of Usher's Well – Graeme and Bewick – The Demon Lover – The Battle of Otterbourne – Johnny Cock – The Cherry Tree Carol – Hugh of Lincoln – Bruton Town – Robin Hood and the Three Squires – The Old Cloak – Wednesbury Cocking – The Night before Larry Was Stretched – The Unquiet Grave – Waly, Waly – The Holy Land of Walsinghame – Loving Mad Tom – The Children in the Wood – The Welsh Buccaneers – The Death of King Edward VII – The Compleat History of Bob of Lyn – The Peeler and the Goat – Boney – Blow the Man Down – Jack o' Diamonds – Jesse James – 'I Want to go Home' – The Top of the Dixie Lid – Two Red Roses across the Moon

Notes: Some copies have an extra spine label tipped in at p.[140].
    In 1971 Haskell House published a photographic facsimile of this edition.

A20b. Second English edition (revised) ([1957]):

ENGLISH | AND SCOTTISH | BALLADS | *Edited with an Introduction* | *and Critical Notes* | *by* | ROBERT GRAVES | [publisher's emblem] | WILLIAM HEINEMANN LTD | MELBOURNE :: LONDON :: TORONTO

Collation: [A]⁸ B−M⁸, 96 leaves.

p.[i] ENGLISH AND SCOTTISH | BALLADS; p.[ii] publisher's advertisements; [frontispiece, back blank]; p.[iii] title-page; p.[iv] publication, publisher's and printer's notices; pp.v−vi CONTENTS; pp.vii−xxvi INTRODUCTION; p.[xxvii] BALLADS; p. [xxviii] blank; pp.1−143 text; p.[144] blank; pp.145−160 NOTES TO THE BALLADS; pp.161−163 INDEX OF TITLES AND FIRST LINES; p. [164] blank.

18.4 × 12.2 cm. Bulk: 0.9/1.3 cm. White wove paper; all edges trimmed. White wove endpapers. Bound in medium-blue simulated cloth boards; front and back blank; spine stamped in gold, top to bottom: *Robert Graves* [ornament] English and Scottish Ballads [ornament] *Heinemann*

Price: 9s. 6d. Number of copies undetermined. Published 6 May 1957 in white dust-jacket printed in black and magenta.

Contents: Introduction − Ballads: 1. The False Knight on the Road − 2. The Twa Sisters of Binnorie − 3. Lord Rendal − 4. Clerk Colvill − 5. Kemp Owyne − 6. Thomas the Rimer − 7. Sir Patrick Spens − 8. The Twa Corbies − 9. Hugh of Lincoln − 10. The Cherry Tree Carol − 11. The Demon Lover − 12. Robin and Gandelyn − 13. The Cleveland Lyke Wake Dirge − 14. The Golden Vanitie − 15. Young Beichan − 16. Johnny of Cockley's Well − 17. The Unquiet Grave − 18. Graeme and Bewick − 19. The Wife of Usher's Well − 20. The Heron − 21. Jonny Faa, the Lord of Little Egypt − 22. King John and the Abbot − 23. Get Up and Bar the Door − 24. Loving Mad Tom − 25. The Dead Brother − 26. Chevy Chase − 27. Waly, Waly − 28. Barbara Allan − 29. Robin Hood and the Three Squires − 30. The Holy Land of Walsinghame − 31. Sir Andrew Barton − 32. Bruton Town − 33. The Death of Robin Hood − 34. The Gaberlunzie Man − 35. Admiral Benbow − 36. Wednesbury Cocking − 37. The Children in the Wood − 38. The Banished Duke of Grantham − Notes to the Ballads − Index of Titles and First Lines

Notes: The introduction is greatly revised from that of A20a.

Both A20b and A20c were printed in Great Britain.

Heinemann continued to issue impressions in paperback under their series title "Poetry Bookshelf" in 1962 and 1963. The 1963 impression has a black wrapper printed in white.

A20c. First American edition (revised text) ([1957]):

ENGLISH | AND SCOTTISH | BALLADS | *Edited with an Introduction* | *and Critical Notes* | *by* | ROBERT GRAVES | THE MACMILLAN COMPANY | NEW YORK

Collation: as A20b.

Remainder as A20b, except p.[ii] blank; p.[vi] printing notice.

Size, bulk, endpapers and binding as A20b, except '*Macmillan*' for '*Heinemann*' on spine.

Price: $2.00. Number of copies undetermined. Published in July 1957 in dust-jacket as A20b.

Note: There was a second impression in 1969 by Barnes and Noble, which had taken over the Macmillan rights in the United States; this impression was simultaneously co-published in Great Britain by Heinemann.

A21   LARS PORSENA   [1927]

a. First edition:

LARS PORSENA | OR | THE FUTURE OF SWEARING | AND IMPROPER LANGUAGE | BY | ROBERT GRAVES | LONDON: | KEGAN PAUL, TRENCH, TRUBNER AND CO., LTD. | NEW YORK: E. P. DUTTON & CO.

Collation: [A]⁸ B−F⁸, 48 leaves, plus 16 pp. publisher's advertisements.
   p.[1] LARS PORSENA; p.[2] series advertisement; p.[3] title-page; p.[4] printer's notice; pp.5−94 text; pp.[95]−[96] blank; 16 pp. publisher's advertisements.
   15.3 × 10.4 cm. Bulk: 1.1/1.4 cm. White laid paper; all edges trimmed. White wove endpapers. Bound in plum boards; back blank; front has white label: [rectangular heavy rule box enclosing all:] | [rectangular light rule box enclosing all:] | LARS PORSENA | OR | THE FUTURE OF SWEARING | *ROBERT GRAVES*; spine has white label: [heavy rule] | [light rule] | LARS | PORSENA | GRAVES | [light rule] | *Kegan Paul* | [heavy rule]

Price: 2s.6d. Number of copies undetermined. Published in February 1927 in white dust-jacket printed in black.

Notes: Impressions: 2nd, April 1927; 3rd, July 1927; 4th, March 1928; 5th, October 1929; 6th, November 1931. In the 5th and later impressions, a note by Graves occupies p.[2], a list of impressions is added on p.[4], and the text occupies pp.5−96 (the extensions are at the end).
   Issued in the To-Day and To-Morrow Series.
   Robert Temple (Catalogue £21, 1982) reports a working copy in Graves' hand which contains revisions incorporated into the later impressions in 1927 with a statement by Graves on the verso of the title-page to that effect (not seen).
   Folcroft Press issued a photocopy reprint of this edition in 1971.

A21b. First American edition: ([1927]):

LARS PORSENA | *or* | THE FUTURE OF SWEARING | AND IMPROPER LANGUAGE | BY | ROBERT GRAVES | NEW YORK | E. P. DUTTON & COMPANY | 681 FIFTH AVENUE

Collation: [1]−[6]⁸, 48 leaves.
   pp.[i]−[ii] blank, pasted down to front cover; pp.[iii]−[iv] blank; p.[v] LARS PORSENA; p.[vi] blank; p.[vii] title-page; p.[viii] copyright and printing notices; p.[1] LARS PORSENA; p. [2] blank; pp.3−77 text; pp.[78]−[86] blank; pp.[87]−[88] blank and pasted down to back cover.
   14.1 × 10.4 cm. Bulk: 1.0/1.6 cm. White wove paper; all edges trimmed. No endpapers. Bound in blue cloth; back blank; front has white label: Lars Porsena | or | THE FUTURE OF SWEARING | AND IMPROPER LANGUAGE | By | ROBERT GRAVES; spine has white label: LARS | PORSENA | [rule] | GRAVES

Price: $1.00. Number of copies: 1,200. Published 12 April 1927 in white dust-jacket printed in red and black.

Notes: Some copies are bound in light olive-green cloth with white labels and others in red-orange cloth with buff labels. In the latter the following variants in the printing of the labels are found. Front: [rectangular box enclosing all:] LARS PORSENA | OR | THE FUTURE OF SWEARING | AND IMPROPER LANGUAGE | [three daggers] | ROBERT GRAVES Spine: [rule] | LARS | PORSENA | [rule] | GRAVES | [rule]
Ellsworth Mason reports a copy measuring 15.0 × 10.9 cm.

A21c. Second edition (revised) (1936):

THE FUTURE | OF SWEARING | AND | IMPROPER LANGUAGE | By | ROBERT GRAVES | [publisher's emblem] | LONDON | KEGAN PAUL, TRENCH, TRUBNER & CO., LTD | BROADWAY HOUSE: 68–74 CARTER LANE, E.C. | 1936

Collation: [A]^8 B–G^8, 56 leaves.
  2 pp. blank; p.[i] THE FUTURE | OF SWEARING; p.[ii] publisher's advertisements; p.[iii] title-page; p.[iv] printer's and edition notices; p.v–vi PREFACE TO | NEW EDITION; pp.1–100 text; p.[101]–[104] blank.
  18.5 × 12.0 cm. Bulk: 1.4/1.8 cm. White wove paper; all edges trimmed. White wove endpapers. Bound in sea-green cloth; front and back blank; spine stamped in gold: [heavy rule] [toward back:] THE FUTURE | [toward front, parallel to previous:] OF SWEARING | [heavy rule] | ROBERT | GRAVES | [heavy rule].

Price: 3s.6d. Number of copies undetermined. Published in March 1936 in white dust-jacket printed in blue-green and black.

Notes: Issued in the Today, Tomorrow and After Series. Some copies have 4 pp. publisher's advertisements following p.[104].

A21d. Third edition ([1972]):

LARS | PORSENA | *Or the Future of Swearing* | *and Improper Language* | ROBERT GRAVES | *Martin Brian & O'Keeffe* | *London*

Collation: [1]^4 [2]–[5]^8, 36 leaves.
  pp.[i]–[ii] blank; p.[iii] LARS PORSENA; p.[iv] blank; p.[v] title-page; p.[vi] publication, publisher's, ISBN, copyright and printer's notices; p.[vii] FOREWORD; p.[viii] blank; pp.1–64 text; pp.65–68 NOTE TO NEW EDITION; pp.[69]–[70] blank; p.[71] limitation and numbering statement and signature; p.[72] blank.
  18.6 × 12.0 cm. Bulk: 1.1/1.2 cm. White laid paper; all edges trimmed. White wove endpapers. Bound in Prussian blue cloth; front and back blank; spine stamped in gold, top to bottom, facing back: Robert Graves Lars Porsena [upright:] MB & O'K

Price: £6.50 limited; £1.50 ordinary. Number of copies: 100 limited edition; 1,000 ordinary edition. Published 27 March 1972. The limited edition was published in a stiff clear plastic dust-jacket and light Prussian blue slipcase and all these copies were signed by Graves; the ordinary edition was published without the slipcase.

A22   IMPENETRABILITY   [1927]

First edition:

IMPENETRABILITY | OR | THE PROPER HABIT OF ENGLISH | ROBERT GRAVES | [publisher's emblem] | *Published by Leonard & Virginia Woolf at The* | *Hogarth Press, 52 Tavistock Square, London, W.C.1* | 1926

Collation: [1]^8 2–4^8, 32 leaves.
    p.[1] IMPENETRABILITY | OR | THE PROPER HABIT OF ENGLISH; p.[2] publisher's advertisements; p.[3] title-page; p.[4] printer's notice; pp.5–61 text; p.[62] text and printer's notice; pp. [63] – [64] publisher's advertisements.
    16.6 × 10.4 cm. Bulk: 0.7/1.0 cm. White wove paper; all edges trimmed. White wove endpapers. Bound in blue-green boards; front and back have ovals containing: Hogarth Essays *and* Second Series plus additional oval and circular designs; spine printed in black from bottom to top: IMPENETRABILITY. By ROBERT GRAVES

Price: 2s. 6d. Number of copies: 1,000. Published in March 1927. Woolmer #93.

Notes: Issued as Hogarth Essays, Second Series, Number III. Cover design by Vanessa Bell. Reprinted in part in Chapter I of A55.
    Woolmer says 1,000 copies were printed of which 400 were pulped.

A23   POEMS (1914–1926)   1927

a. First edition:

POEMS | (1914–26) | By | ROBERT GRAVES | LONDON | WILLIAM HEINEMANN, LTD. | MCMXXVII

Collation: a^2 b^4 B–O^8 P^4 Q^1, 115 leaves.
    p.[i] POEMS (1914–26); p.[ii] blank; p.[iii] title-page; p. [iv] printer's notice; p.v NOTE; p.[vi] TO | N. AND L.; pp. vii–xi CONTENTS; p.xii quotation (7 ll.) from Skelton; p.[1] I | 1914–20; p.[2] blank; pp.3–43 text; p.[44] blank; p.[45] II | WAR | 1915–19; p.[46] blank; pp.47–64 text; p.[65] III | Mainly 1920–23; p.[66] blank; pp.67–118 text; p.[119] IV | MAINLY 1923–25; p.[120] blank; pp.121–78 text; p.[179] V | RECENT POEMS: 1925–26; p.[180] blank; pp.181–216 text; p.217 BIBLIOGRAPHY; p.[218] printer's notice.
    19.1 × 12.8 cm. Bulk: 1.8/2.3 cm. White laid paper watermarked ADELPHI; top edges only trimmed; fore-edges unopened. White wove endpapers. Bound in slick white cloth with black cobbled design; front has blue paper label: POEMS (1914–1926) | *Robert Graves*; back has blue paper label with publisher's emblem; spine has blue paper label: POEMS | 1914 | *to* | 1926 | *Robert* | *Graves* | [rule] | Heinemann

Price: 7s. 6d. Number of copies: 1,000. Published 2 June 1927 in light blue dust-jacket printed in black.

Contents: Note – I: The Poet in the Nursery – In the Wilderness – In Spite – John Skelton – Strong Beer – A Frosty Night – The Troll's Nosegay – A Song for Two

Children – Dicky – Song: One Hard Look – True Johnny – Allie – Loving Henry – Brittle Bones – An English Wood – Henry and Mary – The Country Dance – The Rose and the Lily – Love without Hope – The Traveller's Curse after Misdirection – Mirror, Mirror – What Did I Dream? – The Cupboard – The Beacon – Pot and Kettle – Neglectful Edward – Thunder at Night – Wild Strawberries – Vain and Careless – The Sewing Basket – 'The General Elliott' – A Lover Since Childhood – The Bedpost – Black Horse Lane – Apples and Water – The Finding of Love – II: 1919 – Over the Brazier – The Dead Fox Hunter – Dead Cow Farm – Corporal Stare – Goliath and David – Not Dead – The Last Post – Familiar Letter to Siegfried Sassoon – The Leveller – Escape – The Bough of Nonsense – The Legion – Two Fusiliers – To R. N. – An Occasion – A Dedication of Three Hats – III: Ghost Raddled – The Stake – The Pier-Glass – Reproach – The Gnat – Down – Incubus – The Hills of May – The Coronation Murder: I and II – Lost Love – Return – Ancestors – Richard Roe and John Doe – Burrs and Brambles – Song of Contrariety – The Ridge-Top – Unicorn and White Doe – Sullen Moods – Children of Darkness – The Dialecticians – Old Wives' Tales – Christmas Eve – The Lands of Whipperginny – The Witches' Cauldron – The Snake and the Bull – A Fight to the Death – In Procession – A Crusader – The Turn of a Page – An Idyll of Old Age – A Valentine – The Poet's Birth – The Lord Chamberlain Tells of a Famous Meeting – I am the Star of Morning – A Forced Music – Full Moon – IV: The Bowl and Rim – The Avengers – A History of Peace – Hemlock – Myrrhina – Twin Souls – Diplomatic Relations – The North Window – Attercop: the All-Wise Spider – Witches – Essay on Continuity – Knowledge of God – The Rainbow and the Sceptic – Alice – From Our Ghostly Enemy – The Figure-Head – Ovid in Defeat – To an Editor – The College Debate – A Letter from Wales – The Presence – The Clipped Stater – The Poetic State – Essay on Knowledge – The Corner Knot – Virgil the Sorcerer – To M. in India – V: The Marmosite's Miscellany: with Notes – The Moment of Weakness – Pygmalion to Galatea – In Committee – A Letter to a Friend – This is Noon – The Time of Day – Blonde or Dark? – Boots and Bed – The Taint – Dumpling's Address to Gourmets – Sorrow – The Nape of the Neck – A Visit to Stratford – Pure Death – The Cool Web – Bibliography

A23b. Second English impression (1928):

POEMS | (1914–1926) | By | ROBERT GRAVES | LONDON | WILLIAM HEINEMANN, LTD. | MCMXXVIII

Collation: a^2 b^4 B–O^8 P^4 Q^2, 116 leaves.

Remainder differs from A23a as follows: p.[iv] has impression and printer's notices; pp.[219] – [220] blank.

18.7 × 12.6 cm. Bulk: 1.9/2.4 cm. Paper and binding as A23a; labels are grey-blue with legends as A23a.

Price: 7s. 6d. Number of copies unknown. Published in June 1928.

A23c. American issue (1929):

POEMS | (1914–1926) | By | ROBERT GRAVES | GARDEN CITY NEW YORK | DOUBLEDAY, DORAN & COMPANY | 1929

Collation: [*a*]² *b*⁴ B−O⁸ P⁴ Q², 116 leaves.

Remainder differs from A23b as follows: p.[iv] has printing notice only.

18.0 × 11.6 cm. Bulk: 2.4/2.9 cm. Cream-white laid paper; all edges trimmed. Cream wove endpapers. Bound in maroon cloth; back blank; cream label on front: [rectangular light rule box enclosing all:] *Collected Poems* | 1914−1926 | [rule] | ROBERT GRAVES; cream label on spine: [rectangular single rule box enclosing all:] *Collected* | *Poems* | 1914 | 1926 | [rule] | ROBERT | GRAVES

Price: $2.50. Number of copies unknown. Published 13 September 1929 in cream dust-jacket printed in blue.

Notes: A23a−c were all printed by The Westminster Press, London; but A23a and A24 have 'all', A23b−c have 'All' at p.v, l. 14; and pp.v/[vi], xi/xii and 217/[218] register differently in A23b and A23c, though the material is the same. These differences all occur in preliminary or final matter.

A24   POEMS (1914−1927)   1927

First edition:

POEMS | (1914−1927) | By | ROBERT GRAVES | LONDON | WILLIAM HEINEMANN, LTD. | MCMXXVII

Collation: *a*² *b*⁴ B−P⁸ Q⁴, 122 leaves.

p.[i] POEMS (1914−1927); p.[ii] *This edition is limited to One Hundred* | *and Fifteen copies of which One Hun-* | *dred are for sale.* | *This is No.* [number] | [signature of Graves]; p.[iii] title-page; p.[iv] printer's notice; p.v NOTE; p.[vi] TO | N. AND L.; pp.vii−xi CONTENTS; p.xii quotations (7 ll.) from Skelton; p.[1] I | 1914−20; p.[2] blank; pp.3−43 text; p.[44] blank; p.[45] II | WAR | 1915−19; p.[46] blank; pp.47−64 text; p.[65] III | MAINLY 1920−23; p. [66] blank; pp.67−118 text; p.[119] IV | MAINLY 1923−25; p. [120] blank; pp.121−178 text; p.[179] V | RECENT POEMS: 1925−26; p.[180] blank; pp.181−216 text; p.[217] VI | NINE ADDITIONAL POEMS: 1927; p.[218] blank; pp.219−227 [228 text; p.229 BIBLIOGRAPHY; P. [230] printer's notice; pp.[231]−[232] blank.

22.2 × 14.5 cm. Bulk: 1.8/2.3 cm. White laid paper; top edges only trimmed and gilt; watermarked with a unicorn and: ELLERSLIE. White laid endpapers watermarked with a crown and: Abbey Mills | Greenfield. Bound in white boards with parchment spine stamped in gold: POEMS | 1914−27 | ROBERT | GRAVES | HEINEMANN

Price: 30s. Number of copies: 115. Published in June 1927 in cream-white dust-jacket printed in blue in a plain white slipcase.

Contents: In addition to the contents of A23 the following: The Progress − Hell − The Dead Ship − O Jorrocks, I have promised − The Lost Acres − The Awkward Gardener − To a Charge of Didacticism − The Philatelist-Royal − To be Less Philosophical

A25   JOHN SKELTON (LAUREATE)   [1927]

First edition:

[rectangular heavy rule box enclosing all:] | [rectangular light rule box enclosing all:] | [rectangular broad decorative rule box enclosing all:] | [rectangular light rule box enclosing all:] | *THE AUGUSTAN BOOKS OF | ENGLISH POETRY | SECOND SERIES NUMBER TWELVE* | [rule] | JOHN SKELTON | (LAUREATE) | 1460(?)– 1529 | [rule] | *LONDON: ERNEST BENN, LTD.* | *BOUVERIE HOUSE, FLEET STREET*

Collation: l6 leaves, unsigned, stapled twice at centre.

p.[i] title-page; p.[ii] publisher's advertisement; p.iii NOTE; p.[iv] blank; p.v CONTENTS; p.[vi] blank; [errata slip tipped between [vi] and 7]; pp.7–31 text; p.[32] publisher's advertisements.

22.1 × 14.0 cm. Bulk 0.2 cm. White wove paper; all edges trimmed. Pp.[i] – [ii] and 31 – [32] serve as covers.

Price: 6d. Number of copies unknown. Published October 1927.

Contents: Note – Jane Scroop's Lament for Philip Sparrow – Skelton's Address to Philip Sparrow – From 'On the Death of King Edward the Fourth' – To Mistress Isabel Pennell – From 'The Manner of the World Nowadays' – Prayer to the Father of Heaven – From 'Speak, Parot' – Lullay, Lullay, Like a Child – From 'The Tunning of Elinour Rumming' – To His Wife – Woefully Arrayed

Notes: The first issue lacks the errata slip and contains these three misprints: p.14, l. 3--[blank slug imprinted in front of line; p.22, n. 10--[broken "c" in "can"; p.28-- broken "f" in the title. The second issue contains the errata slip and corrects the first two misprints.

Graves wrote the note (p.iii) and selected and modernised the poems.

A26   LAWRENCE AND THE ARABS   [1927]

a. First edition:

LAWRENCE AND THE | ARABS | *By* | ROBERT GRAVES | [publisher's emblem] | ILLUSTRATIONS EDITED BY | ERIC KENNINGTON | MAPS BY | HERRY PERRY | LONDON | JONATHAN CAPE 30 BEDFORD SQUARE

Collation: [A]⁸ B–2E⁸ 2F⁴, 228 leaves.

p.[i] LAWRENCE AND THE ARABS; p.[ii] quotation (2 ll.) from Jeremiah; p.[1] title-page; p.[2] publication and printer's notices; pp.3–4 LIST OF ILLUSTRATIONS; pp.5–7 INTRODUCTION; p. [8] blank; p.[9] LAWRENCE AND THE ARABS; p.[10] blank; pp. 11–437 text; pp.438–448 appendices; pp.449–454 INDEX. Illustrations face pp.[1], 48, 60, 72, 92, 118, 142, 156, 164, 178, 196, 212, 226, 254, 260, 274, 278, 298, 308, 326, 336, 342, 346, 358, 370, 386, 402, and 428.

20.0 × 13.6 cm. Bulk: 3.0/3.5 cm. White wove paper; all edges trimmed. White wove endpapers. Bound in mustard-orange cloth; front blank; back blind-stamped with publisher's emblem; spine stamped in gold: LAWRENCE | AND THE |

ARABS | [four diamonds in diamond shape] | ROBERT | GRAVES | JONATHAN CAPE

Price: 7s. 6d. Number of copies: 60,000. Published in early November 1927 in white dust-jacket printed in black and blue-green.

Note: This edition had four print runs from October through December of 1927 and the total of all these runs is the figure given above.

Many copies have an order blank for Doughty's *Arabia Deserta* tipped in between pp.448 and 449.

Impressions: 2nd , November 1927; 3rd, November 1927 (in slick brown cloth); 4th, November 1927; 5th 'early' 1928 (50,000 copies).

Carl Hahn reports a binding in deep yellow.

Seven of the illustrations are by Eric Kennington.

This book has been translated into French, German and Japanese.

A26b. First American edition (1928):

LAWRENCE | AND THE ARABIAN | ADVENTURE | By | ROBERT GRAVES | ILLUSTRATIONS BY ERIC KENNINGTON | [rule] | DOUBLEDAY, DORAN & COMPANY, INC. | GARDEN CITY, NEW YORK, 1928

Collation: [1] – [26]^8, 208 leaves.

pp.[i] – [ii] blank; p.[iii] LAWRENCE AND THE ARABIAN ADVENTURE|[publisher's emblem]; p.[iv] quotation (2 ll.) from Jeremiah; [frontispiece, back blank, photograph of Kennington bust]; p.[v] title-page; p.[vi] copyright and printer's notices; pp.[vii] – [viii] LIST OF ILLUSTRATIONS; pp.[ix] – [xi] INTRODUCTION; P.[xii] blank; p.1–400 text; pp.[401] – [404] blank. Illustrations are tipped in facing pp.32, 56, 76, 96, 116, 132, 148, 164, 176, 184, 196, 216, 224, 236, 268, 284, 296, 300, 312, 324, 336, 352, 376.

21.8 × 14.7 cm. Bulk: 3.2/3.6 cm. White wove paper; top edge only trimmed and stained red. White wove endpapers; backs blank; inner sides contain maps in red and blue; front: THE ARAB AREA *and* THE RIDE TO AKABA; back: LAWRENCE'S RIDES *und* THE CAMPAIGN IN THE NORTH. Bound in medium-brown cloth; front and back blank; spine stamped in gold: LAWRENCE | & *THE* | ARABIAN | ADVENTURE | [man with lance on camel] | ROBERT | GRAVES | DOUBLEDAY | DORAN

Price: $3.00. Number of copies: 20,000. Published 30 March 1928 in buff dust-jacket printed in red and blue.

A26c. Concise edition, Florin impression ([1934]):

LAWRENCE AND THE | ARABS | *By* | ROBERT GRAVES | Author of | Good-Bye to All That | [publisher's emblem] | [square bracket] CONCISE EDITION [square bracket] | LONDON | JONATHAN CAPE 30 BEDFORD SQUARE | AND AT TORONTO

Collation: [A]^{16} B–H^{16} I/I*$^{8/8}$, 144 leaves.

p.[1] LAWRENCE AND THE ARABS | [at lower right:] *Florin Books*; p.[2] publisher's advertisement; p.[3] title-page; p. [4] publication, publisher's and printer's notices; p.[5] Note; p.[6] blank; p.[7] map; p.[8] blank; p.[9] LAWRENCE AND THE ARABS; p.[10] blank; pp.11–94 text; p.[95] map; pp.96–146 text; p.[147] map; pp.148–232 text; p.[233] map; pp.234–288 text. A 16 pp. gathering of publisher's advertisements, on cheaper paper than the text, is sewn in at the end.

17.8 × 11.6 cm. Bulk: 1.8/2.2 cm. White wove paper; all edges trimmed. White wove endpapers. Bound in beige cloth; back blank; front stamped in brownish grey: LAWRENCE | AND THE ARABS | ROBERT GRAVES; spine stamped in brownish grey; LAW- | RENCE | AND THE | ARABS | ROBERT | GRAVES | JONATHAN | CAPE

Price: 2s. Number of copies: 10,000. Published in March 1934 in white dust-jacket printed in black and red.

Notes: There were the following impressions: 2nd, April 1934 (5,000 copies); 3rd, February 1935 (5,000 copies); 4th, May 1935 (5,000 copies); 5th, May 1935 (5,000 copies); 6th, July 1935 (5,000 copies); 7th, September 1935 (5,000 copies); 8th, January 1936 (5,000 copies); 9th, September 1937 (5,000 copies); 10th, October 1939 (2,500 copies); and 11th, October 1940 (2,500 copies). A Life and Letters impression was published in May 1935 (2,000 copies) at 4s. 6d.; it was reissued in February 1937 (1,000 copies); this impression (not seen) contained 4 maps and 8 illustrations.

A26d. Concise edition, children's impression ([1935]):

LAWRENCE | AND THE | ARABS | BY | ROBERT GRAVES | [publisher's emblem] | ILLUSTRATIONS EDITED BY | ERIC KENNINGTON | JONATHAN CAPE | THIRTY BEDFORD SQUARE | LONDON

Collation: [A]⁸ B–S⁸, 144 leaves.

p [1] LAWRENCE AND THE ARABS; p.[2] blank; p.[3] title-page; p. [4] publication, publisher's and printer's notices; p.[5] Note; p.[6] blank; p.7 LIST OF ILLUSTRATIONS; p.8 MAPS; p.[9] LAWRENCE AND THE ARABS; p.[10] map; pp.11–94 text; p.[95] map; pp.96–146 text; p.[147] map; pp.148–232 text; p.[233] map; pp.234–288 text. Illustrations face pp.[3], 28, 36, 80, 92, 122, 134, 170, 186, 206, 228, 236, 242, 250, 278, 284.

19.9 × 13.5 cm. Bulk: 2.9/3.5 cm. White wove paper; all edges trimmed. White wove endpapers. Bound in red-orange cloth; front stamped in black open type: LAWRENCE AND THE ARABS; back stamped with large publisher's emblem in black; spine stamped in black open type: LAWRENCE | AND THE | ARABS | ROBERT | GRAVES | JONATHAN | CAPE

Price: 3s.6d. Number of copies: 3,000. Published in November 1935 in white dust-jacket printed in black and green.

Note: Impressions: 2nd, December 1935 (1,000 copies); 3rd, October 1936 (1,000 copies); 4th, March 1937 (1,000 copies).

A26e. English school edition ([1940]):

[rectangular decorative rule box enclosing all:] LAWRENCE AND THE | ARABS | BY | ROBERT GRAVES | CONCISE EDITION PREPARED BY | W. T. HUTCHINS, M. A. | LONGMANS, GREEN AND CO. | LONDON . NEW YORK . TORONTO

Collation: [A]/A*⁸/⁸ B/B*–F/F*⁸/⁸, 96 leaves.

p.[i] [5 ll. flush right:] [lamp with shade on table with book open underneath] | *The Heritage of* | *Literature Series* | [rule] | SECTION A, NO. 36 | LAWRENCE AND THE ARABS; p.[ii] series advertisement; p.[iii] blank; p.[iv] cut of Lawrence; p. [v] title-page; p.[vi] publisher's notices and printer's notice; p.[vii] permission notice; p.[viii] map; pp.ix–xi PROLOGUE; p. [xii] blank; pp.1–8 text; p.[9] portrait of Feisal; p.[10] blank; pp.11–46 text; p.[47] blank; p.[48] portrait of Auda; pp.49–178 text; p.179 EPILOGUE; p.[180] blank.

16.3 × 10.9 cm. Bulk: 1.1/1.4 cm. White wove paper; all edges trimmed. White wove endpapers. Bound in dark yellow-olive cloth; front and back blank; spine stamped in gold: *Lawrence* | *and the* | *Arabs* | [series emblem, as p.[i]] | *Longmans*

Price: 1s. 6d. Number of copies unknown. Published 3 June 1940.

Note: This edition is number 36 in the Heritage of Literature Series, Section A.

A26f. First Canadian edition ([1941]):

LAWRENCE AND THE | ARABS | By | ROBERT GRAVES | Author of | *Good-bye to All That* | [square bracket] CONCISE EDITION [square bracket] | LONDON | JONATHAN CAPE 30 BEDFORD SQUARE | Published in Canada by | THOMAS NELSON AND SONS LIMITED | TORONTO

Collation: [1]^{15}] [2] – [8]^{16} [9]^{17}, 144 leaves.

p.[1] NELSON'S COLLEGIATE CLASSICS | LAWRENCE AND THE ARABS; p. [2] blank; p.[3] title-page; p.[4] publication history, copyright, printing notices; p.[5] Note by R. G.; p.[6] blank; p.[7] map; p.[8] blank; p.[9] NELSON'S COLLEGIATE CLASSICS | LAWRENCE AND THE ARABS; p.[10] blank; pp.11–288 text, with maps on pp.[95], [147], and [233].

16.8 × 11.5 cm. Bulk: 2.5/3.1 cm. White wove paper; all edges trimmed. White wove endpapers. Bound in orange cloth. Front printed in black: LAWRENCE | AND THE ARABS | ROBERT GRAVES; back blank. Spine printed in black: LAW- | RENCE | AND THE | ARABS | ROBERT | GRAVES | NELSON

Price: Undetermined. Number of copies unknown. Published in 1941.

Note: Impressions. 2nd, 1942; 3rd, 1946.

A26g. Australian school edition ([1942]):

[all within a border of open "S" signs:] LAWRENCE AND THE | ARABS | BY | ROBERT GRAVES | CONCISE EDITION PREPARED BY | W. T. HUTCHINS M.A. | LONGMANS, GREEN AND CO. | LONDON :: NEW YORK :: TORONTO

Collation: [A]^{16} B–D^{16} E^{18}, 72 leaves.

pp.[i] – [viii] as A26e; pp.[ix] –x PROLOGUE; pp.1–153 text; p. [154] EPILOGUE.

18.4 × 12.4 cm. Bulk: 1.1 cm. White wove paper; all edges trimmed. White wove endpapers. Bound in tan simulated cloth flexible covers; back blank; front printed in brown: *Lawrence and* | *the Arabs* | [lamp] | LONGMANS

Price: 3s. Number of copies unknown. Published in 1942.

Notes: This edition was entirely set and printed in Australia by Brown, Prior, Anderson of Melbourne.

The illustrations, which are integrated into the text, are by Evelyn Faulds.

A27   THE LESS FAMILIAR NURSERY RHYMES   [1927]

First edition:

[rectangular heavy rule box enclosing all:] | [rectangular light rule box enclosing all:] | [rectangular broad decorative rule box enclosing all:] | [rectangular light rule box enclosing all:] | *THE AUGUSTAN BOOKS OF* | *ENGLISH POETRY* | *SECOND SERIES NUMBER FOURTEEN* | [rule] | THE LESS FAMILIAR | NURSERY | RHYMES | [rule] | *LONDON: ERNEST BENN LTD.* | *BOUVERIE HOUSE, FLEET STREET*

Collation: 16 leaves, unsigned, stapled twice at centre.
    p.[i] title-page; p.[ii] publisher's advertisements; pp.iii–iv FOREWORD; pp.v–vi INDEX; pp.7–31 text; p.[32] publisher's advertisements.
    22.1 × 13.9 cm. Bulk: 0.3 cm. White wove paper; all edges trimmed. Pp. –[ii] and 31–[32] serve as covers.

Price: 6d. Number of copies unknown. Published in November 1927.

Note: Graves wrote the foreword (pp.iii–iv) and selected the poems.

A28   A SURVEY OF MODERNIST POETRY   1927

a. First edition:

A SURVEY OF | MODERNIST POETRY | BY | LAURA RIDING AND ROBERT GRAVES | [publisher's emblem] | LONDON | WILLIAM HEINEMANN LTD. | 1927

Collation: [A]^8 B–S^8 T^4, 148 leaves.
    p.[1] A SURVEY OF | MODERNIST POETRY; p.[2] blank; p.[3] title-page; p.[4] printer's notice; p.[5] NOTE; p.[6] blank; p.[7] CONTENTS; p.[8] blank; pp.9–291 text; p.[292] blank; pp.293–295 INDEX OF | PRINCIPAL PROPER NAMES; p.[296] blank.
    19.0 × 12.4 cm. Bulk: 2.5/2.9 cm. White laid paper; top and fore-edges trimmed. White laid endpapers. Bound in cream boards printed with a red design in columns; black cloth spine stamped in gold: A SURVEY | OF MODERNIST | POETRY | LAURA RIDING | AND | ROBERT GRAVES | HEINEMANN

Price: 7s.6d. Number of copies: 1,000. Published 3 November 1927.

Contents: I. Modernist Poetry and the Plain Reader's Rights – II. The Problem of Form and Subject-Matter in Modernist Poetry – III. William Shakespeare and E. E. Cummings: A Study in Original Punctuation and Spelling – IV. The Unpopularity of Modernist Poetry with the Plain Reader – V. Modernist Poetry and Dead Movements – VI. The Making of the Poem – VII. Modernist Poetry and Civilization – VIII. Variety in Modernist Poetry – IX. The Humorous Element in Modernist Poetry – X. Conclusion – Index

Note: Both A28a and A28b were printed in Great Britain.
    Scholarly Press, St. Clair Shores, Minnesota, issued a photographic reprint in 1972.

A28b. American issue (1928):

A SURVEY OF | MODERNIST POETRY | BY | LAURA RIDING AND ROBERT GRAVES | *Garden City, New York* | DOUBLEDAY, DORAN & COMPANY, INC. | 1928

Collation: as A28a.
18.7 × 12.5 cm. Bulk: 2.3/2.9 cm. White laid paper; all edges trimmed. White laid endpapers. Bound in grey boards; front and back blank; red cloth spine with grey paper label printed in orange: [decorative rule] | A SURVEY | OF MODERNIST | POETRY | [decorative rule] | LAURA RIDING | *and* | ROBERT GRAVES | [decorative rule]

Price: $2.00. Number of copies: 500. Published 28 September 1928.

Note: The title-page is a cancel.

A28c. Second English impression (1929):

A SURVEY OF | MODERNIST POETRY | BY | LAURA RIDING AND ROBERT GRAVES | [publisher's emblem] | LONDON | WILLIAM HEINEMANN LTD. | 1929

Collation: as A28a, except p.[4] has impression and printer's notices.
18.9 × 12.3 cm. Bulk: 2.4/2.9 cm. Cream-white laid paper; top and fore-edges trimmed. Bound in black cloth; front and back blank; spine stamped in gold: A SURVEY | OF MODERNIST | POETRY | LAURA RIDING | AND | ROBERT GRAVES | HEINEMANN

Price: 7s. 6d. Number of copies unknown. Published in September 1929 in cream dust-jacket printed in red.

A29   A PAMPHLET AGAINST ANTHOLOGIES [1928]

a. First edition:

A Pamphlet | AGAINST ANTHOLOGIES | by | LAURA RIDING | AND ROBERT GRAVES | [publisher's emblem] | JONATHAN CAPE | THIRTY BEDFORD SQUARE | LONDON

Collation: [A]⁸ B–M⁸, 96 leaves.
p.[1] A PAMPHLET AGAINST ANTHOLOGIES; p.[2] blank; p.[3] title-page; p.[4] publication and printer's notices; p.5 CONTENTS; p.[6] blank; pp.7–8 FOREWORD; p.[9] A PAMPHLET AGAINST ANTHOLOGIES; p.[10] blank; pp.11–192 text.
19.1 × 12.8 cm. Bulk: 1.5/2.0 cm. White wove paper; all edges trimmed. White wove endpapers. Bound in mustard-brown cloth; front blank; back blind-stamped with publisher's emblem; spine stamped in gold: PAMPHLET | AGAINST | ANTHOLOGIES | [leaf device] | RIDING | & GRAVES | JONATHAN CAPE

Price: 7s. 6d. Number of copies: 1,500. Published in July 1928 in cream dust-jacket printed in red and black.

Contents: Foreword – The True Anthology and the Trade Anthology – Anthologies and the Book Market – The Anthologist in Our Midst – The Popular Poem and the Popular Reader – The Perfect Modern Lyric – 'Best Poems' – Poetry and Anthology Labels – Anthologies and the Living Poet – Conclusion

Note: Both A29a and A29b were printed in Great Britain.

A29b. American issue (1928):

A Pamphlet | AGAINST ANTHOLOGIES | by | LAURA RIDING | AND ROBERT GRAVES | GARDEN CITY, NEW YORK | DOUBLEDAY, DORAN & COMPANY, INC. | 1928

Collation: as A29a, except p.[4] has printer's notice only.
    Size, bulk, paper as A29a. Bound in buff boards with wine cloth spine; front and back blank; white label on spine printed in red: [decorative rule] | A | PAMPHLET | AGAINST | ANTHOLOGIES | [decorative rule] | RIDING | *and* | GRAVES | [decorative rule]

Price: $2.00. Number of copies unknown. Published in January 1929 in light grey dust-jacket printed in red.

Note: AMS Press of New York issued a photographic reprint on 21 May 1970 of 300 copies at the price of $2.00. Although this does not constitute either another edition or state, it may be thought of as an extension of A29b, the American issue of 1928.

A30　MRS FISHER　1928

a. First edition:

MRS FISHER | OR | THE FUTURE OF HUMOUR | BY | ROBERT GRAVES | *Author of 'Lars Porsena, or the Future of* | *Swearing',* etc. | LONDON | KEGAN PAUL, TRENCH, TRUBNER & CO., LTD. | NEW YORK: E. P. DUTTON & CO. | 1928

Collation: [B]⁸ C–G⁸, 48 leaves, plus 10 leaves publisher's advertisements.
    p.[1] MRS FISHER | OR | THE FUTURE OF HUMOUR; p.[2] series advertisements; p.[3] title-page; p.[4] quotation (6 ll.) from Skelton and printer's notice; pp.5–95 text; p.[96] blank; pp. [1] 2–20 publisher's advertisements.
    15.8 × 10.8 cm. Bulk: 1.1/1.5 cm. White laid paper; all edges trimmed. White wove endpapers. Bound in plum boards; back blank; front has white paper label: [rectangular heavy rule box enclosing all:] | [rectangular light rule box enclosing all:] | MRS FISHER | OR | THE FUTURE OF HUMOUR | *ROBERT GRAVES*; spine has white label: [heavy rule] | [light rule] | MRS | FISHER | GRAVES | [light rule] | *Kegan Paul* | [heavy rule]

Price: 2s. 6d. Number of copies undetermined. Published in November 1928 in white dust-jacket printed in black.

Notes: A second impression (November 1928) differs in that the quotation from Skelton appears on the title-page between ll. 7 and 8 of the above; p.[4] has publication data and printer's notice. It measures 15.2 × 10.8 cm. Bulk: 0.9/1.4 cm.

White wove paper and white wove endpapers. Bound in green cloth. Front contains white paper label printed in black: Mrs Fisher | of | THE FUTURE OF | HUMOUR | By | ROBERT GRAVES | *Author of 'Lars Porsena, or the Future of* | *Swearing,' etc.* Back blank; upper spine contains white paper label printed in black: MRS | FISHER | [rule] | Graves. No dust-jacket. This impression was printed by Stephen Austin & Sons, Ltd., Hertford.

Haskell House issued a photographic facsimile of this edition in 1971.

A30b. Second American impression (1928):

MRS FISHER | OR | THE FUTURE OF HUMOUR | BY | ROBERT GRAVES | *Author of "Lars Porsena, or the Future of* | *Swearing", etc.* | [6 ll. quotation from Skelton] | [remainder as A30a]

Collation: As A30, without publisher's advertisements.

pp.[1]–[3] as A30a; p.[4] publisher's and printer's notices; pp. 5–[96] as A30a.

15.7 × 10.6 cm. Bulk: 0.9/1.5 cm. White laid paper; all edges trimmed. White wove endpapers. Bound in apple-green cloth; back blank; front has white paper label printed in black: Mrs Fisher | or | THE FUTURE OF | HUMOUR | By | ROBERT GRAVES | *Author of "Lars Porsena, or the Future of* | *Swearing", etc.* Spine has white paper label printed in black: MRS | FISHER | [rule] | Graves

Price: $1.00. Number of copies unknown. Published in November 1928 in white dust-jacket printed in black and green.

A30.1   THE SEIZIN PRESS   1929

First edition:

THE SEIZIN PRESS | [drawing by Len Lye] | NECESSARY BOOKS | Our plan is to print necessary books | by various particular people. A neces- | sary book may be either a Trouble or a | No Trouble book. A Trouble book | is necessary trouble taking and trouble | making. A No Trouble book is neces- | sary no trouble taking and no trouble | making. | 1929

Collation: A folio sheet folded twice, four leaves connected at the top.

p.[1] title-page; pp.[2]–[3] blank; p.[4] list of Seizin books One to Four; p.[5] BETWEEN DARK AND DARK | [page number '9' at bottom, though it actually appears as page 1 of *Poems 1929*, Seizin Three, 1929]; pp.[6]–[7] blank; p.[8] announcement of forthcoming Seizin books and directions for ordering.

21.8 × 14.8 cm. Bulk: 0.6 cm. White laid paper watermarked with hammer and anvil.

Price: Gratis. Number of copies unknown. Published in 1929.

Note: Printed on Riding and Graves' Seizin press at Hammersmith in 1929. This is the first printing of 'Between Dark and Dark.'

A31 THE SHOUT 1929

First edition:

[rectangular heavy rule box enclosing all:] | [rectangular light rule box enclosing all:] | THE SHOUT | by | ROBERT GRAVES | *being Number Sixteen of* | *The Woburn Books* | [publisher's emblem] | *Published at London in 1929 by* | ELKIN MATHEWS & MAROT

Collation: [A]⁴ B−D⁴, 16 leaves.

p.[1] title-page; p.[2] Five hundred and thirty numbered | copies of this story have been set in | Monotype Pica Bodoni, and printed | by Robert MacLehose & Co. Ltd., at the University Press, Glasgow; | Nos. 1−500 only are for sale and | Nos. 501−530 for presentation. | This is copy No. [number written in by hand] | [signature of Graves]; pp.3−31 [32] text.

19.1 × 13.8 cm. Bulk: 0.5/0.8 cm. Cream wove paper; all edges untrimmed. Grey laid endpapers printed with repeated plume design in purple; inner sides of free endpapers blank. Bound in grey boards printed with wave design in purple; on front cover: THE | SHOUT | By | ROBERT GRAVES; on back: THE WOBURN BOOKS | JGP '28

Price: 6s. Number of copies: 530. Published in November 1929, in grey dust-jacket printed in purple as cover.

Note: A facsimile of this edition was published by R. West in 1973.

A32 GOOD-BYE TO ALL THAT [1929]

a. First edition:

GOOD-BYE TO ALL THAT | An Autobiography | BY | ROBERT GRAVES | [publisher's emblem] | JONATHAN CAPE | THIRTY BEDFORD SQUARE | LONDON

Collation: [A]⁸ B−2E⁸, 224 leaves.

p.[1] GOOD-BYE TO ALL THAT; p.[2] list of works by Graves; [portrait plate, facing title-page, back blank]; p.[3] title-page; p.[4] publication and printer's notices; p.[5] MY DEDICATION IS | AN EPILOGUE; p.[6] blank; pp.7−9 LIST OF ILLUSTRATIONS; p.[10] WORLD'S END; p.[11] GOOD-BYE TO ALL THAT; p.[12] blank; pp.13−437 text, with illustrations facing pp. 152, 190, 246, 262, 296, and 364, all backs blank, and double fold-out plate between pp.322/323, back blank; p.[438] blank; pp.439−443 text; p.[444] blank; pp.445−448 Dedicatory Epilogue | to | Laura Riding   −

20.9 × 13.2 cm. Bulk: 3.0/3.5 cm. White wove paper; top and fore-edges trimmed. White wove endpapers. Bound in salmon cloth; front blank; back blind-stamped with publisher's emblem; spine stamped in gold: GOOD-BYE | TO | ALL THAT | [four diamonds in diamond shape] | ROBERT | GRAVES | JONATHAN CAPE

Price: 10s. 6d. Number of copies: 5,000 [but, see *Notes*]. Published on 18 November

1929 in white photographic dust-jacket printed in black; the photography is by Alfred Cracknell; design is by Len Lye.

Note: Expurgations in later states consist of a short passage on p.290 and a poem by Siegfried Sassoon consisting of the last 4 ll. on p.341 and all of pp.342–343. Faber and Foyle, *Modern First Editions: Points and Values (Second Series)* (London: Foyle, 1931) suggest that less than 100 copies of the first state exist.

This book has been translated into French, German, Spanish and Swedish.

The nature of the changes between A32a and A32b seem to indicate that A32a is merely a pre-publication state, rather than a true first edition; nevertheless, A32a is generally considered the collector's impression.

A32b. Second state (expurgated) ([1929]):

Title-page as A32a.

Collation: as A32a.

Remainder as A32a except that p.290 has a deletion marked by 3 asterisks in a V-shape; p.341 has 3 asterisks in a V-shape at the bottom; pp.342–343 have 4 asterisks in a diamond shape; and there is an erratum slip tipped in between pp.398/399.

Otherwise as A32a.

Note: It would appear that 5,000 copies of this state were printed in November of 1929.

A32c. Second impression ([1929])

Title-page as A32a.

Collation as A32a.

Remainder as A32a except: pp.290–295 reset; as A32a to p.341; then: pp.341–435 text; p.[436] blank; pp.437–441 text; p. [442] blank; pp.443–446 DEDICATORY EPILOGUE | TO | LAURA RIDING; pp.[447]–[448] blank.

Size, bulk and paper as A32a. Binding: red cloth; otherwise as A32a.

Price: 10s 6d. Number of copies: 30,000. Published in November 1929 with dust-jacket as A32a.

Notes: Impressions: 3rd, November 1929; 4th, November 1929; 5th, December 1929.

An erratum slip (as A32b) is tipped in between pp.396/397. Illustrations face as in A32a.

This book sold 20,000 copies in the first week and 30,000 by December.

A32d. First American edition ([1930]):

GOOD-BYE TO ALL THAT | An Autobiography | BY | ROBERT GRAVES | [publisher's emblem] | NEW YORK | JONATHAN CAPE & HARRISON SMITH

Collation: [1] – [27]⁸ [28]⁴, 220 leaves.

p.[i] GOOD-BYE TO ALL THAT; p.[ii] publisher's notice and list of works by Graves; [portrait plate, facing title-page, back blank]; p.[iii] title-page; p.[iv] copyright, printing, printer's and binder's notices; p.[v] MY DEDICATION IS | AN EPILOGUE; p.[vi] blank; pp.[vii]–[viii] LIST OF ILLUSTRATIONS; p.[ix]

WORLD'S END; p.[x] blank; pp.1–426 text, with illustrations facing pp.141, 179, 235, 251, 284, 308 (foldout) and 350; pp.427–430 DEDICATORY EPILOGUE | TO | LAURA RIDING

21.0 × 15.0 cm. Bulk: 3.0/3.7 cm. White wove paper; top edges only trimmed and stained black. White laid endpapers. Bound in maroon cloth; front and back blind-stamped with double-rule rectangular box with double-rule diagonals with publisher's emblem in centre in double rule circle; spine stamped: [heavy rule] | [dashed rule] | GOOD-BYE | TO ALL THAT | [dash] | ROBERT GRAVES | [dashed rule] | [heavy rule] | Jonathan Cape | Harrison Smith

Price: $3.00. Number of copies undetermined. Published in January 1930 in white dust-jacket as A32a; printed in December 1929.

Notes: Impressions: 2nd, December 1929; 3rd, December 1929.
No American edition seen contains the passages expurgated from A32a.

A32e. Life and Letters impression ([1931]):

THE LIFE AND LETTERS SERIES NO. 22 | [swelled rule] | ROBERT GRAVES | GOOD-BYE | TO ALL THAT | An Autobiography | With eight illustrations | London – JONATHAN CAPE – Toronto

Collation: as A32c.
p.[1] [entire at right:] THE LIFE & LETTERS | SERIES, VOLUME 22 | GOOD-BYE | TO ALL THAT | [series emblem]; p.[2] series notice; [frontispiece]; p.[3] title-page; p.[4] publication, publisher's, printer's and papermaker's notices; pp.[7]8–9 LIST OF ILLUSTRATIONS; then as A32c.
19.9 × 13.5 cm. Bulk: 3.0/3.6 cm. White wove paper; all edges trimmed. White wove endpapers. Bound in green cloth; front stamped in gold: [double angular wavy rule] GOOD-BYE [double angular wavy rule] | [rule as before] TO ALL THAT [rule as before] | [at left: series emblem]; back blind-stamped with publisher's emblem; spine stamped in gold: GOOD-BYE | TO ALL | THAT | [series emblem] | ROBERT | GRAVES | JONATHAN CAPE

Price: 4s. 6d. Number of copies: 6,000. Published in July 1931 in a white dust-jacket printed in green.

Notes: Up to 36 pp. of publisher's advertisements are bound in at the end.
Cape also reports a 7s. 6d. issue (not seen) made up of 500 copies from A32c and 350 copies from A32e published in July 1941.

A32f. Blue Ribbon impression ([1931]):

GOOD-BYE TO ALL THAT | An Autobiography | BY | ROBERT GRAVES | [publisher's emblem] | BLUE RIBBON BOOKS | NEW YORK

Collation: as A32d.
p.[i] GOOD-BYE TO ALL THAT; p.[ii] publisher's notice and list of books by Graves; p.[iii] blank; p.[iv] portrait; p.[v] title-page; p.[vi] copyright, impression and printer's notices; p.[vii] MY DEDICATION IS | AN EPILOGUE; p.[viii] blank; then as A32d; no plates.
20.2 × 13.9 cm. Bulk: 2.7/3.4 cm. White wove paper; all edges trimmed. White

wove endpapers. Bound in dark blue cloth; front and back blank; spine stamped: [heavy rule] | [dashed rule] | GOOD-BYE | TO ALL THAT | [dash] | ROBERT GRAVES | [dashed rule] | [heavy rule] | BLUE RIBBON BOOKS

Price: $1.00. Number of copies unknown. Published in 1931.

Note: Printed by the Cornwall Press.

A32g. Second edition (revised) (1957):

Good-bye | to All That | NEW EDITION, REVISED, | WITH A PROLOGUE | AND AN EPILOGUE | Robert Graves | DOUBLEDAY ANCHOR BOOKS | DOUBLEDAY & COMPANY, INC. | GARDEN CITY, NEW YORK, 1957

Collation: 180 leaves, glued at spine.
    p.[i] Good-bye to All That; p.[ii] blank; pp.[iii] – [iv] list of books by Graves; p.[v] title-page; p.[vi] designer's, photographer's, typographer's, LC card, copyright and printing notices; p.[vii] Prologue; p.[viii] blank; p.[ix] Good-bye to All That; p.[x] blank; pp.[1]2–243 text, with pp. [12, 17, 22, 29, 36, 41, 47, 61, 67, 82, 91, 106, 119, 141, 166, 181, 192, 199, 209, 226, 238, 245, 255, 265, 279, 291, 297, 312, 320, 324, 334] unnumbered; pp.[344]345–347 Epilogue; pp. [348] – [350] blank.
    18.1 × 10.5 cm. Bulk: 2.0 cm. White wove paper; all edges trimmed. Bound in white paper covers printed in red, black and blue-grey; front has solid red box upper left, at upper left of which is: A123; below the box is the photo of Graves used on the A32a dust-jacket; below this is a solid blue-grey box reading: *An autobiography* | [publisher's emblem] *A Doubleday Anchor Book*; right-hand side of cover appears as a white column, inside of which: 95c | *Good-* | *bye* | *to* | *All* | *That* | *by Robert Graves* | *A Revised Second Edition*; the last two lines are continuous with the last two lines of the left-hand column. The back has a white column at left, inside of which: *Good-bye* | [blurb of 28 ll.] | *An autobiography*; the right side has a solid blue-grey box at top, inside of which: *to All That* continuous with the rest of the title; below is a photograph of Graves *c.* 1957 in a pose similar to that on front; below this is a solid red box inside of which: *by Robert Graves* | [publisher's emblem] *A Doubleday Anchor Book.* The spine has a red band at top, inside which: *Robert Graves*; below which is white band inside of which: *Good-bye to All That* [from top to bottom]; below is a blue-grey band, inside of which, upright: *Anchor* | *A123*

Price: $0.95. Number of copies: 25,000. Published 7 November 1957.

Notes: The jacket design is by George Giusti; the later photograph is by Susan Greenberg. The 'revisions' make substantially a new book.
    Impression: 2nd, (copies:10,000); later this impression was published in a reduced trim size which measured 17.6 × 10.4 cm., though the bulk is the same; the cover is printed in wine, brown, and pink and the front is a reproduction of "Captain Robert Graves" by Eric Kennington, courtesy of the National Museum of Wales, Cardiff; the imprint now reads: DOUBLEDAY ANCHOR BOOKS | DOUBLEDAY & COMPANY, INC. | GARDEN CITY, NEW YORK, [stet: YORK,]; and there is an extra leaf at the front of the book and three extra leaves at the rear of the book, all blank; the price at this point was $5.95.

A32h. Second English edition (revised) ([1957]):

ROBERT GRAVES | *GOODBYE* | *TO ALL THAT* | *New edition, revised,* | *with a prologue and epilogue* | [publisher's emblem] | CASSELL & COMPANY LTD | LONDON

Collation: [A]⁸ B–T⁸ U⁶, 152 leaves.

p.[i] *GOODBYE TO ALL THAT*; p.[ii] list of books by Graves; p.[iii] title-page; p.[iv] publisher's, copyright and printer's notices; p.v LIST OF ILLUSTRATIONS; p.[vi] blank; p.vii PROLOGUE; p.[viii] blank; pp.1–303 text; pp.304–306 EPILOGUE; pp.[307]–[308] blank; plates, printed on both sides, appear between pp.88/89, 104/105, 216/217 and 232/233.

21.6 × 13.5 cm. Bulk: 2.5/3.1 cm. White wove paper; all edges trimmed. White wove endpapers. Bound in black cloth; front and back blank; spine stamped in gold: ROBERT | GRAVES | Goodbye | to All That | CASSELL

Price: 21s. Number of copies: 6,027. Published 14 November 1957 in white dust-jacket printed in black and yellow.

Note: Impressions: 2nd, May 1958 (2,001 copies); 3rd, November 1961 (1,512 copies); 4th, 1966; 5th, 1969.

Octagon Press issued a photographic reprint of this edition in 1980.

A32i. Third English edition (revised) ([1960]):

ROBERT GRAVES | [swelled rule] | *Goodbye to All That* | PENGUIN BOOKS

Collation: [A]¹⁶ B–I¹⁶, 144 leaves.

p.[1] PENGUIN BOOKS | 1443 | GOODBYE TO ALL THAT | ROBERT GRAVES | [publisher's emblem]; p.[2] blank; p.[3] title-page; p.[4] publisher's, copyright and printer's notices; p.[5] LIST OF ILLUSTRATIONS; p.[6] blank; P. [7] PROLOGUE; p.[8] blank; pp. 9–144 text; [9 pp.illustrations]; pp.145–278 [279] text; pp. 280–281 [282] EPILOGUE; pp.[283]–[288] publisher's advertisements.

17.9 × 11.0 cm. Bulk: 1.4 cm. White wove paper; all edges trimmed. Bound in white paper covers printed in pink, grey and black.

Price: 3s. 6d. Number of copies: 40,000. Published 24 March 1960.

Note: Impressions: 2nd, 1967; 3rd, 1972; 4th, 1973. Reprintings listed by publisher: 1961, 1963, 1965, 1966, 1967, 1969, 1970, 1971 (twice), 1972, 1973 (twice), 1975, 1976, 1977, 1979, 1980, 1981, 1982, 1983 (twice), 1984, 1985; covers vary.

A32j. Fourth English edition (abridged) (1966):

Goodbye To | All That | ROBERT GRAVES | [publisher's emblem] | CASSELL . LONDON

Collation: [A]⁸ B–M⁸, 96 leaves.

pp.[i]–[ii] series advertisements; p.[iii] title-page; p.[iv] publisher's, copyright and printer's notices; p.[v] CONTENTS; p. [vi] blank; pp.1–170 [171] text; p.[172] blank; p.[173] POEMS BY ROBERT GRAVES; p.[174] blank; pp.175–186 text of poems.

18.0 × 12.3 cm. Bulk: 1.3/1.7 cm. White wove paper; all edges trimmed. White wove endpapers. Bound in cloth-simulated boards (white printed in light peach, grey-brown and olive).

Price: 8s. 6d. Number of copies unknown. Published September 1966 without dust-jacket.

Contents: Goodbye to All That (abridged) – Lost Love – Symptoms of Love – Woman and Tree – The Secret Land – Rocky Acres – Spoils – I'm Through with You Forever – Flying Crooked – She Tells Her Love While Half Asleep – Brother

Note: Red Lion Reader No. 1.

A32k. Fourth English edition, Second impression ([1977]):

ROBERT GRAVES | *GOODBYE* | *TO ALL THAT* | CASSELL | LONDON

Collation: [1]⁴ [2]⁸ [3] – [11]¹⁶, 156 leaves.

p.[i] *GOODBYE TO ALL THAT*; p.[ii] list of books by Graves; p.[iii] title-page; p.[iv] publisher's, copyright, rights reservation, edition, ISBN, and printer's notices; p.v PROLOGUE; p.[vi] blank; pp.1–303 text; pp.304–306 EPILOGUE.

21.5 × 13.6 cm. Bulk: 2.4/3.2 cm. Cream wove paper; all edges trimmed. White wove endpapers. Bound in black cloth; front and back blank; spine stamped in silver, top to bottom: ROBERT GRAVES Goodbye To All That Cassell

Price: Price and copies unknown. Published in 1977.

A32l. Fourth English edition (revised) (1981):

[first three lines in shaded type:] ROBERT GRAVES | GOODBYE | TO ALL THAT | Introduced by | RALEIGH TREVELYAN | [publisher's emblem] | London | THE FOLIO SOCIETY | 1981

Collation: [1] – [17]⁸ [18]⁴ [19]⁸, 148 leaves.

p.[1] *GOODBYE TO ALL THAT*; p.[2] frontispiece; p.[3] title-page; p.[4] publisher's, printer's and copyright notices; pp.[5]–6 [in shaded type:] ILLUSTRATIONS; pp.7–12 [in shaded type:] INTRODUCTION; p.[13] [in shaded type:] PROLOGUE; p.[14] blank; pp.15–292 text; pp.[37–38, 47–48, 65–66, 85–86, 105–106, 125–126, 145–146, 168, 191–192, 203–204, 229–230, 253–254, 283–284] unnumbered, being full-page black and white illustrations printed on one side only; pp.293–295 [in shaded type:] EPILOGUE; p.[296] blank.

21.7 × 14.4 cm. Bulk: 1.8/2.4 cm. White wove paper; all edges trimmed, top edge stained mustard. Olive wove endpapers, printed with map of the Western Front. Bound in silver-grey cloth with silkscreen of troops on the Western Front printed in black running from the back across spine onto front. Spine stamped in gold: GOODBYE | TO ALL | THAT | [reversed C, *, ordinary C] | ROBERT | GRAVES | [publisher's emblem]

Price: £8.50 Number of copies: 14,440, in two printings. Published in February 1981.

Note: The second printing of 4,000 copies was in January 1982.

A33   POEMS 1929   1929

First edition:

POEMS 1929 | BY | ROBERT GRAVES | [publisher's emblem] | Printed and published at The Seizin Press | 35a St. Peter's Square Hammersmith | London 1929

Collation: [1] – [3]⁸, 24 leaves.

p.[i] – [ii] pasted down as front endpaper; pp.[iii] – [iv] blank; p.[v] POEMS 1929; p.[vi] 225 numbered copies of SEIZIN THREE have been printed | and this is number [number written in by hand] | [signature of Graves]; p.[vii] title-page; p.[viii] blank; pp.1–31 text; p.[32] blank; p.33 CONTENTS; p.[34] blank; p.[35] publisher's advertisements; pp.[36] – [38] blank; pp.[39] – [40] pasted down as endpaper.

20.3 × 13.4 cm. Bulk: 0.4/0.9 cm. White laid paper; all edges trimmed; watermarked with a hammer and anvil, BS *and* seal: BRITISH HAND MADE enclosing four clasped hands. Bound in yellow-green buckram; front and back blank; spine stamped in gold, from bottom to top: POEMS 1929: ROBERT GRAVES

Price: 12s. 6d. Number of copies: 225. Published in December 1929.

Contents: Between Dark and Dark – In No Direction – In Broken Images – To the Galleys – Warning to Children – A Dismissal – Guessing Black or White – Hector – Against Kind – Midway – Green Cabbage Wit – Castle – Railway Carriage – Back Door – Front Door – The Tow-Path – Repair Shop – Landscape – Sandhills – Pavement – Return Fare – Single Fare – It Was All Very Tidy – A Sheet of Paper – Contents

Notes: "Between Dark and Dark" was published in a one sheet flier in 1929, see B17.1.

A34   TEN POEMS MORE   1930

First edition:

[3 ll. flush left:] TEN | POEMS | MORE | ROBERT |[flush right:] GRAVES | HOURS PRESS | 15, *Rue Guénégaud, PARIS* | 1930

Collation: [1]² [2]⁸ [3]². 12 leaves.

p.[i] *TEN POEMS MORE* | *by* | *Robert Graves* | *Covers* | *by* | *LEN LYE*; p.[ii] blank; p.[iii] title-page; p.[iv] CONTENTS; pp.[1] 2–17 text; p.[18] blank; p.[19] 200 COPIES OF THIS BOOK | SET BY HAND AND PRIVATELY | PRINTED ON HAND-PRESS | EACH COPY HAS BEEN | SIGNED BY THE AUTHOR | THIS IS No [number written in] | [signature of Graves]; p.[20] blank.

28.2 × 19.3 cm. Bulk: 0.3/0.7 cm. White Vidalon Haut wove paper watermarked VIDALON HAUT and a cross and IHSV in a circle; all edges untrimmed. White Vidalon Haut wove endpapers. Bound in boards covered with reproductions of photographs by Len Lye; front rocks and chicken-wire; back pebbles, rocks and basin; spine is green morocco stamped in gold from bottom to top: ROBERT GRAVES 1930 TEN POEMS MORE

Price: 30s. Number of copies: 200. Published in June 1930 in transparent paper wrapper.

Contents: To the Reader over My Shoulder – History of the Word – Interruption – Survival of Love – The Age of Certainty – The Beast – Cracking the Nut against the Hammer – The Terraced Valley – Oak, Poplar, Pine – Act V Scene 5 – Tail Piece: A Song to Make You and Me Laugh

Notes: p.7, l. ult. has 'Rep' for 'Red'; p.7 l. 3 has 'witheld' for 'withheld'; p.10, l. 5 has 'impraticable' for 'impracticable'; p.15, l. 9 has 'futher' for 'further'.

Nancy Cunard (*Book Collector* 13 [1964], 494) says that the publication date was "early spring."

A35 BUT IT STILL GOES ON [1930]

a. First edition:

BUT IT STILL GOES ON | An Accumulation | BY | ROBERT GRAVES | [publisher's emblem] | JONATHAN CAPE | LONDON & TORONTO

Collation: [A]^8 B–U^8, 160 leaves.

2 pp. blank; p.[1] BUT IT STILL GOES ON; p.[2] list of books by Graves; p.[3] title-page; p.[4] publication, publisher's and printer's notices; p.[5] CONTENTS; p.[6] blank; p.[7]FOREWORD; p.[8] blank; p.[9] epigraph (6 ll.) by Laura Riding; p.[10] blank; p.[11] PART ONE; p.[12] blank; pp.13–104 text; p.[105] PART TWO; p.[106] blank; pp.107–207 text; p.[208] blank; p.[209] PART THREE; p.[210] blank; pp.211–315 text; pp.[316] – [318] blank.

19.9 × 13.2 cm. Bulk: 2.4/2.9 cm. White wove paper; all edges trimmed. White wove endpapers. Bound in bright green cloth; front blank; back has blind-stamped publisher's emblem; spine stamped in gold: BUT IT | STILL | GOES ON | [four diamonds in diamond shape] | ROBERT | GRAVES | JONATHAN CAPE

Price: 10s. 6d. Number of copies: 5,000. Published in November 1930 in white dust-jacket printed in blue and black.

Contents: I: Postscript to 'Good-Bye to All That' – Old Papa Johnson – Avocado Pears – The Shout – II: A Journal of Curiosities, with the First and Last Chapters of 'The Autobiography of Baal' – III: But It Still Goes On: A Play

Note: As with A32, the nature of the changes between A35a and A35b seem to indicate that A35a is only a pre-publication state, rather than a true first edition; nevertheless, as with A32a, A35a is generally considered the collector's impression.

William Reese records a copy with a blueish-green dust-jacket with blue lettering.

A35b. Second state ([1930]):

Title-page, collation, paper and binding as A35a; but p.157 has no reference to *The Child She Bare* in the first paragraph and pp.157/158 is a cancel pasted to the stub of K7. Bertram Rota (Catalogue 216, 1979) records a copy in which pp.157/158 is integral (not seen).

A35c. Second impression ([1930]):

As A35b but with no cancel. Some copies of both A35a and A35c are 19.7 × 13.4 cm., the binding correspondingly smaller; but the type-page of both is the same size.

A35d. First American edition ([1931]):

[rectangular single rule box enclosing all:] | [rectangular decorative rule box enclosing all:] | But It Still Goes On | *An Accumulation* | By | ROBERT GRAVES | [publisher's emblem] | New York | Jonathan Cape & Harrison Smith

Collation: [1] – [21]⁸, 168 leaves.

pp.[i] – [ii] blank; p.[iii] BUT IT STILL GOES ON; p.[iv] list of books by Graves and publisher's notices; p.[v] title-page; p. [vi] copyright, publishing and printing notices; p.[vii] epigraph (6 ll.) by Laura Riding; p.[viii] blank; p.[ix] FOREWORD; p.[x] blank; p.[xi] CONTENTS; p.[xii] blank; p.[1] PART ONE; p.[2] blank; pp.[3] 4–98 text with pp.[49, 64, 72] unnumbered; p.[99] PART TWO; p.[100] blank; p.[101] 102–203 text with pp.[170, 192] unnumbered; p.[204] blank; p.[205] PART THREE; p.[206] blank; pp.[207] 208–319 text with pp.[209, 249, 288] unnumbered; pp.[320] – [324] blank, fore-edges unopened.

20.4 × 13.9 cm . Bulk: 2.9/3.5 cm. White wove paper; top and bottom edges trimmed; top edges stained black. White wove endpapers. Bound in dark green cloth; back blank; front blind-stamped with publisher's emblem and circular curlicues above and below; spine stamped in gold: BUT IT | STILL | GOES ON | [swirl] | ROBERT GRAVES | JONATHAN CAPE | HARRISON SMITH

Price: $2.50. Number of copies undetermined. Published 26 January 1931.

Note: p.152 of this edition contains the reference to *The Child She Bare*.

A36 POEMS 1926–1930 1931

First edition:

POEMS | 1926–1930 | BY | ROBERT GRAVES | LONDON | WILLIAM HEINEMANN LTD | MCMXXXI

Collation: [A]⁸ B–F⁸ G⁴, 52 leaves.

p.[i] POEMS 1926–1930; p.[ii] blank; p.[iii]title-page; p.[iv]publication and printer's notices; p.[v]NOTE; p.[vi]blank; p.[vii]quotation (2 ll.) from Laura Riding; p.[viii]blank; pp. [ix] – [xi] CONTENTS; p.[xii]blank; p[1] I; p.[2] blank; pp.3–14 text; pp.[15] – [16]blank; p.[17]II; p.[18]blank; pp.19–34 text; pp.[35] – [36]blank; p.[37]III; p.[38]blank; pp.39–48 text; pp.[49] – [50]blank; p.[51]IV; p.[52] blank; pp.53–74 text; pp.[75] – [76] blank; p.[77] V; p.[78] blank; pp.79–89 text; pp.[90] – [92] blank.

20.2 × 13.4 cm. Bulk: 1.1/1.6 cm. White laid paper; top edge only trimmed. White wove endpapers. Bound in maroon cloth with white cobbled design; back blank; front has maroon label: POEMS (1926–1930) | *Robert Graves*; spine has maroon label: POEMS | 1926 | to | 1930 | *Robert* | *Graves* | [rule] | Heinemann

Price: 3s. 6d. Number of copies: 1,000. Published 9 February 1931 in mauve dust-jacket printed in white and black.

Contents: Note – I: Thief – Saint – Gardener – Ship Master – Philatelist-Royal – Lift-Boy – Brother – II: Castle – Cabbage Patch – Railway Carriage – Front Door – Repair Shop – Landscape – Bay of Naples – Tap Room – Sandhills – Pavement – Quayside – III: To the Reader over My Shoulder – In Broken Images – Flying Crooked – Hector – Interruption – Act V, Scene 5 – Dismissal – Reassurance to a Satyr – IV: Hell – To be Less Philosophical – Synthetic Such – Anagrammagic – Midway – Lost Acres – In No Direction – Guessing Black or White – Warning to Children – Dragons – History of the Word – Against Kind – V: O Love in Me – Return Fare – Single Fare – It was All Very Tidy – The Terraced Valley – The Age of Certainty – The Next Time

Note: An extra spine label is tipped to p.[92] in some copies.

A37 TO WHOM ELSE? 1931

First edition:

TO WHOM ELSE? | BY | ROBERT GRAVES | The Seizin Press | Deya', Majorca | 1931

Collation: [1] – [4]⁴, 16 leaves.
    pp.[i] – [ii] blank, pasted down to front cover; pp.[iii] – [iv] blank; p.[v] A SEIZIN; p.[vi] blank; p.[vii] title-page; p.[viii] blank; pp.1–19 text; p.[20] There are 200 numbered and signed copies of | Seizin 6 hand-set and hand-printed by ourselves | on hand-made paper. The cover is by Len Lye. | [number written in] | [signature of Graves]; pp.[21] – [22] blank; p.[23] – [24] blank, pasted down to back cover.
    27.1 × 19.4 cm. Bulk: 0.3/0.8 cm. White laid paper; top edges only trimmed; watermarked: GUA [design of diamond with bars and crosses] RRO. | . Bound quarter cloth; front and back covered with paper printed in silver, black and dark blue; design on front suggests peacock's tail; design on back is circles and rectangles in rows; spine stamped in silver, from bottom to top: SEIZIN 6 TO WHOM ELSE? ROBERT GRAVES

Price: 25s. Number of copies: 200. Published in July 1931 in glassine dust-jacket attached to buff paper fold-ins tapered at corners.

Contents: Largesse to the Poor – The Felloe' d Year – On Time – On Rising Early – On Dwelling – Of Necessity – The Foolish Senses – Devilishly Disturbed – The Legs – Ogres and Pygmies – To Whom Else? – As It were Poems: I: 'In the legend of Reynard the Fox ...' – II: 'A sick girl went from house to house ...' – III: 'Dear Name, how shall I call you?' – On Portents

A38 NO DECENCY LEFT [1932]

First edition:

NO DECENCY LEFT | BY | BARBARA RICH | [publisher's emblem] | JONATHAN
CAPE | THIRTY BEDFORD SQUARE | LONDON

Collation: [A]⁸ B–S⁸, 144 leaves.

p.[1] NO DECENCY LEFT; p.[2] blank; p.[3] title-page; p.[4] edition, publisher's
printer's, paper supplier's and binder's notices; p.[5] TO | MY PUBLISHER; p.[6]
blank; p[7] NO DECENCY LEFT; p[8] blank; pp.9–287 [288] text.

19.3 × 12.5 cm. Bulk: 2.3/2.8 cm. White wove paper; top and fore-edges trimmed.
White wove endpapers. Bound in flesh cloth; front stamped in blue with a crown;
back blind-stamped with publisher's emblem; spine stamped in blue: NO |
DECENCY | LEFT | [star] | BARBARA | RICH | JONATHAN CAPE

Price: 7s. 6d. Number of copies undisclosed. Published in February 1932 in white
dust-jacket printed in blue, flesh, brown and black.

Notes: Impressions: 2nd, March 1932; 3rd, April 1932; 4th, March 1935, at 2s. 6d.
Thought to be written in collaboration with Laura Riding although she has
subsequently denied authorship (see Laura Riding Jackson, "Some
Autobiographical Corrections of Literary History," _Denver Quarterly_ 8 (1974), 29; but
also see Seymour-Smith, pp.212–213).
    Variant binding: The Library of Congress copy is bound in orange cloth; front and
back blank.

A39 THE REAL DAVID COPPERFIELD [1933]

a First edition:

THE REAL | DAVID COPPERFIELD | BY | ROBERT GRAVES | LONDON |
ARTHUR BARKER, LTD. | 21 GARRICK STREET, COVENT GARDEN

Collation: [1]⁸ 2–26⁸ 27⁴, 212 leaves.

p.[1] THE REAL | DAVID COPPERFIELD; p.[2] blank; p.[3] title-page; p.[4]
printing, copyright and printer's notices; pp. 5–9 FOREWORD; p.[10] blank;
pp.11–418 text; pp.419–424 APPENDIX.

20.4 × 13.8 cm. Bulk: 3.6/4.1 cm. White wove paper; all edges trimmed. White
wove endpapers. Bound in bright medium-blue cloth; front and back blank; spine
stamped in gold: The Real | David | Copperfield | ROBERT | GRAVES | BARKER

Price: 9s. Number of copies unknown. Published in March 1933 in light blue dust-
jacket printed in black and pink.

Note: The appendix reprints Dickens' Chapter LXII, 'A Light Shines on My Way.'
Though the texts of A39a and A39b are for the most part identical, the two books are
not identical in purpose. A39a is a rewriting to produce a 'real' book, while A39b
abandons some of the plot changes made in A39a to make merely an abridged
version of the novel for school use. Compare particularly the beginnings of the two

Chapters XXIII, the scene with Emily at the end of Chapter XXX, the end of Chapter XXXII, Chapters LIII and LIV of the two versions of the epilogue.

Mason records a variant state measuring 21.3 × 14.0 cm., bound in purplish-blue cloth, spine stamped in black, and with black (overall) and tan (spine lettering) on dust-jacket; in all other respects identical. It is possible that the binding was the binding used for most of the copies of this edition issued and that the binding described above was a trial state. However, I have retained the description of the first edition of this bibliography.

A39b. First American edition (1934):

David Copperfield | BY CHARLES DICKENS | *Condensed by Robert Graves* | *Edited by Merrill P. Paine* | DIRECTOR OF ENGLISH, | ELIZABETH, NEW JERSEY | [publisher's emblem] | NEW YORK . CHICAGO | HARCOURT, BRACE AND COMPANY | 1934

Collation: [1]⁸ [2]⁹ [3] – [4]⁸ [5] – [17]¹⁶ [18] – [20]⁸, 265 leaves.

p.[i] David Copperfield; p.[ii] map of David Copperfield's England; p.[iii] title-page; p.[iv] copyright and printing notices; p.[v] CONTENTS; p.[vi] blank; pp.[vii] viii–xxxi INTRODUCTION; p.[xxxii] blank; p.[xxxiii] David Copperfield; p. [xxxiv] blank; pp.[1] 2–474 text; pp.[475] 476–486 STUDY QUESTIONS; pp.[487]–488 GENERAL TOPICS FOR STUDY; PP. [489]–490 SUGGESTIONS FOR ADDITIONAL READING; PP. [491]–[496] blank.

18.6 × 12.5 cm. Bulk: 2.6/3.3 cm. White wove paper; all edges trimmed. White wove endpapers. Bound in blue cloth, printed in orange; on front: David | Copperfield | [decorative swirl]; back blank; on spine: David | Copperfield | BY | CHARLES DICKENS | GRAVES | [decorative dash] | PAINE | HARCOURT, BRACE | AND COMPANY

Price: $1.00. Number of copies undetermined. Published in 1934.

Note: The book was being reprinted as late as 1940. See note to A39a.

The title-page is a cancel, tipped in.

A40   POEMS 1930–1933   1933

First edition:

POEMS | 1930–1933 | BY | ROBERT GRAVES | London: | ARTHUR BARKER LTD. | 21 Garrick Street, W.C.2 | 1933

Collation: [1] – [3]⁸, 24 leaves.

p.[i] POEMS | 1930–1933; p.[ii] blank; p.[iii] title-page; p. [iv] publishing and printer's notices; p.[v] CONTENTS; p.[vi] blank; p.[vii] NOTE; p.[viii] blank; pp.1–38 text; pp. [39] – [40] blank.

21.4 × 13.6 cm. Bulk: 0.6/1.2 cm. White laid paper; all edges trimmed. White wove endpapers. Bound in grey boards with black cloth spine; back blank; front stamped: POEMS | [swelled rule] | BY ROBERT GRAVES | [swelled rule] | *Nineteen Thirty to* | *Nineteen Thirty Three*; spine stamped in gold, near top, running up: POEMS *by* Robert Graves

Price: 5s. Number of copies unknown. Published in May 1933.

Contents: Note – The Bards – Time – Ulysses – Down, Wanton, Down! – The Cell – The Succubus – Nobody – Danegeld – Trudge, Body – On Rising Early – On Necessity – Ogres and Pygmies – Music at Night – The Legs – Without Pause – Devilishly Disturbed – The Clock Men – The Commons of Sleep – The Foolish Senses – What Times are These? – The Felloe'd Year – Largesse to the Poor – On Dwelling – To Whom Else? – On Portents – As It Were Poems I, II, III.

Note: Impressions: 2nd, September 1933.

A41   OLD SOLDIERS NEVER DIE   [1933]

a. First edition:

OLD SOLDIERS | NEVER DIE | BY | PRIVATE | FRANK RICHARDS | D.C.M.,M.M. | *Late of the Second Battalion* | *Royal Welch Fusiliers* | LONDON | FABER & FABER LIMITED | 24 RUSSELL SQUARE

Collation: [A]^8 B–T^8 u/u$^{*2/8}$, 162 leaves.
  p.[1]–[2] blank; p.[3] OLD SOLDIERS NEVER DIE; p.[4] blank; p. [5] title-page; p.[6] publisher's, printer's and rights reservation notices; pp.7–8 CONTENTS; pp.9–324 text.
  18.8 × 12.0 cm. Bulk: 2.6/3.1 cm. White wove paper; all edges trimmed. White wove endpapers. Bound in orange cloth; front and back blank; spine stamped in gold: Old | Soldiers | Never | Die | Frank | Richards | Faber | and Faber

Price: 7s. 6d. Number of copies: 2,000. Published in August 1933.

Notes: This book was rewritten by Graves.
  Impressions: 2nd, September 1933 (2,000 copies); 3rd, October 1933 (2,000 copies); 4th, July 1936 (3,000 copies) at 3s. 6d.
  A paperback reprint of this edition was issued by Anthony Mott Ltd., London, in 1983. It lacks pp.[1]–[4];pp.[5]–[6] have been reset; the remainder appears to be a photographic reprinting. It was published at £4.95.

A41b. First Australian edition (1933):

OLD SOLDIERS | NEVER DIE | By | FRANK RICHARDS, D.C.M., M.M. | Late of the Second Battalion | Royal Welch Fusiliers | AUSTRALIA | ANGUS & ROBERTSON LIMITED | 89 CASTLEREAGH STREET, SYDNEY | 1933

Collation: [A]^8 B–T^8, 152 leaves.
  p.[i] OLD SOLDIERS NEVER DIE; P.[ii] blank; p.[iii] title-page; p.iv printing and copyright notices; pp.[v]–vi CONTENTS; p.[vii] OLD SOLDIERS NEVER DIE; p.[viii] blank; pp. [1] 2–295 text with pp.[6, 14, 22, 41, 53, 58, 88, 97, 116, 125, 134, 146, 160, 172, 181, 192, 201, 208, 217, 235, 242, 250, 260, 269, 276, 285, 290] unnumbered; p.296 text and printer's notice.
  18.2 × 12.2 cm. Bulk: 2.7/3.2 cm. White wove paper; all edges trimmed. White wove endpapers. Bound in bright orange cloth; back blank; front stamped in black: [heavy rule] | [light rule] | [light rule] | Old Soldiers | Never Die | Frank Richards |

[light rule] | [light rule] | [heavy rule]; spine stamped in black: [heavy rule] | [light rule] | [light rule] | Old | Soldiers | Never | Die | Frank | Richards | Angus & | Robertson | [light rule] | [light rule] | [heavy rule]

Price: 6s. Australian. Number of copies: 1,998. Published 17 November 1933.

A41c. Second English edition ([1942]):

Private FRANK RICHARDS | D.C.M., M.M. | *Late of the Second Battalion Royal Welch Fusiliers* | [rule] | OLD SOLDIERS | NEVER DIE | FABER AND FABER LIMITED | 24 Russell Square | London

Collation: [A]^{16} B–H^{16}, 128 leaves.
    p.[i] OLD SOLDIERS NEVER DIE; p.[2] author's advertisement; p. [3] title-page; p.[4] publication, printer's, rights reservation and war economy notices; pp.v–vi CONTENTS; pp.7–256 text, with p.[128] being unnumbered.
    18.3 × 12.5 cm. Bulk: 1.5 cm. White wove paper; all edges trimmed. Bound in white paper covers printed in light blue and black.

Price: 2s. Number of copies: 25,000. Published in May 1943 in white dust-jacket printed in light blue and black as cover.

A41d. First edition, fourth English impression ([1964]):

OLD SOLDIERS | NEVER DIE | BY | PRIVATE | FRANK RICHARDS | D.C.M., M.M. | *Late of the Second Battalion* | *Royal Welch Fusiliers* | *With an introduction by* | ROBERT GRAVES | LONDON | FABER & FABER LIMITED | 24 RUSSELL SQUARE

Collation: π^2 [A]^8 B–T^8 u/u$^{*2/8}$, 164 leaves.
    p.[i] OLD SOLDIERS NEVER DIE; p.[ii] blank; p.[iii] title-page; p.[iv] publication and copyright notices; pp.1–7 INTRODUCTION; p.[8] blank; pp.9–324 text.
    18.4 × 12.0 cm. Bulk: 1.6 cm. White wove paper; all edges trimmed. Bound in white paper covers printed in black, pink and olive-gold.

Price: 7s. 6d. Number of copies: 10,068. Published 26 November 1964.

Note: This is the first impression with an introduction by Graves.

A42 I, CLAUDIUS 1934

a. First edition::

ROBERT GRAVES | [heavy rule] | [light rule] | I, CLAUDIUS | *From the Autobiography of* | TIBERIUS CLAUDIUS | [facsimile signature of Tiberius Claudius] | *Emperor of the Romans* | born B.C. 10 | murdered and deified | A.D. 54 | [publishers's emblem] | 1934 | [light rule] | [heavy rule] | ARTHUR BARKER : LONDON

Collation: [A]^8 B–2H^8, 248 leaves.
    pp.[1]–[2] blank; p.[3] I, CLAUDIUS; p.[4] blank; p.[5] title-page; p.[6] printer's and publication notices; p.[7] quotation (7 ll.) from Tacitus; p.[8] blank; pp.9–10

AUTHOR'S NOTE; P. [11] I, CLAUDIUS; p.[12] blank; pp.13–494 text; [genealogical table tipped to p.[495]; pp.[495]–[496] blank.
21.8 × 13.8 cm. Bulk: 3.5/4.1 cm. White laid paper; top and fore-edges trimmed. White wove endpapers. Bound in black cloth; front and back blank; spine stamped in gold: ROBERT GRAVES | [light rule] | [heavy rule] | I, | CLAUDIUS | BARKER

Price: 8s. Number of copies unknown. Published in May 1934 in white dust-jacket printed in blue, brown, flesh and black.

Notes: The jacket design is by John Aldridge.
This book has been translated into Czech, Danish, Dutch, Finnish, French, German, Greek, Hebrew, Hungarian, Italian, Norwegian, Polish, Portugese, Romanian, Russian, Slovenian, Spanish, Swedish, and Ukranian.
Impressions: 2nd, 3rd, May 1934; 4th, June 1934; 5th, September 1934; 6th, December 1934; 7th, January 1935; 8th, May 1935; 9th, October 1935.
See *Notes* to A43a.
Printed in Great Britain. For a note on the printing of the first edition by two firms see *Bibliographical Notes & Queries* 2, ii (1936), 5.
There was also a "remainder" impression bound in orange cloth to be distributed by W.H.Smith.

A42b. American issue (1934):

I, CLAUDIUS | FROM THE AUTOBIOGRAPHY OF TIBERIUS CLAUDIUS | BORN B.C. 10 . MURDERED AND DEIFIED A.D. 54 | [facsimile signature of Tiberius Claudius] | [medallion of Claudius] | BY ROBERT GRAVES | [rule] | NEW YORK . MCMXXXIV | HARRISON SMITH AND ROBERT HAAS

Collation: [1]–[12]^{16} [13]^8 [14]–[16]^{16}, 248 leaves.
Remainder as A42a.
21.4 × 14.1 cm. Bulk: 3.1/3.7 cm. White wove paper; all edges trimmed. White wove endpapers. Bound in dark slate-blue cloth; back blank; front stamped in gold with medallion of Claudius; spine stamped in gold: I, | CLAUDIUS | [double rule] | Graves | [publisher's emblem]

Price: $2.00. Number of copies undetermined. Published 4 June 1934 in dust-jacket as A42a.

Notes: Impressions: 2nd, 3rd, 4th, June 1934; 5th, July 1934; 6th, 7th, August 1934.
Printed in the U.S.

A42c. Second American edition ([1935]):

I, CLAUDIUS | FROM THE AUTOBIOGRAPHY OF TIBERIUS CLAUDIUS | BORN B.C. 10 . MURDERED AND DEIFIED A.D.54 | [facsimile signature] | [medallion] | BY ROBERT GRAVES | [swelled rule] | GROSSET & DUNLAP | *Publishers* New York

Collation: [1]–[12]^{16} [13]^{12} [14]^{16}, 220 leaves.
p.[i], I, CLAUDIUS; p.[ii] blank; p.[iii] title-page; p.[iv] copyright notice; p.[v] biographical note; p.[vi] blank; p. [vii] quotation (6 ll.) from Tacitus; p.[viii] blank;

pp.ix–x AUTHOR'S NOTE; p.[1] I, CLAUDIUS; p.[2] blank; pp.3–427 text; pp.[428] – [430] blank.
    21.1 × 14.0 cm. Bulk: 2.9/3.6 cm. White wove paper; all edges trimmed; top edges stained blue-green. White wove endpapers. Bound in dark blue cloth; back blank; front blind-stamped with medallion; spine stamped in gold: I, | CLAUDIUS | [double rule] | Graves | GROSSET | & DUNLAP

Price: $1.00. Number of copies unknown. Published on 10 June 1935.

A42d. Cheap English issue (1936):

Title-page as A42a, except for date.

Collation: [A]/A*8/8 B/B* –P/P*8/8 Q8, 248 leaves.
    Remainder as A42a.
    19.7 × 13.2 cm. Bulk: 2.1/2.6 cm. White wove paper; all edges trimmed. White wove endpapers. Bound in grey cloth; front and back blank; spine printed in brown: ROBERT GRAVES | [rule] | [solid brown rectangular box, grey cloth showing through to read 2 ll.:] I, | CLAUDIUS | [rule] | BARKER

Price: 5s. Number of copies unknown. Published in May 1936.

Notes: Impressions: 2nd, November 1936; 3rd, May 1937; 4th, July 1938. In August 1939 the Barker rights were taken over by Methuen, who received 275 copies and 1,000 sheets. Methuen published a 5th impression of 3,000 copies (the '14th edition') in 1940; 2,000 of these were destroyed by enemy action. Subsequent Methuen impressions: 6th, 1941 (3,000 copies); 7th, 1943 (3,000 copies); 8th, 1946 (2,500 copies). The latter three impressions were produced during wartime paper rationing and are slightly smaller (18.7 × 12.4 cm.) and bulk: 2.2/2.6 cm.

A42e. Second American edition, Modern Library issue ([1937]):

[double rule rectangular box (light rule within heavy rule) enclosing all:] I, CLAUDIUS | FROM THE AUTOBIOGRAPHY OF | TIBERIUS CLAUDIUS | BORN B.C. 10 | MURDERED AND DEIFIED A.D.54 [all foregoing in open type] | [rule] | BY | ROBERT GRAVES | [rule] | [publisher's emblem] | [rule] | THE MODERN LIBRARY . NEW YORK

Collation: [1]16 [2] – [7][′32] [8]16, 224 leaves.
    p.[i] THE MODERN LIBRARY | *OF THE WORLD'S BEST BOOKS* | [heavy above light rules] | I, CLAUDIUS; p.[ii] publisher's advertisement; p.[iii] title-page; p.[iv] copyright, publisher's and manufacturer's notices; p.[v] biographical note; p.[vi] blank; p.[vii] quotation (6 ll.) from Tacitus; p.[viii] blank; pp.ix–x AUTHOR'S NOTE; p.[1] I, CLAUDIUS; p.[2] blank; pp. 3–427 text; p.[428] – [430] blank.
    16.5 × 10.6 cm. Bulk: 1.7/2.0 cm. White wove paper; all edges trimmed; top edges stained green. White wove endpapers; first and fourth sides blank; second and third sides printed with brown overall design of books and: ml; publisher's emblem in centre. Bound in green cloth; back blank; front blind stamped: [rectangular single-rule box enclosing all:] | [publisher's emblem stamped in gold in centre] | I, | CLAUDIUS| [rule] | GRAVES | [intermingled script M and L] | MODERN | LIBRARY

Price: $0.95; later $1.25. Number of copies: 89,000 to June 1964. Published 25 February 1937 in white dust-jacket printed in black and gold, with list of Modern Library books printed on inside.

Later in the press-run the binding was changed to red and the printing of the endpapers to grey.

A42f. Second English edition ([1941]):

ROBERT GRAVES | [swelled rule] | I, CLAUDIUS | *From the Autobiography of* | TIBERIUS CLAUDIUS | [facsimile signature] | *Emperor of the Romans* | born B.C. 10 | murdered and deified | A.D. 54 | VOLUME I [II] | [publisher's emblem] | ALLEN LANE | PENGUIN BOOKS | HARMONDSWORTH MIDDLESEX ENGLAND | 41 EAST 28TH STREET NEW YORK U.S.A.

Collation: [both volumes:] [A]/A$^{*8/8}$ B–G^{16}, 112 leaves.

Vol. I: p.[1] blurb; p.[2] portrait of Graves and biographical note; p.[3] title-page; p [4] publication notice, list of books by Graves and printer's notice; p.[5] quotation (6 ll.) from Tacitus; p.[6] the Sibylline verses; pp.[7]–[8] AUTHOR'S NOTE; pp.[9] 10–222 text, with pp.[19, 33, 45, 53, 71, 89, 105, 111, 123, 131, 151, 165, 177, 189, 199, 211] unnumbered and pp.[52, 70, 88, 104, 110, 122, 150, 164, 176, 188] blank; pp.[223]–[224] advertisements.

Vol. II: p.[i] blurb; p.[ii] portrait of Graves and biographical note; p.[iii] title-page; p.[iv] publication notice, list of books by Graves and printer's notice; p.[v] quotation (6 ll.) from Tacitus; p.[vi] blank; pp.[vii]–[viii] AUTHOR'S NOTE; pp.[223] 224–433 text, with pp.[229, 245, 261, 271, 289, 299, 311, 319, 329, 345, 355, 369, 385, 403, 417, 429] unnumbered and pp.[260, 270, 298, 310, 328, 344, 368, 384, 416, 428] blank; pp.[434]–[438] advertisements.

18.0 × 10.6 cm. Bulk: 0.8 cm. White wove paper; all edges trimmed. Bound in paper covers printed in black and orange; inside covers and back covers have advertisements.

Price: 9d. per volume. Number of copies: 55,000. Published in July 1941 in white dust-jacket printed in orange and black.

Notes: These books are Penguins 318 and 319.

Volume I, p.[4] has *"Decdmber"* for *"December"*; volume II has not this misprint. Both volumes, same page, have *"Perany"* for *"Penny"* in the list of Graves' titles.

A42g. Third English edition ([1944]):

ROBERT GRAVES | [swelled rule] | I, CLAUDIUS | *From the Autobiography of* | TIBERIUS CLAUDIUS | [facsimile signature] | *Emperor of the Romans* | born B.C. 10 | murdered and deified | A.D. 54 | VOLUME II | [publisher's emblem] | ALLEN LANE | PENGUIN BOOKS | HARMONDSWORTH MIDDLESEX ENGLAND | 245 FIFTH AVENUE NEW YORK U.S.A.

Collation: Vol. I: unknown; Vol. II [1]^{16} 2–6^{16}, 96 leaves.

Vol. I: unknown.

Vol. II: p.[i] I, CLAUDIUS | VOLUME II | [blurb 7 ll.]; p.[ii] portrait of Graves and biographical note; p.[iii] title-page; p. [iv] publication date and author's advertisement; p.[v] quotation (8 ll.) from Tacitus; p.[vi] blank; pp.[vii]–[viii]

AUTHOR'S NOTE; pp.201–379 text; p.[380] text and printer's notice; pp.[381]–[382] advertisements; pp.[383]–[384] publisher's advertisements.

18.0 × 10.9 cm. Bulk: (I) unknown; (II) 0.8 cm. White wove paper; all edges trimmed. Bound in white paper covers printed in orange and black; inside front and back covers: advertisements.

Price: Unknown. Number of copies: unknown. Published in 1944.

Note: p.[vi] indicates that this edition is merely a reprinting of the 1941 Penguin edition (A42f), but it obviously is not.

A42h. Third American edition ([1944]):

[whole enclosed within double-rule rectangular box:] [4 ll. in left half of page:] PUBLISHED BY ARRANGEMENT WITH | RANDOM HOUSE, INC., NEW YORK | COPYRIGHT, 1934 | BY HARRISON SMITH AND ROBERT HAAS, INC. | [rule, dividing left from right half of page] | [6 ll. in right half of page:] I, CLAUDIUS | by | Robert Graves | *Editions for the Armed Services, Inc.* | A NON-PROFIT ORGANIZATION ESTABLISHED BY | THE COUNCIL ON BOOKS IN WARTIME, NEW YORK | [outside of double-rule box, at lower left:] L-27

Collation: [1]–[12]¹⁶ [13]–18⁸, 240 leaves.

p.[1] title-page; p.[2] quotation (6 ll.) from Tacitus; pp. [3]–[4] AUTHOR'S NOTE; pp.[5] 6–477 text; p.[478] blank; pp. [479]–[480] ABOUT THE AUTHOR.

16.7 × 11.6 cm. Bulk: 1.8 cm. White wove paper; all edges trimmed. Bound in white paper covers with multicolour printing; front has title, author and rights notice; inside front and back covers are publisher's announcements; back cover has blurb.

Note: This edition was never for sale, but only for distribution to members of the U.S. Armed Forces overseas. It is printed in double columns throughout, with the exception of p. [2]; the gatherings are stabbed together with a single staple at the center of the gutter. The Library of Congress copy was received on 24 October 1944.

A42i. Fourth English edition ([1949?]):

ROBERT GRAVES | [double rule] | I, CLAUDIUS | *From the Autobiography of* | TIBERIUS CLAUDIUS | [facsimile signature] | *Emperor of the Romans* | born B.C. 10 | murdered and deified | A.D. 54 | [publisher's emblem] | [double rule] | METHUEN & CO. LTD. LONDON

Collation: [1]⁸ 2/2* –15/15*⁸/⁸, 232 leaves.

p.[i] I, CLAUDIUS; p.[ii] list of books by Graves; p.[iii] title-page; p.[iv] quotation (7 ll.) from Tacitus, edition and printer's notices; pp.v–vi AUTHOR'S NOTE; pp.1–454 text; [fold-out genealogical table tipped to p.[455]]; pp.[455]–[458] blank.

18.4 × 12.2 cm. Bulk: 2.0/2.4 cm. White wove paper; all edges trimmed. White wove endpapers. Bound in grey cloth; front and back blank; spine printed in brown: ROBERT GRAVES | [rule] | [solid rectangular box with cloth showing through for 2 ll.:] | I, | CLAUDIUS | [rule] | METHUEN

Price: 8s. 6d. Number of copies: 3,000. Published in 1949 in dust-jacket as A42a.

Notes: Impressions: 2nd, 1952 (3,250 copies); 3rd, 1956 (3,000 copies); 4th, 1962 (3,000 copies); 5th, 1971.

In 1972 Heron Books, a part of the Edito-Service Group, printed a direct mail order edition offset from this edition. A copy has not been seen.

A42j. Fifth English edition ([1953]):

ROBERT GRAVES | [swelled rule] | I, CLAUDIUS | FROM THE AUTOBIOGRAPHY OF | TIBERIUS CLAUDIUS | [facsimile signature] | EMPEROR OF THE ROMANS | BORN 10 B.C. | MURDERED AND DEIFIED | A.D. 54 | PENGUIN BOOKS

Collation: [A]^{16} B–L^{16} M^8 N^{16}, 200 leaves.

p.[1] PENGUIN BOOKS | 318 | I, CLAUDIUS | ROBERT GRAVES | [publisher's emblem]; p.[2] blank; p.[3] title-page; p.[4] publisher's notice, printing history and printer's notice; p.[5] the Sibylline verses; p.[6] quotation (10 ll.) from Tacitus; pp. 7–[8] *Author's Note*; pp.9–395 [396] text; p.[397] TREE OF THE | IMPERIAL FAMILY AND CONNEXIONS | TO THE YEAR A.D. 41 | GIVING NAMES AS ABBREVIATED | IN THIS BOOK; pp.[398]–[399] genealogical table; p.[400] blank.

18.0 × 11.0 cm. Bulk: 1.9 cm. White wove paper; all edges trimmed. Bound in paper covers printed in black and orange.

Price: 3s. 6d. Number of copies unknown. Published in 1953.

Note: Reported printings: 2nd, 1955; 3rd, 1964; 4th, 1977 (four times); 5th, 1978 (twice); 6th, 1979 (twice); 7th, 1983; 8th, 1984.

A42k. Fourth American edition ([1953]):

I, CLAUDIUS | ROBERT GRAVES | COMPLETE AND UNABRIDGED | [publisher's emblem] | AVON PUBLICATIONS, INC. | 575 MADISON AVENUE . NEW YORK 22, N.Y.

Collation: 224 leaves, glued at spine.

pp.[3]–[4] blurbs; p.[5] title-page; p.[6] copyright, acknowledgement and printing notices; p.[7] I, CLAUDIUS; p.[8] blank; pp.9–445 [446] text; pp.[447]–[448] AUTHOR'S NOTE; pp. [449]–[450] publisher's advertisements.

16.0 × 10.7 cm. Bulk: 2.3 cm. White wove paper; all edges trimmed; all edges stained yellow. Bound in pictorial paper covers.

Price: $0.35. Number of copies: 250,000. Published in October 1953.

Note: This is Avon Red and Gold Library No. AT-68.

A42l. Fifth American edition ([1961]):

[elaborate 10-line rule and decorative rule device] | I, CLAUDIUS | FROM THE AUTOBIOGRAPHY OF | TIBERIUS CLAUDIUS | BORN B.C. X | MURDERED AND DEIFIED A.D. LIV | BY | ROBERT GRAVES | [publisher's emblem] | VINTAGE BOOKS | A DIVISION OF RANDOM HOUSE | NEW YORK

Collation: 224 leaves, glued at spine.

p.[i] [decorative rule] | [rule] | I, CLAUDIUS | [rule]; p.[ii] blank; p.[iii] title-page;

p.[iv] copyright, rights reservation, publisher's and manufacturing notices; p.[v] quotation (10 ll.) from Tacitus; p.[vi] blank; pp.[vii] – [viii] AUTHOR'S NOTE; p.[1] [decorative rule] | I, CLAUDIUS | [rule]; p.[2] blank; pp.[3] 4–432 text; p.[433] biographical and typographical notices; p.[434] – [440] publisher's advertisements.

18.4 × 11.1 cm. Bulk: 2.1 cm. White wove paper; all edges trimmed. Bound in white paper covers printed in red, blue and black.

Price: $1.45. Number of copies undisclosed. Published 13 February 1961.

Note: This book is Vintage Book V-182. After the *Masterpiece Theatre* dramatization was broadcast in the United States this edition was re-issued with a new cover designed by Seymour Chwast, the price was raised to $2.95 and its number was changed to Vintage Book V-536.

A42m. Sixth American edition ([1965]):

[7 ll. magenta:] FROM THE | AUTOBIOGRAPHY | OF TIBERIUS CLAUDIUS | BORN B.C. 10 | MURDERED | AND DEIFIED | A.D. 54 | I, CLAUDIUS | [in magenta:] BY ROBERT GRAVES | WITH A NEW INTRODUCTION | BY THE AUTHOR | [in magenta: publisher's emblem] | TIME READING PROGRAM | SPECIAL EDITION | TIME INCORPORATED, NEW YORK

Collation: 228 leaves, glued at spine.

p.[i] [in magenta:] I, CLAUDIUS; p.[ii] blank; p.[iii] title-page; p.[iv] publisher's emblem, staff credits, copyright, rights reservation and printing notices; pp.[v] – [vi] solid magenta, otherwise blank; pp.vii–xi EDITORS' | PREFACE; p.[xii] solid magenta, otherwise blank; pp.xiii–xvii INTRODUCTION; p. [xviii] blank; p.xix–xx AUTHOR'S | NOTE; p.[xxi] quotation (11 ll.) from Tacitus; p.[xxii] blank; p.[xxiii] [in magenta:] I, CLAUDIUS; p.[xxiv] solid magenta, otherwise blank; pp.1–429 text; p.[430] blank; p.[431] colophon; p.[432] blank.

20.3 × 13.2 cm. Bulk: 2.7 cm. White wove paper; all edges trimmed. Bound in paper covers; inner sides scarlet; outer sides white printed with pictorial design in orange, green, blue, yellow, and black.

Price: $3.95. Number of copies undisclosed. Published in February 1965.

Note: The Introduction (pp.xiii–xvii) has not appeared elsewhere.

A42n. Sixth English edition ([1976]):

ROBERT GRAVES | [thick rule, thin rule] | I, CLAUDIUS | *From the Autobiography of* | TIBERIUS CLAUDIUS | [facsimile signature] | *Emperor of the Romans* | born B.C. 10 | murdered and deified | A.D. 54 | [thin rule, thick rule] | EYRE METHUEN . LONDON

Collation: [1] – [9]^{16}, 144 leaves.

p.[i] I, CLAUDIUS; p.[ii] *by the same author* | CLAUDIUS THE GOD; p.[iii] title-page; p.[iv] quotation from Tacitus, publisher's, ISBN, and printer's notices; pp.v–vi AUTHOR'S NOTE; pp.[1] 2–281 text [fold-out genealogical table tipped in between pp.280–281; p.[282] blank.

21.5 × 13.4 cm. Bulk: 2.2/2.6 cm. White wove paper; all edges trimmed; top edge stained light blue. Bound in navy blue cloth; front and back blank; spine stamped in gold, top to bottom: [2 ll. horizontal:] Robert | Graves | [down spine:] I, CLAUDIUS | [2 ll. horizontal:] EYRE | METHUEN

Price: £3.95. Number of copies: 3,000. Published June 1976.

Note: Book Club Associates in 1978 intended an issue using stock sold by Methuen from this edition, in the event they published an edition using their own setting of the text. A copy of this edition has not been seen.

A limited issue of 100 signed and numbered copies using sheets of this edition purchased from Methuen was specially bound in full purple morroco and issued by David Paradine in 1977 in a slipcase without dust-jacket.

A42o. Seventh English edition ([1978]):

I, Claudius | FROM THE AUTOBIOGRAPHY OF | TIBERIUS CLAUDIUS | EMPEROR OF THE ROMANS | BORN B.C. X | MURDERED AND DEIFIED A.D. LIV | ROBERT GRAVES | METHUEN

Collation: 204 leaves glued at the spine.
   p.[i] I, CLAUDIUS; p.[ii] *by the same author* | CLAUDIUS THE GOD; p.[iii] title-page; p.[iv] publishing, edition, ISBN and printer's notices; p.[v] [7 line quotation from Tacitus]; p. [vi] blank; p.[vii] –viii AUTHOR'S NOTE; p.[ix] I, CLAUDIUS; p.[x] blank; pp.[1]2–395 text, with pp.[10, 24, 36, 43, 59, 76, 91, 96, 107, 115, 134, 147, 158, 168, 178, 190, 201, 207, 222, 236, 245, 263, 272, 282, 290, 299, 313, 323, 336, 351, 368, 380, 391] being unnumbered; [fold-out genealogical tables tipped in between pp. 394–395; pp.[396] – [398] blank.
   21.5 × 13.6 cm. Bulk: 3.0/3.4 cm. White wove paper; all edges trimmed. White wove endpapers. Bound in navy blue cloth, front and back blank; spine stamped in gold: Robert | Graves | [down spine] I, CLAUDIUS | [upright] Methuen.

Price: £7.95. Number of copies: 2,700. Published in September 1978 in white dust-jacket printed in black and gold with colour photograph of Derek Jacobi from the television series on front and back.

Note: Impressions: 2nd, September, 1982 (copies: 2,000).
   Random House produced a book club impression of this edition. It was printed offset in the United States, and the title-page has been reset and it lacks the genealogical tables; it is not perfect bound.

A42p. Seventh American edition ([1982]):

ROBERT GRAVES | [all within a rectangular rule box, printed in black with lettering and one rule in white:] I, CLAUDIUS| FROM THE AUTOBIOGRAPHY OF | TIBERIUS CLAUDIUS | BORN 10 B.C. | MURDERED AND DEIFIED A.D. 54 | [publisher's emblem] | MODERN LIBRARY | NEW YORK

Collation: 224 leaves, glued at spine.
   pp.[i] – [ii] blank; p.[iii] woodcut of Claudius; p.[iv] blank; p.[v] title-page; p.[vi] edition, copyright, rights reservation and publishing notices; p.[vii] [10 ll. quotation from Tacitus]; p.[viii] blank; pp.[ix] – [x] AUTHOR'S NOTE; p.[1] as p.[iii]; p.[2] blank; p.[3]4–432 text; pp.[433] – [436] blank.
   18.2 × 11.8 cm. Bulk: 2.5/3.0 cm. White wove paper; all edges trimmed. White

wove endpapers. Bound in reddish-brown vinyl; back blank; front stamped with publisher's emblem in negative black; spine stamped in gold: I, Claudius | Robert Graves | Modern Library

Price: $8.95. Number of copies undetermined. Published in October 1982 in fawn dust-jacket printed in black and red.

A43   CLAUDIUS THE GOD   1934

a. First edition:

ROBERT GRAVES | [heavy rule] | [light rule] | CLAUDIUS | THE GOD | *and his wife* | MESSALINA | *The troublesome reign of Tiberius Claudius* | *Caesar, Emperor of the Romans (born* | *B.C. 10, died A.D. 54), as described by* | *himself; also his murder at the hands* | *of the notorious Agrippina (mother of* | *the Emperor Nero) and his subsequent* | *deification, as described by others* | [publisher's emblem] | 1934 | [light rule] | [heavy rule] | ARTHUR BARKER: LONDON

Collation: [A]⁸ B–2N⁸, 288 leaves.

p.[1] CLAUDIUS THE GOD | *and his wife* | MESSALINA; p.[2] *By the same Author* | I, CLAUDIUS; p.[3] title-page; p.[4] printer's, publisher's and edition notices; pp.5–6 AUTHOR'S NOTE; p.[7] CLAUDIUS THE GOD; p.[8] blank; pp.9–76 text [genealogical table of the Herods tipped to p.77]; pp.77–302 text; p.303 map; pp.304–553 text; pp.554–559 THREE ACCOUNTS OF CLAUDIUS'S DEATH; pp.560–575 THE PUMPKINIFICATION OF CLAUDIUS; p.[576] blank; [genealogical table of the Roman Imperial Family tipped to p.[576].

21.4 × 13.8 cm. Bulk: 3.7/4.3 cm. White laid paper; top and fore-edges trimmed. White wove endpapers. Bound in black cloth; front and back blank; spine stamped in gold: ROBERT GRAVES | [double rule] | CLAUDIUS | THE GOD | *and his wife* | MESSALINA | BARKER

Price: 10s. 6d. Number of copies unknown. Published in November 1934 in white dust-jacket printed in light and dark blue, pink and red-brown.

Notes: Impressions: 2nd, November 1934; 3rd, December 1934; 4th, January 1935; 5th, December 1935; 6th, May 1936; 7th, 1938 ('cheap' edition).

There are two combined issues of A42 and A43. The first is bound in red morocco, top edges gilt, sheets of A42a and A43a, issued in December 1935 at 25s. the set. The second is bound in three-quarter green leather, top edges gilt, sheets of A42c and the cheap issue of A43a, boxed, issued in November 1936 at 21s. the set. mottled pink and grey endpapers, inside which, front and back, is a heavy binder's sheet of two leaves; spine stamped in gold: [heavy rule] | [light rule] | I, CLAUDIUS | ROBERT GRAVES | [light rule] | [heavy rule] | and | [heavy rule] | [light rule] | CLAUDIUS | THE GOD | ROBERT GRAVES | [light rule] | [heavy rule]

In August 1939 the Barker rights were taken over by Methuen, who received 1,100 copies; of their impression in 1940 (3,000), 1,500 copies were destroyed by enemy action.

Ellsworth Mason reports a copy with "COLONIAL EDITION" ink stamped in black on the front free endpaper, but how many of these copies were produced is not known.

This book has been translated into Bulgarian, Czech, Danish, Dutch, Finnish, French, German, Greek, Hebrew, Hungarian, Italian, Norwegian, Polish, Portugese, Romanian, Russian, Slovenian, Spanish and Swedish.

A43b. First American edition (1935):

BY ROBERT GRAVES | CLAUDIUS *the* GOD | *and his wife Messalina* | [medallion of Claudius] | *The troublesome reign of Tiberius Claudius* | *Caesar, Emperor of the Romans (born B.C. 10,* | *died A.D. 54), as described by himself; also* | *his murder at the hands of the notorious* | *Agrippina (mother of the Emperor Nero)* | *and his subsequent deification, as described* | *by others* | NEW YORK . MCMXXXV | HARRISON SMITH AND ROBERT HAAS

Collation: [1] – [7]^{16} [18^4 [19]^{16}, 292 leaves.

p.[1] CLAUDIUS THE GOD; p.[2] *By the same author* | I, CLAUDIUS; p.[3] title-page; p.[4] copyright, publisher's and printing notices; p.5–6 *Author's Note*; p.[7] CLAUDIUS THE GOD | *and his wife* | *Messalina*; p.[8] blank; pp.9–559 text [genealogical table tipped in facing p.64]; pp.560–565 THREE ACCOUNTS OF CLAUDIUS'S DEATH; pp.566–583 THE PUMPKINIFICATION OF CLAUDIUS; p.[584] blank; [genealogical table, fold-out, tipped to rear endpaper].

21.3 × 14.3 cm. Bulk: 3.5/4.3 cm. White wove paper; all edges trimmed. White wove endpapers. Bound in black cloth; back blank; front stamped in gold with medallion; spine stamped in gold: CLAUDIUS | THE GOD | [double rule] | Graves | [publisher's emblem]

Price: $3.00. Number of copies undetermined. Published 4 March 1935 in dust-jacket as A43a.

Note: Grosset and Dunlap issued an impression of this edition in 1939 at $1.00. The Book of the Month Club issued this book as its selection for March 1935.

A43c. Second English edition ([1943]):

CLAUDIUS THE GOD | *and his wife* | MESSALINA | BY | ROBERT GRAVES | The troublesome reign of Tiberius Claudius Caesar, | Emperor of the Romans (born 10 B.C., died A.D. 54), | as described by himself; also his murder at the hands | of the notorious Agrippina (mother of the Emperor | Nero) and his subsequent deification, as described by | others | VOLUME I [II] | [publisher's emblem] | PENGUIN BOOKS | HARMONDSWORTH MIDDLESEX ENGLAND | 300 FOURTH AVENUE NEW YORK U.S.A.

Collation: [both volumes:] [A]^{16} B–G^{16}, 112 leaves.

Vol. I: p.[1] CLAUDIUS THE GOD | *and his wife* | MESSALINA | VOLUME I; p.[2] list of books by Graves; p.[3] title-page; p. [4] publication history and printer's notices; p.[5] CONTENTS; p.[6] blank; pp.[7] – [8] AUTHOR'S NOTE; pp.9–223 text; p.[224] portrait and biographical note.

Vol. II: p.[i] CLAUDIUS THE GOD | *and his wife* | MESSALINA | VOLUME II; p.[ii] – [viii], as pp.[2] – [8] in Vol. I; pp.225–243 text; p.244 map; pp.245–424 text; pp.425–428 THREE ACCOUNTS OF CLAUDIUS'S DEATH; pp.429–439 THE PUMPKINIFICATION OF CLAUDIUS; p.[440] portrait and biographical note.

I: 17.2 × 10.7 cm.; II: 18.2 × 10.7 cm. Bulk [each volume]: 0.8 cm. White wove paper; all edges trimmed. Bound in paper covers printed in black and red-orange; inside front and back covers and back cover: advertisements.

Price: 9d. per volume. Number of copies unknown. Published in March 1943.

Note: These are Penguin Books Nos. 421–422.

A43d. Third English edition ([1944]):

ROBERT GRAVES | [heavy rule] | [light rule] | CLAUDIUS | THE GOD | *and his wife* | MESSALINA | *The troublesome reign of Tiberius Claudius* | *Caesar, Emperor of the Romans (born* | *10 B.C., died A.D. 54), as described by* | *himself; also his murder at the hands* | *of the notorious Agrippina (mother of* | *the Emperor Nero) and his subsequent* | *deification, as described by others* | [publisher's emblem] | [light rule] | [heavy rule] | METHUEN & CO. LTD. LONDON

Collation: [1]/2$^{8/8}$ 3/4–31/32$^{8/8}$ 33^8, 264 leaves.

    p.[i] CLAUDIUS THE GOD | *and his wife* | MESSALINA; p.[ii] list of books by Graves; p.[iii] title-page; p.[iv] publication, war economy and printing notices; pp.v–vi AUTHOR'S NOTE; pp.1–64 text; [genealogical table tipped to p.65]; pp. 65–272 text; p.273 map; pp.274–499 text; pp.500–504 THREE ACCOUNTS OF CLAUDIUS'S DEATH; pp.505–520 THE PUMPKINIFICATION OF CLAUDIUS; [genealogical table tipped to p.[521]]; p.[521] blank; p.[522] printer's notice [blank in impressions after the third].

    18.4 × 12.2 cm. Bulk: 2.0/2.2 cm. White wove paper; all edges trimmed. White wove endpapers. Bound in grey cloth; front and back blank; spine stamped in blue: ROBERT GRAVES | [rule] | [solid rectangular box with cloth showing through to read 2 ll.:] | CLAUDIUS | THE GOD | [rule] | *Methuen*

Price: 8s. Number of copies: 2,500 Published in 1944 in dust-jacket as 43a.

Notes: Impressions: 2nd, 1946 (2,500 copies); 3rd, 1949 (3,000 copies); 4th, 1951 (3,250 copies); 5th, 1957 (3,000 copies); 6th, 1962 (3,000 copies). The third and subsequent impressions have a slightly larger bulk and a different signing pattern (see A43d in the first edition of this bibliography).

A43e. Fourth English edition ([1954]):

ROBERT GRAVES | CLAUDIUS THE GOD | AND HIS WIFE MESSALINA | [swelled rule] | THE TROUBLESOME REIGN OF TIBERIUS CLAUDIUS | CAESAR, EMPEROR OF THE ROMANS | (BORN 10 B.C., DIED A.D. 54), | AS DESCRIBED BY HIMSELF; | ALSO HIS MURDER AT THE HANDS OF THE | NOTORIOUS AGRIPPINA | (MOTHER OF THE EMPEROR NERO) | AND HIS SUBSEQUENT DEIFICATION, | AS DESCRIBED BY | OTHERS | PENGUIN BOOKS

Collation: [A]^{16} B–O^{16}, 224 leaves.

    pp.[1]–[2] blank; p.[3] PENGUIN BOOKS | 421 | CLAUDIUS THE GOD | ROBERT GRAVES | [publisher's emblem]; p.[4] blank; p.[5] title-page; p.[6] publisher's, publication and printer's notices; pp.7–8 *Author's Note*; pp.9–418 text; p.419 map; p.[420] blank; p.pp.421–425 *Three Accounts* | *of Claudius's Death*; p.[426] blank; pp.427–439 *The Pumpkinification of Claudius*; p.[440] blank; p.[441] THE |

ROYAL FAMILY | OF THE | HERODS; pp.442–443 genealogical table; p.[444] blank; p. [445] publisher's advertisement; p.[446] blank; pp.[447]–[448] publisher's advertisements.

18.0 × 11.0 cm. Bulk: 1.2 cm. (later 1.6 cm.). White wove paper; all edges trimmed. Bound in paper covers printed in black and orange.

Price: 3s. 6d. Number of copies unknown. Published in 1954.

Note: Impressions: 2nd, 31 May 1956; 3rd, 1957; 4th, 1959; 5th, 1961; 6th, 1964; 7th and 8th, 1977; 9th and 10th, 1978; 11th and 12th, 1979; 13th, 1984.

After the BBC television series was broadcast the cover was changed to a colour photograph of Derek Jacobi as Claudius.

A43f. Second American edition (1968):

CLAUDIUS *the* GOD | *and his wife Messalina* | BY | ROBERT GRAVES | THE TROUBLESOME REIGN OF TIBERIUS CLAUDIUS | CAESAR, EMPEROR OF THE ROMANS | (BORN 10 B.C., DIED A.D. 54), | AS DESCRIBED BY HIMSELF; | ALSO HIS MURDER AT THE HANDS OF THE | NOTORIOUS AGRIPPINA | (MOTHER OF THE EMPEROR NERO) | AND HIS SUBSEQUENT DEIFICATION, | AS DESCRIBED BY | OTHERS | [series emblem] | VINTAGE BOOKS | *A Division of Random House* | *New York*

Collation: 296 leaves, unsigned, glued at the spine.

p.[1] CLAUDIUS THE GOD; p.[2] blank; p.[3] title-page; p.[4] copyright, rights reservation, manufacturing and series notices; pp.5–6 *Author's Note*; p.[7] CLAUDIUS THE GOD | *and his wife* | *Messalina*; p.[8] blank; pp.9–559 text; pp.560–565 THREE ACCOUNTS OF CLAUDIUS'S DEATH; pp.566–582 THE PUMPKINIFICATION OF CLAUDIUS; pp.582–583 SEQUEL; pp.[584]–[585] genealogical tables; p.[586] blank; p.[587] biographical note; p.[588] blank; pp.[589]–[592] advertisements for Vintage Books.

18.3 × 10.8 cm. Bulk: 2.5 cm. White wove paper; all edges trimmed. Bound in white paper covers printed in pink, red and black.

Price: $1.95. Number of copies undetermined. Published in 1968.

Notes: Vintage Book V-425. Cover design by George Giusti. After the *Masterpiece Theatre* dramatization was broadcast in the United States this edition was re-issued with a cover desgined by Seymour Chwast, though it is not attributed to him on the cover; the price was changed to $3.95 and it was re-designated as Vintage Book V-537.

A43g. Third American edition ([1982]:

ROBERT GRAVES | [two lines in white in a black rectangle; all within single white rule:] CLAUDIUS | THE GOD | *and his wife* MESSALINA | THE TROUBLESOME REIGN OF TIBERIUS CLAUDIUS | CAESAR, EMPEROR OF THE ROMANS | (BORN 10 B.C., DIED A.D. 54), | AS DESCRIBED BY HIMSELF; | ALSO HIS MURDER AT THE HANDS OF THE | NOTORIOUS AGRIPPINA | (MOTHER TO THE EMPEROR NERO) | AND HIS SUBSEQUENT DEIFICATION. | AS DESCRIBED BY | OTHERS | [publisher's emblem] | MODERN LIBRARY | NEW YORK

Collation: 296 leaves, glued at the spine.

[2 blank pages]; p.[1] woodcut of Claudius; p.[2] blank; p.[3] title-page; p.[4] edition, copyright, rights reservation and manufacturing notices; pp.5–6 *Author's Note*; p.[7] woodcut as on p.[1]; p.[8] blank; pp.9–305 text; p.[306] map; pp. 307–559 text; pp.560–565 THREE ACCOUNTS OF CLAUDIUS'S DEATH; pp. 566–583 THE PUMPKINIFICATION OF CLAUDIUS; pp.[584]–[585] genealogical table; pp.[586]–[590] blank.

18.2 × 12.2 cm. Bulk: 3.3/3.8 cm. White wove paper; all edges trimmed. White wove endpapers. Bound in reddish brown cloth; back blank; front has publisher's emblem in black; spine stamped in gold at top: Claudius | the God | Robert Graves | Modern Library

Price: $8.95. Number of copies undetermined. Published in 1982 in tan dust-jacket printed in black and red.

A44　OLD-SOLDIER SAHIB　[1936]

a. First edition:

OLD-SOLDIER SAHIB | *by* | Private | FRANK RICHARDS | D.C.M., M.M. | *Late of the Second Battalion* | *Royal Welch Fusiliers* | London | FABER & FABER LIMITED | 24 Russell Square

Collation: [A]^8 B–X^8 Y^4, 172 leaves.

p.[1] OLD-SOLDIER SAHIB; p.[2] author's advertisement; p.[3] title-page; p.[4] publisher's and printer's notices; p.[5] To | THE PRAYER-WALLAH | in the hope | that this meets his eye; p.[6] blank; p.7 CONTENTS; p [8] blank; pp.9–341 text; pp. [342]–[344] blank.

18.5 × 12.2 cm. Bulk: 2.6/3.1 cm. White wove paper; all edges trimmed. White wove endpapers. Bound in bright blue cloth; front and back blank; spine stamped in gold: Old- | Soldier | Sahib | Frank | Richards | Faber | and Faber

Price: 7s. 6d. Number of copies: 5,000. Published in April 1936 in yellow dust-jacket printed in blue and red.

Notes: Impressions: 2nd, September 1938 at 3s.6d. (5,000 copies).
Graves rewrote this book.

A44b. First American edition ([1936]):

Old Soldier Sahib | By Private Frank Richards | D.C.M., M.M., LATE OF THE SECOND BATTALION | ROYAL WELCH FUSILIERS | [cut of soldier with rifle; fort with Union Jack at right; native village at left; signed 'Floethe'] | WITH AN INTRODUCTION BY ROBERT GRAVES | [rule] | HARRISON SMITH AND ROBERT HAAS | [rule]

Collation: [1]–[18]^{18} [19]^4 [20]^8, 156 leaves.

p.[1] OLD SOLDIER SAHIB; p.[2] blank; p.[3] title-page; p.[4] copyright and printing notices; p.[5] To | THE PRAYER WALLAH | in the hope | that this meets his eye; p.[6] blank; p.[7] Contents; p.[8] blank; pp.9–18 Introduction; p.[19] OLD

SOLDIER SAHIB; p.[20] blank; pp.21–310 text with pp.[62, 76, 106, 124, 168, 178, 190, 206, 220, 235, 246, 260, 298] blank; pp. [311]–[312] blank.
    21.2 × 14.0 cm. Bulk: 2.7/3.3 cm. White wove paper; all edges trimmed; top edges stained red. White wove endpapers. Bound in buff cloth; front stamped in red with helmet, beneath which is a bayonet and below which is a grenade; back blank; spine stamped in red: RICHARDS | OLD | SOLDIER | SAHIB | [publisher's emblem]

Price: $2.50. Number of copies undetermined. Published 6 April 1936 in white dustjacket printed in red and black.

A44c. Second English edition ([1966]):

OLD-SOLDIER | SAHIB | *by* | Private | FRANK RICHARDS | D.C.M., M.M. | *Late of the Second Battalion* | *Royal Welch Fusiliers* | *With a foreword by ROBERT GRAVES* | London | FABER & FABER LIMITED | 24 Russell Square

Collaltion: 172 leaves, glued at spine.
    p.[1] title-page; p.[2] publisher's, edition and printer's notices: TO | THE PRAYER-WALLAH | in the hope | that this meets his eye: loan restriction notice; pp.3–8 FOREWORD; pp.9–341 text; pp.[342]–[344] blank.
    18 × 12 cm. Bulk: 1.9 cm. White wove paper; all edges trimmed. Bound in white paper covers printed in black, mustard-gold and blue. Inside front cover has blurb; inside back cover has publisher's advertisements.

Price: 7s.6d. Number of copies: 10,000. Published 24 February 1966.

Notes: This is a Faber Papercovered edition; p.[2] gives the publication date, erroneously, as *mcmlxv.*
    In 1983 Anthony Mott Ltd. issued a paperback reprint of this edition. This reprint varies as follows: 2 pp. blank; title-page and publisher, publication, copyright, ISBN, printer's and rights reservation notices on the recto and verso, respectively of an unpaginated leaf; p.[1] dedication; p.[2] blank; pp.3–[342] unchanged; p.[343] publisher's advertisements; p.[344] blank; pp.[345]–[347] publisher's advertisements; p.[348] blank.

A45   ALMOST FORGOTTEN GERMANY   [1936]

First edition:

ALMOST FORGOTTEN | GERMANY | by | GEORG SCHWARZ | Translated by | LAURA RIDING and ROBERT GRAVES | [publisher's emblem] | THE SEIZIN PRESS . DEYÁ MAJORCA | AND | CONSTABLE & CO., LTD. | London

Collation: [A]¹⁶ B–I¹⁶, 144 leaves.
    p.[i] ALMOST FORGOTTEN GERMANY; p.[ii] publisher's advertisements; [plate, back blank, facing title-page, portrait of Schwarz]; p.[iii] title-page; p.[iv] publication and printer's notices; p.v CONTENTS; p.[vi] blank; pp.vii–viii FOREWORD; pp.1–278 text; pp.[279]–[280] blank.
    18.5 × 12.3 cm. Bulk: 3.0/3.5 cm. White wove paper; all edges trimmed. White

wove endpapers. Bound in medium brown cloth; front and back blank; spine stamped in black: ALMOST | FORGOTTEN | GERMANY | GEORG SCHWARZ | Translated by | LAURA RIDING | and | ROBERT GRAVES | [publisher's emblem] | SEIZIN PRESS | AND | CONSTABLE

Price: 7s.6d. Number of copies unknown. Published in April 1936 in white dust-jacket printed in black, red and brown.

Note: This book was issued in the U.S. by Random House.

A46   ANTIGUA, PENNY, PUCE   [1936]

a. First edition:

'ANTIGUA, PENNY, PUCE' | by | ROBERT GRAVES | [publisher's emblem] | THE SEIZIN PRESS-DEYÁ MAJORCA | AND | CONSTABLE & COMPANY LTD | LONDON

Collation: [A]^8 B–U^8, 160 leaves.
  p.[i] 'ANTIGUA, PENNY, PUCE'; p.[ii] list of books by Graves; p.[iii] title-page; p.[iv] publication and printer's notices; p.[v] TO | WILLIAM FULLER | IN GRATITUDE; p.[vi] blank; p.vii CONTENTS; p.[viii] blank; pp.1–311 text; p.[312] blank.
  18.4 × 12.2 cm. Bulk: 2.8/3.2 cm. White wove paper; all edges trimmed. White wove endpapers. Bound in dull maroon cloth; front and back blank; spine stamped in white: ANTIGUA | PENNY | PUCE | a novel by | ROBERT | GRAVES | SEIZIN- | CONSTABLE

Price: 10s. 6d. Number of copies unknown. Published in October 1936 in white dust-jacket printed in black and purplish-brown.

Notes: Impressions: 2nd, April 1938 at 3s. 6d., although Mason reports a dust-jacket of this impression with "7/6 net" printed on it. The first impression, p.100, l. 11 has 'ytyle' for 'style'; p.103, l. 15 has 'being' for 'been'; p.293, ult. has lowered 'l' as last letter; in some copies these misprints have been corrected by hand.
This book has been translated into German, Magyar, Polish, Spanish and Swedish.
  There was a photographic reprint by Cedric Chivers Ltd., Portway, Bath, in 1971 "at the request of the London and Home Counties Branch of the Library Association". Identical in content except for the title-page.

A46a.1. First Canadian impression (1936):

"ANTIGUA, PENNY, PUCE" | by | ROBERT GRAVES | THE MACMILLAN | COMPANY OF | CANADA LTD | TORONTO | 1936
  Remainder as A46a save for "SEIZIN- | CONSTABLE" being replaced on spine with "MACMILLAN"

Price: $2.25. Number of copies unknown. Published in 1936.

Note: All misprints listed in A46a have been corrected in this edition.

A46b. First American edition ([1937]):

[whole enclosed in wavy-rule rectangular box:] | [whole enclosed in single-rule rectangular box:] | THE | ANTIGUA | STAMP | by | Robert Graves | [publisher's emblem] | Random House . New York

Collation: [1] – [21]⁸, 168 leaves.

p.[i] [whole enclosed in wavy-rule rectangular box:] The | Antigua | Stamp; p.[ii] list of books by Graves; p. [iii] title-page; p.[iv] edition, copyright and manufacturing notices; p.[v] TO | WILLIAM FULLER | in gratitude; p.[vi] blank; p.[vii] Contents; p.[viii] blank; p.[1] [whole enclosed in wavy-rule rectangular box] The | Antigua | Stamp; p.[2] blank; pp.3–326 text; pp.[327] – [328] blank.

20.4 × 13.8 cm. Bulk: 2.8/3.4 cm. White wove paper; top edges only trimmed and stained salmon. Buff wove endpapers. Bound in rust-brown cloth; back blank; front has label facsimile of stamp; spine stamped in gold: [double wavy rule] | THE | ANTIGUA | STAMP | [double wavy rule] | ROBERT | GRAVES | RANDOM HOUSE

Price: $2.50. Number of copies undisclosed. Published 8 March 1937 in white dust-jacket printed in oxblood red and black.

A46c. Second English edition ([1948]):

'ANTIGUA, PENNY, PUCE' | BY | ROBERT GRAVES | [publisher's emblem] | PENGUIN BOOKS | WEST DRAYTON MIDDLESEX ENGLAND | 245 FIFTH AVENUE NEW YORK U.S.A.

Collation: [A]¹⁶ B–K¹⁶, 160 leaves.

p.[1] 'ANTIGUA, PENNY, PUCE' | BY ROBERT GRAVES | (605); p.[2] publisher's note; p.[3] title-page; p.[4] publication, publisher's and printer's notices; p.[5] CONTENTS; p.[6] blank; p.[7] TO | WILLIAM FULLER | IN GRATITUDE; p.[8] blank; pp. 9–314 text; pp.[315] – [320] publisher's advertisements.

18.0 × 11.0 cm. Bulk: 1.4 cm. White wove paper; all edges trimmed. Bound in white paper covers printed in orange and black.

Price: 2s. Number of copies: 60,000. Published in January 1948.

A46d. Third English edition ([1968]):

ROBERT GRAVES | 'Antigua, Penny, Puce' | [publisher's emblem] | PENGUIN BOOKS

Collation: [A]¹⁶ B–H¹⁶, 128 leaves.

p.[1] PENGUIN BOOKS | 605 | 'ANTIGUA, PENNY, PUCE' [and blurb]; p.[2] blank; p.[3] title-page; p.[4] publisher's, publication, copyright, manufacturing and sales limitation notices; p.[5] CONTENTS; p.[6] TO | WILLIAM FULLER | IN GRATITUDE; pp.[7] 8–255 text, with pp.[17, 27, 36, 51, 64, 80, 89, 103, 114, 133, 145, 154, 168, 172, 185, 199, 208, 216, 226, 233, 246] unnumbered; p.[256] blank.

18.0 × 11.0 cm. Bulk: 1.3 cm. White wove paper; all edges trimmed. Bound in white paper covers printed in orange, red and black.

Price: 5s. Number of copies unknown. Published in October 1968.

Note: Impressions: 2nd, 1984 (copies: 6,000); 3rd, 1986 (copies: 3,000).

A47   COUNT BELISARIUS   [1938]

a. First edition:

[double rule rectangular box enclosing all:] | *COUNT BELISARIUS* | *By* | ROBERT GRAVES | *Author of* | *'I Claudius' and 'Claudius the God'* | [publisher's emblem] | CASSELL | *and Company Limited* | *London Toronto Melbourne* | *and Sydney*

Collation: [A]⁸ B–2L⁸, 272 leaves.
    p.[i] COUNT BELISARIUS; pp.[ii] – [iii] blank; p.[iv] map; p. [v] title-page; p.[vi] arrangement, publication and printer's notices; pp.vii–ix FOREWORD; p.[x] CONTENTS; pp.1–526 [527] text; p.[528] publisher's advertisement; p.[529] map; p.[530] blank; p.[531] map; p.[532] blank; pp.[533] – [534] maps.
    21.1 × 13.8 cm. Bulk: 2.9/3.6 cm. White wove paper; all edges trimmed; top edge stained reddish brown. White wove endpapers. Bound in dark blue-green cloth; front and back blank; spine stamped in gold: COUNT | BELISARIUS | [medallion] | ROBERT GRAVES | [medallion] | CASSELL

Price: 8s.6d. Number of copies: 16,000. Published in April 1938 in white dust-jacket printed in blue, red-brown, purple, green and black.

Notes: Impressions: 2nd, October 1939 (5s.); 3rd, May 1948 (2,813 copies). The first impression also exists in a brown cloth 'Colonial' binding, of which there were 4,000 copies, making a total of 20,000 copies of the first impression.
    The jacket design is by John Aldridge.
    This work has been translated into Czech, Finnish, German, Greek, Hungarian, Magyar, Polish, Portugese, Romanian, Serbo-Croatian, Spanish and Swedish.

A47b. First American edition ([1938]):

[whole enclosed within rectangular single-rule box:] | [in brown decorative scallop-and-dot box:] | *Robert Graves* | COUNT | BELISARIUIS | [in brown: medallion] | RANDOM HOUSE . NEW YORK

Collation: [1] – [36]⁸, 288 leaves.
    p.[i] [in decorative box:] COUNT BELISARIUS; p [ii] list of works by Graves; p.[iii] title-page; p.[iv] printing and publisher's notices; pp.v–viii FOREWORD; p.[ix] CONTENTS; p. [x] blank; p.[xi] LIST OF MAPS; p.[xii] blank; p.[1] [in decorative box] COUNT BELISARIUS; p.[2] map; pp.3–92 text; p. [93] map; pp.94–114 text; p.[115] map; pp.116–228 text; p. [229] map; pp.230–312 text; p.[313] map; pp.314–564 text.
    21.2 × 14.4 cm. Bulk: 3.4/4.0 cm. White wove paper; all edges trimmed; top edges stained green. White wove endpapers. Bound in dark green cloth; front and back blank; spine stamped in gold: [rule] | [5 ll. on solid rectangular black box:] COUNT | BELISARIUS | [medallion] | ROBERT GRAVES | [medallion] | [rule] | RANDOM HOUSE

Price: $3.00. Number of copies undisclosed. Published 21 November 1938 in white dust-jacket printed in black, pink, blue, brown and green with summary of the book on the back.

Note: There was a second printing of this edition. It can be distinguished by the words "SECOND PRINTING" on the verso of the title-page (the first printing had "FIRST PRINTING" in its place) and by its slightly smaller page measurements (21.1 × 14.3 cm.).

Farrar, Straus and Giroux issued a photographic reprint in paperback of this edition in 1982, with a 2nd impression in 1983; except that p.[ii] is blank and that pp.[iii] – [vi] are reset it is identical in contents and format, though slightly reduced in physical size.

A47c. Literary Guild impression ([1938]):

Robert Graves | COUNT BELISARIUS | [medallion] | LITERARY GUILD . NEW YORK

Collation: [1] – [18]¹⁶, 288 leaves.

Remainder as A47b, except p.[ii] is blank.

21.3 × 14.1 cm. Bulk: 3.5/4.2 cm. White wove paper; all edges trimmed; top edges stained rust. Buff wove endpapers. Bound in rust cloth; front and back blank; spine stamped in gold as A47b, except solid black box is solid cream.

Price: $2.00. Number of copies undisclosed. Published in December 1938 in dust-jacket as A47b with the Literary Guild's advertisements replacing book summary.

A47d. Second English edition ([1955]):

COUNT | BELISARIUS | BY ROBERT GRAVES | [star] | PENGUIN BOOKS

Collation: [A]¹⁶ B–F¹⁶ G²⁴ H–N¹⁶, 216 leaves.

p.[1] PENGUIN BOOKS | 1025 | COUNT BELISARIUS | ROBERT GRAVES | [publisher's emblem]; p.[2] blank; p.[3] title-page; p.[4] publisher's, publication and printer's notices; p.[5] CONTENTS; p.[6] blank; pp.[7]–8 FOREWORD; pp.[9] 10–421 text, with pp. [29, 46, 61, 76, 92, 108, 124, 142, 161, 179, 197, 215, 229, 245, 265, 284, 304, 318, 340, 356, 371, 388, 406] unnumbered; pp. [422] – [426] maps; p.[427] publisher's announcement; p.[428] blank; pp.[429] – [432] publisher's advertisements.

18.0 × 11.0 cm. Bulk: 2.1 cm. White wove paper; all edges trimmed. Bound in white paper covers printed in black and orange; inside front cover: blurb; inside back cover: publisher's advertisements.

Price: 3s.6d. Number of copies: 40,000. Published 24 March 1955.

A47e. Third English edition ([1962]):

Count Belisarius | ROBERT GRAVES | [publisher's emblem] | CASSELL . LONDON

Collation: [1] – [33]⁸ [34]⁶, 270 leaves.

p.[i] COUNT BELISARIUS and blurb; p.[ii] list of novels by Graves; p.[iii] blank; p.[iv] map; p.[v] title-page; p.[vi] publisher's, rights reservation, edition and printing notices; pp.1– [534] as A47a.

19.9 × 13.2 cm. Bulk: 3.6/4.3 cm. White wove paper; all edges trimmed; top edges stained brown. Bound in orange-brown cloth: front and back blank; spine stamped in gold: COUNT | BELISARIUS | [heavy rule] | ROBERT | GRAVES | CASSELL

Price: 18s. Number of copies: 4,000. Published 11 January 1962 in dust-jacket as A47a.

Note: This book is a line-for-line, page-for-page resetting of A47a; printed in Czechoslovakia.

A47f. Second American edition ([1966]):

[entire flush right:] COUNT BELISARIUS | ROBERT GRAVES | [publisher's emblem] | PYRAMID BOOKS . NEW YORK

Collation: 208 leaves, glued at spine.

p.[1] blurb; p.[2] blank; p.[3] title-page; p.[4] title and arrangement, edition, copyright, rights reservations, printing and publishing notices; pp.5–7 FOREWORD; pp.[8]–[12] maps; pp. 13–415 text; p.[416] publisher's advertisements.

18.0 × 10.6 cm. Bulk: 1.8 cm. White wove paper; all edges trimmed and stained orange. Bound in paper covers printed in black, gold and red with a mottled grey background.

Price: $0.85. Number of copies undetermined. Published 15 February 1966.

Note: This is Pyramid Book S-1288.

A47g. Fourth English edition ([1968]):

COUNT | BELISARIUS | BY ROBERT GRAVES | [star] | [publisher's emblem] | PENGUIN BOOKS

Collation: [A]^{16} B–F^{16} G–I^8 K–P^{16}, 216 leaves.

p.[1] PENGUIN BOOKS | 1025 | COUNT BELISARIUS and biographical note; p.[2] blank; p.[3] title-page; p.[4] publisher's, publication, printer's and rights limitation notices; p.[5] CONTENTS; p.[6] blank; pp.[7] 8–421 text, with pp.[9, 29, 46, 61, 76, 92, 108, 124, 142, 161, 179, 197, 215, 229, 245, 265, 284, 304, 318, 340, 356, 371, 388, 406] unnumbered; pp. [422]–[426] maps; p.[427] publisher's advertisements; p.[428] blank; pp.[429]–[432] publisher's advertisements.

18.0 × 11.0 cm. Bulk: 1.5 cm. White wove paper; all edges trimmed. Bound in white paper covers printed in black, brown and orange.

Price: 7s. Number of copies unknown. Published in 1968.

Note: Impressions: 2nd, 1975; 3rd, 1977; 4th, 1978; 5th, 1980; 6th, 1983; 7th, 1986.

A47h. Fifth English edition (1970):

Count Belisarius | ROBERT GRAVES | [publisher's emblem] | CASSELL . LONDON

Collation: [A]^8 B–2L^8, 272 leaves.

p.[i] COUNT BELISARIUS and blurb; p.[ii] list of historical novels by Graves; p.[iii] blank; p.[iv] map; p.[v] title-page; p.[vi] publisher's, copyright, rights reservations, SBN and printer's notices; pp 1–526 [527] text; p.[528] blank; p.[529] map; p.[530] blank; p.[531] map; p.[532] blank; p.[533] map; p.[534] map; pp.[535]–[538] blank.

19.6 × 12.9 cm. Bulk: 3.8/4.3 cm. White wove paper; all edges trimmed. White

wove endpapers. Bound in light brown cloth, front and back blank; spine stamped in gold; top to bottom: Count Belisarius [horizontal rule] ROBERT GRAVES [horizontal rule] CASSELL

Price: £1.75. Number of copies unknown. Published March 1970.

Note: This is a photographically reduced replating of A47a with the Foreword and Contents removed.

A48   COLLECTED POEMS   [1938]

a. First edition.

COLLECTED POEMS | [swelled rule] | ROBERT GRAVES | [publisher's emblem] | CASSELL | AND COMPANY LIMITED | LONDON, TORONTO, MELBOURNE AND SYDNEY

Collation: [a]/a1$^{4/8}$ A–M^8, 108 leaves.
    p.[i] COLLECTED POEMS; p.[ii] blank; p.[iii] title-page; p. [iv] copyright, printing and printer's notices; p.v list of works by Graves; p.vi quotations from Riding (3 ll.) and Skelton (7 ll.); pp.vii–xi CONTENTS; p.[xii] blank; pp.xiii–xxiv FOREWORD; p.[1] –190 text, with pp.[1, 35, 75, 107, 171] being section headings and pp.[2, 36, 74, 76, 106, 108, 170, 172] blank; pp.[191] –[192] blank.
    21.6 × 13.9 cm. Bulk: 1.7/2.3 cm. White wove paper; all edges trimmed. White wove endpapers. Bound in medium green cloth; front and back blank; spine stamped in gold: [first five lines enclosed in oval wreath:] | COLLECTED POEMS | . | Robert | Graves | CASSELL

Price: 10s.6d. Number of copies unknown. Published in November 1938 in buff dust-jacket printed in black and red.

Contents: Foreword – I: The Haunted House – Reproach – The Finding of Love – 'The General Elliott' – Outlaws – One Hard Look – A Frosty Night – Allie – Unicorn and the White Doe – Henry and Mary – Love without Hope – What Did I Dream? – The Country Dance – The Hills of May – Lost Love – Vain and Careless – A English Wood – The Bedpost – The Pier-Glass – Apples and Water – Wanderings of Christmas – Pygmalion and Galatea – Down – Mermaid, Dragon, Fiend – II: In Procession – Angry Samson – Warning to Children – Song: To Be Less Philosophical – Alice – Blonde or Dark? – Richard Roe and John Doe – The Witches' Cauldron – Ancestors – Children of Darkness – The Cool Web – Certain Mercies – The Cuirassiers of the Frontier – Love in Barrenness – The Presence – The Land of Whipperginny – In No Direction – The Castle – Return – Lust in Song – Nobody – Without Pause – Full Moon – Vanity – Pure Death – Sick Love – It Was All Very Tidy – III: Callow Captain – Thief – Saint – The Furious Voyage – Song: Lift Boy – The Next Time – Ulysses – The Succubus – The Stranger – Trudge, Body – The Clock Man – The Reader over My Shoulder – The Smoky House – Green Loving – The Legs – Gardener – Front Door Soliloquy – In Broken Images – On Rising Early – Flying Crooked – The Foolish Senses – Largesse to the Poor – The Goblet – Fiend, Dragon, Mermaid –

Fragment of a Lost Poem – IV: Galataea and Pygmalion – The Devil's Advice to Story-Tellers – Sea Side – Lunch-Hour Blues – Wm. Brazier – Welsh Incident – Vision in the Repair-Shop – Hotel Bed – Progressive Housing – Interruption – Act V, Scene 5 – Midway – Hell – Leda – Synthetic Such – The Florist Rose – Being Tall – Lost Acres – At First Sight – Recalling War – Down, Wanton, Down! – X – A Former Attachment – Nature's Lineaments – Time – The Philosopher – On Dwelling – Parent to Children – Ogres and Pygmies – History of the Word – Single Fare – To Challenge Delight – To Walk on Hills – To Bring the Dead to Life – To Evoke Posterity – The Poets – Defeat of the Rebels – The Grudge – Never Such Love – The Halfpenny – The Fallen Signpost – The China Plate – Idle Hands – The Laureate – A Jealous Man – The Cloak – The Halls of Bedlam – Or to Perish before Day – A Country Mansion – The Eremites – The Advocates – Self-Praise – V: On Portents – The Terraced Valley – The Challenge – To Whom Else? – To the Sovereign Muse – The Ages of Oath – New Legends – Like Snow – The Climate of Thought – End of Play – The Fallen Tower of Siloam – The Great-Grandmother – No More Ghosts – Leaving the Rest Unsaid

Note: Both A48a and A48b were printed in Great Britain.

A48b. American issue ([1939]):

COLLECTED POEMS | [swelled rule] | ROBERT GRAVES | [publisher's emblem] | RANDOM HOUSE | NEW YORK

Collation as 48a.
   21.6 × 13.9 cm. Bulk: 1.7/2.2 cm. White wove paper; all edges trimmed; top edges stained black. White wove endpapers. Bound in dark brick-red cloth; front and back blank; spine stamped in gold: [publisher's emblem in black and gold] | [solid rectangular black box, inside which next 7 ll.:] [rectangular broad rule box, inside which:] | [rectangular light rule box, inside which the next 5 ll.:] | COLLECTED | POEMS | [wedge] | ROBERT | GRAVES | [next 2 ll. at bottom of spine:] RANDOM | HOUSE

Price: $2.50. Number of copies undisclosed. Published 16 March 1939 in a buff dust-jacket printed in black and purple.

A49   T.E. LAWRENCE TO HIS BIOGRAPHER   1938

a. First edition:

[in brown:] T. E. Lawrence | TO HIS BIOGRAPHER, | Robert Graves | INFORMATION ABOUT HIMSELF, IN THE FORM | OF LETTERS, NOTES AND ANSWERS TO QUESTIONS, | EDITED WITH A CRITICAL COMMENTARY. | [in brown: cut of crossed rifles, flags, swords, scimitar and sabre, with leaves] | NEW YORK | Doubleday, Doran & Company, Inc. | MCMXXXVIII

Collation: [1]⁸⁺² [2] – [10]⁸ [11]¹⁰ [12]⁸, 100 leaves.
   one leaf, verso blank, on the recto of which: *This edition | is limited to 1,000 numbered and | signed copies for sale, of which 500 copies | are printed for the United*

States. | *This is number* --- [number written in by hand] | [signature of Graves]; p.[i] T. E. Lawrence | TO HIS BIOGRAPHER, | ROBERT GRAVES; p.[ii] blank; [frontispiece, back blank]; p.[iii] title-page tipped in; p.[iv] printer's, designer's, copyright, rights reservation and edition notices; p.[v] PUBLISHER'S NOTE; p.[vi] blank; pp.vii–viii FOREWORD; p.ix CONTENTS; p.[x] blank; p.[1] PART I | *1920–1926*; p.[2] blank; pp.3–39 text; p.[40] blank; p.[41] PART II | *1927*; p.[42] blank; pp.43–144 text; p.[145] PART III | *1928–1935*; p.[146] blank; pp.147–187 text; p.[188] blank.

22.7 × 15.2 cm. Bulk: 1.7/2.3 cm. Cream laid paper; top edge only trimmed and gilt. Cream laid endpapers. Bound in buff cloth; back blank; front blind-stamped: T. E. LAWRENCE | TO HIS BIOGRAPHER | ROBERT GRAVES; spine stamped: [triple light-heavy-light rule of brown, gold, brown] | triple rule as above] | [triple rule as above] | [brown light rule] | [double heavy gold rule] | [solid brown rectangular box, inside which next 8 ll.:] T. E. | LAWRENCE | TO HIS | BIOGRAPHER | ROBERT | GRAVES | DOUBLEDAY | DORAN | [two heavy gold rules] | [brown light rule] | [eleven triple rules as at top]

Price: $20.00. Number of copies: 500. Published 2 December 1938 in a buff dust-jacket printed in black, brown and green.

Note: Issued with Liddell Hart's book of the same title. The book was designed by A.P. Tedesco. Both volumes were enclosed in a brown slip-case printed in black and brown covering entire front and back.

A49b. First English issue ([1939]):

[in brown:] T. E. Lawrence | TO HIS BIOGRAPHER, | Robert Graves | INFORMATION ABOUT HIMSELF, IN THE FORM | OF LETTERS, NOTES AND ANSWERS TO QUESTIONS, | EDITED WITH A CRITICAL COMMENTARY. | [in brown: cut of crossed rifles, flags, swords, scimitar and sabre, with leaves] | FABER AND FABER LIMITED | 24 Russell Square | London

Collation as A49a.

one leaf, recto blank, on the verso of which: *This edition* | *is limited to 1,000 numbered and* | *signed copies for sale, of which 500 copies* | *are printed for Great Britain.* | *This is number* [number written in by hand] | [signature of Graves]; pp.[i]–[ii] as A49a; p.[iii] title-page tipped in; p.[iv] *First published in December Mcmxxxviii* | *by Faber and Faber Limited* | *24 Russell Square, London,W.C.* | *Printed in the United States of America* | *All Rights Reserved* | DESIGNED BY A.P. TEDESCO | CL | The Publishers are grateful to Messrs. | Jonathan Cape, Ltd. for permission to | include copyright material.; remainder as A49a.

Size, bulk, and paper as A49a . Bound in red cloth; back blank; front stamped with solid grey rectangular box stamped in gold: [three successivly smaller rectangular light rule boxes, inside which:] T.E. LAWRENCE | to his biographer | ROBERT GRAVES; spine stamped with solid grey rectangular box inside which: [three light rules] | T.E. | LAWRENCE | to his | biographer | ROBERT | GRAVES | [light rule] | *Faber and* | *Faber* | [three light rules]

Price: 5 gns. Number of copies: 500. Published 12 January 1939 in glassine wrapper and included in a light grey-green box with Liddell Hart's book.

A49c. Second English edition ([1963]):

T.E. Lawrence | TO HIS BIOGRAPHERS | Robert Graves | AND | Liddell Hart | [publisher's emblem] | CASSELL . LONDON

Collation: [A]⁸ B–P¹⁶, 232 leaves.

p.[i] T.E. Lawrence | TO HIS BIOGRAPHERS | ROBERT GRAVES | AND | LIDDELL HART; p.[ii] blank; [frontispiece, back blank]; p.[iii] title-page; p.[iv] publisher's, copyright, acknowledgement and printer's notices; p.[v] T.E. Lawrence | TO HIS BIOGRAPHER | ROBERT GRAVES | *Information about himself, in the form of letters, notes and answers to* | *questions, edited with a critical commentary.*; p.[vi] PUBLISHER'S NOTE; pp.vii–viii FOREWORD; p.ix CONTENTS; p.[x] blank; p.[1] PART I | *1920–1926*; p.[2] blank; pp.3–39 text; p.[40] blank; p. [41] PART II | *1927*; p.[42] blank; pp.43–144 text; p.[145] PART III | *1928–1935*; p.[146] blank; pp.147–187 text; p. [188] blank; p. *T.E. Lawrence* | *TO HIS BIOGRAPHER* | *LIDDELL HART* | *Information about himself, in the form of letters, notes, answers to* | *questions and conversations*; p.[ii] PUBLISHER'S NOTE; pp.iii–iv FOREWORD; pp.[1] 2–233 text; p. [234] blank; pp.235–260 INDEX; pp.[261]–[262] blank.

21.5 × 13.8 cm. Bulk: 3.1/3.7 cm. White wove paper; all edges trimmed. White wove endpapers. Bound in dark beige cloth; front and back blank; spine stamped in gold: [at top of spine, facing front:] T.E. LAWRENCE | [remainder across spine:] TO HIS | BIOGRAPHERS | ROBERT | GRAVES | & | LIDDELL | HART | CASSELL

Price: 42s. Number of copies: 2,062. Published 7 March 1963 in white dust-jacket printed in black and yellowish grey-green.

Notes: Impressions: 2nd, May 1963 (1,000 copies).
Printed in Great Britain.
Greenwood Press issued a photographic reprint of this edition in 1976.

A49d. Second edition, American issue (1963):

T.E. Lawrence | TO HIS BIOGRAPHERS | Robert Graves | AND | Liddell Hart | [Cassell publisher's emblem] | DOUBLEDAY & COMPANY, INC. | GARDEN CITY, NEW YORK, 1963

Collation as A49c.
Remainder as A49c, except lacks frontispiece and p.[vi] has acknowledgement, LC card, copyright, rights reservation and printing notices.
20.8 × 14.1 cm. Bulk: 3.1/3.7 cm. White wove paper; top and fore-edges trimmed. White wove endpapers. Bound in rust cloth; front and back blank; quarter cloth spine in buff, printed in two rows, top to bottom: [in black:] T.E. LAWRENCE [in rose buff:] TO HIS BIOGRAPHERS | [in black:] *Robert Graves & B.H. Liddell Hart* [in rose buff:] DOUBLEDAY

Price: $6.50. Number of copies: 3,500. Published 16 August 1963 in white dust-jacket printed in black, orange and green.

Notes: Impressions: 2nd, 1963 (2,500 copies); p.[iv] has *'Johnathan'* for *'Jonathan'* in first impression.
Printed in the U.S.

A50 NO MORE GHOSTS [1940]

First edition:

NO MORE GHOSTS | Selected Poems | by | ROBERT GRAVES | Faber and Faber | 24 Russell Square | London

Collation: [A]⁸ B–E⁸, 40 leaves.

p.[1] NO MORE GHOSTS; p.[2] blank; p.[3] title-page; p.[4] publication, printer's and rights reservation notices; p.5 SELECT BIBLIOGRAPHY; p.[6] blank; pp.7–8 CONTENTS; pp.9–79 text; p.[80] blank.

18.7 × 12.4 cm. Bulk: 0.7/1.0 cm. White wove paper; all edges trimmed; watermarked with a crown and Abbey Mills | Greenfield. White wove endpapers. Bound in grey-tan boards; back blank; front printed in blue: *No More* | *Ghosts* | [star] | *Robert* | *Graves*; spine printed in blue from top to bottom: NO MORE GHOSTS BY ROBERT GRAVES FABER

Price: 2s. 6d. Number of copies: 2,000. Published in September 1940 in bright blue dust-jacket printed in black.

Contents: 1. The Haunted House – 2. Apples and Water – 3. Time – 4. On Dwelling – 5. Love in Barrenness – 6. Vain and Careless – 7. In Procession – 8. Angry Samson – 9. Ogres and Pygmies – 10. The Bards – 11. The Cool Web – 12. The Cuirassiers of the Frontier – 13. The Castle – 14. Full Moon – 15. Vanity – 16. Pure Death – 17. Sick Love – 18. The Presence – 19. Nature's Lineaments – 20. The Furious Voyage – 21. Callow Captain – 22. The Beast – 23. A Love Story – 24. The Legs – 25. Flying Crooked – 26. Warning to Children – 27. The Laureate – 28. The Terraced Valley – 29. Recalling War – 30. Certain Mercies – 31. Ulysses – 32. Down, Wanton, Down! – 33. The Florist Rose – 34. The Thieves – 35. Sea Side – 36. The Devil's Advice to Story-Tellers – 37. The Cloak – 38. To Bring the Dead to Life – 39. Defeat of the Rebels – 40. Never Such Love – 41. The Poets – 42. A Jealous Man – 43. The Advocates – 44. On Portents – 45. Like Snow – 46. End of Play – 47. The Fallen Tower of Siloam – 48. The Great-Grandmother – 49. To Sleep – 50. No More Ghosts

Notes: Impressions: 2nd, March 1941 (2,000 copies); 3rd, June 1945 (2,000 copies); 4th, January 1947 (2,000 copies). The cover legend on the second and third reads: *No More Ghosts* | *selected poems* | [star] | *Robert* | *Graves*; the second impression has black printing on the covers; the third has blue.

A51 SERGEANT LAMB OF THE NINTH [1940]

a. First edition:

SERGEANT LAMB | OF THE NINTH | *by* | ROBERT GRAVES | AUTHOR OF | 'I, CLAUDIUS', 'CLAUDIUS THE GOD' | 'COUNT BELISARIUS' ETC. | [publisher's emblem] | METHUEN & CO. LTD. LONDON | *36 Essex Street, Strand, W.C.2*

Collation: π⁶ 1–23⁸ 24⁴, 194 leaves.

p.[i] SERGEANT LAMB | OF THE NINTH; p.[ii] list of regiments; [frontispiece, letter from Lamb, back blank]; p.[iii] title-page; p.[iv] publication and printing notices; pp.v–vi *FOREWORD*; pp.vii–xi ROGER LAMB'S NOTE OF EXPLANATION; p. [xii] blank; pp.1–376 text; [foldout map tipped to p.376 and rear endpaper].

18.5 × 12.3 cm. Bulk: 3.0/3.4 cm. White wove paper; all edges trimmed. White wove endpapers. Bound in plum-red cloth; front and back blank; spine stamped in white: *SERGEANT* | *LAMB* | *OF* | *THE NINTH* | *ROBERT* | *GRAVES* | *METHUEN*

Price: 8s 6d. Number of copies: 10,000. Published 12 September 1940 in white dust-jacket printed in red, black, brown, green and blue.

Notes: Impressions: 2nd, July 1945 (2,500 copies).

The dust-jacket was designed by John Aldridge.

This book has been translated into German and Spanish.

The second impression is called "SECOND EDITION" between ll. 7/8 on the title-page; it collates [1]^{16} 2–11^{16} 11/13$^{2/16}$ [*sic*: 11 *for* 12]; 18.2 × 12.3 cm.

Hutchinson issued a photographic reprint of this edition in 1985. Pp.[i], [iii] – [iv] have been reset; there are two blank leaves after p.376; there is no folding map after p.376; and there is no frontispiece. However, a note, in different type, has been added at the foot of p.vi stating: 'Not reproduced in this edition.' This book is perfect bound and is in white covers printed in black, red, and tan. It measures 21.4 × 13.6 cm. Bulk 2.6 cm.

A51b. First American edition ([1940]):

[rectangular double-rule box enclosing all:] | *Sergeant* LAMB'S | [in red:] AMERICA | [rule] | by Robert Graves | [rule] | [in red: publisher's emblem] | RANDOM HOUSE | *New York*

Collation: [1] – [25]^8, 200 leaves.

2 pp. blank; p.[i] SERGEANT LAMB'S | AMERICA; p.[ii] list of books by Graves; p.[iii] title-page; p.[iv] acknowledgement, printing and copyright notices; p.[v] facsimile of letter by Lamb; p.[vi] transcript of letter facing; pp.vii–viii Foreword; pp.ix–xiii Roger Lamb's Note of *Explanation*; p. [xiv] list of regiments; p.[1] SERGEANT LAMB'S | AMERICA, p.[2] blank; pp.3–380 text; pp.[381] – [384] blank.

21.1 × 14.2 cm. Bulk: 3.4/4.1 cm. White wove paper; all edges trimmed. Rear endpapers blank white wove paper; front endpapers white wove, inner sides printed with map of Lamb's travels. Bound in red cloth; back blank; front has blue paper label with white legend: [double-rule rectangular box enclosing all:] *Sergeant* LAMB'S | AMERICA | [rule] | Robert Graves; spine has blue label with white legend: [double-rule rectangular box enclosing all:] | *Sergeant* LAMB'S | AMERICA | [rule] | ROBERT | GRAVES | Random House

Price: $2.50. Number of copies undisclosed. Published 1 November 1940 in white dust-jacket printed in black, red, green and gold.

Note: There was a second printing of this edition, probably before 1 November 1940, which can be distinguished as follows: on the verso of the title-page the note, "A transcription of Sergeant Lamb's letter appears on reverse side of facing page" and the statement, "Second Printing before publication"; the top edges are stained blue.

A51c. Second English edition ([1950]):

SERGEANT LAMB | OF THE NINTH | [swelled rule with elliptical asterisk in centre] | ROBERT GRAVES | [star] | PENGUIN BOOKS | HARMONDSWORTH . MIDDLESEX

Collation: [A]^{16} B$-$L^{16}, 176 leaves.

p.[1] PENGUIN BOOKS | 725 | SERGEANT LAMB OF THE NINTH | ROBERT GRAVES | [publisher's emblem]; p.[2] publication, publisher's and printer's notices; p.[3] title-page; p.4 list of regiments; p.5 *Foreword*; pp.6–7 [8] ROGER LAMB'S NOTE OF EXPLANATION; pp.9–15 text; pp.[16] – [17] map; pp.18–352 text.

18.1 × 11.1 cm. Bulk: 1.6 cm. White wove paper; all edges trimmed. Bound in white paper covers printed in orange and black.

Price: 1s. 6d. Number of copies: 45,000. Published in February 1950.

A51d. Third English edition ([1961]):

ROBERT GRAVES | [rule] | SERGEANT LAMB | OF THE NINTH | MAY FAIR BOOKS

Collation: [A]^{16} B$-$I^{16} [K]^{16}, 160 leaves.

p.[1] blurb; p.[2] publisher's notice, list of books by Graves, copyright and publication notices; p.[3] title-page; pp.[4] – [5] map; p.6 list of regiments; pp.7–316 text; p.317 *Postcript*; pp.318–320 *Roger Lamb's Note of Explanation*

17.4 × 10.8 cm. Bulk: 1.8 cm. White wove paper; all edges trimmed. Bound in white paper covers printed in green, blue, red, magenta and black; inside of front and back covers blank.

Price: 3s. 6d. Number of copies: 25,000. Published 15 July 1961.

Note: This is May Fair Book no. 12.

A51e. Second American edition ([1962]):

ROBERT GRAVES | [decorative divider] | Sergeant Lamb's | AMERICA | [publisher's emblem] | VINTAGE BOOKS | *A Division of Random House* | New York

Collation: 176 leaves, glued at spine.

p.[i] Sergeant Lamb's | AMERICA; p.[ii] blank; p.[iii] title-page; p.[vi] edition, publisher's copyright and manufacturing notices; pp.[v] –vi Foreword; pp.[vii] viii–xi Roger Lamb's | Note of Explanation; p.[xii] list of regiments; p.[1] Sergeant Lamb's | AMERICA; p.[2] blank; pp.[3] 4–339 text, pp.[92, 105, 119, 147, 241] being unnumbered; p.[340] biographical, typographical, printer's and designer's notices.

18.4 × 11.1 cm. Bulk: 1.6 cm. White wove paper; all edges trimmed. Bound in white paper covers printed in blue, red and black.

Price: $1.45. Number of copies undisclosed. Published 30 April 1962.

A52   THE LONG WEEK-END   [1940]

a. First edition:

THE LONG WEEK-END | A Social History of Great Britain | 1918–1939 | *by* | ROBERT GRAVES | *and* | ALAN HODGE | FABER AND FABER LIMITED | 24 *Russell Square* | *London*

Collation: [A]⁸ B–2F⁸ 2G⁴, 236 leaves.

p.[1] THE LONG WEEK-END | A Social History of Great Britain | 1918–1939; p.[2] blank; p.[3] title-page; p.[4] publication, publisher's and printer's notices; p.[5] To | K. G. | in gratitude for much | hard work; p.[6] blank; p.7 Authors' Note; p.[8] blank; pp.9–10 Contents; pp.11–455 text; pp.456–472 Index.

21.6 × 13.9 cm. Bulk: 2.7/3.2 cm. White wove paper; top and fore-edges trimmed. White wove endpapers. Bound in brown cloth; front and back blank; spine stamped in gold: THE | LONG | WEEK-END | [double rule] | Robert Graves | *and* | Alan Hodge | [double rule] | FABER AND | FABER

Price: 12s. 6d. Number of copies: 4,000. Published in November 1940 in canary dust-jacket printed in red and black.

Contents: Authors' Note – 1. Armistice, 1918 – 2. Revolution Averted, 1919 – 3. Women – 4. Reading Matter – 5. Post-War Politics – 6. Various Conquests – 7. Sex – 8. Amusements – 9. Screen and Stage – 10. Revolution Again Averted – 11. Domestic Life – 12. Art, Literature and Religion – 13. Education and Ethics – 14. Sport and Controversy – 15. The Depression, 1930 – 16. Pacifism, Nudism, Hiking – 17. The Days of the Loch Ness Monster – 18. Recovery, 1935 – 19. The Days of Non-Intervention – 20. 'The Deepening Twilight of Barbarism' – 21. Three Kings in One Year – 22. Keeping Fit and Doing the Lambeth Walk – 23. Social Consciences – 24. 'Markets Close Firmer' – 25. Still at Peace – 26. Rain Stops Play, 1939 – Index

Notes: The 'second edition,' although it is called 'impression' on p.[4], is a photographic reprint of this edition with minor rearrangements in [A]; the dedication has been moved to p.[4]; p.[5] Note to First Edition; pp.6–8 Note to Second Edition; 4,050 copies were published in May 1950 at 16s.

Hutchinson issued a photographic reprint of the 'second edition' in paperback in 1985. pp.[1], [3]–[4] have been reset but the remainder of the contents are the same: the dedication remains on p.[4]. It is 19.8 × 12.6 cm. and bulks 3.5 cm. There are 4 additional blank leaves (pp.[473]–[480]) at the end of the book making the total of 240 leaves, perfect bound.

This book has been translated into Danish and Swedish.

A52b. First American edition (1941):

THE LONG WEEK END | A Social History of Great Britain | 1918–1939 | *by* | ROBERT GRAVES | *and* | ALAN HODGE | *New York* | THE MACMILLAN COMPANY | 1941

Collation: [1]–[13]¹⁶ [14]¹² [15]¹⁶, 236 leaves.

pp.[i]–[ii] blank; p.[iii] THE LONG WEEK END | A Social History of Great

Britain | 1918–1939; p.[iv] publisher's emblem and notice; p.[v] title-page; p.[vi] copyright and printer's notices; p.[vii] To | K.G. | in gratitude for much | hard work; p.[viii] blank; p.[ix] Authors' Note; p.[x] blank; pp. [xi] – [xii] Contents; p.[xiii] THE LONG WEEK END | A Social History of Great Britain | 1918–1939; p.[xiv] blank; pp.1–439 text; p.[440] blank; pp.441–445 Index; pp.[456] – [458] blank.

23.4 × 15.5 cm. Bulk: 3.0/3.5 cm. White wove paper; all edges trimmed. Heavy white wove endpapers. Bound in dark blue cloth; front and back blank; spine stamped in gold: THE | LONG | WEEK END | [double rule] | Robert Graves | *and* | Alan Hodge | [double rule] | MACMILLAN | [long-short-long dashes]

Price: $3.00. Number of copies unknown. Published 27 May 1941 in white dust-jacket printed in red and dark blue.

Note: Impression: 2nd, 1941.

A52c. Readers' Union impression (1941):

THE LONG WEEK-END | A Social History of Great Britain | 1918–1939 | *by* | ROBERT GRAVES | *and* | ALAN HODGE | READERS' UNION LIMITED | *by arrangement with* | FABER AND FABER LIMITED | *London 1941*

Collation: [A]/A*8/8 B/B* –O/O*8/8 P8 Q4, 236 leaves.

pp.[1]–[2] front pastedown endpaper; pp.[3]–[4] blank; p.[5] THE LONG WEEK-END | A Social History of Great Britain | 1918–1939; p.[6] blank; p.[7] title-page; p.[8] printer's, publisher's and dedication notices; p.9 Contents; p.10 Authors' Note; pp.11–472 as A52a.

19.7 × 12.9 cm. Bulk: 2.4/2.8 cm. White wove paper; all edges trimmed. Rear endpapers white wove. Bound in wine-red cloth; front and back blank; spine stamped in silver: *Graves* | [rule] | [rectangular rule box enclosing 2 ll.:] THE LONG | WEEK-END | [rule] | *Hodge* | [remainder blind stamped:] [rule] | [Readers' Union emblem]

Price: 2s. 9d. Number of copies: 19,000. Published in November 1941.

A52d. Second English edition ([1961]):
[7 ll. flush left:] The Long | Week-End | A Social History of Great Britain, | 1918–1939 | ROBERT GRAVES and | ALAN HODGE | [publisher's emblem] | [centred:] FOUR SQUARE BOOKS LTD BARNARD'S INN HOLBORN LONDON EC1

Collation: [A]16 B–N16 [O]16, 224 leaves.

p.[1] [title and publisher flush left:] The Long | Week-End | [centred 3 ll. blurb] | A FOUR SQUARE BOOK; p.[2] publisher's advertisement; p.[3] title-page; p.[4] publication notice, dedication, and publisher's and printer's notices; p.[5] CONTENTS; p.[6] AUTHORS' NOTE and NOTE TO THIS EDITION; pp. 7–448 text.

17.8 × 10.8 cm. Bulk: 2.0 cm. White wove paper; all edges trimmed. Bound in white paper covers printed in magenta, red, blue, gold and black; inner sides blank.

Price: 5s. Number of copies: 20,000. Published in October 1961.

Note: Impressions: 2nd, 4 November 1965 (10,000 copies; price 6s.); the title-page and pagination differ but the collation is the same.

A52e. Second American 'edition' ([1963]):

THE LONG WEEK-END | A Social History of Great Britain | 1918–1939 | *by* | ROBERT GRAVES | *and* | ALAN HODGE | [publisher's emblem] | The Norton Library | W . W . NORTON & COMPANY . INC . | NEW YORK

Collation: 240 leaves, unsigned, glued at spine.
    p.[i] THE LONG WEEK-END | A Social History of Great Britain | 1918–1939; p.[ii] blank; p.[1] biographical notices; p.[2] blank; p.[3] title-page; p.[4] copyright, publication, dedication and printing notices; p.5 Note to the First Edition; pp.6–8 Note to the Second Edition; pp.9–472 as A52a; p.[473] blank; pp.[474]–[477] publisher's advertisements; p.[478] blank.
    19.6 × 12.9 cm. Bulk: 2.2 cm. White wove paper; all edges trimmed. Bound in white paper covers printed in red, blue and black.

Price: $1.95. Number of copies: 53,961, in several printings. Published in 1963.

Note: This book would appear to be a photographic reprint of the second 'edition' of A52a.
    The publishers report the number of copies sold rather than printed and say that this figure, 53,961, was as of 31 March 1985.

A52f. Third English edition (1971):

The Long | Week-end | A SOCIAL HISTORY OF GREAT BRITAIN | 1918–1939 | Robert Graves and | Alan Hodge | [publisher's emblem] | PENGUIN BOOKS

Collation: [1]^{12} 2–6^{12} 7–14^{10} 15–20^{12}, 224 leaves.
    p.[1] PENGUIN BOOKS | THE LONG WEEK-END | [blurb]; p.[2] blank; p.[3] title-page; p.[4] publisher's, publication, copyright and printer's notices, dedication, rights limitation notice; p. [5] CONTENTS; p.[6] AUTHORS' NOTE and NOTE TO THIS EDITION; pp. 7–448 text.
    18.0 × 11.0 cm. Bulk: 2.2 cm. White wove paper; all edges trimmed. Bound in white paper covers printed in cream, orange, brown and blue-grey.

Price: .50p. Number of copies: 17,148 sold by March 1986. Published in July 1971.

A53 PROCEED, SERGEANT LAMB [1941]

a. First edition:

PROCEED, | SERGEANT LAMB | *by* | ROBERT GRAVES | AUTHOR OF | 'SERGEANT LAMB OF THE NINTH' | [publisher's emblem] | METHUEN & CO. LTD. LONDON | *36 Essex Street, Strand, W.C.2*

Collation: π^6 1–19^8 20^6, 164 leaves.
    2 pp. blank, as front pastedown endpaper; p.[i] PROCEED, | SERGEANT LAMB; p.[ii] list of regiments; [frontispiece, back blank]; p.[iii] title-page; p.[iv] publication

and printing notices; pp.v–vii *FOREWORD*; p.[viii] blank; p.[ix] PROCEED, | SERGEANT LAMB; p.[x] blank; pp.1–314 text; p.[315] blank; p.[316] printer's notice; [map tipped to rear endpaper].

18.6 × 12.3 cm. Bulk: 2.3/2.6 cm. White wove paper; all edges trimmed. White wove rear endpaper. Bound in sea-green cloth; front and back blank; spine stamped in white: PROCEED, | SERGEANT | LAMB | ROBERT | GRAVES | METHUEN

Price: 8s. 6d. Number of copies: 10,000. Published 13 February 1941 in white dust-jacket printed in black, red, blue and brown.

Notes: This book has been translated into Spanish.

The dust-jacket was designed by John Aldridge.

According to Methuen, 4,000 copies of signatures 1–16 'were destroyed by enemy action during 1942' and were reprinted.

Hutchinson published a photographic reprint of this edition in 1985. pp.[i], [iii], [iv] have been reset and pp.v–vii either reset or reimposed so that *FOREWORD* is now on pp.[v]–vi and there is no blank p.[viii]. There are no blank pages at the end and there is no map at the end and no frontispiece. However, a note at the foot of p.[v] says: 'Not reproduced in this edition.' The book is perfect bound in white covers printed in black, red, and tan. It measures 21.5 × 13.6 cm. Bulk: 2.1 cm. It is interesting to note that Hutchinson chose to reprint this edition rather than A53c.

A53b. First American edition ([1941]):

[whole enclosed within double-rule rectangular box:] PROCEED, | [in red:] SERGEANT LAMB | [rule] | by Robert Graves | *Author of* | SERGEANT LAMB'S AMERICA | [rule] | [in red: publisher's emblem] | RANDOM HOUSE | *New York*

Collation: [1]–[21]^8, 168 leaves.

p.[i] PROCEED, | SERGEANT LAMB; p.[ii] list of regiments; p.[iii] title-page; p.[iv] publication, printer's and copyright notices; p.[v] facsimile of letter; p.[vi] transcript of letter; pp.vii–xi Foreword; p.[xii] blank; p.[1] PROCEED, | SERGEANT LAMB; p.[2] map; pp.3–322 text; pp.[323]–[324] blank.

21.3 × 14.3 cm. Bulk: 3.0/3.6 cm. White wove paper; all edges trimmed; top edges stained blue. Cream wove endpapers. Bound in red cloth; back blank; blue label on front printed in white: [whole enclosed in double-rule rectangular box:] PROCEED, | SERGEANT | LAMB | [rule] | by Robert Graves; blue label on spine, printed in white: [whole enclosed in double-rule rectangular box:] PROCEED, | SERGEANT | LAMB | [rule] | ROBERT | GRAVES | Random House

Price: $2.50. Number of copies undisclosed. Published 15 October 1941 in white dust-jacket printed in black, red, orange, brown, tan, blue and gold.

Note: The second impression of this edition varies only in changing "First" to "Second Printing" on the verso of the title-page.

A53c. Second English edition ([1947]):

PROCEED, | SERGEANT LAMB | *by* | ROBERT GRAVES | AUTHOR OF | 'SERGEANT LAMB OF THE NINTH' | SECOND EDITION | [publisher's emblem] | METHUEN & CO. LTD. LONDON | *36 Essex Street, Strand, W.C.2*

Collation: [A]⁸ B–L¹⁶, 168 leaves.

p.[i] PROCEED, | SERGEANT LAMB; p.[ii] list of regiments; [frontispiece, back blank]; p.[iii] title-page; p.[iv] publication and printing notices; pp.v–vii *FOREWORD*; pp. viii–ix *NOTE TO SECOND EDITION*; p.[x] blank; pp.1–321 text; p.[322] printer's notice; [map tipped to following page]; pp. [323]–[324] blank; pp.[325]–[326] pasted down to back cover.

18.2 × 12.3 cm. Bulk: 2.1/2.4 cm. White wove paper; all edges trimmed. White wove front endpapers. Bound in sea-green cloth; front and back blank; spine stamped in white: *PROCEED,* | *SERGEANT* | *LAMB* | *ROBERT* | *GRAVES* | *METHUEN*

Price: 8s. 6d. Number of copies: 5,000. Published in February 1947 in white dust-jacket printed in black, red, blue and brown; pictorial portion of jacket as in A53a.

Notes: The last 1,750 sheets of this edition were issued 10 September 1953 at 6s.

The edition notice gives 1946 as the publication date but the work was not issued until the following year.

A53d. Third English edition ([1961]):

ROBERT GRAVES | [rule] | PROCEED, SERGEANT | LAMB | MAY FAIR BOOKS

Collation: [A]¹⁶ B–H¹⁶ [I]¹⁶, 144 leaves.

p.[1] publisher's advertisements; p.[2] list of books by Graves and copyright and printing notices; p.[3] title-page; pp.[4]–[5] map; p.[6] list of regiments; p.[7]–[8] *FOREWORD*; pp.9–288 text.

17.4 × 10.6 cm. Bulk: 1.6 cm. White wove paper; all edges trimmed. Bound in white paper covers printed in blue, magenta and black.

Price: 3s. 6d. Number of copies: 25,000. Published 15 July 1961.

A54 WIFE TO MR. MILTON [1943]

a. First edition:

THE STORY OF MARIE POWELL, | WIFE TO MR. MILTON | by | ROBERT GRAVES | *With two half-tone plates* | [publisher's emblem] | CASSELL AND COMPANY LTD. | London, Toronto, Melbourne | and Sydney

Collation: [A]¹⁶ B–M¹⁶, 192 leaves.

p.[i] WIFE TO MR. MILTON; p.[ii] list of novels by Graves; [frontispiece, back blank]; p.[iii] title-page; p.[iv] economy, publication and printer's notices; p.v CONTENTS; p.vi ILLUSTRATIONS; pp.vii–viii FOREWORD; pp.1–112 text; [plate, facing 112, back blank]; pp.113–346 text; pp.347–357 EPILOGUE; pp.358–363 APPENDIX; pp.364–372 GLOSSARY; pp.[373]–[374] blank, as rear free endpaper; pp.[375]–[376] blank, as rear pastedown endpaper.

18.4 × 12.0 cm. Bulk: 1.6/1.9 cm. White wove paper; all edges trimmed. Front endpapers white wove. Bound in tan cloth; front and back blank; spine printed in black; *Wife to* | *Mr. Milton* | ROBERT | GRAVES | CASSELL

Price: 10s.6d. Number of copies: 9,420. Published 28 January 1943 in white dust-jacket printed in orange and black.

Notes: Impressions: 2nd, January 1943 (2,950 copies); 3rd, June 1949 (3,471 copies). The collation of the 3rd impression is: [A]/A*⁸/⁸ B/B* –M/M*⁸/⁸. The 3rd impression was priced 8s.6d.

The page numbers appear in brackets; on p.33 the right bracket is reversed, and on p.283 the left bracket is missing.

Peter Jolliffe (Catalogue 29) records a copy of the dust-jacket with 'OVERSEAS EDITION' on one of the flaps of the jacket (not seen).

Cedric Chivers, Portway, Bath, published a fascimile of this book in 1985.

This book has been translated into French and Polish.

A54b. First American edition ([1944]):

[in red-brown:] WIFE | [in red-brown:] TO MR. MILTON | The Story of | MARIE POWELL | by | ROBERT GRAVES | [[in red-brown:] [publisher's emblem] | *NEW YORK* | CREATIVE AGE PRESS, INC.

Collation: [1]¹⁰ [2] – [12]¹⁶ [13]⁸, 192 leaves.
p.[i] *WIFE TO MR. MILTON*; p.[ii] list of books by Graves; p.[iii] title-page; p.[iv] economy, copyright, designer's and printer's notices; pp.v – vi *Contents*; pp.vii – viii *Foreword*; p.[1] *WIFE TO MR. MILTON*; p.[2] blank; pp.3 – 356 text; pp.357 – 366 *Epilogue*; pp.367 – 372 *Appendix*; pp.373 – 380 *Glossary*.
20.2 × 13.6 cm. Bulk: 2.2/2.9 cm. White wove paper; all edges trimmed; top edges stained blue. White wove endpapers; inner sides maps. Bound in blue cloth; back blank; front stamped in gold with facsimile signature of Graves; spine stamped in gold: ROBERT GRAVES | [five lines in solid black rectangular box:] | [rule] | WIFE | *to* | MR. MILTON | [rule] | CREATIVE AGE | PRESS

Price: $2.75. Number of copies unknown, but Seymour-Smith says 20,000 plus. Published 22 November 1944 in white dust-jacket printed in pink and blue.

Note: The second impression of this edition can be distinguished by the addition of "SECOND PRINTING" and "ALSO BY GRAVES" with the same list of titles as on p.[ii] following the economy, copyright and other notices on p.[iv]. Its bulk is 2.4/3.1 cm. and the spine lettering of the dust-jacket is light brown.

Farrar, Straus and Giroux issued a photographic reprint of this edition in 1979 under its Octagon Books imprint.

A54c. Second English edition ([1954]):

ROBERT GRAVES | WIFE TO MR MILTON | *The Story of Marie Powell* | PENGUIN BOOKS

Collation: [A]¹⁶ B–F¹⁶ G–H⁸ I–O¹⁶, 208 leaves.
p.[1] PENGUIN BOOKS | 1024 | WIFE TO MR MILTON | ROBERT GRAVES | [publisher's emblem]; p.[2] map; p.[3] title-page; p.[4] publisher's printing and printer's notices; p.[5] CONTENTS; p.[6] blank; pp.[7] – [8] FOREWORD; pp.[9] 10 – 387 text, with pp.[58, 72, 114, 141, 166, 201, 283, 302, 331, 368] being unnumbered; p.[388] blank; pp.[389] 390 – 399 EPILOGUE; p.[400] blank; pp.[401]

402–407 APPENDIX; p.[408] blank; pp.[409] 410–415 GLOSSARY; p.[416] blank.
18.0 × 11.0 cm. Bulk: 1.9 cm. White wove paper; all edges trimmed. Bound in white paper covers printed in orange and black.

Price: 3s.6d. Number of copies: 40,000. Published 27 August 1954.

A54d. Second American issue ([1962]):

WIFE | TO MR. MILTON | The Story of | MARIE POWELL | by | ROBERT GRAVES | [publisher's emblem] | The Noonday Press, a division of | Farrar, Straus & Cudahy New York

Collation: [1] – [12]¹⁶, 192 leaves.
p.[i] *WIFE TO MR. MILTON*; p.[ii] blank; p.[iii] title-page; p.[iv] copyright, publication, designer's and manufacturing notices; pp.v–vi *Contents*; pp.vii–viii *Foreword*; pp.3–356 text; pp.357–366 *Epilogue*; pp.367–372 *Appendix*; pp.373–378 *Glossary*.
20.3 × 13.6 cm. Bulk: 3.0 cm. White wove paper; all edges trimmed. Bound in white paper covers printed in purple, black and red.

Price: $1.95. Number of copies unknown. Published 20 April 1962.

Note: Academy Chicago Ltd. issued a photographic reprint of this edition in 1979.

A54e. Third English edition (1968):

ROBERT GRAVES | *Wife to Mr Milton* | THE STORY OF MARIE POWELL | [publisher's emblem] | PENGUIN BOOKS

Collation: [A]¹⁶ B–N¹⁶, 208 leaves.
p.[1] PENGUIN BOOKS | 1024 | WIFE TO MR MILTON and blurb; p.[2] map; p.[3] title-page; p.[4] publisher's, publication, copyright, printer's and sales limitation notices; p.[5] CONTENTS; p.[6] blank; pp.[7]–8 FOREWORD; pp.[9] 10–408 [409] – [410] text; pp.[411] 412–416 GLOSSARY.
18.0 × 11.0 cm. Bulk: 1.8 cm. White wove paper; all edges trimmed. Bound in white paper covers printed in orange, blue and black.

Price: 7s./35p. Number of copies unknown. Published in October 1968.

Note: Impressions: 2nd, 1968; 3rd, 1984 (copies: 11,000); 4th, 1986 (copies: 4,000).

A55 THE READER OVER YOUR SHOULDER [1943]

a. First edition:

The | READER | OVER YOUR SHOULDER | *A Handbook for Writers* | *of English Prose* | *by* | ROBERT GRAVES | *B. Litt., Oxon, once Professor of English Literature* | *at the Royal Egyptian University* | & | ALAN HODGE | *B.A., Oxon* | *Authors of* The Long Week End | [publisher's emblem] | JONATHAN CAPE | THIRTY BEDFORD SQUARE | LONDON

Collation: [A]⁸ B−2D⁸ 2E⁷, 223 leaves.

p.[1] THE READER OVER YOUR SHOULDER; p.[2] blank; p.[3] title-page; p.[4] publication, publisher's, war economy, printer's, papermaker's and binder's notices; pp.5−6 CONTENTS; p.7 ACKNOWLEDGEMENTS; p.[8] _To_ | _JENNY NICHOLSON_; pp.9−446 text.

21.8 × 14.4 cm. Bulk: 2.3/2.6 cm. White wove paper; top and fore-edges trimmed; top edges stained blue. White wove endpapers. Bound in blue cloth; front and back blank; spine stamped in gold: THE READER | OVER YOUR | SHOULDER | [decorative swirl] | ROBERT | GRAVES | & | ALAN | HODGE | [publisher's emblem].

Price: 18s. Number of copies: 2,800. Published 17 May 1943 in grey dust-jacket printed in black and blue.

Contents: Part I: The Reader over Your Shoulder: I. The Peculiar Qualities of English − II. The Present Confusion of English Prose − III. Where is Good English to be Found? − IV. The Use and Abuse of Official English − V. The Beginnings of English Prose − VI. The Ornate and Plain Styles − VII. Classical Prose − VIII. Romantic Prose − IX. Recent Prose − X. The Principles of Clear Statement I − XI. The Principles of Clear Statement II − XII. The Principles of Clear Statement III − XIII. The Graces of Prose − Part II: Examinations and Fair Copies: Sir Norman Angel − Irving Babbitt − Earl Baldwin of Bewdley − Clive Bell − Viscount Castlerosse (now the Earl of Kenmare) − Bishop of Chichester − G.D.H. Cole − Marquess of Crewe − Dr. Hugh Dalton, M.P.− Daphne du Maurier − Sir Arthur Eddington − T.S. Eliot − Lord Esher − Admiral C.J. Eyres − Negley Farson − Major-Gen. J.F.C. Fuller − Major-Gen. Sir Charles Gwynn − Viscount Halifax − Cicely Hamilton − 'Ian Hay' − Ernest Hemingway − Aldous Huxley − Prof. Julian Huxley − Paul Irwin − Sir James Jeans − Prof. C.E.M. Joad − Senator Hiram Johnson − J.M. Keynes (now Lord Keynes) − Com. Stephen King-Hall − Dr. F.R. Leavis − Cecil Day Lewis − Desmond MacCarthy − Brig.-Gen. J.H. Morgan, K.C. − J. Middleton Murry − Sir Cyril Norwood − 'Observator' − An Editor of The Oxford English Dictionary − 'Peterborough' − Ezra Pound − J.B. Priestly − D.N. Pritt, K.C., M.P.− Herbert Read − I.A. Richards − Bertrand Russell − Viscount Samuel − G.B. Shaw − Stephen Spender − J.W.N. Sullivan − Helen Waddell − Sir Hugh Walpole − H.G. Wells − Prof. A. N. Whitehead − Sir Leonard Woolley

Note: Printed in Great Britain.

A55b. American issue (1943):

The | READER | OVER YOUR SHOULDER | _A Handbook for Writers_ | _of English Prose_ | _by_ | ROBERT GRAVES | _B. Litt., Oxon, once Professor of English Literature_ | _at the Royal Egyptian University_ | & | ALAN HODGE | _B.A., Oxon_ | _Authors of_ The Long Week End | NEW YORK | THE MACMILLAN COMPANY | 1943

Collation: [1]−[28]⁸, 224 leaves.

p.[1] THE READER OVER YOUR SHOULDER; p.[2] publisher's device and notice; p.[3] title-page; p.[4] publisher's device and copyright and first printing and printer's notices; pp.5−[6] CONTENTS; p.7 ACKNOWLEDGEMENTS; p.[8] _To_ | _JENNY NICHOLSON_; pp.9−446 text; pp.[447]−[448] blank.

21.3 × 14.1 cm. Bulk: 2.7/3.1 cm. White wove paper; all edges trimmed. White wove endpapers. Bound in grey-green cloth; front and back blank; spine stamped in blue: THE READER | OVER YOUR | SHOULDER | [decorative swirl] | ROBERT | GRAVES | & | ALAN | HODGE | MACMILLAN | [long-short-long dashes]

Price: $3.00. Number of copies unknown. Published 16 November 1943 in a grey dust-jacket printed in black and blue.

Note: Printed in the United States.

A55c. Readers Union impression (1944):

The | READER | OVER YOUR SHOULDER | *A Handbook for Writers* | *of English Prose* | *by* | ROBERT GRAVES | *B. Litt., Oxon, once Professor of English Literature* | *at the Royal Egyptian University* | & | ALAN HODGE | *B.A., Oxon* | *Authors of* The Long Week End | [Readers Union emblem] | *LONDON:* 1944 | READERS UNION/JONATHAN CAPE

Collation: [A]/A*$^{8/8}$ B/B* −O/O*$^{8/8}$, 224 leaves.

Remainder as A55a except p.[4] has war economy, printer's and Readers Union notices and pp.[447] – [448] blank.

21.4 × 13.7 cm. Bulk: 1.5/1.9 cm. White wove paper; all edges trimmed; top edges stained purple. White wove endpapers. Bound in maroon cloth; front and back blank; spine printed in white: *GRAVES* | *and* | *HODGE* | THE | READER | OVER | YOUR | SHOULDER | [in red: Readers Union emblem].

Price: 7s.6d. Number of copies unknown. Published in July 1944.

A55d. Abridged impression ([1947]):

Title-page as A55a.

Collation: [A]^8 B−O^8, 112 leaves.

Remainder as A55a, except that p.[4] has publication, printer's and binder's notices, p.[6] is blank, pp.9–221 are text and pp.[222] – [224] are blank.

22.2 × 14.1 cm. Bulk: 1.7/2.4 cm. White wove paper; top and fore-edges trimmed; top edge stained green. White wove endpapers. Bound in green cloth; front and back blank; spine stamped in gold: THE | READER | OVER | YOUR | SHOULDER | [decorative swirl] | GRAVES | & | HODGE | [publisher's emblem].

Price: 10s.6d. Number of copies: 3,000. Published 19 May 1947 in tan dust-jacket printed in black and red.

Notes: Impressions: 2nd, October 1947 (2,000 copies); 3rd, October 1948 (2,000 copies); 4th, April 1952 (2,000 copies).

Contents: Part I: The Reader over Your Shoulder: I. The Peculiar Qualities of English – II. The Present Confusion of English Prose – III. Where is Good English to be Found? – IV. The Use and Abuse of Official English – V. The Principles of Clear Statment, I – VI. The Principles of Clear Statement, II – VII. The Principles of Clear Statement, III – VIII. The Graces of Prose – Part II: Examinations and Fair

Copies: Sir Norman Angell – Viscount Castlerosse (later the Earl of Kenmare) – Bishop of Chichester – T.S. Eliot – Major-Gen. J.F.C. Fuller – Earl Halifax – Sir James Jeans – J.M. Keynes (later Lord Keynes) – Sir Cyril Norwood – J.B. Priestly – D.N. Pritt, K.C., M.P.– I.A. Richards – Bertrand Russell – G. B. Shaw – H.G. Wells – Prof. A.N. Whitehead – Sir Leonard Woolley

A55e. Second American impression (1961):

Title-page as A55b, except date is 1961.

Collation as A55b.
    Remainder as A55b except p.[2] is blank, p.[4] lacks the publisher's emblem and adds a statement of edition and pp.[5] and [7] are unnumbered.
    21.0 × 13.7 cm. Bulk: 2.6 cm. White wove paper; all edges trimmed. Bound in white paper covers printed in black, yellow and dull mustard.

Price: $2.25. Number of copies unknown. Published 27 March 1961.

Contents: As A55a.

A55f. Second English edition ([1962]):

[bar] | THE READER OVER | YOUR SHOULDER | [rule] | [flush right:] *by* | [rule] | [flush right:] Robert Graves & | [flush right:] Alan Hodge | [bar] | [flush right:] [publisher's emblem] A MAYFLOWER BOOK

Collation: [A]^{16} B–G^{16} [H]^{16}, 128 leaves.
    p.[1] title and blurbs; p.[2] title and publication, copyright, permission, publisher's and printer's notices; p.[3] title-page; p.[4] blank; pp.5–256 text.
    18.0 × 11.3 cm. Bulk: 1.6 cm. White wove paper; all edges trimmed. Bound in paper covers.

Price: 3s.6d. Number of copies unknown. Published 4 May 1962.

Contents: As A55d.

A55g. Third English edition ([1965]):

ROBERT GRAVES & | ALAN HODGE | The Reader | Over Your Shoulder | A HANDBOOK FOR WRITERS | OF ENGLISH PROSE | JONATHAN CAPE | THIRTY BEDFORD SQUARE LONDON

Collation: [A]^8 B–O^8 [P]^6, 118 leaves.
    p.[1] [vase with fruit] | JONATHAN CAPE | PAPERBACK | JCP 27 | THE READER OVER YOUR SHOULDER; p.[2] blank; p.[3] title-page; p.[4] publication, sales limitation and printer's notices; p.5 CONTENTS; p.[6] blank; p.7 ACKNOWLEDGEMENTS; p.[8] *To* | *JENNY NICHOLSON*; pp.9–221 text; pp.[222] – [224] blank; pp.[225] – [236] publisher's advertisements.
    19.6 × 12.4 cm. Bulk: 1.7 cm. White wove paper; all edges trimmed. Bound in white paper covers printed in blue, red, purple and black.

Price: l0s.6d. Number of copies: 4,000. Published 25 January 1965.

Contents: As A55d.

Note: There was a second impression in l967 (3,500 copies).

A55h. Third American impression (1966):

[13 ll. as A55b, then:] COLLIER BOOKS, NEW YORK

Collation: As A55b.
  p.[1] THE READER OVER YOUR SHOULDER; p.[2] blank; p.[3] title-page; p.[4] copyright, rights reservation and printing notices; pp.[5] – [6]; CONTENTS; p.[7] ACKNOWLEDGEMENTS; p.[8] *To | JENNY NICHOLSON*; pp.9–446 text; pp.[447] – [448] blank.
  13.5 × 10.3 cm. Bulk: 2.9 cm. White wove paper; all edges trimmed. Bound in white paper covers printed in green, blue and black.

Price: $2.95. Number of copies unknown. Published in 1966.

Contents: As A55a.

A55i. Fourth American edition [1979]:

THE | READER | OVER YOUR | SHOULDER | *A Handbook for Writers | of English Prose* | [short rule] | SECOND EDITION | Revised and Abridged by the Authors | ROBERT GRAVES | AND | ALAN HODGE | [publisher's emblem] | RANDOM HOUSE | New York

Collation: [1] – [7]^{16} [8]^8 [9] – [10]^{16}, 152 leaves.
  p.[i] [short rule] | THE | READER | OVER YOUR | SHOULDER | [short rule]; p.[ii] blank; p.[iii] title-page; p.[iv] rights reservations, copyright, LC card and printing notices; p.[v] CONTENTS; p.[vi] blank; p.[vii] Acknowledgements; p.[viii] blank; p.[ix] *To | Jenny Nicholson*; p.[x] blank; p.[1] section title; p.[2] blank; pp.[3]4–290 text, with pp.[17, 31, 46, 66, 88, 111, 142, 175] being unnumbered, p.[173] an unnumbered section title and p.[174] blank; p.[291] biographical notes; pp.[292] – [294] blank.
  20.9 × 13.8 cm. Bulk: 2.2/2.8 cm. White wove paper; all edges trimmed. White wove endpapers. Bound in black cloth; front and back blank; spine stamped in gold: [top to bottom, facing back, in two lines:] THE READER OVER YOUR SHOULDER | *Graves & Hodge* | [upright at foot:] [publisher's emblem] | RANDOM | HOUSE

Price: $9.95. Number of copies undetermined. Published 30 April 1979.

Note: This edition was simultaneously issued in paperback at $3.95.

Contents: As A55d.

A56   ROBERT GRAVES   [1943]

First edition:

[whole enclosed within green-filled double-rule with scallops:] | [whole enclosed in rectangular single-rule box:] | [green-filled:] THE AUGUSTAN POETS | [green-filled tent with hangings] | [green-shaded fancy design with next two lines inside:] ROBERT | GRAVES | [green-shaded] 9^D. | [double branch] | EYRE & SPOTTISWOODE

Collation: 16 leaves, stapled in centre.
p.[i] biographical note; p.ii TO | EDWARD THOMPSON | in happy memory of the Islip village football | team, canoeing on the Ray, and the children | who have now grown up.; p.iii CONTENTS; p.[iv] blank; pp.2–30 [31] text; p.[32] blank.
18.5 × 12.5 cm. Bulk: 0.3 cm. White wove paper; all edges trimmed. Bound in wine-red cloth-effect paper; outside front cover transcribed as title-page; inside front and back covers blank; outside back cover cloth-effect print only.

Price: 9d. Number of copies: 5,000. Published in November 1943.

Contents: Rocky Acres – In the Wilderness – Outlaws – Reproach – Allie – The Haunted House – Love without Hope – The Troll's Nosegay – Song of Contrariety – Sullen Moods – A Crusader – An English Wood – Henry and Mary – A Frosty Night – One Hard Look – Lost Love – The Return – Ancestors – The Presence – What Did I Dream? – The Country Dance – The Hills of May – Unicorn and the White Doe – The Land of Whipperginny – The 'General Elliott' – The Bedpost – Love in Barrenness – Vain and Careless – In Procession – Apples and Water – Vanity

Note: This is Augustan Poets Series, no. 2.

A57   THE GOLDEN FLEECE   [1944]

a. First edition:

THE GOLDEN FLEECE | *By* | ROBERT GRAVES | [publisher's emblem] | CASSELL AND COMPANY LTD. | London, Toronto, Melbourne and Sydney

Collation: [A]/A*8/8 B/B* –L/L*8/8 M/M*2/8, 186 leaves.
p.[1] THE GOLDEN FLEECE; p.[2] list of novels by Graves; p.[3] title-page; p.[4] economy, publication and printer's notices; p. 5 quotation (9 ll.) from Diodorus Siculus; p.6 list of maps, table and illustrations; pp.7–8 CONTENTS; pp.9–27 INTRODUCTION, with pp.[16]–[17] being a genealogical table; p.28 INVOCATION; pp.29–44 text; p.45 map; pp.46–116 text; p.117 illustrations; pp.118–260 text; p.[261] illustrations; pp.262–370 [371] text; p.[372] blank.
21.7 × 13.3 cm. Bulk: 2.1/2.4 cm. White wove paper; all edges trimmed. White wove endpapers; outer sides of free endpapers blank; inner sides are maps, front of the outward voyage, back of the return voyage, of the *Argo*. Bound in medium blue cloth; front and back blank; spine stamped in orange: THE | GOLDEN | FLEECE | ROBERT | GRAVES | CASSELL

Price: 12s. 6d. Number of copies: 11,073. Published in October 1944 in white dust-jacket printed in black and brown.

Notes: Impressions: 2nd, January 1948 (1,966 copies).

There may also have been impressions in 1944 and 1945 but I have been unable to determine this.

This book has been translated into Croatian, Czech, Danish, Dutch, French, German, Hebrew, Polish, Russian, Spanish and Swedish.

A57b. First American edition ([1945]):

[two lines in blue:] HERCULES, | MY SHIPMATE | *A Novel By* | ROBERT GRAVES | [in blue: publisher's emblem] | *NEW YORK* | CREATIVE AGE PRESS, INC

Collation:[[1]^8 [2] – [15]^{16} [16]^8 24 leaves.

p.[i] *HERCULES, MY SHIPMATE*; p.[ii] blank; p.[iii] list of novels by Graves; p.[iv] map in blue; p.[v] title-page; p.[vi] economy, copyright and printer's notices; p.[vii] quotation (8 ll.) from Diodorus Siculus; p.[viii] blank; pp.ix–x *Contents*; p [1] *HERCULES, MY SHIPMATE*; p.[2] *Invocation*; pp.3–445 text; p.[446] blank; pp.447–464 *Historical Appendix*, with pp.[456] – [457] being a genealogical table; pp.[465] – [470] blank.

20.2 × 13.6 cm. Bulk: 3.0/3.6 cm. White wove paper; all edges trimmed and sprinkled with blue. White wove endpapers are maps; first and fourth sides of endpapers blank; second and third sides of front show outward, of rear return, voyage of the *Argo*. Bound in buff cloth; back blank; front printed with solid blue rectangular box around which is stamped a gold rule border and inside which is stamped a facsimile signature of Graves; spine has gold stamping and blue printing: [five-rule crossbar design of two gold rules, blue decorative rule and two gold rules] | [solid blue rectangular box, in which:] ROBERT GRAVES | [three gold rules] | [solid blue rectangular box, inside which three lines:] HERCULES | *my* | SHIPMATE | [three gold rules] | [solid blue rectangular box, inside which two lines:] | CREATIVE AGE | PRESS | [a series of three five-rule devices, as at top] | [solid blue rectangular box, in which: publisher's emblem] | [five-rule device, as at top].

Price: $3.00. Number of copies unknown. Published 7 September 1945 in white dust jacket printed in black, red and gold-brown.

Note: Greenwood Press issued a photographic facsimile of this edition in 1979.

A57b.1. Second English edition ([1951]):

[all within rule and leaf border printed in brown:] THE | GOLDEN | FLEECE | [leaf and arrow emblem] | ROBERT | GRAVES

Collation: [A]^{16} B–S^{16}, 288 leaves.

p.[1] THE GOLDEN FLEECE; p.[2] Pocket Library series title-page; p.[3] title-page; p.[4] edition and printing notices; p.[5] quotation (6 ll.) from Diodorus Siculus; p.[6] list of maps, tables, and illustrations; pp.[7] – [8] CONTENTS; pp.[9] 10–35 INTRODUCTION; p.[36] INVOCATION; pp.[37] 38–560 text, with pp.[50,

65, 77, 89, 107, 108, 118, 130, 140, 148, 159, 174, 182, 191, 203, 212, 220, 228, 235, 246, 254, 267, 277, 287, 295, 301, 311, 319, 326, 335, 349, 360, 372, 384, 393, 404, 413, 425, 437, 448, 458, 469, 478, 488, 498, 507, 519, 522, 532, 544] being unnumbered and pp.[48–49, 64, 172, 272–273, 392] containing maps and illustrations and being unnumbered; pp.561–576 HISTORICAL APPENDIX.

15.9 × 10.7 cm. Bulk: 2.4 cm. White wove paper. Binding not seen.

Price: 7s.6d. Number of copies undetermined. Published in May 1951.

Note: This is one of the Cassell Pocket Library series.

A57c. Second American impression ([1957]):

[at right, facing spine, from top to bottom:] ROBERT GRAVES | [3 ll. flush left:] HERCULES | MY SHIPMATE | GROSSET & DUNLAP . NEW YORK | [at right, facing spine, from top to bottom:] Grosset's UNIVERSAL Library

Collation: 240 leaves, glued at spine.
Remainder as A57b, except p.[1] publisher's advertisement, pp [ii] – [iii] are front endpaper maps of A57b, p.[iv] map in black, p.[vi] has copyright and printing notices, pp. [466] – [467] are rear endpaper maps of A57b.
20.2 × 13.4 cm. Bulk: 2.2 cm. White wove paper; all edges trimmed. Bound in white paper covers printed in red, blue and black.

Price: $1.25. Number of copies undisclosed. Published 22 April 1957.

Note: This book is Grosset's Universal Library no. UL-19.

A57d. Third American impression ([1957]):

HERCULES, | MY SHIPMATE | *A Novel By* | ROBERT GRAVES | *NEW YORK* | FARRAR, STRAUS AND CUDAHY

Collation: [1] – [15]^{16}, 240 leaves.
Remainder as A57c, except p.[i] 25 A57b, p.[vi] copyright and printing notices.
20.2 × 13.7 cm. Bulk: 2.3/2.9 cm. White wove paper; all edges trimmed. Bound in cloth-simulating orange and grey paper; front and back blank; spine stamped: ROBERT | GRAVES | Hercules, | My | Shipmate | FARRAR | STRAUS | CUDAHY

Price: $4.50. Number of copies unknown. Published in August 1957 in white dust-jacket printed in black, brown and orange.

A57e. Second American edition ([1966]):

[2 ll. left of center:] HERCULES, | MY SHIPMATE | [flush left:] ROBERT GRAVES | [series emblem] PYRAMID BOOKS . NEW YORK

Collation: 232 leaves, glued at spine.
p.[1] blurbs; p.[2] blank; p.[3] title-page; p.[4] publication and publisher's notices; p.[5] quotation from Diodorus Siculus, with translation; pp.[6] – [10] maps; p.[11] *Contents*; p.[12] table of contents; p.13 *Invocation*; p. [14] blank; pp.15–463 text, with p.[26] being blank and pp. [252] – [253] being genealogical tables; p.[464] publisher's advertisements.

18.0 × 10.5 cm. Bulk: 2.1 cm. White wove paper; all edges trimmed and stained orange. Bound in white paper covers printed in gold, red, green, brown and black.

Price: $0.85. Number of copies undetermined. Published 15 April 1966.

A57f. Third English edition ([1983]):

THE | GOLDEN | FLEECE | ROBERT | GRAVES | HUTCHINSON | London Melbourne Sydney Auckland Johannesburg

Collation: [1] – [20]^{12}, 240 leaves.

p.[i] THE GOLDEN FLEECE | [publisher's emblem]; pp.[ii] – [iv] maps; p.[v] title-page; p.[vi] publisher's, copyright, rights reservation, printer's, BL card and ISBN notices; p.[vii] quotation from Diodorus Siculus with translation; p.[viii] blank; pp.[ix] – [x] CONTENTS; p.[xi] invocation; p.[xii] blank; p.[1] *HERCULES, MY SHIPMATE*; p.[2] blank; pp.3–445 text; p.[446] blank; pp.447–464 *Historical Appendix*, with pp.[456] – [457] being genealogical tables; p.[465] blank; pp.[466] – [467] map; p.[468] blank.

21.4 × 13.6 cm. Bulk: 2.4 cm. White wove paper; all edges trimmed. Bound in white paper covers printed in black, white, red and light brown; 'The Pyrrhic Dance' by Sir Lawrence Alma-Tadema is reproduced on front.

Price: £4.95. Number of copies undetermined. Published early in 1983.

Note: The contents say that the 'Invocation' appears on p.[2] but it is actually on p.[xi], p.[2] is blank.

A58 POEMS 1938–1945 [1945]

a. First edition:

ROBERT GRAVES | POEMS | [elaborate red circular design, inside which:] 1938–1945 | CASSELL & COMPANY LTD. | [heavy rule] | [light rule] | LONDON, TORONTO, MELBOURNE | AND SYDNEY

Collation: [A] – [B]^4 C–F^4, 24 leaves.

p.[i] ROBERT GRAVES | POEMS (1938–1945); p.[ii] blank; p.[iii] title-page; p.[iv] publication and printer's notices; p. [v] – [vi] CONTENTS p.[vii] FOREWORD p.[viii] blank pp.1–40 text.

18.4 × 11.9 cm. Bulk: 0.4/0.7 cm. Cream laid paper; all edges trimmed; watermarked with a crown and Abbey Mills | Greenfield. White wove endpapers. Bound in blue-green cloth; front and back blank; spine stamped in gold, bottom to top: [light-heavy-light rules] CASSELL [four-pointed star] POEMS (1938–1945) [four-pointed star] ROBERT GRAVES [light-heavy-light rules]

Price: 5s. Number of copies: 3,000. Published November 1945 in a sea-green dust-jacket printed in black.

Contents: Foreword – POEMS: 1. A Love Story – 2. Dawn Bombardment – 3. The Worms of History – 4. The Beast – 5. A Withering Herb – 6. The Shot – 7. The Thieves – 8. Lollocks – 9. To Sleep – 10. Despite and Still – 11. The Suicide in the

Copse – 12. Frightened Men – 13. A Stranger at the Party – 14. The Oath – 15. Language of the Seasons – 16. Mid-Winter Waking – 17. The Rock at the Corner – 18. The Beach – 19. The Villagers and Death – 20. The Door – 21. Under the Pot – 22. Through Nightmare – 23. To Lucia – 24. Death by Drums – 25. She Tells Her Love while Half Asleep – 26. Instructions to the Orphic Adept – 27. Theseus and Ariadne – 28. Lament for Pasiphaë – 29. The Twelve Days of Christmas – 30. Cold Weather Proverb – 31. To Juan at the Winter Solstice – SATIRES AND GROTESQUES: 32. Dream of a Climber – 33. The Persian Version – 34. The Weather of Olympus – 35. Apollo of the Physiologists – 36. The Oldest Soldier – 37. Grotesques i–v – 38. The Eugenist – 39. 1805 – 40. At the Savoy Chapel

Notes: Impression 2nd April 1946 Number of copies: 4,387.

Drafts of poem 31 ("To Juan at the Winter Solstice") were reproduced in facsimile in P.J. Croft's *Autograph Poetry of the English Language·* (London: Cassell, 1973), II, 182–183.

A58b. First American edition ([1946]):

POEMS | 1938–1945 | [double rule] | BY | ROBERT GRAVES | [double rule] | NEW YORK | CREATIVE AGE PRESS

Collation: [1] – [2]^8 [3]^{10} [4]^8, 34 leaves.

p.[i] POEMS | 1938–1945 | [double rule]; p.[ii] blank; p.[iii] title-page; p.[iv] copyright, designer's and printer's notices; p.[v] FOREWORD; p.[vi] blank; pp.[vii]–[ix] CONTENTS; p.[x] blank; p.[1] POEMS; p.[2] blank; pp.3–42 text; p.[43] SATIRES AND GROTESQUES; p.[44] blank; pp.45–58 text.

21.4 × 13.8 cm. Bulk: 0.5/1.1 cm. White wove paper; all edges trimmed. Cream wove endpapers. Bound in red cloth; front and back blank; spine stamped in silver, top to bottom: POEMS 1938–1945 [floral decoration] Robert Graves [floral decoration] CREATIVE AGE PRESS [floral decoration]

Price: $2.00. Number of copies: 5,500. Published in June 1946 in white dust-jacket printed in black, grey and blue.

Note: Impression: 2nd, 1967. 2,000 copies at $4.95, issued by Farrar, Straus and Cudahy who had taken over Creative Age Press.

A59 KING JESUS [1946]

a. First edition:

KING | JESUS | By | *Robert Graves* | *New York* | CREATIVE AGE PRESS, INC.

Collation: [1]^8 [2] – [13]^{16} [14] – [15]^8 216 leaves.

p.[*i*] KING | JESUS; p.[*ii*] blank; p.[*iii*] list of books by Graves; p.[*iv*] map of Palestine; p.[*v*] title-page; p.[*vi*] copyright and printing notices; pp. *vii–viii* CONTENTS; p.[1] KING | JESUS; p.[2] quotation from Clement of Alexandria (11 ll.) and Lexicon Talmudicum (8 ll.); pp.3–418 text, with pp.[156, 268] being blank and p.[33] an illustration; pp.419–424 HISTORICAL COMMENTARY.

20.2 × 13.4 cm. Bulk: 2.3/2.9 cm. White wove paper; all edges trimmed. White

wove endpapers. Bound in buff cloth; back blank; front stamped with octagonal green box inside which are various animals, a wall, a seven-branched candelabrum, etc.; spine stamped with three solid green rectangular boxes printed in gold: [ten lines in first box:] [heavy rule] | [light rule] | [decorative rule] | [light rule] | King | Jesus | [light rule] | [decorative rule] | [light rule] | [heavy rule] | [four lines in second box:] [heavy rule-rectangular border] | [light-rule rectangular border] | ROBERT | GRAVES | [remainder in third box:] [heavy-rule rectangular border] | [light-rule rectangular border] | CREATIVE | AGE | PRESS

Price: $3.00. Number of copies unknown. Published 30 September 1946 in white dust-jacket printed in flesh and green.

Note: This book has been translated into Czech, Danish, German, Hungarian, Spanish and Swedish.

A59b. First English edition ([1946]):

KING JESUS | ROBERT GRAVES | [publisher's emblem] | CASSELL | AND COMPANY LIMITED | LONDON . TORONTO . MELBOURNE . SYDNEY

Collation: [A]/A*8/8B/B* – K/K*8/8 L/L*/L**2/8/8, 178 leaves.
  p.[1] KING JESUS; p.[2] list of novels by Graves; p.[3] title-page; p.[4] economy, publication and printer's notices; p. 5 CONTENTS; p.6 quotations from Clement of Alexandria (10 ll.) and Lexicon Talmudicum (7 ll.); pp.7–31 text; p.[32] description of facing plate; [plate, back blank]; pp.33–351 text; pp.352–355 [356] HISTORICAL COMMENTARY; [map, tipped to rear endpaper].
  21.6 × 13.3 cm. Bulk: 2.0/2.6 cm. White wove paper; all edges trimmed. White wove endpapers. Bound in ochre cloth; front and back blank; spine stamped in gold: [double rule] | [solid rectangular box] | [double rule] | CASSELL; box contains, in relief, in ochre: KING | JESUS | ROBERT | GRAVES

Price: 12s. 6d. Number of copies: 10,152. Published 28 November 1946 in buff dust-jacket printed in black and brown.

Notes: Impressions: 2nd and 3rd, February 1960 (6,042 copies); 4th, 28 April 1960 (2,780 copies); 5th, September 1960 (1,492 copies); 6th, June 1962 (2,000 copies). The publisher confirms the discrepancies between these dates and those on versos of title-pages.

A59c. Second American impression ([1955]):

KING | JESUS | By | *Robert Graves* | *New York* | FARRAR, STRAUS & CUDAHY, INC.

Collation: [1] – [12]16 [13]8 [14]16 216 leaves.
  Remainder as A59a.
  20.2 × 13.5 cm. Bulk: 3.0/3.7 cm. Paper and endpapers as A59a. Bound in tan cloth stamped in blue; back and front as A59a; spine stamped with rules and legend as A59a without solid boxes; at bottom: FARRAR, | STRAUS AND | CUDAHY

Price: undetermined. Number of copies unknown. Published in 1955.

Note: There appear to have been five further impressions of this book by 1984, the date of the fifth, but it has not been possible to determine the dates of the intervening ones.

A59d. Third American impression ([1967]:)

KING | JESUS | *By* | *Robert Graves* | MINERVA PRESS

Collation: 216 leaves, glued at spine.
  Remainder as A59a.
  20.3 × 13.1 cm. Bulk: 2.5 cm. White wove paper; all edges trimmed. Bound in white paper covers printed in yellow and brown.

Price: $2.50. Number of copies undetermined. Published in 1967.

A59e. Second American edition [unknown, 1970?]:

[all set flush right:] *King Jesus* | ROBERT GRAVES | beacon | [publisher's emblem] | envoy

Collation: 192 leaves, glued at spine.
  p.[i] list of works by Graves; p.[ii] map of Palestine; p.[1] title-page; p.[2] copyright, rights reservation, arrangement and publisher's notices; pp.[3]–[4] CONTENTS; p.[5] KING | JESUS; p.[6] quotations from Clement of Alexandria (12 ll.) and Lexicon Talmudicum (8 ll.); pp.7–377 text; pp.378–382 HISTORICAL COMMENTARY.
  18 × 10.6 cm. Bulk: 2.5 cm. White wove paper; all edges trimmed and stained yellow. Bound in white paper covers printed in yellow, red, blue and black.

Price: $0.75. Number of copies unknown. Publication date unknown.

Note: This is Envoy book E-101.

A59f. Second English edition ([1983])

KING JESUS | ROBERT GRAVES | HUTCHINSON | London Melbourne Sydney Auckland Johannesburg

Collation: 216 leaves, glued at the spine.
  p.[i] KING JESUS | [publisher's emblem]; p.[ii] map; p.[iii] title-page; p.[iv] publisher's, copyright, rights reservation, printer's, BL card and ISBN notices; pp.[v]–vi CONTENTS; p.[1] quotations from Clement of Alexandria (11 *ll.*) and *Lexicon Talmudicum* (8 *ll.*); p.[2] blank; pp.3–418 text, with p. [33] being illustrations and pp.[156, 268] being blank; pp. 419–424 HISTORICAL COMMENTARY; pp.[425]–[426] blank.
  21.6 × 13.5 cm. Bulk: 2.2 cm. White wove paper; all edges trimmed. Bound in white paper covers printed in black, red and white, with colour photograph of 6th century mosaic of Christ from the Archepiscopal Chapel in Ravenna on front.

Price: £4.95. Number of copies undetermined. Published in April 1983.

A60   COLLECTED POEMS (1914–1947)   [1948]

First edition:

COLLECTED POEMS | (1914–1947) | [swelled rule] | ROBERT GRAVES | [publisher's emblem] | CASSELL | AND COMPANY LIMITED | LONDON, TORONTO, MELBOURNE AND SYDNEY

Collation: π⁸ A/A* –G/G*⁸/⁸ H⁸, 128 leaves.

4 pp. blank, as front endpapers; p.[i] COLLECTED POEMS; p.[ii] blank; p.[iii] title-page; p.[iv] publication and printer's notices; pp.v–x CONTENTS; p.xi–xii FOREWORD; pp.[1] 2–239 [240] text, with pp.[1, 37, 71, 95, 151, 169, 207] being section headings and pp.[2, 36, 38, 72, 96, 152, 170, 208] being blank.

21.6 × 13.7 cm. Bulk: 1.5/2.0 cm. Cream wove paper; all edges trimmed. Rear endpapers white wove. Bound in dark olive-green cloth; front and back blank; spine stamped in gold: [5 ll. enclosed within gold wreath:] COLLECTED | POEMS | . | 1914– | 1947 | Robert | Graves | CASSELL

Price: 12s.6d. Number of copies: 2,962. Published in April 1948 in cream dust-jacket printed in red and black.

Contents: Foreword – I: In the Wilderness – The Haunted House – Reproach – The Finding of Love – 'The General Elliott' – Rocky Acres – Outlaws – One Hard Look – A Frosty Night – Allie – Unicorn and the White Doe – Henry and Mary – Love Without Hope – What Did I Dream? – The Country Dance – The Troll's Nosegay – The Hills of May – Lost Love – Vain and Careless – An English Wood – The Bedpost – The Pier-Glass – Apples and Water – Angry Samson – Down – Mermaid, Dragon, Fiend – II: In Procession – Warning to Children – Alice – Richard Roe and John Doe – The Witches' Cauldron – Ancestors – Children of Darkness – The Cool Web – Love in Barrenness – Song of Contrariety – The Presence – The Land of Whipperginny – In No Direction – The Castle – Return – Lust in Song – Nobody – Without Pause – Full Moon – Vanity – Pure Death – Sick Love – It Was All Very Tidy – III: Callow Captain – Thief – Saint – The Furious Voyage – Song: Lift-Boy – The Next Time – Ulysses – The Succubus – Trudge, Body – The Clock Man – The Reader over My Shoulder – Green Loving – The Legs – Gardener – Front Door – Soliloquy – In Broken Images – On Rising Early – Flying Crooked – Largesse to the Poor – Fragment of a Lost Poem – IV: Galatea and Pygmalion – The Devil's Advice to Story-Tellers – Sea Side – Wm. Brazier – Welsh Incident – Vision in the Repair-Shop – Interruption – Act V, Scene 5 – Midway – Hell – Leda – Synthetic Such – The Florist Rose – Lost Acres – At First Sight – Recalling War – Down, Wanton, Down! – A Former Attachment – Nature's Lineaments – Time – The Philosopher – On Dwelling – Parent to Children – Ogres and Pygmies – History of the Word – Single Fare – To Walk on Hills – To Bring the Dead to Life – To Evoke Posterity – The Poets – Defeat of the Rebels – Never Such Love – The Fallen Signpost – The China Plate – Certain Mercies – The Cuirassiers of the Frontier – The Laureate – A Jealous Man – The Cloak – The Halls of Bedlam – Or to Perish before Day – A Country Mansion – The Eremites – The Advocates – Self-Praise – V: On Portents – The Terraced Valley – The Challenge – To the Sovereign Muse – The Ages of Oath –

New Legends – Like Snow – The Climate of Thought – End of Play – The Fallen Tower of Siloam – The Great-Grandmother – No More Ghosts – VI: A Love Story – Dawn Bombardment – The Worms of History – The Beast – A Withering Herb – The Shot – The Thieves – Lollocks – To Sleep – Despite and Still – The Suicide in the Copse – Frightened Men – A Stranger at the Party – The Oath – Language of the Seasons – Mid-Winter Waking – The Rock at the Corner – The Beach – The Villagers and Death – The Door – Under the Pot – Through Nightmare – Lucia at Birth – Death by Drums – She Tells Her Love while Half Asleep – Theseus and Ariadne – The Twelve Days of Christmas – Three Short Poems: Cold Weather Proverb – To Poets under Pisces – June – 1805 – At the Savoy Chapel – The Last Day of Leave(1916) – To be Named a Bear – VII: Satires and Grotesques: Dream of a Climber – The Persian Version – The Weather of Olympus – Apollo of the Physiologists – The Oldest Soldier – Grotesques i, ii, iii, iv, v – The Eugenist – A Civil Servant – Gulls and Men – Magical Poems: To Juan at the Winter Solstice – The Allansford Pursuit – The Alphabet Calendar of Amergin – The Siren's Welcome to Cronos – Dichetal do Chennaib – The Battle of the Trees – The Song of Blodeuwedd – Intercession in Late October – Instructions to the Orphic Adept – Lament for Pasiphaë – The Tetragrammaton – Nuns and Fish – The Destroyer – Return of the Goddess. [The final three poems are separated in the table of contents from the 'Magical Poems.']

A61   THE WHITE GODDESS   [1948]

a First edition:

THE | WHITE GODDESS | *A historical grammar* | *of poetic myth ·* | *by* | ROBERT GRAVES | FABER AND FABER LIMITED | 24 Russell Square | London

Collation: π⁸ A–2C⁸ 2D⁴, 216 leaves.

   p.[1] THE WHITE GODDESS; p.[2] list of books by Graves; p.[3] title-page; p.[4] publication, publisher's and printer's notices; p.[5] IN DEDICATION; p.[6] blank; pp.7–[8] CONTENTS; pp.9–12 FOREWORD; pp.13–412 text; pp.413–430 INDEX; pp. [431]–[432] blank.

   21.8 × 13.6 cm. Bulk: 2.4/2.8 cm. White wove paper; all edges trimmed; top edges stained brown; watermarked with a crown and in Gothic: Abbey Mills | Greenfield. White wove endpapers. Bound in medium blue cloth; front and back blank; spine stamped in gold: [triple rule] | THE | WHITE | GODDESS | [triple rule] | ROBERT | GRAVES | FABER

Price: 30s. Number of copies: 2,340. Published 21 May 1948 in canary dust-jacket printed in black and red.

Contents: 'In Dedication' – Foreword – I. Poets and Gleemen – II. The Battle of the Trees – III. Dog, Roebuck and Lapwing – IV. The White Goddess – V. Gwion's Riddle – VI. A Visit to Spiral Castle – VII. Gwion's Riddle Solved – VIII. Hercules on the Lotus – IX. Gwion's Heresy – X. The Tree-Alphabet(I) – XI. The Tree-Alphabet(2) – XII. The Song of Amergin – XIII. Palamedes and the Cranes – XIV. The Roebuck in the Thicket – XV. The Seven Pillars – XVI. The Holy Unspeakable

Name of God – XVII. The Lion with the Steady Hand – XVIII. The Bull-Footed God – XIX. The Number of the Beast – XX. A Conversation at Paphos–A.D.43 – XXI. The Waters of the Styx – XXII. The Triple Muse – XXIII. Fabulous Beasts – XXIV. The Single Poetic Theme – XXV. War in Heaven – Index.

Notes: 'In Dedication' is 10 lines long.
Impressions: 2nd, October 1948 (1,500 copies).
A ballet based upon this work was performed at the Royal Opera House, Covent Garden in 1983.

A61b. First American edition (1948):

The WHITE | GODDESS | *A historical grammar of poetic myth* | Robert Graves | [design of star and three cranes] | Creative Age Press, New York, 1948

Collation: [1]^8 [2] – [13]^{16} [14]^4 [15]^8, 212 leaves.
p.[i] THE WHITE GODDESS; p.[ii] list of books by Graves; p. [iii] title-page; p.[iv] copyright, edition and printer's notices; p.[v] IN DEDICATION; p.[vi] blank; pp.vii–viii CONTENTS; pp.ix–xii FOREWORD; p.[1] THE WHITE GODDESS; p.[2] blank; pp.3–392 text; pp.393–412 SUBJECT INDEX.
21.5 × 14.8 cm. Bulk: 2.7/3.3 cm. White laid paper; top edges only trimmed. White wove endpapers. Bound in brown cloth; back blank; front stamped with three-quarter box, open toward spine, containing three cranes and star below, the edges of the box aligning with rules on spine; spine stamped in black: [rule] | GRAVES | THE | WHITE | GODDESS | CREATIVE AGE | [rule]

Price: $4.50. Number of copies unknown. Published 26 August 1948 in white dust-jacket printed in brown, black and yellow.

A61c. Second English edition ([1952]):

THE | WHITE GODDESS | *A historical grammar* | *of poetic myth* | *by* | ROBERT GRAVES | *amended and enlarged edition* | FABER AND FABER LIMITED | 24 Russell Square | London

Collation: [A]^8 B–2H^8, 248 leaves.
p.[1] THE WHITE GODDESS; p.[2] list of books by Graves; p.[3] title-page; p.[4] publication, publisher's and printer's notices; p.[5] IN DEDICATION; p.[6] blank; pp.7–[8] CONTENTS; pp.9–15 FOREWORD; p.[16] blank; pp.17–478 text; pp.479–496 INDEX.
21.9 × 14.0 cm. Bulk: 2.6/3.1 cm. White wove paper, all edges trimmed. White wove endpapers. Remainder as in A61a, except no edges are stained.

Price: 35s. Number of copies: 2,000. Published in October 1952, in yellow dust-jacket printed in red and black. A new list of books is printed on rear cover.

Contents: As A61a, but the 'Foreword' has been revised and Chapter XXVI (The Return of the Goddess) is new; 'In Dedication' has 22 lines.

Note: Impressions: 2nd, February 1959 (2,000 copies).

A61d. Second American impression ([1958]):

The WHITE | GODDESS | *A historical grammar of poetic myth* | Robert Graves | [design as A61b] | Farrar Straus and Cudahy, Inc.

Collation as A61b.
Remainder as A61b, except p.[iv] has copyright and printing notices only.
20.3 × 13.5 cm. Bulk: 2.1/2.7 cm. White wove paper; all edges trimmed. White wove endpapers. Binding as A61b, except spine reads: [rule] | GRAVES | THE | WHITE | GODDESS | [rule] | FARRAR, | STRAUS | and | CUDAHY

Price: $5.00. Number of copies unknown. Published in 1958 in white dust-jacket printed in black, yellow and brown.

Note: This impression is a photographic reproduction of A61b.

A61e. Second American edition (1958):

A historical grammar of poetic myth | THE | WHITE | GODDESS | *Amended and enlarged edition* | BY | ROBERT | GRAVES | *Vintage Books: New York: 1958*

Collation: 288 leaves, glued at the spine.
    p.[i] *The White Goddess;* p.[ii] blank; p.[iii] title-page; p.[iv] publisher's, arrangement, copyright and manufacturing notices; p.[v]vi–xi *Foreword;* p.[xii] *Contents;* p.[1] *The White Goddess;* p.[2] *In Dedication;* pp.[3] 4–541 text, with pp.[15, 35, 50, 66, 91, 110, 121, 140, 168, 196, 215, 236, 262, 278, 294, 329, 342, 375, 384, 402, 424, 455, 471, 495, 526] unnumbered; p.[542] blank; pp.[i] ii–xix *Index;* p.[xx] biographical note and printer's, papermaker's and designer's notices; pp.[xxi] – [xxii] publisher's advertisements.
    18.4 × 11.0 cm. Bulk: 2.6 cm. White wove paper; all edges trimmed. Bound in white paper covers printed in black, light blue, medium blue and brown.

Price: $1.25. Number of copies unknown. Published 10 February 1958.

Notes: This edition is Vintage Book K-56. The text is that of A61c.
    Impressions: Paper: 2nd, March 1966 (4,500 copies); 3rd, March 1969 (2,000 copies); 4th, December 1969 (2,000 copies); 5th, November 1970 (3,000 copies); 6th, April 1972 (3,000 copies); 7th, April 1973 (4,000 copies). All paper impressions were Noonday paperbacks priced at $3.45 and the book was neither reset nor revised. Bindings may vary.
    Cloth: 1st, March 1966 (3,500 copies), price: $5.95; 2nd, April 1972 (5,000 copies), price: $12.95. Published by Octagon Books.

A61f. Third English edition ([1961]):

THE | WHITE GODDESS | *A historical grammar* | *of poetic myth]* | *by* | ROBERT GRAVES | *amended and enlarged edition* | FABER AND FABER LIMITED | 24 Russell Square | London

Collation: [A]^{16} B–Q^{16}, 256 leaves.

Remainder differs from A61d as follows: pp.17–492 text; pp. 493–511 INDEX; p.[512] blank.

21.0 × 13.4 cm. Bulk: 1.9 cm. White wove paper; all edges trimmed. Bound in paper covers printed in blue and brown.

Price: 12s.6d. Number of copies: 10,000. Published in March 1961.

Contents: As A61d, with the addition of Chapter XXVII (Postscript 1960); 'In Dedication' has 22 lines.

Notes: There are omissions as well as additions throughout the text; the revisions of A61d are retained.

Impressions: 2nd, March 1963 (8,000 copies); 3rd, 1967 (8,000 copies); 4th, 1970 (8,000 copies); 5th, March 1975 (8,080 copies); 6th, October 1977 (10,096 copies); 7th, December 1981 (5,975 copies); 8th, June 1984 (7,383 copies). There was also a hardbound impression in 1970 (2,000 copies).

A62   WATCH THE NORTH WIND RISE   1949

a First Edition:

Robert Graves | [three lines within rectangular box of decorative band:] WATCH THE | NORTH WIND RISE | A NOVEL | *Creative Age Press* | NEW YORK . 1949

Collation: [1] – [16]⁸ [17]⁴ [18] – [19]⁸, 148 leaves
p.[i] [decorative band] | WATCH THE NORTH WIND RISE; p.[ii] list of books by Graves; p.[iii] title-page; p.[iv] copyright, printer's and designer's notices; pp.v–vi *Contents*; pp. 1–290 text.

20.0 × 13.4 cm. Bulk: 2.3/2.8 cm. White wove paper; all edges trimmed. White wove endpapers. Bound in cloth-textured grey paper; front and back blank; spine black cloth stamped in gold in solid blue rectangular box: [decorative band] | *Graves* | WATCH THE | NORTH WIND | RISE | *Creative Age* | [decorative band]

Price: $3.00. Number of copies unknown. Published 18 March 1949 in white dust-jacket printed in olive, yellow, red, blue and black.

Notes: This book has been translated into Hebrew, Italian, Spanish, and Swedish.
Some copies of this edition were issued with a tipped-in leaf signed by Graves (not seen).

A62b. First English edition ([1949]):

SEVEN DAYS IN | NEW CRETE | *A Novel* | by | ROBERT GRAVES | [publisher's emblem] | CASSELL & COMPANY LIMITED | LONDON . TORONTO . MELBOURNE | SYDNEY . WELLINGTON

Collation: [1]/1*8/8 2/2* –9/9*8/8, 144 leaves.
p.[i] SEVEN DAYS IN NEW CRETE; p.[ii] list of books by Graves; p.[iii] title-page; p.[iv] publication and printer's notices; p.[v] CONTENTS; p.[vi] blank; pp.1–281 text; p.[282] blank.

18.3 × 12.3 cm. Bulk: 1.9/2.3 cm. White wove paper; all edges trimmed. White

wove endpapers. Bound in black cloth; front and back blank; spine stamped in gold: SEVEN | DAYS | IN | NEW | CRETE | [nine rules in downward-pointing triangle, plus dot] | ROBERT | GRAVES | CASSELL

Price: 9s.6d. Number of copies: 12,257. Published 29 September 1949 in white dustjacket printed in red, yellow, grey and green.

Notes: Robert Temple, Catalogue no. 9 (1979) reports a copy with CONTENTS page numbered 'v' at foot; not seen. In Catalogue no. 42 (1985) Robert Temple argues that the state, or issue, with the CONTENTS page numbered 'v' is typical of the first state, or printing.

A photographic reprint of this edition was published in 1971 by Cedric Chivers Ltd., Portway, Bath, "at the request of the London & Home Counties Branch of the Library Association." It differs in that p.[1] has a blurb, the title-page and its verso are altered to describe the reprinting, and it contains sixteen pages of publisher's advertisements following p.[282]

A62c. Second American edition ([1963]):

[entire flush left:] [four lines of caps and lower case same size:] WaTcH | THe | NOrTHWIND | rIse | ROBERT | GRAVES

Collation: 128 leaves, glued at spine.

p.[1] summary and blurbs; p.[2] blank; p.[3] title-page; p. [4] copyright, publication, and publisher's notices; pp.[5]–[6] CONTENTS; pp.7–254 text; pp.[255]–[256] publisher's advertisements.

16.3 × 10.9 cm. Bulk: 1.7 cm. White wove paper; all edges trimmed and stained green. Bound in white paper covers printed in yellow, green, blue, pink and black.

Price: $0.75. Number of copies undisclosed. Published 18 July 1963.

Note: This edition is Avon Book V-2075.

A62d. Second English edition ([1975]):

SEVEN DAYS IN NEW CRETE | [publisher's emblem] | ROBERT GRAVES | QUARTET BOOKS LONDON

Collation: [1]⁸ 2–18⁸, 144 leaves.

p.[i] SEVEN DAYS IN NEW CRETE; p.[ii] blank; p.[iii] title-page; p.[iv] publisher's copyright, ISBN, printer's and rights reservation notices; p.[v] CONTENTS; p.[vi] blank; pp. 1–281 text; p.[282] blank.

17.7 × 10.1 cm. Bulk: 1.7 cm. White wove paper, all edges trimmed. Bound in paper covers, black printed in blue, white, red and yellow.

Price: .75p. Number of copies: 7,500. Published in 1975.

A62e. Second Impression of the First American edition ([1982]):

Robert Graves | [3 ll. within rectangle of curved ornaments:] WATCH THE | NORTH WIND RISE | A NOVEL | FARRAR . STRAUS . GIROUX | NEW YORK

Collation: 152 leaves, glued at the spine.

[2 pp.] blank; p.[i] [curved ornament] | WATCH THE NORTH WIND RISE; p.[ii] blank; p.[iii] *By the Same Author* | [within a rectangle of curved ornaments; a list of 11 titles by Graves]; p [iv] blank; p.[v] title-page; p.[vi] [within rectangle of curved ornaments:] copyright, rights reservation, LC card, and printer's notices; pp.vii–[viii] [angle of curved ornaments] *Contents* [angle of curved ornaments]; p.[ix] [as p.[i]] p.[x] blank; pp.1–290 text; pp.[291]–[292] blank.

20.0 × 13.5 cm. Bulk: 2.0 cm. White wove paper, all edges trimmed. Bound in white paper covers printed in tan, orange, yellow, cream, and black.

Price: $7.95. Number of copies unknown. Published in 1982.

Note: This appears to be a re-imposition of A62a.
 The cover was designed by Honi Werner.

A62f. Third English edition (1983):

ROBERT GRAVES | *Seven Days in New Crete* | [decorative rule] | *Introduced by* | MARTIN SEYMOUR-SMITH | OXFORD UNIVERSITY PRESS | 1983

Collation: 152 leaves glued at the spine.
 p.[i] SEVEN DAYS IN NEW CRETE and biographical notes; p.[ii] blank; p.[iii] title-page; p.[iv] publisher's, copyright, rights reservation, BL cataloguing and printer's notices; p.[v] CONTENTS; p.[vi] blank; pp.[vii]viii–xxii INTRODUCTION; pp.[1]2–281 text; p.[282] blank.

19.6 × 13.0 cm. Bulk: 2.1 cm. White wove paper; all edges trimmed. Bound in white paper cover printed in light blue, green, red, yellow and brown.

Price: £2.95. Number of copies: 5,000. Published 20 October 1983.

Notes: The cover illustration is by Paul Allen.
 The following classified advertisement appeared in the *Times Literary Supplement* on 13 September 1985 (p. 1016) under the heading of Announcements:

Oxford University Press

regrets the distress caused to Mrs Laura (Riding) Jackson by the introduction to their edition of *Seven Days in New Crete* by Robert Graves. In his introduction, Martin Seymour-Smith expresses certain views of people and events, which may be read as statements of fact. Mrs Laura (Riding) Jackson completely repudiates these views and regards them as malicious. Mr Seymour-Smith has agreed, in the light of these objections, to revise his introduction for any future impression.

A63   THE COMMON ASPHODEL   [1949]

First edition:

THE | COMMON | ASPHODEL | *COLLECTED ESSAYS ON POETRY* | 1922–1949 | by | ROBERT GRAVES | [publisher's emblem] | HAMISH HAMILTON | LONDON

Collation: [A]⁸ B–X⁸ Y⁶, 174 leaves.

p.[i] THE COMMON ASPHODEL; p.[ii] blank; [frontispiece, back blank]; p.[iii] title-page; p.[iv] publication and printer's notices; p.v–vi CONTENTS; pp.vii–xi INTRODUCTION; p.[xii] blank; pp.1–329 text, with pp.[50, 60, 168, 196, 224, 326] blank; p.[330] blank; pp.331–335 INDEX; p.[336] blank.

21.3 × 13.6 cm. Bulk: 2.4/2.9 cm. White wove paper; all edges trimmed. White wove endpapers. Bound in orange-red cloth; front and back blank; spine stamped in gold: [six lines enclosed in rectangular decorative rule box:] THE | COMMON | ASPHODEL | [star] | ROBERT | GRAVES | [publisher's emblem]

Price: 15s. Number of copies undisclosed. Published in September 1949 in white dust-jacket printed in black and powder blue.

Contents: Introduction – Observations on Poetry (1922–1925): I. The Poetic Trance – II. Prose and Poetry – III. Fake Poetry and Bad Poetry – IV. Schools – V. Rhyme – VI. Ariphrades – VII. *Vers Libre* – VIII. The Hounds of Spring – IX. The Outward and Inward Ears – X. Secondary Elaboration – XI. The Arrogance of Poets – XII. Scientific English – XIII. Texture – XIV. Fashions in Poetry – XV. 'Bread I Dip in the River' – XVI. *He'las, C'est Victor Hugo ·* – *XVII. Shakespeare's Fair Copies* – *XVIII. The Grosser Senses* – *XIX. Centenaries* – *XX Hamlet* – The Sources of *The Tempest* (1925) – The Future of Poetry (1926) – Modernist Poetry (with Laura Riding, 1926): I. Modernist Poetry and the Plain Reader's Rights – II. The Problem of Form and Subject-Matter – III. A Study in Original Punctuation and Spelling – IV. The Unpopularity of Modernist Poetry – V. Dead Movements – VI. The Making of the Poem – VII. Modernist Poetry and Civilization – VIII. Variety in Modernist Poetry – IX. The Humorous Element – Anthologies (with Laura Riding, 1927): I. True Anthologies and Popular Anthologies – II. The Perfect Modern Lyric – Loving Mad Tom (1927) – Rudyard Kipling (1928) – Essays from *Epilogue* (1935–1937): I. Nietzsche – II. Coleridge and Wordsworth – III. Keats and Shelley – IV. The Pastoral – V. Official and Unofficial Literature – VI. Lucretius and Jeans – VII. Poetry and Politics (with Laura Riding) – VIII. Poetic Drama (with Laura Riding) – How Poets See (1939) – The Poets of World War II (1942) – 'Mad Mr. Swinburne' (1945) – The Ghost of Milton (1947) – The Common Asphodel (1949) – Index.

A64   THE ISLANDS OF UNWISDOM   1949

a. First edition:

The Islands of Unwisdom | BY ROBERT GRAVES | [publisher's emblem] | DOUBLEDAY & COMPANY, INC. | *Garden City, New York*, 1949

Collation: [1] – [11]^{16}, 176 leaves.

2 pp. blank; p.[i] The Islands of Unwisdom; p.[ii] list of novels by Graves; p.[iii] title-page; p.[iv] copyright and printer's notices; p.[v] epigraphs (3 ll. and 5 ll.); p.[vi] blank; pp.vii–viii Contents; pp.ix–xi MEMBERS OF THE EXPEDITION | MENTIONED BY NAME; p.[xii] blank; pp.xiii–xv Introduction; p.[xvi] blank; pp.[1] 2–328 text, with pp.[10, 23, 35, 51, 62, 76, 91, 102, 113, 128, 141, 153, 167, 179, 192, 205, 218, 230, 245, 258, 274, 287, 299, 311, 320, 327] unnumbered; pp. [329] – [332] blank.

21.1 × 14.3 cm. Bulk: 2.3/2.9 cm. White wove paper; top edges only trimmed and stained brown gold. White wove endpapers with identical maps back and front; inner free sides blank. Bound in wine-red cloth; front and back blank; spine stamped in gold: ROBERT | GRAVES | [decorative rule] | The | Islands | of | Un- | wisdom | [decorative rule] | DOUBLEDAY

Price: $3.50. Number of copies: 12,000 (in two printings). Published 3 November 1949 in white dust-jacket printed in black and multi-colour, browns predominating.

Note: This book has been translated into Finnish, German, Italian, Polish, Spanish and Swedish.

A64b. First English edition ([1950)]:

THE | ISLES OF UNWISDOM | *by* | ROBERT GRAVES | [publisher's emblem] | CASSELL AND COMPANY LIMITED | LONDON . TORONTO . MELBOURNE | SYDNEY AND WELLINGTON

Collation: [1]^{16} 2–13^{16} 14^8, 216 leaves.
  p.[i] THE ISLES OF UNWISDOM; p.[ii] list of books by Graves; p. [iii] title-page; p.[iv] publication, printing and printer's notices; p.v CONTENTS; pp.vi–vii MEMBERS OF THE EXPEDITION; pp. [viii]–[ix] map; p.[x] epigraph (7 ll.); pp.xi–xiv INTRODUCTION; pp.1–415 text; pp. 416–417 HISTORICAL EPILOGUE; p. [418] blank.
  18.4 × 12.3 cm. Bulk: 2.5/2.9 cm. White wove paper; all edges trimmed. White wove endpapers. Bound in black cloth; front and back blank; spine stamped in gold: [heavy rule] | [light rule] | *THE ISLES* | *of* | *UNWISDOM* | *ROBERT* | *GRAVES* | [light rule] | [heavy rule] | *CASSELL*

Price: 10s.6d. Number of copies: 14,988. Published 20 April 1950 in white dust-jacket printed in red, blue, yellow and black.

A64c. Readers Union impression (1952):

Robert Graves | [decorative swirl] | THE ISLES | OF UNWISDOM | London [Readers Union emblem] 1952 | READERS UNION . CASSELL

Collation: [1]^8 [2]^{16} 3/3* –14/14$^{*8/8}$, 216 leaves.
  p.[i] ISLES OF UNWISDOM; p.[ii] list of novels by Graves; p. [iii] title-page; p.[iv] edition notice, colophon, and acknowledgement; remainder as A64b.
  17.2 × 11.1 cm. Bulk: 1.5/1.9 cm. White wove paper; all edges trimmed. White wove endpapers. Bound in light blue cloth; front and back blank; spine stamped in yellow: [heavy rule] | [light rule] | ROBERT | GRAVES | *The* | *Isles of* | *Unwisdom* | [light rule] | [two heavy rules] | [light rule] | [Readers Union emblem] | [light rule] | [heavy rule]

Price: 4s.6d. Number of copies: more than 25,000. Published in May 1952.

Note: At least one copy collates 2/2*$^{8/8}$

A64d. Second American edition ([1962]):

[entire text flush right; first word above floral design:] THE ISLANDS OF | UNWISDOM | ROBERT GRAVES | [rule]

Collation: 160 leaves, glued at spine.

p.[1] publisher's advertisements; p.[2] publisher's notices; p. [3] title-page; p.[4] epigraph, copyright and arrangement notices; p.[5] CONTENTS; pp.[6] – [7] map; pp.[8] – [9] list of characters; p.[10] blank; pp.[11] – [13] Introduction; p.[14] blank; pp.15 – 317 text; pp.318 – 319 HISTORICAL EPILOGUE; p.[320] blank.

18.1 × 10.7 cm. Bulk: 1.6 cm. White wove paper; all edges trimmed and stained green. Bound in paper covers, inner sides blank.

Price: $0.75. Number of copies undisclosed. Published in 1962.

Note: This edition is Avon Book V-2062.

A65 OCCUPATION: WRITER 1950

a. First edition:

ROBERT GRAVES | [decorative rule] | *Occupation: Writer* | [decorative rule] | CREATIVE AGE PRESS | NEW YORK: 1950

Collation: [1] – [9]^{16} [10]^8 [11]^{16}, 168 leaves.

p.[i] [decorative rule] | *Occupation: Writer* | [decorative rule]; p.[ii] list of books by Graves; p.[iii] title-page; p. [iv] copyright notice; pp.v – viii *Introduction* p.ix *Contents*; p.[x] blank; p.[xi] [decorative rule] | *Occupation: Writer* | [decorative rule]; p.[xii] blank; pp. 1 – 320 text; pp.[321] – [324] blank.

20.3 × 13.2 cm. Bulk: 2.5/3.2 cm. White wove paper; all edges trimmed. White wove endpapers. Bound in buff cloth; front and back blank; brown quarter cloth spine stamped in gold: ROBERT | GRAVES | [facing back:] *OCCUPATION: WRITER* | CREATIVE | AGE

Price: $4.00. Number of copies unknown. Published 23 February 1950 in white dust-jacket printed in brown and black.

Contents: Introduction – Lars Porsena – Mrs. Fisher – The Shout – Avocado Pears – Old Papa Johnson – Interview with a Dead Man – Thames-Side Reverie – -Ess – Charity Appeals – But It Still Goes On: a Play – The Cult of Tolerance – Horses: a Play – Colonel Blimp's Ancestors – The Search for Thomas Atkins – It Was a Stable World – Caenis on Incest – *'Esta En Su Casa'* – How Mad are Hatters? – Pharaoh's Chariot Wheels – Dead Man's Bottles – Occupation: Writer.

A65b. First English edition (1951):

Occupation: | WRITER | [centred decorative rule with sunburst] | ROBERT GRAVES | [publisher's emblem] | MCMLI | CASSELL & CO. LTD | LONDON

Collation: [A]^6 B – Q^8 R/R$^{*2/8}$ S^8, 144 leaves.

pp.[i] – [ii] blank; p.[iii] OCCUPATION: WRITER; p.[iv] list of books by Graves; p.[v] title-page; p.[vi] publisher's, publication and printer's notices; p.vii

CONTENTS; p.[viii] blank; pp.ix–xi INTRODUCTION; p.[xii] blank; pp.1–276 text, with pp.[102, 174] being blank and p.[221] being a genealogical table.

21.5 × 13.8 cm. Bulk: 2.1/2.7 cm. White wove paper; all edges trimmed; top edges stained grey. Bound in wine-brown cloth; front and back blank; spine stamped in gold: [five lines in a rectangular decorative rule box:] Occupation: | WRITER | [star] | ROBERT | GRAVES | CASSELL

Price: 12s.6d. Number of copies: 7,500. Published 27 September 1951 in cream dust-jacket printed in maroon and purple-grey.

Notes: 'Dead Man's Bottles' of the American edition is here called 'Bins K to T.'
There was an "Overseas Edition' and it is reported by Mason.
A photographic reprint was issued in 1974 by Cedric Chivers, Portway, Bath, 'at the request of the London and Home Counties Library Association.' It is identical save for title-page and verso and a blurb on p.[iii].

A65c. Second American impression ([1951]):

ROBERT GRAVES | *Occupation: Writer* | The Universal Library | GROSSET & DUNLAP | NEW YORK [publisher's emblem faces last three lines]

Collation as A65a.
p.[i] biographical note; p.[ii] blank; p.[iii] title-page; pp. [iv]–[x] as A65a; p.[xi] OCCUPATION WRITER; p.[xii] blank; pp. 1–320 text; p.[321] publisher's advertisements; pp.[322]–[324] blank.

20.3 × 13.7 cm. Bulk: 2.1 cm. White wove paper; all edges trimmed. Bound in paper covers; inner sides blank.

Price: $1.25. Number of copies undisclosed. Published in 1951.

Note: This impression is Universal Library U-53.

A66   THE GOLDEN ASS   [1950]

a. First edition:

THE | TRANSFORMATIONS OF LUCIUS | OTHERWISE KNOWN AS | THE GOLDEN ASS | BY LUCIUS APULEIUS | TRANSLATED BY | ROBERT GRAVES | [star] | PENGUIN BOOKS | HARMONDSWORTH . MIDDLESEX

Collation: [A]⁸ B–K¹⁶ L⁸, 152 leaves.
pp.[1]–[2] blank; p.[3] THE PENGUIN CLASSICS | EDITED BY E. V. RIEU | LII | [publisher's emblem]; p.[4] blank; p.[5] title-page; p.[6] publication, publisher's and printer's notices; p.[7] CONTENTS; p.[8] blank; pp.[9] 10–21 INTRODUCTION; p.[22] blank; p.[23] THE | TRANSFORMATIONS OF LUCIUS | OTHERWISE KNOWN AS | THE GOLDEN ASS | [star]; p.[24] blank; p.[25] *Apuleius's Address to the Reader*; p.[26] blank; pp.[27] 28–293 text, with pp.[42, 61, 73, 88, 99, 114, 124, 138, 158, 175, 193, 212, 228, 239, 249, 262, 274, 288] being unnumbered; p.[294] blank; pp.[295] 296–298 APPENDIX; pp.[299]–[302] publisher's advertisements; pp. [303]–[304] blank.

18.0 × 11.1 cm. Bulk: 1.2 cm. White wove paper; all edges trimmed. Bound in paper covers; front cover: [solid rectangular purple border, inside which:] [rectangular decorative rule border, inside which:] APULEIUS | THE | GOLDEN ASS | [roundel of Cupid and Psyche] | A NEW TRANSLATION BY | ROBERT GRAVES | [swelled purple rule] | THE PENGUIN | CLASSICS | [overprinted in lower left corner of border:] 1/6; back cover: solid and decorative borders as front, inside which are publisher's advertisements; spine: [purple band] | [decorative band] | [up spine:] THE GOLDEN ASS | [publisher's emblem] | [up spine:] APULEIUS | [purple band, inside which:] LII; inner sides of both covers blank.

Price: 1s.6d. Number of copies unknown. Published in April 1950.

Notes: Impression: 2nd, 1951; 3rd, 1956; 4th, 1958; 5th, 1960; 6th, 1964; 7th, 1969; 8th, 1972.

This book was also issued hardbound (two printings in 1950); it differs as follows: 18.0 × 10.8 cm. Bulk: 1.4/1.9 cm. White wove endpapers. Bound in bright red cloth; front and back blank. Spine stamped in gold: [rule] | [design of decorative rule, 14 rules forming an oval with a star inside and decorative rule] | APULEIUS | [dash] | *The Golden* | *Ass* | [series of 3 designs (4 decorative rules only) as above] | [publisher's emblem] | design as at top] | [rule]. Price: 7s.6d. Number of copies unknown. Published in 1950 in cream dust-jacket printed in red and grey. The hardbound edition was also reissued in 1956.

A66b. Limited issue (1951):

THE | TRANSFORMATIONS OF LUCIUS | OTHERWISE KNOWN AS | THE GOLDEN ASS | BY LUCIUS APULEIUS | TRANSLATED | BY ROBERT GRAVES | [star] | 1950 | PENGUIN BOOKS | HARMONDSWORTH . MIDDLESEX

Collation: [A]⁸ B–S⁸ T⁷, 151 leaves.

pp.[1] – [2] blank; p.[3] publisher's emblem in red; p.[4] blank; p.[5] title-page; p.[6] blank; p.[7] CONTENTS; p.[8] blank; pp.[9] 10–298 as A66b; p.[299] [signature of Graves] | This edition of Apuleius' | GOLDEN ASS, | translated by Robert Graves, | was first published in 1951. | The typography and the binding were | designed by Jan Tschichold. | It is set in Monotype Lutetia, | and printed by Silk & Terry Ltd, | London and Birmingham, | on Blue-White Wove paper | made by Wiggins, Teape & Co, Ltd. | The binding, with a marbled paper | supplied by Douglas Cockerell & Son, | is by James Burn & Co, London. | This edition is limited to | 2,000 copies numbered and signed | by the translator | of which this is No. [number]; pp.[300] – [302] blank.

19.2 × 11.3 cm. Bulk: 1.5/1.9 cm. White wove paper; all edges trimmed; top edges gilt. Heavy grey laid endpapers watermarked: Charles I. Bound in marbled boards with parchment spine stamped in gold: The | Golden | Ass | [heavy rule] | [light rule].

Price: 30s. Number of copies: 2,000. Published in December 1951 in buff dust-jacket printed in black; boxed; box printed in red and black.

Note: p.299 is a cancel and Mason reports an uncancelled state of this page from his collection, now at the University of Tulsa.

A66c. First American edition ([1951]):

THE TRANSFORMATIONS OF | LUCIUS OTHERWISE KNOWN AS | THE GOLDEN ASS | A NEW TRANSLATION BY | ROBERT GRAVES *from* APULEIUS | FARRAR, STRAUS & YOUNG . NEW YORK

Collation: [1] – [10]^{16}, 160 leaves.
  2 pp. blank; p.[i] [flush right:] THE GOLDEN ASS; p.[ii] [flush left:] list of books by Graves; p.[iii] title-page; p.[iv] copyright, manufacturer's and designer's notices and publisher's emblem; p.[v] [flush right:] CONTENTS; p.[vi] blank; p.[vii] [flush right:] APULEIUS'S ADDRESS TO THE READER; p.[viii] blank; pp. xi–xxii [flush right:] INTRODUCTION; p.[1] [flush right:] THE GOLDEN ASS; p.[2] blank; pp.3–288 text; pp.289–293 APPENDIX; pp.[294] – [296] blank.
  20.2 × 13.4 cm. Bulk: 1.9/2.5 cm. White wove paper; all edges trimmed. White wove endpapers. Bound in yellow cloth; front and back blank; spine stamped in brown: [decorative rule] | [solid box, inside which 8 lines:] GRAVES | THE | GOLDEN | ASS | FARRAR | STRAUS | AND | YOUNG | [decorative rule]

Price: $3.50. Number of copies unknown. Published 11 September 1951 in white dust-jacket printed in brown and gold.

Note: This book was designed by Stefan Salter.

A66d. Second American edition ([1952]):

CARDINAL [cardinal] EDITION | [decorative rule] | THE GOLDEN ASS | OF APULEIUS | [decorative rule] | A NEW TRANSLATION BY | ROBERT GRAVES | [decorative rule] | POCKET BOOKS, INC. . NEW YORK

Collation: 144 leaves, glued at spine.
  p.[i] quotations from reviews; p.[ii] list of books by Graves; p.[iii] title-page; p.[iv] publication, publisher's, copyright and acknowledgement notices; p.[v] CONTENTS; p.[vi] APULEIUS'S ADDRESS TO THE READER; pp.vii–xix INTRODUCTION; p.[xx] blank; p.[1] [decorative rule] THE GOLDEN ASS; p.[2] blank; pp.3–259 text; p.[260] blank; pp.261–264 APPENDIX; pp.[265] – [267] publisher's advertisements; p.[268] blank.
  16.3 × 10.6 cm. Bulk: 1.5 cm. White wove paper; all edges trimmed. Bound in white paper covers with multicolour printing.

Price: $0.35. Number of copies: 150,753. Published in September 1952.

Notes: Impressions: 2nd, 48,715 copies.
  This book was also issued in a Pocket Library impression which differs as follows: lacks first line of title-page; final line: THE POCKET LIBRARY | [publisher's emblem]; covers printed in grey, blue, gold and black; all edges stained gold. Published in May 1954, with four printings subsequently, for a total of five printings of 126,129 copies.

A66e. Second English edition (1960):

THE | TRANSFORMATIONS OF LUCIUS | OTHERWISE KNOWN AS | THE GOLDEN ASS | BY LUCIUS APULEIUS | TRANSLATED BY ROBERT GRAVES |

LITHOGRAPHS BY MICHAEL AYRTON | LONDON | THE FOLIO SOCIETY | 1960

Collation: [A]⁸ B–N⁸, 154 leaves.
[plate, back blank, facing title-page]; p.[1] title-page; p. [2] acknowledgement, printer's and binder's notices; p.[3] CONTENTS; p.[4] ILLUSTRATIONS; pp.5–13 INTRODUCTION; p.[14] blank; p.[15] THE | TRANSFORMATIONS OF LUCIUS | OTHERWISE KNOWN AS | THE GOLDEN ASS; p.[16] blank; p.[17] APULEIUS'S ADDRESS TO | THE READER; p.[18] blank; pp.19–208 text, with plates facing pp.49, 64, 76, 97, 112, 141, 180, 195.
24.6 × 15.3 cm. Bulk: 1.5/2.1 cm. White wove paper; all edges trimmed; top edge stained brown. White wove illustrated endpapers, inner sides blank. Bound in parchment with front and back stamped at top and bottom with brown illustrative bands; spine stamped in gold: APULEIUS | The | Golden | Ass | GRAVES | [elongated figure of ass] | The | Folio | Society

Price: 22s.6d. Number of copies undisclosed. Published in January 1960 without dust-jacket in blank marbled-effect grey-green box.

A66f. Second American impression ([1966]):

The Transformations of Lucius | Otherwise Known as | THE | GOLDEN ASS | [urn] | A New Translation by | ROBERT GRAVES | from Apuleius | Farrar, Straus & Giroux [publisher's emblem] New York

Collation: [1]–[10]¹⁶, 160 leaves.
pp.[i]–[ii] blank; p.[iii] *The Golden Ass*; p.[iv] blank; p.[v] title-page; p.[vi] copyright, rights reservation, LC card and printing notices; p.[vii] *Contents*; p.[viii] blank; p.[ix] *Apuleius's Address to the Reader*; p.[x] blank; pp.xi–xxii *Introduction*; p.[1] *The Golden Ass*; p.[2] blank; pp.3–293 text; pp.[294]–[296] blank.
20.3 × 13.6 cm. Bulk: 2.1/2.7 cm. White wove paper; all edges trimmed. White wove endpapers. Bound in black cloth; front and back blank; spine stamped in gold, top to bottom, facing back: THE GOLDEN ASS | [under title:] *ROBERT GRAVES* [remainder upright on spine:] [publisher's emblem] | *Farrar* | *Straus* | *Giroux*

Price: $4.75. Number of copies: 1,000. Published in November 1966 in white dust-jacket printed in yellow and black.

Notes: Impressions: 2nd, April 1967 (4,000 copies); 3rd, January 1969 (2,000 copies); 4th, September 1969 (2,000 copies); 5th, February 1970 (3,500 copies); 6th, October 1970 (5,000 copies); 7th, October 1971 (5,000 copies).

A66g. Third American impression (1972):

Title-page as A66f.

Collation: 160 leaves, glued at spine.
Paged as A66f.
20.1 × 13.0 cm. Bulk 2.2 cm. White wove paper; all edges trimmed. Bound in white paper covers printed in canary and black.

Price: $2.25. Number of copies: 7,500. Published in November 1972.

Note: This impression is Noonday Book 305.

The publisher reports that the 18th impression had been reached by 1983, but whether this includes the seven impressions of A66f or not is unknown.

A66h. Third English edition ([1976]):

THE | TRANSFORMATIONS OF LUCIUS | OTHERWISE KNOWN AS | THE GOLDEN ASS | BY LUCIUS APULEIUS | TRANSLATED | BY ROBERT GRAVES | [publisher's emblem] | PENGUIN BOOKS

Collation: 128 leaves, glued at the spine.

p.[1] THE PENGUIN CLASSICS | FOUNDER EDITOR (1944–64): E. V. RIEU | *Editor: Betty Radice* | [blurb]; p.[2] blank; p.[3] title-page; p.[4] publisher's, imprintings, copyright, printer's and rights reservations notices; p.[5] CONTENTS; p.[6] blank; pp.[7] 8–17 INTRODUCTION; p.[18] blank; p.[19] THE | TRANSFORMATIONS OF LUCIUS | OTHERWISE KNOWN AS | THE GOLDEN ASS; p.[20] blank; p.[21] *Apuleius's Address to the Reader*; p. [22] blank; pp.[23] 24–247 text, with pp.[36, 52, 63, 75, 84, 97, 105, 117, 134, 148, 163, 179, 192, 201, 210, 221, 231, 243] being unnumbered; p.[248] blank; pp.[249] 250–252 APPENDIX; p. [253] publisher's advertisement; p.[254] blank; pp.[255] – [256] publisher's advertisement.

18.1 × 11.0 cm. Bulk: 1.4 cm. White wove paper; all edges trimmed. Bound in paper covers, inner sides blank, outer sides black printed in white.

Price: 80p. Number of copies: 10,000. Published in 1976.

Note: Impressions: 2nd, 1980 (copies:10,000); 3rd, 1984 (copies: 5,000); 4th, 1985 (copies: 4,000).

A 67   POEMS AND SATIRES   1951

First edition:

ROBERT GRAVES | [star] | [in red:] POEMS | AND | [in red:] SATIRES | 1951 | CASSELL & COMPANY LTD | [heavy rule] | [light rule] | LONDON

Collation: [A]⁶ B–F⁴, 26 leaves.

p.[i] POEMS AND SATIRES; p.[ii] blank; p.[iii] title-page; p. [iv] publisher's, publication and printer's notices; pp.[v] – [vi] CONTENTS; pp.vii–x FOREWORD; p.[xi] POEMS; p.[xii] blank; p. 1–21 text; p.[22] blank; p.[23] SATIRES; p.[24] blank; pp. 25–33 text; p.[34] blank; p.[35] REVISIONS; p.[36] blank; pp. 37–40 text.

18.3 × 11.7 cm. Bulk: 0.4/0.7 cm. Cream wove paper; all edges trimmed; watermarked: Basingwerk Parchment. White wove endpapers. Bound in green cloth; front and back blank; spine stamped in gold, bottom to top: [light rule] [heavy rule] [light rule] CASSELL [four-pointed star] POEMS AND SATIRES 1951 [four-pointed star] ROBERT GRAVES [light rule] [heavy rule] [light rule]

Price: 7s.6d. Number of copies: 3,100 (1,100 wasted). Published 30 November 1951 in cream dust-jacket printed in light maroon.

Contents: Foreword – POEMS: 1. The White Goddess – 2. The Chink – 3. Counting the Beats – 4. The Jackals' Address to Isis – 5. The Death Room – 6. The Young Cordwainer – 7. Your Private Way – 8. My Name and I – 9. Conversation Piece – 10. The Ghost and the Clock – 11. Advice on May Day – 12. For the Rain It Raineth Every Day – 13. Questions in a Wood – 14. The Portrait – 15. Darien – 16. The Survivor – 17. Prometheus – SATIRES: 18. Queen Mother to New Queen – 19. Secession of the Drones – 20. Damocles – 21. Homage to Texas – 22. The Dilemma – 23. General Bloodstock's Lament for England – 24. ≪ iWellcome, to the Caves of Artá!≫ – 25. To a Poet in Trouble – REVISIONS: 26. The Progress – 27. Traveller's Curse after Misdirection – 28. Sergeant-Major Money – 29. Brother

A68   POEMS 1953   1953

a. First edition:

ROBERT GRAVES | POEMS | 1953 | CASSELL & COMPANY LTD | [heavy rule] | [light rule] | LONDON

Collation: [1] – [5]⁴, 20 leaves.

   p.[i] POEMS 1953; p.[ii] list of books by Graves; p.[iii] title-page; p.[iv] publisher's, publication and printer's notices; pp.v–vi CONTENTS; p.vii FOREWORD; p.[viii] blank; pp. 1–30 text; pp.[31] – [32] blank.

   18.4 × 12.0 cm. Bulk: 0.3/0.7 cm. White wove paper; all edges trimmed. White wove endpapers. Bound in sea-green cloth; front and back blank; spine stamped in gold, bottom to top: [light rule] [heavy rule] [light rule] CASSELL [four-pointed star] POEMS 1953 [four-pointed star] ROBERT GRAVES [light rule] [heavy rule] [light rule]

Price: 7s.6d. Number of copies: 1,777. Published 24 September 1953 in light tan dust-jacket printed in brown.

Contents: Foreword – To Calliope – The Straw – The Foreboding – Cry Faugh! – Hercules at Nemea – Dialogue on the Headland – Lovers in Winter – Esau and Judith – The Mark – With the Gift of a Ring – Liadan and Curithir – The Sea Horse – The Devil at Berry Pomeroy – Reproach to Julia – Dethronement – Cat-Goddess – The Blue-Fly – Rhea – The Hero – Marginal Warning – The Encounter – I'm Through with You for Ever – With Her Lips Only – The Blotted Copy-book – The Sacred Mission – From the Embassy – Sirocco at Deya' – Leaving the Rest Unsaid

A68b. Limited issue (1953):

Title-page as A68a.

Collation as A68a.

   Remainder as A68a through p.30; p.[31] THIS EDITION ON HAND-MADE PAPER | IS LIMITED TO 250 COPIES FOR SALE, | NUMBERED 1 TO 250 AND SIGNED BY | THE AUTHOR | This is Number [number] | [signature of Graves]; p.[32] blank.

Size, bulk and paper as A68a. Bound in bright green boards with white cloth spine stamped in gold, from middle to top, up spine: ROBERT GRAVES: POEMS 1953

Price: 15s. Number of copies: 260. Published 24 September 1953 in transparent parchment dust-jacket.

A69 THE NAZARENE GOSPEL RESTORED 1953

a. First edition:

THE | NAZARENE GOSPEL | RESTORED | *By* | ROBERT GRAVES | AND | JOSHUA PODRO | [publisher's emblem] | CASSELL AND COMPANY LIMITED | LONDON | MCMLIII

Collation: [1]/1*8/8 2/2* −32/32*8/8 33/33*4/8,524 leaves
    p [i] THE NAZARENE GOSPEL RESTORED; p.[ii] list of books by Graves; p.[iii] title-page; p.[iv] publisher's, publication and printer's notices; pp.v−ix CONTENTS; p.[x] blank; pp.xi−xxiii FOREWORD; p.[xxiv] blank; p.[1] PART ONE; p.[2] blank; pp.3−41 text; p.[42] blank; p.[43] PART TWO; p.[44] blank; pp.45−827 text; p.[828] blank; p.[829] PART THREE; p.[830] blank; pp.831−833 SUMMARY OF CRITICAL PRINCIPLES; p.[834] blank; p.[835] THE NAZARENE GOSPEL; pp.836−1011 text; p.[1012] blank; p.[1013] CHAPTER INDEX; p.[1014] blank; pp.1015−1021 CHAPTER INDEX; pp. [1022] −[1024] blank.
    24.2 × 15.4 cm. Bulk: 3.4/4.0 cm. White wove paper; all edges trimmed. White wove endpapers. Bound in black cloth; front and back blank; spine stamped in gold: [heavy rule] | [light rule] | [decorative rule] | THE | NAZARENE | GOSPEL | RESTORED | [decorative rule] | [light rule] | [heavy rule] | ROBERT GRAVES | AND | JOSHUA PODRO | CASSELL

Price: 63s. Number of copies: 2,981. Published 22 October 1953 in white dust-jacket printed in grey, red and black.

Contents: Foreword − Part One: I. Curiosities of New Testament Criticism − II. The Pauline Heresy − III. The Hand of Simon Magus − IV. The Process of Gospel-Making − Part Two: [parallel texts of the Gospels, commentary and reconstruction] − Part Three: Summary of Critical Principles − Prolegomena to the Nazarene Gospel − The Nazarene Gospel [in 53 chapters] − Epilegomena by James the Just unto the Faithful − Chapter Index

A69b. First American edition (1954):

THE | NAZARENE GOSPEL | RESTORED | *by* | ROBERT GRAVES | *and* | JOSHUA PODRO | [publisher's emblem] | *Garden City, New York* | DOUBLEDAY & COMPANY, INC. | 1954

Collation: [1] − [30]^16 [31]^8 [32]^16, 504 leaves.
    p.[i] THE | NAZARENE GOSPEL | RESTORED; p.[ii] blank; p.[iii] title-page; p.[iv] copyright, printer's and publication notices; pp.v−xvii FOREWORD; p.[xviii] blank; pp.xix−xxiv CONTENTS; p. [1] *Part One*; p.[2] blank; pp.[3]4−42 text; p.[43]

Part Two; p.[44] blank; pp.[45]46–790 text with p.[118] being a genealogical table; p.[791] *Part Three*; p.[792] blank; pp. [793] 794–795 text; p.[796] blank; pp.[797]–[798]799–975 text; p.[976] blank; pp.[977]978–982 CHAPTER INDEX; pp.[983]–[984] blank; unnumbered pages throughout each chapter.

23.2 × 15.4 cm. Bulk: 4.7/5.3 cm. White wove paper; all edges trimmed; top edges stained red. White wove endpapers. Bound in grey cloth; front and back blank; spine stamped in gold: [ten lines in solid black rectangular box:] [light rule] | [heavy rule] | [light rule] | THE | NAZARENE | GOSPEL | RESTORED | [light rule] | [heavy rule] | [light rule] | ROBERT GRAVES | AND | JOSHUA PODRO | DOUBLEDAY

Price: $10.00. Number of copies: 5,000. Published 15 July 1954 in white dust-jacket printed in light grey-green, red and black.

A69c. Partial edition (1955):

THE | NAZARENE GOSPEL | *by* | ROBERT GRAVES and JOSHUA PODRO | Being PART III (text only) | of their | NAZARENE GOSPEL RESTORED | [publisher's emblem] | CASSELL AND COMPANY LIMITED | LONDON | MCMLV

Collation: [1]⁸ 2–12⁸, 96 leaves.

p.[i] THE NAZARENE GOSPEL; p.[ii] list of books by Graves; p. [iii] title-page; p.[iv] publisher's, printer's and copyright notices; pp.v–vi CONTENTS; pp.vii–ix SUMMARY OF CRITICAL PRINCIPLES; p.x NOTE; p.xi PROLEGOMENA; p.[xii] blank; pp. 1–175 text; pp.[176]–[178] blank.

24.6 × 15.4 cm. Bulk: 1.4/2.0 cm. White wove paper; all edges trimmed. White wove endpapers. Bound in black cloth; front and back blank; spine stamped in gold: [heavy rule] | [light rule] | THE | NAZARENE | GOSPEL | [light rule] | [heavy rule] | ROBERT | GRAVES | AND | JOSHUA | PODRO | CASSELL

Price: 15s. Number of copies: 756. Published 24 February 1955 in cream dust-jacket printed in black and red.

Contents: Part III only of A69a.

Note: Doubleday was permitted to import copies of this edition into the United States as late as 1972.

A69.1 TO MAGDALENA MULET, MARGITA MORA AND LUCIA GRAVES 1954

First edition:

To | [flush left:] *Magdalena Mulet,* | *Margita Mora* | [flush right:] *& Lucia Graves* | *May 4th, 1954*

Collation: A single sheet folded, 2 leaves.

p.[1] title-page; pp.[2]–[3] text (without title; at foot of p. [3]: ROBERT GRAVES and text in English on p.[2] and in Spanish on p.[3]; p.[4] blank.

17.5 × 13.6 cm. Bulk: 0.1 cm. Cream wove paper; deckled edges. Issued as a greeting card, not bound.

Price: Not for sale. Number of copies undetermined. Published 4 May 1954.

A70 THE CROSS AND THE SWORD [1954]

a. First edition:

[p.*ii*:] *Manuel de Jesús Galván's* | *"Enriquillo"* | THE CROSS | UNESCO COLLECTION OF REPRESENTATIVE WORKS: | LATIN AMERICAN SERIES. PUBLISHED WITH | THE COOPERATION OF THE ORGANIZATION OF | AMERICAN STATES. p.[*iii*] AND THE SWORD | *translated by Robert Graves* | INDIANA UNIVERSITY PRESS | BLOOMINGTON

Collation: [1]⁸ [2] – [12]¹⁶ [13]⁸, 192 leaves.
   p.[*i*] THE CROSS AND THE SWORD; p.[*ii*] – [*iii*] title-page; p.[*iv*] copyright, UNESCO and permission notices; pp.[*v*] – *vi* CONTENTS; pp.[*vii*] *viii–xi* FOREWORD p.[*xii*] blank; pp.[*xiii*] *xiv–xvii* TRANSLATOR'S NOTE; p.[*xviii*] PREFACE TO THE 1894 EDITION; p.[1] *Part One*; p.[2] map; pp.[3] 4–80 text; p.[81] *Part Two*; p. [82] blank; pp.[83] 84–189 text; p.[190] blank; p.[191] *Part Three*; p.[192] blank; pp.[193] 194–352 text; pp.[353] 354–364 *Notes*; pp.[365] –366 CAST OF CHARACTERS.
   20.7 × 13.6 cm. Bulk: 2.7/3.3 cm. White wove paper; top and fore-edges only trimmed; top edge stained black. White wove endpapers. Bound in green cloth; back blank; front blind-stamped in lower left with arrow overlaid with compass; spine stamped in bronze, top to bottom: THE CROSS AND THE SWORD [upright:] *Galván* [as title:] INDIANA

Price: $3.75. Number of copies: 2,000. Published 29 October 1954, in white dust-jacket printed in brown, blue and turquoise.

Note: Printed in the United States.

A70b. First English issue (1956):

THE CROSS | AND THE SWORD | *by* | MANUEL DE JESUS GALVAN | *Translated by* | ROBERT GRAVES | LONDON | VICTOR GOLLANCZ LTD | 1956

Collation: [A]/A*⁸/⁸ B/B* –M/M*⁸/⁸, 192 leaves.
   p.[i] THE CROSS AND THE SWORD; p.[ii] *The original title* | *of this book is* | *ENRIQUILLO*; p.[iii] title-page; p. [iv] acknowledgements and printer's and publisher's notices; remainder as A70a, except page-numbers in the preliminaries are not italics.
   19.4 × 12.6 cm. Bulk: 1.8/2.1 cm. White wove paper; all edges trimmed. White wove endpapers. Bound in wine-red cloth; front and back blank; spine stamped in gold: THE | CROSS | AND | THE | SWORD | BY | MANUEL | DE JESUS | GALVAN | GOLLANCZ

Price: 15s. Number of copies undisclosed. Published 11 June 1956 in cream dust-jacket printed in red, blue, yellow, green, brown and black.

Note: This issue appears to be largely a photographic reproduction of the American edition. The type-page of the American text is 16.8 × 10.1 cm., that of the English 16.2 × 9.7 cm.

Printed in Great Britain.

A71   HOMER'S DAUGHTER   [1955]

a. First edition:

HOMER'S DAUGHTER | by | ROBERT GRAVES | [publisher's emblem] | CASSELL & COMPANY LTD | LONDON

Collation: [A]⁸ B–O⁸, 112 leaves.

p.[i] HOMER'S DAUGHTER; p.[ii] list of novels by Graves; p. [iii] title-page; p.[iv] publisher's, publication and copyright notices; p.[v] To Selwyn Jepson, of course; p.[vi] blank; p. vii CONTENTS; p.[viii] blank; pp.ix–xvii PROLOGUE; p.[xviii] blank; pp.1–204 text; pp.[205]–[206] blank.

18.4 × 12.3 cm. Bulk: 1.9/2.3 cm. White wove paper; all edges trimmed. White wove endpapers. Bound in black cloth; front and back blank; spine stamped in gold: Homer's | Daughter | ROBERT | GRAVES | CASSELL

Price: 10s.6d. Number of copies: 15,000. Published 24 February 1955 in eggshell dust-jacket printed in black, yellow and matt olive.

Notes: This book has been translated in Croatian, German, Italian, Magyar, Polish, Russian and Swedish.

A new impression, on slightly larger white wove paper (19.6 × 12.6 cm.) was issued by Cassell in 1973. Aside from the paper the other alterations were: last line of the title-page reads: CASSELL . LONDON; the verso of the title-page has been brought up to date; the book is in 16's ([A] B–G); and it is bound in canary cloth, front and back blank, spine stamped in green: HOMER'S | DAUGHTER | a novel by | ROBERT | GRAVES | CASSELL. The price was £1.75 and it was published in August 1973.

A71b. First American edition (1955):

[entire flush left:] HOMER'S | DAUGHTER | by Robert Graves | DOUBLEDAY & COMPANY, INC., GARDEN CITY, NEW YORK, 1955

Collation: [1]–[9]¹⁶, 144 leaves.

p.[i] HOMER'S | DAUGHTER; p.[ii] blank; p.[1] list of novels by Graves; p.[2] blank; p.[3] title-page; p.[4] copyright, printer's, designer's and edition notices; p.[5] *To Selwyn Jepson, of course*; p.[6] blank; pp.[7]8–9 HISTORICAL NOTE; p. [10] blank; pp.[11]–12 CONTENTS; p.[13] HOMER'S | DAUGHTER; p. [14] blank; pp.[15]16–283 text, with pp.[27, 34, 48, 71, 89, 104, 119, 137, 154, 168, 186, 199, 214, 231, 246, 267] being unnumbered; pp.[284]–[286] blank.

20.8 × 13.9 cm. Bulk: 2.3/2.8 cm. White wove paper; all edges trimmed. White wove endpapers. Bound in black cloth; back blank; front stamped in orange at middle near spine with figure of Greek warrior and horse; spine stamped in orange, top to bottom: Robert Graves [in second row, toward back:] HOMER'S [in centre:

figure of Greek warrior and horse] DAUGHTER [in second row, toward front:] DOUBLEDAY

Price: $3.95. Number of copies: 12,500 (in three printings). Published 24 February 1955 in white dust-jacket printed in red, brown, yellow, green, blue, grey and black.

Note: Academy Chicago issued a photographic reprint in paperback in 1982; it omits pp.[i] – [ii] so that the arabic pagination is continuous.

A71c. Second American edition (1966):

[2 ll. flush left:] HOMER'S | DAUGHTER | [flush right:] ROBERT GRAVES | [publisher's emblem] PYRAMID BOOKS NEW YORK

Collation: 128 leaves, glued at spine.
   p.[1] blurbs; p.[2] blank; p.[3] title-page; p.[4] dedication and publisher's, printing, copyright, LC card and publisher's notices; p.[5] CONTENTS; p.[6] blank; pp.7–9 HISTORICAL NOTE; p.[10] blank; pp.11–254 text, with p.[22] being blank; pp. [255] – [256] publisher's advertisements.
   18.0 × 10.8 cm. Bulk: 1.6 cm. White wove paper; all edges trimmed and stained orange. Bound in white paper covers printed in gold, black, light purple and brown.

Price: $0.85. Number of copies undetermined. Published 15 March 1966.

A72   THE GREEK MYTHS   [1955]

a. First edition:

ROBERT GRAVES | THE GREEK MYTHS | VOLUME ONE[TWO] | PENGUIN BOOKS

Collation: I: [A]¹⁶ B–M¹⁶, 192 leaves; II: [A]¹⁶ B–N¹⁶, 208 leaves.
   I: 2 pp. blank; p.[1] PENGUIN BOOKS | 1026 | THE GREEK MYTHS | VOLUME ONE | ROBERT GRAVES | [publisher's emblem]; p.[2] blank; p.[3] title-page; p.[4] publisher's, edition and printer's notices; pp.[5]6 -7 CONTENTS OF VOLUME ONE; p.[8] frontispiece; pp.[9] 10–13 [14] – [15] 16–23 INTRODUCTION, with pp.[14] – [15] being a map; p.[24] blank; p.[25] THE GREEK MYTHS | VOLUME ONE; p.[26] blank; pp.[27]28–370 text, with pp.[48, 83, 89, 101, 131, 151, 281, 319, 349, 356] being unnumbered; pp.[371] – [382] publisher's advertisements, with p.[372] being blank.
   II: p.[1] PENGUIN BOOKS | 1027 | THE GREEK MYTHS | VOLUME TWO | ROBERT GRAVES | [publisher's emblem]; p.[2] blank; p.[3] title-page; p.[4] publisher's and printer's notices ; pp.[5] –6 CONTENTS OF VOLUME TWO; p.[7] THE GREEK MYTHS | VOLUME TWO; p. [8] blank; pp.[9]10–376 text, with pp.[25, 40, 80, 113, 145, 207, 241, 290, 313, 346] being unnumbered; pp.377–412 INDEX; pp. [413] – [416] publisher's advertisements; [folding map tipped to outside edge of inner back cover].
   18 × 11.2 cm. Bulk: I: 1.8 cm.; II: 2.0 cm. White wove paper; all edges trimmed. Bound in paper covers; front has brown columns down each side with publisher's

emblem half-way down in right-hand column; middle white space reads: [in brown:] PENGUIN BOOKS | [heavy rule across whole cover] | ROBERT GRAVES | [brown rule] | The Greek | Myths | VOLUME ONE [TWO] | [brown rule] | [summary of 9 ll.] | [heavy rule across whole cover] | [in brown:] 3/6; back has same arrangement of brown columns, the publisher's emblem being in the left-hand column; middle white space reads: [in brown:] PENGUIN BOOKS [heavy rule] | [photo of Graves] | [biographical note of 25 ll.] | [heavy rule] | *Not for sale 3/6 in the U.S.A.* [price only in brown]; spine has brown bands top and bottom, inside which the heavy rule; at bottom, upright: 1026 [1027]; spine reads from bottom to top: Robert Graves [publisher's emblem upright in brown] The Greek Myths . Volume 1 [2]; inside front covers is blurb; inside back cover has advertisement for *Count Belisarius*.

Price: 3s.6d. per volume. Number of copies unknown. Published 24 February 1955 in white dust-jacket printed in brown and black like cover.

Notes: Impressions: 2nd, November 1955; 3rd, 1957.
   This book has been translated into Dutch, French, German, Hungarian, Italian, Japanese, Polish and Serbo-Croatian.

A72b. First American issue ([1955]):

ROBERT GRAVES | THE GREEK MYTHS | VOLUME ONE [TWO] | PENGUIN BOOKS | BALTIMORE . MARYLAND

Collation: I: [1] – [12]^{16}, 192 leaves; II: [1] – [13]^{16}, 208 leaves.
   Remainder as A72a, except pp.I.[4] and II.[4] have publication, publisher's, copyright and printing notices and pp.I.[382] and II.[416] are blank.
   Measurements and paper as A72a. Covers as A72a

Price: $0.85 per volume. Number of copies: 35,000. Published 17 June 1955.

Note: Impressions: 2nd, January 1957; 3rd, June 1959; 4th, May 1961.
   There is also an American issue bound in red simulated cloth boards; back blank; front stamped in gold with facsimile signature of Graves; spine stamped in gold: ROBERT | GRAVES | [rule] | THE | GREEK | MYTHS | I [II]; top edges stained black; white wove endpapers; price: $6.50 per volume; 3,000 copies published in 1955 in a slipcase without dust-jacket.

A72c. Second American 'edition' (1957):

ROBERT GRAVES | THE GREEK MYTHS | VOLUME ONE [TWO] | GEORGE BRAZILLER, INC. | NEW YORK | 1957

Collation: I: [1] – [9]^{16} [10]^{12} [11] – [12]^{16}, 188 leaves, but retaining also the signing of the English issue A72a; II: [A]^{16} B–N^{16}, 208 leaves.
   I: 2pp. blank; p.[1] THE GREEK MYTHS | VOLUME ONE | ROBERT GRAVES; p.[2] blank; p.[3] title-page; p.[4] publication, copyright, LC card and printing notices; pp.[5]6–7 CONTENTS OF VOLUME ONE; p.[8] blank; illustration, verso blank; p.[9]10–370 as A72a; pp.[371] – [372] blank.
   II: p.[1] THE GREEK MYTHS | VOLUME TWO | ROBERT GRAVES; p.[2] blank; p.[3] title-page; p.[4] publication, copyright, LC card and printing notices;

pp.[5]6–412 as A72a; pp.[413] – [416] blank; [map pasted to inside back cover].
18.0 × 11.2 cm. Bulk: I: 1.7/2.2 cm.; II: 1.8/2.3 cm. White wove paper; all edges trimmed; top edges stained green. White wove endpapers. Bound in black cloth; front and back blank; spine stamped in gold: ROBERT | GRAVES | [rule] | THE | GREEK | MYTHS | [rule] | I [II]

Price: $6.50 for two volumes. Number of copies undetermined. Published in 1957.

Note: There is also a one-volume issue, which differs as follows: no map; top edges stained blue; grey cloth spine stamped: *Robert Graves* | [rectangular single-rule box enclosing 3 ll.:] THE | GREEK | MYTHS | *George Braziller*; front and back covers simulated black leather; price $4.75; published 28 October 1957.

A72d. Second English 'edition' ([1958]):

GREEK MYTHS | [rule] | ROBERT GRAVES | [publisher's emblem] | CASSELL & COMPANY LTD | LONDON

Collation: [A]/A2$^{8/8}$ B/B2–Z/Z2$^{8/8}$ 2A/2A2$^{8/8}$ 2B^6, 390 leaves.
p.[1] GREEK MYTHS; p.[2] blank; p.[3] title-page; p.[4] publisher's, publication, copyright and printer's notices; pp. [5]6–9 CONTENTS; p.[10] illustration; pp.[11]12–24 INTRODUCTION; two leaf map, first recto and last verso blank; p. [25] GREEK MYTHS; p.[26] blank; pp.[27]28–738 text, with pp.[48, 83, 89, 101, 131, 151, 281, 319, 349, 356, 371, 387, 402, 442, 475, 507, 569, 603, 652, 675, 708] being unnumbered; [map pasted to p.[739]]; pp.[739]740–774 NAME INDEX; pp.[775] – [776] blank.
20.3 × 13.0 cm. Bulk: 3.1/3.7 cm. White wove paper; all edges trimmed. White wove endpapers. Bound in rust cloth; front and back blank; spine stamped in gold: [double-rule rectangular box enclosing 2 ll.:] | GREEK | MYTHS | ROBERT | GRAVES | CASSELL

Price: 30s. Number of copies: 2,999. Published 6 March 1958 in white dust-jacket printed in yellow, chestnut and black.

Notes: Impressions: 2nd, 15 November 1958 (1,500 copies); 3rd, November 1962.
The introduction has been revised for this edition; and note 4 of Chapter 104 is new.

A72e. Second English 'edition', Pelican impression ([1960]):

ROBERT GRAVES | THE GREEK MYTHS | VOLUME ONE [TWO] | PENGUIN BOOKS

Collation as A72a.
I: 2 pp. blank; p.[1] PELICAN BOOKS | A508 | THE GREEK MYTHS | VOLUME ONE | ROBERT GRAVES | [series emblem]; pp.[2] – [8] as A72a; pp.[9] – 10 FOREWORD; pp.[11]12–24 INTRODUCTION; pp. [25]26–370 as A72a; p.[371] MAP OF THE GREEK WORLD; pp. [372] – [373] map; p.[374] blank; pp.[375] – [382] publisher's advertisements, with p.[376] being blank.
II: as A72a.
18.0 × 10.7 Cm. Bulk: I: 1.8 cm. II: 2.1 cm. White wove paper; all edges trimmed. Bound in white paper covers printed in blue and black.

Price: 5s. per volume. Number of copies: I: 25,000; II: 24,000. Published in 1960.

Notes: Impressions: 2nd, 1962; 3rd, 1964; 4th, 1972; 5th, 1973; 6th, 1974; 7th, 1975; 8th, 1977; 9th, 1978; 10th, 1979; 11th, 1980; 12th, 1981; 13th, 1982; 14th, 1983; 15th, 1984; 16th, 1985.

From 1961 Penguin also published this 'edition' in the United States altering only the price on the front cover, the imprint, and the printing and manufacturing notices. There were impressions in 1961, 1964, 1966, 1968. These impressions were printed in the United States.

The text is that of A72d.

A72f. Third English 'edition', Condensed edition ([1981]):

Robert Graves | [geometric designed rule, in grey] | GREEK | MYTHS | [geometric designed rule, in grey] | *Illustrated Edition* | CASSELL | LONDON

Collation: [1] – [3]⁸ [4]⁴ [5] – [13]⁸ [14]⁴ [15]⁸, 112 leaves.

p.[1] [geometric designed rule, in grey] | GREEK | MYTHS | [geometric designed rule, in grey]; p.[2] frontispiece; p.[3] title-page; p.[4] publisher's, copyright, rights reservation, publishing, condensor's, ISBN, printer's and picture credit notices; pp.[5] – [8] CONTENTS; p.[9] [geometric designed rule, in grey] | ACKNOWLEDGEMENTS | [geometric designed rule, in grey]; pp.[10] 11–215 text, with pp.[18, 19, 20, 26, 27, 30, 31, 44, 50, 51, 54, 55, 78, 79, 83, 86, 87, 106, 107, 111, 114, 115, 128, 134, 142, 143, 146, 147, 150, 151, 170, 171, 174, 175, 182, 183, 191, 202, 203, 206, 207] being unnumbered; pp.[216]217–224 [geometric designed rule, in grey] | INDEX | [geometric designed rule, in grey].

24.5 × 18.8 cm. Bulk: 1.6/2.1 cm. White wove paper; all edges trimmed. White wove endpapers. Bound in navy blue cloth; front and back blank. Spine stamped in silver, top to bottom: GREEK MYTHS ROBERT GRAVES

Price: £9.95. Number of copies unknown. Published 27 August 1981.

Note: The condensation was carried out by John Buchanan-Brown.

A73 COLLECTED POEMS 1955   1955

First edition:

COLLECTED POEMS | 1955 | by Robert Graves | 1955 | DOUBLEDAY & COMPANY, INC. | GARDEN CITY, NEW YORK

Collation: [1] – [10]¹⁶, 160 leaves.

p.[i] COLLECTED POEMS | 1955; p.[ii] blank; p.[iii] list of books by Graves; p.[iv] blank; p.[v] title-page; p.[vi] LC card, copyright, printer's and designer's and first edition notices; p.vii TO CALLIOPE; p.[viii] blank; p.[ix] ACKNOWLEDGEMENTS; p.[x] blank; pp.xi–xii FOREWORD; pp.xiii–xx CONTENTS; pp.[1] – [2]3–291 text, with pp.[1, 37, 71, 97, 157, 175, 209, 241, 261] being section headings and pp.[2, 36, 38, 70, 72, 98, 156, 158, 176, 210, 242, 260, 262] being blank; p.[292] blank; pp.293–298 INDEX; pp.[299] – [300] blank.

20.8 × 13.8 cm. Bulk: 2.5/3.2 cm. White wove paper; all edges trimmed; top edges stained light blue. Bound in light blue cloth; front and back blank; spine stamped in blue: *Collected* | *Poems* | 1955 | [decorative rule] | ROBERT | GRAVES

Price: $4.50. Number of copies: 3,500 (in two printings). Published 30 June 1955 in white dust-jacket printed in light and dark blue.

Contents: To Calliope – Foreword – I: In the Wilderness – The Haunted House – Reproach – The Finding of Love – 'The General Elliott' – Rocky Acres – Outlaws – One Hard Look – A Frosty Night – Allie – Unicorn and the White Doe – Henry and Mary – Love without Hope – What Did I Dream? – The Country Dance – The Troll's Nosegay – The Hills of May – Lost Love – Vain and Careless – An English Wood – The Bedpost – The Pier-Glass – Apples and Water – Angry Samson – Down – Mermaid, Dragon, Fiend – II: In Procession – Warning to Children – Alice – Richard Roe and John Doe – The Witches' Cauldron – Ancestors – Children of Darkness – The Cool Web – Love in Barrenness – Song of Contrariety – The Presence – The Land of Whipperginny – In No Direction – The Castle – Return – The Bards – Nobody – The Progress – Full Moon – Vanity – Pure Death – Sick Love – It Was All Very Tidy – III: Callow Captain – Thief – Saint – The Furious Voyage – Song: Lift-Boy – Traveller's Curse after Misdirection – The Last Day of Leave – The Next Time – Ulysses – The Succubus – The Reader over My Shoulder – The Legs – Gardener – Front Door Soliloquy – In Broken Images – The Devil at Berry Pomeroy – On Rising Early – Flying Crooked – Fragment of a Lost Poem – Brother – IV: Galatea and Pygmalion – The Devil's Advice to Story-Tellers – Sergeant-Major Money – Sea Side – Wm. Brazier – Welsh Incident – Vision in the Repair-Shop – Interruption – Act V, Scene 5 – Midway – Hell – Leda – Synthetic Such – The Florist Rose – Lost Acres – At First Sight – Recalling War – Down, Wanton, Down! – A Former Attachment – Nature's Lineaments – Time – The Philosopher – On Dwelling – Parent to Children – Ogres and Pygmies – History of the Word – Single Fare – To Walk on Hills – To Bring the Dead to Life – To Evoke Posterity – Any Honest Housewife – Defeat of the Rebels – Never Such Love – The Fallen Signpost – The China Plate – Certain Mercies – The Cuirassiers of the Frontier – The Laureate – A Jealous Man – The Cloak – The Foreboding – With Her Lips Only – The Halls of Bedlam – Or to Perish before Day – A Country Mansion – The Eremites – Lovers in Winter – Advocates – Self-Praise – V: On Portents – The Terraced Valley – The Challenge – The Chink – The Ages of Oath – New Legends – Like Snow – End of Play – The Climate of Thought – The Fallen Tower of Siloam – The Great-Grandmother – No More Ghosts – VI: A Love Story – Dawn Bombardment – The Worms of History – The Glutton – A Stranger at the Party – The Shot – The Thieves – Lollocks – To Sleep – Despite and Still – The Suicide in the Copse – Frightened Men – The Oath – Language of the Seasons – Mid-Winter Waking – The Rock at the Corner – The Beach – The Villagers and Death – The Door – Under the Pot – Through Nightmare – To Lucia at Birth – Death by Drums – She Tells Her Love While Half Asleep – Theseus and Ariadne – Pethesileia – Cold Weather Proverb – The Death Room – To Juan at the Winter Solstice – To Be Called a Bear – VII: My Name and I – 1805 – At the Savoy Chapel – Dream of a Climber – The Persian Version – The Weather of Olympus – Apollo of the Physiologists – The Oldest Soldier – Grotesques i–vi – The Eugenist – A Civil Servant – Gulls and Men -- Conversation Piece – Queen-Mother to New Queen

– General Bloodstock's Lament for England – 'iWellcome, to the Caves of Arta'!' –
I'm Through with You for Ever – The Sacred Mission – Poets' Corner –
Coronation Address – Beauty in Trouble – Sirocco at Deya' – From the Embassy
– VIII: The White Goddess – The Allansford Pursuit – Amergin's Charm – The
Battle of the Trees – The Song of Blodeuwedd – Instructions to the Orphic Adept
– Lament for Pasiphaë – The Sirens' Welcome to Cronos – Intercession in Late
October – The Jackals' Address to Isis – The Destroyer – Return of the Goddess –
IX: With the Gift of a Ring – Counting the Beats – The Young Cordwainer – Your
Private Way – The Survivor – Questions in a Wood – Darien – The Portrait –
Prometheus – The Straw – Cry Faugh! – Hercules at Nemea – Dialogue on the
Headland – The Mark – Liadan and Curithir – The Sea Horse – Reproach to Julia
– Dethronement – Cat-Goddesses – The Blue-Fly – A Lost Jewel – The Window
Sill – Spoils – Rhea – Leaving the Rest Unsaid – Index

Note: The second printing does not contain the "first edition" notice on p.[vi] and
the blue of the binding and stained edge is darker.

A74   ADAM'S RIB   [1955]

a. First edition:

[in brown:] ADAM'S RIB | *and other anomalous elements in* | *the Hebrew Creation
Myth* | *a new view by* | ROBERT GRAVES| *with wood engravings by James Metcalf* |
TRIANON PRESS

Collation: [1]⁴ [2]⁸ [3]¹⁰ [4] – [5]⁸ [6]⁴, 42 leaves.

p.[i] ADAM'S RIB; p.[ii] blank; p.[iii] statement of edition, printer's, designer's and
publisher's notices; p.[iv] blank; p. [v] title-page; p.[vi] publisher's, distributor's and
printing notices; p.[vii] CONTENTS; p.[viii] blank; pp.1–19 ARGUMENT; p.[20]
blank; p.[21] THE GENESIS VERSION; p.[22] blank; pp. 23–35 text; p.[36] blank;
p.[37] THE HEBRON ICONS; pp.38–72 [73] text and illustrations, text on even-
numbered pages, illustrations facing on unnumbered pages, that part of the book
being printed in brown; pp.[74] – [76] blank.

27.4 × 19.0 cm. Bulk: 1.1/1.7 cm. White wove paper; all edges trimmed. White
wove endpapers. Bound in brick red cloth; front and back blank; spine stamped in
gold, top to bottom: ADAM'S RIB *by Robert Graves* TRIANON

Price: 31s.6d. Number of copies: 1,750. Published 22 July 1955 in grey dust-jacket
printed in black.

A74b. Limited issue ([1955]):

Title-page as A74a.

Collation as A74a.

Remainder as A74a, except p.[ii]: This is Number [letter or number written in] of
the Signed Edition | [signature of Graves] | [signature of Metcalf].

Size, paper and binding as A74a.

Price: 52s.6d. Number of copies: 250 numbered; 26 lettered A–Z (*hors commerce*).
Published as A74a, but in a grey unprinted slip-box.

A74c. First American edition ([1958]):

[in brown:] ADAM'S RIB | *and other anomalous elements in* | *the Hebrew Creation Myth* | *a new view by* | ROBERT GRAVES| *with wood engravings by James Metcalf* | NEW YORK . THOMAS YOSELOFF

Collation: [1]⁶ [2] – [6]⁸, 46 leaves
  2pp. blank, front pastedown endpaper; 2 pp. blank, front free endpaper; p.[i] – [ii] as A74a; p.[iii] designer's and illustrator's notices; p.[iv] blank; p.[v] title-page; p.[vi] copyright, edition, publisher's, LC card and publication notices; pp.[vii] – [76] as A74a; 2 pp.blank, rear free endpaper; 2 pp. blank, rear pastedown endpaper.
  27.3 × 19.0 cm. Bulk: 0.7/1.2 cm. White wove paper; all edges trimmed. Bound in medium red cloth; front and back blank; spine stamped in gold, down spine: ADAM'S RIB *by Robert Graves* [to front:] THOMAS [to back, parallel to previous:] YOSELOFF

Price: $6.00. Number of copies: 2,000. Published in September 1958 in grey dust-jacket printed in black.

Note: 1,000 English sheets of A74a were distributed by Yoseloff at the same price; A74b was also distributed by Yoseloff at $7.50; A74a–b were issued in March 1958.

A75   THE CROWNING PRIVILEGE   [1955]

a. First edition:

THE CROWNING | PRIVILEGE | THE CLARK LECTURES | 1954–1955 | ALSO VARIOUS ESSAYS ON POETRY | AND | SIXTEEN NEW POEMS | *by* | *ROBERT GRAVES* | [publisher's emblem] | CASSELL & COMPANY LTD | LONDON

Collation: [A]⁸ B–P⁸, 120 leaves.
  p.[i] THE CROWNING PRIVILEGE; p.[ii] list of books by Graves; p.[iii] title-page; p.[iv] publisher's, copyright, publication and printer's notices; p.[v] *To the Masters and Fellows of* | *Trinity College, Cambridge* | *in gratitude;* p.[vi] blank; pp.vii–viii CONTENTS; p.ix FOREWORD; p.[x] blank; p.[1] THE CLARK LECTURES | 1954– 1955; p.[2] blank; pp.3–135 text; p. [136] blank; p.[137] VARIOUS ESSAYS | ON POETRY; p.[138] blank; pp.139–214 text; p.215–230 SIXTEEN NEW POEMS
  21.3 × 15.7 cm. Bulk: 1.6/2.1 cm. White wove paper; all edges trimmed. White wove endpapers. Bound in black cloth; front and back blank; spine stamped in gold: The | Crowning | Privilege | ROBERT | GRAVES | CASSELL

Price: 15s. Number of copies: 3,012. Published 22 September 1955 in cream dust-jacket printed in green and black.

Contents: Foreword – The Clark Lectures, 1954–1955: 1. The Crowning Privilege – 2. The Age of Obsequiousness – 3. The Road to Rydal Mount – 4. Harp, Anvil, Oar – 5. Dame Ocupacyon – 6. These Be Your Gods, O Israel! – Various Essays on Poetry: Mother Goose's Lost Goslings – The Old Black Cow – The Essential E.E. Cummings – Juana de Asbaje – Poems by Juana de Asbaje, with translations – The Poet and His Public – Best Man, Bore, Bamboozle, Etc. – Theft – Kynge Arther is Nat Dede – Dr Syntax and Mr Pound – Sixteen New Poems: The

Clearing – A Lost Jewel – The Three Pebbles – The Question – The Window Sill – The Sea Horse – Spoils – Beauty in Trouble – Poets' Corner – End of the World – Penthesileia – To a Pebble in My Shoe – The Tenants – Coronation Address – My Moral Forces – Interview.

Note: Contents differ from those in A75b–c.

A75b. First American edition (1956):

[four lines flush right:] The | Crowning | Privilege | COLLECTED ESSAYS ON POETRY | [two lines flush left:] by ROBERT GRAVES | DOUBLEDAY & COMPANY, INC., GARDEN CITY, NEW YORK, 1956

Collation: [1] – [10]^{16}, 160 leaves.

pp.[i]-[iv] blank; p.[1] [flush right:] THE CROWNING PRIVILEGE; p.[2] blank; p.[3] list of books by Graves; p.[4] blank; p. [5] title-page; p.[6] [flush right:] publisher's, copyright, printer's, designer's and edition notices; p.p.[7] [flush right:] *To the Masters and Fellows | of Trinity College, Cambridge; in gratitude*; p.[8] blank; p.[9] [flush right:] FOREWORD; p.[10] blank; pp.11–12 [flush right:] CONTENTS; p. [13] [flush right:] THE CLARK LECTURES | 1954–1955; p.[14] blank; pp.[15]16–142 text, with pp.[36, 55, 79, 100, 119] being unnumbered; p.[143] [flush right:] VARIOUS ESSAYS ON POETRY; p. [144] blank; pp.[145]146–218 text, with pp.[160, 166, 171, 189, 196, 201, 210, 216] being unnumbered; p.[219] [flush right:] THE COMMON ASPHODEL; p.[220] blank; pp.[221]222–311 text. with pp. [239, 280, 293, 296, 308] being unnumbered; pp.[312] – [316] blank.

20.9 × 13.9 cm. Bulk: 2.3/2.8 cm. White wove paper; all edges trimmed. White wove endpapers. Bound in yellow cloth; front and back blank; spine printed in blue: THE | CROWNING | PRIVILEGE | [in red: device of thirteen winged crowns about circle] | Robert | Graves | DOUBLEDAY

Price: $5.00 Number of copies: 4,000 (in two printings). Published 5 July 1956 in white dust-jacket printed in dark olive, yellow and reddish purple.

Contents: Omits poems of A75a and adds the following essays from A63: Loving Mad Tom – Nietzsche – Coleridge and Wordsworth – Keats and Shelley – Lucretius and Jeans – How Poets See – 'Mad Mr. Swinburne' – The Ghost of Milton – The Common Asphodel.

Note: A photographic reprint of this edition was published by Books for Libraries Press, Freeport, New York, in 1970.

A75c. Second British edition ([1959]):

THE | CROWNING PRIVILEGE | *Collected Essays on Poetry by* | ROBERT GRAVES | PENGUIN BOOKS

Collation: [1]^8 2–22^8, 176 leaves.

p.[1] PELICAN BOOKS | A451 | THE CROWNING PRIVILEGE | ROBERT GRAVES | [publisher's emblem]; p.[2] blank; p.[3] title-page; p.[4] publisher's, publication, copyright and printer's notices; p.[5] TO THE MASTERS AND FELLOWS | OF TRINITY COLLEGE CAMBRIDGE | IN GRATITUDE; p.[6] blank;

p.[7] CONTENTS; p.[8] blank; p. [9] FOREWORD; p.[10] blank; p.[11] THE CLARK LECTURES | 1954–1955; p.[12] blank; pp.13–157[158] text, with pp.[36, 58, 85, 109, 131] being unnumbered; p.[159] VARIOUS ESSAYS ON POETRY; p.[160] blank; pp.161–243[244] text, with pp.[177, 183, 189, 201, 210, 218, 224, 234, 241] being unnumbered; p. [245] THE COMMON ASPHODEL; p.[246] blank; pp.247–346[347] text, with pp.[266, 313, 327, 330, 343] being unnumbered; p.[348] blank; p.[349] publisher's advertisement; p.[350] blank; pp. [351]–[352] publisher's advertisements.

18.0 × 11.0 cm. Bulk: 1.6 cm. White wove paper; all edges trimmed. Bound in white paper covers printed in blue and black.

Price: 4s. Number of copies: 25,000. Published 28 May 1959.

Contents: As A75b.

A76   THE INFANT WITH THE GLOBE   [1955]

a. First edition:

PEDRO ANTONIO DE ALARCON | THE INFANT | WITH THE | GLOBE | *translated* | *with an introduction by* | ROBERT GRAVES | TRIANON PRESS

Collation: [1]^{16} 2–7^{16} 8/8$^{*16/2}$, 130 leaves.

p.[i] THE INFANT WITH THE GLOBE; p.[ii] blank; p.[iii] title-page; p.[iv] publisher's and printer's notices; p.[v] *Contents*; p.[vi] blank; pp.[vii]viii–xviii *Introduction*; pp.[1]2–240 text, with pp.[4, 8, 15, 23, 27, 29, 33, 41, 45, 56, 63, 74, 86, 91, 99, 104, 111, 129, 148, 169, 189, 198, 208, 216, 227] being unnumbered; pp.[241]–[242] blank.

18.4 × 12.3 cm. Bulk: 1.6/1.9 cm. White wove paper; all edges trimmed. White wove endpapers. Bound in rust cloth; front and back blank; spine stamped in gold: ALARCON | [star] | THE | INFANT | WITH THE | GLOBE | [star] | GRAVES | TRIANON | PRESS

Price: 15s. Number of copies unknown. Published 11 November 1955 in white dust-jacket printed in red and black.

76b. American issue ([1955]):

[nine lines flush left of centre:] ROBERT | GRAVES | THE | INFANT | WITH | THE | GLOBE | *From the Spanish of* | *Pedro Antonio de Alarcón* | [publisher's emblem left of remaining] | [two lines flush left:] NEW YORK . LONDON | THOMAS YOSELOFF

Collation as A76a.

Remainder as A76a except p.[iv] edition, publisher's, LC card, copyright, publication and printing notices.

18.3 × 12.3 cm. Bulk: 1.6/2.2 cm. Paper as A76a. Bound in orange cloth; front and back blank; spine printed: [down spine to front:] ROBERT | [down spine to back:] GRAVES | [down spine centred:] THE INFANT WITH THE GLOBE | [down spine, to back, beginning below 'B' of 'GLOBE':] *Alarcón* | [remainder upright:] [publisher's emblem] | THOMAS | YOSELOFF

Price: $4.25. Number of copies: 1,500, Trianon sheets. Published 29 October 1959 in white dust-jacket printed in blue, orange and black.

A77   WINTER IN MAJORCA   [1956]

a. First edition:

WINTER | IN MAJORCA | by | GEORGE SAND | WITH | JOSÉ QUADRADO'S | *Refutation of George Sand* | TRANSLATED AND ANNOTATED | BY | ROBERT GRAVES | [publisher's emblem] | *CASSELL & COMPANY LTD* | *LONDON*

Collation: [A]⁸ B–M⁸ N/*²/⁸, 106 leaves.

pp.[i] – [ii] blank; p.[iii] WINTER IN MAJORCA; p.[iv] list of books by Graves; p.[v] title-page; p.[vi] publisher's, printer's, copyright and publication notices; p.vii CONTENTS; p. [viii] blank; p.ix ILLUSTRATIONS; p.[x] blank; pp.xi–xii FOREWORD; p.[1] WINTER IN MAJORCA | *by* | GEORGE SAND; p.[2] blank; p.3 *AUTHOR'S NOTE*; p.[4] blank; pp.5–9 text; p. [10] map; pp.11–52 text; [plate, printed both sides]; pp.53–68 text; [plate, printed both sides]; pp.69–174 text; pp.175–185 *HISTORICAL SUMMARY*; p.[186] blank; pp.187–200 *TO GEORGE SAND: A REFUTATION*.

21.5 × 13.8 cm. Bulk: 1.5/2.0 cm. White laid paper; all edges trimmed. White wove endpapers. Bound in red cloth; front and back blank; spine stamped in gold: Winter | in Majorca | GEORGE | SAND | *Translated and* | *annotated by* | ROBERT | GRAVES | CASSELL

Price: 15s. Number of copies: 1,370. Published 9 February 1956 in white dust-jacket printed in red, black and olive-tan.

Note: Impression: 2nd, April 1956 (1,003 copies).

Academy Chicago announced a photographic reprint of this edition before 1979 but no copy has been seen.

A77b. Majorcan issue ([1956]):

WINTER | IN MAJORCA | by | GEORGE SAND | WITH | JOSÉ QUADRADO'S | *Refutation of George Sand* | TRANSLATED AND ANNOTATED | BY | ROBERT GRAVES | *VALLDEMOSA EDITION* | *MALLORCA*

Collation as A77a.

Remainder as A77a, except p.[vi] copyright, publication and printing notices.

21.8 × 14.2 cm. Bulk: 1.3 cm. White wove paper; all edges trimmed. Bound in yellow paper cover; back blank; front cover: [four lines in red: WINTER | IN MAJORCA | by GEORGE SAND | with José Quadrado's *Refutation of George Sand* | [cut of George Sand] | [in red:] TRANSLATED & ANNOTATED BY | ROBERT GRAVES; spine: [at top of spine, from bottom to top, in red: WINTER IN MAJORCA | [in lower third of spine, upright:] George | Sand | translated | and |

annotated | by | Robert | Graves | Valldemosa | edition | Mallorca; inner sides of front and back covers blank.

Price: undetermined. Number of copies: 2,009. Published 9 February 1956.

A78   ¡CATACROK!   [1956]

First edition:

¡CATACROK! | Mostly Stories, Mostly Funny | by | ROBERT GRAVES | [publisher's emblem] | CASSELL & CO LTD | LONDON

Collation: [A]⁸ B−N⁸, 104 leaves.

p.[1] ¡CATACROK!; p.[2] blank; p.[3] title-page; p. [4] publisher's, publication, copyright and printer's notices; pp.5−6 CONTENTS; pp.7−8 FOREWORD; pp.9−203 text; pp. [204] − [208] blank.

21.5 × 15.7 cm. Bulk: 1.9/2.4 cm. White wove paper; all edges trimmed. White wove endpapers. Bound in light blue cloth; front and back blank; spine stamped in gold: ROBERT | GRAVES | ¡CATACROK! | CASSELL; title runs downward across spine.

Price: 15s. Number of copies: 4,015. Published 8 November 1956 in white dust-jacket printed in yellow, robin's egg and black.

Contents: Foreword − Varro's Four Hundred and Ninety Books − Treacle Tart − The Full Length − An Appointment for Candlemass − The Devil Is a Protestant− Trín-Trín-Trín − Earth to Earth − Epics Are Out of Fashion − School Life in Majorca − Bulletin of the College of St Francis of Assisi − New Light on Dream-Flight − Period Piece − Protocols of Kitsch − Trouistic Circular K37 − They Say...They Say − Week-End at Cwm Tatws − 6 Valiant Bulls 6 − He Went Out to Buy a Rhine − A Man May Not Marry His... − God Grant Your Honour Many Years − The White Horse, or 'The Great Southern Ghost Story' − A Bomb under My Monument − Thy Servant and God's − Ever Had a Guinea Worm? − Sappy Blancmange − Cambridge Upstairs − The Five Godfathers − Kill Them! Kill Them! − The Abominable Mr Gunn − Harold Vesey at the Gates of Hell − Flesh-Coloured Net Tights − 'Ha, Ha!' Chort-led Nig-ger − Life of the Poet Gnaeus Robertulus Gravesa − Ditching in a Fishless Sea − The Whitaker Negroes − Bathunst at Bathurst

Note: This book has been translated into Swedish.

A79   PHARSALIA   [1956]

a. First edition:

LUCAN | PHARSALIA | DRAMATIC EPISODES OF THE | CIVIL WARS | [star] | TRANSLATED | BY ROBERT GRAVES | [heavy rule] | [three successively shorter light rules] | PENGUIN BOOKS

Collation: [1]¹⁶ 2−3¹⁶ 4−6⁸ 7−9¹⁶, 120 leaves.

p.[1] THE PENGUIN CLASSICS | EDITED BY E. V. RIEU | L66 | [publisher's emblem]; p.[2] blank; p.[3] title-page; p.[4] publisher's, publication and printer's notices; p.[5] CONTENTS; p.[6] blank; pp.7–23[24] INTRODUCTION; pp.25–238[239] text, with pp.[46, 66, 86, 106, 128, 149, 173, 196, 224] being unnumbered; p.[240] blank.

18.0 × 11.1 cm. Bulk: 1.1 cm. White wove paper; all edges trimmed. Bound in paper covers; front cover: [solid rectangular purple border, inside which:] | [rectangular decorative rule border, inside which:] | LUCAN | PHARSALIA | DRAMATIC | EPISODES OF THE | CIVIL WARS | [roundel] | A NEW TRANSLATION BY | ROBERT GRAVES | [swelled purple rule] | THE PENGUIN | CLASSICS | [at right:] 2/6; back cover: solid and decorative borders as front, inside which are publisher's advertisements; spine: [purple band] | [decorative band] | [up spine:] PHARSALIA | [publisher's emblem] | [up spine:] LUCAN | L66 | [decorative band] | [purple band]; inner sides of both covers blank.

Price: 2s.6d. Number of copies: 30,000. Published 29 November 1956.

A79b. First American issue ([1957]):

Title-page as A79a.

Collation: [1] – [3]¹⁶ [4] – [5]¹² [6] – [8]¹⁶, 120 leaves.

Remainder as A79a.

20.3 × 13.6 cm. Bulk: 1.5/2.1 cm. White wove paper; all edges trimmed; top edges stained blue; other edges spattered. White wove endpapers. Bound in red cloth-simulated boards; back blank; front stamped in gold with facsimile signature of Graves; spine stamped in gold, top to bottom: LUCAN . PHARSALIA

Price: $4.00 Number of copies: 3,000. Published in June 1957 in white dust-jacket printed in purple and black.

Notes: There is a second issue which omits 'L66' on p.[1].

There is an American paper-bound issue, identical with A79a, except on better paper; 20,000 copies were printed in the United States and sold for $0.95 each.

A79c. Second English edition ([1961]):

THE BELLE SAUVAGE LIBRARY | LUCAN | PHARSALIA | DRAMATIC EPISODES OF THE | CIVIL WARS | TRANSLATED BY | ROBERT GRAVES | [publisher's emblem] | CASSELL . LONDON

Collation: [1] – [11]⁸ [12]⁹ [13]⁸ [14]² [15]⁴ [16]⁸, 119 leaves, the final leaf of [12] being tipped in and [14] being unsewn and pasted between [13] and [15].

p.[i] PHARSALIA; p.[ii] blank; p.[iii] title-page; p.[iv] publisher's, copyright, publication and printing notices; pp. v–xxii INTRODUCTION; pp.1–214[215] text, with pp.[22, 42, 62, 82, 104, 125, 149, 172, 200] being unnumbered; p.[216] blank.

20.6 × 14.7 cm. Bulk: 1.3/1.8 cm. White wove paper; all edges trimmed. White wove endpapers. Bound in dark buff cloth; front and back blank; spine stamped in copper: [star] | [rule] | LUCAN | *Pharsalia* | [rule] | [star] | *Translated* | *by* | ROBERT | GRAVES | [star] | [rule] | *Cassell* | [rule] | [star]

Price: 12s.6d. Number of copies undisclosed. Published 12 October 1961 in white dust-jacket printed in orange, brown and black.

A80 THE TWELVE CAESARS [1957]

a. First edition:

[whole enclosed within oval of medallions of the twelve Caesars:] THE | TWELVE | CAESARS | – | *Gaius Suetonius* | *Tranquillus* | – | TRANSLATED BY | ROBERT GRAVES | – | *Penguin Books*

Collation: [A]^{16} B–K^{16}, 160 leaves.
　　p.[1] THE PENGUIN CLASSICS | EDITED BY E. V. RIEU | L72 | [publisher's emblem]; p.[2] blank; p.[3] title-page; p.[4] publisher's, publication and printer's notices; p.[5] CONTENTS; p.[6] description of cover design; pp.[7] –8 FOREWORD; pp. [9]10–309 text, with pp.[50, 148, 180, 208, 242, 262, 294] being blank and pp.[51, 109, 149, 181, 209, 243, 255, 263, 273, 287, 295] being unnumbered; pp.[310] – [311] genealogical tables; p. [312] blank; pp.[313]314–315 descriptions of the medallions on the title page; p.[316] blank; p.[317] publisher's advertisement; p.[318] blank; pp.[319] – [320] publisher's advertisements.
　　18.1 × 11.1 cm. Bulk: 1.5 cm. White wove paper; all edges trimmed. Bound in paper covers; front cover: [solid rectagular purple border, inside which: | [rectangular decorative rule border, inside which:] | SUETONIUS | THE | TWELVE | CAESARS | [roundel] | TRANSLATED BY | ROBERT GRAVES | [swelled purple rule] | THE PENGUIN | CLASSICS] [at right:] 3/6; back cover: solid and decorative borders as front, inside which are publisher's advertisements; spine: [purple band] | [decorative band] | [down spine:] SUETONIUS | [publisher's emblem] | [down spine:] THE TWELVE CAESARS | L72 | [decorative band] | [purple band]; inner sides of covers blank.

Price: 3s.6d. Number of copies: 40,000. Published 28 March 1957.

A80b. First American issue ([1957]):

Title-page as A80a.

Collation: [1] – [10]^{16}, 160 leaves.
　　Remainder as A80a, except p.[4] publication, publisher's, copyright and printing notices.
　　20.2 × 13.4 cm. Bulk: 1.9/2.5 cm. White wove paper; all edges trimmed; top edges stained blue. Bound in red cloth-simulated boards; back blank; front stamped in gold with facsimile signature of Graves; spine stamped in gold, top to bottom: SUETONIUS . THE TWELVE CAESARS

Price: $4.50. Number of copies: 3,000. Published 19 July 1957 in white dust-jacket printed in black and mustard-gold.

Note: There is an American paper-bound issue, identical with A80a, except on better paper; 20,000 copies were printed in the United States and were sold at $0.95 each.

A80c. Second English edition ([1962]):

THE BELLE SAUVAGE LIBRARY | THE TWELVE | CAESARS | *Gaius Suetonius* | *Tranquillus* | TRANSLATED BY | ROBERT GRAVES | [publisher's emblem] | CASSELL . LONDON

Collation: [1] – [18]^8 [19]^6, 150 leaves.

p.[i] THE TWELVE CAESARS; p.[ii] blank; p.[iii] title-page; p. [iv] publisher's, copyright, edition and printing notices; p.[v] CONTENTS; p.[vi] blank; pp.vii–viii FOREWORD; pp.1–285 text, with pp.[94, 160, 218, 230, 238, 262, 270] being blank and p. [269] being unnumbered; pp.286–287 genealogical tables; p.[288] blank; pp.289–291 THE COIN PORTRAITS OF THE TWELVE CAESARS; p. [292] blank.

20.4 × 14.4 cm. Bulk: 1.8/2.2 cm. White wove paper; all edges trimmed. White wove endpapers. Bound in light blue cloth; front and back blank; spine stamped in gold: [flower] | [rule] | *The* | *Twelve* | *Caesars* | [rule] | [flower] | SUETONIUS | *Translated by* | *Robert* | *Graves* | [flower] | [rule] | *Cassell* | [rule] | [flower]

Price: 15s. Number of copies: 3,104. Published 22 February 1962 in white dust-jacket printed in pink, blue, purple and black.

A80d. Third English edition (1964):

GAIUS SUETONIUS | TRANQUILLUS | THE | TWELVE CAESARS | TRANSLATED BY ROBERT GRAVES | WOOD-ENGRAVINGS BY RAYMOND HAWTHORN | LONDON | THE FOLIO SOCIETY | MCMLXIV

Collation: [A]^8 B–N^8 [O]^8 P–Q^4 [R]^8 S–U^8, 160 leaves.

p.[1] THE TWELVE CAESARS; p.[2] blank; p.[3] title-page; p. [4] copyright, printing, printer's, binder's and typographical notices; p.[5] CONTENTS; p.[6] blank; pp.[7]–8 INTRODUCTION; pp.[9]–[11]12–318 text, with pp.[9, 51, 109, 149, 181, 209, 243, 257, 267, 279, 295, 303] being section headings, pp.[10, 52, 110, 150, 182, 210, 244, 258, 268, 280, 296, 304] being woodcuts, pp.[53, 111, 151, 183, 211, 245, 259, 269, 281, 297, 305] being unnumbered and pp.[148, 256, 267, 294] being blank; pp.[319]–[320] blank.

24.6 × 15.6 cm. Bulk: 2.3/3.0 cm. White wove paper; all edges trimmed; top edges stained blue. Endpapers printed with map of Roman Empire in deep blue with white lines and lettering; inner sides of free endpapers blank. Bound in brown-rust cloth; front and back stamped in gold at fore-edge with twelve medallions, six front and six back; spine stamped in gold: Suetonius | [solid rectangular blue box with triangles above and below, all bordered with gold, printed from bottom to top:] THE TWELVE CAESARS | Folio

Price: 29s.6d. Number of copies undisclosed. Published in March 1964 in grey-blue box without dust-jacket.

A80e. Fourth English edition ([1979]):

[whole enclosed within oval medallions of the twelve Caesars:] THE | TWELVE | CAESARS | – | *Gaius Suetonius* | *Tranquillus* | – | TRANSLATED BY | ROBERT GRAVES | *Revised with an Introduction by* | MICHAEL GRANT | – | *Penguin Books*

Collation: [1]^{12} 2–6^{12} 7–10^{10} 11^{12} [12]^{12} 13–15^{12} [16]^{12}, 184 leaves.

p.[1] THE PENGUIN CLASSICS | FOUNDER EDITOR (1944–64): E. V. RIEU | *Editor: Betty Radice* | [blurb]; p.[2] blank; p.[3] title-page; p.[4] publisher's, edition, copyright, printer's, and rights restrictions notices; p.[5] CONTENTS; p.[6] blank; pp.[7]8–11 FOREWORD; p.[12] blank; pp.[13]14–314 text, with pp.[54, 113, 153, 185, 213, 247, 259, 267, 278, 292, 299] unnumbered; [315]–[317] GENEALOGICAL TABLES; p.[318] blank; pp. [319]320–321 THE COIN PORTRAITS OF THE | TWELVE CAESARS; p.[322] blank; pp.[323]324–328 KEY TO TERMS; p.[329] DATES OF THE TWELVE CAESARS; p.[330] blank; p.[331] SOME BOOKS ABOUT SUETONIUS; p.[332] blank; pp.[333]334–339 KEY TO PLACE NAMES; p.[340] blank; pp.[341]–[351] MAPS; p.[352] blank; pp. [353]354–363 INDEX OF PERSONAL NAMES | AND PEOPLES; p.[364] blank; pp.[365]–[368] publisher's advertisements, with p.[366] being blank.

17.7 × 10.8 cm. Bulk: 1.8 cm. White wove paper; all edges trimmed. Bound in paper covers; front: [green printed in black:] Penguin [publisher's emblem] Classics | SUETONIUS | [bled rule] | THE TWELVE CAESARS | [in gold, photograph of the reverse of an *aureus* of the reign of Octavian]; back cover: [black printed in white:] Penguin [publisher's emblem] Classics | SUETONIUS | [bled rule] | THE TWELVE CAESARS | TRANSLATED BY ROBERT GRAVES | [publisher's advertisement] | [4 ll. lower left corner:] United Kingdom £1.50 | Australia $4.95 (recommended) | Canada $2.95 | U. S. A. $2.95 | [5 lines lower right corner:] HISTORY | & ARCHAEOLOGY/ | LITERATURE | ISBN 014 | 044. 072 0

Price: £1.50. Number of copies: 35,000. Published in 1979.

A80f. Fifth English edition ([1979]):

Gaius Suetonius Tranquillus | [rule] | THE TWELVE CAESARS | TRANSLATED BY ROBERT GRAVES | REVISED WITH AN INTRODUCTION BY MICHAEL GRANT | [photograph of the Altar of Peace, running entirely across page and across facing page (p.[2])] | ALLEN LANE

Collation: [1]–[18]⁸, 144 leaves.

p.[1] publisher's emblem; p.[2] photograph of Altar of Peace running entirely across this page and facing page; p.[3] title-page; p.[4] publisher's, copyright, ISBN and printer's notices; p.[5] CONTENTS; p.[6] map of Rome; pp.[7]8–9 INTRODUCTION; p.[10] illustration (Julius Caesar); pp.[11]12–272 text, with pp.[18, 24, 28, 46, 47, 66, 68, 88, 99, 100, 101, 114, 116, 117, 129, 134, 135, 160, 161, 185, 210, 211, 219, 222, 223, 224, 225, 230, 231, 232, 235, 240, 241, 245, 252, 253, 255, 258, 260, 261, 270, 271] being unnumbered and with four leaves of colour illustrations bound between pp.56–57, 104–105, 152–153, 216–217; p.[273] photograph of Timgad continued from previous page; p.[274] blank; p.[275] GENEALOGICAL TABLES; p.[276] blank; p.[277] DATES OF THE TWELVE CAESARS; p.[278] blank; pp. [279]280–281 KEY TO TERMS; p.[282] blank; p.[283] LIST OF BOOKS ABOUT SUETONIUS; p.[284]285–287 INDEX; p.[288] ACKNOWLEDGEMENTS.

24.4 × 18.9 cm. Bulk: 2.2/3.0 cm. White wove paper; all edges trimmed. Buff laid endpapers; watermarked: [crown] | Abbey Mills | Greenfield; map of the Roman Empire at the death of Augustus printed in black on the outward facing endpapers. Bound in dark blue cloth; front and back blank. Spine stamped in gold: [vertical row of 6 circles] | SUETONIUS | THE | TWELVE | CAESARS | TRANSLATED | BY | ROBERT | GRAVES | [vertical row of 6 circles] | [publisher's emblem].

Price: £9.95. Number of copies: 11,500. Published 25 October 1979.

Notes: The text of this edition is that of A80e.

A Penguin paperback issue of the sheets of this edition was published in October 1979, containing a blurb on p.[1], lacking the endpaper maps. The cover is black printed in white and green, with a photograph of a statue of Augustus superimposed on a photograph of the Roman Theatre at Merida, Spain on the front. This issue was published at £4.95 (copies: 10,000), with subsequent impressions: 2nd, 1980 (copies: 5,000); 3rd, 1982 (copies: 10,000); 4th, 1984 (copies: 6,000).

A81   JESUS IN ROME   [1957]

First edition:

JESUS IN ROME | A HISTORICAL CONJECTURE | by | ROBERT GRAVES | and | JOSHUA PODRO | [publisher's emblem] | CASSELL & COMPANY LTD | LONDON

Collation: [A]^8 B–F^8, 48 leaves.

p.[i] JESUS IN ROME; p.[ii] list of books by Graves; p.[iii] title-page; p.[iv] publisher's, copyright, publication and printer's notices; p.[v] *Contents*; p.[vi] blank; pp. [1]2–89 text, with pp.[16, 38, 54, 68, 88] being unnumbered; p. [90] blank.

18.4 × 12.5 cm. Bulk: 0.8/1.2 cm. White wove paper; all edges trimmed. White wove endpapers. Bound in black cloth; front and back blank; spine stamped in gold: Jesus | in | Rome | *Robert* | *Graves* | *and* | *Joshua* | *Podro* | *Cassell*

Price: 8s.6d. Number of copies: 3,006. Published 11 April 1957 in grey dust-jacket printed in red and black.

A82   THEY HANGED MY SAINTLY BILLY   [1957]

a. First edition:

THEY HANGED | MY SAINTLY BILLY | by | ROBERT GRAVES | *With twenty-three illustrations* | *in the text* | [publisher's emblem] | CASSELL & COMPANY LTD | LONDON

Collation: [A]^8 B–R^8 S^6, 142 leaves.

p.[i] THEY HANGED MY SAINTLY BILLY; p.[ii] list of books by Graves; p.[iii] title-page; p.[iv] publisher's, printer's, copyright and publication notices; p.v CONTENTS; p.[vi] blank; p.vii LIST OF ILLUSTRATIONS; p.[viii] blank; pp.ix–xi FOREWORD; p.[xii] blank; p.1–269 text; pp.[270]–[272] blank.

21.6 × 13.8 cm. Bulk: 2.2/2.8 cm. White wove paper; all edges trimmed. White wove endpapers. Bound in black cloth; front and back blank; spine stamped in gold: THEY | HANGED | MY | SAINTLY | BILLY | ROBERT | GRAVES | CASSELL

Price: 21s. Number of copies: 5,370. Published 23 May 1957 in white dust-jacket printed in canary and black.

Notes: This book has been translated into Italian, Spanish and Swedish.

A photographic facsimile of this edition was published on 28 September 1971 by Cedric Chivers Ltd, Portway, Bath, "at the request of the London & Home Counties Branch of the Library Association". Except for the blurb on p.[i], the title-page and its verso and sixteen pages of publisher's advertisments following p.[270] it is identical to the original edition.

A82b. First American edition (1957):

[all flush left:] THEY HANGED | MY | SAINTLY BILLY | *The Life and Death* | *of* | *Dr. William Palmer* | *by* | *Robert Graves* | GARDEN CITY, NEW YORK, 1957 | DOUBLEDAY & COMPANY, INC.

Collation: [1] – [13]^{12}, 156 leaves.

p.[1] [all flush left:] THEY HANGED | MY | SAINTLY BILLY; p.[2] list of books by Graves; p.[3] title-page; p.[4] LC card, copyright and printing notices; pp.[5]6–7 *FOREWORD*; pp. [8] – [9] *CONTENTS*; p.[10] blank; pp.[11]12–312 text, with pp.[19, 32, 45, 60, 69, 86, 99, 112, 123, 133, 146, 162, 173, 183, 198, 210, 223, 237, 254, 265, 274, 294, 305] being unnumbered.

20.8 × 13.8 cm. Bulk: 2.3/2.8 cm. White wove paper; top and bottom edges trimmed; top edges stained red. White wove endpapers. Bound in buff cloth; front and back blank; spine stamped in red: [rule] | [rule] | [broad decorative rule of rectangles and dot-chains] | [rectangular solid box, in which flush left the remainder in silver:] *They* | *Hanged* | *My* | *Saintly* | *Billy* | *Robert* | *Graves* | *Doubleday*

Price: $3.95. Number of copies: 11,500 (in two printings). Published 23 May 1957 in white dust-jacket printed in red, pink, blue-green and black.

Note: Academy Chicago Limited published a paperback photographic reprint of this edition in 1980; pp.[1] – [4] have been reset.

A82c. Second American edition ([1959]):

ROBERT GRAVES | [rule] | They Hanged | My Saintly | Billy | *The Life and Death* | *of* | *Dr. William Palmer* | AVON BOOK DIVISION | The Hearst Corporation | 575 Madison Avenue – New York 22

Collation: 128 leaves, glued at spine.

p.[1] blurbs; p.[2] *Complete and Unabridged*; p.[3] title-page; p.[4] copyright, publication and printing notices; pp.5–7 *FOREWORD*; p.[8] blank; pp.9–253 text; p.[254] biographical note; pp.[255] – [256] blank.

17.9 × 10.5 cm. Bulk: 1.5 cm. White wove paper; all edges trimmed; all edges stained yellow. Bound in white paper covers printed in purple, cerise, yellow, blue and black.

Price: $0.50. Number of copies undisclosed. Published 15 October 1959.

Note: This book is Avon Book G1037.

A82d. Second English edition ([1962]):

THEY HANGED | MY SAINTLY BILLY | ROBERT GRAVES | [publisher's emblem] | ARROW BOOKS

Collation: [A]^{16} B–I^{16}, 144 leaves.

p.[i] THEY HANGED MY SAINTLY BILLY; p.[ii] blank; p.[iii] title-page; p.[iv] publisher's, edition, copyright, printer's and binder's notices; p.[v] CONTENTS; p.[vi] blank; p.[vii] ILLUSTRATIONS; p.[viii] blank; pp.ix–xi FOREWORD; p.[xii] blank; p.[xiii] THEY HANGED MY SAINTLY BILLY; p.[xiv] blank; pp.1–270 text; pp.[271]–[274] publisher's advertisements.

17.7 × 11.0 cm. Bulk: 1.9 cm. White wove paper; all edges trimmed. Bound in paper covers printed in black and cerise.

Price: 5s. Number of copies: 7,500. Published 8 January 1962.

Note: This edition is Grey Arrow Book No. G104.

A82e. Third English edition ([1972]):

Robert Graves | [swelled rule] | The Hanged My Saintly Billy | [series emblem] | ARROW BOOKS

Collation: 138 leaves, glued at the spine.

p.[i] THEY HANGED MY SAINTLY BILLY and blurb; p.[ii] blank; p. [iii] title-page; p.[iv] publisher's, printing, sales restriction, copyright and printer's notices; p.v CONTENTS; p. [vi] blank; p.vii LIST OF ILLUSTRATIONS; p.[viii] blank; pp. ix–xi FOREWORD; p.[xii] blank; pp.1–269 text; pp.[270]–[276] blank.

21.5 × 13.5 cm. Bulk: 2.4 cm. White wove paper; all edges trimmed. Bound in paper covers printed in red, yellow and black.

Price: 60p. Number of copies: 2,300. Published 3 April 1972.

Note: This 'edition' is partially made up of sheets from A82d which Hutchinson acquired when they took over Howard Baker.

A83   POEMS SELECTED BY HIMSELF   [1957]

a. First edition [1957]:

ROBERT GRAVES | [swelled rule] | *Poems Selected by Himself* | PENGUIN BOOKS

Collation: [A]^{16} B^{16} C/C* –D/D$^{*4/16}$ E–F^{16}, 104 leaves.

p.[1] THE PENGUIN POETS | D39 | ROBERT GRAVES | [publisher's emblem]; p.[2] blank; p.[3] title-page; p.[4] publisher's, publication and printer's notices; p.[5] *Foreword*; p.[6] blank; pp.7–11 *Contents*; p.[12] blank; pp.13–198 text; pp. 199–204 *Index of First Lines*; p.[205] publisher's advertisement; p.[206] blank; pp.[207]–[208] publisher's advertisements.

18.1 × 11.1 cm. Bulk: 1.0 cm. White wove paper; all edges trimmed. Bound in paper covers printed with over-all background of elongated diamonds and triangles in green and black; on front, as if label: [rectangular box of green light-heavy-light rules enclosing all:] *Robert* | *Graves* | [six-pointed star in green] | SELECTED BY

HIMSELF | [publisher's emblem in green] | THE PENGUIN | POETS | [at right:] 3/6; back has the same design front cover and in small rectangular box near bottom: NOT FOR SALE IN THE U.S.A.; spine has the same design and white box, as if label near top, in which: [light-heavy-light rules in green] | D39 | [light green rule] | [down spine:] Robert Graves | [light green rule] | D39 | [light-heavy-light rules in green]; inner sides of covers blank.

Price: 3s.6d. Number of copies: 24,600. Published 29 August 1957.

Contents: Foreword – In the Wilderness – The Haunted House – Reproach – The Finding of Love – 'The General Elliott' – Rocky Acres – Outlaws – One Hard Look – A Frosty Night – Allie – Henry and Mary – Love without Hope – What Did I Dream? – The Country Dance – The Troll's Nosegay – The Hills of May – Lost Love – Vain and Careless – An English Wood – The Bedpost – The Pier-Glass – Apples and Water – Angry Samson – Down – Mermaid, Dragon, Fiend – In Procession – Warning to Children – Alice – Ancestors –The Cool Web – Love in Barrenness – Song of Contrariety – The Presence – The Land of Whipperginny – In No Direction – The Castle – Return – The Bards – Nobody – Full Moon – Vanity – Pure Death – Sick Love – It Was All Very Tidy – Thief – The Furious Voyage – Song: Lift Boy – Ulysses – The Succubus – The Reader over My Shoulder – The Legs – Gardener – In Broken Images – On Rising Early – Flying Crooked – Fragment of a Lost Poem – The Devil's Advice to Story-Tellers – Sea Side – Wm. Brazier – Welsh Incident – Hell – Synthetic Such – The Florist Rose – Lost Acres – At First Sight – Recalling War – Down, Wanton, Down! – A Former Attachment – Nature's Lineaments – Time – The Philosopher – On Dwelling – Parent to Children – Ogres and Pygmies – To Walk on Hills – To Bring the Dead to Life – To Evoke Posterity – Any Honest Housewife – Defeat of the Rebels – Never Such Love – The China Plate – Certain Mercies – The Cuirassiers of the Frontier – The Laureate – A Jealous Man – The Cloak – The Foreboding – With Her Lips Only – The Halls of Bedlam – A Country Mansion – Lovers in Winter – Advocates – On Portents – The Terraced Valley – The Chink – The Ages of Oath – Like Snow – End of Play – The Fallen Tower of Siloam – The Great-Grandmother – No More Ghosts – A Love Story – Dawn Bombardment – The Shot – The Thieves – Lollocks – To Sleep – Despite and Still – The Suicide in the Copse – Frightened Men – Language of the Seasons – Mid-Winter Waking – The Beach – The Villagers and Death – The Door – Under the Pot – Through Nightmare – She Tells Her Love While Half Asleep – Theseus and Ariadne – The Death Room – To Juan at the Winter Solstice – To Be Called a Bear – My Name and I – 1805 – The Persian Version – The Weather of Olympus – Grotesques i–vi – Conversation Piece – I'm Through with You For Ever – Beauty in Trouble – Sirocco at Deya' – From the Embassy – The White Goddess – The Song of Blodeuwedd – Instructions to the Orphic Adept – Lament for Pasiphaë – Intercession in Late October – Counting the Beats – Your Private Way – The Survivor – Questions in a Wood – Darien – The Portrait – Prometheus – The Straw – Dialogue on the Headland – The Mark – The Sea Horse – Dethronement – Cat-Goddesses – The Blue-Fly – A Lost Jewel – The Window Sill – Spoils – Rhea – Leaving the Rest Unsaid – Index of First Lines

Note: This book has been translated into Serbo-Croatian.

A83b. Revised edition ([1961]):

Title-page as A83a.

Collation: [A]^{16} B^{16} C–F^{12} G–H^{16}, 112 leaves.

p.[1] THE PENGUIN POETS | D39 | ROBERT GRAVES | [publisher's emblem]; p.[2] blank; p.[3] title-page; p.[4] publisher's, edition, copyright and printer's notices; p.5 *Foreword*; p. [6] blank; pp.7–12 *Contents*; pp.13–214 text; pp.215–220 *Index of First Lines*; p.[221] publisher's advertisements; p. [222] blank; pp.223–224 publisher's advertisements.

18.1 × 11.1 cm. Bulk: 1.1 cm. White wove paper; all edges trimmed. Bound as A83a except overall design is black and white and price is changed to 4s.

Price: 4s. Number of copies unknown. Published in 1961.

  Contents: As A83a except as follows: . . . Rhea – The Face in the Mirror – Gratitude for a Nightmare – The Naked and the Nude – A Slice of Wedding Cake – Call it a Good Marriage – Around the Mountain – Symptoms of Love – The Visitation – Apple Island – Troughs of Sea – The Starred Coverlet – Turn of the Moon – Seldom Yet Now – Here Live Your Life Out! – Burn It! – Leaving the Rest Unsaid – Index of First Lines

A83c. Third English edition ([1966]):

ROBERT GRAVES | [swelled rule] | *Poems Selected by Himself* | [publisher's emblem] | PENGUIN BOOKS

Collation: As A83b.

  p.[1] THE PENGUIN POETS | D39 | ROBERT GRAVES; p.[2] blank; p. [3] title-page; p.[4] publisher's, edition, copyright, printer's and circulation restriction notices; p.[5] Foreword; p.[6] blank; pp.7–11 Contents; p.[12] blank; pp.13–216 text; pp. 217–222; Index of First Lines; p.[223] publisher's advertisements; p. [224] blank.

  18.1 × 11.0 cm. Bulk: 0.9 cm. White wove paper; all edges trimmed. Bound in white paper covers printed with overall abstract design composed (on front cover) of red vertical stripes over light and mottled-dark-brown background on left half, and blue upper third, purple lower two-thirds of right half, winding around spine to reverse the order on back cover. Front cover: [at left:] [a penguin] [at right:] Robert Graves | [blue thin rule] | [at left:] 5'– | [at right in green:] Selected by himself. Back cover: [at left:] Robert Graves [at right:] [a penguin] | blue thin rule] | [at left, two lines in green:] Cover design by Stephen Russ | Not for sale in the U.S.A. Inner sides of covers blank.

Price: 5s. Number of copies unknown. Published in August 1966.

Contents: Foreword – The Haunted House – Reproach – The Finding of Love – Rocky Acres – Outlaws – One Hard Look – A Frosty Night – Allie – Love without Hope – What Did I Dream? – The Troll's Nosegay – The Hills of May – Lost Love – Vain and Careless – The Pier-Glass – Apples and Water – Angry Samson – Down – In Procession – Warning to Children – Alice – Ancestors –The Cool Web – Love in Barrenness – Song of Contrariety – The Presence – The Land of Whipperginny – In No Direction – The Castle – Return – The Bards – Nobody – Full Moon – Vanity – Pure Death – Sick Love – It Was All Very Tidy –

Thief – The Furious Voyage – Song: Lift Boy – Ulysses – The Reader over My
Shoulder – The Legs – Gardener – In Broken Images – On Rising Early – Flying
Crooked – Fragment of a Lost Poem – The Devil's Advice to Story-Tellers – Sea
Side – Wm. Brazier – Welsh Incident – Hell – Synthetic Such – Lost Acres – At
First Sight – Down, Wanton, Down! – A Former Attachment – Nature's
Lineaments – Time – The Philosopher – On Dwelling – Ogres and Pygmies – To
Walk on Hills – To Bring the Dead to Life – To Evoke Posterity – Any Honest
Housewife – Never Such Love – The Cuirassiers of the Frontier – The Laureate –
A Jealous Man – The Cloak – The Foreboding – With Her Lips Only – The Halls
of Bedlam – A Country Mansion – Advocates – On Portents – The Terraced
Valley – The Chink – The Ages of Oath – Like Snow – End of Play – The Fallen
Tower of Siloam – The Great-Grandmother – No More Ghosts – A Love Story –
Dawn Bombardment – The Shot – The Thieves – Lollocks – To Sleep – Despite
and Still – The Suicide in the Copse – Frightened Men – Language of the Seasons
– Mid-Winter Waking – The Beach – The Villagers and Death – The Door –
Under the Pot – Through Nightmare – She Tells Her Love While Half Asleep –
Theseus and Ariadne – The Death Room – To Juan at the Winter Solstice – To Be
Called a Bear – My Name and I – 1805 – The Persian Version – Grotesques i–vi –
Conversation Piece – Beauty in Trouble – Sirocco at Deyá – The White Goddess –
The Song of Blodeuwedd – Instructions to the Orphic Adept – Lament for
Pasiphaë – Counting the Beats – Your Private Way – The Survivor – Questions in
a Wood – Darien – The Portrait – Prometheus – The Straw – Dialogue on the
Headland – The Sea Horse – Cat-Goddesses – The Blue-Fly – A Lost Jewel –
The Window Sill – Spoils – Rhea – The Face in the Mirror – Gratitude for a
Nightmare – The Naked and the Nude – A Slice of Wedding Cake – Call it a
Good Marriage – Around the Mountain – Symptoms of Love – The Visitation –
Apple Island – Troughs of Sea – The Starred Coverlet – Turn of the Moon –
Seldom Yet Now – Leaving the Rest Unsaid – I'd Die for You – Horizon – Lion
Lover – The Wreath – In Her Praise – A Restless Ghost – Beware, Madam! –
Hedges Freaked With Snow – In Time – She Is No Liar – A Last Poem – To
Beguile and Betray – I Will Write – Bird of Paradise – Song: Sword and Rose –
The Green Castle – Not to Sleep – Above the Edge of Doom – Black – Whole
Love – The Impossible – Iron Palace – Everywhere is Here – Song: The Far Side
of Your Moon – Conjunction – Index of First Lines.

Note: Impression: 2nd, 1968.

A83d. Fourth English edition ([1972]):

Title-page as A83c except swelled rule is split in middle.

Collation: [1] – [12]^8, 96 leaves.
    p.[1] THE PENGUIN POETS | ROBERT GRAVES | [biographical note]; p.[2]
blank; p.[3] title-page; p.[4] publisher's, edition, copyright, printer's and circulation
restriction notices; p.[5] Foreword; p.[6] blank; pp.7–12[13] Contents; p.[14] blank;
pp. 15–179 text; pp.180–185[186]; Index of First Lines; p.[187] publisher's
advertisements; p.[188] blank; pp.[189] – [192] publisher's advertisements.
    Size, bulk and paper as A83c. Bound in white paper covers printed in black, grey,
red, brown and blue. Front cover: [at left:] [a penguin] [at right, two lines:] Robert

Graves | Poems selected by himself | [in colour, left profile face of Graves by John Aldridge]. Back cover: [at left, three lines:] Robert Graves | The cover shows a detail from a portrait of Robert Graves | by John Aldridge, in the National Portrait Gallery | [in colour, left profile face of Graves by John Aldridge] [overprinted in black in upper left, five lines:] United Kingdom 35p. | Australia $1.20 (recommended) | New Zealand $1.20 | South Africa RO,90 | Canada $1.50. [overprinted in black in lower right, three lines:] POETRY | ISBN 0 14 | 042.039 8 | [at lower edge:] For copyright reasons this edition is not for sale in the U.S.A. Spine [running down:] ROBERT GRAVES [two lines:] ISBN 0 14 | 042.039 8. Inner sides of covers blank.

Price: 35p. Number of copies unknown. Published in 1972.

Note: Impressions: 2nd, 1974 (copies: 10,000); 3rd, 1976 (copies: 10,000).

Contents: Foreword – The Haunted House – Reproach – The Finding of Love – Rocky Acres – Outlaws – One Hard Look – A Frosty Night – Allie – Love without Hope – What Did I Dream? – The Troll's Nosegay – The Hills of May – Lost Love – Vain and Careless – The Pier-Glass – Angry Samson – Apples and Water – Down – Thief –In Procession – Warning to Children – The Cool Web – Alice – The Bards – Ancestors – Love in Barrenness – Song of Contrariety – The Presence – The Land of Whipperginny – In No Direction – The Castle – Return – Nobody – Full Moon – Conjunction – Vanity – Pure Death – It Was All Very Tidy – Theseus and Ariadne – The Furious Voyage – Song: Lift Boy – Ulysses – The Reader over My Shoulder – The Legs – Flying Crooked – Gardener – Fragment of a Lost Poem – In Broken Images – On Rising Early – The Devil's Advice to Story-Tellers – Sea Side – Wm. Brazier – Welsh Incident – A Former Attachment – Hell – Lost Acres – At First Sight – Synthetic Such – Down, Wanton, Down! – Any Honest Housewife – Nature's Lineaments – Time – The Philosopher – On Dwelling – Ogres and Pygmies – Never Such Love – To Walk on Hills – On Portents – To Bring the Dead to Life – To Evoke Posterity – The Cuirassiers of the Frontier – The Laureate – Like Snow – A Jealous Man – The Cloak – The Foreboding – With Her Lips Only – The Halls of Bedlam – A Country Mansion – Advocates – The Terraced Valley – The Chink – The Ages of Oath – End of Play – The Fallen Tower of Siloam – The Great-Grandmother – No More Ghosts – A Love Story – Dawn Bombardment – The Shot – The Thieves – Lollocks – To Sleep – Despite and Still – The Suicide in the Copse – Frightened Men – Language of the Seasons – Mid-Winter Waking – The Beach – The Villagers and Death – The Door – Under the Pot – Through Nightmare – She Tells Her Love While Half Asleep – To Juan at the Winter Solstice – The Death Room – To Be Called a Bear – My Name and I – The Persian Version – 1805 – Conversation Piece – Grotesques i–vi – The Survivor – Beauty in Trouble – Sirocco at Deyá – Your Private Way – The White Goddess – The Song of Blodeuwedd – Instructions to the Orphic Adept – Lament for Pasiphaë Counting the Beats – Questions in a Wood – Darien – The Portrait – Prometheus – The Straw – Dialogue on the Headland – A Lost Jewel – The Sea Horse – Cat-Goddesses – The Blue-Fly – The Window Sill – Spoils – Rhea – Gratitude for a Nightmare – The Naked and the Nude – A Slice of Wedding Cake – Call it a Good Marriage – Around the Mountain – The Face in the Mirror – Symptoms of Love – The Visitation – Troughs of Sea – The Starred Coverlet – Turn of the

Moon – Seldom Yet Now – Apple Island – Horizon – I'd Die For You – The Wreath – Lion Lover – In Her Praise – A Restless Ghost – Beware, Madam! – Hedges Freaked With Snow – In Time – She Is No Liar – A Last Poem – To Beguile and Betray – I Will Write – Bird of Paradise – Song: Sword and Rose – Above the Edge of Doom – The Green Castle – Not to Sleep – Whole Love – The Impossible – Iron Palace – Everywhere is Here – Song: The Far Side of Your Moon – Leaving the Rest Unsaid – Dead Hand – Lure of Murder – Arrears of Moonlight – What Did You Say? – All Except Hannibal – Stolen Jewel – The Snapped Thread – Ecstasy of Chaos – Dancing Flame – Birth of Angels – Fortunate Child – Loving True, Flying Blind – The Near Eclipse – Like Owls – On Giving – In Perspective – The P'eng that was a K'un – Bower-Bird – The Utter Rim – Unicorn and the White Doe – A Dream of Hell – Our Self – Perfectionists – The Necklace – Bites and Kisses – Spite of Mirrors – A Bracelet – Hooded Flame – The Crane – Her Brief Withdrawal – Strangeness – Song: Though Once True Lovers – Song: The Palm Tree – Song: Dewdrop and Diamond – Song: Just Friends – Song: Sullen Moods – Possibly – Is Now the Time? – Twins – Sail and Oar – Gooseflesh Abbey – Wigs and Beards – Astymelusa – To Be In Love – Fact of the Act – Within Reason – She To Him – The Yet Unsayable – The Olive-Yard – The Narrow Sea – Index of First Lines.

A83e. Fifth English edition ([1978]):

ROBERT GRAVES | [swelled rule split at middle] | *Poems Selected by Robert Graves* | and *Anthony Thwaite* | [publisher's emblem] | PENGUIN BOOKS

Collation: 95 leaves, glued at spine.

[pagination begins at p.[3]] p.[3] THE PENGUIN POETS | ROBERT GRAVES | [biographical note] ; p.[4] blank; p.[5] title-page; p.[6] publisher's, copyright, printer's and rights reservations notices; pp.7–12[13] *Contents*; p.[14] *Foreword* [as A83d] and note on revision; pp.15–188 text; pp.189–194 *Index of First Lines*.

18.1 × 11.1 cm. Bulk: 1.2 cm. White wove paper; all edges trimmed. Bound in white paper covers printed in black. Front: [at left:] [publisher's emblem] Robert Graves | Poems selected by himself. Back: [blurb] | [cover credit] | [price left, publisher's emblem and ISBN right]. Spine: [top to bottom:] Robert Graves [publisher's emblem, in two lines:] ISBN 0 14 | 042.039 8

Price: £2.25. Number of copies: 11,000. Published in 1978.

Note: Impressions: 2nd, 1981 (copies: 5,000); 3rd, 1983 (copies: 5,000).

Contents: As in A83d with the following additions: Here Live Your Life Out! – Surgical Ward: Men – Joan and Darby – Dance of Words – Broken Neck – The Uncut Diamond – The Risk – Tilth – A Dream of Frances Speedwell – Age Gap – Fools – Work Drafts – L.s.d. – Ours is No Wedlock.

A84   5 PENS IN HAND   1958

First edition:

5 | PENS | IN | HAND | by Robert Graves | DOUBLEDAY & COMPANY, INC. GARDEN CITY, NEW YORK | 1958

Collation: [1]–[15]^{12}, 180 leaves.
    p.[1] 5 Pens in Hand; p.[2] blank; p.[3] list of books by Graves; p.[4] blank; p.[5] title-page; p.[6] acknowledgement, copyright, printing, edition and designer's notices; p.[7] FOREWORD; p.[8] blank; pp.[9]10–11 CONTENTS; p.[12] blank; pp. [13]–[15]16–360 text, with pp.[13, 31, 91, 145, 287, 331] being section-headings, pp.[14, 30, 32, 92, 144, 146, 286, 288, 332] being blank and pp.[33, 54, 73, 93, 100, 104, 107, 114, 118, 123, 129, 137, 147, 152, 157, 161, 165, 175, 179, 184, 189, 194, 197, 202, 206, 211, 215, 219, 223, 227, 232, 235, 239, 243, 248, 253, 257, 264, 275, 289, 299, 317, 333] being unnumbered.
    20.7 × 13.8 cm. Bulk: 2.7/3.3 cm. White wove paper; top and bottom edges trimmed. White wove endpapers. Bound in red-brown cloth with buff quarter-cloth spine; back blank; front has blue rule one-third from bottom across entire cover; spine stamped in brown and printed in blue: [two lines in brown:] *Robert* | *Graves* | [four lines in blue:] 5 | *PENS* | *IN* | *HAND* | [blue rule] | [in brown:] *Doubleday*

Price: $4.50. Number of copies: 4,500. Published 20 March 1958, in white dust-jacket printed in black, orange and green.

Contents: I. FOREWORD: Why I Live in Majorca – II. AMERICAN LECTURES: Legitimate Criticism of Poetry – The White Goddess – Diseases of Scholarship, Clinically Considered – III. CRITICAL ESSAYS: Pandora's Box and Eve's Apple – The Gold Roofs of Sinadon – Numismatics for Student Christians – An Eminent Collaborationist – Answer to a Religious Questionnaire – Paul's Thorn – Don't Fidget, Young Man! – Religion: None; Conditioning: Protestant – Colonel Lawrence's *Odyssey* – IV. MOSTLY STORIES, MOSTLY FUNNY: Varro's Four Hundred and Ninety Books – Treacle Tart – The Full Length – An Appointment for Candelmas – The Devil Is a Protestant – Trín-Trín-Trín – Earth to Earth – Epics Are Out of Fashion – New Light on Dream-Flight – Period Piece – They Say . . . They Say – Week-End at Cwm Tatws – 6 Valiant Bulls 6 – He Went out to Buy a Rhine – A Man May Not Marry His . . . – God Grant Your Honour Many Years – The White Horse or 'The Great Southern Ghost Story' – The Five Godfathers – Kill Them! Kill Them! – The Abominable Mr Gunn – Harold Vesey at the Gates of Hell – Life of the Poet Gnaeus Robertulus Gravesa – Ditching in a Fishless Sea – I Hate Poems – The French Thing – Evidence of Affluence – A Bicycle in Majorca – V. HISTORICAL ANOMALIES: The Fifth Column at Troy – The Whitaker Negroes – A Dead Branch on the Tree of Israel – VI. POEMS 1955–1957: Prologue to a Poetry Reading at the Massachusetts Institute of Technology, Boston – The Face in the Mirror – Forbidden Words – Song for New Year's Eve – A Ballad of Alexander and Queen Janet – The Coral Pool – Gratitude for a Nightmare – Friday Night – The Naked and the Nude – Woman and Tree – Destruction of Evidence – Hotel Bed at Lugano – The Clearing – The Second-Fated – End of the World – Bitter Thoughts on Receiving a Slice of Cordelia's Wedding Cake – The Question – A Plea to Boys and Girls – A Bouquet from a Fellow Roseman – Yes – The Outsider

A85   THE POEMS OF ROBERT GRAVES   1958

First edition:

THE POEMS | OF | ROBERT GRAVES | *Chosen by Himself* | Doubleday Anchor Books | Doubleday & Company, Inc. | Garden City, New York | 1958

Collation: 320 pp., glued at spine.
   p.[i] THE POEMS OF ROBERT GRAVES | [series emblem]; p.[ii] blank; p.[iii] biographical note; p.[iv] blank; p.[v] title-page; p.[vi] designer's, typographer's, copyright, printing and acknowledgement notices; p.[vii] FOREWORD; p. [viii] blank; p.[ix] TO CALLIOPE; p.[x] blank; pp.xi–xviii CONTENTS; p.[1] – [2]3–289 text, with pp.[1, 35, 67, 93, 151, 169, 203, 235, 255] being section-headings and pp.[2, 36, 68, 94, 152, 168, 170, 204, 234, 236, 254, 256] being blank; p.[290] blank; pp.291–296 INDEX OF TITLES; pp.297–302 INDEX OF FIRST LINES.
   18.1 × 10.5 cm. Bulk: 1.8 cm. White wove paper; all edges trimmed. Bound in paper covers; front has grey background with Hera of Samos overprinted with: [at left:] A 139 [at right:] $1.25 | THE | POEMS | OF | ROBERT | GRAVES | [in red:] *Chosen by himself* | A DOUBLEDAY [series emblem] ANCHOR BOOK; back printed in red and black with blurb; spine has grey background, printed top to bottom: THE POEMS OF ROBERT GRAVES [three words in red:] *Chosen by himself* | Anchor | A139; inner sides of front and back covers blank.

Price: $1.25. Number of copies: 25,000. Published 5 June 1958.

Contents: Foreword – To Calliope – I: In the Wilderness – The Haunted House – Reproach – The Finding of Love – 'The General Elliott' – Rocky Acres – Outlaws – One Hard Look – A Frosty Night – Allie – Unicorn and the White Doe – Henry and Mary – Love without Hope – What Did I Dream? – The Country Dance – The Troll's Nosegay – The Hills of May – Lost Love – Vain and Careless – An English Wood – The Bedpost – The Pier-Glass – Apples and Water – Angry Samson – Down – Mermaid, Dragon, Fiend – II: In Procession – Warning to Children – Alice – Richard Roe and John Doe – The Witches' Cauldron – Ancestors – Children of Darkness – The Cool Web – Love in Barrenness – Song of Contrariety – The Presence – The Land of Whipperginny – In No Direction – The Castle – Return – The Bards – Nobody – The Progress – Full Moon – Vanity – Pure Death – Sick Love – It Was All Very Tidy – III: Callow Captain – Thief – Saint – The Furious Voyage – Song: Lift-Boy – Traveller's Curse after Misdirection – The Last Day of Leave – The Next Time – Ulysses – The Succubus – The Reader over My Shoulder – The Legs – Gardener – Front Door Soliloquy – In Broken Images – The Devil at Berry Pomeroy – On Rising Early – Flying Crooked – Fragment of a Lost Poem – Brother – IV: Galatea and Pygmalion – The Devil's Advice to Story-Tellers – Sergeant-Major Money – Sea Side – Wm. Brazier – Welsh Incident – Vision in the Repair-Shop – Interruption – Act V, Scene 5 – Midway – Hell – Leda – Synthetic Such – The Florist Rose – Lost Acres – At First Sight – Recalling War – Down, Wanton, Down! – A Former Attachment – Nature's Lineaments – Time – The Philosopher – On Dwelling – Parent to Children – Ogres and Pygmies – History of the Word – Single Fare – To Walk on Hills – To Bring the Dead to Life – To Evoke Posterity – Any Honest Housewife – Defeat of the Rebels – Never Such Love – The Fallen Signpost – The China Plate – Certain Mercies – The Cuirassiers of the Frontier – The Laureate – A Jealous

Man – The Cloak – The Foreboding – With Her Lips Only – The Halls of Bedlam – Or to Perish before Day – A Country Mansion – The Eremites – Lovers in Winter – Advocates – Self-Praise – V: On Portents – The Terraced Valley – The Challenge – The Chink – The Ages of Oath – New Legends – Like Snow – End of Play – The Climate of Thought – The Fallen Tower of Siloam – The Great Grandmother – No More Ghosts – VI: A Love Story – Dawn Bombardment – The Worms of History – The Glutton – A Stranger at the Party – The Shot – The Thieves – Lollocks – To Sleep – Despite and Still – The Suicide in the Copse – Frightened Men – The Oath – Language of the Seasons – Mid-Winter Waking – The Rock at the Corner – The Beach – The Villagers and Death – The Door – Under the Pot – Through Nightmare – To Lucia at Birth – Death by Drums – She Tells Her Love While Half Asleep – Theseus and Ariadne – Penthesileia – Cold Weather Proverb – The Death Room – To Juan at the Winter Solstice – To Be Called a Bear – VII: My Name and I – 1805 – At the Savoy Chapel – Dream of a Climber – The Persian Version – The Weather of Olympus – Apollo of the Physiologists – The Oldest Soldier – Grotesques i–vi – The Eugenist – A Civil Servant – Gulls and Men – Conversation Piece – Queen-Mother to New Queen – General Bloodstock's Lament for England – 'ÍWellcome, to the Caves of Artá!' – I'm Through with You Forever – The Sacred Mission – Poet's Corner – Coronation Address – Beauty in Trouble – Sirocco at Deya' – From the Embassy – VIII: The White Goddess – The Allansford Pursuit – Amergin's Charm – The Battle of the Trees – The Song of Blodeuwedd – Instructions to the Orphic Adept – Lament for Pasiphaë – The Sirens' Welcome to Cronos – Intercession in Late October – The Jackals' Address to Isis – The Destroyer – Return of the Goddess – IX: With the Gift of a Ring – Counting the Beats – The Young Cordwainer – Your Private Way – The Survivor – Questions in a Wood – Darien – The Portrait – Prometheus – The Straw – Cry Faugh! – Hercules at Nemea – Dialogue on the Headland – The Mark – Liadan and Curithir – The Sea Horse – Reproach to Julia – Dethronement – Cat-Goddesses – The Blue-Fly – A Lost Jewel – The Window Sill – Spoils – The Coral Pool – The Naked and the Nude – Woman and Tree – Bitter Thoughts on Receiving a Slice of Cordelia's Wedding-Cake – A Bouquet from a Fellow Roseman – Rhea – Leaving the Rest Unsaid – Index of Titles – Index of First Lines

A86   STEPS   [1958]

First edition:

STEPS | *Stories* | *Talks* | *Essays* | *Poems* | *Studies in History* | BY | ROBERT GRAVES | [publisher's emblem] | CASSELL . LONDON

Collation: [A]⁸ B–W⁸ X/X*²/⁸ Y⁸, 178 leaves.

pp.[i]–[ii] blank; p.[iii] STEPS; p.[iv] blank; p.[v] title-page; p.[vi] publisher's, copyright, publication and printer's notices; pp.vii–ix *Contents*; p.[x] blank; p.xi *Foreword*; p.[xii] blank; pp.[1]–[2]3–343 text, with pp.[1, 61, 155, 229, 263] being section headings and pp.[2, 60, 62, 154, 156, 228, 230, 264] being blank; p.[344] blank.

21.6 × 13.8 cm. Bulk: 2.8/3.4 cm. White wove paper; all edges trimmed. White

wove endpapers. Bound in sea-green cloth; front and back blank; spine stamped in gold: [light-heavy-light rules] | STEPS | [light rule] | [longer heavy rule] | [light rule] | ROBERT | GRAVES | [light-heavy-light rules] | CASSELL

Price: 30s. Number of copies: 2996. Published 13 November 1958 in blue-grey dust-jacket printed in green and black.

Contents: Foreword – STORIES: A Bicycle in Majorca – Evidence of Affluence – The Viscountess and the Short-Haired Girl – A Toast to Ava Gardner – TALKS: Legitimate Criticism of Poetry – The White Goddess – Sweeney among the Blackbirds – The Making and Marketing of Poetry – Pulling a Poem Apart – ESSAYS: Pandora's Box and Eve's Apple – The Gold Roofs of Sinadon – An Eminent Collaborationist – Don't Fidget, Young Man! – Colonel Lawrence's *Odyssey* – Maenads, Junkies and Others – The Language as Spoken – It Ended with a Bang – Legends of the Bible – And the Children's Teeth are Set on Edge – Progessive Puericulture – POEMS: Preface to a Reading of New Poems at the University of Michigan – The Face in the Mirror – Song for New Year's Eve – Alexander and Queen Janet – The Coral Pool – Gratitude for a Nightmare – Friday Night – The Naked and the Nude – Woman and Tree – Forbidden Words – Hotel Bed at Lugano – The Enlisted Man – A Slice of Wedding Cake – A Plea to Boys and Girls – Trudge, Body! – Mike and Mandy – The Christmas Robin – Nothing – Call It a Good Marriage – Read Me, Please! – The Second-Fated – The Twin of Sleep – Around the Mountain – STUDIES IN HISTORY: The Fifth Column at Troy – A Dead Branch of the Tree of Israel – Was Benedict Arnold a Traitor? – The Cultured Romans – New Light on an Old Murder – What Food the Centaurs Ate

Note: p.315, *ll*.3–4 has 'Whole,/some' for 'Whole-/some'.

A87   COLLECTED POEMS 1959   [1959]

First edition:

ROBERT GRAVES | COLLECTED | POEMS | 1959 | [publisher's emblem | CASSELL . LONDON

Collation: [A]^8 B–U^8 X/X$^{*2/8}$, 170 leaves.
   p.[i–ii] blank; p.[iii] COLLECTED POEMS | 1959; p.[iv] blank; [frontispiece, back blank]; p.[v] title-page; p.[vi] publisher's, copyright, publication and printer's notices; p.[vii] TO CALLIOPE; p.[viii] blank; p.[ix] FOREWORD; p.[x] blank; pp.xi–xix CONTENTS; p.[xx] blank; p.[1]–[2]3–320 text, with pp.[1, 41, 75, 101, 161, 181, 215, 247, 261, 299] being section-headings and pp.[2, 40, 42, 76, 102, 162, 180, 182, 216, 246, 248, 262, 298, 300] being blank; p.[290] blank.
   21.5 × 15.0 cm. Bulk: 2.5/2.9 cm. White wove paper; all edges trimmed. White wove endpapers. Bound in bright green cloth; back blank; front stamped in gold: COLLECTED | POEMS | 1959; spine stamped in gold: ROBERT | GRAVES | [rule] | COLLECTED | POEMS | 1959 | CASSELL

Price: 25s. Number of copies: 3,037. Published 23 April 1959 in white dust-jacket printed in bright green and black.

Contents: To Calliope – Foreword – I: In the Wilderness – The Haunted House –
Reproach – The Finding of Love – 'The General Elliott' – Rocky Acres – Outlaws
– One Hard Look – A Frosty Night – Allie – Unicorn and the White Doe –
Henry and Mary – Love Without Hope – What Did I Dream? – The Country
Dance – The Troll's Nosegay – The Hills of May – Lost Love – Vain and Careless
– An English Wood – The Bedpost – The Pier-Glass – Apples and Water –
Angry Samson – Mermaid, Dragon, Fiend – II: In Procession – Warning to
Children – Alice – Richard Roe and John Doe – The Witches' Cauldron –
Ancestors – Children of Darkness – The Cool Web – Love in Barrenness – Song
of Contrariety – The Presence – The Land of Whipperginny – In No Direction –
The Castle – Return – The Bards – Nobody – The Progress – Full Moon – Vanity
– Pure Death – Sick Love – It Was All Very Tidy – III: Callow Captain – Thief –
Saint – The Furious Voyage – Song: Lift Boy – Traveller's Curse after Misdirection
– The Last Day of Leave – The Next Time – Ulysses – The Succubus – The
Reader over My Shoulder – The Legs – Gardener – Front Door Soliloquy – In
Broken Images – Trudge, Body! – The Christmas Robin – On Rising Early –
Flying Crooked – Fragment of a Lost Poem – Brother – IV: Galatea and Pygmalion
– The Devil's Advice to Story-Tellers – Sergeant-Major Money – Sea Side – Wm.
Brazier – Welsh Incident – Vision in the Repair-Shop – Interruption – Act V,
Scene 5 – Midway – Hell – Leda – Synthetic Such – The Florist Rose – Lost
Acres – At First Sight – Recalling War – Down, Wanton, Down! – A Former
Attachment – Nature's Lineaments – Time – The Philosopher – On Dwelling –
Hotel Bed at Lugano – Ogres and Pygmies – History of the Word – Single Fare –
To Walk on Hills – To Bring the Dead to Life – To Evoke Posterity – Any Honest
Housewife – Defeat of the Rebels – Never Such Love – The Fallen Signpost – The
China Plate – Certain Mercies – The Cuirassiers of the Frontier – The Laureate –
A Jealous Man – The Cloak – The Foreboding – With Her Lips Only – The Halls
of Bedlam – Or to Perish before Day – A Country Mansion – Lovers in Winter –
Advocates – V: On Portents – The Terraced Valley – Alexander and Queen Janet –
The Chink – The Ages of Oath – New Legends – Like Snow – End of Play – The
Climate of Thought – The Fallen Tower of Siloam – The Great-Grandmother – No
More Ghosts – VI: A Love Story – Dawn Bombardment – The Worms of History
– The Glutton – The Shot – The Thieves – Lollocks – To Sleep – Despite and
Still – The Suicide in the Copse – Frightened Men – The Oath – Language of the
Seasons – Mid-Winter Waking – The Rock at the Corner – The Beach – The
Villagers and Death – The Door – Under the Pot – Through Nightmare – To Lucia
at Birth – Death by Drums – She Tells Her Love While Half Asleep – Theseus and
Ariadne – Penthesileia – The Death Room – To Juan at the Winter Solstice – To Be
Called a Bear – VII: My Name and I – 1805 – At the Savoy Chapel – Dream of a
Climber – The Persian Version – The Weather of Olympus – Apollo of the
Physiologists – The Oldest Soldier – Grotesques i–vi – The Eugenist – A Civil
Servant – Gulls and Men – Conversation Piece – General Bloodstock's Lament for
England – 'iWellcome, to the Caves of Artá!' – I'm Through with You Forever –
The Sacred Mission – Poet's Corner – Beauty in Trouble – Sirocco at Deyá' –
From the Embassy – VIII: The White Goddess – Amergin's Charm – The Battle of
the Trees – The Song of Blodeuwedd – Instructions to the Orphic Adept – Lament
for Pasiphaë – The Sirens' Welcome to Cronos – Intercession in Late October –

The Jackals' Address to Isis – The Destroyer – Return of the Goddess – IX: With the Gift of a Ring – Counting the Beats – The Young Cordwainer – Your Private Way – The Survivor – Questions in a Wood – Darien – The Portrait – Prometheus – The Straw – Cry Faugh! – Hercules at Nemea – Dialogue on the Headland – The Mark – Liadan and Curithir – The Sea Horse – Reproach to Julia – Dethronement – Cat-Goddesses – The Blue-Fly – A Lost Jewel – The Window Sill – Spoils – Rhea – X: The Face in the Mirror – The Coral Pool – Gratitude for a Nightmare – Friday Night – The Naked and the Nude – Woman and Tree – Forbidden Words – The Enlisted Man – A Slice of Wedding Cake – A Plea to Boys and Girls – Nothing – Call It a Good Marriage – Read Me, Please! – The Second-Fated – The Twin of Sleep – Around the Mountain – Leaving the Rest Unsaid

Note: Impressions: 2nd, September 1959 (number of copies unknown); 3rd, November 1961 (1,971 copies); 4th, January 1962 (2,000 copies). The binding colour is changed to maroon in the 2nd impression; the frontispiece is altered to only a bust.

A88   FABLE OF THE HAWK AND THE NIGHTINGALE   1959

First edition:

FABLE OF THE HAWK AND THE NIGHTINGALE | TRANSLATED FROM HESIOD'S WORKS | AND DAYS [fourteen characters in red:] (lines 202–212) BY ROBERT GRAVES | PRINTED IN LEXINGTON KENTUCKY AT | THE STAMPERIA DEL SANTUCCIO M . CM . LIX

Collation: 4 leaves, sewn at centre.
  p.[1] title-page; pp.[2] – [4] blank; p.[5] text, printed in blue, red and black; p.[6] blank; p.[7] biographical note about Hesiod, statement of edition and typographical notice; p.[8] blank.
  26.7 × 19.8 cm. Bulk: 0.2/0.7 cm. White wove paper; all edges untrimmed. Bound in grey or brown boards with a label running from front to back across spine; on front, in red: STAMPERIA DEL SANTUCCIO | BROADSIDE NUMBER I | M . CM . LIX; label on back blank; on spine, bottom to top, first word and virgule in red: HESIOD/GRAVES

Price: $6.00. Number of copies: 100, plus at least 10 gratis out of series. Published midsummer 1959.

Note: Carl Hahn reports a variant binding in brick-red boards with separate cover and spine labels made by cutting the wrap-around label descibed above.

A89   THE ANGER OF ACHILLES   1959

a. First edition:

[four lines flush left:] The | Anger | of | Achilles | [slightly right of centre:] HOMER'S

ILIAD | [remainder flush left:] *Translated by* ROBERT GRAVES | *Illustrations by* RONALD SEARLE | *Doubleday & Company, Inc., Garden City, New York, 1959*

Collation: [1]^{12} 2^{12} [3]^{12} 4−6^{12} [7] − [8]^{12} 9−16^{12}, 192 leaves.

p.[1] THE ANGER OF ACHILLES; pp.[2] − [3] list of books by Graves; p.[4] blank; p.[5] title-page; p.[6] copyright, printing and designer's notices; p.[7] To Kenneth Gay | in gratitude for twenty-five years | of patient critical help.; p.[8] blank; pp.[9] −10 Contents; pp.[11] −12 Illustrations; pp.[13]14−35 Introduction; P.[36] blank; p.[37] THE ANGER OF ACHILLES; p.[38] blank; pp.[39]40−383 text, with pp.[54, 86, 100, 120, 144, 188, 234, 246, 308, 340, 384] being blank and pp.[55, 75, 87, 101, 121, 133, 145, 159, 175, 189, 207, 217, 235, 247, 263, 281, 295, 309, 317, 327, 341, 351, 367] being unnumbered; p.[384] blank; illustrations, all backs blank, face pp.24, 48, 73, 97, [120], [144], 168, 216, 240, 264, 288, 313, 336, 361.

23.2 × 15.2 cm. Bulk: 3.1/3.9 cm. White wove paper; all edges trimmed. White wove endpapers. Bound in black cloth; back blank; front stamped in gold with figure of Achilles; spine stamped in gold, top to bottom: The Anger of Achilles | [three lines upright:] HOMER'S *ILIAD* | *Translated by* | ROBERT GRAVES |[down spine:] *Doubleday*

Price: $4.95. Number of copies: 11,000 (in two printings). Published 5 November 1959 in white dust-jacket printed in black, brown, yellow, brick-red, green, violet and blue.

Note: Signatures appear quite close to the gutter opposite the final line of text; others than shown may therefore show in other copies.

This book has been translated into Swedish.

A89b. First English edition ([1960]):

[entire enclosed within rectangular decorative band box:] THE ANGER | OF | ACHILLES | *Homer's Iliad* | *translated by* | ROBERT GRAVES | CASSELL . LONDON

Collation: [A]^{16} B−K^{16} L^4 M−N^{16}, 196 leaves.

p.[i] THE ANGER | OF | ACHILLES; p.[ii] blank; p.[iii] title-page; p.[iv] publisher's, copyright, publication and printer's notices; pp.[v] − [vi] CONTENTS; p.[vii] To Kenneth Gay | in gratitude for twenty-five years | of patient critical help; pp.[viii] − [ix] map; p.[x] blank; pp.xi−xxxiv INTRODUCTION; pp. 1−357 text; p.[358] blank.

21.4 × 13.8 cm. Bulk: 2.7/3.3 cm. White wove paper; all edges trimmed. White wove endpapers. Bound in brown cloth; front and back blank; spine stamped in gold: ROBERT | GRAVES | [decorative band] | THE ANGER | OF | ACHILLES | [decorative band] | CASSELL

Price: 30s. Number of copies: 3,967. Published 10 March 1960 in cream dust-jacket printed in brown and black.

Note: Impression: 2nd, April 1960 (2,507 copies).

A89c. Readers Union issue (1961):

[entire enclosed within rectangular decorative band box:] THE ANGER | OF | ACHILLES | *Homer's Iliad* | *translated by* | ROBERT GRAVES | READERS UNION . CASSELL | *London* 1961

Collation: As A89a.
    Remainder as A89a, except p.[iv] has copyright and edition notices and p.[357] unnumbered.
    21.2 × 13.6 cm. Bulk: 2.6/3.1 cm. White wove paper; all edges trimmed. White wove endpapers. Bound in light grey cloth; front and back black; spine stamped in gold: The | Anger | of | Achilles | [light rule] | [broad rule] | [light rule] | HOMER'S ILIAD | TRANSLATED BY | ROBERT | GRAVES | [Readers Union emblem]

Price: 16s. Number of copies: 2,500. Published in October 1961.

A89d. Second English edition ([1962]):

HOMER | [swelled rule] | THE ANGER OF ACHILLES | (ILIAD) | TRANSLATED FROM THE GREEK BY | ROBERT GRAVES | [publisher's emblem] | A FOUR SQUARE CLASSIC *Collation:* [A]^{16} B–L^{16}, 176 leaves.
    p.[i] FOUR SQUARE CLASSICS | GENERAL EDITOR: ILSA BAREA; p.[ii] list of works in the series; p.[iii] title-page; p.[iv] publication, copyright, edition, conditions of sale and printer's notices; p.[v] To Kenneth Gay | in gratitude for twenty-five years | of patient critical help; pp.vi–[vii] CONTENTS; pp. [viii] – [ix] map; p.[x] blank; pp.xi–xxx INTRODUCTION; pp.1–322 text.
    18.0 × 10.8 cm. Bulk: 1.8 cm. White wove paper; all edges trimmed. Bound in paper covers.

Price: 6s. Number of copies undisclosed. Published 15 November 1962.

A90 FOOD FOR CENTAURS 1960

First edition:

Food for Centaurs: | *Stories, Talks, Critical* | *Studies, Poems by* | *Robert Graves* | [cut of centaur] | DOUBLEDAY & COMPANY, INC. | GARDEN CITY, NEW YORK | 1960

Collation: [1]^{12} 2–16^{12}, 192 leaves.
    p.[1] *Food for Centaurs*; p.[2] blank; p.[3] list of books by Graves; p.[4] blank; p.[5] title-page; p.[6] copyright, printing and edition notices; p.[7] FOREWORD; p.[8] To Mildred Lockwood Lacey | in gratitude for her | generous heart; pp.[9] – [10] CONTENTS; pp.[11] – [12]13–382 text, with pp.[11, 95, 147, 295, 351] being section-headings and pp.[12, 96, 146, 148, 294, 296, 350, 352] being blank; pp.[383] – [384] blank.
    20.8 × 13.7 cm. Bulk: 2.8/3.4 cm. White wove paper; top and bottom edges trimmed. White wove endpapers. Bound in black cloth with green quarter-cloth spine; front and back blank; spine stamped in silver, printed in purple: *Robert* | *Graves* | [purple enclosing device facing down] | [purple rectangular solid box,

inside which, top to bottom:] *FOOD for CENTAURS* | [purple enclosing device facing up] | *Doubleday*

Price: $4.95. Number of copies: 5,500 (in two printings). Published 6 May 1960 in white dust-jacket printed in black, green, pink and blue.

Contents: Foreword – *Stories:* The Viscountess and the Short-Haired Girl – A Toast to Ava Gardner – She Landed Yesterday – The Lost Chinese – You Win, Houdini! – *Talks on Poetry:* Sweeney among the Blackbirds – The Making and Marketing of Poetry – Pulling a Poem Apart – *Studies in History:* To be a Goy – A Dead Branch on the Tree of Israel – Was Benedict Arnold a Traitor? – The Cultured Romans – New Light on an Old Murder – To Minorca! – The Dour Man – Praise Me and I Will Whistle to You! – What Was That War Like, Sir? – Centaurs' Food – The Fifth Column at Troy – *Critiques of New Books:* Maenads, Junkies and Others – It Ended with a Bang – Legends of the Bible – Puck, Mab, the Billy Blin – The Pirates Who Captured Caesar – The Butcher and the Cur – Two Studies in Scientific Atheism – The Archetypal Wise Old Man – *Poems:* Preface to a Reading of Poems – Trudge, Body! – The Christmas Robin – Twice of the Same Fever – Nothing – Call It a Good Marriage – Read Me, Please! – The Twin of Sleep – Established Lovers – The Quiet Glades of Eden – Heroes in Their Prime – Catkind – The Young Goddess – Here Live Your Life Out – Joan and Darby – Superman on the Riviera – The Picture Nail – Old World Dialogue – The Were-Man – The Person from Porlock – Around the Mountain

Note: The second issue of this edition lacks the edition notice on the verso title-page and measures 20.7 × 13.9 cm Bulk: 2.5/3.2 cm.

A91   GREEK GODS AND HEROES   1960

a. First edition:

ROBERT GRAVES | [three lines in brown:] GREEK GODS | AND | HEROES | ILLUSTRATED BY DIMITRIS DAVIS | 1960 | DOUBLEDAY & COMPANY, INC. | GARDEN CITY, NEW YORK

Collation: [1] – [10]⁸, 80 leaves.
    p.[1] GREEK GODS AND HEROES; p.[2] illustration of Pan in brown and black; p.[3] title-page; p.[4] copyright, printing and designer's notices; pp.5–6 INTRODUCTION; pp.[7] – [8] CONTENTS; p.[9] GREEK GODS AND HEROES; p.[10] blank; p.[11] THE PALACE OF OLYMPUS and illustration in brown and black; p.[12] blank; p.13–155 text, with pp.[15, 24, 27, 31, 33, 35, 39, 41, 46, 49, 52, 55, 58, 62, 66, 69, 71, 73, 77, 81, 85, 90, 99, 104, 106, 110, 114, 121, 126, 131, 137, 142, 147, 152] being illustrations in black and brown; pp.156–160 INDEX.
    23.3 × 15.3 cm. Bulk: 1.0/1.5 cm. White wove paper; all edges trimmed. White wove endpapers; both front and back have illustrations in brown of centaur, nymph, satyr, mermaid and offspring; inner free sides blank. Bound in brownish grey cloth; back blank; front stamped in brown at upper right with vase; spine stamped in brown: Robert | Graves | [down spine:] GREEK GODS AND HEROES | Doubleday

Price: $2.95. Number of copies: 37,500 (in five printings). Published 9 November 1960 in white dust-jacket printed in yellow, orange, brown and green.

Note: This book has been translated into Dutch and Polish.

A91b. First English edition ([1961]):

ROBERT GRAVES | MYTHS OF | ANCIENT | GREECE | ILLUSTRATED BY JOAN KIDDELL-MONROE | CASSELL . LONDON

Collation: [A]⁸ B−K⁸, 80 leaves.

p.[1] MYTHS OF ANCIENT GREECE; p.[2] illustration; p.[3] title-page; p.[4] publisher's, copyright, publication and printer's notices; pp.5−6 INTRODUCTION; pp.[7]−[8] CONTENTS; p.[9] MYTHS OF ANCIENT GREECE; p.[10] blank; p.[11] THE PALACE OF OLYMPUS and illustration; p.[12] blank; p.13−155 text, with pp.[15, 19, 25, 28, 32, 35, 40, 45, 48, 51, 54, 57, 61, 65, 68, 71, 75, 79, 83, 88, 93, 98, 104, 108, 112, 117, 121, 125, 130, 134, 137, 142, 147, 152] being illustrations in black and brown; pp.[156]−[160] INDEX.

21.5 × 14.0 cm. Bulk: 1.4/2.0 cm. White wove paper; all edges trimmed. White wove endpapers. Bound in grey cloth-textured boards; front and back blank; spine stamped in silver: Robert | Graves | [up spine:] Myths of Ancient Greece | Cassell

Price: 13s.6d. Number of copies: 5,946. Published 9 November 1961 in white dust-jacket printed in brown and purple.

Note: Impressions: 2nd, January 1962 (3,011 copies); 3rd, December 1962 (2,931 copies); 4th, August 1964 (5,000 copies); 5th, 1970 (number of copies unknown).

A91c. Second American edition ([1965]):

GREEK GODS | AND HEROES | [concave rule] | ROBERT GRAVES | [at right:] [series emblem]

Collation: 64 leaves, glued at spine.

p.[1] publisher's advertisements and blurb; p.[2] list of books in this series; p.[3] title-page; p.[4] publisher's, copyright, series, rights reservation, arrangement, edition and printing notices; pp.[5]−[6] CONTENTS; pp.[7]8−9 Introduction; p.[10] blank; pp.[11]12−116 text, with pp.[22, 32, 43, 94, 98, 103, 114] being unnumbered; pp.[117]118−127 Index; p.[128] publisher's advertisement.

16.1 × 10.6 cm. Bulk: 0.6 cm. White wove paper; all edges trimmed; all edges stained blue. Bound in white paper covers printed in gold, pink, yellow and black; inner sides blank.

Price: $0.45. Number of copies: 75,000. Published 11 November 1965.

Note: This is Dell Laurel-Leaf Library 3221

A92 THE PENNY FIDDLE [1960]

a. First edition:

[whole has four children, dog and cat in pink and black, one child holding bow across bass viol, inside which nine lines:] THE | PENNY | FIDDLE | *Poems for* | *Children* | *by* | *Robert Graves* | *Illustrated by* | *Edward Ardizzone* | [remainder below viol.:] *Cassell — London*

Collation: [A]^8 B–D^8, 32 leaves.

p.[1] *The Penny Fiddle*; p.[2] blank; p.[3] title-page; p.[4] publisher's, copyright, publication and printer's notices; p.[5] *To* | TOMÁS | *on his eighth birthday*; p.[6] blank; p.[7] *Contents*; pp.8–[64] text and illustrations, with pp.[9–10, 12, 14–15, 17–18, 21–22, 24–26, 28, 30, 32, 34–35, 39, 41–42, 46, 49, 53–54, 56–58. 61, 63–64] being unnumbered.

21.5 × 16.3 cm. Bulk: 0.6/1.0 cm. White wove paper; all edges trimmed. White wove endpapers. Bound in green cloth-simulated boards; front and back blank; spine stamped in gold, bottom to top: CASSELL [decorative device] *The Penny Fiddle* [decorative device] ROBERT GRAVES

Price: 12s.6d. Number of copies: 6,238. Published 10 November 1960 in white dust-jacket printed in black, green, pink and light blue.

Contents: The Penny Fiddle – Allie – Robinson Crusoe – The Six Badgers – One Hard Look – Jock o'Binnorie – What Did I Dream? – Lift-Boy – Henry and Mary – Dicky – Love without Hope – The Hills of May – In the Widerness – 'The General Elliott' – Vain and Careless – The Forbidden Play – The Bedpost – The Well-Dressed Children – The Magical Picture – The *Alice Jean* – A Boy in Church – How and Why – Warning to Children

Note: Impression: 2nd, September 1961 (3,067 copies).
Printed in Great Britain.

A92b. American issue ([1961]):

Title-page as A92a, except below viol: *DOUBLEDAY & COMPANY, INC.* | *Garden City, New York*

Collation: [1]–[4]^8, 32 leaves.

Remainder as A92a, except p.[4] publisher's emblem and copyright, printing and edition notices.

23.3 × 15.5 cm. Bulk: 0.5/1.1 cm. Paper as A92a. Bound in green cloth; front blank; back stamped with white publisher's emblem in lower right corner; spine stamped in white, top to bottom: ROBERT GRAVES THE PENNY FIDDLE DOUBLEDAY

Price: $2.50. Number of copies: 9,000 (including 3,000 institutional). Published 8 September 1961 in dust-jacket as A92a.

Note: This issue uses slightly brighter colours and darker inking than A92a.
Printed in the United States.

A93   MORE POEMS 1961   [1961]

First edition:

ROBERT GRAVES | MORE POEMS | 1961 | [publisher's emblem] | CASSELL .
LONDON

Collation: [A]⁴ B−D⁸, 28 leaves.

Collation: [A]^4 B−D^8, 28 leaves.

pp.[i] − [ii] blank; p.[iii] MORE POEMS | 1961; p.[iv] blank; p.[v] title-page; p.[vi] publisher's, copyright, publication and printer's notices; p.[vii] FOREWORD; p.[viii] blank; pp.[ix] − [x] CONTENTS; p.[1] XI; p.[2] blank; pp.3−26 text; p.[27] XII; p.[28] blank; pp.29−45 text; p.[46] blank.

21.6 × 15.0 cm. Bulk: 0.5/1.1 cm. White wove paper; all edges trimmed. White wove endpapers. Bound in maroon cloth; front and back blank; spine stamped in gold, bottom to top: *Cassell Robert Graves* MORE POEMS 1961

Price: 10s.6d. Number of copies: 3,913. Published 11 May 1961 in white dust-jacket printed in black and brick-cherry.

Contents: Foreword − XI: Lyceia − Symptoms of Love − The Sharp Ridge − Under the Olives − The Visitation − Fragment − Apple Island − The Falcon Woman − Troughs of Sea − The Laugh − The Death Grapple − In Single Syllables − The Starred Coverlet − The Intrusion − Patience − The Cure − Hag-Ridden − Turn of the Moon − The Secret Land − Seldom Yet Now − To Myrto of Myrtles − Anchises to Aphrodite − XII: Two Children − A Lost World − The Dangerous Gift − Twice of the Same Fever − Surgical Ward: Men − Nightfall at Twenty Thousand Feet − The Simpleton − The Were-Man − Two Rhymes about Fate and Money − The Two Witches − The Person from Porlock − Established Lovers − The Quiet Glades of Eden − Here Live Your Life Out! − Burn It! − Joan and Darby − Song: Come, Enjoy Your Sunday!

A94   SELECTED POETRY AND PROSE   [1961]

First edition:

Selected Poetry and Prose of | ROBERT GRAVES | *Chosen, introduced and* | *annotated by* | JAMES REEVES | [publisher's emblem] | HUTCHINSON EDUCATIONAL

Collation: [A]¹⁶ B−F¹⁶ G−I⁸ 120 leaves.

Collation: [A]^{16} B−F^{16} G−I^8 120 leaves.

p.[1] HUTCHINSON ENGLISH TEXTS | Selected Poetry and Prose of | ROBERT GRAVES; p.[2] list of books in this series; p.[3] title-page; p.[4] publisher's, publication, copyright and printer's notices; p.[5]; HANC OLGAM GRAVEM | OLGAE MINIME GRAVI | D. D. ROBERTUS GRAVES; p.[6] ACKNOWLEDGEMENTS; pp.[7] − [10] Contents; pp.11−20 Robert Graves: His Life and Writings; p.[21] Selected Poetry and Prose of | ROBERT GRAVES; pp.[22] blank; pp.23−215 text, with pp.[76, 130, 184] being blank; p.[216] blank; p.[217] NOTES; p.[218] blank; pp.219−240 notes.

18.5 × 12.3 cm. Bulk: 1.5/1.8 cm. White wove paper; all edges trimmed. White wove endpapers. Bound in green cloth; back blank; front blind-stamped with publisher's emblem; spine stamped in silver: Edited by | JAMES | REEVES | [decorative rule] | [top to bottom, near front:] Selected Poetry and Prose | [top to bottom, parallel with preceding line, near back:] of Robert Graves | [decorative rule] | [publisher's emblem interlocked with oval inside which is script *HEJ*]

Price: 9s.6d. Number of copies: 6,000. Published 15 May 1961 without dust-jacket.

Contents: Acknowledgements – Robert Graves: His Life and Writings – Pollux Boxes with King Amycus (*Golden Fleece*) – The Passage of the Bosphorus (*Golden Fleece*) – A Gladiatorial Combat (*I, Claudius*) – Public Works by the Emperor Claudius (*Claudius the God*) – The Expedition against Carthage (*Count Belisarius*) – Poems I: The Alice Jean – Diplomatic Relations – Welsh Incident – The Discovery of the Marquesas Islands (*The Isles of Unwisdom*) – The Execution of Charles I (*Wife to Mr. Milton*) – A Troopship Sails for the American Colonies, 1776 (*Sergeant Lamb of the Ninth*) – Poems II: The Haunted House – Retrospect: Jests of the Clock – The Pier-Glass – Outlaws – An English Wood – Rocky Acres – Lost Acres – In No Direction – The Next Time – The Legs – On Dwelling – The Cloak – The Beach – Vanity – Nature's Lineaments – Old Papa Johnson (*Occupation: Writer*) – The Abominable Mr. Gunn (*Catacrok*) – War on the Western Front, 1915 (*Good-Bye to All That*) – On Leave, 1916 (*Good-Bye to All That*) – Poems III: Lost Love – Love without Hope – Love in Barrenness – At First Sight – Time – The Great-Grandmother – To Lucia at Birth – Under the Pot – John Skelton – The Twin of Sleep – The Cool Web – Gardener – Flying Crooked – My Name and I – Any Honest Housewife – The Laureate – A Plea to Boys and Girls – Brother and Sister (*Antigua, Penny, Puce*) – A Stamp Auction (*Antigua, Penny, Puce*) – Poems IV: 1805 – 'The General Elliott' – Nobody – Traveller's Curse after Misdirection – To Bring the Dead to Life – The China Plate – Lollocks – Act V, Scene 5 – Brother – A Village Conflict – A History of Peace – Warning to Children – To Evoke Posterity – Notes

A95   COLLECTED POEMS   1961

First edition:

ROBERT GRAVES | COLLECTED | POEMS | DOUBLEDAY & COMPANY, INC. | GARDEN CITY, NEW YORK | 1961

Collation: 1–2¹² [3] – [5]¹² 6–7¹² [8] – [15]¹², 180 leaves.
   p.[1] COLLECTED POEMS; p.[2] blank; p.[3] list of books by Graves; p.[4] blank; p.[5] title-page; p.[6] acknowledgement, copyright, printing and edition notices; p.[7] TO CALLIOPE; p.[8] blank; p.[9] FOREWORD; p.[10] blank; pp.11–20 CONTENTS; pp.[21] – [22]23–350 text, with pp.[21, 53, 87, 111, 167, 185, 219, 245, 263, 291, 307, 333] being section headings and pp.[22, 54, 88, 112, 166, 184, 186, 218, 220, 244, 246, 262, 264, 290, 292, 308, 332, 334] being blank; pp.351–358 INDEX OF FIRST LINES; pp.[359] – [360] blank.
   20.8 × 13.9 cm. Bulk: 2.6/3.2 cm. White wove paper; top and bottom edges trimmed. White wove endpapers. Bound in grey cloth; back blank; front stamped in silver: [decorative rule] | [solid brown rectangular box, inside which two lines:]

COLLECTED | POEMS | [decorative rule]; spine stamped in silver: [decorative rule] | [solid brown rectangular box, inside which four lines:] COLLECTED | POEMS | *Robert | Graves* | [decorative rule] | DOUBLEDAY

Price: $5.95. Number of copies: 6,000 (in two printings). Published 21 July 1961 in white dust-jacket printed in grey, black and light and dark brown.

Contents: To Calliope – Foreword – I: In the Wilderness – The Haunted House – Reproach – The Finding of Love – 'The General Elliott' – Rocky Acres – Outlaws – One Hard Look – A Frosty Night – Allie – Unicorn and the White Doe – Henry and Mary – Love Without Hope – What Did I Dream? – The Country Dance – The Troll's Nosegay – The Hills of May – Lost Love – Vain and Careless – An English Wood – The Bedpost – The Pier-Glass – Apples and Water – Angry Samson – Down – Mermaid, Dragon, Fiend – II: In Procession – Warning to Children – Alice – Richard Roe and John Doe – The Witches' Cauldron – Ancestors – The Coronation Murder – Children of Darkness – The Cool Web – Love in Barrenness – Song of Contrariety – The Presence – The Land of Whipperginny – In No Direction – The Castle – Return – The Bards – A Lost World – Nobody – The Progress – Full Moon – Vanity – Pure Death – Sick Love – It Was All Very Tidy – III: Callow Captain – Thief – The Furious Voyage – Song: Lift-Boy – Traveller's Curse after Misdirection – The Last Day of Leave – The Next Time – Ulysses – The Succubus – The Reader over My Shoulder – The Legs – Gardener – Front Door Soliloquy – In Broken Images – Trudge, Body! – The Christmas Robin – On Rising Early – Flying Crooked – Fragment of a Lost Poem – Brother – IV: Galatea and Pygmalion – The Devil's Advice to Story-Tellers – Sergeant-Major Money – Sea Side – Wm. Brazier – Welsh Incident – Vision in the Repair-Shop – Interruption – Act V, Scene 5 – Midway – Hell – Leda – Synthetic Such – The Florist Rose – Lost Acres – At First Sight – Recalling War – Down, Wanton, Down! – A Former Attachment – Nature's Lineaments – Time – The Philosopher – On Dwelling – Hotel Bed at Lugano – Ogres and Pygmies – History of the Word – Single Fare – To Walk on Hills – To Bring the Dead to Life – To Evoke Posterity – Any Honest Housewife – Defeat of the Rebels – Never Such Love – The Fallen Signpost – The China Plate – Certain Mercies – The Cuirassiers of the Frontier – The Laureate – A Jealous Man – The Cloak – The Foreboding – With Her Lips Only – The Halls of Bedlam – Or to Perish before Day – A Country Mansion – Lovers in Winter – Advocates – V. On Portents – The Terraced Valley – Alexander and Queen Janet – The Chink – The Ages of Oath – New Legends – Like Snow – End of Play – The Climate of Thought – The Fallen Tower of Siloam – The Great-Grandmother – No More Ghosts – VI: A Love Story – Dawn Bombardment – The Worms of History – The Glutton – The Shot – The Thieves – Lollocks – To Sleep – Despite and Still – The Suicide in the Copse – Frightened Men – The Oath – Language of the Seasons – Mid–Winter Waking – The Rock at the Corner – The Beach – The Villagers and Death – The Door – Under the Pot – Through Nightmare – To Lucia at Birth – Death by Drums – She Tells Her Love While Half Asleep – Theseus and Ariadne – Penthesileia – Cold Weather Proverb – The Death Room – To Juan at the Winter Solstice – To Be Called a Bear – VII: My Name and I – 1805 – At the Savoy Chapel – Dream of a Climber – The Persian Version – The Weather of Olympus – Apollo of the Physiologists – The Oldest Soldier – Grotesques i–vi – The Eugenist – A Civil Servant – Gulls and Men – Conversation Piece – General Bloodstock's Lament for England – 'iWellcome, to the Caves of Artá!' – I'm Through with You Forever – The Sacred Mission – Poets' Corner – Beauty in Trouble – Sirocco at Deyá – From the Embassy – VIII: The White Goddess – Amergin's Charm – The Battle of the Trees – The Song of Blodeuwedd – Instructions to the Orphic Adept – Lament for Pasiphaë – The Sirens' Welcome to Cronos – Intercession in Late October – The Jackals' Address to Isis – The Destroyer – Return of the Goddess – IX: Counting the Beats – The Young Cordwainer – Your Private Way – The Survivor – Questions in a Wood – Darien – The Portrait – Prometheus – The Straw – Cry Faugh! – Hercules at Nemea – Dialogue on the Headland – The Mark – Liadan and Curithir – The Sea Horse – Reproach to Julia – Dethronement – Cat-Goddesses – The Blue-Fly – A Lost Jewel – The Window Sill – Spoils – Rhea – X: The Face in the Mirror – The Coral Pool – Gratitude for a Nightmare – Friday Night – The Naked and the Nude – Woman and Tree – Forbidden Words – A Slice of Wedding Cake – A Plea to Boys and Girls – Nothing – Call It a Good Marriage – The Second-Fated – The Twin of Sleep – Around the Mountain – XI: Lyceia – Symptoms of Love – The Sharp Ridge – Under the Olives – The Visitation – Fragment – Apple Island – The Falcon Woman – Troughs of Sea – The Laugh – The Death Grapple – In Single Syllables – The Starred Coverlet – The Intrusion – Patience – Hag-Ridden – The Cure – Turn of the Moon – Seldom, Yet Now – Anchises to Aphrodite – The Secret Land – To Myrto of Myrtles – XII: Two Children – The Dangerous Gift – Twice of the Same Fever – Surgical Ward: Men – Nightfall at Twenty Thousand Feet – The Simpleton – The Were-Man – The Person from Porlock – Established Lovers – The Quiet Glades of Eden – Here Live Your Life Out! – Burn It! – Joan and Darby – Ruby and Amethyst – Song: Come, Enjoy Your Sunday! – Leaving the Rest Unsaid – Index of First Lines.

Note: There is a variant of the dust-jacket which has the letters C.P. printed above the price.

A96   THE MORE DESERVING CASES   1962

First edition:

THE MORE | DESERVING CASES | Eighteen Old Poems | for | Reconsideration | by | ROBERT GRAVES | Marlborough College Press | 1962

Collation: [1] – [5]⁴, 20 leaves.

    pp.[1] – [2] blank; p.[3] THE MORE DESERVING CASES; p.[4] portrait of Graves; p.[5] title-page; p.[6] blank; p.[7] FOREWORD; p.[8] blank; p.[9] CONTENTS; p.[10] blank; p.[11] – [37] text; p.[38] colophon and signature of Graves; pp.[39] – [40] blank.

    24.7 × 15.2 cm. Bulk: 0.3/1.0 cm. Heavy white wove paper; all edges trimmed; top edges gilt. Wove endpapers with watered design; innersides blank. Bound in red morocco; back and spine blank; front stamped in gold: THE MORE | DESERVING CASES | ROBERT GRAVES

Price: 3 gns. Number of copies: 400. Published 1 February 1962 without dust-jacket.

Contents: Foreword – 1. Sullen Moods 1922 – 2. The Dialecticians 1922 – 3. A Village Feud 1923 – 4. The Clipped Stater 1923 – 5. Epitaph on an Unfortunate Artist 1923 – 6. The Corner Knot 1924 – 7. Death of the Farmer 1924 – 8. Virgil the Sorcerer 1924 – 9. Pygmalion to Galatea 1925 – 10. Diplomatic Relations 1925 – 11. The Philatelist Royal 1929 – 12. To be Less Philosophical 1931 – 13. Variables of Green 1931 – 14. Devilishly Provoked 1933 – 15. The Miller's Man 1934 – 16. July 24th 1942 – 17. Safe Receipt of a Censored Letter 1942 – 18. The Blotted Copy-Book 1952

Note: An issue in blue buckram has white wove endpapers without design and the top edges are not gilt; price: 2 gns.; number of copies: 350; signed by Graves. Carl Hahn reports a copy in red morroco numbered 510 which may mean that the sheets for both the original issue and the blue buckram issue became mixed during the binding process.
The portrait of Graves is by H. A. Freeth.

A97 OXFORD ADDRESSES ON POETRY [1962]

a. First edition:

OXFORD ADDRESSES | ON POETRY | by | ROBERT GRAVES | *Professor of Poetry, Oxford University* | 1961 | [publisher's emblem] | CASSELL . LONDON

Collation: [A]^8 B–H^8 I/I$^{*2/4}$, 70 leaves.
      p.[i] OXFORD ADDRESSES ON POETRY; p.[ii] blank; p.[iii] title-page; p.[iv] publisher's, copyright, edition and printer's notices; p.[v] AD COLL. SANCT. JOH. BAPT. ALUMNO | CANO REDEUNTI BENIGNISSAM; p.[vi] blank; p.[vii] table of contents; p.[viii] blank; pp.[ix] – [x] *Foreword*; pp.[1] – [2]3–129 text, with pp.[1, 27, 55, 83, 97, 109] being section-headings and pp.[2, 26, 28, 54, 56, 82, 84, 98, 108, 110] being blank; p.[130] blank.
      21.6 × 13 9 cm. Bulk: 1.2/1.7 cm. White wove paper; all edges trimmed. White wove endpapers. Bound in dark blue cloth; front and back blank; spine stamped in gold: [at bottom:] CASSELL | [up spine:] Robert Graves [enclosed in double-rule box with swirls and diamond top and bottom] OXFORD ADDRESSES ON POETRY

Price: 18s. Number of copies: 2,951. Published 26 April 1962 in grey-blue dust-jacket printed in black and medium blue.

Contents: Foreward – The Dedicated Poet – The Anti-Poet – The Personal Muse – Poetic Gold – The Word 'Béraka' – The Poet's Paradise.

Note: A photographic reprint of this edition was published in 1974 by Cedric Chivers, Portway, Bath, "at the request of the London and Home Counties Branch of The Library Association;" it is identical except for title-page and blurb on p.[iii].

A97b. First American edition (1962):

[at left:] *Robert Graves* | (PROFESSOR OF POETRY, OXFORD UNIVERSITY) 1961 | OXFORD | ADDRESSES | ON POETRY | [decorative device] | [three lines at left:] *Doubleday & Company, Inc.* | *Garden City, New York* | *1962*

Collation: $1-3^{12}$ [4] $-[6]^{12}$, 72 leaves, first gathering being signed on p.24.
   p.[1] OXFORD | ADDRESSES | ON POETRY; pp.[2]–[3] list of books by Graves; p.[4] blank; p.[5] title-page; p.[6] dedication (as A97a, p.[v]), LC card, copyright, printing and edition notices; p.[7]–8 *Contents*; pp.[9]–10 *Foreword*; pp.[11]–[12]13–141 text, with pp.[11, 37, 65, 95, 109, 121] being section headings, pp.[12, 38, 66, 96, 110, 122] being unnumbered and pp.[94, 120] being blank; pp.[142]–[144] blank.
   20.8 × 13.7 cm. Bulk: 1.1/1.5 cm. White wove paper; top and bottom edges trimmed. White wove endpapers. Bound in three-quarter grey cloth with black cloth spine; front and back blank; spine stamped in silver, top to bottom: [near front:] OXFORD ADDRESSES ON POETRY [near back:] Robert Graves [near front:] Doubleday

Price: $3.95. Number of copies: 4,000 (in two printings). Published 21 September 1962 in white dust-jacket printed in grey, dark blue and black.

Note: Greenwood Press issued a photographic reprint of this edition in 1968 and again in 1972.

A98   THE COMEDIES OF TERENCE   1962

a First edition:

THE COMEDIES OF | TERENCE | [swelled rule] | Edited, with a Foreword, by | ROBERT GRAVES | ANCHOR BOOKS | DOUBLEDAY & COMPANY, INC. | GARDEN CITY, NEW YORK | 1962

Collation: 180 leaves, glued at spine.
   p.[i] THE COMEDIES OF | TERENCE | [series emblem]; p.[ii] blank; p.[iii] biographical note; p.[iv] blank; p.[v] title-page; p.[vi] LC card, copyright, printing and edition notices; p.[vii] CONTENTS; p.[viii] blank; pp.[ix]x–xiv FOREWORD; p.[xv] THE COMEDIES OF | TERENCE; p.[xvi] blank; pp.[1]–334 text, with pp.[1–3, 15, 25, 34, 46, 59–61, 67, 72, 84, 94, 103–105, 113, 123, 133, 148, 161–163, 170, 182, 194, 208, 223–225, 231, 240, 255, 266, 283–285, 290, 298, 309, 323] being unnumbered and pp.[58, 160] being blank; pp.[335]–[344] publisher's advertisements.
   18.1 × 10.6 cm. Bulk: 1.9 cm. White wove paper; all edges trimmed. Bound in white paper covers printed in blue and black; front has woman holding a large mask with series number, price, title and series credits; back has blurb; spine: [top to bottom:] THE COMEDIES OF TERENCE EDITED BY ROBERT GRAVES | ANCHOR | A305 | [triangle]; inner sides of front and back covers blank.

Price: $1.45. Number of copies: 10,000. Published 18 May 1962

Contents: Foreword – The Fair Andrian – The Mother-in-Law – The Self-Tormentor – The Eunuch – The Tricks of Phormio – The Brothers

Note: The cover design is by Eugene Berman.
This edition is Anchor Book A305.
The text is revised from the seventh edition of Echard's translation.

A98b. Second American issue ([1962]):

THE COMEDIES OF | TERENCE | [swelled rule] | Edited, with a Foreword, by | ROBERT GRAVES | ALDINE PUBLISHING COMPANY/CHICAGO

Collation: [1] – [11]^{16}, 176 leaves.
  p.[i] THE COMEDIES OF | TERENCE | AN ALDINE LIBRARY EDITION; pp.[ii] – [v] as A98a; p.[vi] copyright, LC card, publication, publisher's and printing notices; pp.[vii] –334 as A98a; pp.[335] – [336] blank.
  20.9 × 13.9 cm. Bulk: 2.3/3.0 cm. White wove paper; all edges trimmed. White wove endpapers. Bound in maroon cloth; front and back blank; spine stamped in silver: [down spine, near front:] THE COMEDIES | [down spine, near back, parallel to preceding line:] OF TERENCE | [remainder upright: GRAVES | ALDINE | [publisher's emblem]

Price: $5.95. Number of copies: 2,000. Published 26 July 1962 in white dust-jacket printed in black and mauve as cover of A98a.

A98c. First English edition ([1963]):

THE BELLE SAUVAGE LIBRARY | THE COMEDIES OF | TERENCE | ECHARD'S TRANSLATION | EDITED, WITH A FOREWORD, BY | ROBERT GRAVES | [publisher's emblem] | CASSELL . LONDON

Collation: [1]^8 2–11^8 12^6 13–20^8 21/21a$^{2/4}$ 22^8, 174 leaves.
  p.[i] THE COMEDIES OF TERENCE; p.[ii] blank; p.[iii] title-page; p.[iv] publisher's, copyright, publication and printing notices; p.[v] CONTENTS; p.[vi] blank; pp.[vii]viii–xii FOREWORD; pp.[1] – [3]4–335 text, with pp.[1, 59, 103, 161, 223, 283] being title pages, pp.[2–3, 15, 25, 34, 46, 60–61, 67, 72, 84, 94, 104–105, 113, 123, 133, 148, 162 –163, 170, 182, 194, 207, 224 –225, 231, 240, 255, 266, 284–285, 291, 299, 310, 324] being unnumbered and pp.[58, 160, 222] being blank; p.[336] blank.
  20.4 × 14.6 cm. Bulk: 2.6/3.3 cm. White wove paper; all edges trimmed. White wove endpapers. Bound in brownish-grey cloth; front and back blank; spine stamped in gold: [star] | [light rule] | *The* | *Comedies of* | *Terence* | [light rule] | [star] | *Edited by* | ROBERT | GRAVES | [star] | [heavy rule] | *Cassell* | [heavy rule] | [star]

Price: 16s. Number of copies: 2,866. Published 13 June 1963 in white dust-jacket printed in black and dark yellow-green.

A98d. Third American impression ([1969]):

THE | COMEDIES | OF | TERENCE | *Edited, with a Foreword by* | ROBERT GRAVES | [publisher's emblem] | FREDERICK UNGAR PUBLISHING CO. | *NEW YORK*

Collation: [1] – [11]¹⁶, 176 leaves.

p.[i] THE COMEDIES OF TERENCE; p.[ii] blank; p.[iii] biographical note; p.[iv] blank; p.[v] title-page; p.[vi] publication, printing and LC card notices; p.[vii] CONTENTS; p.[viii] blank; pp.[ix]x–xiv FOREWORD; p.[xv] THE COMEDIES OF | TERENCE; p.[xvi] blank; pp.[1] – [3] 4 – [336] text, with pp.[15, 25, 34, 46, 59, 60, 61, 67, 72, 84, 94, 103 – 105, 113, 123, 133, 148, 161 – 163, 170, 182, 194, 208, 223 – 225, 231, 240, 255, 266, 283 – 285, 290, 309, 323] being unnumbered and pp.[58, 160, 335 – 336] being blank.

21.2 × 13.5 cm. Bulk: 2.1/2.8 cm. White wove paper; all edges trimmed; white wove endpapers. Bound in apple-green cloth; front and back blank; spine printed in black, top to bottom, facing back: THE COMEDIES | OF TERENCE | [two lines lower on spine:] Edited by | Robert Graves | [upright on spine: UNGAR

Price: $6.50 Number of copies: 1,000. Published in early 1969 in white dust-jacket printed in black and olive-gold.

Note: The copyright notice says that the date of this impression is 1968 but Ungar confirms the later date.

A99   ORATIO CREWEIANA   1962

ORATIO CREWEIANA | MDCCCCLXII

Collation: 6 leaves, stapled twice at centre.

p.[1] title-page; pp.2, 4, 6, 8, 10 text of oration in Latin; pp.3, 5, 7,9, 11 paraphrase in English; p.[12] printer's notice.

21.5 × 14.0 cm. Bulk: 0.04 cm. White wove paper; all edges trimmed.

Not for sale; distributed gratis. Number of copies: 1,400. Published 27 June 1962 by Oxford University Press.

A100   THE BIG GREEN BOOK   [1962]

a. First edition:

Robert Graves | THE BIG GREEN BOOK | [illustration of boy lying on bed reading with woolly dog observing] | illustrated by Maurice Sendak | THE CROWELL-COLLIER PRESS

Collation: [1] – [4]⁸, 32 leaves.

p.[1] THE BIG GREEN BOOK | [illustration of boy sitting on hassock reading]; p.[2] publisher's advertisements; p.[3] title-page; p.[4] edition, copyright and printing notices; p.[5] – [63] text and illustrations; p.[64] blank.

28.6 × 19.0 cm. 0.8/1.3 cm. White wove paper; all edges trimmed. Green wove er dpapers. Bound in slick green cloth; spine blank; front printed: [in white:] ROBERT GRAVES | THE BIG GREEN BOOK | [white rectangular border, inside which, in black over chartreuse, is illustration of little old man, woolly dog, aunt and uncle] | [in white:] illustrated by Maurice Sendak | A MODERN MASTERS BOOK FOR CHILDREN; back printed with blurb and publisher's advertisement.

Price: $1.95. Number of copies unknown. Published 15 October 1962 without dust-jacket.

Notes: Most copies have a silver label reading $1^{95} stuck at upper right front corner of cover. The same book was issued in England on 2 October 1963 with an English price label (15s).

Mason records a variant with the spine printed in black, running down: THE BIG GREEN BOOK | Robert Graves | THE CROWELL-COLLIER PRESS

This work has been translated into Danish, German and Swedish.

A100b. Second American impression (1968):

Robert Graves | THE BIG GREEN BOOK | [illustration as A100a] | illustrated by Maurice Sendak | Crowell-Collier Press, New York | Collier-Macmillan Limited, London

Collation: [1] – [4]^8, 32 leaves.

p.[1] title-page; p.[2] LC card, publisher's, printer's and edition notices; pp.[3] – [64] text and illustrations, with pp.[4, 64] blank.

21.5 × 15.0 cm. Bulk: 0.5/1.1 cm. White wove paper; all edges trimmed. Bound in bright green cloth printed in dark green; front with picture as A100a; back (at lower right) printed 63671; spine printed in black, facing back: GRAVES/SENDAK THE BIG GREEN BOOK CROWELL-COLLIER PRESS

Price: $3.95. Number of copies unknown. Published in 1968 in white dust-jacket printed in black, olive and light green.

Note: Macmillan (U.S.A.) reissued this book in the spring of 1985 at $12.95.

A100c. First English edition (1978):

Robert Graves | THE BIG GREEN BOOK | [illustration as A100a] | illustrated by Maurice Sendak | PUFFIN BOOKS

Collation: 32 leaves glued at spine.

p.[1] PUFFIN BOOKS | *Editor: Kaye Webb* | THE BIG GREEN BOOK | [blurb] | [illustration of boy sitting on hassock reading]; p.[2] blank; p.[3] title-page; p.[4] publisher's, copyright, printer's and rights reservation notices; p.[5] – [63] text and illustrations; p.[64] blank.

19.8 × 13.0 cm. Bulk: 0.5 cm. White wove paper; all edges trimmed. Bound in olive wove paper covers printed in white, black and yellow.

Price: 45p. Number of copies: 30,000. Published 30 March 1978.

Notes: Impressions: 2nd, 1980 (copies: 10,000); 3rd, 1982 (copies: 12,000); 4th, 1986 (copies: 10,000).

The cover illustration, old man under a tree talking to aunt, uncle and dog, is not used in the text of the book.

A100d. Second issue of First English edition (1979):

Title-page as A100c except last line: KESTREL BOOKS

Collation: [1]–[4]⁸, 32 leaves.

　　p.[1] title-page; p.[2] publisher's, copyright, rights reservation, ISBN and printer's notices; p.[3] illustration of boy sitting on hassock reading; p.[4] blank; pp.[5]–[63] text and illustrations; p.[64] blank.

　　21.5 × 14.3 cm. Bulk: 0.5/1.1 cm. White wove paper; all edges trimmed. White wove endpapers. Bound in greenish-yellow cloth; front and back blank. Spine stamped in florescent green, top to bottom: [geometric design] THE BIG GREEN BOOK KESTREL BOOKS

Price: £1.95. Number of copies unknown. Published in March 1979 in white dust-jacket printed in black, olive and light green.

A101　NEW POEMS 1962　[1962]

a. First edition:

ROBERT GRAVES | NEW POEMS | 1962 | [publisher's emblem] | CASSELL . LONDON

Collation: [A]⁸ B⁸ C/C*²/⁸, 26 leaves.

　　pp.[i]–[ii] blank; p.[iii] NEW POEMS | 1962; p.[iv] blank; p.[v] title-page; p.[vi] publisher's, publication and printer's notices; p.[vii] FOREWORD; p.[viii] blank; pp.[ix]–[x] CONTENTS; p.[1] XIII; p.[2] blank; pp.3–25 text; p.[26] blank; p.[27] XIV; p.[28] blank; pp.29–42 text.

　　21.4 × 14.8 cm. Bulk: 0.4/1.0 cm. White wove paper; all edges trimmed. White wove endpapers. Bound in orange-rust cloth; front and back blank; spine stamped in gold, bottom to top: *Cassell Robert Graves* NEW POEMS 1962

Price: 12s.6d. Number of copies: 3,082. Published 18 October 1962 in white dust-jacket printed in black and orange-brown.

Contents: Foreword – XIII: Ruby and Amethyst – Recognition – Variable of Green – The Watch – Name Day – Uncalendared Love – The Meeting – Lack – Not at Home – Horizon – Golden Anchor – Lion Lover – Ibycus in Samos – Possessed – The Winged Heart – In Trance at a Distance – The Wreath – In Her Praise – The Alabaster Throne – A Restless Ghost – Between Moon and Moon – XIV: Beware, Madam! – The Cliff Edge – The Miller's Man – Acrobats – Ouzo Unclouded – The Broken Girth – Inkidoo and the Queen of Babel – Three Songs for the Lute: I. Truth Is Poor Physic – II. In Her Only Way – III. Hedges Freaked with Snow – The Ambrosia of Dionysus and Semele – The Unnamed Spell

Notes: Impression: 2nd, August 1963 (1,500 copies).

A101b. First American edition (1963):

NEW POEMS | [swelled decorative rule] | ROBERT GRAVES | DOUBLEDAY & COMPANY, INC., GARDEN CITY, NEW YORK, 1963

Collation: [1] – [3]¹², 36 leaves.

p.[*i*] NEW POEMS; p.[*ii*] blank; p.[*iii*] title-page; p.[*iv*] acknowledgement, LC card, copyright, printing and edition notices; p.[*v*] FOREWORD; p.[*vi*] blank; pp.*vii*–*viii* CONTENTS; pp.1–64 text, with pp.[4, 6, 8, 10, 12, 14, 16, 20, 24, 28, 34, 36, 38, 40, 42, 46, 48, 50, 52, 58, 62] being blank.

20.8 × 13.7 cm. Bulk: 0.6/1.1 cm. White wove paper; all edges trimmed. White wove endpapers. Bound in black cloth; back blank; front stamped with signature of Graves in gold; spine stamped in gold, top to bottom: *NEW POEMS* Robert Graves *DOUBLEDAY*

Price: $2.95. Number of copies: 3,500. Published 21 June 1963 in white dust-jacket printed in black and green.

A102   THE SIEGE AND FALL OF TROY   [1962]

a. First edition:

THE SIEGE | AND FALL | OF TROY | *by* | ROBERT GRAVES | *Illustrated by* | WALTER HODGES | [publisher's emblem] | CASSELL . LONDON

Collation: [A]⁸ B–I⁸, 72 leaves.

p.[i] *The Siege and Fall of Troy*; p.[ii] list of children's books by Graves; p.[iii] blank; p.[iv] illustration; p.[v] title-page; p.[vi] publisher's, copyright, edition and printer's notices; p.vii CONTENTS; p.[viii] blank; pp.ix–x INTRODUCTION; p.[xi] blank; pp.[xii] – [xiii] map; p.[xiv] illustration; pp.1–119 text, with pp.[4, 12, 22, 32, 42, 50, 60, 68, 80, 92, 100, 108] being illustrations and pp.[11, 21, 41, 59, 99] being blank; p.[120] blank; p.[121] *Index*; p.[122] blank; pp.123–128 index; pp.[129] – [130] blank.

21.6 × 14.0 cm. Bulk: 1.4/2.0 cm. White wove paper; all edges trimmed. White wove endpapers. Bound in brown cloth-simulated boards; front and back blank; spine stamped in gold: ROBERT | GRAVES | [up spine:] The Siege and Fall of Troy | CASSELL

Price: 15s. Number of copies: 7,553. Published 8 November 1962 in white dust-jacket with multicolour Trojan horse scene and author and title in yellow.

Note: Impression: 2nd, November 1964 (3,000 copies).

This book has been translated into Dutch and Serbo-Croatian.

A102b. First American edition ([1963]):

[first four lines in pseudo-Celtic type:] ROBERT GRAVES | THE | SIEGE AND FALL | OF TROY | ILLUSTRATED BY C. WALTER HODGES | DOUBLEDAY & COMPANY, INC. | GARDEN CITY, NEW YORK

Collation: 64 leaves, glued to tape at spine.

p.[1] THE SIEGE AND FALL OF TROY; p.[2] frontispiece; p.[3] title-page; p.[4] LC card, copyright, printing and edition notices, with publisher's emblem to left of all; p.[5] list of books for children by Graves; p.[6] blank; p.[7] CONTENTS; p.[8] blank; pp.9–10 INTRODUCTION; p.[11] THE SIEGE AND FALL OF TROY; pp.[12] – [13] map; p.[14] blank; pp.15–120 text, with pp.[17, 22, 31, 35, 47, 53, 62, 71, 83, 91, 99,

106, 117] being illustrations, and pp.[42, 58, 74, 96, 110] being blank; p.[121] INDEX; p.[122] blank; pp.123–128 index. Illustrations, frontispiece and map are printed in red.

23.3 × 15.0 cm. Bulk: 0.9/1.4 cm. White wove paper; all edges trimmed. Cream wove endpapers. Bound in rust-brown cloth; front and back blank; spine stamped in gold, top to bottom: [near front:] Robert | [near back, parallel to preceding line:] Graves| [in pseudo-Celtic type:] THE SIEGE AND FALL OF TROY | [remainder upright:] [publisher's emblem] | Doubleday

Price: $3.50. Number of copies: 20,000 (including 5,000 institutional). Published 4 October 1963 in white dust-jacket printed in yellow, orange, brown and black.

A102c. Second American edition ([1965]):

THE SIEGE AND | FALL OF TROY | [concave rule] | ROBERT GRAVES | [at right:] [series emblem]

Collation: 64 leaves, glued at spine.

p.[1] publisher's advertisements and blurb; p.[2] list of books in this series; p.[3] title-page; p.[4] publisher's, copyright, series, rights reservation, arrangement, edition and printing notices; p.[5] CONTENTS; p.[6] blank; pp.[7]8–9 Introduction; p.[10] blank; p.[11] THE SIEGE AND | FALL OF TROY; p.[12] blank; pp.[13]14–112 text, with pp.[16, 22, 30, 39, 47, 54, 61, 68, 78, 89, 95, 102] unnumbered; pp.[113]114–124 Index; pp.[125] – [128] publisher's advertisements.

16.1 × 10.5 cm. Bulk: 0.6 cm. White wove paper; all edges trimmed; all edges stained blue. Bound in white paper covers printed in blue, yellow, red, brown and black.

Price: $0.45. Number of copies: 75,000. Published 11 November 1965.

Note: This book is Dell Laurel-Leaf Library 7885.

A103   NINE HUNDRED IRON CHARIOTS   [1963]

First edition:

[two words in grey:] Robert Graves Nine Hundred Iron Chariots | The Twelfth Arthur Dehon Little Memorial Lecture, Massachusetts Institute of Technology | Delivered in Kresge Auditorium, Cambridge Massachusetts, on Wednesday, May 14, 1963 | [rule]

Collation: 12 leaves, stapled twice in centre.

p.[1] title-page; p.[2] copyright notice; pp.[3] – [21] text; p.[22] photograph of Graves and biographical note; p.[23] history of the lectures and list of lecturers; p.[24] blank.

22.9 × 15.3 cm. Bulk: 0.25 cm. White wove paper; all edges trimmed. Stiff white paper wrapper printed black; back only; front as title-page in white, with author's name in red and in the centre an eclipse with white corona with sun being Zeus in green; inner sides of both covers blank.

Price: Not for sale; distribution gratis. Number of copies: 4,500; 3,000 issued 7

October 1963; 1,500 issued 30 October 1963 by Massachusetts Institute of Technology Press.

Note: The design is by W. John Lees.

A103.1   A NEW POEM   [1963]

First edition:

A NEW POEM BY ROBERT GRAVES | WITH BEST WISHES | FOR A MERRY CHRISTMAS | FROM DOUBLEDAY

Collation: 2 leaves in a single fold.
   p.[1] title-page; p.[2] THE BIRD OF PARADISE; p.[3] illustration by Leonard Baskin; p.[4] copyright, illustrator and printer's notices.
   19.6 × 13.7 cm. Bulk: 0.06 cm. White wove paper printed in black.

Price: Not for sale; given by Doubleday as Christmas card. Number of copies unknown. Published December 1963.

Note: This is the first printing of "The Bird of Paradise."

A104   MAMMON   1964

First edition:

MAMMON | ORATION DELIVERED AT THE | LONDON SCHOOL OF ECONOMICS | AND POLITICAL SCIENCE | ON FRIDAY, 6 DECEMBER 1963 | BY | ROBERT GRAVES | THE LONDON SCHOOL OF ECONOMICS | AND POLITICAL SCIENCE | 1964

Collation: 14 leaves, sewn at centre with cover.
   p.[1] title-page; p.[2] copyright notice; pp.3–25 text; p.[26] printer's notice; pp.[27]–[28] blank.
   21.0 × 13.8 cm. Bulk: 0.2 cm. White wove paper; all edges trimmed. Bound in light blue paper covers; front printed as title-page; spine and back blank.

Price: Not for sale; supplied only to those present at the oration. Number of copies: 500. Published in March 1964.

A105   THE HEBREW MYTHS   [1964]

a. First edition:

HEBREW MYTHS | THE BOOK OF GENESIS | *by* | ROBERT GRAVES | *and* | RAPHAEL PATAI | MCMLXIV | DOUBLEDAY & COMPANY, INC. | GARDEN CITY, NEW YORK

Collation: 1–13^{12}, 156 leaves.

p.[1] HEBREW MYTHS | THE BOOK OF GENESIS; p.[2] blank; pp.3–4 lists of books by Graves and Patai; p.[5] title-page; p.[6] LC card, copyright, printing and edition notices; pp.7–8 CONTENTS; p.[9] HEBREW MYTHS | THE BOOK OF GENESIS; p.[10] blank; pp.11–19 INTRODUCTION; p.[20] blank; pp.21–279 text, with pp.[123, 131, 239] being maps; p.[280] blank; pp.281–294 ABBREVIATIONS, SOURCES AND ANNOTATED BIBLIOGRAPHY; pp.295–311 INDEX; p.[312] blank.

23.4 × 15.3 cm. Bulk: 2.4/3.1 cm. White wove paper; top and bottom edges trimmed. White wove endpapers printed deep mustard with designs of facing dragons; inner sides both blank. Bound in light grey cloth; back blank; front stamped with a scroll in blue, the unrolled portion forming a box inside which is stamped in gold: HEBREW MYTHS | The Book of Genesis; spine stamped with solid blue rectangular box stamped in gold: HEBREW | MYTHS | · | *Robert* | *Graves* | *&* | *Raphael* | *Patai* | [at bottom, outside of box:] DOUBLEDAY

Price: $4.95. Number of copies: 6,500. Published 20 March 1964 in white dust-jacket printed in grey, blue and mustard-gold.

Note: Printed in the U.S.
This book has been translated into Hebrew, Hungarian, Italian and Slovenian.

A105b. English issue ([1964]):

HEBREW MYTHS | THE BOOK OF GENESIS | *by* | ROBERT GRAVES | *and* | RAPHAEL PATAI | [publisher's emblem] | CASSELL . LONDON

Collation: [A]⁴ B–U⁸, 156 leaves.
Remainder as A105a except p.[6] publisher's, copyright, publication and printer's notices.

24.6 × 15.3 cm. Bulk: 2.8/3.6 cm. White wove paper; all edges trimmed. White wove endpapers. Bound in bright blue cloth; front blank; back blind-stamped with a script *L* near spine at bottom; spine stamped in gold: [heavy rule] | [light rule] | Hebrew | Myths | ROBERT | GRAVES & | RAPHAEL | PATAI | [light rule] | heavy rule] | CASSELL

Price: 36s. Number of copies: 4,022. Published 8 October 1964 in slick white dust-jacket printed in black and blue with multicoloured illustration of Adam and Eve on front.

Notes: Impression: 2nd, 17 May 1965 (3,150 copies).
Printed in Great Britain.

A105c. Second American impression ([1966]):

[all flush right:] [stylized sunflower design] Hebrew Myths: | The Book of Genesis | Robert Graves and Raphael Patai | McGraw-Hill Book Company | New York

Collation: 160 leaves, glued at spine.
p.[1] blurbs; p.[2] blank; p.[3] HEBREW MYTHS | THE BOOK OF GENESIS; p.[4] blank; p.[5] title-page; p.[6] copyright, edition and LC card notices; pp.7–8 CONTENTS; p.[9] HEBREW MYTHS | THE BOOK OF GENESIS; p.[10] blank;

pp.11–19 INTRODUCTION; p.[20] blank; pp.21–279 text, with pp.[123, 131, 239] being maps and pp.[196, 209, 220] unnumbered; p.[280] blank; pp.281–294 notes; pp.295–311 INDEX; p.[312] blank; p.[313] list of books by Graves; p.[314] list of books by Patai; pp.[315]–[320] blank.

20.2 × 13.6 cm. Bulk: 1.5 cm. White wove paper; all edges trimmed. Bound in white paper covers printed in blue, green and red geometric design.

Price: $2.95. Number of copies: 10,000 (in four printings). Published in September 1966.

A105d. Third American impression [1983]:

[all set flush right:] Hebrew Myths: | The Book of Genesis | Robert Graves and Raphael Patai | Greenwich House | Distributed by Crown Publishers, Inc. | New York

Collation: [1]–[10]^{16}, 160 leaves.

p.[1] Hebrew Myths: | The Book of Genesis; p.[2] blank; p.[3] title-page; p.[4] copyright, rights reservation, arrangement, manufacturing, LC and ISBN notices; pp.5–7 CONTENTS; p.[8] blank; p.[9] Hebrew Myths: | The Book of Genesis; p.[10] blank; pp.11–19 INTRODUCTION; p.[20] blank; pp.21–279 text, with pp.[123, 131, 239] being maps and pp.[196, 209, 220] unnumbered; p.[280] blank; p.[280] ABBREVIATIONS, | SOURCES | AND | ANNOTATED | BIBLIOGRAPHY; p.[281] blank; pp.283–296 notes; p. [297] INDEX; p.[298] blank; pp.299–315 index; pp.[316]–[320] blank.

22.7 × 14.8 cm. Bulk: 1.5/2.3 cm. White wove paper; all edges trimmed. White wove endpapers. Bound in navy blue cloth; front blank; back stamped in gold, lower right: ISBN 0-517-413663; spine stamped in gold, down spine: Hebrew Myths [vertical rule] [two lines:] The Book | of Genesis [vertical rule] [remainder upright:] Graves | & | Patai | GREENWICH | HOUSE

Price: undetermined. Number of copies undetermined. Published in 1983 in white dust-jacket printed in tan, red and black.

Note: Although much of this book appears to be a photographic reprint of earlier editions, it appears to be sufficiently different to consitute a separate issue.

A106   COLLECTED SHORT STORIES   1964

a. First edition:

Robert Graves | [swelled rule] | COLLECTED | SHORT | STORIES | DOUBLEDAY & COMPANY, INC. | GARDEN CITY, NEW YORK | 1964

Collation: [1]^{12} 2–7^{12} [8]–[14]^{12}, 168 leaves.

p.[i] COLLECTED SHORT STORIES; p.[ii] blank; pp.[iii]–iv list of books by Graves; p.[v] title-page; p.[vi] acknowledgement, LC card, copyright, rights reservation, printing and edition notices; pp.[vii]–viii CONTENTS; pp.[ix]–x [flush left:] INTRODUCTION; p.[xi] COLLECTED SHORT STORIES; p.[xii] blank; pp.[1]–323 text, with pp.[1, 133, 175] being section headings, pp.[2, 132, 134, 176] being blank and pp.[3, 25, 37, 43, 48, 54, 58, 63, 68, 71, 80, 85, 90, 95, 100, 119, 135, 141, 154, 177, 183, 189, 202, 208, 221, 226, 250, 265, 286, 302] being unnumbered; p.[324] blank.

20.7 × 13.6 cm. Bulk: 2.4/2.9 cm. White wove paper; top and bottom edges trimmed. White wove endpapers. Bound in grey cloth; front and back blank; spine printed, top to bottom: [near front:] ROBERT | [near back, parallel to preceding line:] GRAVES | [in blue, near front:] COLLECTED | [near back, parallel to preceding line:] SHORT STORIES | [upright:] DOUBLEDAY

Price: $4.95. Number of copies: 7,000 (in two printings). Published 17 April 1964 in white dust-jacket printed in grey, black, blue and chartreuse.

Contents: Introduction – ENGLISH STORIES: The Shout – Old Papa Johnson – Treacle Tart – The Full Length – Earth to Earth – Period Piece – Week-End at Cwm Tatws [in contents: Cwn] – He Went Out to Buy a Rhine – Kill Them! Kill Them! – The French Thing – A Man May Not Marry His … – An Appointment for Candlemas – The Abominable Mr Gunn – Harold Vesey at the Gates of Hell – Christmas Truce – You Win, Houdini! – ROMAN STORIES: Epics Are Out of Fashion – The Apartment House – The Myconian – MAJORCAN STORIES: They say … They Say – 6 Valiant Bulls 6 – A Bicycle in Majorca – The Five Godfathers – Evidence of Affluence – God Grant Your Honour Many Years – The Viscountess and the Short-Haired Girl – A Toast to Ava Gardner – The Lost Chinese – She Landed Yesterday – The Whitaker Negroes

Notes: Printed in the U.S.
This collection has been translated into Polish and Romanian.

A106b. English issue ([1965]):

Robert Graves | [swelled rule] | COLLECTED | SHORT | STORIES | [publisher's emblem] | CASSELL . LONDON *Collation:* [1] – [9]^{16} [10]^8 [11]^{16}, 168 leaves.

p.[*i*] COLLECTED SHORT STORIES | [blurb (14 ll.)]; p.[*ii*] blank; pp.[*iii*] – [*iv*] list of books by Graves; p.[*v*] title-page; p.[*vi*] acknowledgement, copyright, rights reservation, publication and printer's notices; remainder as A106a.

19.5 × 13.2 cm. Bulk: 2.4/3.0 cm. White wove paper; all edges trimmed. White wove endpapers. Bound in medium blue cloth-simulated boards; front and back blank; spine stamped in gold: [heavy rule] | [light rule] | Collected | Short | Stories | ROBERT | GRAVES | [light rule] | [heavy rule] | CASSELL

Price: 25s. Number of copies: 3,000. Published 18 November 1965 in white dust-jacket printed in slate blue, drab gold and black.

Notes: Impressions: 2nd, November 1965 (2,000 copies); 3rd, 1966 (2,000 copies); 4th, 1971 (number of copies unknown).
'The Apartment House' of A106a is here called 'The Tenement: A Vision of Imperial Rome'.
Printed in Great Britain.

A106c. Second English edition ([1968]):

ROBERT GRAVES | *Collected Short Stories* | [publisher's emblem] | PENGUIN BOOKS

Collation: [1]^{12} 2^{12} 3–6^{10} 7–8^{12} 9–12^{10} 13–14^{12}, 152 leaves.

p.[1] PENGUIN BOOKS | 2881 | COLLECTED SHORT STORIES | OF ROBERT GRAVES and biographical note; p.[2] blank; p.[3] title-page; p.[4] publisher's, publication, acknowledgement, printer's and sales limitation notices; pp.[5]–[6] CONTENTS; p.[7] INTRODUCTION; p.[8] blank; p.[9] section title; p.[10] blank; pp.[11]12–300 text; with pp.[31, 42, 47, 57, 61, 65, 69, 72, 80, 84, 89, 94, 99, 116, 131, 136, 148, 167, 169, 174, 179, 191, 196, 208, 212, 234, 248, 268, 282] unnumbered and pp.[128, 130, 132, 168] blank; pp.[301]–[304] publisher's advertisements.

18.0 × 11.3 cm. Bulk: 1.4 cm. White wove paper; all edges trimmed. Bound in white paper covers printed in black, orange and green.

Price: 30p. Number of copies unknown. Published in October 1968.

Notes: Impressions: 2nd, January 1971; 3rd, 1978; 4th, 1979; 5th, 1984 (copies: 10,000); 6th, 1986 (copies: 4,000).

The 2nd and 3rd impressions were issued in the United States by Viking.

In the 3rd impression the title was changed to *The Shout and Other Stories* with consequent changes in the contents of pp.[1]–[3]. It would appear that in the United Kingdom the front cover was changed to a colour photograph of Alan Bates shouting and a colour photograph of Bates and Susannah York was added to the back cover, while in the United States the cover has an illustration of Bates shouting in grey, black and orange by Neil Stuart;the claim: NOW A STUNNING FILM is on the front cover on both sides of the Atlantic. With the 5th impression the title was changed back to *Collected Short Stories* and the size changed to 19.8 × 12.9 cm.; bulk 1.7 cm., and the John Aldridge painting of Graves from the National Portrait Gallery was used on the cover.

A107   MAN DOES, WOMAN IS   1964

a. First edition:

ROBERT GRAVES | [light rule] | MAN DOES, | WOMAN IS | 1964 | [publisher's emblem] | CASSELL . LONDON

Collation: [A]^{10} B–D^{8} E/E$^{*2/8}$, 44 leaves.

pp.[i]–[ii] blank; p.[iii] MAN DOES, WOMAN IS | 1964; p.[iv] blank; p.[v] title-page; p.[vi] publisher's, copyright, publication and printer's notices; p.[vii] FOREWORD; p.[viii] blank; pp.[ix]–[xi] CONTENTS; p.[xii] blank; p.[1] XV; p.[2] blank; pp.3–26 text; p.[27] XVI; p.[28] blank; pp.29–53 text; p.[54] blank; p.[55] XVII; p.[56] blank; pp.57–74 text; pp.[75]–[76] blank.

21.5 × 15.0 cm. Bulk: 0.8/1.4 cm. White wove paper; all edges trimmed. White wove endpapers. Bound in ultramarine cloth; front and back blank; spine stamped in gold, bottom to top: *Cassell Robert Graves* MAN DOES, WOMAN IS

Price: 16s. Number of copies: 4,010. Published 17 April 1964 in white dust-jacket printed in black and French blue.

Contents: Foreword – XV: A Time of Waiting – Expect Nothing – No Letter – The Why of the Weather – In Time – Fire Walker – Deed of Gift – At Best, Poets – She is No Liar – A Last Poem – The Pearl – The Leap – Bank Account – Judgement of Paris – Man Does, Woman Is – The Ample Garden – To Myrto About Herself – The Three-Faced – Dazzle of Darkness – Myrrhina – Food of the Dead – Eurydice – To Beguile and Betray – I Will Write – XVI: Bird of Paradise – The Metaphor – Song: A Phoenix Flame – Secrecy – Joseph and Mary – An East Wind – Dance of Words – A Blind Arrow – The Oleaster – The Septuagenarian – *Non Cogunt Astra* – Song: Sword and Rose – Endless Pavement – In Disguise – A Measure of Casualness – In Time of Absence – The Green Castle – Not to Sleep – The Hearth – That Other World – The Beds of Grainne and Diarmuid – Rain of Brimstone – Consortium of Stones – The Black Goddess – XVII: Broken Neck – O – Woman of Greece – The Colours of Night – Between Trains – To the Teumessian Vixen – The Hung Wu Vase – *La Mejicana* – Lamia in Love – After the Flood – A Late Arrival – Song: With No Return – All I Tell You From My Heart – The Undead

Notes: Impression: 2nd, January 1965 (number of copies unknown).

'The Colours of Night' was reprinted in a Spanish translation in *El Vol De L'Alosa Els Poetes Mallorquins A Joan Miro'* (Mallorca, 1973).

A107b. Limited issue (1964):

Title-page as A107a.

Collation as A107a.

Remainder as A107a except p.[i] *Of this edition | there have been printed | 175 copies for sale, numbered 1–175 | and 26 copies not for sale, lettered A–Z | all signed by the author | this is No.* [number written in] | [signature of Graves]

21.6 × 14.7 cm. Bulk: 0.8/1.4 cm. Buff laid paper; all edges trimmed; watermarked with crown and a script Glastonbury. Buff laid endpapers. Bound in buff linen with ultramarine quarter cloth spine with gold rules front and back near buff cloth; front and back otherwise blank; spine stamped in gold, bottom to top: *Cassell Robert Graves* MAN DOES, WOMAN IS

Price: 50s. Number of copies: 201. Published 18 June 1964 in transparent glassine wrapper.

A107c. American issue (1964):

ROBERT GRAVES | [light rule] | MAN DOES, | WOMAN IS | 1964 | Doubleday & Company, Inc. | Garden City, New York

Collation: 48 leaves, glued at spine.

pp.[i]–[iv] blank; p.[v] MAN DOES, WOMAN IS | 1964; p.[vi] blank; pp.[vii]–[viii] list of books by Graves; p.[ix] title-page; p.[x] *ACKNOWLEDGMENTS* and LC card, copyright, rights reservation, printing and edition notices; p.[xi] FOREWORD; p.[xii] blank; pp.[xiii]–[xv] CONTENTS; p.[xvi] blank; p.[1]–74 as A107a; pp.[75]–[80] blank.

20.7 × 14.0 cm. Bulk: 0.6/1.2 cm. White wove paper; top and bottom edges trimmed. Cream wove endpapers. Bound in three-quarter black cloth with slick black cloth spine; front and back blank; spine stamped in silver, top to bottom: Man Does, Woman Is *by Robert Graves* Doubleday

Price: $3.95. Number of copies: 4,500. Published 20 November 1964 in white dust-jacket printed in black, scarlet and lake.

A108   EL FENOMENO DEL TURISMO   1964

First edition:

ROBERT GRAVES | EL FENOMENO | DEL TURISMO | ATENEO | MADRID | 1964 | XXV Aniversario | de la Paz Expañola

Collation: [1]⁸ [2]⁴ [3]⁸, 20 leaves.
   2 pp. blank; p.[i] EL FENOMENO DEL TURISMO; p.[ii] blank; p.[iii] title-page; p.[iv] [entire flush right:] Conferencia pronunciada en el Ate- | neo de Madrid el 3 de marzo de 1964; pp.1–31 text; p.[32] blank; p.[33] ACABÓSE DE IMPRIMIR EN MADRID, | EN LOS TALLERES GRÁFICOS DE | BOLAÑOS Y AGUILAR, S. L., EL | DÍA 18 DE JUNIO DE 1964; p.[34] blank.
   19.3 × 11.5 cm. Bulk: 0.3 cm. White wove paper; all edges trimmed. Bound in white paper covers printed in medium cobalt blue and black.

Price: 20 ptas. Number of copies undetermined. Published 3 March 1964.

Notes: This book is no. 21 of the Coleccion Ateneo.
   'Postscript, 1965' in *Majorca Observed* [A112a] is largely a translation of this speech.

A109   ORATIO CREWEIANA   1964

First edition:

ORATIO | CREWEIANA | [ornament] | MDCCCCLXIV

Collation: 8 leaves, stapled twice at centre.
   p.[1] title-page; pp.2, 4, 6, 8, 10, 12 text of oration in Latin; pp.3, 5, 7, 9, 11, 13 paraphrase in English; p.[14] printer's notice; pp.[15] – [16] blank.
   21.5 × 13.8 cm. Bulk: 0.08 cm. Cream-white wove paper; all edges trimmed.

Price: Not for sale; distributed gratis. Number of copies: 1,400. Published 24 June 1964 by Oxford University Press.

A110   ANN AT HIGHWOOD HALL   [1964]

a. First edition:

[entire related to cut in green and black of Ann having her portrait painted] | [three lines in rectangular white box:] ANN AT HIGHWOOD | HALL | *Poems for Children* | [remainder in rectangular white box:] [broken rule] | *by* | [broken rule] | *Robert Graves* | *Illustrated by* | *Edward Ardizzone* | [broken rule] | *Cassell – London*

Collation: [A]⁸ B–C⁸, 24 leaves.

p.[i] *Ann at Highwood Hall*; p.[ii] blank; p.[iii] title-page; p.[iv] publisher's, copyright, publication and printer's notices; p.[v] *Contents*; p.[vi] blank; p.[vii] *To my grandchildren* | Georgina and David Graves | *with love*; p.[viii] blank; pp.1–38[39] text, with pp.[2–3, 4, 6–7, 9–12, 15–16, 19–20, 22, 24, 26, 28–33, 35, 37] being unnumbered; p.[40] illustration.

21.6 × 16.2 cm. Bulk: 0.4/1.1 cm. White wove paper; all edges trimmed. White wove endpapers. Bound in powder-blue cloth-simulated boards; front and back blank; spine stamped in gold, bottom to top: CASSELL Ann at Highwood Hall ROBERT GRAVES

Price: 13s.6d. Number of copies: 5,000. Published 8 October 1964 in white dust-jacket printed in black, blue, green and orange-pink.

Contents: Ann at Highwood Hall – St Valentine's Day – George II and the Chinese Emperor – I Have a Little Cough, Sir – The Sewing Basket – Joseph and Jesus – Caroline and Charles

A110b. American issue ([1964]):

[entire related to cut in green and black of Ann having her portrait painted] | [three lines in rectangular white box:] ANN AT HIGHWOOD | HALL | *Poems for Children* | [remainder in rectangular white box:] [broken rule] | *by* | [broken rule] | *Robert Graves* | *Illustrated by* | *Edward Ardizzone* | [broken rule] | DOUBLEDAY & COMPANY, INC. | GARDEN CITY, NEW YORK

Collation: [1] – [3]⁸, 24 leaves.

p.[1] *Ann at Highwood Hall*; p.[2] blank; p.[3] title-page; p.[4] LC card, copyright, rights reservation, printer's and edition notices; p.[5] *To my grandchildren* | Georgina and David Graves | *with love*; p.[6] blank p.[7] *Contents*; p.[8] blank; pp.1–46[47] text, with pp.[10, 12, 14–15, 17–20, 23–24, 27–28, 30, 32, 34, 36–41, 43, 45] being unnumbered; p.48 biographical notes on Graves and Ardizzone.

23.4 × 15.4 cm. Bulk: 0.4/1.0 cm. White wove paper; all edges trimmed. Blue wove endpapers, sides white. Bound in yellow-green cloth; front and back blank; spine stamped in gold, top to bottom: *Robert Graves* ANN AT HIGHWOOD HALL *Doubleday*

Price: $2.95. Number of copies undetermined. Published in 1964 in white dust-jacket printed in black, blue, green and orange-pink.

Note: This edition was printed in the U.S.

Carl Hahn reports a 'Doubleday Prebound Edition' which is bound in pictorial papercovered boards (not seen).

A111   MAMMON AND THE BLACK GODDESS   [1965]

a. First edition:

MAMMON AND THE | BLACK GODDESS | by | ROBERT GRAVES | [publisher's emblem] | CASSELL . LONDON

Collation: [A]⁸ B–L⁸, 88 leaves.

p.[i] MAMMON AND THE BLACK GODDESS; p.[ii] blank; p.[iii] title-page; p.[iv] publisher's, copyright, publication, acknowledgement and printer's notices; p.[v] table of contents; p.[vi] blank; p.[vii] *Foreword*; p.[viii] blank; pp.[1]–165 text, with pp.[1, 27, 53, 99, 115, 141] being section-headings and pp.[2, 26, 28, 52, 54, 100, 114, 116, 140, 142] being blank; pp.[166]–[168] blank.

21.4 × 13.9 cm. Bulk: 1.8/2.4 cm. White wove paper; all edges trimmed. White wove endpapers. Bound in slick grey cloth; front and back blank; spine stamped in gold, bottom to top: [at bottom, upright:] CASSELL | [up spine:] Robert Graves [ornament] [inside double rule rectangular box:] MAMMON AND THE BLACK GODDESS [ornament]

Price: 21s. Number of copies: 3,000. Published 8 March 1965 in grey dust-jacket printed in black and sea-green.

Contents: Foreword – Mammon – Nine Hundred Iron Chariots – Three Oxford Lectures on Poetry (Some Instances of Poetic Vulgarity; Technique in Poetry; The Poet in a Valley of Dry Bones) – Real Women – Moral Principles in Translation – Intimations of the Black Goddess

Note: Printed in Great Britain.

A111b. American issue (1965):

MAMMON AND THE | BLACK GODDESS | by | ROBERT GRAVES | Doubleday & Company, Inc., Garden City, New York | 1965

Collation: [1]–[11]⁸, 88 leaves.
Remainder as A111a, except p.[iv] LC card, copyright, printing and edition notices.
20.8 × 13.8 cm. Bulk: 1.1/1.6 cm. White wove paper; top and bottom edges trimmed. Blue wove endpapers, inner sides white. Bound in black cloth with light blue quarter-cloth spine; front and back blank; spine stamped, top to bottom: [in blue:] ROBERT GRAVES [in black:] MAMMON AND THE BLACK GODDESS [in blue:] DOUBLEDAY

Price: $3.95. Number of copies: 4,000. Published 18 June 1965 in white dust-jacket printed in light blue and black.

Note: Printed in the U.S.

A112   MAJORCA OBSERVED   [1965]

a. First edition:

[entire flush left:] MAJORCA OBSERVED | by Robert Graves | & Paul Hogarth | [publisher's emblem] | CASSELL – LONDON

Collation: [1]–[10]⁸, 80 leaves.
2 pp. blank; p.[1] [flush right:] MAJORCA OBSERVED; p.[2] frontispiece; p.[3] title-page; p.[4] publisher's, copyright, designer's and printer's notices; p.[5] [flush left:] Contents; p.[6] illustration; pp.7–150 text, with pp.[55, 83, 91, 99, 109, 117, 125,

133] being section-headings, pp.[25], 31, [40] – [41], 42, 45, [50], 59, 73, 79, [94], [123], 128, [131] containing text and illustrations and pp.[10, 12, 15–16, 18–20, 24, 27–28, 30, 32, 35–38, 43–44, 46, 48, 52–54, 56, 63–64, 66, 69–70, 74, 76, 80–82, 84, 89–90, 92, 97–98, 100, 104, 106, 108, 110, 115–116, 118, 121, 124, 126, 132, 134, 136, 140, 143, 146, 148] being illustrations only; pp.[151] – [152] illustrations; pp.[153] – [158] blank.

24.1 × 16.7 cm. Bulk: 1.3/2.1 cm. White laid paper; all edges trimmed. White wove endpapers. Bound in rust cloth; front and back blank; spine stamped in gold: Robert | Graves | & Paul | Hogarth | [up spine:] MAJORCA OBSERVED | CASSELL

Price: 36s. Number of copies: 4,935. Published 13 May 1965 in white dust-jacket printed in black and light orange-buff.

Contents: Why I Live in Majorca 1953 – Postscript, 1965 – A Dead Branch of the Tree of Israel – Trín-Trín-Trín – School Life in Majorca 1955 – Bulletin of the College of St Modesto of Bobbio – God Grant Your Honour Many Years – Thy Servant and God's – Ditching in a Fishless Sea – George Sand in Majorca

Note: Both A112a and A112b were printed in England.
This book has been translated into Swedish.

A112b. American issue ([1965]):

MAJORCA OBSERVED | by Robert Graves | & Paul Hogarth | DOUBLEDAY & COMPANY, INC. | GARDEN CITY NEW YORK

Collation as A112a.
Remainder as A112a, except p.[6] publisher's, copyright, designer's and printing notices.
Size, bulk, paper, endpapers and binding as A112a, except spine has DOUBLEDAY for CASSELL.

Price: $10.00. Number of copies: 1,624. Published 17 September 1965 in dust-jacket as A112a.

A113   LOVE RESPELT   [1965]

a. First edition:

[entire enclosed within abstract branch and circle design:] [two lines flush left:] Love | Respelt | by | [flush left:] Robert Graves | [rule] | [flush left:] Cassell, London

Collation: [1] – [3]⁸, 24 leaves.

pp.[1] – [2] blank; p.[3] Of this book | there have been printed | 250 copies, numbered 1–250 | all signed by the author | This is No. [number written in] | [signature of Graves]; p.[4] blank; p.[5] [two lines flush left:] Love | Respelt | by | [flush left:] Robert Graves | [rule]; p.[6] blank; p.[7] title-page; p.[8] publisher's, copyright, publication and printer's notices; p.[9] table of contents; p.[10] blank; pp.[11] – [42] text, with pp.[11, 14, 19, 34] having illustrations or designs as well as text; p.[43] design; p.[44] blank; p.[45] text; pp.[46] – [48] blank.

21.5 × 17.0 cm. Bulk: 0.4/1.1 cm. White laid paper; all edges trimmed. White laid endpapers. Bound in three-quarter grey pepper-and-salt cloth with slick black cloth spine; front and back blank; spine stamped in gold script, bottom to top: Cassell Love Respelt Robert Graves

Price: 50s. Number of copies: 250 plus 30 copies out of series. Published 16 July 1965 in white dust-jacket printed in black.

Contents: 1. The Red Shower – 2. Above the Edge of Doom – 3. Wild Cyclamen – 4. Gift of Sight – 5. Batxóca – 6. The Snap-Comb Wilderness – 7. Change – 8. A Court of Love – 9. Black – 10. Between Hyssop and Axe – 11. Gold and Malachite – 12. Ambience – 13. The Vow – 14. The Frog and the Golden Ball – 15. Those Who Came Short – 16. Whole Love – 17. This Holy Month – 18. The Blow – 19. The Impossible – 20. The Fetter – 21. Iron Palace – 22. True Joy – 23. Tomorrow's Envy of Today – 24. The Hidden Garden – 25. The Wedding – 26. What Will Be, Is – 27. Son Altesse – 28. Everywhere Is Here – 29. Song: The Far Side of Your Moon – 30. Deliverance – 31. Conjunction – 32. Nothing Now Astonishes – 33. Postscript

Note: The printing throughout, except for pp.[3, 8], is a reproduction of Graves' MSS.

The illuminations are by Aemilia Laraçuen.

There is a reprint of 18 copies, lettered A–R, not for sale.

A113b. First American edition (1966):

LOVE RESPELT | [flourish] | ROBERT GRAVES | 1966 | DOUBLEDAY & COMPANY, INC. | GARDEN CITY, NEW YORK

Collation: [1]^4 [2]^{12} [3]^8, 24 leaves.

p.[i] LOVE RESPELT; p.[ii] portrait of Graves by Aemilia Laraçuen; p.[iii] title-page; p.[iv] LC card, copyright, printing and edition notices; p.[v] FOREWORD; p.[vi] blank; pp.vii–viii CONTENTS; p.[1] XVIII; p.[2] blank; pp.3–35 text; p.[36] blank; p.[37] flourish; pp.38–44 text; pp.[45]–[48] blank.

20.9 × 13.6 cm. Bulk: 0.1/1.1 cm. White wove paper; all edges trimmed. White wove endpapers. Bound in grey-brown cloth; front and back blank; spine stamped in gold, top to bottom: ROBERT GRAVES [fleuron] [title in dark brown rectangular box:] LOVE RESPELT [fleuron] DOUBLEDAY.

Price: $2.95. Number of copies: 4,000. Published 4 April 1966 in white dust-jacket printed in red, green, blue, grey and black.

Contents: The Red Shower – Above the Edge of Doom – Wild Cyclamen – Gift of Sight – Batxóca – The Snap-Comb Wilderness – A Shift of Scene – Change – A Court of Love – Black – Between Hyssop and Axe – *Son Altesse* – Gold and Malachite – Ambience – The Vow – The Frog and the Golden Ball – Those Who Came Short – Whole Love – This Holy Month – The Impossible – The Fetter – Iron Palace – True Joy – Tomorrow's Envy of Today – The Hidden Garden – The Wedding – Everywhere Is Here – What Will Be, Is – *Song:* The Far Side of Your Moon – Deliverance – Conjunction – Nothing Now Astonishes – Postscript – The Gorge – Arrears of Moonlight – The Tangled Thread – Lure of Murder – Fortunate Child – Loving True, Flying Blind – Dancing Flame.

A114   COLLECTED POEMS 1965   1965

First edition:

ROBERT GRAVES | COLLECTED | POEMS | 1965 | [publisher's emblem] | CASSELL . LONDON

Collation: [A]^8 B–2E^8 2F^4 2G^8, 236 leaves.

pp.[i] – [ii] blank; p.[iii] COLLECTED POEMS | 1965; p.[iv] blank; p.[v] title-page; p.[vi] publisher's, copyright, publication and printer's notices; pp.[vii] – [viii] FOREWORD; pp.[ix] – [xxii] CONTENTS; p.[1] I; p.[2] blank; pp.3–436 text, with pp.[31, 67, 87, 135, 151, 181, 199, 209, 237, 255, 277, 287, 311, 327, 353, 379, 403] being section headings and pp.[30, 32, 66, 68, 88, 134, 136, 152, 180, 182, 200, 208, 210, 236, 238, 256, 278, 288, 312, 328, 354, 380, 404] being blank; pp.[437] – [438] blank; p.[439] INDEX TO FIRST LINES OF POEMS; p.[440] blank; pp.441–449[450] index.

21.5 × 14.8 cm. Bulk: 2.9/3.6 cm. White wove paper; all edges trimmed. White wove endpapers. Bound in bright ultramarine cloth; back blank; front stamped in gold: COLLECTED | POEMS | 1965; spine stamped in gold: ROBERT | GRAVES | [rule] | COLLECTED | POEMS | 1965 | CASSELL

Price: 42s. Number of copies: 5,135. Published 23 September 1965 in white dust-jacket printed in black and purplish ultramarine.

Contents: Foreword – I: In the Wilderness – The Haunted House – Reproach – The Finding of Love – Rocky Acres – Outlaws – One Hard Look – A Frosty Night – Allie – Henry and Mary – Love Without Hope – What Did I Dream? – The Troll's Nosegay – The Hills of May – Lost Love – Vain and Careless – The Pier-Glass – Apples and Water – Angry Samson – Down – II: In Procession – Warning to Children – Alice – Richard Roe and John Doe – I'd Die for You – Ancestors – The Coronation Murder – Children of Darkness – The Cool Web – Love in Barrenness – Song of Contrariety – The Presence – The Land of Whipperginny – In No Direction – The Castle – Return – The Bards – Nobody – The Progress – Full Moon – Vanity – Pure Death – Sick Love – It Was All Very Tidy – III: Thief – The Furious Voyage – *Song*: Lift-Boy – The Next Time – Ulysses – The Succubus – The Reader over My Shoulder – The Legs – Gardener – Front Door Soliloquy – In Broken Images – Trudge, Body! – The Christmas Robin – On Rising Early – Flying Crooked – Fragment of a Lost Poem – Brother – IV: The Devil's Advice to Story-Tellers – Sea Side – Wm. Brazier – Welsh Incident – Interruption – Hell – Leda – Synthetic Such – The Florist Rose – Lost Acres – At First Sight – Down, Wanton, Down! – A Former Attachment – Nature's Lineaments – Time – The Philosopher – On Dwelling – Ogres and Pygmies – Single Fare – To Walk on Hills – To Bring the Dead to Life – To Evoke Posterity – Any Honest Housewife – Never Such Love – Certain Mercies – The Cuirassiers of the Frontier – The Laureate – A Jealous Man – The Cloak – The Foreboding – With Her Lips Only – The Halls of Bedlam – Or to Perish before Day – A Country Mansion – Lovers in Winter – Advocates – V: On Portents – The Terraced Valley – The Chink – The Ages of Oath – New Legends – Like Snow –

End of Play – The Climate of Thought – The Fallen Tower of Siloam – The Great-Grandmother – No More Ghosts – VI: A Love Story – Dawn Bombardment – The Shot – The Thieves – Lollocks – To Sleep – Despite and Still – The Suicide in the Copse – Frightened Men – The Oath – Language of the Seasons – Mid-Winter Waking – The Beach – The Villagers and Death – The Door – Under the Pot – Through Nightmare – To Lucia at Birth – Death by Drums – She Tells Her Love While Half Asleep – Theseus and Ariadne – Penthesileia – The Death Room – To Juan at the Winter Solstice – To Be Called a Bear – VII: My Name and I – 1805 – The Persian Version – The Weather of Olympus – Apollo of the Physiologists – The Oldest Soldier – Grotesques i–vi – Beauty in Trouble – Sirocco at Deyá – From the Embassy – VIII: The White Goddess – The Song of Blodeuwedd – Instructions to the Orphic Adept – Lament for Pasiphaë – Return of the Goddess – IX: Counting the Beats – The Young Cordwainer – Your Private Way – The Survivor – Questions in a Wood – Darien – The Portrait – Prometheus – The Straw – Cry Faugh! – Hercules at Nemea – Dialogue on the Headland – Liadan and Curithir – The Sea Horse – Cat-Goddesses – The Blue-Fly – A Lost Jewel – The Window Sill – Spoils – Rhea – X: The Face in the Mirror – Gratitude for a Nightmare – Friday Night – The Naked and the Nude – Woman and Tree – Forbidden Words – A Slice of Wedding Cake – A Plea to Boys and Girls – Nothing – Call It a Good Marriage – The Second-Fated – The Twin of Sleep – Around the Mountain – Leaving the Rest Unsaid – XI: Lyceia – Symptoms of Love – The Sharp Ridge – Under the Olives – The Visitation – Fragment – Apple Island – The Falcon Woman – Troughs of Sea – The Laugh – The Death Grapple – The Starred Coverlet – Patience – The Cure – Hag-Ridden – Turn of the Moon – The Secret Land – Seldom, Yet Now – XII: A Lost World: The Dangerous Gift – Twice of the Same Fever – Surgical Ward: Men – The Two Witches – The Quiet Glades of Eden – Joan and Darby – *Song*: Come, Enjoy Your Sunday! – XIII: Ruby and Amethyst – Recognition – Variables of Green – The Watch – Name Day – Uncalendared Love – The Meeting – Lack – Not at Home – Horizon – Golden Anchor – Lion Lover – Ibycus in Samos – Possessed – The Winged Heart – In Trance at a Distance – The Wreath – In Her Praise – A Restless Ghost – Between Moon and Moon – XIV: Beware, Madam! – The Cliff Edge – The Miller's Man – Acrobats – Ouzo Unclouded – The Broken Girth – Inkidoo and the Queen of Babel – Three Songs for the Lute: I. Truth is Poor Physic – II. In Her Only Way – III. Hedges Freaked With Snow – The Ambrosia of Dionysus and Semele – The Unnamed Spell – XV: A Time of Waiting – Expect Nothing – No Letter – The Why of the Weather – In Time – Fire Walker – Deed of Gift – At Best, Poets – She is No Liar – A Last Poem – The Pearl – The Leap – Bank Account – Judgement of Paris – Man Does, Woman Is – The Ample Garden – To Myrto About Herself – The Three-Faced – Dazzle of Darkness – Myrrhina – Food of the Dead – Eurydice – To Beguile and Betray – I Will Write – XVI: Bird of Paradise – The Metaphor – *Song*: A Phoenix Flame – Secrecy – Joseph and Mary – An East Wind – Dance of Words – A Blind Arrow – The Oleaster – The Septuagenarian – *Non Cogunt Astra* – *Song*: Sword and Rose – Endless Pavement – In Disguise – A Measure of Casualness – In Time of Absence – The Green Castle – Not to Sleep – The

Hearth – That Other World – The Beds of Grainne and Diarmuid – Consortium of Stones – The Black Goddess – XVII: Broken Neck – O – Woman of Greece – The Colours of Night – Between Trains – To the Teumessian Vixen – The Hung Wu Vase – *La Mejicana* – Lamia in Love – After the Flood – All I Tell You From My Heart – The Undead – Grace Notes – Good Night to the Old Gods – The Sweet-Shop Round the Corner – Double Bass – Descent into Hell – The Pardon – Point of No Return – XVIII: The Red Shower – Above the Edge of Doom – Wild Cyclamen – Gift of Sight – *Batxóca* – The Snap-Comb Wilderness – A Shift of Scene – Change – A Court of Love – Black – Between Hyssop and Axe – *Son Altesse* – Gold and Malachite – Ambience – The Vow – The Frog and the Golden Ball – Those Who Came Short – Whole Love – This Holy Month – The Impossible – The Fetter – Iron Palace – True Joy – Tomorrow's Envy of Today – The Hidden Garden – The Wedding – Everywhere is Here – What Will Be, Is – *Song*: The Far Side of Your Moon – Deliverance – Conjunction – Nothing Now Astonishes – Index of First Lines.

Note: An abridged Polish edition, *Wiersze*, based on this collection was published in 1965.

A115 SEVENTEEN POEMS MISSING FROM LOVE RESPELT 1966

First edition:

Robert | GRAVES | SEVENTEEN | POEMS | *MISSING FROM* | LOVE | RESPELT | PRIVATELY PRINTED | 1966

Collation: [1] – [3]^8, 24 leaves.
   2 pp. blank; p.[i] half-title; p.[ii] blank; p.[iii] title-page; p.[iv] copyright, printer's, distributor, series record and signature notices; p.v FOREWORD; p.[vi] blank; p.vii CONTENTS; p.[viii] blank; pp.1–17 text, with only the odd-numbered pages being paged; pp.[18] – [22] blank. Page numbers are enclosed in square brackets.
   25.4 × 16.4 cm. Bulk: 0.4/0.7 cm. White laid paper; no edges trimmed. White laid endpapers. Bound in paper boards with blue-grey wrapper jacket as cover. Back blank; front printed in black and *red*: *ROBERT* | *GRAVES* | SEVENTEEN | *POEMS* | MISSING FROM | *LOVE* | *RESPELT*; spine printed in red, top to bottom: ROBERT GRAVES / SEVENTEEN POEMS

Price: 63s. Number of copies: 330, 300 numbered and signed. Published 6 June 1966.

Contents: Cock in Pullet's Feathers – Dead Hand – Arrears of Moonlight – What Did You Say? – Lure of Murder – The Gorge – Ecstasy of Chaos – Stolen Jewel – The Eagre – The Snapped Thread – Fortunate Child – Loving True, Flying Blind – The Near Eclipse – Dancing Flame – Birth of Angels – Clothed in Silence – On Giving.

Notes: There is an orange illustration of a fragmenting sun at the foot of p.7[=13] by Aemilia Laraçuen.
   The contents of this edition were collected in A122, *Collected Poems, 1965–1968*.
   This edition was published by Bertram Rota, Ltd.

A116   TWO WISE CHILDREN   [1966]

a. First edition:

[7 lines in rectangular single-rule box, left of centre, flush left:] *Robert Graves* |
Two | Wise | Children | [bucket] | *Pictures by* | *Ralph Pinto* | [remainder centered:] *A
Harlin Quist Book*

Collation: [1] – [3]⁸, 24 leaves.

 p.[1] TWO WISE CHILDREN; p.[2] blank; p.[3] title-page; p.[4] dedication and
publisher's, LC card, copyright and printing notices; pp.[5] – [48] text and
illustrations.

 21.0 × 14.0 cm. Bulk: 0.3/0.9 cm. White wove paper; all edges trimmed. Dull
yellow-green wove endpapers. Bound in green paper-covered boards printed in
dark green; cloth spine stamped in gold, top to bottom: *Robert Graves* TWO WISE
CHILDREN QUIST

Price: $2.75. Number of copies undisclosed. Published in November 1966 in cream
dust-jacket printed in green, red, blue and black.

Note: Carl Hahn reports a variant binding which is full green cloth and the spine
lettering is in black. He believes that this was an 'institutional issue' (not seen).

A116b. First English edition ([1967]):

Title-page as A116a.

Remainder as A116a.
 21.0 × 14.0 cm. Bulk: 0.3/0.9 cm. Remainder as A116a, except spine: *Quist*

Price: 10s.6d. Number of copies undisclosed. Published in 1967 in cream dust-jacket
printed as A116a.

A117   POETIC CRAFT AND PRINCIPLE   [1967]

First edition:

POETIC CRAFT AND | PRINCIPLE | *Lectures and Talks by* | ROBERT GRAVES |
Professor of Poetry at Oxford University | [publisher's emblem] | CASSELL .
LONDON

Collation: [A]⁸ B–M⁸ N/N*²/⁴, 98 leaves.

 p.[i] POETIC CRAFT AND PRINCIPLE; p.[ii] blank; p.[iii] title-page; p.[iv]
publisher's, copyright, publication and printer's notices; p.[v] table of contents;
p.[vi] *Acknowledgement*; pp.vii – [viii] *Foreword*; p.[1] section title; p.[2] blank;
pp.3–194[195] text, with pp.[31, 63, 95, 123, 151, 181] being unnumbered and pp.[32,
64, 96, 122, 124, 152, 180, 182] being blank; p.[196] blank.

 21.5 × 13.5 cm. Bulk: 1.6/2.4 cm. White wove paper; all edges trimmed. White
wove endpapers. Bound in lake cloth; front and back blank; spine stamped in gold,
up spine, facing front: Robert Graves [remainder in double-rule rectangular box
with decorative ends:] POETIC CRAFT AND PRINCIPLE

Price: 30s. Number of copies unknown. Published April 1967 in grey dust-jacket printed in black and magenta.

Contents: Foreword – Oxford Chair of Poetry 1964: Lecture One – Lecture Two – Lecture Three – Oxford Chair of Poetry 1965: Lecture One – Lecture Two – Lecture Three – The Word 'Romantic'

A118   COLOPHON TO LOVE RESPELT   1967

Robert | GRAVES |[swelled rule] | COLOPHON | TO | LOVE | RESPELT | PRIVATELY PRINTED | 1967

Collation: [1]⁴ [2] – [3]⁸, 20 leaves.
    p.[1] title page; p.[2] copyright, printer's and distributor's notices and copy number and signature of Graves; p. half-title; p.[ii] blank; p.[iii] CONTENTS; p.[iv] blank; p.v FOREWORD; p.[vi] blank; pp.1–32 text [page numbers are enclosed in square brackets].
    25.4 × 16.5 cm. Bulk: 0.4/0.7 cm. White laid paper; no edges trimmed. White laid endpapers. Bound in paper boards with dark green wrapper jacket as cover. Back blank; front printed in black and *red*: ROBERT | GRAVES | *COLOPHON* | *TO* | LOVE | RESPELT; spine printed, top to bottom: ROBERT GRAVES / COLOPHON TO LOVE RESPELT

Price: 63s. Number of copies: 386 (350 numbered and signed). Published 10 July 1967.

Contents: Foreword – The P'eng that was a K'un – Like Owls – In Perspective – The Utter Rim – Unicorn and the White Doe – Bower Bird – Mist – The Word – Perfectionists – Prison Walls – A Dream of Hell – Our Self – Bites and Kisses – Sun-Face and Moon-Face – Freehold – The Necklace – A Bracelet – Blackening Sky – Blessed Sun – Lion Gentle – *Song*: The Palm Tree – Spite of Mirrors – Pride of Love – Hooded Flame – Injuries – Her Brief Withdrawal – The Crane – Strangeness.

Notes: These poems were later collected in A122 *Poems 1965–1968*.
    Printed at the Stellar Press by Bill Hummerstone; distributed by Bertram Rota Ltd.

A119   SIXTEEN POEMS   1967

[all flush left:] SIXTEEN POEMS | BY ROBERT GRAVES | COLLEGE OF TECHNOLOGY | OXFORD | 1967

Collation: [1] – [3]⁸, 24 leaves.
    p.[1] [flush left:] SIXTEEN POEMS; p.[2] blank; p.[3] title-page; p.[4] blank; p.[5] table of contents; p.[6] blank; pp.[7] – [22] text; p.[23] blank; p.[24] [unjustified right margin:] Designed, printed and bound in an edition of 75 copies | at the College of Technology, Oxford, 1967 by kind | permission of Mr. Robert Graves. | With the exception of 'In Single Syllables' and 'The Intrusion' published in *More Poems 1961*, This selection | has been made from *Collected Poems 1965* Robert Graves.

18.4 × 12.2 cm. Bulk: 0.2/0.4 cm. Grey laid paper, watermarked with a crown and Abbey Mills | Greenfield; all edges trimmed. White laid endpapers, watermarked as text paper. Bound in dark reddish-violet cloth; back and spine blank; front stamped in gold, flush left: SIXTEEN POEMS:

Price: undetermined. Number of copies: 75. Published October 1967.

Contents: Symptoms of Love – The Cure – Troughs of Sea – The Death Grapple – The Falcon Woman – The Starred Coverlet – Apple Island – Under the Olives – Patience – The Laugh – In Single Syllables – The Intrusion – Hag-Ridden – Seldom Yet Now – The Visitation – The Sharp Ridge.

A120   THE RUBAIYYAT OF OMAR KHAYAAM   [1967]

a. First edition:

THE RUBAIYYAT OF | OMAR KHAYAAM | A new translation | with critical commentaries | by | ROBERT GRAVES | and | OMAR ALI-SHAH | CASSELL . LONDON

Collation: [1] – [6]⁸, 48 leaves.
    p.[i] THE RUBAIYYAT OF | OMAR KHAYAAM; p.[ii] blank; p.[iii] title-page; p.[iv] publisher's, copyright, publication and printing notices; p.[v] CONTENTS; p.[vi] blank; pp.1–31 THE FITZ-OMAR CULT | ROBERT GRAVES; pp.32–45[46] HISTORICAL PREFACE | OMAR ALI-SHAH; p.[47] THE RUBAIYYAT; p.[48] NOTE; pp.49–76 text; pp.77–81 NOTES; pp.82–83 TWO COMPARATIVE RENDERINGS; pp.84–86 bibliographies; pp.[87] – [90] blank.
    21.5 × 15.1 cm. Bulk: 0.8/1.5 cm. White wove paper; all edges trimmed. Light sage-green wove endpapers, watermarked: ja-Bülten and a blade of grass. Bound in new-blue cloth; front and back blank; spine stamped in gold, bottom to top: *Cassell The Rubaiyyat of* OMAR KHAYAAM.

Price: 21s. Number of copies unknown. Published 9 November 1967 in dark buff laid dust-jacket printed in blue and black and watermarked with a crown and: Lonbury.

Note: Extracts were published in the *Weekend Telegraph* on 13 October 1967.

A120b. First American edition (1968):

THE ORIGINAL | *Rubaiyyat* | *of Omar Khayaam* | [swelled rule with centre dot] | A NEW TRANSLATION | WITH CRITICAL COMMENTARIES | BY | *Robert Graves* | AND | *Omar Ali-Shah* | DOUBLEDAY & COMPANY, INC. | GARDEN CITY, NEW YORK | 1968

Collation: [1] – [6]⁸, 48 leaves.
    p.[i] The Original Rubaiyyat of Omar Khayaam | [French rule]; p.[ii] blank; p.[iii] title-page; p.[iv] LC card, copyright, and edition notices; p.[v] CONTENTS; p.[vi] blank; p.[vii] as p.[i] p.[viii] blank; pp.1–31 The Fitz-Omar Cult; pp.32–45[46] Historical Preface; p.[47] THE RUBAIYYAT; p.[48] NOTE; pp.49–76 text; pp.77–86 NOTES; pp.[87] – [88] blank.
    23.1 × 15.4 cm. Bulk: 0.7/0.9 cm. White wove paper; top and bottom edges

trimmed. White wove endpapers outer sides printed yellow. Bound in black cloth with white cloth spine; front and back blank; spine printed in black, top to bottom: *The Original Rubaiyyat of Omar Khayaam* ROBERT GRAVES *and* OMAR ALI-SHAH DOUBLEDAY

Price: $5.00. Number of copies: 12,000. Published 17 May 1968 in white dust-jacket printed in yellow, purple and black.

Note: There was also a limited issue, called a 'Limited Edition' of this edition. It has an additional leaf before p.[i]: *This is a limited edition of five hundred autographed copies | of which this is number* [line with number written on it] | [signatures of Shah and Graves]. It also has an extra free front endpaper. The endpapers are white wove paper with grey-green marbling printed on outer sides. It is bound in the same marbled paper with a quarter black cloth spine with gold stamping identical to that of the ordinary issue's black printing. It was issued in a slipcase covered in the same marbled paper with a tan wove paper label printed in red and black pasted on the front.

A120c. Second English edition ([1972]):

RUBAIYYAT OF | OMAR | KHAYAAM | *A new translation with | critical commentaries* | by *Robert Graves and | Omar Ali-Shah* | [publisher's emblem] | *Penguin Books*

Collation: [A]^{16} B–C^{16}, 48 leaves.
    p.[1] PENGUIN BOOKS | THE RUBAIYYAT OF | OMAR KHAYAAM; p.[2] blank; p.[3] title-page; p.[iv] publisher's, publication, copyright, printer's and rights reservation notices; p.[5] CONTENTS; p.[6] blank; pp.7–30 THE FITZ-OMAR CULT; pp.31–42 HISTORICAL PREFACE; p.[43] THE RUBAIYYAT; p.[44] NOTE; pp.45–67 text; p.[68] blank; pp.69–78 NOTES; pp.79–95 Fitzgerald's translation; p.[96] blank.
    18.0 × 11.0 cm. Bulk: 0.5 cm. White wove paper; all edges trimmed. Bound in white paper pictorial covers printed in orange, black, pink and blue-green.

Price: 25p. Number of copies: 28,146 (several impressions) sold by March 1986. Published 27 April 1972.

A120d. Second American edition (1972):

THE ORIGINAL | *Rubaiyyat | of Omar Khayaam* | [swelled rule with centre dot] | A NEW TRANSLATION | WITH CRITICAL COMMENTARIES | BY | *Robert Graves* | AND | *Omar Ali-Shah* | OMEN PRESS, INC. | TUCSON, ARIZONA | 1972

Collation: 48 leaves, glued at spine.
    p.[i] title-page; p.[ii] printing, publisher's, ISBN and copyright notices; p.[iii] *The Original Rubaiyyat of Omar Khayaam* | [French rule]; p.[iv] blank; p.[v] as p.[iii]; p.[vi] blank; p.[vii] CONTENTS; p.[viii] blank; pp.1–31 The Fitz-Omar Cult; pp.32–45[46] Historical Preface; p.[47] THE RUBAIYYAT; p.[48] blank; pp.49–76 text; pp.77–86 NOTES; pp.[87]–[88] blank.

20.1 × 12.7 cm. Bulk: 0.7 cm. White wove paper; all edges trimmed. Bound in white paper covers printed in orange, pink and blue.

Price: $2.25. Number of copies: undisclosed. Published in 1972.

A121 THE POOR BOY WHO FOLLOWED HIS STAR [1968]

a. **First edition**:

[in roman and **shaded** type] **THE POOR BOY** | **WHO FOLLOWED HIS** | **STAR** | AND CHILDREN'S POEMS | [illustration] | *by* **ROBERT GRAVES** | *illustrated by Alice Meyer-Wallace* | CASSELL . LONDON

Collation: A⁸ [B]⁸ C⁸, 24 leaves.
     p.[i] THE POOR BOY WHO FOLLOWED HIS STAR | *and Children's Poems*; p.[ii] blank; p.[iii] title-page; p.[iv] publisher's, copyright, ISBN and printer's notices; p.1 CONTENTS; p.[2] illustration, running onto p.[3]; pp.[3]4–44 text, with pp.[28, 30–31, 40] being unnumbered, pp.[6] 10, [22], 26, [32], 35, [41], 42 containing illustrations and no text.
     21.8 × 14.9 cm. Bulk: 0.4/0.8 cm. White wove paper; all edges trimmed. White wove endpapers. Bound in light blue cloth; front and back blank; spine stamped in gold, bottom to top: Cassell [device] THE POOR BOY WHO FOLLOWED HIS STAR [device] Robert Graves

Price: 18s. Number of copies unknown. Published in 1968 in white dust-jacket printed in black, blue and yellow.

Contents: Hide and Seek – The Hero – The Poor Boy Who Followed His Star – At Seventy-Two.

Notes: The illustrations are in black and white and appear on every page.
     This book has been translated into Afrikaans.
     In the title poem and in "At Seventy-Two" the old man in the illustration is Graves.
     Carl Hahn reports a copy in dark blue cloth, or perhaps simulated cloth (not seen).

A121b. First American edition [1969]:

[set left:] *The* | [set one space further left:] *Poor Boy* | *Who* [star] | *Followed* | [set right:] *His Star* | Robert Graves | Illustrated by Alice Meyer-Wallace | *Doubleday & Company, Inc., Garden City, New York*

Collation: [1] – [3]¹⁶, stabbed not sewn, 24 leaves.
     2 pp. blank; p.[1] [set right:] *The* | *Poor Boy* | *Who* [star] | *Followed* | *His Star*; p.[2] blank; p.[3] title-page; p.[4] LC card, copyright, rights reservation, printing, edition and source notices; p.[5] as p.[1]; p.[6] illustration; pp.7–40 [41] text, with pp.[10, 17. 22, 26, 32, 35, 41] containing illustrations and no text and pp.[13, 16, 19, 20, 24, 28, 30, 34, 36, 39] being unnumbered; p.[42] blank; p. 43 *About the Author*; pp.[44] – [46] blank.

23.4 × 15.3 cm. Bulk: 0.5/1.0 cm. White wove paper; all edges trimmed. White wove endpapers. Bound in slick white cloth; back blank; front printed in blue, yellow, green, and black, in centre of star-burst design at top, black printed on yellow field: *The Poor Boy | Who Followed | His Star |* [at foot in sea, printed in blue and black on white field:] [in blue:] *Robert Graves |* [in black:] Illustrated by Alice Meyer Wallace; spine printed in black and blue: [down spine:] *The Poor Boy Who Followed His Star* [remainder in blue:] *Robert Graves Doubleday*

Price: $3.50. Number of copies undetermined. Published in 1969 in white dust-jacket printed as binding with photograph of Graves by Marion Morehouse on back.

Notes: Illustrations appear on every page of text.

A122   GREEK MYTHS AND LEGENDS   [1968]

First edition:

Greek Myths | and Legends | ROBERT GRAVES | [series emblem] | CASSELL . LONDON

Collation: [A]⁶ B−N⁸, 102 leaves.

pp.[i] − [ii] front pastedown endpaper, blank; pp.[iii] − [iv] front free endpaper, blank; p.[v] RED LION READER NO. 9 | Greek Myths and Legends and description of book; p.[vi] series advertisement; p.[vii] title-page; p.[viii] publisher's, copyright, publication, printing and printer's notices; pp.[ix] − [x] Contents; pp.1 − 182 text, with pp.[2] − [3] and [108] − [109] being maps; pp.183 − 190 Index; pp.[191] − [192] rear free endpaper, blank; pp.[193] − [194] rear pastedown endpaper, blank.

18.3 × 12.3 cm. Bulk: 1.3/1.7 cm. White wove paper; all edges trimmed. White wove endpapers. Bound in orange cloth printed in green and brown. Front has title, author, series, temple, trees, rocks; back has list of books in series. Spine printed bottom to top, facing front: CASSELL GREEK MYTHS AND LEGENDS ROBERT GRAVES

Price: 8s.6d. Number of copies unknown. Published January 1968 without dust-jacket.

Contents: A combination of A91 and A102.

A123   POEMS 1965–1968   [1968]

a. First edition:

ROBERT GRAVES | [one line in open letters] POEMS 1965−1968 | [publisher's emblem] | CASSELL . LONDON

Collation: [A]⁸ B−G⁸, 56 leaves.

2 pp. blank; p.[i] POEMS 1965−1968; p.[ii] blank; p.[iii] title-page; p.[iv] publisher's, printing and copyright notices; p.v FOREWORD; p.[vi] blank; pp.vii−x CONTENTS; p.[1]2−97 text; pp.[98] − [100] blank.

21.5 × 14.7 cm. Bulk: 1.1/1.5 cm. White wove paper; all edges trimmed. White wove endpapers. Bound in light blue cloth. Front and back blank; spine stamped in gold, bottom to top: *Cassell Robert Graves* POEMS 1965–1968

Price: 25s. Number of copies unknown. Published 25 July 1968 in white dust-jacket printed in black and blue.

Contents: Foreword – Cock in Pullet's Feathers – Dead Hand – Arrears of Moonlight – What Did You Say? – Lure of Murder – The Gorge – Ecstasy of Chaos – Stolen Jewel – The Snapped Thread – Fortunate Child – Loving True, Flying Blind – The Near Eclipse – Dancing Flame – Birth of Angels – On Giving – The P'eng that was a K'un – Like Owls – In Pespective – The Utter Rim – Unicorn and the White Doe – Bower Bird – Mist – The Word – Perfectionists – Prison Walls – A Dream of Hell – Our Self – Bites and Kisses – Sun-Face and Moon-Face – Freehold – The Necklace – A Bracelet – Blackening Sky – Blessed Sun – Lion-Gentle – Spite of Mirrors – Pride of Love – Hooded Flame – Injuries – Her Brief Withdrawal – The Crane – Strangeness – *Song*: How Can I Care? – *Song*: Though Once True Lovers – *Song*: Cherries or Lilies – *Song*: Crown of Stars – *Song*: The Palm Tree – *Song*: Fig Tree in Leaf – *Song*: Dewdrop and Diamond – *Song*: Sullen Moods – *Song*: Just Friends – *Song*: Of Course – *Song*: Three Rings for Her – *Sincèrement* – *Dans un Seul Lit* – Possibly – Is Now the Time? – Twins – Sail and Oar – Gooseflesh Abbey – The Home-coming – With the Gift of a Lion's Claw – Wigs and Beards – Personal Packaging, Inc. – Work Room – The Ark – All Except Hannibal – The Beggar Maid and King Cophetua – For Ever – *Jugum Improbum* – *De Arte Poetica* – *Sit Mihi Terra Levis* – Astymelusa – Tousled Pillow – To Be in Love – Fact of the Act – To Ogmian Hercules – Arrow Shots – She to Him – Within Reason – The Yet Unsayable – None the Wiser – The Narrow Sea – The Olive Yard.

Note: 'The Beggar Maid and King Cophetua', 'Work Room', 'Is now the Time?', 'To Ogmian Hercules', 'The Narrow Sea', and 'Possibly' were published in the *Daily Telegraph* Magazine, 26 July 1968, p.9.

A123b. First American impression (1969):

Robert Graves | [curlicue] | [one line in open lettering:] POEMS 1965–1968 | Doubleday & Company, Inc. | Garden City, New York | 1969

Collation: [1] – [7]⁸, 56 leaves.

Remainder as A122a, except p.[iv] LC card, copyright, printing and edition notices.

20.7 × 13.8 cm. Bulk: 0.8/1.2 cm. White wove paper; all edges trimmed. Olive-green wove endpapers, inner sides white. Bound in brown cloth with quarter black cloth spine. Front and back blank; spine stamped in gold, top to bottom: ROBERT GRAVES POEMS 1965–1968 DOUBLEDAY

Price: $4.95. Number of copies undetermined. Published in 1969 in white dust-jacket printed in black, blue and brown, with photographs front and back.

A124   LOVE RESPELT AGAIN   [1969]

First edition:

[floral design in black and white on whole page; large oval set right; in facsimile of Graves' handwriting:] Love Respelt | Again | by | Robert Graves | [short rule] | Doubleday, N.Y.

Collation: [1] – [4]⁸, 32 leaves.

pp.[1] – [2] blank; p.[3] statement of number of copies printed, numbering, and Graves' signature; p.[4] blank; p.[5] [in facsimile of Graves' handwriting:] Love Respelt | Again | by | Robert Graves | [short rule]; p.[6] blank; p.[7] title-page; p.[8] LC card, copyright, rights reservation, edition and printer's notices; p.[9] [running bottom to top along left margin in facsimile of Graves' handwriting:] The Poems Contents — The Poems — Contents — p.[10] running vertically bottom to top in facsimile of Graves' handwriting:] Additions to the Original Sequence: 1966; pp.[11] – [61] text, with pp.[11, 14, 19, 34] having black and white illustrations around poems and p.[43] having black and white illustration and no poem; pp.[62] – [64] blank.

20.6 × 17.1 cm. Bulk: 0.6/1.1 cm. White laid paper; all edges trimmed. White wove endpapers. Bound in black cloth; front and back blank; spine stamped in gold in facsimile of Graves' handwriting, bottom to top: Doubleday Love Respelt Again Robert Graves

Price: $15.00. Number of copies: 1,000. Published in 1969 in white dust-jacket printed in black and grey.

Contents: The Red Shower – Above the Edge of Doom – Wild Cyclamen – Gift of Sight – Batoxca – The Snap-Comb Wilderness – Change – A Court of Love – Black – Between Hyssop and Axe – Gold and Malachite – Ambience – The Vow – The Frog and the Golden Ball – Those Who Came Short – Whole Love – This Holy Month – The Blow – The Impossible – The Fetter – Iron Palace – True Joy – Tomorrow's Envy of Today – The Hidden Garden – The Wedding – What Will Be, Is – Son Altesse – Everywhere Is Here – Song: The Far Side of Your Moon – Deliverance – Conjunction – Nothing Now Astonishes – Postscript – Cock in Pullet's Feathers – Dead Hand – Arrears of Moonlight – What Did You Say? – Lure of Murder – The Gorge – Ecstasy of Chaos – Stolen Jewel – The Eagre – The Snapped Thread – Fortunate Child – Loving True, Flying Blind – The Near-Eclipse – Dancing Flame – Birth of Angels – Clothed in Silence – On Giving.

Notes: Entire contents of the book are in facsimile of Graves' handwriting, only pp.[3, 8] are in type.

There is no attribution of the illustrations.

A125   THE CRANE BAG   [1969]

First edition:

THE CRANE BAG | and other | disputed subjects | [rule] | ROBERT GRAVES | CASSELL . LONDON

Collation: [A]⁸ B–Q⁸, 128 leaves.

p.[i] THE CRANE BAG; p.[ii] blank; p.[iii] title-page; p.[iv] publisher's, copyright and printer's notices; pp.[v]–[vi] CONTENTS; p.[vii]–viii FOREWORD; p.[ix] ACKNOWLEDGEMENTS; p.[x] blank; pp.[1]2–243 text; pp.[244]–[246] blank.

20.8 × 13.8 cm. Bulk: 2.5/2.8 cm. White wove paper; all edges trimmed. White wove endpapers. Bound in olive-green cloth; front and back blank; spine stamped in gold, bottom to top: [upright:]CASSELL | [down spine, facing front:] THE CRANE BAG [vertical rule] Robert Graves

Price: 42s. Number of copies unknown. Published in 1969 in white dust-jacket printed in olive and dark green.

Contents: Foreword – The Crane Bag – The Language of Monsters – Two Studies in Scientific Atheism – The Dour Man – Praise Me, and I will Whistle to You! – What was that War like, Sir? – The Case for Xanthippe – The Lost Atlantis – Reincarnation – The *New English Bible* – Mr. Nabokov's Democratic Eclecticism – A *Goy* in Israel – Forgotten Loyalists – Do You Remember Albuhera? – The Pirates Who Captured Caesar – A Significant Lecture at Mount Holyoke – Tyger, Tyger – Five Score and Six Years Ago – The Decline of Bullfighting – The Phenomenon of Mass-tourism – The Idiom of the People – My Best Christmas – Charterhouse Flourishes – Miss Briton's Lady-Companion – The Uses of Superstition – Witches Today – Translating the *Rubaiyyat* – An Absolute Criminal.

Note: Impression: 2nd, May 1970

A126   ON POETRY   1969

First edition:

ON POETRY: | *Collected Talks and Essays* | [floral ornament] | *by Robert Graves* | *Doubleday & Company, Inc., Garden City New York* | 1969

Collation: [1]–[25]¹², 300 leaves.

p.[1] *ON POETRY:* | *Collected Talks and Essays*; p.[2] blank; p.[3] title-page; p.[4] designer's, LC card, copyright, rights reservation, printing and edition notices; pp.[5]–6 *Foreword*; pp.[7]–8 *Contents*; p.[9] *ON POETRY:* | *Collected Talks and Essays*; p.[10] blank; pp.[11]12–597 text, with pp.[33, 55, 83, 107, 127, 153, 157, 175, 195, 201, 227, 249, 273, 279, 301, 323, 347, 359, 367, 383, 397, 413, 427, 449, 473, 501, 529, 551, 575] being unnumbered and pp.[32, 54, 82, 106, 156, 174, 226, 248, 346, 358, 396, 412, 426, 448, 472, 574] being blank; pp.[598]–[600] blank.

23.2 × 15.1 cm. Bulk: 2.8/3.2 cm. White wove paper; top and bottom edges trimmed. White wove endpapers, inner sides printed olive green. Bound in three-quarter dark red cloth; front and back blank; spine bound in brown cloth and stamped in gold and black: [two rows, top to bottom, down spine:] [two words in gold:] ROBERT GRAVES [vertical rule] ON POETRY: | COLLECTED TALKS AND ESSAYS | [upright at foot, in gold:] DOUBLEDAY

Price: $10.00. Number of copies undetermined. Published 25 July 1969 in white dust-jacket printed in black, gold, red and grey.

Contents: Foreword – The Crowning Privilege – The Age of Obsequiousness – The Road to Rydal Mount – Harp, Anvil, Oar – Dame Ocupacyon – These Be Your Gods, O Israel! – Dr. Syntax and Mr. Pound – Mother Goose's Lost Goslings – Juana de Asbaje – The Old Black Cow – Legitimate Criticism of Poetry – The White Goddess – Sweeney Among the Blackbirds – Pulling a Poem Apart – The Dedicated Poet – The Anti-Poet – The Personal Muse – Poetic Gold – The Word 'Báraka' – The Poet's Paradise – Some Instances of Poetic Vulgarity – Technique in Poetry – The Poet in a Valley of Dry Bones – Intimations of the Black Goddess – Standards of Craftsmanship – A Favourite Cat Drowned – A Pretty Kettle of Fish – The Dueude – Munta, Mammon, Marxism – Ecstasy

A127   BEYOND GIVING   1969

First edition:

Robert | GRAVES | [swelled rule] | BEYOND GIVING | *POEMS* | PRIVATELY PRINTED | 1969

Collation: [1] – [3]⁸, 24 leaves.

p.[i] BEYOND GIVING | Poems; p.[ii] blank; p.[iii] title-page; p.[iv] [copyright symbol] Robert Graves 1969 | This edition consists of 536 copies | of which 500 numbered and signed by | the author are for sale. | Printed in Great Britain at | THE STELLAR PRESS, HATFIELD | by Bill Hummerstone | Number | [number] | [signature] | DISTRIBUTED BY | Bertram Rota (Publishing) Ltd, | 4, 5 & 6 Savile Row London W1; p.[v] – [vi] table of contents; p.[vii] FOREWORD; p.[viii] blank; p.[1] PART I; p.[2] blank; pp.3–19 text; p.[20] blank; p.[21] PART II; p.[22] blank; pp.23–40 text. [page numbers are in square brackets].

25.3 × 16.3 cm. Bulk: 0.4/0.7 cm. White laid paper, untrimmed and unopened. White laid endpapers. Plain white card covers with dull lemon wrapper as cover; printed in red and black; back blank; front: ROBERT | GRAVES | [two lines in red:] BEYOND | GIVING | POEMS | [in red:] 1969; spine, top to bottom, facing back, in red: ROBERT GRAVES / BEYOND GIVING / POEMS

Price: £3.50. Number of copies: 536 (500 signed and numbered). Published 19 October 1969.

Contents: PART I: Song: To a Rose – Dream Warning – Song: Beyond Giving – Trial of Innocence – Poisoned Day – Leave-taking – In the Name of Virtue – What We Did Next – Compact – Song: New Year Kisses – The Clocks of Time – Gold Cloud – Basket of Blossom – Wherever We May Be – What is Love? – Song: The Promise – Song: Yesterday Only. PART II: Semi-Detached – Iago – Against Witchcraft – Troublesome Fame – Tolling Bell – The Hero – Blanket Charge – The Strayed Message – Song: The Sundial's Lament – Poem: A Reminder – *Antorcha y Corona* – Torch and Crown – Armistice Day, 1918 – The Motes

TREASURE BOX

—

BY

ROBERT GRAVES

GOLIATH AND DAVID

—

BY

ROBERT GRAVES

The title pages of Treasure Box *(A4)* and Goliath and David *(A2)*

Transformations of I, Claudius *(clockwise from top left): A42e, A42p, A42o, A42l in its post-television dramatization covers, and of A42m*

Transformations of Claudius the God *(clockwise from top left): A43e in dustjacket, and A43g, A43e and A43f in their post-television dramatization covers*

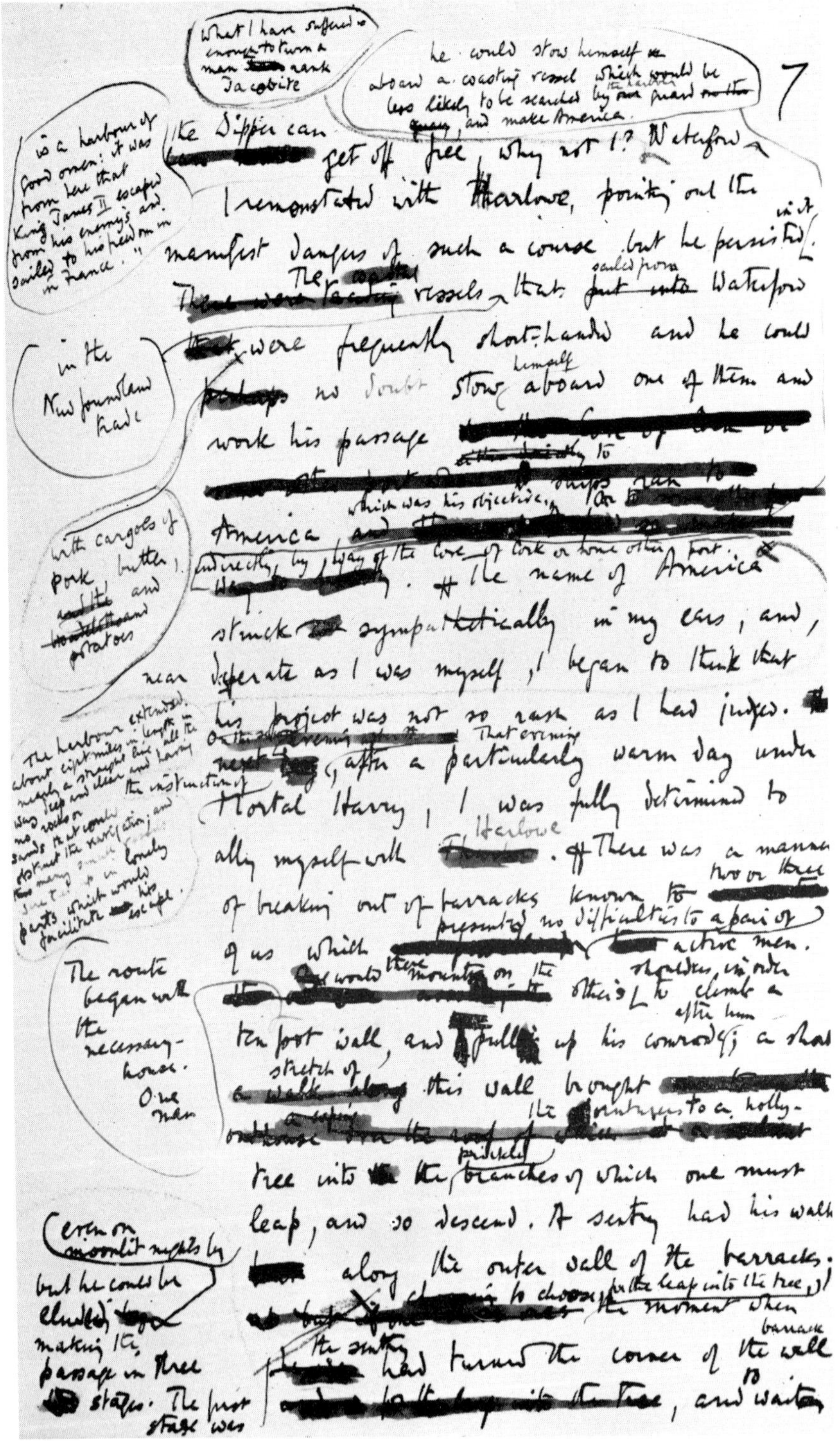
What I have suffered is enough to turn a man rank Jacobite
he would stow himself aboard a coasting vessel which would be less likely to be searched by the harbour guard and make America.
7
is a harbour of good omen: it was from here that King James II escaped from his enemy's and sailed to his freedom in France."
the Dipper can [redacted] get off free, why not I? Waterford
I remonstrated with Harlowe, pointing out the manifest dangers of such a course but he persisted in it.
The vessels that sailed from Waterford were frequently short-handed and he could no doubt stow himself aboard one of them and
in the Newfoundland trade
work his passage [redacted]
[redacted]
with cargoes of pork butter and potatoes
America which was his objective, [redacted]
indirectly by way of the Cove of Cork or some other port.
The name of America struck sympathetically in my ears, and, near desperate as I was myself, I began to think that his project was not so rash as I had judged.
The harbour extended about eight miles in length in nearly a straight line all the way deep and clear and having no rocks or sands that could obstruct the navigation, and ... lonely parts which would facilitate his escape.
That evening, after a particularly warm day under the instruction of Mortal Harry, I was fully determined to ally myself with Harlowe. There was a manner of breaking out of barracks known to two or three of us which presented no difficulties to a pair of active men.
The route began with the necessary-house. One man
[redacted] would there mount on the other's shoulders in order to climb a ten foot wall, and after him pull up his comrade; a short stretch of this wall brought the adventurers to a holly-tree into the prickly branches of which one must leap, and so descend. A sentry had his walk [redacted] along the outer wall of the barracks.
even on moonlit nights by
but he could be eluded making the passage in three stages. The first stage was
[redacted] to choose for the leap into the tree, the moment when the sentry had turned the corner of the barrack wall [redacted], and waiting

Part of a page of the MS of Sergeant Lamb of the Ninth *(A51)*

The covers of the American issue of the fourth and fifth impressions of Collected Short Stories, *the title of which was changed in the third and fourth impressions only to* The Shout and Other Stories *(A106c)*

POEMS:-
ABRIDGED
FOR
DOLLS
AND
PRINCES
by
ROBERT GRAVES

The title page, first page of text and last page of MS from Poems: Abridged for Dolls and Princes *(A131)*

The Mirror

Mirror Mirror
Tell me
Am I pretty or
plain?
Or am I downright
ugly
And ugly to
remain?

THE END

Performed by
Captain Robert
Graves at the
World's End
Islip. Oxon
1922

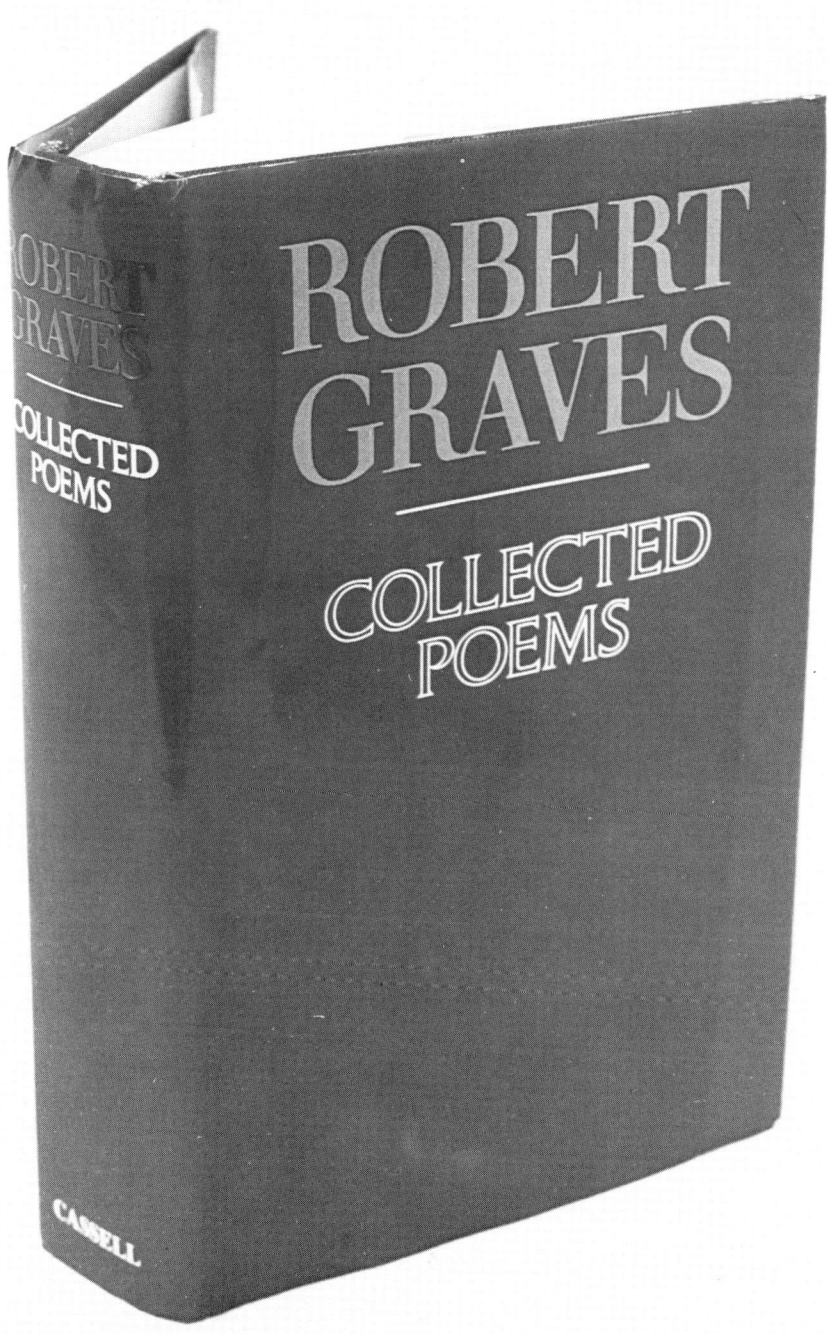

The dustjacket from the 1975 edition of Collected Poems *(A138)*

A Country Mood

Take now a country mood,
Resolve, distil it:—
Nine acre swaying alive,
Jane flowers that fill it,

Spicy sweet-briar bush,
The uneasy wren
Fluttering from ash to birch
And back again,

Milkwort on its low stem,
Spread hawthorn tree,
Sunlight patching the wood,
A hive bound bee,

Girls riding nim-nim-nim,
Ladies, trot-trot,
Gentlemen hard at gallop,
Shouting, steam hot.

Now over the rough turf
Bridles go jingle
And theres a well-loved pool
By Fox's Dingle

Where Sweetheart my to
Old Glory's daughter
May loll her leathern tong

MS of 'A Country Mood' (C76)

A128 POEMS ABOUT LOVE [1969]

a. First edition:

Robert Graves' | *Poems* | *About Love* | [double curlicue] | DOUBLEDAY AND COMPANY, INC., GARDEN CITY, NEW YORK

Collation: [1] – [8]¹², 96 leaves.

   p.[1] *Robert Graves' Poems About Love*; p.[2] blank; p.[3] title-page; p.[4] LC card, copyright, rights reservation and printing notices; pp.5–7 *Foreword*; p.[8] blank; pp.9–15 *Contents*; p.[16] blank; pp.17–181 text; p.[182] blank; pp.183–189 *Index*; pp.[190] –[192] blank.

   23.2 × 15.2 cm. Bulk: 1.4/2.0 cm. White wove paper; top and bottom edges trimmed. Wove endpapers, green outer and white inner sides. Bound in maroon cloth; back blank; front stamped in gold: [all within curly monogram design encorporating 'R' of first line:] ROBERT | GRAVES' | POEMS | ABOUT | LOVE; spine stamped in gold, top to bottom: ROBERT GRAVES' POEMS ABOUT LOVE | [upright:] DOUBLEDAY

Price: $5.00. Number of copies undetermined. Published in late 1969 in white dust-jacket printed in black, dark green, red and light green.

Contents: Foreword – I: The Finding of Love – One Hard Look – Sullen Moods – Love Without Hope – The Troll's Nosegay – Unicorn and the White Doe – The Hills of May – Lost Love – Love in Barrenness – Song of Contrariety – Full Moon – Vanity – Pure Death – Sick Love – Ulysses – The Succubus – The Christmas Robin – Fact and Act – At First Sight – Down, Wanton, Down! – Never Such Love – A Jealous Man – The Foreboding – With Her Lips Only – II: On Portents – The Terraced Valley – Like Snow – End of Play – A Love Story – Dawn Bombardment – The Thieves – To Sleep – The Oath – Mid-Winter Waking – The Door – Through Nightmare – She Tells Her Love While Half Asleep – Theseus and Ariadne – To Juan at the Winter Solstice – To Be Called a Bear – Beauty in Trouble – The Song of Blodeuwedd – Lament for Pasiphaë – Counting the Beats – The Young Cordwainer – The Survivor – III: Questions in a Wood – The Portrait – The Straw – Hercules at Nemea – Dialogue on the Headland – Cat-Goddesses – The Blue-Fly – A Lost Jewel – The Window Sill – Spoils – Rhea – The Face in the Mirror – Forbidden Words – Possibly – A Slice of Wedding Cake – Call It a Good Marriage – Around the Mountain – IV: Lyceia – Symptoms of Love – The Sharp Ridge – Under the Olives – The Visitation – Fragment – The Falcon Woman – Troughs of Sea – The Death Grapple – The Starred Coverlet – Turn of the Moon – Seldom Yet Now – *Song*: A Lost World – The Dangerous Gift – Twice of the Same Fever – V: Ruby and Amethyst – Recognition – Variables of Green – The Meeting – Not at Home – Horizon – Golden Anchor – Lion Lover – The Winged Heart – In Her Praise – A Restless Ghost – Between Moon and Moon – Beware, Madam! – Acrobats – Ouzo Unclouded – The Broken Girth – Inkidoo and the Queen of Babel – Three Songs for the Lute: I. Truth is Poor Physic – II. In Her Only Way – III. Hedges Freaked With Snow – A Time of Waiting – Expect Nothing – No Letter – The Why of the Weather – In Time – *Jugum-Improbum* – At Best, Poets – She is No Liar – The Leap – Judgement of Paris – Man Does, Woman Is – The Three-Faced – Dazzle of Darkness – Myrrhina – Food of the

Dead – I Will Write – VI: Bird of Paradise – The Metaphor – Secrecy – Joseph and Mary – The Oleaster – *Non Cogunt Astra* – *Song*: Sword and Rose – Endless Pavement – In Disguise – A Measure of Casualness – In Time of Absence – The Green Castle – Not to Sleep – The Hearth – The Beds of Grainne and Diarmuid – The Black Goddess – Between Trains – To the Teumessian Vixen – The Hung Wu Vase – *La Mejicana* – Lamia in Love (*revision*) – *Song*: All I Tell You From My Heart – The Undead – Grace Notes – VII: Above the Edge of Doom – Wild Cyclamen – *Batxóca* – The Snap-Comb Wilderness – Change – A Court of Love – Black – Between Hyssop and Axe – Gold and Malachite – Ambience – The Vow – The Frog and the Golden Ball – Those Who Came Short – Whole Love – This Holy Month – The Blow – The Impossible – The Fetter – Iron Palace – True Joy – The Hidden Garden – Son Altesse – Everywhere is Here – *Song*: The Far Side of Your Moon – Deliverance – Conjunction – Nothing Now Astonishes – Postscript – VIII: Cock in Pullet's Feathers – Arrears of Moonlight – What Did You Say? – Lure of Murder – The Gorge – Extacy of Chaos – Stolen Jewel – The Snapped Thread – Fortunate Child – Loving True, Flying Blind – The Near-Eclipse – Dancing Flame – Birth of Angels – On Giving – IX: The Perfectionists – Lion-Gentle – The Word – The Necklace – A Bracelet – While the Sky Blackens – Sun-Face and Moon-Face – Prison Walls – A Dream of Hell – Our Self – Hooded Flame – Crown of Stars – Pride of Love – *Song*: The Palm Tree – If and When – *In Perspective* – Injuries – The Bower Bird – Mist – Bites and Kisses – Spite of Mirrors – Her Brief Withdrawal – The Crane – Strangeness – She to Him – *Song*: Cherries or Lilies – For Ever – *Song*: Dew-Drop and Diamond – To Be in Love – The Olive Yard – The Yet Unsayable – The Narrow Sea – Within Reason – Index.

A128b. First British impression ([1969]):

Title-page as A128a except CASSELL . LONDON for Doubleday.

　　Remainder as A128a, printed in 12s but gathered in 24s, and p.[4] copyright, restiction and publication notices.

　　22.2 × 14.9 cm. Bulk: 1.6/2.2 cm. White wove textured paper; all edges trimmed. White wove endpapers. Bound in maroon cloth; front and back blank; spine stamped in gold: ROBERT | GRAVES | [rule] | Poems | about Love | CASSELL

Price: 30s. Number of copies unknown. Published in November 1969 in white dust-jacket printed in black, royal purple and yellow-orange.

Notes: The 'press figure': J50 at the lower left of p.189 is the same as that found in A128a.

　　Statement on p.[4] says: Reprinted offset in Great Britain by the Camelot Press Ltd., London and Southampton.

A129 POEMS 1968–1970 [1970]

a. First edition:

ROBERT GRAVES | POEMS 1968–1970 | [publisher's emblem] | CASSELL . LONDON

Collation: [A] – [B]⁸ C–E⁸ F/F*²/⁸, 50 leaves.

p.[i] POEMS | 1968–1970; p.[ii] blank; p.[iii] title-page; p.[iv] publisher's, copyright, rights reservation, ISBN and printer's notices; p.v FOREWORD; p.[vi] blank; pp.vii–ix CONTENTS; p.[x] blank; p.[1] section head; p.[2] blank; pp.3–90 text, with pp.[17, 26, 45, 71] being unnumbered section headings and pp; [16, 44, 46, 72] being blank.

21.5 × 15.3 cm. Bulk: 0.9/1.5 cm. White wove paper; all edges trimmed. White wove endpapers. Bound in dull yellow-green cloth; front and back blank; spine stamped in gold, bottom to top: *Cassell Robert Graves* POEMS 1968–1970

Price: 30s. Number of copies unknown. Published 12 October 1970 in white dust-jacket printed in green and black.

Contents: Foreword – XXIII: *Song*: Dream Warning – *Song*: Beyond Giving – *Song*: The Sigil – *Song*: Basket of Blossom – *Song*: Yesterday Only – *Song*: Twinned Heart – *Song*: Olive Tree – *Song*: Once More – *Song*: The Promise – *Song*: Victims of Calumny – *Song*: To a Rose – *Song*: The Clocks of Time – *Song*: Wherever We May Be – XXIV: Gold Cloud – Compact – Trial of Innocence – Love Gifts – Mankind and Ocean – Poisoned Day – Virgin Mirror – What Is Love? – Secret Theatre – How It Started – Brief Reunion – The Judges – Love and Night – Child with Veteran – Superstition – Purification – Powers Unconfessed – Pandora – Solomon's Seal – To Put It Simply – In the Name of Virtue – To Tell and Be Told – The Theme of Death – At the Well – XXV: Logic – Robbers' Den – The Accomplice – First Love – Through a Dark Wood – In the Vestry – When Love Is Not – The Reiteration – Semi-Detached – Iago – Against Witchcraft – Man of Evil – The Raft – Tolling Bell – The Hero – Blanket Charge – The Uncut Diamond – The Strayed Message – The Co-Walker – The Risk – Something to Say – Troublesome Fame – OCCASIONALIA: Research and Development: Classified – The Imminent Seventies – Carol of Patience – Invitation to Bristol – The Primrose Bed – Poem: A Reminder – The Strangling in Merrion Square – *Song*: The Sundial's Lament – *Antorcha y Corona, 1968:* – Torch and Crown, 1968 – The Awakening – Armistice Day, 1918.

A129b. First American edition (1971):

Robert Graves | [flourish] | POEMS 1968–1970 | Doubleday & Company, Inc. | Garden City, New York | 1971

Collation: 56 leaves, unsigned.

4 pp. blank; p.[i] POEMS | 1968–1970; p.[ii] blank; p.[iii] title-page; p.[iv] LC card, copyright, rights reservation, printing and edition notices; p.v FOREWORD; p.[vi] blank; pp.vii–ix CONTENTS; p.[x] blank; p.[1] section head; p.[2] blank; pp.3–90 text, with pp.[17, 26, 45, 71] being section heads and pp.[16, 44, 46, 72] being blank; pp.[91] – [98] blank.

20.8 × 13.7 cm. Bulk: 0.7/1.3 cm. White wove paper; all edges trimmed. White wove endpapers, inner sides slate blue. Bound in three-quarter dull grey-blue cloth with black cloth spine stamped in gold, top to bottom: ROBERT GRAVES POEMS 1968–1970 DOUBLEDAY

Price: $5.95. Number of copies: 4,500. Published 22 October 1971 in white pictorial dust-jacket printed in black, green and red.

A130   THE GREEN-SAILED VESSEL   1971

First edition:

Robert | GRAVES | [swelled rule] | THE | GREEN-SAILED | VESSEL | *POEMS* | PRIVATELY PRINTED | 1971

Collation: [1] – [2]⁸ [3]¹⁰, 26 leaves.

pp.[1] – [2] blank; p. half-title; p.[ii] blank; p.[iii] title-page; p.[iv] copyright, printing and distribution notices, number and signature location; pp.[v] – [vi] CONTENTS; p.vii FOREWORD; p.viii DEDICATORY; p.[ix] PART I; p.[x] blank; pp.3–21 text; p.[22] blank; p.[23] PART II; p.[24] blank; pp.25–41 text; p.[42] blank. [page numbers are in square brackets].

25.2 × 16.5 cm. Bulk: 0.5/0.8 cm. White laid paper; top edge only trimmed. White laid endpapers. Bound in olive-yellow cloth; front and back blank; spine stamped in gold, top to bottom: ROBERT GRAVES . THE GREEN-SAILED VESSEL

Price: £5.00. Number of copies: 536 (500 numbered and signed). Published 2 August 1971 in a light orange dust-jacket printed in red and blue.

Contents: Foreword – Dedicatory – PART I: The Wand – Five: *Quinque* – Arrow on the Vane – Gorgon Mask – To be Poets – With a Gift of Rings – Casse-Noisette – The Garden – The Green-Sailed Vessel – Dreaming Children – The Prohibition – Serpent's Tail – Until We Both – The Miracle – The Rose – Testament – The Crab Tree – Three Locked Hoops – Cliff and Wave – PART II: Those Blind from Birth – Fools – The Gateway – Advice from a Mother – A Reduced Sentence – The Gentlemen – Complaint and Reply – My Ghost – Song: Reconciliation – Knobs and Levers – The Virus – Druid Love – Problems of Gender – Confess, Marpessa – Jus Primae Noctis – Work Drafts.

Note: Published and distributed by Bertram Rota Ltd.

In the table of contents Part I is labelled: *Love Poems* and Part II: *Mainly Satires* although these designations are not found on the section title-pages.

A131 POEMS: ABRIDGED FOR DOLLS AND PRINCES [1971]

First edition:

[in facsimile of Graves' handwriting:] POEMS:— | ABRIDGED | FOR | DOLLS | AND | PRINCES | by | ROBERT GRAVES

Collation: [1] – [8]⁸ [9]⁴ [10]⁸, 76 leaves.

[printed on rectos only and with no pagination] pp.[1] – [2] blank; p.[3] title-page; p.[4] blank; pp.[5] – [147] text; p.[148] blank; p.[149] colophon: THE END | [short rule] | Performed by | Captain Robert | Graves at the | World's End | 1922 Islip. Oxon; p.[150] blank; p.[151] printing, copyright, rights reservation, ISBN and printer's notices; p.[152] blank.

13.0 × 9.5 cm. Bulk: 1.0/1.3 cm. White wove coated paper; all edges trimmed. White wove endpapers. Bound in blue cloth; front and back blank; spine stamped in gold: Robert | Graves | POEMS: | Abridged | for Dolls | and | Princes | Cassell

Price: £1.40. Number of copies unknown. Published in November 1971 in blue dust-jacket printed in white and yellow with photograph of the manuscript volume on front.

Contents: The Mirror – Henry & Mary – What did I dream? – Vain & Careless – One Hard Look – Love Without Hope – In the Wilderness – Song for Two Children – The Stake – Song of Contrariety – Lost Love – The Finding of Love – The Philosophers.

Note: This is an enlarged photographic facsimile of the miniature volume done by Graves in 1922 for the Library of Queen Mary's Dolls House at Windsor Castle.

Martin Seymour-Smith, *Robert Graves His Life and Work* (London: Hutchinson, 1982), p580, lists a Doubleday edition of this book in the United States in 1971 but no copy has been observed. However, it would appear that Doubelday did issue or publish a 'limited edition' of this book in the United States; limited to 500 copies (not seen). It may be this 'limited edition' to which Seymour-Smith refers.

A132 DEYA, A PORTFOLIO 1972

ROBERT GRAVES AND PAUL HOGARTH | DEYÁ | A portfolio | of five poems and lithographs | MOTIF EDITIONS LONDON, 1972

Collation: 9 loose leaves, each leaf separated by tissue.

[sheet 1] DEYÁ | five poems; [sheet 2] title-page; [sheet 3] introduction by the publisher, Edward Booth-Clibborn; [sheets 4–8] text and lithographs; [sheet 9] colophon: This limited edition consists of seventy-five | portfolios numbered and signed by the author, ROBERT GRAVES | Each of the five lithographs in the portfolio | are numbered and signed by the artist, | PAUL HOGARTH | Published by Motif Editions, 58 Firth Street, London W.1 England | [copyright symbol] 1972 First Run Limited [copyright symbol] 1972 Poems Robert Graves | Printed in Paris by Mourlot, 43 rue Barrault, Paris XIII, France | on Arches paper | completed on the twenty-second day of November 1972 | [signature] | Number | [number]

53.5 × 75.5 cm. In portfolio case three-quarter green paper and one-quarter tan monks' cloth; spine and back blank; front stamped in gold: ROBERT GRAVES & PAUL HOGARTH | DEYÁ

Price: £325.00. Number of copies: 75. Published November 1972.

Contents: [first lines, titles are not given] Ours has no bearing on quotidian love − Love makes poor sense in either speech or letters: − No one can understand our habit of love − Is there another man − Confess, sweetheart, confess.

Note: The lithographs are in colour; the poems are printed in facsimile of Graves' handwriting.

A133   DIFFICULT QUESTIONS, EASY ANSWERS   [1972]

a. First edition:

DIFFICULT QUESTIONS, | EASY ANSWERS | ROBERT GRAVES | CASSELL . LONDON

Collation: [A]⁸ B−O⁸, 112 leaves.
   p.[i] DIFFICULT QUESTIONS, EASY ANSWERS; p.[ii] blank; p.[iii] title-page; p.[iv] publisher's, copyright, rights reservation, ISBN and printer's notices; p.[v] *Foreword*; p.[vi] blank; p.vii *Contents*; p.[viii] blank; pp.1−213 text; pp.[214]−[216] blank.
   21.4 × 13.7 cm. Bulk: 1.7/2.3 cm. White wove paper; all edges trimmed. White wove endpapers. Bound in light brown cloth; front and back blank; spine stamped in gold, top to bottom, each set of two lines parallel: *DIFFICULT | QUESTIONS | EASY | ANSWERS | Robert | Graves |* [upright:] CASSELL

Price: £3.00. Number of copies unknown. Published in November 1972 in white dust-jacket printed in tan and brown.

Contents: Foreword − Address to the Poets of Hungary − Genius − Arts and Crafts − The Bible in Europe − Poetry and Obscenity − Goddesses and Obosoms − The Universal Paradise − Mushrooms and Religion − The Two Births of Dionysus − What Has Gone Wrong? − Rationality − The Greek Tradition − Ovid and the Libertines − Birds and Men − The Kaiser's War − Fighting Courage − A Soldier's Honour − The Absentee Fusilier − The Inner Ear − The Pentagram of Isis − Solomon's Seal − The Heart Shape − The Sufic Chequer-board − The Nine of Diamonds − Speaking Freely.

A133b. First American edition (1973):

[all in shaded type:] Difficult Questions | Easy Answers | By Robert Graves | Doubleday & Company, Inc. | Garden City, New York | 1973

Collation: [1]−[7]¹⁶, 112 leaves.
   p.[i] [in shaded type:] Difficult Questions | Easy Answers; p.[ii] blank; p.[iii] title-page; p.[iv] ISBN, LC card, copyright, rights reservation, printing and edition notices; p.v *Foreword*; p.[vi] blank; p.vii *Contents*; pp.[viii]−[x] blank; pp.1−213 text; p.[214] blank.

20.9 × 13.7 cm. Bulk: 1.4/1.9 cm. White wove paper; all edges trimmed. Reddish-brown wove endpapers, inner sides white. Bound in dark maroon cloth; front and back blank; spine printed in orange, top to bottom: [two lines upright:] Robert | Graves | [down spine, in shaded type:] Difficult Questions Easy Answers | [upright:] Doubleday

Price: $6.95. Number of copies undetermined. Published 24 September 1973 in white pictorial dust-jacket printed in black and golden brown.

Contents: As A133a.

A134   POEMS 1970–1972   [1972]

a. First edition:

ROBERT GRAVES | POEMS 1970–1972 | [publisher's emblem] | CASSELL . LONDON

Collation: [A]⁸ B–F⁸, 48 leaves.
   p.[i] POEMS | 1970–1972; p.[ii] blank; p.[iii] title-page; p.[iv] publisher's, copyright, rights reservation, publication, ISBN and printer's notices; pp.v–vi FOREWORD; pp.vii–ix CONTENTS; p.[x] blank; p.[1] section head; p.[2] blank; pp.3–85 text, with p.[47] being section head and p.[48] being blank; p.[86] blank.
   21.6 × 15.1 cm. Bulk: 0.8/1.4 cm. White wove paper; all edges trimmed. White wove endpapers. Bound in ultramarine cloth; front and back blank; spine stamped in silver, bottom to top: *Cassell Robert Graves* POEMS 1970–1972

Price: £1.90. Number of copies unknown. Published 16 November 1972 in white dust-jacket printed in red and blue.

Contents: XXVI: The Hoopoe Tells us How – The Wand – Five Quinque – Arrow on the Vane – Gorgon Mask – To be Poets – With a Gift of Rings – *Casse-Noisette* – The Garden – The Green-Sailed Vessel – Dreaming Children – The Prohibition – Serpent's Tail – Until We Both . . . – The Rose – Testament – The Crab Tree – Three Locked Hoops – Cliff and Wave – Her Beauty – Always – Desert Fringe – The Title of Poet – Depth of Love – Breakfast Table – The Half-Finished Letter – The Hazel Grove – Pity – Silent Visit – Coronet of Moonlight – *Song:* To Become Each Other – Heaven – Growing Pains – Friday Night – The Pact – Poor Others – A Toast to Death – The Young Sibyl – Records – The Flowering Aloe – Circus Ring – Ageless Reason – As When the Mystic – Unposted Letter (1963) – XXVII: Birth of a Goddess – Beatrice and Dante – The Dilemma – The Gentleman – The Wall – Women and Masks (translation) – Tilth – The Last Fistful – The Traditionalist – The Prepared Statement – St Antony of Padua – Broken Compact – A Dream of Frances Speedwell – The Encounter – Age Gap – Nightmare of Senility – Research and Development: Classified – Fools – Those Blind from Birth – The Gateway – Advice from a Mother – A Reduced Sentence – Absent Crusader – Complaint and Reply – My Ghost – *Song*: Reconciliation – Knobs and Levers – The Virus – Druid Love – Problems of Gender – *Jus Primae Noctis* – Confess, Marpessa – Dream Recalled on Waking – Work Drafts – Colophon.

A134b. First American edition (1973):

Robert Graves | [flourish] | POEMS 1970–1972 | DOUBLEDAY & COMPANY, INC. | GARDEN CITY, NEW YORK | 1973

Collation: [1]–[4]^{12}, 48 leaves.

    p.[i] POEMS | 1970–1972; p.[ii] blank; p.[iii] title-page; p.[iv] LC card, copyright, rights reservation, printing and edition notices; pp.v–vi FOREWORD; pp.vii–x CONTENTS; p.[xi] as p.[i]; p[xii] blank; p.[1] section head; p.[2] blank; pp.3–83 text, with pp.[35, 65] being section heads and pp.[36, 66] being blank; p.[84] blank.

    20.7 × 13.7 cm. Bulk: 0.7/1.2 cm. White wove paper; top and bottom edges trimmed. White wove endpapers; inner sides gold. Bound in three-quarter black cloth with brown-mustard spine stamped in gold, top to bottom: ROBERT GRAVES POEMS 1970–1972 DOUBLEDAY

Price: $5.95. Number of copies: 4,500. Published 5 January 1973 in white dust-jacket printed in gold and black.

Contents: XXVI: The Hoopoe Tells Us How – The Wand – Five Quinque – Arrow on the Vane – Gorgon Mask – To be Poets – With a Gift of Rings – *Casse-Noisette* – The Garden – The Green-Sailed Vessel – Dreaming Children – The Prohibition – Serpent's Tail – Until We Both . . . – The Rose – Testament – The Crab-Tree – Three Locked Hoops – Cliff and Wave – Her Beauty – The Title of Poet – Gift of Sleep – Depth of Love – Breakfast Table – The Half-Finished Letter – The Hazel Grove – Silent Visit – Coronet of Moonlight – Song: To Become Each Other – Heaven – Growing Pains – XXVII: The Pact – Poor Others – A Toast to Death – The Young Sibyl – Records – The Flowering Aloe – Circus Ring – Ageless Reason – As When the Mystic – Birth of a Goddess – Beatrice and Dante – The Dilemma – The Gentleman – The Wall – Women and Masks (translation) – Tilth – The Last Fistful – The Traditionalist – The Prepared Statement – St. Antony of Padua – Broken Compact – A Dream of Frances Speedwell – The Encounter – Age Gap – Nightmare of Senility – Research and Development: Classified – Fools – XXVIII: Those Blind from Birth – The Gateway – Advice from a Mother – A Reduced Sentence – Absent Crusader – Complaint and Reply – My Ghost – Song: Reconciliation – Knobs and Levers – The Virus – Druid Love – Problems of Gender – *Jus Primae Noctis* – Confess, Marpessa – Dream Recalled on Waking – Work Drafts.

Note: An issue in two volumes was projected and announced, but was never published.

A135   TIMELESS MEETING   1973

First edition:

Robert | GRAVES | [swelled rule] | TIMELESS MEETING | *POEMS* | PRIVATELY PRINTED | 1973

Collation: [1]–[3]^{8}, 24 leaves.

    2 pp. blank; p.[i] half-title; p.[ii] blank; p.[iii] title-page; p.[iv] copyright notice:

This edition consists of 536 copies | of which 500 numbered and signed by | the author are for sale, printing notice: Number | [signature of Graves], distribution notice; p.[v] CONTENTS; p.[vi] blank; p.vii FOREWORD; p.[viii] blank; pp.1–19 [/1–37] text [poems printed on rectos only, all versos unpaged and blank]; p.[38] blank. [page numbers in square brackets].

    25.0 × 16.5 cm. Bulk: 0.5/0.8 cm. White laid paper; top edge only trimmed. White laid endpapers. Bound in blue cloth; front and back blank; spine stamped in gold, top to bottom: ROBERT GRAVES . TIMELESS MEETING

Price: £5.00. Number of copies: 536. Published 22 June 1973 in light blue dust-jacket printed in dark blue.

Contents: The Promised Ballad – The Impossible Day – The Poet's Curse – Where is the Truth – Love as Lovelessness – The Scared Child – As All Must End – Touch My Shut Lips – The Moon's Last Quarter – True Evil – When and Why – The Window Pane – Unposted Letter (1963) – Pride of Progeny – That Was the Night – Song: The Queen of Time – Should I Care – Timeless Meeting – Envoi.
    Notes: Distributed by Bertram Rota Ltd.
    These poems were simultaneously published in *The Daily Telegraph Magazine*, 22 June 1973.

A136   SONG OF SONGS   [1973]

First edition:

THE SONG OF SONGS | Text and Commentary | by ROBERT GRAVES | Illustrated by HANS ERNI | [publisher's emblem] | *Clarkson N. Potter, Inc.* / *Publisher* NEW YORK | DISTRIBUTED BY CROWN PUBLICATIONS

Collation: [A]⁸ B–D⁸, 32 leaves [endpapers integral with gatherings].
    pp.[i] – [ii] as pastedown endpapers, blank; pp.[iii] – [iv] as free endpapers, blank; p.[v] THE SONG OF SONGS; p.[vi] colour illustration in brown and blue; p.[vii] title-page; p.[viii] [facsimile of Graves' handwriting:] — *In Commendation of Hans Erni* – :[signature of Graves] designer's, copyright, rights reservation, publisher's, LC card, ISBN, printing and edition notices; p.[ix] black and white illustration; p.[x] blank; pp.1–16 INTRODUCTION, with pp [8] and [13] being full-page black and white illustrations; p.[17] THE SONG OF SONGS, CALLED SOLOMON'S [lower right: black and white illustration]; p.[18] black and white illustration; pp.[19] – [49] text, with pp.[21, 23, 24, 27, 28, 31, 33, 35, 37, 38, 41, 43, 45, 46, 48] being full-page black and white illustrations; p.[50] black and white illustration; pp.[51] – [52] as free endpapers, blank; pp.[53] – [54] as pastedown endpapers, blank.
    26.8 × 20.0 cm. Bulk: 0.7/1.2 cm. White laid paper; all edges trimmed. Bound in black cloth; back blank; front gold stamped illustration as p.[33]; spine stamped in gold, top to bottom: ROBERT GRAVES THE SONG OF SONGS . Illustrated by HANS ERNI POTTER

Price: $5.95. Number of copies: 10,000. Published in October 1973 in a white dust-jacket printed in brown and blue.

Notes: Collins issued this edition in the United Kingdom at £2.95, identical in all respects save for Collins appearing on the imprint and spine instead of Potter and the appropriate changes to the copyright notices.

This edition was designed by Felix Gluck Press and was printed in Great Britain.

A137   AT THE GATE   1974

First edition:

Robert | GRAVES | [swelled rule] | AT THE GATE | *POEMS* | PRIVATELY | PRINTED | 1974

Collation: [1] – [3]^8, 24 leaves.

p.[1] Robert Graves | AT THE GATE | Poems; p.[2] blank; p.[3] title-page; p.[4] copyright, printer's, number and signature and publisher's notices; p.[5] CONTENTS; p.[6] blank; pp.7–47 text, with all versos unnumbered and blank; p.[48] blank.

24.8 × 15.9 cm. Bulk: 0.4/0.8 cm. White laid paper; all edges trimmed. White wove endpapers. Bound in red cloth; front and back blank; spine stamped in gold, top to bottom: ROBERT GRAVES . AT THE GATE

Price: £6.00. Number of copies: 536 (500 signed and numbered). Published in 1974 in grey dust-jacket printed in red and purple.

Contents: Ours is no Wedlock – The Discarded Love Poem – Earlier Lovers – Fast Bound Together – L.s.d. – Three Words Only – True Magic – The Tower of Love – The Love Letter – Song: Seven Fresh Years – As A Less Than Robber – Singleness in Love – Love Charms – At The Gate – The Moon's Tear – Song: From Otherwhere or Nowhere – Name Two Disciplines – The Ugly Secret – Three Years Waiting

Note: Published and distributed by Bertram Rota, Ltd.

A138   COLLECTED POEMS 1975   1975

a. First edition:

ROBERT GRAVES | COLLECTED POEMS | 1975 | CASSELL . LONDON

Collation: [1] – [19]^{16} [20]^8, 312 leaves.

pp.[i] – [ii] blank; p.[iii] COLLECTED POEMS | 1975; p.[iv] blank; p.[v] title-page; p.[vi] publisher's, copyright, edition, ISBN and printer's notices; p.[vii] FOREWORD; p.[viii] blank; p.[ix] – [xxxi] CONTENTS; p.[xxxii] blank; p.[1] section head; p.[2] blank; pp.3–551 text, with pp.[25, 51, 67, 105, 119, 141, 155, 163, 185, 199, 215, 223, 241, 253, 267, 285, 299, 325, 335, 355, 373, 383, 395, 417, 437, 453, 483, 509, 521, 537] being section headings and pp.[26, 52, 68, 106, 120, 142, 156, 164, 186, 200, 216, 224, 242, 254, 268, 286, 300, 326, 336, 356, 374, 384, 396, 418, 438, 454, 484, 510, 522, 538] being blank; p.[552] blank; p.[553] INDEX OF TITLES; p.[554] blank; pp.555–572 index; p.[573] INDEX TO FIRST LINES OF POEMS; p.[574] blank; pp.575–592 index.

21.5 × 13.7 cm. Bulk: 4.1/4.7 cm. White wove paper; all edges trimmed. White

wove endpapers. Bound in dull myrtle cloth; front and back blank; spine stamped in gold: ROBERT | GRAVES | [rule] | COLLECTED | POEMS | 1975 | CASSELL

Price: £8.50. Number of copies: unknown. Published in September 1975 in white dust-jacket printed in green and gold.

Contents: Foreword – I: In the Wilderness – The Haunted House – Reproach – The Finding of Love – Rocky Acres – Outlaws – One Hard Look – A Frosty Night – Allie – Henry and Mary – Love Without Hope – What Did I Dream? – The Troll's Nosegay – The Hills of May – Lost Love – Vain and Careless – The Pier-Glass – Apples and Water – Angry Samson – Down – II: In Procession – Warning to Children – Alice – Richard Roe and John Doe – I'd Die for You – Ancestors – The Coronation Murder – Children of Darkness – The Cool Web – Love in Barrenness – Song of Contrariety – The Presence – The Land of Whipperginny – In No Direction – The Castle – Return – The Bards – Nobody – The Progress – Full Moon – Vanity – Pure Death – Sick Love – It Was All Very Tidy – III: Thief – The Furious Voyage – *Song*: LiftBoy – The Next Time – Ulysses – The Succubus – The Reader over My Shoulder – The Legs – Gardener – Front Door Soliloquy – In Broken Images – Trudge, Body! – The Christmas Robin – On Rising Early – Flying Crooked – Fragment of a Lost Poem – Brother – IV: The Devil's Advice to Story-Tellers – Sea Side – Wm. Brazier – Welsh Incident – Interruption – Hell – Leda – Synthetic Such – The Florist Rose – Lost Acres – At First Sight – Down, Wanton, Down! – A Former Attachment – Nature's Lineaments – Time – The Philosopher – On Dwelling – Ogres and Pygmies – Single Fare – To Walk on Hills – To Bring the Dead to Life – To Evoke Posterity – Any Honest Housewife – Never Such Love – Certain Mercies – The Cuirassiers of the Frontier – The Laureate – A Jealous Man – The Cloak – The Foreboding – With Her Lips Only – The Halls of Bedlam – Or to Perish before Day – A Country Mansion – Lovers in Winter – Advocates – V: On Portents – The Terraced Valley – The Chink – The Ages of Oath – New Legends – Like Snow – End of Play – The Climate of Thought – The Fallen Tower of Siloam – The Great-Grandmother – No More Ghosts – VI: A Love Story – Dawn Bombardment – The Shot – The Thieves – Lollocks – To Sleep – Despite and Still – The Suicide in the Copse – Frightened Men – The Oath – Language of the Seasons – Mid-Winter Waking – The Beach – The Villagers and Death – The Door – Under the Pot – Through Nightmare – To Lucia at Birth – Death by Drums – She Tells Her Love While Half Asleep – Theseus and Ariadne – Penthesileia – The Death Room – To Juan at the Winter Solstice – To Be Called a Bear – VII: My Name and I – 1805 – The Persian Version – The Weather of Olympus – Apollo of the Physiologists – The Oldest Soldier – Grotesques i, ii, iii, iv, v, vi – Beauty in Trouble – Sirocco at Deyá – From the Embassy – VIII: The White Goddess – The Song of Blodeuwedd – Instructions to the Orphic Adept – Lament for Pasiphaë – Return of the Goddess – IX: Counting the Beats – The Young Cordwainer – Your Private Way – The Survivor – Questions in a Wood – Darien – The Portrait – Prometheus – The Straw – Cry Faugh! – Hercules at Nemea – Dialogue on the Headland – Liadan and Curithir – The Sea Horse – Cat-Goddesses – The Blue-Fly – A Lost Jewel – The Window Sill – Spoils – Rhea – X: The Face in the Mirror – Gratitude for a Nightmare – Friday Night – The Naked and the Nude – Woman and Tree –

Forbidden Words – A Slice of Wedding Cake – A Plea to Boys and Girls – Nothing
– Call It a Good Marriage – The Second-Fated – The Twin of Sleep – Around the
Mountain – Leaving the Rest Unsaid – XI: Lyceia – Symptoms of Love – The
Sharp Ridge – Under the Olives – The Visitation – Fragment – Apple Island –
The Falcon Woman – Troughs of Sea – The Laugh – The Death Grapple – The
Starred Coverlet – Patience – The Cure – Hag-Ridden – Turn of the Moon – The
Secret Land – Seldom, Yet Now – XII: A Lost World – The Dangerous Gift –
Twice of the Same Fever – Surgical Ward: Men – The Two Witches – The Quiet
Glades of Eden – Joan and Darby – *Song*: Come, Enjoy Your Sunday! – XIII: Ruby
and Amethyst – Recognition – Variables of Green – The Watch – Name Day –
Uncalendared Love – The Meeting – Lack – Not at Home – Horizon – Golden
Anchor – Lion Lover – Ibycus in Samos – Possessed – The Winged Heart – In
Trance at a Distance – The Wreath – In Her Praise – A Restless Ghost – Between
Moon and Moon – XIV: Beware, Madam! – The Cliff Edge – The Miller's Man –
Acrobats – Ouzo Unclouded – The Broken Girth – Inkidoo and the Queen of
Babel – Three Songs for the Lute: I. Truth is Poor Physic – II. In Her Only Way –
III. Hedges Freaked With Snow – The Ambrosia of Dionysus and Semele – The
Unnamed Spell – XV: A Time of Waiting – Expect Nothing – No Letter – The
Why of the Weather – In Time – Fire Walker – Deed of Gift – At Best, Poets – She
is No Liar – A Last Poem – The Pearl – The Leap – Bank Account – Judgement of
Paris – Man Does, Woman Is – The Ample Garden – To Myrto About Herself –
The Three-Faced – Dazzle of Darkness – Myrrhina – Food of the Dead – Eurydice
– To Beguile and Betray – I Will Write – XVI: Bird of Paradise – The Metaphor –
Song: A Phoenix Flame – Secrecy – Joseph and Mary – An East Wind – Dance of
Words – A Blind Arrow – The Oleaster – The Septuagenarian – *Non Cogunt Astra*
– *Song*: Sword and Rose – Endless Pavement – In Disguise – A Measure of
Casualness – In Time of Absence – The Green Castle – Not to Sleep – The
Hearth – That Other World – The Beds of Grainne and Diarmuid – Consortium
of Stones – The Black Goddess – XVII: Broken Neck – O – Woman of Greece –
The Colours of Night – Between Trains – To the Teumessian Vixen – The Hung
Wu Vase – *La Mejicana* – Lamia in Love – After the Flood – All I Tell You From My
Heart – The Undead – Grace Notes – Good Night to the Old Gods – The Sweet-
Shop Round the Corner – Double Bass – Descent into Hell – The Pardon – Point
of No Return – XVIII: The Red Shower – Above the Edge of Doom – Wild
Cyclamen – Gift of Sight – *Batxóca* – The Snap-Comb Wilderness – A Shift of
Scene – Change – A Court of Love – Black – Between Hyssop and Axe – *Son
Altesse* – Gold and Malachite – Ambience – The Vow – The Frog and the Golden
Ball – Those Who Came Short – Whole Love – This Holy Month – The
Impossible – The Fetter – Iron Palace – True Joy – Tomorrow's Envy of Today –
The Hidden Garden – The Wedding – Everywhere is Here – What Will Be, Is –
Song: The Far Side of Your Moon – Deliverance – Conjunction – Nothing Now
Astonishes – XIX: Cock in Pullet's Feathers – Dead Hand – Arrears of Moonlight
– What Did You Say? – Lure of Murder – The Gorge – Ecstasy of Chaos – Stolen
Jewel – The Snapped Thread – Fortunate Child – Loving True, Flying Blind – The
Near Eclipse – Dancing Flame – Birth of Angels – On Giving – XX: P'eng that
was a K'un – Like Owls – In Perspective – The Utter Rim – Unicorn and the
White Doe – Bower-Bird – Mist – The Word – Perfectionists – Prison Walls – A
Dream of Hell – Our Self – Bites and Kisses – Sun-Face and Moon-Face –

Freehold – The Necklace – A Bracelet – Blackening Sky – Blessed Sun – Lion-gentle – Spite of Mirrors – Pride of Love – Hooded Flame – Injuries – Her Brief Withdrawal – The Crane – Strangeness – XXI: *Song*: How Can I Care? – *Song*: Though Once True Lovers – *Song*: Cherries or Lilies – *Song*: Crown of Stars – *Song*: The Palm Tree – *Song*: Fig Tree in Leaf – *Song*: Dewdrop and Diamond – *Song*: Sullen Moods – *Song*: Just Friends – *Song*: Of Course – *Song*: Three Rings for Her – *Sincèrement* – *Dans un Seul Lit* – Possibly – Is Now the Time? – Twins – Sail and Oar – Gooseflesh Abbey – The Home-coming – With the Gift of a Lion's Claw – Wigs and Beards – Personal Packaging, Inc. – Work Room – The Ark – All Except Hannibal – The Beggar Maid and King Cophetua – For Ever – *Jugum Improbum* – *De Arte Poetica* – *Sit mihi terra levis* – XXII: Astymelusa – Tousled Pillow – To Be In Love – Fact of the Act – To Ogmian Hercules – Arrow Shots – She to Him – Within Reason – The Yet Unsayable – None the Wiser – The Narrow Sea – The Olive-Yard – XXIII: *Song*: Dream Warning – *Song*: Beyond Giving – *Song:* The Sigil – *Song*: Basket of Blossom – *Song*: Yesterday Only – *Song*: Twinned Heart – *Song*: Olive Tree – *Song*: Once More – *Song*: The Promise – *Song*: Victims of Calumny – *Song*: To a Rose – *Song*: The Clocks of Time – *Song*: Wherever We May Be – XXIV: Gold Cloud – Compact – Trial of Innocence – Love Gifts – Mankind and Ocean – Poisoned Day – Virgin Mirror – What Is Love? – Secret Theatre – How It Started – Brief Reunion – The Judges – Love and Night – Child with Veteran – Superstition – Purification – Powers Unconfessed – Pandora – Solomon's Seal – To Put It Simply – In the Name of Virtue – To Tell and Be Told – The Theme of Death – At the Well – XXV: Logic – Robbers' Den – The Accomplice – First Love – Through a Dark Wood – In the Vestry – When Love Is Not – The Reiteration – Semi-Detached – Iago – Against Witchcraft – Man of Evil – The Raft – Tolling Bell – The Hero – Blanket Charge – The Uncut Diamond – The Strayed Message – The Risk – Something to Say – Troublesome Fame – OCCASIONALIA: The Imminent Seventies – Carol of Patience – H – Invitation to Bristol – The Primrose Bed – Poem: A Reminder – The Strangling in Merrion Square – *Song*: The Sundial's Lament – *Antorcha y Corona, 1968:* Torch and Crown, 1968 – The Awakening – Armistice Day, 1918 – XXVI: The Hoopoe Tells Us How – The Wand – Five: Quinque – Arrow on the Vane – Gorgon Mask – To be Poets – With a Gift of Rings – *Casse-Noisette* – The Garden – The Green-Sailed Vessel – Dreaming Children – The Prohibition – Serpent's Tail – Until We Both . . . – The Rose – Testament – The Crab-Tree – Three Locked Hoops – Cliff and Wave – Her Beauty – Always – Desert Fringe – The Title of Poet – Depth of Love – Breakfast Table – The Half-Finished Letter – The Hazel Grove – Pity – Silent Visit – Coronet of Moonlight – *Song*: To Become Each Other – Heaven – Growing Pains – Friday Night – The Pact – Poor Others – A Toast to Death – The Young Sibyl – Records – The Flowering Aloe – Circus Ring – Ageless Reason – As When the Mystic – Unposted Letter (1963) – XXVII: Birth of a Goddess – Beatrice and Dante – The Dilemma – The Gentleman – The Wall – Women and Masks (translation) – Tilth – The Last Fistful – The Traditionalist – The Prepared Statement – St Antony of Padua – Broken Compact – A Dream of Frances Speedwell – The Encounter – Age Gap – Nightmare of Senility – Research and Development: Classified – Fools – Those Blind From Birth – The Gateway – Advice from a Mother – A Reduced Sentence – Absent Crusader – Complaint and Reply – My Ghost – *Song*: Reconciliation – Knobs and Levers –

The Virus – Druid Love – Problems of Gender – *Jus Primae Noctis* – Confess, Marpessa – Dream Recalled on Waking – Work Drafts – Colophon – XXVIII: The Promised Ballad – The Impossible Day – The Poet's Curse – Seven Years – Love as Lovelessness – The Scared Child – As All Must End – Touch My Shut Lips – The Moon's Last Quarter – True Evil – When and Why – The Window Pane – Pride of Progeny – That Was the Night – *Song*: The Queen of Time – Should I Care – Timeless Meeting – Envoi – XXIX: Ours Is No Wedlock – The Crystal – The Discarded Love Poem – A Charm for Sound Sleeping – Earlier Lovers – Fast Bound Together – The New Eternity – History of the Fall – L.s.d. – Three Words Only – True Magic – The Tower of Love – The Love Letter – *Song*: Seven Fresh Years – Love Charms – Elsewhere – As a Less Than Robber – What Can We Not Ask? – Two Crucial Generations – To Come of Age – XXX: Singleness in Love – September Landscape – Crucibles of Love – At the Gate – Woman Poet and Man Poet – The Field-Postcard – If No Cuckoo Sings – The Moon's Tear – *Song*: From Otherwhere or Nowhere – Name – Two Disciplines – The Ugly Secret – Mountain Lovers – Three Times in Love – Three Years Waiting – The Sentence – Spring 1974 – Advent of Summer – The Unpenned Poem – The Green Woods of Unrest – Index of Titles – Index of First Lines.

Notes: There is a cancel title-page in some copies of this edition.

Impressions: 2nd, February 1978.

A138b. First American edition (1977):

Robert Graves | NEW | COLLECTED | POEMS | Introduction by | JAMES McKINLEY | 1977 | Doubleday & Company, Inc. | Garden City, New York

Collation: [1] – [20]^{12}, 240 leaves.

p.[i] NEW | COLLECTED | POEMS; p.[ii] blank; p.[iii] title-page; p.[iv] LC card, copyright, rights reservation, printing and edition notices; p.[v] *FOREWORD*; p.[vi] blank; pp. vii–xix *CONTENTS*; p.[xx] blank; pp.xxi–xxxi *INTRODUCTION*; p.[xxxii] blank; p.[xxxiii] NEW | COLLECTED | POEMS; p.[xxxiv] blank; p.1–403 text, with two leaves of photographic plates inserted between pp.62/63, 158/159, 254/255, 350/351; p.[404] blank; p.[405] *INDEX OF TITLES*; p.[406] blank; pp.407–423 index; p.[424] blank; p.[425] *INDES TO FIRST LINES OF POEMS* ; p.[426] blank; pp.427–442 index; pp. [443] – [446] blank.

20.8 × 13.8 cm. Bulk: 3.3/3.8 cm. White wove paper; top and bottom edges only trimmed. White wove endpapers. Bound in grey-blue paper boards with black cloth spine. Front and back blank; spine printed in silver, down spine, in two parallel lines: *ROBERT GRAVES* NEW | COLLECTED POEMS | [upright at foot:] DOUBLEDAY.

Price: $10.00. Number of copies undetermined. Published in January 1977.

Contents: As A138a except for the Introduction by McKinley.

A139   TWIN TO TWIN   1977

First edition:

Twin to Twin | Two poems | by | ROBERT GRAVES | SIDCOT | The Gruffyground Press | 1977

Collation: 1 French folded leaf, sewn at centre.
p.[1] title-page; pp.[2] – [3] text; p.[4] publisher's, printer's and limitations notices.
18 × 12.2 cm. Bulk: .01 cm. White Hosho handmade paper. Sewn with red thread in to French folded red Tumba Ingres mould-made paper covers, printed in black on front: Twin to Twin | ROBERT GRAVES

Price: Not for sale. Number of copies: 25. Published in September 1977.

Contents: Considine – Twin to Twin.

A140   ADVICE TO COLONEL VALENTINE   [1979]

First edition:

[all set flush left:] *Advice to* | *Colonel Valentine* | Two poems | by | ROBERT GRAVES | SIDCOT | The Gruffyground Press | 1979

Collation: single sheet folded in half and stitched to inner cover, 2 leaves.
p.[1] title-page; pp.[2] – [3] text; p.[4] colophon: *Designed, handset in Palatino types and printed on | Japanese hand-made paper by Kenneth Hardacre | at the Kit-Cat Press, 17 Lauderdale Road, | Hunton Bridge, King's Langley, Hertforshire | Published by Anthony Baker at the | Gruffyground Press, Ladram, Sidcot, | Winscombe, Somerset | The edition is limited to twenty-five copies*
17.6 × 12.6 cm. Bulk: .02 cm. White laid paper; top edge only trimmed. Bound in quarto fold of mustard yellow paper and that covered to two single wrap folds. Back cover blank; front printed in black: [all set flush left:] Advice to | Colonel Valentine | ROBERT GRAVES

Price: gratis. Copies: 25. Published autumn 1979.

Contents: Hippopotamus' Address to the Freudians – Advice to Colonel Valentine.

Note: No copyright permissions or protections are recorded in this edition

A141   ROBERT GRAVES POEMS   1980

First edition:

[all within red box rule; inside which a pale yellow ground; upon which printed in black and **red**:]ROBERT | GRAVES | **POEMS** | *Selected and Introduced by* | ELAINE KERRIGAN | *Illustrated by* | PAUL HOGARTH | **The Limited Editions Club** | **New York . 1980**

Collation: [1] – [9]⁸ [10]⁴ [11]⁸, 184 leaves.
pp.[i] – [ii] blank; p.[iii] *Poems by Robert GRAVES*; p.[iv] blank; p.[v] title-page;

p.[vi] copyright notice; pp.vii–xiii *Introduction*; p.[xiv] blank; pp.xv–xvii *Contents*; p. [xviii] blank; pp.xix–xx *The Artist's Notes on the Illustrations·*; *p.*[1] *Poems by Robert GRAVES*; p.[2] blank; pp.3–144 text, with two leaf colour plates on coated paper bound in between pp.12/13, 28/29, 44/45, 60/61, 76/77, 92/93, 108/109, 124/125; p.[145] blank; p.[146] Two thousand copies of this edition of | *Poems by Robert Graves* | have been made for the members of | The Limited Editions Club | at The Stinehour Press in | Lunenburg Vermont | from the typographic plans of | Freeman Keith | [dot] | This is copy number | [number written in] | and it is here signed by | [signatures of Keith and Hogarth]; pp.[147]–[148] blank.

25.3 × 17.0 cm. Bulk: 2.6/3.2. Heavy cream laid paper, unwatermarked; all edges trimmed and top gilt. Dark tan textured wove endpapers. Bound in 3/4 dark tan paper printed in type-ornament designs in red and black; spine dark brown buckram stamped in gold, top to bottom: ROBERT GRAVES [diamond] POEMS

Price: Undetermined. Number of copies: 2,000. Published in 1980 in glassine dust-jacket and in a slip case covered in paper as the binding with dark brown buckram on top and bottom ends.

Contents: Introduction – Seldom Yet Now – The Starred Coverlet – The Visitation – Spoils – The Sea Horse – Broken Neck – Black – Gold and Malachite – La Mejicana – Lamia in Love – The Black Goddess – Consortium of Stones – The Snap-Comb Wilderness – Change – The Pardon – Between Trains – In Disguise – A Measure of Casualness – An East Wind – The Three-Faced – The Ample Garden – Fire Walker – A Time of Waiting – The White Goddess – In Her Praise – The Wreath – Lion Lover – Golden Anchor – Name – Recognition – Ruby and Amethyst – The Falcon Woman – Good Night to the Old Gods – A Last Poem – At Best, Poets – She Is No Liar – Expect Nothing – Possessed – Turn of the Moon – Full Moon – Tomorrow's Envy of Today – Song: The Far Side of Your Moon – What Will Be, Is – Nothing Now Astonishes – Between Moon and Moon – Song of Contrariety – The Presence – Pure Death – The Vow – Son Altesse – Whole Love – Gift of Sight – Batxóca – A Court of Love – The Door – I'd Die for You – A Jealous Man – It was All Very Tidy – The Beds of Grainne and Diarmuid – Secrecy – The Suicide in the Copse – Under the Olives – Darien – The Straw – The Winged Heart – Apple Island – Rhea – The Weather of Olympus – The Naked and the Nude – The Terraced Valley – Wild Cyclamen – The Oleaster – Leaving the Rest Unsaid – The Face in the Mirror – My Name and I – The Foreboding – The Cloak – Return – In No Direction – The Progress – Point of No Return – What Did I Dream? – Gratitude for a Nightmare – To Sleep – Reproach – The Pier-Glass – In Procession – The Castle – The Green Castle – Prometheus – The Twin of Sleep – The Succubus – Outlaws – A Lost Jewel – Lack – Nobody – The Thieves – Thief – Beware, Madam! – Those Who Came Short – All I Tell You from My Heart – To the Teumessian Vixen – I Will Write – Eurydice – To Beguile and Betray – Food of the Dead – Myrrhina – 3 Songs for the Lute: Truth is Poor Physic – In Her Only Way – Hedges Freaked with Snow – The Hearth – That Other World – In Time of Absence – Judgement of Paris – Joan and Darby – A Lost World – The Secret Land – The Cure – Woman and Tree.

Note: The Introduction is dated "Mallorca, 1980."

A142   AN ANCIENT CASTLE   [1980]

First edition:

ROBERT GRAVES | An Ancient Castle | *Illustrated by* | Elizabeth Graves | [dot] | With an Afterword by | William David Thomas | [publisher's emblem] | PETER OWEN . LONDON

Collation: π 1 [1]^8 [2]^{14} χ 1, 38 leaves.
   [Note that π 1 is the front free endpaper and χ 1 is the rear free endpaper.]
   pp.[i] – [ii] blank; p.[1] An Ancient Castle; p.[2] blank; p.[3] title-page; p.[4] ISBN, rights reservation, publisher's, copyright and printer's notices; p.[5] Contents; p.[6] black and white illustration; pp.7–66 text and illustrations, with p.[56] being unnumbered; pp.67–69 Afterword; pp.[70] – [74] blank.
   21.5 × 13.7 cm. Bulk: 0.7/1.0 cm. White wove paper; all edges trimmed. White wove endpapers, pastedowns only. Bound in brown simulated cloth; front and back blank; spine stamped in silver, top to bottom: Robert Graves AN ANCIENT CASTLE *Peter Owen*

Price: £3.95. Number of copies: 1,000. Published in October 1980 in white dust-jacket printed in black, green and yellow.

Note: The manuscript from which this edition was produced was sold by Graves, through Bertram Rota, to the University of British Columbia, Victoria, Canada, in 1975.
   This work has been translated into Spanish.

A143   IN BROKEN IMAGES   [1982]

First edition:

IN | BROKEN IMAGES | *Selected Letters of Robert Graves* | *1914–1946* | Edited, with a commentary, by | Paul O'Prey | HUTCHINSON | London Melbourne Sydney Auckland Johannesburg

Collation: [1] – [10]^{16} [11]^{10} [12]^{16}, 186 leaves.
   p.[1] [set flush right:] IN BROKEN IMAGES | [publisher's emblem]; p.[2] blank; p.[3] title-page; p.[4] publisher's, copyright, printer's, BL cataloguing and ISBN notices; p.[5] CONTENTS; p.[6] blank; p.[7] ILLUSTRATIONS; p.[8] blank; p.[9] quotation from Graves, *incipit*: He continues quick and dull; p.[10] blank; pp.11–13[14] INTRODUCTION; pp.15–18[19] CORRESPONDENTS; p.[20] blank; pp.21–22[23] BIOGRAPHICAL NOTES; p.[24] blank; pp.[25] – [26]27–344[345] text, with pp.[25, 109 185, 283] being section titles and pp.[26, 108, 110, 183, 184, 186, 282, 284, 301] being unnumbered; p.[346] blank; p.347 APPENDIX A [letter from Sassoon]; pp.348–349 APPENDIX B [historical reconstruction in *I, Claudius*]; pp.350–367 NOTES; p.[368] blank; pp.369–371[372] INDEX
   23.2 × 15.3 cm. Bulk: 2.9/3.5 cm. White wove paper; all edges trimmed. White wove endpapers. Bound in navy blue cloth; front and back blank; spine stamped in silver: IN | BROKEN | IMAGES | [ornamental rule] | *Selected* | *Letters of* | *Robert* | *Graves* | *1914–1946* | [ornamental rule] | Edited by | PAUL | O'PREY | [publisher's emblem] | HUTCHINSON

Price: £12.95. Number of copies: 2,463. Published 10 May 1982 in navy blue dust-jacket printed in white.

Note: A portion of this edition was published in *The Observer,* 9 May 1982.

A144   TWO POEMS BY ROBERT GRAVES   1982

First edition:

Two Poems by | *ROBERT GRAVES* | *with a Dutch translation by]* | *Willem Kramer* | *Mercator Pers 1982*

Collation: [1]¹⁰, 10 leaves.
pp.[1] – [4] blank; p.[5] ,,*And Robert Graves lives on";* p. [6] blank; p.[7] title-page; pp.[8] –14[15] text; p.[16] blank; p.[17] COLOPHON | *In honour of Robert Graves these two poems* | *were hand-set in Cancellaresca Bastarda* | *and printed on Zerkall Bü-tten in 1982;* | *45 copies are a humble contribution* | *to the 'Drukken' project; 30 are* | *presents for friends of the* | *Mercator Press.* | [ornament;] pp.[18] – [20] blank.
16.4 × 10.5 cm. Bulk: 0.3 cm. White laid paper, unwatermarked; top edge only trimmed. Bound in heavy grey paper wrappers; back and spine blank; front printed in black: *Two Poems by* | *ROBERT GRAVES* | *with a Dutch translation by* | *Willem Kramer* | [large printer's ornament (3.9 × 3.5 cm.) upper female body with heavy swirls].

Price: gratis. Number of copies: 45. Published in late 1982.

Contents: Ulysses – Despite and Still.

Notes: The English text appears on versos and the Dutch translation on rectos. No pages are numbered. No copyright permissions or protections are recorded in this book, and the text of both poems is that found in A138, except for the capitalisation of 'Despite' and 'Still' in line 12 of the latter poem.

A145   ELEVEN SONGS   [1983]

Eleven Songs / Robert Graves | [design in tan of figures]

Collation: 14 double folds with open ends stabbed, 14 [28] leaves.
pp.[1] – [2] blank; p.[3] A New Seizin; p.[4] blank; p.[5] title-page; p.[6] blank; pp.[7] – [20] text; pp.[21] – [22] blank; p.[23] Index; p.[24] blank; p.[25] Colophon | New Seizin 1 has been hand-set in | 20 point Monotype Bemb and | hand-printed on 'La Pedalette', | a 1910 cylinder press, by Tibor Szántó | and Tomás Graves at The New | Seizin Press, Deiá, Mallorca, in | September 1983. The paper is made | by Hahnemühle and the covers | by Fabriano. The illustration on the cover | and title-page is the work of Junyer. | There are 100 copies signed by | the printers and by the illustrator. | This is copy number [number written in] | [3 signatures]; pp.[26] – [28] blank, but p. [27] has embossed at top: [within a shield] DEIA
24.5 × 17.6 cm. Bulk: .9/1 cm. White laid paper, bottom edge only trimmed. Bound in pale olive wrappers stabbed through rear edge. Back and spine blank; front printed in black: ELEVEN SONGS | ROBERT GRAVES | [blind stamped design as on title-page]

Price: Undetermined. Number of copies: 100. Published in September 1983.

Contents: Just Friends – Of Course – The Palm Tree – How Can I Care? – Fig Tree in Leaf – Though Once True Lovers – Three Rings for Her – Dew Drop and Diamond – Cherries or Lilies – Sullen Moods – Crown of Stars.

Note: An errata slip is laid-in noting correction to the final line of 'Sullen Moods'.

A146   BETWEEN MOON AND MOON   [1984]

First edition:

BETWEEN | MOON AND | MOON | *Selected Letters of Robert Graves* | *1946–1972* | Edited, with a commentary and notes, by | Paul O'Prey | HUTCHINSON | London Melbourne Sydney Auckland Johannesburg

Collation: [1] – [10]^{16}, 160 leaves.
    [free endpaper reckoned as pp.1–2]; p.[3] [all set flush right:] BETWEEN MOON AND MOON | [publisher's emblem]; p.[4] blank; p.[5] title-page; p.[6] publisher's, copyright, typography, printer's, BL cataloguing and ISBN notices; p.[7] CONTENTS; p.[8] blank; p.[9]–10 INTRODUCTION; pp.11–[12] ACKNOWLEDGEMENTS; pp.13–15[16] CORRESPONDENTS; pp.17–[18] BIOGRAPHICAL NOTES | 1946–1982, including principal | publications; p.[19] PART ONE | 1946–1951; p.[20] blank; pp. 23–286[287] text, with pp.[98, 167] being unnumbered, pp.[99, 169, 229] being section titles and pp.[100, 168, 170, 230] being blank; p.[288] blank; p.[289] APPENDIX | 'Summary of | Critical Principles' | from *The Nazarene* | *Gospel Restored*; p. [290] blank; pp.291–293[294] text; pp.295–317 NOTES; p.[318] blank; pp.319–323 Index; P. [324] blank.
    23.2 × 15.4 cm. Bulk: 2.2/2.8 cm. White wove paper; all edges trimmed. White wove endpapers. Bound in dark green cloth; front and back blank; spine stamped in silver: BETWEEN | MOON | AND | MOON | [decorative rule] | *Selected* | *Letters* *of* | *Robert Graves* | *1946–1972* | [decorative rule] | Edited by | PAUL O'PREY | [publisher's emblem] | HUTCHINSON

Price: £14.95. Number of copies: 1,726. Published in November 1984 in white dust-jacket printed in green and white.

Notes: Pages 21–22 do not exist and the pagination skips from p.[20] to p.23.
    The 'Biographical Notes' (pp.17–[18]) say that they cover the years 1946–1982, but the latest date given in them is 1978.

B. Books containing contributions by Robert Graves

A complete listing of first book publications only is intended. No attempt has been made to include the many anthology reprintings of material already published by Graves in his own books, nor are partial quotations or passing references or brief citations from Graves included.

B1 WELSH POETRY OLD AND NEW 1912

WELSH POETRY | OLD AND NEW | IN ENGLISH VERSE | BY | ALFRED PERCEVAL GRAVES, M.A. | ('CANWR CILARNÉ') | PRESIDENT OF THE IRISH LITERARY SOCIETY | LONDON REPRESENTATIVE OF THE COUNCIL OF THE CELTIC ASSOCIATION | MEMBER OF THE EXECUTIVE COMMITTEES OF THE FOLK SONG SOCIETY | AND OF THE WELSH AND IRISH FOLK SONG SOCIETIES | AND MEMBER OF THE HONOURABLE SOCIETY OF CYMMRODORION | LONGMANS, GREEN, AND CO. | 39 PATERNOSTER ROW, LONDON | NEW YORK, BOMBAY, AND CALCUTTA | 1912 | *All rights reserved*

Collation: [a]⁶ b − c⁸ B − L⁸ M⁶, 108 leaves.

2pp. blank; p.[i] WELSH POETRY OLD AND NEW; p.[ii] blank; p.[iii] title-page; p.[iv] blank; p.[v] dedication; p.[vi] blank; pp.[vii] − viii FOREWORD; p.[ix]x − xv PREFACE; p.[xvi] blank; pp.[xvii]xviii − xx CONTENTS; pp.[xxi]xxii − xlii INTRODUCTION; pp.[1]2 − 134 text, with pp.[13, 23, 42, 53, 64, 84, 97, 116] unnumbered; pp.[135]136 − 144 A NOTE ON WELSH METRES; pp.[145]146 − 170 BIOGRAPHICAL AND CRITICAL NOTES; pp.[171] − [172] blank.

18.5 × 12.4 cm. Bulk: 1.5/1.9 cm. White wove paper; all edges trimmed. White wove endpapers. Bound in medium dull green cloth; back blank; front stamped: WELSH POETRY | OLD AND NEW | IN ENGLISH VERSE | ALFRED PERCEVAL GRAVES | [near bottom, at right:] [two concentric circles, inside which a solid circular black box, in which a red lion rampant]; spine stamped: [double rule] | WELSH | POETRY | OLD AND NEW | IN ENGLISH | VERSE | A.P. | GRAVES | LONGMANS | [double rule]

Price: 2s.6d. Number of copies: 2,000. Published 15 July 1912.

Note: Graves' contribution (p.139) is an englyn called 'The Will O' the Wisp'.

B2 THE BRITISH SOLDIER 1918

[all flush left:]'THE BRITISH SOLDIER' | AN EXHIBITION OF PICTURES | BY ERIC H. KENNINGTON | (An Official Artist on the Western Front) | WITH A PREFACE BY | ROBERT GRAVES | ERNEST BROWN & PHILLIPS | THE LEICESTER GALLERIES | LEICESTER SQUARE, LONDON | JUNE–JULY, 1918. *Collation*: 8 leaves, unsigned, sewn three times in centre.

p.[1] title-page; p.[2] advertisement for artists' supplies; pp.3–6 THE BRITISH SOLDIER; pp.7–16 *Catalogue*

13.1 × 10.6 cm. Bulk: 0.2 cm. White wove paper; all edges trimmed. Bound in grey paper wrappers printed in black; front cover: ENTRANCE GALLERY AND REYNOLDS ROOM | [rectangular single rule box enclosing all but final line:] | [six lines flush left:] 'THE BRITISH SOLDIER' | AN EXHIBITION OF PICTURES | BY ERIC H. KENNINGTON | (An Official Artist on the Western Front) | WITH A PREFACE BY | ROBERT GRAVES | ERNEST BROWN & PHILLIPS | (W.L.PHILLIPS, C.L. PHILLIPS, O.F. BROWN) | THE LEICESTER GALLERIES | LEICESTER SQUARE, LONDON | EXHIBITION HO. 260.JUNE–JULY, 1918. PRICE THREEPENCE. [*sic* 'HO']; inside front cover: advertisement for exhibit of watercolours by Capt. E. Handley-Read; inside back cover: advertisements for *Colour*; back cover: advertisement for official war publications.

Price: 3d. Number of copies: *c*. 1,200. Published in June 1918.

Note: Graves' contribution is 'The British Soldier' (pp.3–6).

B3 GEORGIAN POETRY 1918–1919 1919

GEORGIAN | POETRY | 1918–1919 | [three leaves] | [two leaves] | [leaf] | THE POETRY BOOKSHOP | 35 Devonshire Street | Theobalds Road | W.C. | MCMXIX

Collation: [1]–[13]⁸, 104 leaves.

p.[i] GEORGIAN POETRY; p.[ii] publication notice; p.[iii] title-page; p.[iv] TO | THOMAS HARDY; p.[v] PREFATORY NOTE; p.[vi] blank; pp.[vii]–[x] CONTENTS; p.[1] section heading; p.[2] blank; pp.3–191 text, with pp.[9, 15, 27, 37, 47, 57, 71, 79, 91, 95, 105, 113, 123, 127, 139, 155, 163, 177] being section headings and pp.[8, 10, 14, 16, 28, 38, 48, 58, 72, 80, 92, 96, 106, 114, 124, 126, 128, 140, 156, 164, 178] being blank; p.[192] blank; pp.193–196 BIBLIOGRAPHY; pp.[197]–[198] publisher's advertisements.

18.7 × 12.8 cm. Bulk: 1.4/1.9 cm. White laid paper watermarked with a crown and: Abbey Mills | Greenfield; top edges only trimmed and gilt; fore-edges unopened. White wove endpapers. Bound in goldish yellow cloth; back blank; front stamped in gold: GEORGIAN POETRY | 1918–1919 | THE POETRY BOOKSHOP; spine stamped in gold: Georgian | Poetry | 1918–1919 | [inside a solid blue shield:] P [diamond] B

Price: 6s. Number of copies undetermined. Published 15 November 1919.

Notes: Graves' contribution is attributed in the index to *Country Sentiment* (A5). But in fact that book was not published until March 1920. This is therefore the first book publication of the following poems: 'A Ballad of Nursery Rhyme' (pp.81–83), 'A

Frosty Night' (p.84), 'True Johnny' (pp.85–86), 'The Cupboard' (p.87), 'The Voice of Beauty Drowned' (pp.88–89), and 'Rocky Acres' (p.90).
The title-page in some copies is a cancel.

B4   OXFORD POETRY 1921   1921

OXFORD POETRY | 1921 | EDITED BY | ALAN PORTER RICHARD HUGHES | ROBERT GRAVES | OXFORD BASIL BLACKWELL | MCMXXI

Collation: [A]⁴ B–E⁸, 36 leaves.
p.[i] OXFORD POETRY | 1921; p.[ii] publisher's advertisements; p.[iii] title-page; p.[iv] printer's notice; p.[v] note; pp.[vi] – [vii] CONTENTS; p.[viii] blank; pp.1–64 text.
18.4 × 12.5 cm. Bulk: 0.6 cm. White wove paper; all edges trimmed. Bound in dark blue paper wrapper; back blank; front has white paper label at top left: [rectangular single rule box enclosing all:] Oxford | Poetry | 1921 | Oxford | Basil Blackwell

Price: 2s. Number of copies: 1,500. Published 21 November 1921.

Notes: Graves' contribution (pp.21–29) is 'Cynics and Romantics', 'Unicorn and the White Doe', 'Sullen Moods', 'Henry and Mary', 'On the Ridge' and 'A Lover Since Childhood'.
There was also a hardbound issue at 3s.6d., slightly larger (19.0 × 12.7 cm.), the top edges unopened and the fore- and bottom edges untrimmed.

B5   A MISCELLANY OF POETRY   [1922]

A Miscellany of Poetry | 1920–1922 | *Edited by* | *William Kean Seymour* | London | JOHN G.WILSON | 350 *Oxford Street,* | W. 1

Collation: π² [a]⁴ b – o⁸ p², 112 leaves.
2 pp. blank; p.[i] *A Miscellany of Poetry* | 1920–1922; p.[ii] publisher's advertisements; p.[iii] title-page; p.[iv] rights reservation notice and: Fifteen hundred copies of this book | were printed in December, 1922, | by the Westminster Press; pp.v–vi PREFATORY NOTE; pp.vii–x CONTENTS; pp.1–203 text; p.[204] blank; p.[205] BIBLIOGRAPHY; pp.206–210 bibliography; p.[211] printer's notice; p.[212] blank.
18.5 × 12.7 cm. Bulk: 1.3/1.7 cm. White laid paper; top edges trimmed; fore-edges unopened; bottom edges untrimmed. White wove endpapers. Bound in grey-blue boards with yellow cloth spine; white label on front: [double-rule rectangular box enclosing all:] *A Miscellany* | *of Poetry* | 1920–1922 | [decorative swirl] | *Edited by* | *William Kean Seymour*; back blank; spine stamped in gold: A | Miscellany | of Poetry | 1920–1922 | William | Kean Seymour | J.G. | Wilson

Price: 6s. Number of copies: 1,500. Published in December 1922.

Note: Graves' contribution is 'The Manifestation in the Temple' (pp. 67–68), 'The Avengers' (p.69) and 'A False Report' (p.70).

B6 CENOTAPH [1923]

CENOTAPH | A BOOK OF REMEMBRANCE IN POETRY AND | PROSE FOR NOVEMBER THE ELEVENTH | COMPILED & EDITED BY | THOMAS MOULT | [publisher's emblem] | *The frontispiece from* | *a drawing by* | JOSEPH PIKE | JONATHAN CAPE | ELEVEN GOWER STREET LONDON

Collation: [A]⁸ B−O⁸, 112 leaves.

p.[1] CENOTAPH; p.[2] epigraphs from Euripides (3 ll.) and Shakespeare (7 ll.); [plate, back blank, facing title-page, of cenotaph in Whitehall]; p.[3] title-page; p.[4] publication, rights reservation and printer's notices; pp.5−7 *Contents*; p.[8] blank; pp.9−11 *Introductory Note*; p.[12] blank; p.[13] transcription of memorial to the unknown soldier; p.[14] blank; pp.5−223 text; p.[224] blank.

17.9 × 10.3 cm. Bulk: 2.4/2.8 cm. Heavy white wove paper; top and fore-edges only trimmed. White wove endpapers. Bound in plum-brown cloth; back blind-stamped with publisher's emblem; front stamped in gold with a wreath; spine stamped in gold: [broad decorative rule] | CENOTAPH | JONATHAN CAPE | [broad decorative rule].

Price: 5s. Number of copies undisclosed. Published in November 1923.

Note: Graves' contribution is 'Peace' (p.52); it is listed here as having appeared in *Fairies and Fusiliers* (A3); but it did not appear in that book.

B7 THE BEST POEMS OF 1923 [1924]

The | BEST POEMS | *of* 1923 | [publisher's emblem] | *Selected* | *by* THOMAS MOULT *&* | *Decorated by* | PHILIP HAGREEN | *Jonathan Cape, Eleven Gower Street* | LONDON

Collation: [A]⁸ B−I⁸, 72 leaves.

4 pp. as pastedown and free endpapers, second and third sides printed with three designs of three leaves each, top and bottom, first and fourth sides blank; p.[1] THE BEST POEMS OF 1923; p.[2] design of two nymphs dancing; p.[3] title-page; p.[4] publication and printer's notices; p.[5] *To* | THE MEMORY | *of* | MAURICE HEWLETT | *and* | HERBERT TRENCH; p.[6] blank; pp.7−12 *Contents*; pp.13−14 *INTRODUCTION*; p.[15] THE BEST POEMS OF 1923 | [cut of fat baby in grass]; p.[16] blank; pp.17−135 text; pp.[136] − [137] blank; pp.[138] − [139] insides of free and pastedown endpapers, as front; p.[140] blank and pasted down.

18.6 × 12.5 cm. Bulk: 1.1/1.5 cm. White laid paper; top edges only trimmed; fore-edges unopened. Bound in royal blue cloth-textured paper with 22 × 14 rows of circular gold designs overall; spine has white label at top: *The* | BEST POEMS | *of* | 1923

Price: 6s. Number of copies undisclosed. Published in February 1924.

Note: Graves' contribution is 'Twin Souls' (pp.68−69).

B8   GRACE AFTER MEAT   1924

GRACE AFTER MEAT | JOHN CROWE RANSOM | *With an Introduction by Robert Graves* | Printed and published by Leonard & Virginia | Woolf at the Hogarth Press 52 Tavistock | Square London W.C. | 1924

Collation: [1] – [8]⁴, 32 leaves.

2 pp. blank, pasted to front cover; 2 pp. blank; p.[1] title-page; p.[2] blank; p.[3] *To* | *ROBERT GRAVES*; p.[4] blank; p.[5] CONTENTS; p.[6] blank; pp.7–11 Introduction; p.[12] blank; pp.13–57 text; p.[58] blank; pp.[59] – [60] blank, pasted to back cover.

21.5 × 13.7 cm. Bulk: 0.5 cm. White wove paper; all edges trimmed. Bound in gold-yellow boards with 24 × 16 designs of white and green with red centres; back and spine blank; yellow label on front: [rectangular single-rule box enclosing all:] GRACE | AFTER MEAT | JOHN CROWE RANSOM

Price: 4s.6d. Number of copies: 400. Published 30 October 1924. Woolmer 51.

Note: Graves' contribution is the introduction (pp.7–11) including "Philosophers" (see C131).

B9   THE BEST POEMS OF 1924   [1925]

The | BEST POEMS | *of* 1924 | [publisher's emblem] | *Selected by* | THOMAS MOULT | *& decorated by* | PHILIP HAGREEN | *Jonathan Cape, Ltd., Thirty Bedford Square* | LONDON

Collation: [A]⁸ B–I⁸, 72 leaves.

p.[i] THE BEST POEMS OF 1924 | [interwoven J and C]; p.[ii] cut of basket of flowers; p.[iii] title-page; p.[iv] publication and printer's notices; p.[v] *To* | THE MEMORY | *of* | ANATOLE FRANCE | *and* | JOSEPH CONRAD | *Poets*; p.[vi] blank; pp.vii–xii *Contents*; pp.xiii–xv *INTRODUCTION*; p.[xvi] blank; pp.1–127 text; pp.[128] blank.

18.8 × 12.6 cm. Bulk: 1.2/1.7 cm. White laid paper; top edges only trimmed; fore-edges unopened. White laid endpapers; inner sides printed with floral and vine design at each corner; first and fourth sides blank. Bound in boards covered in rough green paper printed in dark blue with design of splotches and spiderweb; spine has white label at top: *The* | BEST POEMS | *of* | 1924

Price: 6s. Number of copies undisclosed. Published in February 1925.

Note: Graves' contribution is 'Burrs and Brambles' (pp.102–103).

B10   COLLINS' CHILDREN'S ANNUAL   [1926]

[first 4 ll. in red:] COLLINS' | CHILDREN'S ANNUAL | [to right:] TWELFTH YEAR | OF ISSUE | [14 ll. to left in cream box, mainly rectangular:] [in red:] AUTHORS | ROBERT | GRAVES | BARRY | PAIN | KATHARINE | TYNAN | [in red:] ARTISTS | WINIFRED | ACKROYD | ANNE | ANDERSON | DOROTHY | REES | [in centre and to right of cream box is red, yellow and blue picture of tot fishing for golliwog doll] | [publisher's emblem] | LONDON & GLASGOW | COLLINS' CLEAR-TYPE PRESS

Collation: π² [A]⁴ B−P⁶, 90 leaves.

p.[1] book-plate page; p.[2] coloured frontispiece; p.[3] title-page; p.[4] cut of caravan; pp.5−10 lists of contents; pp.11−183[184] text, with pp.[15, 19, 22, 25, 31, 44, 49, 55, 62, 67, 71, 74, 79, 86, 91, 98, 103, 109, 110, 115, 122, 127, 134, 139, 146, 151, 158, 163, 170, 184] unnumbered and pp.[27/28] and [37/38] being included in the pagination, though plates (first blank recto, second verso) not included in collation.

27.3 × 21.3 cm. Bulk: 3.5/4.3 cm. Heavy white wove paper; all edges trimmed. White wove endpapers; inner sides printed in pink and grey with picture of a boy and girl swinging; first and fourth sides blank. Bound in cream boards; back blank; front has picture of boy and girl playing and in gold at top: COLLINS' | CHRISTMAS ANNUAL; light tan cloth spine printed in blue: *Collins'* | *Childrens'* | *Annual* | [rectangular box with picture of two girls and a boy] | COLLINS; [*sic Childrens'*]

Price: 5s. Number of copies unknown. Published in August 1926.

Note: Graves' contribution is 'The Story Teller' (p.11) and 'The Penny Fiddle' (p.12).

B11 MERCURY BOOK I 1926

.. THE .. | MERCURY BOOK | Being selections from Volumes I & II | of the *London Mercury*, made by | H.C.M. | LONDON: | WILLIAMS & NORGATE, LTD., | 14 HENRIETTA STREET, COVENT GARDEN, W.C.2 | [rule] | 1926

Collation: [A]⁸ B−U⁸, 160 leaves.

p.[i] THE MERCURY BOOK; p.[ii] blank; [frontispiece, recto blank]; p.[iii] title-page; p.[iv] blank; p.[v] PREFATORY NOTE; pp.[vi] −[vii] EDITOR'S NOTE; pp.[viii] − [ix] CONTENTS; p.[x] blank; pp.1−309 text, with pp.[33, 65, 86, 136, 170, 204, 254, 291] being unnumbered; p.[310] blank.

21.3 × 16.8 cm. Bulk: 3.3/3.9 cm. Heavy white wove paper; top edges only trimmed. White wove endpapers. Bound in light orange cloth; back blind-stamped with publisher's emblem; front stamped in black: THE | MERCURY BOOK | [head of Mercury]; spine stamped in black: THE| MERCURY | BOOK | WILLIAMS & | NORGATE

Price: 7s.6d. Number of copies unknown. Published in November 1926 in light orange dust-jacket printed in black.

Note: Graves' contribution is 'A Country Mood' (p.205).

B11.1 THE BEST POEMS OF 1926 1926

THE BEST POEMS | OF 1926 | EDITED BY | L.A.G. STRONG | Editor of "The Best Poems of 1923," | "The Best Poems of 1924," "The | Best Poems of 1925" | [publisher's emblem] | DODD, MEAD & COMPANY | NEW YORK 1926

Collation: [see Notes], 132 leaves.

p.[i] BEST POEMS OF 1926; p.[ii] BOOKS BY L.A.G. STRONG; p.[iii] title-page; p.[iv] copyright and printer's notices; pp.v–vii ACKNOWLEDGMENTS; p.[viii] blank; pp.ix–xviii INTRODUCTION; pp.xix–xxv CONTENTS; p.[xxvi] blank; p.[xxvii] THE BEST POEMS OF 1926; p.[xxviii] blank; pp.1–225 text; p.[226] blank; pp.227–228 APPENDIX; pp.229–234 INDEX OF FIRST LINES; pp.[235]–[236] blank.

16.3 × 11.4 cm. Bulk: 1.9/2.4 cm. White wove paper; all edges trimmed. White wove endpapers. Bound in dark blue cloth; front stamped in gold: [within a decorative border:] The Best Poems | of | 1926; back blank; spine stamped in gold: The Best | Poems | of | 1926 | DODD, MEAD | & COMPANY

Price: $2.00. Number of copies unknown. Published December 1926.

Notes: Graves' contribution is 'The Corner Knot'.

Mason reports this edition but I have been unable to see a copy of this book and Dodd, Mead & Company report that a search of their "library of press copies and old books [provides no] printing history for this book."

B12   THE BEST POEMS OF 1926   1927

The | BEST POEMS | *of* 1926 | [publisher's emblem] | *Selected by* | THOMAS MOULT | *& decorated by* | JOHN AUSTEN | *Jonathan Cape, Ltd., Thirty Bedford Square* | 1927

Collation: [A]⁸ B–H⁸, 68 leaves.

p.[i] THE BEST POEMS OF 1926 | [cut of cloud, moon, stars, dale with trees and house]; p.[ii] cut of village in valley with two trees in foreground]; p.[iii] title-page; p.[iv] printer's notices; p.[v] *To* | THE MEMORY | *of* | CHARLES MONTAGU DOUGHTY | EVA GORE-BOOTH | ISRAEL ZANGWILL | *Poets* | [design of rose with three large leaves]; p.[vi] blank; pp.vii–xi *Contents*; p.[xii] stylized urban skyline; pp.xiii–xiv *INTRODUCTION*; pp.1–120 text; pp.[121] blank; p.[122] printer's notice.

18.6 × 12.6 cm. Bulk: 1.1/1.5 cm. White laid paper; top edges only trimmed; fore-edges unopened. White laid endpapers; inner sides printed with four masks, one at each corner, and piping child in centre; first and fourth sides blank. Bound in boards covered in pinkish brick-red paper printed with tree and flower modernistic design; spine has white label at top: *The* | BEST | POEMS | *of* | 1926

Price: 6s. Number of copies undisclosed. Published in January 1927.

Note: Graves' contribution is 'Four Children' (p.1).

B13   LOVING MAD TOM   [1927]

LOVING MAD TOM | *Bedlamite Verses* | *Of the XVI and XVII Centuries* | With | FIVE ILLUSTRATIONS BY | NORMAN LINDSAY | [double flower and leaf device] | *Foreword By* ROBERT GRAVES | *The Texts Edited with Notes By* JACK LINDSAY | *Musical Transcriptions By* PETER WARLOCK | [double flower and leaf device] | THE FANFROLICO PRESS | FIVE BLOOMSBURY SQUARE | LONDON

Collation: [1]⁶ [2] – [14]⁴, 58 leaves.

p.[i] blank; p.[ii] *This Edition is limited to* | 375 *copies, of which this is* | *No.* [number written in over dots]; p.[iii] LOVING MAD TOM; p.[iv] blank; p.[1] title-page; p.[2] blank; p.[3] illustration; p.[4] blank; pp.[5] – [6] CONTENTS; p.[7] THE REDISCOVERY OF | 'LOVING MAD TOM'; p.[8] blank; pp.9–20 text; p.[21] THE POEMS; p.[22] blank; pp.23–26 text; p.[27] illustration; pp.28–30 text; p.[31] illustration; pp.32–40 text; p.[41] illustration; pp.42–54 text; p.[55] THE MUSICKS; p.[56] blank; pp.[57] – [60] music; p.[61] NOTES AND COMMENTARY; p.[62] blank; pp.63–110 text; p.[111] colophon; p.[112] blank.

28.2 × 22.0 cm. Bulk: 1.1/1.7 cm. White wove paper; top edges only trimmed and gilt. White wove endpapers. Both watermarked: 927 UNBLEACHED ARNOLD and MADE IN ENGLAND LINEN FIBRE. Bound in quarter vellum; front and back in light olive-green laid paper; back blank; front stamped in gold with picture of Mad Tom derived from illustration on p.[41]; spine stamped in gold: LOVING | MAD | TOM

Price: 42s. Number of copies: 375. Published in December 1927.

Note: Graves' contribution is 'The Rediscovery of "Loving Mad Tom" (pp.9–20).

B14   SCRUTINIES   1928

SCRUTINIES | By VARIOUS WRITERS | Collected by | EDGELL RICKWORD | LONDON | WISHART & COMPANY | 1928

Collation: [1]⁸ 2–13⁸, 104 leaves.

p.[i] SCRUTINIES; p.[ii] blank; p.[iii] title-page; p.[iv] printer's and copyright notices; pp.v –vii FOREWORD; p.[viii] blank; p.ix CONTENTS; p.[x] blank; pp.1–196[197] text, with pp.[15, 29, 41, 51, 73, 95, 109, 131, 145, 161, 181] being unnumbered section headings and pp.[14, 28, 94, 144, 180] being blank; p.[198] printer's notice.

19.0 × 13.2 cm. Bulk: 1.8/2.3 cm. White laid paper; top and fore-edges trimmed; watermarked SAVORY Antique. White wove endpapers. Bound in black cloth; front and back blank; spine stamped in gold: [broad rule] | [box in shape of squared-off shield, inside which 7 ll.:] SCRUTINIES | [rule] | *Critical Essays* | *by* | VARIOUS | WRITERS | [dot] | [box inside which:] WISHART | [broad rule].

Price: 7s.6d. Number of copies unknown. Published in March 1928.

Note: Graves' contribution is an essay on Kipling (pp.74–93). Reprinted in A63.

B15   THE OXFORD BOOK OF CAROLS   1928

The | Oxford Book of | Carols | By | Percy Dearmer | R. Vaughan Williams | Martin Shaw | Oxford University Press | London: Humphrey Milford | 1928

Collation: [a]⁸ b/b2²/⁸ B/B2–Q/Q2²/⁶ R⁴, 142 leaves.

p.[i] The | Oxford Book of | Carols; p.[ii] blank; p.[iii] title-page; p.[iv] edition and publisher's notices; pp.[v]vi–xxxiv PREFACE; pp.[xxxv] –xxxvi ACKNOWLEDGEMENTS; pp.[1]2–237 text; p.[238] blank; pp.[239] –240 INDEX

OF AUTHORS, SOURCES, &c.; pp.[241]242–245 INDEX OF FIRST LINES; pp.[246]247–248 INDEX OF TITLES.

16.7 × 11.3 cm. Bulk: 1.7/2.1 cm. White wove paper; all edges trimmed. White wove endpapers. Bound in light cherry cloth; front and back blind-stamped with design of five circles with bells and large cross; spine stamped in gold: The | Oxford | Book of | Carols | Oxford

Price: 4s.6d. Number of copies unknown. Published in April 1928.

Notes: Graves' contributions are No. 80 'Three Kings', translation of a Flemish carol, and No. 84 'The Candle', translation of an Austrian carol.

The book exists in three editions: a complete music edition, a complete words edition and a cheap edition (words only, without notes). The complete words edition is described above; it precedes the others by some six months.

B16   THE ENORMOUS ROOM   [1928]

THE | ENORMOUS ROOM | By | E. E. CUMMINGS | With an | Introduction | by | ROBERT GRAVES | [publisher's emblem] | JONATHAN CAPE 30 BEDFORD SQUARE | LONDON

Collation: [A]⁸ B–X⁸, 168 leaves.

p.[1] THE ENORMOUS ROOM; p.[2] blank; p.[3] title-page; p.[4] publication and printer's notices; p.5 CONTENTS; p.[6] blank; pp.7–15 INTRODUCTION; p.[16] blank; pp.17–23 FOREWORD (1922); P.[24] blank; p.[25] THE ENORMOUS ROOM; p.[26] blank; pp.27–332 text; pp.[333]–[336] blank.

20.2 × 12.9 cm. Bulk: 3.0/3.5 cm. White wove paper; top and fore-edges trimmed. White wove endpapers. Bound in dull plum cloth; front blank; back blind-stamped with publisher's emblem; spine stamped in gold: THE | ENORMOUS | ROOM | [decorative leaf] | E. E. CUMMINGS | JONATHAN CAPE   ˙

Price: 7s.6d. Number of copies undisclosed. Published in July 1928.

Notes: Graves' contribution is the introduction (pp.7–15).

This book was reprinted twice in 1928; in 1930 a Life and Letters Series impression was issued; the introduction has not appeared in American editions of this work.

B17   THE HOGARTH ESSAYS   1928

THE HOGARTH ESSAYS | [publisher's emblem] | DOUBLEDAY, DORAN & COMPANY | INC. *GARDEN CITY, NEW YORK* 1928

Collation: [1]–[20]⁸ [21]⁴ [22]⁸, 172 leaves.

p.[i] THE HOGARTH ESSAYS; p.[ii] blank; p.[iii] title-page; p.[iv] rights reservation, printer's and edition notices; pp.v–vi *Publisher's Note*; p.[vii] *Contents*; p.[viii] blank; p.[1] section heading; p.[2] blank; pp.3–336 text, with pp.[31, 49, 67, 109, 133, 161, 195, 241, 277, 305] being unnumbered section headings and pp.[30, 48, 50, 110, 132, 134, 160, 162, 194, 196, 198, 240, 242, 278, 304, 306] being blank and pp.[32] and [68] being unnumbered epigraphs.

20.4 × 13.8 cm. Bulk:2.7/3.2 cm. White wove paper; top edges only trimmed. Cream wove endpapers; insides printed with watermark-like design in grey of waved chain and wire lines. Bound in cream boards with light gunmetal-blue cloth spine; back blank; front printed with basket of flowers in purple and green; spine has cream paper label: [in purple:] THE | [in green:] HOGARTH | [in purple:] ESSAYS

Price: $3.00 Number of copies unknown. Published 28 September 1928.

Note: Graves' contribution is 'The Future of the Art of Poetry' (pp.163–193), a revision of *Another Future of Poetry* (A19).

B17.1   THE SEIZIN PRESS   1929

THE SEIZIN PRESS | [device] | NECESSARY BOOKS | [blurb] | 1929

Collation: half-sheet folded twice, 4 leaves.
   p.[1] title-page; p.[2] blank; p.[3] list of books; p.[4] blank; p.[5] 'Between Dark and Dark'; pp.[6] – [7] blank; p.[8] publisher's announcements. p.[5] numbered '9'.
   22.0 × 14.2 cm. White laid paper watermarked with hammer and anvil; uncut and untrimmed.

Price: gratis. Number of copies unknown. Published early spring 1929.

Note: Graves' contribution is 'Between Dark and Dark' (p.[5]), see A33.

B18   TO RETURN TO ALL THAT   [1930]

TO RETURN TO ALL THAT | AN AUTOBIOGRAPHY | BY | ALFRED PERCEVAL GRAVES | LITT.D. DUBLIN, F.R.S.L. | [publisher's emblem] | London . Jonathan Cape . Toronto

Collation: [A]⁸ B–Y⁸, 176 leaves.
   p.[1] TO RETURN TO ALL THAT; p.[2] blank; [plate, back blank]; p.[3] title-page; p.[4] publication, publisher's and printer's notices; p.5 CONTENTS; p.[6] blank; p.7 LIST OF ILLUSTRATIONS and acknowledgements; p.[8] blank; p.[9] TO RETURN TO ALL THAT; p.[10] blank; pp.11–343 text; p.[344] blank; p.[345] BIBLIOGRAPHY; p.[346] blank; pp.347–350 bibliography; pp.[351] – [352] blank.
   20.1 × 13.4 cm. Bulk: 2.3/2.8 cm. White wove paper; top and fore-edges trimmed. White wove endpapers. Bound in maroon cloth; front blank; back blind-stamped with publisher's emblem; spine stamped in gold: TO RETURN | TO | ALL THAT |[decorative floral divider] | ALFRED | PERCEVAL | GRAVES | JONATHAN CAPE

Price: 7s.6d. Number of copies undisclosed. Published in July 1930 in white dust-jacket printed in black.

Note: Graves' contributions are 'The Hushu Bird' (p.320), 'The Montrose Quagga' (pp.320–321), 'Zachaeus Zerites' (p.321) and the war letters printed in the *Spectator* in 1919 (C34).

B19   THE SECOND OMNIBUS BOOK   [1930]

THE | SECOND | OMNIBUS BOOK | Containing three full-length Novels, | as well as Short Stories, Plays, | Parodies and Poems | by | J.B. PRIESTLY | W. SOMERSET MAUGHAM | MAURICE BARING | ROBERT GRAVES | EDNA FERBER | J.C. SQUIRE | CHRISTOPHER BUSH | and | AUGUSTUS CARP | Edited by | RUPERT HART-DAVIS | [publisher's emblem] | LONDON | WILLIAM HEINEMANN LIMITED

Collation: [A]⁶ B–T⁸ U⁴ W–2U¹⁶, 538 leaves.

pp.[i] – [ii] blank; p.[iii] THE SECOND OMNIBUS BOOK; p.[iv] publisher's advertisement; p.[v] title-page; p.[vi] reprinting, publication and printer's notices; p.[vii] EDITOR'S NOTE; p.[viii] blank; pp.[ix] – [x] CONTENTS; pp.[xi] – [xii] half-title for Priestly contribution; pp.1–292[293] Priestly text; pp.[294] – [296] blank; 2 pp., Maugham half-title; pp.115–147[148] Maugham text; p.[156] blank; 2 pp., Baring half-title; pp.1–8, 49–59[60], 149–155[156] Baring text; pp.[1] – [2] Ferber half-title; p.3–34 Ferber text; 2pp., Squire half-title; pp.77–82, 86–88, 100 Squire text; 2 pp., Carp half-title; pp.1–274 Carp text; 2 pp., Graves half-title; pp.1–10 Graves text; 2 pp. Bush half-title; pp.1–312 Bush text.

18.7 × 12.5 cm. Bulk: 3.7/4.1 cm. White wove paper; all edges trimmed. White wove endpapers printed with map showing contributions as locations; first and fourth sides blank. Bound in dark olive cloth; front and back blank; spine stamped in gold: THE SECOND | OMNIBUS | BOOK | [star] | [two vertical parallel rules joined top and bottom] | [star] | HEINEMANN

Price: 8s.6d. Number of copies unknown. Published in August 1930.

Note: Graves' contributions consist of ten poems, six reprinted from *Poems 1914–1927* (A24), and four new: 'To the Reader Over My Shoulder', 'The Beast', 'The Terraced Valley' and 'Tail Piece: A Song to Make You and Me Laugh'.

B20   THE YEAR'S POETRY   [1934]

THE YEAR'S POETRY | A REPRESENTATIVE SELECTION | [large solid dot] | Compiled by | DENYS KILHAM ROBERTS | GERALD GOULD . JOHN LEHMANN | JOHN LANE THE BODLEY HEAD | LONDON

Collation: [a]⁸ b–i⁸, 72 leaves.

p.[1] THE YEAR'S POETRY; p.[2] blank; p.[3] title-page; p.[4] printer's and publication notices; pp.5–7 PREFACE; p.[8] blank; p.9–12 CONTENTS; p.[13] THE YEAR'S POETRY; p.[14] blank; pp.15–144 text.

18.7 × 12.2 cm. Bulk: 1.1/1.5 cm. White wove paper; all edges trimmed; top edges stained red. White laid endpapers. Bound in tan cloth; front and back blank; spine stamped in red: THE | YEAR'S | POETRY | [solid dot] | THE | BODLEY HEAD

Price: 6s. Number of copies unknown. Published 4 December 1934.

Note: Contains 'Midsummer Duet, 1934' (pp.139–144) by Laura Riding and Robert Graves; not reprinted by Graves, but in Riding's *Collected Poems*; the 'Second Voice' is Graves.

B21 LIVES OF THE ROMAN EMPRESSES 1935

LIVES OF THE | ROMAN EMPRESSES | THE HISTORY OF THE LIVES AND SECRET | INTRIGUES OF THE WIVES, SISTERS AND | MOTHERS OF THE CAESARS | By | JACQUES BOERGAS DE SERVIEZ | With An Introduction by | ROBERT GRAVES | *Author of 'I, Claudius', 'Claudius the God', etc.* | *Illustrated* | [publisher's emblem] | WM. H. WISE & CO. | 1935 [BOERGAS]

Collation: [1] – [27]^{16}, 432 leaves.

  2 pp., uncounted (recto: LIVES OF THE | ROMAN EMPRESSES; verso: blank); [frontispiece, back blank, tipped to p.[i]]; p.[i] title-page; p.[ii] copyright and printing notices; pp.iii–iv CONTENTS; p.vi LIST OF ILLUSTRATIONS; pp.vii–ix INTRODUCTION TO THE | *LIVES OF THE ROMAN EMPRESSES* | By ROBERT GRAVES; pp.xv–xvi AUTHOR'S PREFACE; pp.xvii–xxiii historical note and chronological table; p.[xxiv] blank; p.[1] LIVES OF THE | ROMAN EMPRESSES; p.[2] blank; pp.3–812 text; pp.813–834 INDEX; pp.[835] – [838] blank; illustrations face pp.6, 38, 166, 198, 294, 326, 486, 518, 678, 710.

  21.1 × 13.9 cm. Bulk: 4.7/5.5 cm. White wove paper; all edges trimmed; top edges stained purple. White wove endpapers. Bound in purple cloth; back blank; front blind-stamped with fasci and a vertical band of dancing nymphs; spine has blind-stamped fasci, circles, rules and solid rectangular boxes and is printed in silver: LIVES | of the | ROMAN EMPRESSES | DE SERVIEZ | WISE & CO.

Price: $2.90. Number of copies unknown. Published in August 1935 in powder-blue dust-jacket printed in orange-red and purple.

Note: Graves' contribution is the introduction (pp.vii–xiv).

B22 EPILOGUE I 1935

EPILOGUE | A Critical Summary | *Volume I – Autumn* 1935 | [swelled rule] | *Editor:* | Laura Riding | *Assistant-Editor:* | Robert Graves | [swelled rule] | Contributors to this Issue: | [ten names in two columns:] MADELEINE VARA LAURA RIDING | JAMES REEVES ROBERT GRAVES | THOMAS MATTHEWS HONOR WYATT | JOHN CULLEN JOHN ALDRIDGE | LEN LYE WARD HUTCHINSON | [swelled rule] | THE SEIZIN PRESS . DEYA MAJORCA | AND | CONSTABLE & CO LTD | LONDON

Collation: [A]^8 B–Q^8, 128 leaves.

  p.[i] EPILOGUE; p.[ii] blank; p.[iii] title-page; p.[iv] printer's notice; p.v CONTENTS; p.[vi] epigraph of 3 ll.; pp.1–218 text; [gathering of 4 leaves of coated paper, all versos blank]; pp.219–236 text; [plate of photograph tipped in, verso blank]; pp.237–245 text; p.[246] Seizin Press advertisement; pp.[247] – [248] blank; pp.[249] – [250] blank as pastedown endpaper.

  21.6 × 13.6 cm. Bulk: 1.7/2.1 cm. White laid paper; all edges trimmed. White laid front endpaper. Bound in buff boards printed in black; back blank; front: [at left:] Twice a Year [at right:] Volume I | EPILOGUE | A CRITICAL SUMMARY | [cut of stage with temple prop, scroll, clouds] | AUTUMN 1935 | Laura Riding [turned rule] Editor | Robert Graves [turned rule] Associate Editor | THE SEIZIN PRESS . DEYA

MAJORCA | AND | CONSTABLE & CO. LTD. | LONDON | *Seven Shillings and Sixpence net*; spine: EPILOGUE | A | CRITICAL | SUMMARY | I | AUTUMN | 1935

Price: 7s.6d. Number of copies unknown. Published in November 1935.

Note: Graves' contributions are 'A Poem Sequence: To the Sovereign Muse' ('The Challenge', 'Fiend, Dragon, Mermaid', 'To the Sovereign Muse', 'Green Loving', 'Like Snow') (pp.87–92), 'Germany' (signed M[adeleine] V[ara], a house pseudonym, and reprinted as 'Nietzsche' [A63 and A75b–c]) (pp.113–125), 'Coleridge and Wordsworth, Keats and Shelley' (pp.157–174) and 'A Note on the Pastoral' (reprinted as 'The Pastoral' [A63]) (pp. 200–207). Madeleine Vara was a house pseudonym, but see Laura (Jackson) Riding, *Denver Quarterly* (1974), 5–6: 'This name … I introduced into *Epilogue* as other-signature for writings of *mine* A piece of writing on Nietzsche in *Epilogue* [i.e. B22] is included in Robert Graves' collection of "his" critical writings The signature of the piece is "M.V.". It was of my writing, as was everything else of that signature, full or abbreviated.'

B23   THE FABER BOOK OF MODERN VERSE   [1936]

THE FABER BOOK | OF MODERN VERSE | *edited by* | MICHAEL | ROBERTS | *London* | FABER AND FABER | *24 Russell Square*

Collation: π⁸ A–Y⁸, 184 leaves.
    pp[i] – [ii] blank; p.[iii] THE FABER BOOK | OF MODERN VERSE; p.[iv] blank; p.[v] title-page; p.[vi] publication, publisher's and rights notices; p.vii EDITOR'S NOTE; p.[viii] blank; pp.ix–xvi CONTENTS; pp.1–35 INTRODUCTION; p.[36] blank; p.[37] POETRY | [rule]; p.[38] blank; pp.39–342 text; p.[343] ACKNOWLEDGEMENTS | [rule]; p.[344] blank; pp.345–350 ACKNOWLEDGEMENTS; pp.351–352 INDEX OF AUTHORS.
    18.5 × 11.8 cm. Bulk: 2.0/2.5 cm. White wove paper; all edges trimmed; top edges stained rust-brown. White wove endpapers. Bound in bright blue cloth; front and back blank; spine stamped in gold: THE | FABER | BOOK | OF | MODERN | VERSE | *edited by* | MICHAEL | ROBERTS | FABER AND | FABER

Price: 7s.6d. Number of copies: 3,080. Published in February 1936.

Note: Contains thirteen poems by Graves (pp.224–233) of which 'To Bring the Dead to Life' is first published here.

B24   EPILOGUE II   1936

EPILOGUE | A Critical Summary | *Volume II – Summer* 1936 | [swelled rule] | *Editor:* | Laura Riding | *Associate Editor:* | Robert Graves | [swelled rule] | Contributors to this Issue: | [ten names in two columns:] ALAN HODGE HONOR WYATT | JAMES REEVES KENNETH ALLOTT | MADELEINE VARA LAURA RIDING | WARD HUTCHINSON ROBERT GRAVES | KATHERINE BURDEKIN GORDON GLOVER | [swelled rule] | THE SEIZIN PRESS . DEYA MAJORCA | AND | CONSTABLE & CO LTD | LONDON

Collation: [A]⁸ B–Q⁸ R¹, 129 leaves.

p.[i] EPILOGUE; p.[ii] publisher's advertisements; p.[iii] title-page; p.[iv] publisher's, publication and printer's notices; p.v CONTENTS; p.[vi] epigraph of 3 ll.; pp.1–251 text; p.[252] text and printer's notices.

21.6 × 13.6 cm. Bulk: 1.8/2.2 cm. White laid paper; all edges trimmed. White laid endpapers. Bound in light green boards printed in black; back blank; front: [at left:] Twice a Year [at right:] Volume II | EPILOGUE | A CRITICAL SUMMARY | [cut of stage with temple prop, scroll, clouds] | SUMMER 1936 | Laura Riding [turned rule] Editor | Robert Graves [turned rule] Associate Editor | THE SEIZIN PRESS . DEYA MAJORCA | AND | CONSTABLE & CO. LTD. | LONDON | *Seven Shillings and Sixpence net*; spine: EPILOGUE | A | CRITICAL | SUMMARY | II | SUMMER | 1936

Price: 7s.6d. Number of copies unknown. Published in July 1936.

Note: Graves' contributions are 'Official and Unofficial Literature' (pp.57–61), 'Stealing' (reprinted as 'Theft' in A75) (pp.67–75), a note on a homiletic study 'Enthusiasm' (p.89), 'The Exercise of English' (pp.127–134), 'To Walk on Hills', 'Never Such Love', 'The Climate of Thought' (pp.145–147), 'Lucretius and Jeans' (p.208–220) and 'Neo-Georgian Eternity' (pp.231–242).

B25   EPILOGUE III   1937

EPILOGUE | A Critical Summary | *Volume III – Spring* 1937 | [swelled rule] | *Editor:* | Laura Riding | *Associate Editor:* | Robert Graves | [swelled rule] | Contributors to this Issue: | [sixteen names in two columns:] MADELEINE VARA ALAN HODGE | NORMAN CAMERON HONOR WYATT | SALLY GRAVES KARL GOLDSCHMIDT | BASIL TAYLOR ROBIN HALE | LUCIE BROWN JOHN ALDRIDGE | WILLIAM ARCHER HARRY KEMP | LAURA RIDING ROBERT GRAVES | WARD HUTCHINSON THOMAS MATTHEWS | [centre:] JAMES REEVES | [swelled rule] | THE SEIZIN PRESS . DEYA MAJORCA | AND | CONSTABLE & CO LTD | LONDON

Collation: [A]⁸ B–L⁸ M–N¹⁰ O–Q⁸, 132 leaves.

p.[i] EPILOGUE; p.[ii] IN APOLOGY; p.[iii] title-page; p.[iv] publisher's, publication and printer's notices; p.v CONTENTS; p.[vi] epigraph of 3 ll.; pp.1–190 text; [gathering of 4 leaves of coated paper, versos blank]; pp.191–257 text; p.[258] text and printer's notices.

21.6 × 13.6 cm. Bulk: 2.0/2.4 cm. White laid paper; all edges trimmed. White laid endpapers. Bound in light red boards printed in black; back blank; front: [at left:] Twice a Year [at right:] Volume III | EPILOGUE | A CRITICAL SUMMARY | [cut of stage with temple prop, scroll, clouds] | Spring 1937 | Laura Riding [turned rule] Editor | Robert Graves [turned rule] Associate Editor | THE SEIZIN PRESS . DEYA MAJORCA | AND | CONSTABLE & CO. LTD. | LONDON | *Seven Shillings and Sixpence net*; spine: EPILOGUE | A | CRITICAL | SUMMARY | III | Spring | 1937

Price: 7s.6d. Number of copies unknown. Published in April 1937.

Note: Graves' contributions are 'Politics and Poetry' (with Harry Kemp and Laura Riding, reprinted as 'Poetry and Politics' [A63]) (pp.6–53), 'The Theme of Fame' (with Laura Riding, as Madeleine Vara, but see Note to B22) (pp.75–99), 'From a Private Correspondence on Reality' (with Laura Riding) (pp. 107–130), 'At the

Marble Table', 'Parent to Children', 'The Exile', 'A Jealous Man', 'End of Play', 'The Halfpenny' (pp.164–169), 'Drama' (with Alan Hodge and Laura Riding, reprinted as 'Poetic Drama' [A63]) and 'Book-Advertising' (pp.239–246).

B26   T.E. LAWRENCE BY HIS FRIENDS   [1937]

T.E. LAWRENCE | BY HIS FRIENDS | EDITED BY | A.W. LAWRENCE | [publisher's emblem] | JONATHAN CAPE | THIRTY BEDFORD SQUARE | LONDON

Collation: [A]⁸ B–2N⁸ 2O/2O*²/⁸, 298 leaves.
   p.[1] T.E. LAWRENCE BY HIS FRIENDS; p.[2] blank; [frontispiece, back blank]; p.[3] title-page; p.[4] publication, publisher's, printer's papermaker's and binder's notices; pp.5–6 PREFACE; pp.7–10 CONTENTS; pp.11 ILLUSTRATIONS; p.[12] blank; p.13 DATES IN THE LIFE OF T.E. LAWRENCE; p.[14] blank; pp.[15]–[596] text, with pp.[15, 23, 39, 71, 109, 129, 151, 175, 203, 217, 239, 309, 323, 337, 359, 381, 393, 399, 421, 457, 511, 531, 563, 567, 583] being unnumbered and pp.[16, 24, 38, 40, 70, 110, 128, 130, 152, 174, 176, 204, 216, 218, 238, 240, 308, 310, 322, 324, 338, 358, 360, 380, 382, 394, 400, 420, 422, 456, 458, 512, 530, 532, 564, 568, 582, 584, 596] being blank; illustrations, all backs blank, face pp.48, 154, 190, 234, 266, 376, 572.
   21.6 × 14.5 cm. Bulk: 3.3/4.0 cm. White wove paper; top and fore-edges trimmed; top edges stained maroon. White wove endpapers. Bound in maroon cloth; front and back blank; spine stamped in gold: T.E. LAWRENCE | BY | HIS FRIENDS | [publisher's emblem].

Price: 15s. Number of copies undisclosed. Published 21 May 1937.

Note; Graves' contribution (pp.325–331) is an essay largely adapted from *Lawrence and the Arabs* (A26). The abridged edition of B23 published by Cape in 1954 also contains this essay.

B27   THE MODERN POET   [1938]

The Modern Poet | an Anthology chosen and edited | by | GWENDOLEN MURPHY | London: Sidgwick & Jackson, Ltd. | 44 Museum Street, W.C.1

Collation: π¹⁰ 1–13⁸, 114 leaves.
   p.[i] The Modern Poet; p.[ii] blank; p.[iii] title-page; p.[iv] publication and printer's notices; p.v PREFACE; p.[vi] blank; pp.vii–x INDEX OF AUTHORS; pp.xi–xiv ACKNOWLEDGEMENTS; pp.xv–xx THE MODERN POET; pp.[1]2–143 text; p.[144] blank; pp.145–203 COMMENTARY; p.[204] blank; pp.205–208 INDEX OF FIRST LINES.
   18.4 × 12.3 cm. Bulk: 1.4/1.9 cm. White wove paper; all edges trimmed. White wove endpapers. Bound in medium blue cloth; back blank; front blind-stamped with heavy-rule rectangular box; inside light-rule rectangular box, inside which, stamped in white: THE | MODERN POET | an Anthology | Gwendolen Murphy; spine stamped in white: [heavy rule] | [light rule] | THE | MODERN | POET | [four dots] | Gwendolen | Murphy | Sidgwick | & Jackson | [light rule] | [heavy rule]

Price: 3s.6d. Number of copies: 30,000 (in many printings). Published 25 May 1938.

Note: Graves' contribution (pp.78–84) includes the first appearance of 'The Wretch' (p.81), later 'The Laureate'; there are also some notes on 'The Wretch' (pp.182–183).

B28 THE WORLD AND OURSELVES [1938]

THE WORLD | AND OURSELVES | Laura Riding | [epigraph of 9 ll.] | CHATTO & WINDUS | LONDON

Collation: [A]^6 B–2K^8 2L/L$^{*2/8}$, 272 leaves.

p.[i] THE WORLD AND OURSELVES; p.[ii] note; p.[iii] title-page; p.[iv] publisher's, printing and rights reservation notices; pp.v–viii *Contents*; pp.ix–xi *Foreword*; p.[xii] blank; pp.[1]–529 text, with pp.[1, 45, 131, 221, 369] being section headings and pp.[2, 46, 130, 132, 222, 368, 370] being blank; p.[530] blank; p.[531] printer's notice; p.[532] blank.

21.8 × 13.7 cm. Bulk: 3.8/4.4 cm. White laid paper; top and fore-edges trimmed; top edge stained maroon. White wove endpapers. Bound in maroon cloth; front and back blank; spine stamped in gold: THE | WORLD AND | OURSELVES | [swirl] | Laura Riding | CHATTO | AND WINDUS

Price: 15s. Number of copies undetermined. Published in November 1938.

Note: Graves' contribution is a letter (pp.120–126).

B29 THE LEFT HERESY IN LITERATURE AND LIFE [1939]

THE LEFT HERESY IN | LITERATURE AND LIFE | BY | HARRY KEMP, LAURA RIDING | AND OTHERS | [publisher's emblem] | METHUEN PUBLISHERS LONDON | ESSEX STREET STRAND W.C.2

Collation: π^4 [1]^8 2–17^8, 140 leaves.

p.[i] THE LEFT HERESY IN | LITERATURE AND LIFE; p.[ii] blank; p.[iii] title-page; p.[iv] publication and printing notices; p.v FOREWORD; p.[vi] blank; pp.vii–viii CONTENTS; p.[1] section heading; p.[2] blank; pp.3–270 text, with pp.[63, 121, 177, 213, 255] being section headings, pp.[65, 257] being unnumbered and pp.[64, 122, 178, 214, 256] being blank; p.[271] blank; p.[272] printer's notice.

18.5 × 12.0 cm. Bulk: 2.3/2.8 cm. White wove paper; all edges trimmed. White wove endpapers. Bound in dull orange cloth; front and back blank; spine stamped in red: *THE LEFT* | *HERESY* | *In Literature* | *and Life* | *HARRY KEMP,* | *LAURA RIDING* | *and others* | *METHUEN*

Price: 7s.6d. Number of copies undetermined. Published May 1939 in white dust-jacket printed in black and red.

Note: Sections V and VI of this book are a revised reprint of 'Politics and Poetry' from *Epilogue* III (B25).

B29.1   THE TURNING PATH   [1939]

THE TURNING PATH | BY | RONALD BOTTRALL | [publisher's emblem] | LONDON | ARTHUR BARKER LTD. | 12 ORANGE STREET, W.C.2

Collation: [A]⁸ B−C⁸ D⁴, 28 leaves.
   p.[i] THE TURNING PATH; p.[ii] list of works by Bottrall; p.[iii] title-page; p.[iv] publication and printer's notices; p.[v] TO | LAURA RIDING; p.vi ACKNOWLEDGMENTS; p.vii PREFATORY NOTE; p.[viii] blank; p.ix CONTENTS; p.[x] blank; pp.xi−xii letter from Graves; pp.1−41[42] text, with pp.[1, 15, 29] being section headings and pp.[2, 14, 16, 30] being blank; pp.[43] − [44] blank.
   21.4 × 13.6 cm. Bulk: 0.7/1.15 cm. White laid paper; top and bottom edges trimmed. White wove endpapers. Bound in light green paper-covered boards with black quarter-cloth spine; front and back blank; spine stamped in gold, middle to top, facing front: THE TURNING PATH | Ronald Bottrall

Price: 5s. Number of copies unknown. Published in May 1939.

Note: Graves' contribution is the letter (pp.xi−xii), dated March 1939 from Montaubon-de-Bretagne.

B30   WORK IN HAND   [1942]

WORK IN HAND | ALAN HODGE | NORMAN CAMERON | ROBERT GRAVES | *The New Hogarth Library* | Vol. VI | THE HOGARTH PRESS | 37 MECKLENBURGH SQUARE | LONDON, W.C.1

Collation: [A]⁸ B−D⁸, 32 leaves.
   p.[1] ALAN HODGE, NORMAN CAMERON, ROBERT | GRAVES: WORK IN HAND; p.[2] list of books by the three authors, publication and distribution notices; p.[3] title-page; p.[4] AUTHORS' NOTE and printer's notice; p.5 contents page for Hodge; p.[6] blank; pp.7−25 text of Hodge; p.[26] blank; p.27 contents page for Cameron; p.[28] blank; pp.29−41 text of Cameron; p.[42] blank; p.[43] contents page for Graves; p.[44] blank; pp.45−64 text of Graves.
   18.1 × 11.9 cm. Bulk: 0.5/0.8 cm. White wove paper; all edges trimmed. White wove endpapers. Bound in sea-green cloth; front and back blank; spine stamped in red, bottom to top: HODGE, CAMERON, GRAVES [star] Work in Hand

Price: 2s.6d. Number of copies undetermined. Published 26 March 1942 in sand-orange dust-jacket printed in blue-green.

Note: The Graves contents are: A Love Story − Dawn Bombardment − The Worms of History − The Beast − A Withering Herb − The Shot − Dream of a Climber − The Thieves − Lollocks − To Sleep − Despite and Still − The Suicide in the Copse − Frightened Men − A Stranger at the Party − The Oath − Language of the Seasons − Mid-Winter Waking − The Rock at the Corner.

B31 LONDON CALLING 1942

[flush left:] LONDON | [flush right:] CALLING | EDITED BY | Storm Jameson |
[publisher's emblem] | HARPER & BROTHERS . *PUBLISHERS* | New York and
London | 1942

Collation: [1] – [21]⁸, 168 leaves.
    p.[i] *London Calling*; p.[ii] title and list of authors; p.[iii] title-page; p.[iv] copyright,
printing, rights reservation and edition notices; pp.v – vi *Contents*; p.[vii] *London
Calling* p.[viii] blank; pp.1 – 308 text; pp.309 – 322 biographical notes; p.[323]
designer's, manufacturer's and publisher's notices; pp.[324] – [328] blank.
    20.6 × 13.8 cm. Bulk: 2.7/3.2 cm. White wove paper; top edges only trimmed.
White wove endpapers. Bound in chestnut cloth; back blank; front blind-stamped
at lower right with publisher's emblem; spine stamped in gold, printed in grey:
[solid grey rectangular box, inside which five lines:] | [rectangular gold single-rule
box enclosing solid chestnut box, inside which two lines:] | London | Calling | [2 ll.
in gold:] Edited by | STORM JAMESON | [in grey:] HARPER

Price: $2.50. Number of copies: 2,000. Published 13 November 1942 in white dust-
jacket printed in green, tan and black.

Note: Graves' contribution is *Horses: A Play Chiefly for Children* (pp.177 – 198).

B32 AN OLD SAYING 1945

AN OLD SAYING | *BY* | ALGERNON CHARLES SWINBURNE | [decorative
swirl] | *With a Foreword by* | ROBERT GRAVES | [decorative swirl] | JOHN S. MAYFIELD |
1945

Collation: 6 leaves, stapled twice at centre.
    pp.[1] – [2] blank; p.[3] title-page; p.[4] copyright and printer's notices; p.[5]
NOTE; p.[6] blank; pp.[7] – [8] FOREWORD; p.[9] AN OLD SAYING | [decorative
swirl]; p.[10] blank; p.[11] text of poem; p.[12] blank.
    19.7 × 11.7 cm. Bulk: 0.1 cm. White laid paper; all edges trimmed. Bound in
cream laid wrappers; back blank; front printed: AN OLD SAYING | *BY* |
ALGERNON CHARLES SWINBURNE

Price: Not for sale. Number of copies: 35. Published in late summer 1945.

Notes: Graves' contribution is the foreword (pp.[7] – [8]); reprinted in A63.
    John S. Mayfield, in his note to the 1947 edition of this work, says that the true
first edition is a mimeographed one, done in spring 1945 on Saipan for interim
copyright purposes only. That interim edition is as follows: AN OLD SAYING |
by | Algernon Charles Swinburne | with a Foreword by Robert Graves | John S.
Mayfield | In the Marianas Islands | 1945

Collation as above.
    Pp.[1] title-page; p.[2] copyright notice; p.[3] NOTE [by Mayfield]; p.[4] blank;
pp.[5]/[7] FOREWORD; p.[8] blank; p. [9] An Old Saying; p.[10] blank; p.[11] text of
poem; p.[12] blank.
    20.2 × 13.4 cm. Bulk: 0.1 cm. Wove paper. Bound in pink wrappers; back and

spine blank; front mimeographed: AN OLD SAYING | by | Algernon Charles Swinburne

B33   HA! HA! AMONG THE TRUMPETS   [1945]

HA! HA! AMONG THE | TRUMPETS | *Poems in Transit* | *by* | ALUN LEWIS | *Foreword by* | ROBERT GRAVES | *London* | *George Allen & Unwin Ltd*

Collation: [1] – [5]⁸, 40 leaves.

2 pp. blank; p.[1] HA! HA! AMONG THE TRUMPETS *Poems in Transit·*; p.[2] publisher's advertisements; [frontispiece, back blank]; p.[3] title-page; p.[4] publication and rights notices, epigraph (3 ll.), edition notice (Edition limited to 50 copies of which | this is No. [number written in]), war economy and printer's notices; pp.[5] – [6] Contents; pp.[7] – [12] Foreword; pp.13–75 text; p.[76] publisher's notice.

18.4 × 12.4 cm. Bulk: 0.7/1.0 cm. Heavy white wove paper; top edges trimmed and gilt; fore-edge trimmed; watermarked with a shell with a lion and: HANDMADE. Bound in dark blue cloth; front and back blank; spine stamped in gold, bottom to top: *Ha! Ha! among the Trumpets* ALUN LEWIS; at bottom of spine, upright: G | A | & | U; the book is fitted with a dark blue ribbon bookmark.

Price: 10s.6d. Number of copies: 50. Published 19 July 1945.

Note: Graves' contribution is the foreword (pp.[7] – [12]). An ordinary edition of this book (5,000 copies) was published at the same time, price 5s.6d.

B34   BRITISH THOUGHT 1947   1947

[whole enclosed within single-rule rectangular box:] BRITISH | THOUGHT | 1947 | *With an introduction by* IVOR BROWN | [publisher's emblem] | *THE GRESHAM PRESS* | PUBLISHERS | NEW YORK . 1947

Collation: [1] – [14]¹⁶ [15]⁸, 232 leaves.

p.[i] BRITISH THOUGHT 1947; p.[ii] blank; p.[iii] title-page; p.[iv] copyright, manufacturing and rights reservations notices; pp.v–vii *TABLE OF CONTENTS*; p.[viii] blank; pp.9–17 INTRODUCTION; pp.18–22 *PUBLISHER'S NOTE*; p.[23] BRITISH THOUGHT 1947; p.[24] blank; pp.25–456 text; pp.457–461 *NOTES ON AUTHORS*; pp.[462] – [464] blank.

21.6 × 15.2 cm. Bulk: 2.9/3.7 cm. White wove paper; all edges trimmed. White wove endpapers. Bound in scarlet cloth; front and back blank; spine stamped in silver: [broad rule] | [light rule] | BRITISH | THOUGHT | 1947 | [swelled rule] | INTRODUCTION | BY | IVOR BROWN | THE | GRESHAM | PRESS | [light rule] | [broad rule].

Price: $3.75. Number of copies unknown. Published summer 1947.

Note: Graves' contribution is 'It Was a Stable World' (pp.226–235).

B35   EXPOSICIÓN GRUPO DE LOS SIETE   1948

EXPOSICIÓN | [2 ll. in red:] GRUPO DE LOS | SIETE | [seven circles with a top hat in each] | GALERIAS QUINT | 12 a 25 de Junio | Palma, 1948

Collation: 4 leaves, stapled twice at centre.
    pp.1–3 PRESENTACIÓN Y JUSTIFICACIÓN | DEL GRUPO DE LOS SIETE; p.4 PRISMA; pp.5–7 LOS SIETE DEL GRUPO EN | EL «GRUPO DE LOS SIETE»; p.[8] blank.
    21.3 × 15.5 cm. Bulk: 0.1 cm. White wove paper; all edges trimmed. Bound in green paper wrapper transcribed as title-page; inside front cover blank; inside back cover: CATÁLOGO; outside back cover: printer's notice.

Price: undetermined. Number of copies undetermined. Published 12 June 1948.

Note: Graves' contribution is the presentation (pp.1–3).

B36   SATURDAY BOOK 8   [1948]

[flush left:] *The Saturday* | [left of centre:] *Book* | [7 ll. in mirror on stand:] *being* | *the eighth annual* | *issue of this celebrated* | *cabinet of curiosities* | *and looking-glass of* | *past and* | *present* | [remainder flush left:] *edited by* | LEONARD RUSSELL | *the book designed by* | *LAURENCE SCARFE* | HUTCHINSON *are the publishers*

Collation:[A]^8 [B] – [C]^4 x^8 D–M^8 [N]^4 O^8 [P]^4 Q–T^8, 144 leaves.
    p.[1] *The Saturday Book 8th Year*; p.[2] calligraphic portrait; p.[3] title-page; p.[4] epigraph, table of contents, publication, printer's and engraver's notices; pp.5–128 text, with pp.[15]–[48] and [97]–[112] being unnumbered; [foldout four-colour plate wrapped around H]; pp.129–288 text, with pp.[217–225, 233] being unnumbered.
    22.9 × 14.9 cm. Bulk: 1.7/2.2 cm. White wove paper; all edges trimmed; signatures [A, B, C, x, G, N, P] on coated paper. Bound in bright orange cloth; front and back blank; spine stamped in gold: edited | by | Leonard | Russell | [down spine:] The Saturday Book — 8 | [upright:] HUTCHINSON

Price: 21s. Number of copies: 20,000. Published in October 1948.

Note: Graves' contribution is 'The Place for a Holiday' (pp.90–94), about Deyá.

B37   ROBERT ROSS   [1952]

Robert Ross | Friend of Friends | Letters to Robert Ross, Art Critic | and Writer, together with extracts | from his published articles | *Edited by* | MARGERY ROSS | [publisher's emblem] | JONATHAN CAPE | THIRTY BEDFORD SQUARE | LONDON

Collation: [A]^8 B–Z^8, 184 leaves.
    p.[1] ROBERT ROSS: FRIEND OF FRIENDS; p.[2] blank; [frontispiece, back blank]; p.[3] title-page; p.[4] publication, Dewey decimal, printer's and binder's notices; p.[5] ILLUSTRATIONS; p.[6] *To* | *William, and the Friends of* | *Robert Ross*;

p.[7] twelve-line poem, 'To Robert Ross' by Siegfried Sassoon; p.[8] blank; pp.9–14 INTRODUCTION; pp.15–16 ACKNOWLEDGMENTS; p.[17] ROBERT ROSS: FRIEND OF FRIENDS; p.[18] blank; pp.19–345 text; pp.346–360 appendixes; pp.361–367 INDEX; p.[368] blank; illustrations face pp.20, 22, 24/25, 35, 47, 80, 125, 180, 224, 276, 284.

21.8 × 14.0 cm. Bulk: 2.3/2.8 cm. White wove paper; top and fore-edges trimmed; top edges stained green. White wove endpapers. Bound in sea-green cloth; front and back blank; spine stamped in gold: ROBERT | ROSS | [star] | FRIEND | OF | FRIENDS | [curled decorative rule] | MARGERY | ROSS | [publisher's emblem]

Price: 30s. Number of copies undisclosed. Published 17 March 1952 in grey dust-jacket printed in red and black.

Note: Graves' contribution is letters *passim*.

B38   EDDIE MARSH   [1953]

Eddie Marsh | SKETCHES FOR A COMPOSITE LITERARY PORTRAIT OF | SIR EDWARD MARSH K.C.V.O., C.B., C.M.G. | *Compiled by* | CHRISTOPHER HASSALL | *and* | DENIS MATHEWS | *Published by* LUND HUMPHRIES | *for the* | CONTEMPORARY ART SOCIETY | *The Tate Gallery, London SW 1*

Collation: [1] – [2]⁸ [3]¹⁰, 26 leaves.

p.[1] EDDIE MARSH; p.[2] facsimile of MS; p.[3] title-page; p.[4] publication and printer's notices; p.5 CONTENTS; p.6 ILLUSTRATIONS; pp.7–8 NOTE; p.9 FOREWORD; pp.10–11 Introduction; p.[12] blank; pp.13–51 text; p.[52] blank; plates as follows: one leaf, printed both sides, tipped between pp.16/17; two leaves, printed four sides, sewn between pp.24/25; one leaf, printed both sides, tipped between pp.32/33; two leaves, printed four sides, sewn between pp.42/43.

22.8 × 15.1 cm. Bulk: 0.6 cm. Cream wove paper watermarked: BASINGWERK PARCHMENT; all edges trimmed. Issued in white paper covers with white wrapper printed in black and light yellow-green; front printed with a photo of Marsh, below which in a green band: [in white:] Eddie Marsh | SKETCHES FOR A COMPOSITE LITERARY PORTRAIT OF | SIR EDWARD MARSH, K.C.V.O., C.B., C.M.G. | [bar] | *Lund Humphries*; back blank; spine, top to bottom: [in white to dot] EDDIE MARSH . *Sketches for a Composite Literary Portrait*

Price: 7s.6d. Number of copies: 2,500. Published 5 May 1953.

Note: Graves' contribution is a biographical memoir (pp. 25–26).

B38.1   IDEAS AND PLACES   [1953]

IDEAS | AND | PLACES | BY | CYRIL CONNOLLY | [six pointed star] | *. . . et nous errions, nourris du vin des Palermes et | du biscuit de la route, moi presse' de trouver le lieu | et la formule.* | RIMBAUD | *LONDON* | WEIDENFELD & NICOLSON | LIMITED

Collation: [1]¹⁰ [2] – [18]⁸, 146 leaves.

p.[i] IDEAS AND PLACES; p.[ii] To *L. L.*; p.[iii] title-page; p.[iv] publication, acknowledgements and printer's notices; pp. [v]–vi CONTENTS; pp.[vii] viii–x INTRODUCTION; pp.[1] 2–280 text, with pp.[203, 220, 228, 238, 253, 271] being unnumbered; pp.[281]–[282] blank.

20.8 × 13.5 cm. Bulk: 2.1/2.6 cm. White wove paper; all edges trimmed. White wove endpapers. Bound in rusty orange cloth; front and back blank; spine stamped in gold: [two decorative devices as rules] | IDEAS | AND | PLACES | [two decorative devices as rules] | CYRIL | CONNOLLY | WEIDENFELD | & NICOLSON

Price: 16s. Number of copies undetermined. Published 15 May 1953.

Note: Graves' contribution is a reply to the questionnaire "The Cost of Literature" (pp. 89–90). Reprinted in C330.1.

B39   NEW POEMS 1953   [1953]

New Poems | [swelled rule, at centre of which is a fancy circular device, inside which:] 1953 | *A P.E.N. Anthology* | Edited by | ROBERT CONQUEST | MICHAEL HAMBURGER | HOWARD SERGEANT | *Introduction by* | C.V. WEDGWOOD | PRESIDENT OF THE P.E.N. | [publisher's emblem] | *London* | MICHAEL JOSEPH

Collation: [A]⁸ B–K⁸ L⁶, 86 leaves.

p.[1] NEW POEMS | [fancy circular device, inside which:] 1953; p.[2] publisher's advertisement; p.[3] title-page; p.[4] publisher's and printer's notices; pp.[5]–[12] *Contents*; pp. [13] 14–16 *Introduction*; pp.[17]–18 *Foreword*; p.[19] section heading; p.[20] blank; pp.21–160 text, with pp.[41, 59, 79, 103, 121, 141] being section headings and pp.[40, 42, 60, 80, 104, 122, 140, 142] being blank; pp.161–172 *The Contributors*.

20.2 × 13.0 cm. Bulk: 1.0/1.4 cm. White wove paper; all edges trimmed. White wove endpapers. Bound in white boards with red and black designs (11 × 6); black cloth spine stamped in silver: *New* | *Poems* | [swelled decorative rule] | *1953* | [swelled decorative rule] | *a* | *P.E.N.* | *Anthology* | [publisher's emblem] | MICHAEL | JOSEPH

Price: 10s.6d. Number of copies: 3,000. Published 18 May 1953.

Note: Graves' contributions are 'Dialogue on the Headland' (pp. 25–26), 'The Straw' (p. 26), 'The Foreboding' (p. 27) and 'The Survivor' (pp. 27–28).

B39.1   CHOPIN'S WINTER IN MAJORCA   1955

LUIS RIPOLL | [one line in red:] CHOPIN'S | WINTER IN MAJORCA | 1838–1839 | FOREWORD BY ROBERT GRAVES | *Translated by Alan Sillitoe* | PALMA DE MALLORCA | 1955

Collation: [1]–[3]⁸ [4]⁴ [5]–[6]⁸ [7]⁴ [8]–[9]⁸ [10]², 66 leaves.

p.[i] [all in red:] SIURELL | [device] | LIBRARY; p.[ii] blank; p.[iii] CHOPIN'S | WINTER IN MAJORCA | 1838–1839; p.[iv] list of works by Ripoll; p.[v] title-page; p.[vi] rights reservation, copyright, edition and printer's notices; p.[vii] *To my wife*; p.[viii] blank; pp.[ix]–x ILLUSTRATIONS; pp. [xi] xii–xiv *FOREWORD*; pp.[xv]–xvi introduction; pp.[1] 2–109 text, with pp.[9, 15, 23, 31, 43, 51, 61, 69, 81,

93, 99, 103] being unnumbered and pp.[42, 80, 98] being blank; p. [110] blank; pp.[111]–112 BIBLIOGRAPHY: pp.[113] 114–115 chronologies; pp.[116] blank; 8 pp. illustrations between each of pp.40–41, 72–73 and 104–105.
16.5 × 11.2 cm. Bulk: 1.2/1.3 cm. White wove paper; all edges trimmed. White wove endpapers. Bound in boards covered with pink paper with webbed design in white; back and spine otherwise blank; front has portrait of George Sand in black in simulated white quadrilateral box.

Price: Unknown. Number of copies unknown. Published in 1955 in white dust-jacket printed in black and blue.

Note: Graves' contribution is the foreword (pp.[xi] xii–xiv).
The printer is Imprenta Mossén Alcover, Calatrava 68, Palma de Mallorca.

B40 BATTLE FOR THE MIND [1957]

WILLIAM SARGANT | [star] | *Battle for the Mind* | A PHYSIOLOGY OF CONVERSION | AND BRAIN-WASHING | [publisher's emblem] | HEINEMANN | MELBOURNE LONDON TORONTO

Collation: [A]⁸ B–R⁸, 136 leaves.
    p.[i] *Battle for the Mind* | A PHYSIOLOGY OF CONVERSION | AND BRAIN-WASHING; p.[ii] blank; [frontispiece, back blank]; p. [iii] title-page; p.[iv] publisher's, publication and printer's notices; p.[v] *Contents*; p.[vi] blank; pp.vii–viii *List of Illustrations*·; p.[ix] *Acknowledgements*; p.[x] epigraph (20 ll.)from George Salmon; pp.xi–xii [xiii] *Foreword*; p. [xiv] blank; pp.xv–xxiv *Introduction*; pp.1–236 text; pp. 237–240 *Bibliography*; pp.241–248 *Index*; illustrations in two gatherings, sewn between I and K.
21.4 × 13.8 cm. Bulk: 2.3/3.0 cm. White laid paper; all edges trimmed. White wove endpapers. Bound in salt-and-pepper cloth; front blank; back stamped in lower right with a maroon publisher's emblem; spine stamped with a solid maroon rectangular box at top printed in silver: *Battle* | *for the* | *Mind* | [star] | WILLIAM | SARGANT; solid maroon rectangular box at bottom printed in silver: HEINEMANN

Price: 25s. Number of copies undetermined. Published 15 April 1957 in white dust-jacket printed in red and black.

Note: Graves' contribution is Chapter 8, 'Brain-Washing in Ancient Times' (pp. 166–176).

B41 COLLECTED POEMS OF NORMAN CAMERON 1957

THE | COLLECTED POEMS | OF | NORMAN CAMERON | 1905–1953 | [star] | With an Introduction by | ROBERT GRAVES | LONDON | THE HOGARTH PRESS | 1957

Collation: [A]⁴ B–E⁸, 36 leaves.
    p.[1] COLLECTED POEMS; p.[2] blank; [frontispiece, back blank]; p.[3] title-

page; p.[4] publisher's, printer's and rights notices; pp.[5] – [7] CONTENTS; p.[8] NOTE; pp.9 – 24 *Introduction*; pp.25 – 72 text.

21.4 × 13.8 cm. Bulk: 0.5/1.0 cm. White laid paper; all edges trimmed. White wove endpapers. Bound in boards covered in dusty mauve paper; back blank; front printed in blue: [broad decorative rule rectangular box enclosing all:] *The | Collected Poems of |* NORMAN | CAMERON | [decorative rule] | 1905 – 1953 | [decorative rule] | *With | an Introduction by |* ROBERT GRAVES | *The Hogarth Press*; spine printed in blue, top to bottom: COLLECTED POEMS [star] Norman Cameron *The Hogarth Press*

Price: 15s. Number of copies: 750. Published 11 June 1957 in mauve laid dust-jacket printed in blue, as cover.

Note: Graves' contribution is the introduction (pp.9 – 24).

B42 MEMORY AND HER NINE DAUGHTERS 1957

MEMORY AND HER NINE DAUGHTERS, THE MUSES, | a pretext for printing cast into the mould | of a dialogue in four chapters, by victor hammer. | GEORGE WITTENBORN, INC. | 1018 madison avenue, new york city, 21— new york. | MDCCCCLVII

Collation: π⁴ a – i⁶, 58 leaves.

2 pp. blank; 1 p., title-page; 1 p., rights reservation notice; p.i half-title; pp.ij – iij translation of vv.53 – 84 of Hesiod's *Theogony*; p.iv diagram; pp.1 – 103 text; pp.104 – 107 NOTES AND REMARKS; p.[108] colophon: two-hundred and fifty-two copies | have been printed at the hand press by | carolyn r. hammer | victor hammer has set the pages | number [square bracket] [number written in] [square bracket] | A + M + D + G

24.7 × 15.5 cm. Bulk: 1.4/2.1 cm. White laid paper; top edges only trimmed. Endpapers are a blank four-leaf sheet, top unopened, sewn in separately. Bound in paper-covered boards; front printed in black, blue and rust with 34 ll. of text and catchword; back printed with 35 ll. of text in rust and black with catchword; spine printed in rust, up spine. hammer : 4 dialogues

Price: $9.50. Number of copies: 252. Published in midsummer 1957 in light tan laid dust-jacket printed in black.

Note: Graves' contribution is the translation from Hesiod (pp.ij – iij).

B43 NEW POEMS 1957 [1957]

New Poems | [swelled rule with fancy circular device in centre, inside which:] 1957 | *Edited by* | KATHLEEN NOTT | C. DAY LEWIS | THOMAS BLACKBURN | [publisher's emblem] | *London* | MICHAEL JOSEPH

Collation: [A]⁸ B – H⁸ I⁶, 70 leaves.

p.[1] NEW POEMS | [fancy circular device, inside which:] 1957; p.[2] blank; p.[3] title-page; p.[4] publisher's, printer's, papermaker's and binder's notices; pp.[5] – [7]

Contents; p. [8] blank; pp.[9]–10 *Introduction*; p.[11] *The Poems*; p. [12] blank; pp.13–132 text; pp.[133] 134–140 *The Contributors*.
    20.1 × 13.0 cm. Bulk: 1.0/1.4 cm. White wove paper; all edges trimmed. White wove endpapers. Bound in boards covered with paper in 5 1/2 × 3 floral design; yellow cloth spine stamped in black: *New | Poems | [swelled decorative rule] | 1957 | [swelled decorative rule] | a | P.E.N. | Anthology | [publisher's emblem] | MICHAEL | JOSEPH*

Price: 15s. Number of copies: 2,000. Published 21 October 1957.

Note: Graves' contribution is 'The Coral Pool' (p.56).

B44   YOU COUL HEAR THE SNOW MELTING   [1958]

piero heliczer | [row of 19 solid circular spots] | YOU COUL HEAR THE SNOW MELTING & | DRIPPING INTO THE DEERS MOUTH | [COUL] [DEERS]

Collation: 12 leaves, unsigned, stapled twice in the centre.
    p.[1] blank; p.[2] letter from Graves, dated 7 March 1958; pp. [3]–[23] text; p.[24] blank, with photograph of Heliczer pasted in upper left corner.
    15.9 × 15.7 cm. Bulk: 0.2 cm. Grey laid paper; top and bottom edges trimmed. Issued in yellow paper wrapper; across back: you coul hear the snow dripping | [on front, continuous:] and falling into the deers mouth; front has splotchy orange overprinting; inside of front cover is title-page, flush right; inside back cover: *by piero heliczer | GIRL BODY | available through the dead language | [row of 13 solid circular spots] | title by siggy wessberg | photograph by harold chapman | press work by the dead language paris | dixhuit rue descartes*

Price: undetermined. Number of copies undetermined. Published in 1958.

Note: Graves' contribution is the letter (p.[2]).

B45   A GOLDEN LAND   [1958]

A | GOLDEN LAND | *Stories, Poems, Songs | New and Old* | [cut of woman cradling child in arms] | *Edited by* JAMES REEVES | *Illustrated by* GILLIAN CONWAY | *and others* | CONSTABLE AND COMPANY LTD | *London*

Collation: π^8 A–2H^8, 256 leaves.
    p.[i] A GOLDEN LAND; p.[ii] blank; p.[iii] title-page; p.[iv] copyright, acknowledgement, publisher's and printer's notices; p.[v] TO THE MEMORY OF | WALTER DE LA MARE | 1873–1956 | *'The best in this kind are but shadows'*; p.[vi] blank; pp.vii–x CONTENTS; pp.xi–xiv INTRODUCTION; pp.xv–xvi ACKNOWLEDGMENTS; pp.1–489 text; pp.490–496 indexes.
    23.5 × 15.6 cm. Bulk: 3.2/3.9 cm. White wove paper; all edges trimmed; top edges stained light orange. Mustard-orange wove endpapers. Bound in medium blue cloth; front and back blank; spine stamped in gold: A | Golden | Land | [swelled rule] | JAMES | REEVES | *Constable*

Price: 25s. Number of copies undetermined. Published 9 October 1958 in white dust-jacket printed in black, orange, blue and green.

Notes: Graves' contributions are 'The Six Badgers' (p.260) and 'The Pumpkin' (p.286).
The jacket-design is by Jane Paton.

B45.1   TRIBUNE 21   [1959]

[flush centre:] Tribune 21 | [rule] | [remainder flush centre:] *Edited by Elizabeth Thomas* | London | MACGIBBON & KEE | 1958

Collation: [A]¹⁶ B–K¹⁶, 160 leaves.

p.[1] [entire flush right:] Tribune 21 | [rule] | *Edited by Elizabeth Thomas*·; p.[ii] blank; p.[iii] title-page; p.[iv] copyright and printer's notices; pp.[v] – [viii] Contents; pp.[1] --312 text with pp.[2, 3, 4, 13, 14, 16, 54, 55, 56, 116, 117, 118, 201, 202, 251, 252, 309, 310] being unnumbered.

19.5 × 12.8 cm. Bulk: 1.6/2.1 cm. White wove paper; all edges trimmed. White wove endpapers. Bound in black cloth-simulated boards; front and back blank; spine stamped in gold, top to bottom, facing back: Tribune 21 | [upright on spine] MacGibbon & Kee.

Price: 18s. Number of copies unknown. Published 19 January 1959 in white dust-jacket printed in black and red.

Note: Graves' contribution is '"Yet once more, O ye laurels"' (pp.157–159).
Although this edition is dated 1958 on both pp.[iii] and [iv] it was not published until 19 January 1959.

B46   LOVER MAN   [1959]

[all but cut flush left:] Lover Man | by Alston Anderson | [cut of boy and girl holding hands] | Cassell . London

Collation: [A]⁸ B–M⁸, 96 leaves.

p.[i] [flush left:] Lover Man; p.[ii] blank; p.[iii] title-page; p.[iv] publisher's, copyright, edition and printer's notices; p.[v] For Marshall, with thanks; p.[vi] blank; pp.vii–xi [flush left:] Foreword by | Robert Graves; p.[xii] [flush left:] Illustrations by | Denys and Judith Valentine; p.[xiii] [flush left:] Contents; p.[xiv] blank; pp.[1] 2–177 [178] text, with pp. [5, 16, 17, 20, 28, 29, 46, 49, 56, 57, 65, 72, 73, 77, 89, 105, 115, 128, 140, 141, 170, 171, 178] being unnumbered.

20.2 × 12.5 cm. Bulk: 1.1/1.5 cm. White wove paper; all edges trimmed. White wove endpapers; inner sides black. Bound in black cloth; front and back blank; spine stamped in white ANDERSON | [solid rectangular box, inside which, up spine, black showing through:] LOVER MAN | CASSELL

Price: 16s. Number of copies undetermined. Published 9 April 1959 in white dust-jacket printed in black, yellow, light blue and red.

Notes: Graves' contribution is the foreword (pp.vii–xi).
Mason reports a Doubleday edition, or issue, which varies, aside from the imprint, by having a LC card and fiction disclaimer on p.[iv]; measures 20.7 × 14.0 cm. Bulk: 1.3/1.9 cm.; only top and bottom edges trimmed; and spine stamped in red, running down: *LOVER MAN* | *Alston Anderson* | *Doubleday* This may precede the Cassell issue.

B47   THE LAST PHARISEE   [1959]

THE LAST | PHARISEE | THE LIFE AND TIMES OF | RABBI JOSHUA BEN HANANYAH | A FIRST-CENTURY IDEALIST | *By* | JOSHUA PODRO | *Foreword by* | ROBERT GRAVES | [publisher's emblem] | VALLENTINE, MITCHELL | 37 Furnival Street, London, EC4

Collation: [A]^{16} B–D^{16}, 64 leaves.
    p.[1] THE LAST PHARISEE; p.[2] blank; p.[3] title-page; p.[4] copyright notice, author's advertisement, printer's and binder's notices; p.5 CONTENTS; p.[6] blank; pp.7–10 FOREWORD; pp.11–117 text; pp.118–119 APPENDIX; pp.120–124 A SELECT BIBLIOGRAPHY; pp.125–128 INDEX.
    21.5 × 13.9 cm. Bulk: 0.9/1.4 cm. White wove paper; all edges trimmed. White wove endpapers. Bound in dull red cloth; front and back blank; spine stamped in gold: [rule] | [swelled decorative rule] | [rule] | The | Last | Pharisee | [rule] | JOSHUA | PODRO | Vallentine | Mitchell

Price: 16s. Number of copies: 2,000 (not all bound up). Published 1 June 1959 in yellow-brown dust-jacket printed in dark brown.

Note: Graves' contribution is the foreword (pp.7–10).

B48   EDWARD MARSH   [1959]

EDWARD MARSH | PATRON OF THE ARTS | *A Biography* | BY | CHRISTOPHER HASSALL | [publisher's emblem] | LONGMANS

Collation: π^8 1+/1*–22+/22$^{*8/8}$ 23+/*/$^{**2/4/8}$, 374 leaves.
    p.[i] EDWARD MARSH | PATRON OF THE ARTS; p.[ii] blank; [frontispiece, back blank]; p.[iii] title-page; p.[iv] publisher's, copyright, publication, manufacturing and printer's notices; p.v CONTENTS; p.[vi] blank; pp.vii–viii ILLUSTRATIONS; pp.ix–xvi PREFACE; pp.1–680 text; pp.681–703 appendixes; pp.704–707 ACKNOWLEDGEMENTS; p.[708] blank; pp.709–732 INDEX; illustrations appear between pp.64/65, 96/97, 224/225, 256/257, 416/417, 448/449, 626/627.
    22.2 × 14.5 cm. Bulk: 4.0/4.8 cm. White wove paper; all edges trimmed; top edges stained light blue. White wove endpapers. Bound in navy-blue cloth; back blank; front stamped in gold with facsimile autograph of Marsh; spine has light grey solid rectangular box near top, inside which: [rectangular decorative rule box enclosing 6 ll.:] EDWARD | MARSH | *A Biography* | [three diamonds] | CHRISTOPHER | HASSALL | LONGMANS

Price: 42s. Number of copies: 9,870. Published 8 June 1959 in white dust-jacket printed in light blue and black.

Note: Graves' contribution is letters, *passim*.

B49   LAROUSSE ENCYCLOPEDIA OF MYTHOLOGY   [1959]

LAROUSSE | ENCYCLOPEDIA OF | [in red-brown:] MYTHOLOGY | [cut of frieze] | *With an Introduction by* | ROBERT GRAVES | LONDON | BATCHWORTH PRESS LIMITED

Collation: [1] – [31]⁸ [32] – [33]⁴, 256 leaves.

   p.[i] LAROUSSE | ENCYCLOPEDIA OF | MYTHOLOGY; p.[ii] blank; p.[iii] title-page; p.[iv] series, translator's, publication, publisher's and copyright notices; pp.v–viii INTRODUCTION; pp.[ix] – [x] CONTENTS; p.[xi] LIST OF COLOUR PLATES; p.[xii] cut; pp.[1] 2–492 text, with pp.[8–9, 12–13, 15, 18, 20–23, 29, 33, 38–39, 44–45, 49, 61, 64–65, 73, 87, 89–90, 93–95, 97, 101, 108, 110, 112, 114, 116, 127, 134, 143, 145, 147, 152–153, 156–157, 161–163, 166–168, 176–177, 179, 185, 188, 192–195, 202–205, 208–209, 213, 223–224, 228–230, 234–235, 251, 253, 256–257, 262–263, 280–281, 293, 295, 306–308, 311–314, 321–323, 334–335, 339–341, 344, 356–357, 369–375, 382, 385, 387–391, 393, 406–407, 412–413, 432–433, 441, 448–449, 456–459, 466–467, 470–471, 473, 480, 483, 490, 493, 495] being unnumbered and with colour plates facing pp.36, 100, 212, 244, [356], 404, 420, 452; pp.[493] –494 A SELECTED LIST FOR FURTHER READING; pp.[495] 496–500 INDEX OF NAMES.

   28.7 × 20.2 cm. Bulk: 2.8/3.5 cm. White wove paper; all edges trimmed. Photographic white wove endpapers; inner sides of free endpapers blank. Bound in mustard cloth; back blank; front stamped with bull and with black band at right, mustard spelling out MYTHOLOGY from top to bottom; spine stamped in black: M | Y | T | H | O | L | O | G | Y | BATCH- | WORTH | PRESS

Price: 63s. Number of copies: unknown. Published 4 September 1959 in white dust-jacket printed in red, black and yellow.

Note: Graves' contribution is the introduction (pp.v–viii).

B50   THE ST. TRINIAN'S STORY   [1959]

[in wiggly Searle letters:] The St Trinian's Story | The whole ghastly dossier compiled by | Kaye Webb | with contributions by | SIRIOL HUGH-JONES | MALCOLM ARNOLD BERTOLT BRECHT | JOHNNY DANKWORTH MICHAEL FLANDERS | SIDNEY GILLIAT ROBERT GRAVES | JAMES LAVER C. DAY LEWIS | G.W. STONIER DONALD SWANN | D.B. WYNDHAM LEWIS | and | Ronald Searle | [publisher's emblem] | PERPETUA BOOKS

Collation: [1] – [7]⁸ [8]⁴, 60 leaves.

   p.[1] Searle drawing; p.[2] Searle cartoon; p.[3] title-page; p.[4] edition, publisher's, distributor's, copyright and printer's notices; p.[5] dedication; p.[6] acknowledgements and sketch; p.[7] sketch and *Contents*; p.[8] reproduction of newspaper clipping; pp.[9] 10–117 [118] text with pp.[12, 16, 20, 25, 26, 30, 31, 36, 37, 38, 40, 41, 42, 43, 47, 48, 52, 56, 59, 61, 63, 69, 71, 73, 77, 79, 85, 88, 93, 102, 105, 107, 109, 111, 113, 114] unnumbered; pp.[119] – [120] blank.

   24.6 × 18.4 cm. Bulk: 1.2/1.8 cm. White wove paper; all edges trimmed. Yellow wove endpapers printed in black; first and fourth sides blank. Bound in black cloth;

back blank; front stamped in gold: The St Trinian's Story and a trumpeting angel; spine stamped in gold, top to bottom: [to front:] *Compiled by* | [parallel to previous line, to back:] *Kaye Webb* | [in single column:] THE ST. TRINIAN'S STORY *Perpetua*

Price: 21s. Number of copies: 16,500. Published 23 November 1959.

Note: Graves' contribution is 'School Hymn for St. Trinian's' (p.49) with music by Johnny Dankworth facing; the introduction says the poem was 'originally composed as a flamenco for the Deya Girls' Choir'.

B50.1   BEST POEMS OF 1958   1960

BEST POEMS | of 1958 | BORESTONE MOUNTAIN | POETRY AWARDS | 1959 | *A Compilation of Original Poetry* | *published in* | *Magazines of the English-speaking World* | *in 1958* | ELEVENTH ANNUAL ISSUE | [publisher's device] | PACIFIC BOOKS, PUBLISHERS . PALO ALTO, CALIFORNIA | 1960

Collation: [1] – [4]^{16}, 64 leaves.
  pp.[i] – [ii] blank; p.[iii] *Best Poems of 1958*; p.[iv] blank; p.[v] title-page; p.[vi] publisher's, copyright, printing and LC card notices; p.[vii] ROBERT THOMAS MOORE; p.[viii] blank; pp.[ix] – [x] ANNOUNCEMENT OF AWARDS AND ACKNOWLEDGMENTS; pp.[xi] – [xv] CONTENTS; p.[xvi] blank; p.[1] *Best Poems of 1958*; p.[2] blank; pp.[3] 4 – 110 text; pp.[111] – [112] blank.
  21.5 × 13.8 cm. Bulk: 0.8/1.4 cm. White wove paper; all edges trimmed. White wove endpapers. Bound in light tan cloth; front and back blank; spine stamped in blue: [down spine:] Best Poems of 1958 | [upright:] [publisher's emblem].

Price: $3.50. Number of copies: 1,024. Published in 1960.

Note: Graves' contribution is 'Call It a Good Marriage' (p.30).

B51   HODGKINSON   [1960]

HODGKINSON

Collation: 4 leaves, unnumbered, stapled twice at centre.
  front cover: title-page; inside front-cover: 'The Intruders' by Graves; p.[1] biographical sketch of Hodgkinson by Alan Bowness; p.[2] list of paintings; p.[3] biographical data; p.[4] reproduction of painting; inside back cover, near bottom: 20th April–7th May 1960 | Daily 10 am––6 pm Except Sunday | Private View on Tuesday 19th April 1960 | 7–9 pm Cocktails; back cover: [flush left:] drian gallery | 7 porchester place marble arch london w2 pad9473
  22.8 × 17.7 cm. White laid paper; all edges trimmed; pp.[1] – [4] coated.

Price: undetermined. Number of copies: 1,000. Published in April 1960.

Note: Graves' contribution is 'The Intruders' (inside front cover).

B52   EXPLORATIONS IN COMMUNICATION   1960

[entire flush left:] EXPLORATIONS | IN COMMUNICATION | *An Anthology* | Edited by Edmund Carpenter and Marshall McLuhan | Beacon Press Beacon Hill Boston

Collation: [1] − [3]¹⁶ [4] − [5]⁸ [6] − [8]¹⁶, 112 leaves.

p.[1] [flush left:] EXPLORATIONS IN COMMUNICATIONS; p.[ii] list of contributors; p.[iii] title-page; p.[iv] copyright, LC card and printing notices; pp.v−vi [at left:] ACKNOWLEDGMENTS; pp.vii−viii CONTENTS; pp.ix−xii [at left:] INTRODUCTION; p.[xiii] [flush left:] EXPLORATIONS IN COMMUNICATION; p.[xiv] blank; pp.1−208 text; pp.209−210 [at left:] NOTES ON CONTRIBUTORS.

20.2 × 13.7 cm. Bulk: 1.5/2.0 cm. White wove paper; all edges trimmed. White wove endpapers. Bound in dark brown cloth; back blank; front blind-stamped with publisher's emblem; spine stamped in white, down spine, in two lines and three ranks: [near front:] CARPENTER EXPLORATIONS IN BEACON [near back:] MCLUHAN COMMUNICATION PRESS

Price: $4.00. Number of copies undisclosed. Published in May 1960 in white dust-jacket printed in red and black.

Note: Graves' contribution (pp.155−161) is 'Comments on "Lineal and Non-Lineal Codifications of Reality"', reprinted from C541.

B52.1   SWINBURNIAN COINCIDENCES   1960

SWINBURNIAN | COINCIDENCES | *BY* | CARL HERTZOG | *PRINTER* | [swirl] | EL PASO DEL NORTE | MIXLX

Collation: 24 leaves stapled at centre.

p.[i] SWINBURNIAN | COINCIDENCES; p.[ii] blank; p.[iii] limitation notice and publisher's emblem [in orange]; p.[iv] blank; p.[v] title-page; p.[vi] blank; p.[vii] EPISODES; p.[viii] blank; pp.1−39 [40] text, with pp.[2, 4, 6, 10, 12, 14, 16, 20, 30, 32, 34, 40] blank and pp.[13, 15, 33, 35−39] being unnumbered.

21.4 × 13.5 cm. Bulk: 0.4/0.7 cm. White wove paper watermarked: Utopian; all edges trimmed. Endsheets pasted to white paper cover which is tipped to grey unprinted boards, which are covered in maroon wrappers; spine and back blank, front printed in silver: SWINBURNIAN | COINCIDENCES.

Price: Undetermined. Number of copies: 200. Published in 1960.

Note: Graves' contributions are: Foreword to John Mayfield's publication of Swinburne's 'An Old Saying' (pp.17−18); a letter to his daughter Jenny Nicholson Clifford dated from Deyá, June 12, 1947 (p.27); and a letter to Hertzog dated from Deyá, June 12, 1947 (p.28).

B53   VIVA CAMENA   1961

VIVA | CAMENA | LATINA HVIVS AETATIS CARMINA | COLLECTA ET EDITA AB | IOSEPHO EBERLE | CVM COMMENTARIOLO | IOSEPHI ET LINAE

IJSEWIJN-JACOBS | DE LITTERIS RECENTIORIBUS | IN AEDIBVS ARTEMIDOS | TVRICI ET STVTTGARDIAE | MCMLXI

Collation: [1] – [2]⁸ 3–14⁸ 15⁴, 116 leaves.

p.[1] VIVA CAMENA; p.[2] blank; p.[3] title-page; p.[4] copyright notice; pp.5–14 PRAEFATIO; p.15 AD LIBRVM; p.[16] blank; p.[17] METRA; p.[18] blank; pp.19–140 text; p.[141] RHYTHMI; p.[142] blank; pp.143–182 text; p.[183] COMMENTARIOLVS | AVCTORES ET ANNOTATIONES | TITVLI ET INITIA CARMINVM | INDEX; p.[184] blank; pp.185–199 text; p.[200] blank; pp.201–221 text; p.[222] blank; pp.223–229 index of first lines and titles; p.[230] blank; p.[231] INDEX; p.[232] rights reservation, printer's and printing notices.

20.8 × 12.0 cm. Bulk: 1.5/2.0 cm. White wove paper; all edges trimmed. Tan laid endpapers watermarked with a crown and, in Gothic: Abbey Mills | Greenfield. Bound in boards covered with very light Venetian red wove paper; front and back blank, spine stamped in gold, bottom to top, near top: VIVA CAMENA

Price: 18.50 DM. Number of copies: 2,550. Published 7 September 1961 in brownish grey dust-jacket printed in black and reddish brown.

Note: Graves' contribution is a two-line Latin poem 'Turdo Merula' (p.59); it contains the misprint 'tarde' for 'turde' in l. 2.

B54   THE ARTISTS' AND WRITERS' COOKBOOK [1961]

[3 ll. in the centre of a swelled braided rug and doily design:] THE | ARTISTS' & WRITERS' | COOKBOOK | EDITED BY | BERYL BARR | AND | BARBARA TURNER SACHS | DESIGNED BY | NICHOLAS SIDJAKOV | [swelled decorative rule] | CONTACT | EDITIONS | SAUSALITO, CALIFORNIA | [swelled decorative rule] [All text and decorative rules in purple; upper design only in black]

Collation: [1]¹⁰ [2] – [19]⁸ 20¹⁰, 164 leaves.

p.[i] cut of quills and printing press; p.[ii] LC card, typographer's, printer's, publisher's, copyright and printing notices; p.[iii] title-page; p.[iv] blank; p.[v] [device] | dedicated | to the art of imperfection | in the kitchen | [device]; p.[vi] blank; pp.[vii] – [xiv] TABLE OF CONTENTS; p.[xv] FOREWORD; pp.[xvi] – [xx] text of foreword; pp.1–288 text; p.[289] – [294] FROM THE EDITORS; pp.[295] – [307] CONTRIBUTORS; p.[308] blank.

24.3 × 18.5 cm. Bulk: 2.6/3.3 cm. White wove paper; all edges trimmed. White wove endpapers. Bound in white cloth printed overall with names of contributors in purple and olive.

Price: $10.00. Number of copies: at least 20,000. Published 1 November 1961 in grey box with arrangement of old cuts (3 × 4) and title on one side and title, authors, designer, introducer, publisher and price on other; spine blank.

Note: Graves' contribution is a recipe for Sevillian yellow plum conserve (p.284).

B55   X   [1961]

[in red:] X | VOLUME ONE 1960–61 | EDITED BY DAVID WRIGHT | AND PATRICK SWIFT | [publisher's emblem] | BARRIE AND ROCKLIFF | LONDON

Collation: π^4 [1]^8 2–5^8 [6]^8 7–10^8 [11]^8 12–14^8 15^4 16^8 [17]^8 18^8 19^{*4} 20^4 21–22^8, 168 leaves.

p.[i] [in red:] X | VOLUME ONE; p.[ii] blank; p.[iii] title-page; p.[iv] copyright, publisher's, printer's and edition notices; p.[v]–[vi] PREFACE; pp.[vii]–[viii] CONTENTS; pp.[1]–328 text, with pp.[2, 45, 76, 81–84, 143, 161–164, 247, 249–252, 325, 327] being unnumbered; plate of 1 leaf between pp.32/33, 34/35, 62/63, 200/201, 280/281, 288/289 and of 2 leaves between pp.136/137, 184/185.

26.0 × 16.4 cm. Bulk: 3.1/3.8 cm. White wove paper; all edges trimmed; top edge stained brick-red. White wove endpapers. Bound in cream boards; back blank; front stamped with large gold X; spine stamped in gold: X | VOLUME | ONE | BARRIE | & | ROCKLIFF

Price: 32s.6d. Number of copies: 800. Published 10 November 1961.

Note: Graves' contribution is 'November 5th Address' (pp.171–176).

B55.1   THE VIOLENT SEASON   1961

[across two facing pages:] [on left, flush right:] BY Robert Goulet | [on right:] *The Violent Season* | *GEORGE BRAZILLER*, NEW YORK, 1961

Collation: [1]–[12]^{16}, 192 leaves.

p.[1] [flush left] *The Violent Season*; pp.[2]–[3] title-pages; p.[4] copyright, rights reservation, LC card and printing notices; p.[5] dedication; p.[6] fiction disclaimer; p.[7] quotation from George Washington Cable and comment signed: R.G.; p.[8] blank; pp.9–383 text, with pp.[24, 48, 112, 140, 178, 198, 218, 256, 268, 286, 334, 374, 378] being blank; p.[384] blank.

20.9 × 13.7 cm. Bulk: 3.2/3.9 cm. White wove paper; all edges trimmed; top edges only stained grey. White wove endpapers. Bound in tan cloth, back blank; front stamped in black in lower right with facsimile signature of Robert Goulet; spine stamped in black: [in irregular letters] *THE* | *VIOLENT* | *SEASON* | [rule] | [in orange irregular letters] *Robert Goulet* | [black rule] | [in orange irregular letters] *GEORGE BRAZILLER*

Price: $4.50. Number of copies undetermined. Published in 1961 in white dust-jacket printed in purple, red, yellow and orange.

Notes: Graves' contribution is the advertisement on p.[7] and a letter from Graves to Braziller on the back of the dust-jacket.

This replaces B56 in the first edition of this bibliography, which incorrectly listed the W. H. Allen edition as the earliest.

B56 See B55.1

B57   LE MORTE D'ARTHUR   [1962]

Sir Thomas Malory's | [in white, in a black band, in mock-Celtic type:] LE MORTE D'ARTHUR | King Arthur and the | Legends of the Round Table | *A RENDITION IN MODERN IDIOM BY* | [in Gothic:] Keith Baines | *WITH AN INTRODUCTION BY* | [in Gothic:] Robert Graves | *DECORATIVE ILLUSTRATIONS BY ENRICO ARNO* | *BRAMHALL HOUSE* | *NEW YORK*

Collation: [1] – [16]¹⁶, 256 leaves.

p.[*i*][in Gothic:] Le Morte d'Arthur; p.[*ii*] cut of castle, ladies and two knights jousting; p.[*iii*] title-page; p.[*iv*] edition, copyright, rights reservation, LC card and printing notices; p.[*v*] [in Gothic:] For Anna; p.[*vi*] cut of knight with raised sword; pp.*vii – viii* preface; pp.*ix – x* [in Gothic:] Introduction; pp.*21 – 507* text and illustrations; pp.*508 – 512* [in Gothic:] Appendix.

23.5 × 15.5 cm. Bulk: 2.3/2.9 cm. White wove paper; all edges trimmed. White wove endpapers. Bound in brown-grey cloth; front and back blank; spine printed in brown: [down spine, in Gothic:] Sir Thomas Malory Le Morte d'Arthur | [remainder upright:] [publisher's emblem] | BRAMHALL | HOUSE

Price: $6.00 Number of copies undisclosed. Published in July 1962 in tan cream wove dust-jacket printed in black and brown.

Note: Graves' contribution is the introduction (pp.*ix – xx*).

B58   LETTERS TO T.E. LAWRENCE   [1962]

LETTERS | to | [in red:] T.E. LAWRENCE | Edited by | A.W. LAWRENCE | [publisher's emblem] | LONDON | JONATHAN CAPE 30 BEDFORD SQUARE

Collation: [A]⁸ B – O⁸, 112 leaves.

p.[1] LETTERS TO T.E. LAWRENCE; p.[2] blank; p.[3] title-page; p.[4] edition, copyright, printer's, papermaker's and binder's notices; pp.[5] – [6] CONTENTS; pp.[7] – [8] PREFACE; p.[9] LETTERS TO T.E. LAWRENCE; p.[10] NOTE; pp.11 – 24 text; 2 pp.reproductions of MS, part of the signature, not included in the enumeration; pp.25 – 120 text; 2 pp.reproductions of MS, not included in the enumeration; pp.121 – 160 text; 2 pp.reproductions of MS, not included in the enumeration; pp.161 – 214 text; pp.215 – 216 INDEX; pp.[217] – [218] blank.

22.8 × 15.4 cm. Bulk: 1.7/2.2 cm. White wove paper; all edges trimmed; top edge stained brown. White wove endpapers printed with grey background for facsimile signatures of contributors; first and fourth sides blank. Bound in dark mustard cloth; front and back blank; spine stamped in gold: LETTERS | TO | T.E. LAWRENCE | [4 diamonds in diamond shape] | [publisher's emblem]

Price: 35s. Number of copies undisclosed. Published 16 July 1962.

Note: Graves' contribution is letters (pp.107 – 115). There are references to him *passim*.

B59   IN THE CLEARING   [1962]

IN THE | CLEARING | BY | ROBERT | FROST | [publisher's emblem] | [swelled rule] | HOLT, RINEHART AND WINSTON | LONDON

Collation: [1]^8 2^8 [3]^8 4–5^8 6^4 7^8, 52 leaves.

p.[1] IN THE CLEARING BY ROBERT FROST; p.[2] blank; p.[3] title-page; p.[4] publication, copyright and printer's notices; pp.[5]–[6] CONTENTS; pp.7–10 INTRODUCTION | by | ROBERT GRAVES; p.[11] IN THE CLEARING | *'And wait to watch the water clear, I may'*; p.[12] blank; pp.13–31 text; p.[32] blank; p.[33] CLUSTER OF FAITH; pp.34–39 text; p.[40] blank; pp.41–90 text; p.[91] QUANDARY; pp.92–101 text; pp.[102]–[104] blank.

22.9 × 15.3 cm. Bulk: 0.9/1.4 cm. White wove paper; all edges trimmed. Cream-white textured wove endpapers. Bound in grey cloth; front and back blank; spine stamped in silver, top to bottom: ROBERT FROST / IN THE CLEARING *Holt . Rinehart . Winston*

Price: 21s. Number of copies: 5,000. Published 28 September 1962 in white dust-jacket printed in black and red.

Note: Graves' contribution is the introduction (pp.7–10).

B60   POET'S CHOICE   1962

POET'S | CHOICE | [fancy swelled rule] | EDITED BY | Paul Engle and Joseph Langland | [publisher's emblem] | THE DIAL PRESS NEW YORK 1962

Collation: [1]–[8]^{16} [9]^4 [10]–[11]^{16}, 164 leaves.

[2 pp. blank]; p.[i] POET'S | CHOICE | [fancy swelled rule]; p.[ii] blank; p.[iii] title-page; p.[iv] copyright, rights reservation, LC card, designer's and manufacturer's notices and acknowledgements; pp.v–vii acknowledgements; p.[viii] blank; pp.ix–xi table of contents; p.[xii] blank; pp.xiii–xvii [flush left:] THE POET ON HIS POEM; p.[xviii] blank; p.[xix] POET'S | CHOICE | [fancy swelled rule]; p.[xx] blank; pp.1–291 text; p.[292] blank; pp.293–303 BRIEF BIOGRAPHIES; pp.[304]–[306] blank.

23.1 × 15.5 cm. Bulk: 2.0/2.7 cm. White wove paper; top edges only trimmed. Rust wove endpapers. Bound in maroon cloth; front and back blank; spine stamped in gold: [decorative device] | [down spine:] POET'S CHOICE | [remainder upright:] | EDITED BY | ENGLE | AND | LANGLAND [with a fancy G] | [publisher's emblem] | DIAL

Price: $6.95. Number of copies: 10,000. Published 29 October 1962 in cream dust-jacket printed in rust, gold and black.

Note; Graves' contribution is a comment (pp.29–30) on 'The Troll's Nosegay', also printed here.

B60.1   MONITOR   [1962]

MONITOR | *An Anthology* | *Edited by* | HUW WHELDON | MACDONALD: LONDON *Collation*: [A]⁸ B−K⁸ L⁴ M/M*²/⁴, 90 leaves.

p.[1] Monitor; p.[2] blank; p.[3] title-page; p.[4] arrangement with BBC, copyright, edition and publisher's notices; p.5 Contents; pp.6−8 List of Illustrations; pp.9−14 Foreword; pp.15−16 Directors; pp.17−178 text; pp.[179]−[180] blank; [photographic plates tipped in between pp.[2]/[3], 16/17, 24/25, 32/33, 40/41, 48/49, 56/57, 64/65, 72/73, 80/81, 96/97, 104/105, 112/113, 120/121, 128/129, 136/137, 144/145, 152/153, 160/161, 168/169, 174/175].

21.3 × 13.8 cm. Bulk: 1.6/2.0 cm. White wove paper; all edges trimmed. White wove endpapers. Bound in black cloth; front and back blank; spine stamped in gold, down spine, over solid light blue rectangular box: MONITOR HUW WHELDON MACDONALD

Price: 18s. Number of copies unknown. Published in 1962 in white dust-jacket printed in black and light blue, with photograph of Wheldon on front.

Note: Graves' contribution is an interview with Wheldon at Deyá and three pages of photographs of Graves (pp.89−96).

B60.2   PARTY OF TWENTY   1963

[in script type:] Party of Twenty | [in roman:] INFORMAL ESSAYS | FROM HOLIDAY MAGAZINE | EDITED AND | WITH AN INTRODUCTION BY | [remainder of page in script type:] Clifton Fadiman | Simon and Schuster . New York 1963

Collation: [1]−[8]¹⁶, 128 leaves.

p.[1] publisher's emblem; p.[2] other books by Clifton Fadiman; p.[3] title-page; p.[4] copyright, LC card, printer's and printing notices and acknowledgements; p.[5] *FOR JIM CERRUTI* | *AS FRIEND AND AS EDITOR ·* | *HORS CONCOURS*; p.[6] blank; pp.7−8 Contents; p.[9] *Party of Twenty*; p.[10] blank; pp.11−21 INTRODUCTION; p.[22] blank; pp.23−252 text; p.[253] About the Editor; pp.[254]−[256] blank.

20.3 × 13.5 cm. Bulk: 1.9/2.5 cm. White wove paper; all edges trimmed; top edge stained light brown. Light brown endpapers. Bound in light brown boards with orange cloth spine. Back blank; front stamped in gold, in script type, at bottom, flush right: *Party of Twenty*; spine stamped in gold, over solid light brown rectangular box in script type: *Party* | *of* | *Twenty* | [rule] | *edited* | *by* | *Clifton* | *Fadiman* | [at foot:] *Simon and* | *Schuster*

Price: $4.50. Number of copies undetermined. Published in 1963 in white dust-jacket printed in black, brown, light blue and red.

Notes: Graves' contribution is 'Talking About Hexes' (pp.155−156).

B60.3   SELECTED POETRY OF ROBERT FROST   [1963]

Selected Poems of | ROBERT FROST | WITH INTRODUCTION BY ROBERT GRAVES | [rule] | *Holt, Rinehart and Winston, Inc.* | New York . Chicago . San Francisco . Atlanta . Dallas | Montreal . Toronto

Collation: 164 leaves, glued at spine.

   p.[i] title-page; p.[ii] copyright and acknowledgements; pp.iii–viii Contents; pp.ix–xiv Introduction by Robert Graves; pp.xv–xvi Robert Frost: A Biographical Note; pp.xvii–xxiv Bibliography; pp.1–321 text; pp.322–326 Index of Titles; pp.[327] – [328] publisher's advertisement.

   18.3 × 12.1 cm. Bulk: 1.6 cm. White wove paper; all edges trimmed. Bound in white paper covers printed in grey, black and green.

Price: $1.45. Number of copies undetermined. Published in 1963.

Note: Graves' contribution is the introduction (pp.ix–xiv). It is so thoroughly revised a version of the introduction in B59 as to constitute a new work.

B61   THE SUFIS   1964

[flush left:] THE | [flush right:] SUFIS | *Idries Shah* | [flush left:] *Introduction by* | [flush right:] *Robert Graves* | DOUBLEDAY & COMPANY, INC. | GARDEN CITY, NEW YORK, 1964

Collation: [1]^{12} 2–9^{12} [10] – [18]^{12}, 216 leaves.

   p.[i] [flush left:] THE | [flush right:] SUFIS; p.[ii] example of 'Sufi illustrative calligraphy'; p.[iii] title-page; p.[iv] LC card, copyright, rights reservation, printing and edition notices; pp.[v] – vi CONTENTS; p.[vii] THE SITUATION; p.[viii] blank; pp.[ix]x–xxii INTRODUCTION; pp.[xxiii]xxiv–xxvi AUTHOR'S PREFACE; pp.[1]2–365 text, with pp.[11, 34, 56, 98, 104, 115, 137, 147, 164, 172, 182, 192, 206, 217, 225, 228, 235, 249, 261, 286, 308, 317, 326, 345, 356] being unnumbered; pp.[366]367–400 ANNOTATIONS; pp.[401]402–403[404] appendixes; pp.[405] – [406] blank.

   20.8 × 13.7 cm. Bulk: 3.1/3.7 cm. White wove paper; top and bottom edges trimmed. White wove endpapers. Bound in grey cloth; back blank; front blind-stamped with calligraphic emblem; spine stamped THE | SUFIS | *Idries* | *Shah* | DOUBLEDAY

Price: $5.95. Number of copies: 4,000 (in two printings). Published 17 January 1964 in white dust-jacket printed in black, yellow, red and magenta.

Notes: Graves' contribution is the introduction (pp.[ix] x–xxii).

   There were English hardcover and paperback issues of this edition, the former by W.H. Allen and the latter by Cape. In the case of the hardback both book and dust-jacket were manufactured in the United States. The paperback appears to have used the plates of the American edition.

B62 GOLDENSHEEP [1964]

[entire flush left:] KEITH BAINES | Goldensheep | *A Sequence of Poems to Judith* | [publisher's emblem] | *Longmans*

Collation: [A]^8 B−C^8, 24 leaves.

p.[1] [flush left:] title and blurb; p.[2] blank; p.[3] title-page; p.[4] [flush right:] publisher's, edition, copyright and printer's notices; p.[5] [flush left:] CONTENTS; p.[6] blank; p.[7] [flush left:] PROLOGUE; p.[8] blank; pp.9−48 text.

21.7 × 13.9 cm. Bulk: 0.3/0.9 cm. White wove paper; all edges trimmed. Grey laid endpapers watermarked with a crown, below which in Gothic: Glastonbury. Bound in mustard canary cloth; back blank; front stamped: [heavy orange rule] | [in gold:] GOLDEN-SHEEP | [heavier orange rule]; spine stamped in gold, top to bottom: GOLDENSHEEP . KEITH BAINES LONGMANS

Price: 18s. Number of copies: 750. Published 7 September 1964 in white dust-jacket printed in black and yellow.

Note: Graves' contributions are the blurb on p.[1], which is repeated on the front flap of the dust-jacket, and the prologue (p.7).

B63 AS IT WAS [1964]

AS IT WAS | *Terence Hards* | *with an Introduction by Robert Graves* | The Seizin Press, Deyá, Mallorca | distributed by | HEINEMANN : LONDON

Collation: [1] − [6]^4, 24 leaves.

p.[1] AS IT WAS; p.[2] blank; p.[3] title-page; p.[4] publisher's, distributor's, publication, copyright and printer's notices; p.[5] Contents; p.[6] blank; pp.7−8 FOREWORD; pp.9−48 text.

21.5 × 13.4 cm. Bulk: 0.4/0.9 cm. White laid paper; top and fore-edges only trimmed; watermarked with a crown and in Gothic: Abbey Mills | Greenfield. White wove endpapers. Bound in black cloth; front and back blank; spine stamped in gold, top to bottom: Hards AS IT WAS Seizin — Heinemann

Price: 12s.6d. Number of copies undetermined. Published 21 September 1964 in grey-blue dust-jacket printed in black.

Note: Graves' contribution is the foreword (pp.7−8).

B64 THE COLLECTED POEMS OF FRANK PREWETT [1964]

THE | COLLECTED | POEMS OF | FRANK | PREWETT | [publisher's emblem] | CASSELL . LONDON

Collation: [A]^8 B−C^8 D^4 E^8, 36 leaves.

p.[i] THE COLLECTED POEMS | OF FRANK PREWETT; p.[ii] blank; [frontispiece, back blank]; p.[iii] title-page; p.[iv] publisher's, copyright, edition, rights reservation and printer's notices; pp.v−vi CONTENTS; pp.vii−[viii] INTRODUCTION; pp.1−46 text of poems; p.[47] *Three Broadcast Talks (1954)* | FARM

LIFE IN ONTARIO | FIFTY YEARS AGO; p.[48] blank; pp.49–63 text of talks; p.[64] blank.

    21.6 × 14.9 cm. Bulk: 0.6/1.1 cm. White wove paper; all edges trimmed. White wove endpapers. Bound in deep blue cloth; front and back blank; spine stamped in gold, bottom to top: CASSELL THE COLLECTED POEMS OF FRANK PREWETT

Price: 21s. Number of copies: 500. Published in November 1964 in white dust-jacket printed in blue, olive and black.

Notes: Graves' contribution is the introduction (pp.vii–[viii]). Graves is also quoted on the front of the dust-jacket and the inside front flap.

    The dust-jacket was designed by Edward Ripley.

B65 OPINIONS AND PERSPECTIVES 1964

OPINIONS | AND PERSPECTIVES | from | The New York Times Book Review | EDITED AND WITH AN INTRODUCTION | BY FRANCIS BROWN | [publisher's emblem] | HOUGHTON MIFFLIN COMPANY BOSTON | [in Gothic:] The Riverside Press Cambridge | 1964

Collation: [1] – [12]^{16} [13]^4 [14] – [15]^{16}, 228 leaves.

    p.[i] OPINIONS AND PERSPECTIVES | from | The New York Times Book Review; p.[ii] blank; p.[iii] title-page; p.[iv] printing, copyright, permission, rights reservation, LC card and printing notices; pp.[v]vi–viii Contents; pp.[ix]x–xiii Introduction; p.[xiv] blank; pp.[1]–427 text, with pp.[1, 61, 111, 205, 255, 305, 375] being section-headings and pp.[2, 62, 112, 206, 256, 306, 376] being blank and 62 pp.being unnumbered; p.[428] blank; p.[429] INDEX; p.[430] blank; pp.[431]432–441 index; p.[442] blank.

    21.4 × 14.6 cm. Bulk: 2.9/3.4 cm. White wove paper; top and bottom edges trimmed. White wove endpapers. Bound in forest green cloth; back blank; front stamped in gold: OPINIONS | AND PERSPECTIVES | from | The New York Times Book Review; spine stamped in gold: OPINIONS | AND | PERSPEC- | TIVES | BROWN | HMCO

Price: $6.95. Number of copies undetermined. Published 18 November 1964 in white dust-jacket printed in bright green and black.

Note: Graves' contribution is 'Mostly It's Money That Makes a Writer Go, Go, Go' (pp.[257]258–262).

B66 THE VALLEY OF THE LATIN BEAR 1965

[p.2:] *The Valley of the* | [part of cut of village and hills] | [flush left:] *Foreword by Robert Graves* | NEW YORK [turned rule] 1965
[p.3:]*Latin Bear* | [remainder of cut] | *by* ALEXANDER LENARD | [flush right:] *with pen-and-ink sketches by the author* | E.P. DUTTON & CO., INC.

Collation: [1] – [7]^{16}, 112 leaves.

    p.[i] blank; p.[ii] author's advertisement; p.[1] [flush right:] The Valley of the Latin Bear; pp.[2] – [3] title-pages; p.[4] author's disclaimer, copyright, rights reservation, publication, LC card and edition notices and publisher's emblem; pp.5–7 FOREWORD; p.[8] blank; p.[9] [flush right:] The Valley of the Latin Bear; p.[10] blank; pp.11–219 text, with pp.[30–31, 66, 118–119, 138, 194–195] being unnumbered; pp.[220]–[222] blank.

20.2 × 13.6 cm. Bulk: 1.7/2.2 cm. White wove paper; all edges trimmed. White wove endpapers. Bound in orange boards with blue-green cloth spine; back blank; front printed in black with sketch of house; spine printed in black: The | Valley | of | the | Latin | Bear | LENARD | DUTTON

Price: $4.95. Number of copies: 7,000. Published 19 May 1965 in white dust-jacket printed in turquoise-green, black, red, yellow and blue.

Note: Graves' contribution is the foreword (pp.5–7).

B67 SCAN 1965

KENNETH ALLSOP | SCAN | [publisher's emblem] | HODDER AND STOUGHTON

Collation: [A]^8 B–N^8 O^4 P^8, 116 leaves.

p.[1] SCAN; p.[2] *By the same Author*; p.[3] title-page; p.[4] acknowledgements, copyright, printing and printer's notices; pp.5–8 *Introduction*; pp.9–10 *Contents*; p.[11] CONVERSATIONS; p.[12] blank; pp.13–320 text, with pp.[102, 104, 180] being blank and pp.[103, 179] being section titles; pp.[231]–[232] blank.

20.3 × 13.5 cm. Bulk: 1.7/2.3 cm. White wove paper; all edges trimmed. White wove endpapers. Bound in maroon cloth; front and back blank; spine stamped in gold: [4 rules] | SCAN | Kenneth | Allsop | [4 rules] | [publisher's emblem]

Price 25s. Number of copies undetermined. Published in 1965 in white dust-jacket printed in black, grey and yellow.

Note: Graves' contribution is 'The Poet and Peasant', a narrative interview with Graves at age 68 in Maida Vale (pp.29–33).

B68 WESTMINSTER ABBEY, OCCASIONAL PAPER NO. 18 1967

[JOHN MASEFIELD, O.M. 1885–1967]

WESTMINSTER ABBEY | OCCASIONAL PAPER No. 18 | November, 1967 | [wood engraving by Simon Brett] | CONTENTS | [6 lines set flush left, with 2 and 3, 5 and 6 indented three spaces:] *Profile of the High Steward* | The Rt. Hon. The Lord Clitheroe | P.C., M.A., F.S.A. | *Profile of the High Bailiff* | The Rt. Hon. The Lord Redcliffe- | Maud, G.C.B., C.B.E. | [6 lines set right opposite other column, with lines 3 and 5 indented two spaces:] *Reflections on the Monuments* | *The Muniments of Westminster·* | *Abbey* | *Address at Memorial Service for* | John Masefield, O.M. | *Domestic Notes* | SIXPENCE

Collation: 12 leaves, stapled twice.

p.[1] title-page; p.[2] blank; pp.3–4 THE HIGH STEWARD; pp. 5–6 THE HIGH

BAILIFF; pp.7–11 REFLECTIONS ON THE MONUMENTS; pp. 12–16 THE MUNIMENTS OF WESTMINSTER ABBEY; pp.17–20 Address Given by Mr. ROBERT GRAVES at the Memorial Service to | John Masefield, June 20th, 1967 | JOHN MASEFIELD, O.M. | 1885–1967; p.21 DOMESTIC NOTES; pp.[22]–[23] blank; p.[24] printer's notice.

21.4 × 13.9 cm. Bulk: 0.2 cm. Cream laid paper, watermarked with a crown and, in Gothic: Abbey Mills | Greenfield; all edges trimmed. Not bound; the outer bifolium serves as wrapper as well as title-page.

Price: 6d. Number of copies unknown. Published November 1967.

Notes: Graves' contribution is the address (pp.17–20).
   For other printings of this address see C814 and C820.
   This pamphlet was printed by The Hove Shirley Press Ltd.

B68.1   WILFRED OWEN COLLECTED LETTERS   1967

WILFRED | OWEN | *COLLECTED LETTERS* | *Edited by* | Harold Owen and John Bell | *London* | OXFORD UNIVERSITY PRESS | NEW YORK TORONTO | 1967

Collation: [1]–[20]^{16}, 320 leaves.
   p.[i] WILFRED OWEN | Collected Letters; p.[ii] blank; frontispiece, rector blank; p.[iii] title-page; p.[iv] publisher's and copyright notices; p.[v] CONTENTS; p.[vi] blank; p.[vii] PLATES; p.[viii] blank; pp.1–8 INTRODUCTION; pp.9–16 BIOGRAPHICAL TABLE; p.17 THE OWEN AND SHAW FAMILIES; p. [18] blank; p.[19] BIRKENHEAD AND SHREWSBURY | 1898–1911; p. [20] blank; pp.21–591 text, with pp.[89, 193, 307, 373, 419, 523] being sectional titles, pp.[90, 194, 196, 306, 308, 372, 374, 420, 522, 524] being blank, and black-and-white plates between pp.24/25, 56/57, 248/249, 280/281, 440/441, 472/473; p. [592] blank; p.593 APPENDIX A; p.594 APPENDIX B; pp.595–596 APPENDIX C; p.597 APPENDIX D; p.[598] blank; p.[599] INDEX | *Compiled by R. E. Thompson*; p.[600] blank; pp.601–629 text of index; p.[630] blank; p.[631] *Printed in Great Britain by* | W. & J. Mackay & Co. Ltd, *Chatham, Kent*; p.[632] blank.
   24.8 × 15.4 cm. Bulk: 4.2/4/8 cm. White wove paper, all edges trimmed and top edge stained green. Yellow-green endpapers. Bound in olive-green cloth; front and back blank, spine: [gold stamped rules around red printed rectangle; gold stamped within rectangle:] WILFRED | OWEN | *COLLECTED* | *LETTERS* | [flower] | OXFORD

Price: 84s. Number of copies undetermined. Published in 1967.

Note: Graves' contribution is two letters in Appendix C (pp. 595–596), *ca.* 17 October 1917 and *ca.* 22 December 1917.

B69   AUTHORS TAKE SIDES ON VIETNAM   [1967]

[4 lines flush left:] AUTHORS | TAKE | SIDES | ON VIETNAM | Two Questions | on the War in Vietnam | Answered by the Authors | of Several Nations | Edited by |

CECIL WOOLF and | JOHN BAGGULEY | [flush left:] [publisher's emblem] SIMON AND SCHUSTER, NEW YORK

Collation: [1] – [3]^{16}, 48 leaves.

p.[1] publisher's emblem flush right; p.[2] THE QUESTIONNAIRE; p.[3] title-page; p.[4] [flush right:] rights, copyright, LC card, designer's, publisher's and printer's notices; p.[5] [flush right:] Editors' dedication | To the memory of Nancy Cunard | who conceived and compiled | *Authors Take Sides on the Spanish War*; p.[6] blank; p.[7] [flush left:] Acknowledgements; p.[8] blank; pp.[9] – [11] Contents; p.[12] blank; pp.[13] 14 – 15 Introduction; p.[16] blank; pp.17–77 text; p.[78] blank; pp.[79]80–92 biographical notes; p.[93] The 1937 Questionnaire; p.[94] blank; p.[95] Excerpts from *Authors Take Sides on the Spanish War*; p.[96] blank.

28.0 × 21.6 cm. Bulk: 0.6 cm. White wove paper; all edges trimmed. Bound in white paper covers printed in black and red.

Price: $1.95. Number of copies undetermined. Published in 1967.

Note: Graves' contribution is his answer to the questionnaire (pp.53–54).

B70   BULFINCH'S MYTHOLOGY   [1968]

[cut of Zeus] | BULFINCH'S | [flush with 'L' in preceding line:] MYTHOLOGY | [four lines flush with 'M' in preceding line:] THE AGE OF FABLE *With a Foreword by* | Robert Graves | *Illustrated by JOSEPH PAPIN* | DOUBLEDAY & COMPANY, INC. GARDEN CITY, NEW YORK

Collation: [1] – [17]^{12}, 204 leaves.

p.[i] BULFINCH'S MYTHOLOGY | *The Age of Fable*; p.[ii] blank; p.[iii] title-page; p.[iv] copyright, rights reservation and printing notices; pp.[v]vi–viii AUTHOR'S PREFACE; pp.[ix]x–xii FOREWORD; pp.[xiii]xiv–xvi CONTENTS; p.[xvii] biographical note on Bulfinch; p.[xviii] blank; p.[xix] BULFINCH'S MYTHOLOGY | *The Age of Fable*; p.[xx] blank; pp.[1]2–376 text, with pp.[13, 21, 30, 40, 48, 55, 65, 72, 79, 84, 95, 102, 111, 120, 127, 135, 144, 150, 157, 166, 173, 184, 192, 202, 211, 219, 234, 243, 254, 265, 273, 283, 295, 308, 319, 327, 338, 347, 354, 362, 371, 374] being unnumbered; p.[377] INDEX OF NAMES; pp.378–383 index; pp.[384] – [388] blank.

20.7 × 13.7 cm. Bulk: 3.0/3.7 cm. White wove paper; top and bottom edges trimmed. White wove endpapers; inner sides blue. Bound in light ochre cloth; front and back blank; spine stamped in black: THE AGE | OF FABLE | [light rule] | [heavy rule] | [down spine:] BULFINCH'S MYTHOLOGY | [upright:] [heavy rule] | [light rule] | DOUBLEDAY

Price: Undetermined. Number of copies undetermined. Published in 1968.

Note: Graves' contribution is the foreword (pp.[xi]x–xii).

B71 POEMS OF ST. JOHN OF THE CROSS [1968]

THE POEMS | of | ST. JOHN | OF THE CROSS | ORIGINAL SPANISH TEXT | AND | English versions newly revised and rewritten | by | John Frederick Nims | With an essay *A Lo Divino* by Robert Graves | Grove Press, Inc. New York

Collation: [1] – [4]^{16} [5]^4 [6]^{16}, 84 leaves.

p.[i] THE POEMS | of | ST. JOHN OF THE CROSS ; p.[ii] blank; p.[iii] title-page; p.[iv] copyright, LC card, edition, printing and manufacturing notices; p.[v] ACKNOWLEDGMENTS; p.[vi] blank; pp.[vii] – [viii] CONTENTS; pp.[ix] – [xv] A LO DIVINO; p.[xvi] blank; p.[1] section head; pp.2 – 151 text, with pp.[83, 97, 117] being section heads and pp.[82, 96, 116, 118] being blank; p.[152] blank.

20.2 × 13.3 cm. Bulk: 1.3/1.9 cm. White wove paper; all edges trimmed. White wove endpapers. Bound in black cloth; front and back blank; spine stamped in gold, down spine: The Poems of St. John of the Cross John Frederick Nims [remainder upright:] Grove | Press

Price: $5.00. Number of copies unknown. Published in 1968.

Note: Graves' contribution is 'A Lo Divino' (pp.[ix] – [xv]).

B72 GREECE GODS AND ART [1968]

ALEXANDER LIBERMAN | GREECE | GODS | AND ART | INTRODUCTION BY ROBERT GRAVES | TEXT AND COMMENTARIES ON | THE PHOTOGRAPHS BY IRIS C. LOVE | COLLINS | ST JAMES'S PLACE, LONDON

Collation: [1]^4 [2] – [4]^6 [5]^2 [6] – [7]^4, 32 leaves.

p.[1] [at foot:] GREECE, GODS, AND ART; p.[2] [at foot:] ALSO BY ALEXANDER LIBERMAN: THE ARTIST IN HIS STUDIO; p.[3] title-page; p.[4] ACKNOWLEDGEMENTS, copyright, publishing, rights reservation and printer's notices; p.[5] CONTENTS; p.[6] map; pp.7 – 9 INTRODUCTION; p.[10] *To Dolly and Nico Goulandris*; pp.11 – 61 text [1 leaf black and white plate between pp.14 – 15; 16 leaves of colour plates between pp.20 – 21, 24 – 25; 8 leaves of colour plates between pp.30 – 31; 17 leaves of colour plates between pp.44 – 45; 6 leaves of colour plates between pp.48 – 49; 5 leaves of colour plates between pp.56 – 57; 10 leaves of colour plates between pp.60 – 61]; pp.62 – 64 INDEX

32.4 × 23.9 cm. Bulk: 1.6/2.3 cm. White wove paper, all edges trimmed. White wove endpapers. Bound in light blue cloth; front and back blank, spine stamped in gold: LIBERMAN | [down spine:] GREECE GODS AND ART | [upright:] COLLINS

Price: 6 gns. Number of copies undetermined. Published in 1968 in white dust-jacket printed in black, yellow, orange, red, lavender, blue, purple and green.

Note: Graves' contribution is the Introduction (pp.7 – 9).

B72.1 OUT ON A LIMB [1969]

OUT ON A LIMB | *selected poems by* | DAVID SUTTON | *Rapp + Whiting* London

Collation: [1] – [3]⁸, 24 leaves.

    p.[1] OUT ON A LIMB; p.[2] [set left:] *For Gillian*; p.[3] title-page; p.[4] acknowledgements, copyright, publisher's, printer's and rights reservation notices; pp.[5] – [6] FOREWORD; pp.[7] – [47] text; p.[48] blank.

    21.5 × 13.8 cm. Bulk: O.5/1.0 cm. White wove paper, all edges trimmed. White wove endpapers. Bound in light blue cloth; front and back blank; spine stamped in gold, top to bottom: [six-ended cross ornament] out on a limb david sutton rapp + whiting

Price: 25s. Number of copies undetermined. Published in 1969 in white dustjacket printed in purplish blue and black.

Notes: Graves' contribution is the Foreword on pp.[5] – [6].

    There was a simultaneous paperback issue of this book.

B72.2 JOHN ALDRIDGE WATER-COLOURS 1931–1968 1969

JOHN ALDRIDGE | *Water-colours 1931–1968* | [black-and-white reproduction of landscape painting, 11 × 15.2 cm.] | 19 UPPER GROSVENOR GALLERIES | 19 UPPER GROSVENOR STREET | LONDON, W.1 | 01-493 3091 | *7th–24th May 1969*

Collation: White card folded once, 2 leaves.

    p.[1] title-page; p.[2] Introduction; pp.[3] – [4] numbered lists of water-colours and drawings.

    20.2 × 16.5 cm. Not bound.

Price: gratis. Number of copies undetermined. Published in May 1969.

Notes: Graves' contribution is the Introduction on p.[2].

    Most copies have the '24th' neatly crossed out by hand and the '31st' added.

B73 WITHOUT HARDWARE 1970

WITHOUT | HARDWARE | BY | C. R. DALTON | FIRST EDITION | NICHOLSON PRINTS & PUBLISHING | CANBERRA — AUSTRALIA | 1970

Collation: [1] – [15]⁸, 120 leaves.

    p.[i] title-page; p.[ii] DEDICATION [signed C.D. and R.G.], printer's notice; p.[iii] statement by Catherine Dalton; p.[iv] rights reservation notice; p.[v] PREFACE; p.[vi] blank; pp. vii–xii INTRODUCTION; pp.1–226 text, with pp.[4, 14, 24, 72, 82, 114, 194, 220] being unnumbered and blank and p.[113] being an unnumbered section title; p.[227] blank; p.[228] printer's notice.

    24.1 × 17.6 cm. Bulk: 1.5/2.0 cm. White wove paper, all edges trimmed. White wove endpapers. Bound in navy blue pebble-grained cloth; back and spine blank; front stamped in gold: WITHOUT | Hardware | BY | C. R. DALTON

Price: Undetermined. Number of copies undetermined. Published in 1970.

Note: Graves' contribution is the "Preface" (p.[vi]).

B74 MILLIGAN'S ARK [1971]

[all flush left of center:] MILLIGAN'S | ARK | Edited by Spike Milligan and Jack Hobbs | Foreword by HRH. The Prince Philip, Duke of Edinburgh | KG, PC, KT, GMBE, FRS. | Margaret and Jack Hobbs | [drawing of an elephant]

Collation: [1] – [7]⁸, 56 leaves.
  p.[1] Milligan's Ark; p.[2] edition, copyright, designer's, publisher's, printer's and distributor's notices; p.[3] title-page; p.[4] Acknowledgements; pp.5–6 text and pictures; p.[7] blank; pp.8[9] – [10] list of contributors; p.[11] letter from The Prince Philip; p.[12] – [14] blank; p.[15] TO ALL WILDLIFE; pp.16–111[112] text and pictures, with pp.[31, 36, 37, 44, 56, 65, 90, 91] being unnumbered.
  25.6 × 20.1 cm. Bulk: 0.7/1.2 cm. White wove paper; all edges trimmed. White wove endpapers; pastedown white; inner sides of free endpapers printed with bookworm and hole, front disappearing down hole, rear emerging. Bound in boards covered with paper printed in blue, green, yellow, orange, brown and purple, pictorially. Down spine in white: MILLIGAN'S ARK/HOBBS

Price: £1.25. Number of copies undetermined. Published in November 1971.

Note: Graves' contribution is a drawing of a camelopard (p.99).

B75 THE SONNETS OF WILLIAM SHAKESPEARE 1975

THE SONNETS | WILLIAM SHAKESPEARE | Preface by Robert Graves | with drawings by | Clarke Hutton | [publisher's device] | LONDON: THE SWALLOW PRESS : 1975

Collation: [1]² [2] – [12]⁸, 90 leaves.
  pp.[1] – [2] blank; p.[3] THE SONNETS: WILLIAM SHAKESPEARE; p. [4] blank; p [5] title-page; p.[6] publisher's, printer's, copyright and ISBN notices; p.[7] CONTENTS; p.[8] blank; pp. [9] – [17] THE PREFACE; p [18] blank; pp.[19] – [173] text, with plates after sonnets 1, 9, 17, 25, 33, 41, 49, 57, 65, 73, 81, 89, 97, 105, 113, 121, 129, 137, 145, 153; p.[176] blank; p. [177] numbering statement and signatures; pp.[178] – [180] blank. *N.B.* No pages are numbered.
  34 × 24.4 cm. Bulk: 2.1/2.9 cm. White laid paper; watermarked: Glastonbury. White wove endpapers, outsides printed in purple with angular gold designs. Bound in full niger leather with single rule blind stamping on edges of boards; back blank; front gold stamped star burst and crescent design; spine stamped in gold: [as a monogram:] WS | [raised band] | [up spine:] THE SONNETS | [raised band] | [publisher's emblem]

Price: £260.00 (copies 1–40) £175.00 (copies 41–300). Number of copies: 300. Published in 1975 in slip case covered in paper printed as outside endpapers.

Note: Graves' contribution is the Preface (pp.[9] – [17]).

B76   IRISH STRATEGIES   [1976]

[flush left:] IRISH STRATEGIES | [large shamrock in orange, green and brown]

Collation: [1] – [11]⁴, 44 leaves.

p.[1] title-page; p.[2] [three lines in brown:] This first edition consists of | three hundred and fifty copies | of which this is number [number written in] | [signature of Anthony Kerrigan] | [signature of Diarmaid O'Suilleabhain] | [signature of B. Childs]; p.[3] description of contents and statement of edition [Dolmen Editions xxi] and publisher's emblem, printed in brown and black; p.[4] statement on reproduction of illustrations; p.[5] [in brown and black:] contents; p.[7] [flush left, printed facsimile of manuscript:] God does not love | Ulster as he did in the | time of Cuchulain | — Robert Graves — | [printed in brown type:] Penned for this book | in the Cafe Formentor, Palma. | Friday 19 January 1973.; p.[8] blank; pp.[9] – [10] [in brown:] mnemonic note to these histories; p.[11] chapter headings in brown and colour illustrations in green; p.[12] 5 ll. quote from Yeats' 'Nineteen Hundred and Nineteen' and, printed in brown, the citation; p.[13] colour illustration in brown, green, and orange; pp.14–23 text; pp.[24] – [25] text and colour illustrations in brown and orange; p.[26] blank; p.[27] chapter heading in brown and colour illustration in brown, green and orange; pp.28–42 text; p.[43] text and colour illustration in brown, green and orange; p.[44] blank; pp.45–49 text; p.[50] borges on revolution [printed in brown and black]; p.[51] section heading in brown and black and colour illustration in black, green and orange; pp.52–87 text; p.88 printing and limitations of sale statement.

24.0 × 16.6 cm. Bulk: .73/1.3 cm. White laid paper; all edges trimmed. Green laid endpapers. Bound in green paper covered boards with brown morocco spine; front and back blank; spine stamped in gold, top to bottom: borges [publisher's emblem] irish strategies.

Price: £15.00. Number of copies: 350. Published in 1976.

Note: Graves' contribution is the statement about Ulster (p.[7]).

B77   AN ANGLE ON HUNGARY   1977

[title-page printed black with lettering in white:] An | Angle | on | Hungary

Collation: [1] – [8]⁶ [9]⁴, 52 leaves.

p.[1] An | Angle | on | Hungary; p.[2] *An album | of photographs by | Thelma Dufton | Introduction by | Robert Graves | Corvina Press*; p.[3] title-page; p.[4] copyright and ISBN notices; pp.[5] – [7] Preface; pp.[8] – [99] text, 95 black and white photographs with poems printed black on beige printed pages (pp.[10–11, 16, 20–21, 26, 30, 36, 40, 42, 46, 48, 51, 53, 64, 71, 74, 81, 86, 88, 98]) and printed in white on black at foot of photographs on pp.[24, 32, 83]; p.[100] blank; p.[101] Postscript; p.[102] Sources | of the | Poems; p. [104] designer's and printer's notices; [two-leaf fold-out, printed in beige which black printing: List of | Photographs | [arrow] tipped to p.[104]].

23.1 × 20.4 cm. Bulk: 0.7/1.2 cm. White wove coated paper; all edges trimmed. White wove endpapers; outer sides printed beige. Bound in charcoal-grey cloth; back blank; front printed in white: [within blind-stamped rectangle:] An | Angle |

T. Dufton on *R. Graves* | Hungary; spine printed in white: [down spine:] *T. Dufton —
R. Graves* An Angle on Hungary

Price: Undetermined. Number of copies undetermined. Published in 1977.

Note: Graves' contribution is the Preface (pp.[5] – [7]).

B77.1   JACKS OR BETTER   [1977]

[rule, thick rule] | JACKS OR BETTER | [thick rule, rule] | A Narrative by T.S.
Matthews | HARPER & ROW, PUBLISHERS | New York, Hagerstown, San
Francisco, London

Collation: [1]^{16} [2]^8 [3] – [12]^{16}, 184 leaves.
   p.[i] [light rule, heavy rule] | JACKS OR BETTER | [heavy rule, light rule]; p.[ii] list
of Matthews' books; p.[iii] title-page; p.[iv] acknowledgements, copyright, edition,
designer's, LC card, and register notices; p.[v] *To Pam, the happy ending·*; p.[vi]
blank; p.vii [light rule, heavy rule] CONTENTS | [heavy rule, light rule]; p.[viii]
blank; p.[ix] Opening Remarks; p.[x] blank; p.[xi] [light rule, heavy rule] JACKS OR
BETTER | [heavy rule, light rule]; p.[x] blank; pp.1–345 text, with pp [3, 69, 115, 159,
199, 221, 255, 275, 307] being sectional titles, pp.[4, 68, 70, 116, 158, 160, 198, 200,
222, 254, 256, 274, 276, 308] being blank and pp.[12, 64, 103, 120, 142] being full-page
black-and-white illustrations; p. [346] blank; pp.347–355 INDEX; pp.[355] – [356]
blank.
   23.x × 15,8 cm. Bulk: 2.5/3.2 cm. White wove paper; top and bottom edges
trimmed. Purple wove endpapers. Bound in off-white cloth; back blank; front blind-
stamped: [rule] | T.S. MATTHEWS | [rule]; sprine stamped in black: [down spine:]
JACKS OR BETTER | T.S. MATTHEWS | [upright:] HARPER | & ROW

Price; $12.50. Number of copies undetermined. Published in 1977.

Notes: Graves' contribution are two letters on pp.283–84. There is also a photograph
of Graves on p.[120].

B78   SELECTED POEMS OF ALUN LEWIS   [1981]

[all set flush left:] Selected Poems | of | Alun Lewis | *Selected by* | JEREMY I IOOKER
and GWEND LEWIS | *Foreword by* | ROBERT GRAVES | *Afterword by* | JEREMY
HOOKER | London | UNWIN PAPERBACKS | Boston Sydney

Collation: 56 leaves, glued at the spine.
   p.[1] blurb; p.[2] other books by Lewis; p.[3] title-page; p. [4] publication,
copyright, BL cataloguing and printer's notices; pp. 5–6 FOREWORD; p.[7]
BIOGRAPHICAL NOTE; p.[8] blank; pp.9–10 CONTENTS; pp.11–100 text;
pp.101–111 AFTERWORD; p.112 publisher's advertisements.
   19.6 × 12.6 cm. Bulk: 0.9 cm. White wove paper, all edges trimmed. Bound in
white paper covers printed in black and grey.

Price: £2.50. Number of copies undetermined. Published in 1981.

Note: Graves' contribution is the Foreword (pp.5–6).

B79   AS I WALKED DOWN NEW GRUB STREET   [1982]

As I Walked Down | New Grub Street | [ornament] | *Memories of a Writing Life* | WALTER
ALLEN | HEINEMANN

Collation: [1] – [9]^{16}, 144 leaves.
    p.[i] *As I Walked Down New Grub Street*; p.[ii] blank; p. [iii] title-page; p.[iv]
publisher, copyright, Arts Council, ISBN and printing notices; p.[v] *to Peggy*; p.[vi];
blank; pp.1–271 text; p.[272] blank; pp.273–276 [277] Index; pp. [278] – [282] blank.

    21.5 × 13.5 cm. Bulk: 2.1/2.4 cm. White wove paper; all edges trimmed. White
wove endpapers. Binding not seen.

Price: £8.95. Number of copies undetermined. Published early in 1982.

Notes: Graves' contribution is the portion of a letter on p.223.
    Although the copyright statement states the publication date as 1981 the book was
not published until 1982.

C. Contributions to Press and periodicals

Notes:

(1) Poems are starred.

(2) An indication of content is given when a title is not self-explanatory and the article has not been reprinted.

(3) 'Reprinted' often means 'reprinted with revisions'.

(4) Articles, letters, and reviews to which Graves' contributions are replies are listed here in conjunction with the relevant entries.

1911

C1　　　*Mountain Side at Evening. *Carthusian* 10: 425 June.

1912

C2　　　Why Jigsaws Went out of Fashion. [With Rosaleen Graves.] *Westminster Gazette*, 21 December, p.2; *Saturday Westminster Gazette*, 21 December, p.9 [A short story]

1913

C3　　　Ragtime. *The Greyfriar* 6: 86–88 April. [Not signed; acknowledged.]

C4　　　One Hundred Years Ago. *The Green Chartreuse*, July, p.2. [Not signed; acknowledged.]

C5　　　*The King's Son. *The Green Chartreuse*, July, p.3.

C6　　　My New-Bug's Exam. *The Green Chartreuse*, July, p.4.

C6.1　　Origin of Words in use at Charterhouse. *The Green Chartreuse*, July, p.10.

C7	How to Do Things. *The Green Chartreuse*, July, p.11. [Not signed; acknowledged.]
C7.1	Honey and Flowers. *The Green Chartreuse*, July, p.12.
C8	*The Miser of Shenham Heath. *The Green Chartreuse*, July p.13.
C8.1	To the Editor of the *The Green Chartreuse*. *The Green Chartreuse*, July, p.14 [Signed 'Pollux.' For the attribution of C4–C8.1 see Mason.]
C9	*Jolly Yellow Moon. *Carthusian* 11: 173–174 October.
C10	*Rondeau: The Clouds. *Carthusian* 11: 174 October.
C11	*Love and Black Magic. *Carthusian* 11: 187 November.
C12	*Am and Advance: A Cockney Study. *Carthusian* 11: 188 November.
C13	*Peeping Tom. *Spectator* 111: 758, 8 November.
C14	*Ballad of the White Monster. *Carthusian* 11: 205 December. [Signed 'Z'; in the Lockwood notebook]
C15	*Alcaics Addressed to My Study Fauna. *Carthusian* 11: 206 December [Signed 'Z'; in the Lockwood notebook.]
C16	*The Future. *Carthusian* 11: 206 December.
C17	*Pan Set at Nought. *Carthusian* 11: 207 December.
C18	*The Cyclone. *Carthusian* 11: 207 December.

1914

C19	*The Ape God. *Carthusian* 11: 229 February.
C20	*Lament in December. *Carthusian* 11: 231 February.
C21	*Ghost Music. *Carthusian* 11: 232 February.
C22	*Merlin the Diviner. *Carthusian* 11: 233 February. [Signed 'Z'; in Lockwood and Berg notebooks.]
C23	*A Day in February. *Carthusian* 11: 247 March.
C24	*The Wasp. *Carthusian* 11: 248 March.
C25	*Five Rhymes: My Hazel Twig – After the Rain – Envy – Triolet: The King's Highway – The Glorious Harshness of the Parrot's Voice. *Carthusian* 11: 252 March.
C26	[Letter about the General Library Committee]. *Carthusian* 11: 263 March.
C27	*Two Moods. *Carthusian* 11: 267–268 April. [Signed 'Z'; in the Lockwood notebook.]

C28	*Youth and Folly. *Carthusian* 11: 268–269 April. [Signed 'Peccavi'.]
C29	[Letter about triolets.] *Carthusian* 11: 284 April.
C30	The Druid's Club. *The Greyfriar* 6: 127–129 April.
C31	*The Briar Burners. *Carthusian* 11: 286 June.
C32	*The Tyranny of Books. *Carthusian* 11: 311 July. [Unsigned; in the Lockwood notebook.]
C33	*The Organ Grinder. *The Greyfriar* 6: 149 July.

1915

C34	Some Trench Scenes. *Spectator* 115: 329–331, 11 September. [Reprinted in A.P. Graves' *To Return to All That* (B18); see also references in A32.]

1916

C35	*Between La Bassée and Bethune. *Westminster Gazette*, 6 March, p.2.
C36	*The Morning before the Battle. *Westminster Gazette*, 13 March, p.2.
C37	*The Dead Fox-Hunter. *Westminster Gazette*, 20 September, p.2; *Saturday Westminster Gazette*, 23 September, p.17.
C38	*The Cottage. *Carthusian* 12: 14 November.

1917

C39	*The Dead Boche. *Cambridge Magazine* 6: 302, 10 February.
C40	*The Last Post (June, 1916). *Nation* (London) 20: 735, 3 March. [With 'Died of Wounds' by Siegfried Sassoon with the title 'Two Poems by Soldiers'.]
C41	*Not Dead. *Carthusian* 12: 69 April.
C42	*The Lady Visitor in the Pauper's Ward. *Carthusian* 12: 69 April.
C43	*The Last Post. *Living Age* 293: 130, 21 April.

1918

C44	*Country at War. *Colour* 8: 39 March.
C45	*The Two Brothers: An Allegory. *Colour* 8: 80 May.

C46	*Jonah. *Literary Digest*. 57: 40, 4 May.
C47	*The Picture Book. *New Statesman* 11: 213, 15 June.
C48	*Peace. *New Statesman* 11: 213, 15 June.
C49	*A Pinch of Salt – The Lady Visitor in the Pauper Ward – When I'm Killed – To Lucasta on Going to the Wars for the Fourth Time – The Shivering Beggar – Escape – The Last Post. *Literary Digest* 59: 36–38, 16 November.
C50	*True Johnny. *Land and Water* 2955: 11, 26 December.

1919

C51	*The Leveller. *New Statesman* 12:302, 11 January.
C52	*Neglectful Edward. *Land and Water* 2958: 14, 16 January.
C53	*Sospan Fach. *Reveille* 3: 473–474 February.
C54	*Bazentin, 1916. *Land and Water* 2961: 31, 6 February.
C55	*Country at War. *Land and Water* 2963: 15, 20 February.
C56	*The Leveller. *Literary Digest* 60: 39, 8 March.
C57	*Hate Not, Fear Not. *New Statesman* 12: 552, 22 March.
C58	*True Johnny. *Living Age* 300: 768, 22 March.
C59	Parodies and Prisoners. *Daily Herald*, 12 April, p.8. [Review of E. de Stein's *The Poets in Picardy* and Alec Waugh's *The Prisoners of Mainz*].
C60	Foreword. *The Owl* 1: [3] May. [Probably by Graves, the literary editor.]
C61	*Ghost Raddled. *The Owl* 1: 8 May.
C62	*A Frosty Night. *The Owl* 1: 9 May.
C62.1	*Careless Lady. *The Owl* 1: [in drawing facing p. 12] May. [Part of 'Vain and Careless'.]
C63	*Sospan Fach. *Living Age* 301: 335, 10 May.
C64	*Loving Henry. *Land and Water* 2976: 36, 22 May.
C65	A Nine-Year-Old Looks at the World. *Daily Herald*, 28 May, pp.8–9. [Review of Daisy Ashford's *The Young Visiters*.]
C66	*The Boy out of Church. *Land and Water* 2979: 25, 12 June.
C67	*The Kiss. *Century* 98: 417 July.
C68	An Old Friend. *Daily Herald*, 16 July, p.8. [Review of Samuel Butler's *The Way of All Flesh*.]

C69	*Dicky – Hawk and Buckle – The Cupboard. *Poetry* 14: 252–255 August.
C69.1	*The Dancing Green. *The Vineyard* n.s.4: 175 Harvest.
C70	A Master Singer of Joy and Pity. *Daily Herald*, 3 September, p.2. [Review of *Collected Poems of W. H. Davies*.]
C71	*Ghost Raddled. *Living Age* 302: 640, 6 September.
C72	*A Frosty Night. *Living Age* 302: 768, 20 September.
C73	*Advice to Lovers. *The Owl* 2: 8 October.
C73.1	*Vain Man. *The Owl* 2: [in drawing facing p. 9] October. [Part of 'Vain and Careless'.]
C74	*One Hard Look. *The Owl* 2: 9 October.
C75	*Becker's Ghost. *Nation* (London) 26: 392, 13 December.

1920

C76	*Country Mood. *London Mercury* 1: 272 January.
C77	*The Treasure Box. *New Statesman* 14: 436, 17 January.
C78	*Catherine Drury. *Land and Water* 3011: 13, 22 January.
C79	*The Personal Touch. *Spectator* 124: 110, 24 January. [Signed 'Tom Fool'; reprinted in A7.]
C80	*Song: The Ring and Chain. *Voices* 3: 16 February.
C81	*The Treasure Box. *Living Age* 304: 473, 21 February.
C82	*Country Mood. *Living Age* 304: 496, 21 February.
C83	*The Troll's Nosegay. *To-Day* 7: 2 March.
C84	*Words to the Tune of 'Black Horse Lane'. *Spectator* 124: 308, 8 March.
C85	Books at Random. *Woman's Leader and the Common Cause* 12: 159, 19 March. [Signed 'FUZE'; acknowledged. About the dropping of compulsory Greek at Oxford, Hardy's honorary degree and John Masefield.]
C86	*The Hills of May. *Woman's Leader* 12: 176, 26 March.
C87	*Lost Love. *The Apple of Beauty and Discord* 1: 86 2nd Quarter.
C88	Books at Random. *Woman's Leader* 12: 209, 1 April. [Signed 'FUZE'. See C85. Review of Aldous Huxley's *Limbo* and speculations about who buys books.]

C89   Books at Random. *Woman's Leader* 12: 230, 9 April.
            [Signed 'FUZE'. See C85. On the 'holiness' of books, the bad effect of
            booksellers on publishers and E.B. Browning.]

C90   *Reproach. *Athenaeum* 94: 508, 16 April.

C91   Books at Random. *Woman's Leader* 12: 252, 16 April.
            [Signed 'FUZE'. See C85. On literary back-scratching.]

C92   Books at Random. *Woman's Leader* 12: 300, 30 April.
            [Signed 'FUZE'. See C85. About his library and reorganizing his
            bookshelves.]

C93   Books at Random. *Woman's Leader* 12: 348, 14 May.
            [Signed 'FUZE'. See C85. About Mabel Nicholson and referring to
            women artists by their married names.]

C94   Books at Random. *Woman's Leader* 12: 373, 21 May.
            [Signed 'FUZE'. See C85. About children's literature.]

C95   *Words to the Tune of 'Black Horse Lane'. *Living Age* 305: 496, 22 May.

C96   *The Troll's Nosegay. *Literary Digest* 65: 46, 22 May.

C97   Books at Random. *Woman's Leader* 12: 393, 28 May.
            [Signed 'FUZE'. See C85. About slang.]

C98   *Kit Logan and Lady Helen. *Oxford and Cambridge Miscellany* (June
            1920), p.1.

C99   *The Stake. *London Mercury* 2: 138 June.

C100   [Review of Robert Nichols' *Aurelia*]. *Isis* 563: 11, June.

C101   Books at Random. *Woman's Leader* 12: 439, 11 June.
            [Signed 'FUZE'. See C85. About *Irene Iddesleigh*.]

C102   Books at Random. *Woman's Leader* 12: 462–463, 18 June.
            [Signed 'FUZE'. See C85. About Traherne, Campion, Donne, Douglas,
            Henryson, Darley, Clare and Skelton: 'neglected and recently rescued'
            poets.]

C103   *Storm: At the Farm Window. *Spectator* 124: 828, 19 June.

C104   *The Pier-Glass. *Athenaeum* 94: 823, 25 June.

C105   Books at Random. *Woman's Leader* 12: 486, 25 June.
            [Signed 'FUZE'. See C85. On blasphemy in art.]

C106   Books at Random. *Woman's Leader* 12: 585, 30 July.
            [Signed 'FUZE'. See C85. A 'holiday letter' from Hwch Goch.]

C107   *Lady Student: A Study in Norman Influences.
            Anglo-French Review 4: 52–53 August.

C108   *Incubus. *Spectator* 125: 336, 11 September.

C109   *Lady Student: A Study in Norman Influences. *Living Age* 306: 682, 11 September.

C110   *The Traveller's Curse after Misdirection (from the Welsh). *Saturday Review of Literature* 1: 121, 20 September.

C111   *Delilah's Parrot: From the *Coronation Murder* Cycle. *Carthusian* 13: 32 October.

C112   Isis Idol: Mr. T.E. Lawrence (Arabia and All Souls). *Isis* 567: 5, 27 October.
[Unsigned; acknowledged.]

1921

C113   *The Finding of Love. *London Mercury* 3: 254–255 January.

C114   *Raising the Monolith. *Athenaeum*, 7 January, p.8.

C115   *The Magical Picture. *Saturday Westminster Gazette*, 22 January, p.10.

C116   *The Magical Picture. *Living Age* 309: 124, 9 April.

C117   *'The General Elliott'. *Spectator* 126: 491, 16 April.

C118   *Song of Contrariety. *Outlook* 47: 393, 7 May.

C119   *Cynics and Romantics. *To-Day* 8: 154 June.

C120   *Records for Wonder. *Saturday Westminster Gazette*, 4 June, p.10.

C121   *Raising the Monolith. *Living Age* 309: 586, 4 June.

C122   *Song of Contrariety. *Living Age* 309: 794, 25 June.

C122.1   *A Vehicle, to Wit, a Bicycle. *New Statesman* 17: 414, 16 July.
[Formerly C195; reprinted in A8.]

C123   *On the Ridge. *Nation* (London) 29: 613, 23 July.

C124   *The Lands of Whipperginny. *Voices* 5: 110 Autumn.

C125   *Sullen Moods – A Lover Since Childhood – The Bedpost – Old Wives' Tales. *London Mercury* 4: 455–458 September.

C126   *Lawyer's Tale. *New Republic* 28: 103, 21 September.

C127   A Parable. *Form* n.s.1: 17–20 October.
[Reprinted A7, Sec. VIII.]

C128   *Old Wives' Tales. *Literary Digest* 71: 32, 22 October.

C129   *A Lover Since Childhood. *Literary Digest* 71: 134, 29 October.

C130   The Dangers of Definition. *SPE Tract* 6, pp.23–26.

C131   *Philosophers. *Form* 1: 56 November–December.

C132   *The Sewing Basket (A Wedding Present from Jenny Nicholson to Winifred Roberts). *Spectator* 127: 595–596, 5 November.

C133   Poets and anthologies. *TLS*, 1 December, p.789.
[Letter commending T.S. Eliot's complaint about anthologies.]

C134   How English Is Taught. *Daily Herald*, 14 December, p.7.
[Review of *The Teaching of English in England* by a committee of the President of the Board of Education.]

C135   *Christmas Eve. *New Republic* 29: 125, 28 December.

1922

C136   Inspiration and the Pattern. *Form* 1: 103 January.

C137   *Old Lob-Lie-by-the-Fire. *Spectator* 128: 15, 7 January.

C138   *On Preserving a Poetical Formula – Epitaph on an Unfortunate Artist. *Spectator* 128: 175, 11 February.

C139   *The Red Ribbon Dream. *New Republic* 30: 43, 8 March.

C140   *Philosophers. *Harpers* 144: 722 May.

C141   *The Rock Below. *London Mercury* 6: 17 May.

C142   *Whipperginny (as 'Wipperginny'). *London Mercury* 6: 129 June.

C143   Answers to a Questionnaire. *Chapbook* 27: 11–14 July.

C144   *On D – A Lover Who Died in an Accident. *Spectator* 129: 16, 1 July.

C145   The Illogic of Stoney Stratford and of Poetry. *Spectator* 129: 87, 15 July.

C146   *Whipperginny. *Literary Digest* 74: 36, 15 July.

C147   Poetic Catharsis and Modern Psychology. *Spectator* 129: 151–152, 29 July.

C148   Alexander Pope. *Daily Herald* 30 August, p.7.
[Short biographical and critical note.]

C149   *A Forced Music. *Spectator* 129: 305, 2 September.

C150   *Return. *Saturday Review* 134: 420, 16 September.

C151   Mr Graves Replies. *Literary Review* [of *New York Evening Post*], 7 October, p.98.
[Review by Joseph Wood Krutch, 12 August, p.868.]

C152   *A Forced Music. *Living Age* 315: 56, 7 October.

C153   *Return. *Independent* 109: 236, 28 October.

C154   *An English Wood. *New Republic* 32: 248, 1 November.

C155   *Children of Darkness. *New Republic* 33: 11, 29 November.

C156   *Mirror, Mirror – Return. *Bookman* (New York) 56: 448 December.

C157   *On the Poet's Birth. *Fugitive* 1: 103 December.

C158   *A Valentine. *Fugitive* 1: 112 December.

1923

C159   *The Avengers. *The Observer*, 14 January, p.13.

C160   *Children of Darkness. *Bookman* (New York) 56: 718 February.

C161   *The Lord Chamberlain Tells of a Famous Meeting. *Poetry* 21: 257–261 February.

C162   *The Snake and the Bull. *Chapbook* 35: 19–21 March.

C163   *A Dewdrop. *Harpers* 146: 526 March.

C164   *A Dewdrop. *Spectator* 130: 406, 10 March.

C165   *Lost Love. *Living Age* 317: 116, 14 April.

C165.1   *The Haunted House. *The Challenge* 2: 149, 18 May.
         [The manuscript of this poem was sold at Sotheby's, 4 December 1973, lot 180.]

C166   The Eagle and the Wren. *Nation and Athenaeum* 33: 272–273, 26 May.
         [Review of Edith Sitwell's *Bucolic Comedies* and C.M. Doughty's *Mansoul*.]

C167   *Twin Souls. *Saturday Review* 135: 733, 2 June.

C168   *Misgivings, on Reading a Popular 'Outline of Science'. *Lyric* 3: 1 July.

C169   Mr Hardy and the Pleated Skirt. *Nation and Athenaeum* 33: 451–452, 7 July.

C170   *Twin Souls. *Living Age* 318: 330, 18 August.

C171   What Is Bad Poetry? *North American Review* 218: 353–368 September.

C171.1   How Many Miles to Babylon? *Broom* 5: 164–166 October.

C172   *The Safe, or Erewhon Redivivus. *Winter Owl* [November], pp.18–19.
         [Signed 'John Doyle'.]

C172.1   Mr. Belloc. *Winter Owl* [November], [facing p.19]. [A drawing signed 'John Doyle'.]

C173   Interchange of Selves [As by B.K. Mallik.] *Winter Owl* [November], pp.28–43.

C174   *Full Moon. *Winter Owl* [November], pp.44–45.

C175   *The Knowledge of God. *Winter Owl* [November], p.59.

C176   *British* or *English*. SPE Tract 15, p.22. [About usage of the two words.]

C177   A Poetess and Five Poets. *Nation and Athenaeum* 34: 278–279, 17 November.
[Review of *Trentaremi and Other Moods* by Sir Rennell Rodd, *Poems* by W.S. Blunt, *Autumn Midnight* by Frances Cornford, *The Day's Delight* by Geoffrey Deamer, *A Devonshire Garden* by R.H. Foster and *Plummets* by Henry Allsopp.

C178   *Henry and Mary. *Current Opinion* 75: 736 December.

C179   A 'Galileo of mares' nests.' *Spectator* 131: 949–950, 15 December.
[On Samuel Butler.]

C180   'The Victorian Pageant.' *Nation and Athenaeum* 34: 492–493, 29 December.
[Review of John Drinkwater's *Victorian Poetry* and Frances M. Sim's *Robert Browning: Poet and Philosopher*.]

1924

C180.1   The Illogic of Stoney Stratford and of Poetry. *Double Dealer* 6: 18–19 January.
[Not seen.]

C181   *Northward from Oxford: An Architectural Progress. *Nation and Athenaeum* 34: 516, 5 January.

C182   *The Kingfisher's Return from Being Stuffed. [With Molly Adams.] *Spectator* 132: 52, 12 January.

C183   A 'Galileo of mares' nests.' *Living Age* 321: 180–183, 26 January.

C184   *The Cost. *Oxford Outlook* 6: 76–77 February.

C185   Ejaculations before Reviewing. *Nation and Athenaeum* 34: 670–671, 9 February.
[Review of *At Dawn* by Hon. Evan Morgan, *An Offering of Swans* by Oliver Gogarty, *The Death of Itylus* by Edward Glyn-Jones, *The Wise Men Come to Town* by William Jeffrey and *Frogs at Twilight* by Helen Nicholson.]

C186   Mr. Hardy and the Pleated Skirt. *New Republic* 38: 77–79, 12 March.

C187   'The Freeing of Ariel.' *Nation and Athenaeum* 34: 891–892, 22 March.
[Review of *Ariel: A Shelley Romance* by André Maurois.]

C188   Wanted: Poetic Value Charts. *Nation and Athenaeum* 35: 20, 5 April.
[Review of *The Chilswell Book of English Poetry*, ed. Robert Bridges.]

C189   Kensington Gardens to Looking Glass Land. *Nation and Athenaeum* 35: 88, 19 April. [Review of *Kensington Gardens* by Humbert Wolfe, *The Pilgrim of Festus* by Conrad Aiken and *The Sleeping Beauty* by Edith Sitwell.]

C190   *At the Games. *English Life* 2: 348–350, May.

C191   The Cup Final. *Nation and Athenaeum* 35: 144, 3 May.
[Aston Villa v. Newcastle.]

C192   Eleven Plays. *Nation and Athenaeum* 35: 250, 24 May.
[Review of *Tunnel Trench* by Hubert Griffith, *Krishna Kumari* by Edward Thompson, *First Blood* by Allan Monkhouse, *The Fanatics* by Miles Malleson, *The Three Barrows* by Charles McEvoy, *The Forest* by John Galsworthy, *Far above Rubies* by Alfred Sutro, *Taffy* by Caradoc Evans, *Beyond the Horizon* and *Gold* by Eugene O'Neill and *Punchinello* by Alfred Rosenberg.]

C193   Critical Limitations. *Nation and Athenaeum* 35: 542, 544, 6 July.
[Review of *The Awakening and Other Poems* by Don Marquis, *Selected Poems* and *New Hampshire* by Robert Frost, *The White Stallion* by F.V. Branford, *Tally Ho! and Other Hunting Noises* by J.B. Morton, *Visiting Winds* by Eric N. Batterham, and *Wayfaring* by William Force Stead.]

C194   *Sergeant-Major Money: An Economic Allegory. *Nation and Athenaeum* 35: 476, 12 July.

C195   ENTRY CANCELLED, SEE C122.1

C196   *Modern Poetry: 'That This House Approves the Trend of Modern Poetry.' *Adelphi* 2: 288–290 September.

C197   *Allie – Burrs and Brambles. *London Mercury* 10: 459–461 September.

C198   Gold and Iron. *Nation and Athenaeum* 35: 723, 13 September.
[Review of H.J. Massingham's *In Praise of England*.]

C199   Anthologies Private and Public. *Nation and Athenaeum* 35: 751, 20 September.
[Review of N.G. Royde-Smith's *A Private Anthology* and John Buchan's *The Northern Muse*.]

C200   *A History. *Decachord* 1: 146 November-December.

C201   Poets in War and Peace. *Saturday Review of Literature* I: 250, 1 November.
[About Hardy, Doughty and the young 'War-poets'.]

C202   *The Presence. *Nation and Athenaeum* 36: 266, 15 November.

C203   Eleven Pounds Weight of Verse. *Nation and Athenaeum* 36: 333–334, 29 November.
[Review of *Flame and Shadow* by Sara Teasdale, *April Twilights* by Willa Cather, *The Wayland-Dietrich Saga* by Katherine M. Buck, *Collected Works* and *Selected Poems* by Herbert Trench, *The Magic Grape* by Reginald Cripps, *Poems* by Henry Derozio, *The Well of Memory* by E.E. Speight and *Miss Bedell* by C.C. Abbott.]

C204   *From Our Ghostly Enemy. *London Mercury* 11: 128–129 December.

C205   Muscular Poetry. *Saturday Review of Literature* I: 412, 27 December.
[Review of John Crowe Ransom's *Chills and Fever*.]

1925

C206   *From Our Ghostly Enemy. *Literary Digest* 84: 31, 3 January.

C207   'Beastly' Skelton. *Nation and Athenaeum* 36: 614–615, 31 January.
         [Review of Richard Hughes' edition of Skelton.]

C208   Such Stuff As Dreams. *Saturday Review* 139: 80, 24 January.
         [Letter in reply to review of A11, 139:32–33, 10 January.]

C209   Sensory Vehicles of Poetic Thought. *Saturday Review of Literature* 1:
         489–490, 31 January.

C210   *The Clipped Stater – Essay on Knowledge – A Letter from Wales.
         Calendar 1: 23–31 March.

C211   Mr. Santayana, Mr. Freeman and Others. *Nation and Athenaeum* 36:
         815–816, 14 March.
         [Review of Santayana's *Lucifer*, John Freeman's *The Grove* and Thomas
         Moult's *Best Poems of 1924*.]

C212   Poetic 'Control' by Spirits. *Southwest Review* 10: 55–62 April.

C213   *Ballad of Tilly Kettle. *Nation and Athenaeum* 37: 15, 4 April.

C214   *Passing of the Farmer. *London Mercury* 12: 8–9 May.

C215   Tarantula barbipes and Some Poets. *Nation and Athenaeum* 37: 140, 142,
         2 May.
         [Review of *Poems and Fables* by R.C. Trevelyan, *An Essex Harvest* by H.H.
         Abbott, *Collected Poems* by Maurice Baring, *The Spirit of Happiness* by
         Lord Gorell, *Parallax* by Nancy Cunard, *Complete Poems* by Emily
         Dickinson, *First Poems* by Edwin Muir and *Adriatica* by Ferenc Békássy.]

C216   *A Letter: Richard Rolls to His Friend, Captain Abel Wright. *Southwest
         Review* 10: 87–91 July.

C216.1   Trial Voices and Irish Ears. *Irish Statesman*[Dublin] 4: 525–526 July.
         [Review of AE's *Voices of the Stones*.]

C217   *The Marmosite's Miscellany. *Calendar* 2: 1–14 September.
         [Signed 'John Doyle'. See A18.]

C218   An Oxford Guide Book. *Nation and Athenaeum* 37: 735–736, 19
         September.
         [Review of L. Rice-Oxley's *Oxford Renowned*.]

C219   Keats and Mr. Murry. *Calendar* 2: 131–135 October.
         [Review of John Middleton Murry's *Keats and Shakespeare*.]

C220   *Ovid in Defeat. *London Mercury* 12: 568–569 October.

C221   *An Occasion. *Nation and Athenaeum* 38: 150, 24 October.

C222   Mr. George Pontifex and More Recent Travellers. *Nation and Athenaeum*
         38: 184, 31 October.
         [Review of *The Little World* by Stella Benson.]

C223   *Ancestors. *Chapbook* 40: 51 [November].

C223.1   [Review of Winifred Ashton's *Naboth's Vineyard.*]
          Calendar 2: 211–213 November.

C224   *Four Children. *Spectator* 135: 972, 28 November.

C225   On Foul and Blasphemous Tongues. *Calendar* 2: 248–257 December.

C226   *The Corner Knot. *Fugitive* 4: 124 December.

C227   Donnybrook Fair and Seven Poets. *Nation and Athenaeum* 38: 442, 444, 19
          December.
          [Review of *Poems* by Barrington Gates, *The Old Gods and Other Poems* by
          Richard Rowley, *The Cattle Drive in Connaught* by Austin Clarke, *I Heard
          a Sailor* by Wilfred Gibson, *Selected Poems* by Aldous Huxley, *Songs of
          Salvation, Sin and Satire* by Herbert E. Palmer and *Poems, Brief and New*
          by William Watson.]

C228   *The Hobby Horse.
          [An extempore poem included in C227.]

C229   *Bargain. *Spectator* 135: 1143, 19 December.

1926

C230   [Review of Edward Thompson's *The Other Side of the Medal.*] *Calendar* 2:
          364–366 January.

C231   *Four Children. *Literary Digest* 88: 28, 2 January.

C232   *Bargain. *Literary Digest* 88: 34, 23 January.

C233   *Virgil the Sorcerer. *Calendar* 2: 376–378 February.

C234   The Future of English Poetry. *Fortnightly Review* 119: 289–302 March;
          119. 443–453 April.
          [Reprinted in A63.]

C235   *Pygmalion to Galatea. *London Mercury* 14: 10–11 May.

C236   *Toads. *London Mercury* 14: 232–233 July.

C237   *Pygmalion to Galatea. *Living Age* 330: 27–28, 3 July.

C238   *The Corner Knot. *Literary Digest* 90: 34, 14 August.

C239   Piping Peter and Others. *Nation and Athenaeum* 39: 617, 28 August.
          [Review of *The Green Bough* by Ann Allnutt Knox, *The Laburnum Branch*
          by Naomi Mitchison, *Martha-Wish-You-Ill* by Ruth Manning-Sanders,
          Collected Poems by A.E., *Poems 1902–1925* by Edward Thompson and
          Chorus of the Newly Dead by Edwin Muir.]

C240   *The Taint. *Harpers* 153: 502 September.

C241   The State of Poetry. *Saturday Review of Literature* 3: 129–130, 25 September.
[Shortened version of C234.]

C242   Mother Poetry. *Nation and Athenaeum* 40: 30, 32, 9 October.
[Review of *Poets and Their Art* by Harriet Monroe.]

C243   *Dumpling's Address to Gourmets. *Nation and Athenaeum* 40: 113, 23 October.

C244   *Boots and Bed. *Harpers* 153: 758 November.

C245   *Pure Death. *Nation* (New York) 123: 509, 17 November.

C246   Impenetrability I. *Fortnightly Review* 120: 781–792 December.

C247   *The Cool Web. *London Mercury* 15: 127 December.

C248   *A Dedication of Three Hats. *Saturday Review of Literature* 3: 445, 18 December.

1927

C249   Impenetrability II. *Fortnightly Review* 127: 59–73 January.

C250   The Anthologist in Our Midst. [With Laura Riding.] *Calendar* 4: 22–36 April.

C251   *In the Beginning Was a Word – The Cool Web – The Bait. *Poetry* 30: 16–18 April.

C252   [Review of Malinowski's *Crime and Custom in Savage Society* and *Myth in Primitive Psychology* and W.H.R. Rivers' *Ethnology*] *Criterion* 5: 247–252 May.

C253   *An Independent. *Saturday Review of Literature* 3: 939, 2 July.

C253.1   Lawrence of Arabia — a reply to A. T. Wilson. *Sunday Times* 31 July, p.13.
[letter]

C254   [Note on Poe.] *Bookman* (London) 72: 258 August.

C255   Mallory of Everest. *Nation and Athenaeum* 41: 723, 3 September.
[Review of *George Leigh Mallory: A Memoir* by David Pye.]

C256   [Letter in answer to a review of Laura Riding's *The Close Chaplet.*] *Criterion* 6: 357–359 October.
[Review by John Gould Fletcher, 6: 168–172 August; rejoinder by Fletcher 6: 546–547 December.]

C257   *O Jorrocks I Have Promised. *transition* 7: 132–133 October.

C258   *The Dead Ship. *London Mercury* 17: 14 November.

C258.1   The Lawrence Legend: A Reply to Mr. St.J. Philby. *Observer*, 27 November, p.10.
[letter]

1928

C259   Thomas Hardy. *Sphere* 112: 129, 28 January.

C260   New Tales about Lawrence of Arabia. *World's Work* 55: 389–398 February.

C261   Lawrence of Arabia as a Buck Private. *World's Work* 55: 508–516 March.

C262   The Real Col. Lawrence. *World's Work* 55: 663–670 April.

C263   The Making of a Conqueror. *World's Work* 56: 100–111 May.

C264   A Letter from W[illiam] W[ordsworth]. *Life and Letters* 1: 208–211 August.

C265   Patronage and the English Poets. *Fortnightly Review* 130: 400–408 September.

C266   'The Enormous Room': A Note by Robert Graves. *Now and Then* 29: 25–26 Autumn.
[Review of *The Enormous Room* by E. E. Cummings; see B16]

C267   Trench History. *Nation and Athenaeum* 44: 420, 15 December.
[Review of *Ten Years Ago* by R.H. Mottram and *Undertones of War* by Edmund Blunden.

C268   The Future of Humour. *Nation and Athenaeum* 44: 441, 22 December.
[Letter in reply to E.V. Knox's review of A30 in 44: [379], 8 December.

1929

C269   Romantic Criticism. [With Laura Riding.] *Times Literary Supplement*, 3 January, p.12.
[Letter supporting the *TLS* review of Humbert Wolfe's *Dialogues and Monologues*.]

C269.1   Why Should a Wife Lose Her Own Name? *Evening Standard*, 19 February, p.7.

C270   By a Thames Window. *Evening News*, 26 February, p.11.
[Reprinted as 'Thames-Side Reverie'; see A65.]

C271   On Charity. *Manchester Guardian*, 8 February, p.20.
[Reprinted as 'Charity Appeals'; see A65.]

C271.1   The Egg-Cup Mystery. *Daily Express*, 8 March, p.10.

C271.2   *Warning to Children. *The New Era*, 1: 545–546, 1 April.

C272   I Solve Man's Dress Problem for Myself, At Least – and Nobody Jeers! *Evening News*, 24 July, p.11.

C272.1   A Poet Defends St. Swithin. *Daily Mail*, 5 August, p.8.
           [Letter.]

C272.2   Modernist Poetry. *Nation and Athenaeum* 45: 621, 10 August.
           [A letter about A28.]

C273   More War Books. *Nation and Athenaeum* 45: 629–630, 10 August.
           [Review of *A Subaltern's War* by Charles Edmonds and *The Wet Flanders Plain* by Henry Williamson.]

C274   Robert Graves Replies. *Daily Mail*, 16 December, p.10.
           [Reprinted in A35.]

C275   Troops Who Stuck It Out. *Daily Mail*, 17 December, p.10.

C276   Soldier-Poet Hits Back at Critics. *Daily Herald*, 23 December, pp.1, 6.

1930

C277   The Jocks. *Daily Mail*, 2 January, p.8.
           [Letter in answer to a letter signed 'Black Watch' (*Daily Mail*, 19 December, p.10) about a supposed German rating of British divisions.]

C278   The Cheshire Regiment. *Morning Post*, 23 January, p.9.
           [Letter in answer to Sir Hastings Anderson, *Morning Post*, 3 January, p.4, about the Royal Welch Fusiliers' rivalry with the Cheshire.]

C279   What It Feels Like to be Famous. *Daily Herald*, 7 February, p.4.

C280   A Brass Hat in No Man's Land. *Now and Then* 36: 7–9 Summer.
           [Review of book of same title by Brig. Gen. F.P. Crozier.]

C281   The Garlands Wither. *Times Literary Suppplement*, 26 June, p.534.
           [Letter about war novels.]

C281.1   [Letter about Sassoon's *Memoirs of an Infantry Officer*.] *Daily Herald*, 20 September, p.7.

1931

C282   Modern Riddles. [With Laura Riding.] *Times Literary Supplement*, 26 February, p.154.
           [Letter in answer to review of A34, *TLS*, 1 January, p.8.]

C283   Salute of Guns. *Now and Then* 38: 36–37 Spring.
           [Review of war book of same title by Donald Boyd.]

C284   An Incomplete Complete Skelton. *Adelphi* n.s. 3: [146] 147–158 December.
[This was reprinted in A.S.G. Edwards, *John Skelton: The Critical Heritage* (1981).]

1933

C284.1   The Real David Copperfield. *New Statesman* 5: 475, 15 April.
[Letter about A39.]

C284.2   The Two Abbeys. *Week-end Review* 7: 471–472, 29 April.

C285   'Old Soldiers Never Die.' *Times Literary Supplement*, 14 September, p.611.
[Letter about review of A41, *TLS*, 31 August, p.571; rejoinder *TLS*, 28 September, p.651.]

C285.1   [A letter denying authorship of *The Gold Falcon*.] *New York Times Book Review*, 5 November, p.24.

1934

C285.2   Quot Homines. *Spectator* 152: 19, 5 January.
[Letter signed by Graves, among others, protesting a review of Laura Riding's *Poet: A Lying Word* by John Sparrow.]

C285.3   Lawrence and the Arabs. *New Statesman* 7: 482, 31 March.
[Letter about David Garnett's review of A26.]

C285.4   I, Claudius.' *Spectator* 152: 780, 19 May.
[Letter in response to a review by Graham Greene.]

C286   'I, Claudius.' *Bookman* (London) 86: 201 July.
[Reply to review by Jack Lindsay, *Bookman* 86: 166 June.]

C287   English Epigrams. *Times Literary Supplement*, 19 July, p.511.
[Letter ascribing an epigram to Skelton, not Herrick; rejoinder, *TLS*, 2 August, p.541.]

C288   [Answers to questionnaire on poetry.] *New Verse* 11: 5–6 October.

C288.1   American Poetry. *Listener* 12: 664, 17 October.
[Letter on this subject.]

C289   Mr. Lindsay's Rome. *Bookman* (London) 87: 123 November.
[Review of Jack Lindsay's *Caesar Is Dead*.]

C289.1   Caligula the Good. *Observer* 11 November, p.12.
[Review of J.P.V.D. Balsdon's *The Emperor Gaius (Caligula)*.]

C290   Mr. Graves and Mr. Lindsay. *Bookman* (London) 87: 197 December.
[Reply to Lindsay, *Bookman* 87: 66 October. See C289.]

1935

C290.1   [Letter from Deyá.] *Focus I*, January, pp. 4–5.

C290.2   [Letter from Deyá.]*Focus II*, February–March, pp.12–15.

C290.3   [Letter from Deyá.] *Focus III*, April–May, pp.27–28

C290.4   How This Document Was Written. *Evening Standard*, 20 May, p.1.
[Obituary notice on T.E. Lawrence accompanying Lawrence's self-written obituary 'Myself'.]

C290.5   [Letter about the composition of *I, Claudius* and Graves' continued writing of poetry]. *Liverpool Daily Post*, 25 June, p.4.

C290.6   Hadrian: With Emendations. *Observer*, 27 October, p.8.
[Review of Sulamith Ishkishor's *Magnificent Hadrian*.]

C290.7   [Letter defending use of 'shall' and 'will' in *I, Claudius*.] *Red Tape* 25: 31–32 October.

C291   A Letter from Robert Graves. *Left Review* 2: [128] –129 December.
[Reply to Montagu Slater, 'The Turning Point', *Left Review* 2: 15–23 October.]

C291.1   [Letter from Deyá.] *Focus IV*, December, pp. 29–30.

C291.2   *Majorcan Letter, 1935. [With Laura Riding] *Focus IV*, December, pp.1–9.

C291.3   *Christmas. *Focus IV*, December, pp.18–19.

C291.4   Robert's 'Likes'. *Focus IV*, December, pp.40–42.

1936

C291.5   Taxi and Gin Shorthand. *Observer*, 9 February, p.13.
[Letter with Laura Riding.]

C291.6   A Roman Triumph. *Daily Telegraph*, 21 May, p.16.
[Letter about Abyssinia.]

C291.7   The Naval Officer. *Observer*, 28 June, p.6.
[Review of A. Hillgarth's *Davy Jones*.]

C292   [Letter about the Lawrence-Feisal letters in reply to front-page article of 16 June.] *News Chronicle*, 29 June, p.15.

C292.1   [Letter about the Seizin Press.] *John O'London's Weekly*, 6 November, p.262.

1937

C292.2 [Letter about economic provisions for poets.] [With Laura Riding.] *Daily Telegraph*, 27 May, p.16.

C292.3 [Letter about ways of providing patronage for poets.] [With Laura Riding.] *Daily Telegraph*, 15 June, p.16.

C292.4 [Letter on druidical sea-serpents' eggs.] *Daily Telegraph*, 11 October, p.11.

1938

C293 Powerless in the Matter. *Spectator* 160: 510–511, 25 March. [About trouble with ministries.]

C293.1 [Letter about character of Belisarius in *Count Belisarius*.] *Sunday Times*, 17 April, p.8.

C293.2 [Letter about historicity of *Count Belisarius*.] *Sunday Times*, 15 May, p.16.

C294 English Humorists. *Times Literary Supplement*, 28 May, p.369. [Letter about neglect of Skelton.]

1939

C294.1 [Letter about Laura Riding's poetry.] *Time and Tide*, 21 January, pp.70–71.

C294.2 [Letter in reply to review of Graves' *Collected Poems*.] *Serpent* 23: 55–56 February [Review by J.B.W. 23: 50–51.]

C294.3 [Letter in reply to review of Graves' *Collected Poems* and Laura Riding's *Collected Poems*.] *Time and Tide*, 4 February, p.138.

C294.4 [Letter on returning to poetry and W.B. Yeats.] *Daily Mail*, 8 February, p.10.

C294.5 [Letter about modern poetry.] [With Laura Riding.] *Sunday Times*, 19 February, p.16.

C295 Ubu Empereur: La Mort de Caligula. *Les Annales politiques et littéraires* 113: 446–453, 25 April. [Reprinted from the French translation of *I, Claudius*.]

C295.1 [Letter by Graves in:] Bunker Blaise, 'The Mark Twain Society.' *Saturday Review of Literature* 20: 11–12, 15 July.

C296 The Mad Caligula Humors Himself. *Reader's Digest* 35: 68–70 September. [Condensed from A42.]

C296.1   Nation Gone Mad! *Sunday Graphic*, 8 October, p.8.
               [About German character.]

1940

C297   *On Rising Early – One Hard Look. *Scholastic* 35: 25–26E, 30 October.

C297.1   Long Week End. *New Statesman* 20: 653, 21 December.
               [Letter.]

C298   Leave, 1915. *Lilliput* 8: 278–279 April.
               [Memoirs. Mason reports a *Lilliput Annual* for 1941 as an addition to the
               B section but his would appear to be only a binding-up of the issues of
               this journal for 1941; 1939/40 was the last time this journal was issued in
               book form.]

C299   Thursday Morning and Our Long Week-End. [With Alan Hodge.]
               Readers News, October.
               [Seen only as extracted clipping.]

C300   War Poetry in This War. *Listener* 26: 566–567, 23 October.
               [Reprinted as 'The Poets of World War II'.]

C300.1   What I Believe About Ghosts. *Picture Post* 13: 22–25, 27 December.

1942

C301   Common Sense about Ghosts. *Atlantic* 169: 752–755 June.

C302   [Letter on patience.] *The Times*, 18 August, p.5.

C302.1   George Washington. *Daily Telegraph*, 10 September, p. 16.
               [letter.]

C303   *The Eugenist. *Eugenics Review* 34: 84 October.

C304   *1805. *Listener* 28: 494, 15 October.
               [Reprinted in *Sunday Times*, 23 October 1955.]

C305   [Letter on Scipio and Belisarius.] *The Times*, 29 October, p.5.

C305.1   Cartoonist's Joke Becomes Film Hero. *Picture Post* 17: 14–17, 19
               December.

1943

C306   'Wife to Mr. Milton.' *Times Literary Supplement*, 2 February, p.67.
               [Reply to review, *TLS*, 30 January, p.53.]

C306.1   'Wife to Mr. Milton.' *Listener*, 29: 275–276, 4 March.
               [Letter.]

C307   [Letter about fourth terms for U.S. Presidents.] *The Times*, 12 March, p.5.

C307.1   'Wife to Mr. Milton.' *Listener* 29: 365, 25 March.
[Letter.]

C307.2   What Can It Possibly Mean? *New Statesman* 25: 354, 29 March.
[Letter about *The Reader Over Your Shoulder* and *The Real David Copperfield*.]

C307.3   English Prose. *Sunday Times*, 30 May, p.4.
[Letter.]

C308   *The Persian Version − Apollo of the Physiologists − The Beach − The Villagers and Death − The Oldest Soldier − Grotesques (i−v) − The Weather of Olympus. *New Writing and Daylight* (Summer), pp.74−77.

C309   Eyes on the Reader. *Times Literary Supplement*, 19 June, p.295.
[Reply to review of A55, *TLS*, 12 June, p.283; rejoinder, 3 July, p.319; further reply by Graves, 3 July, p.319.]

C310   It Happened in 537 A.D. *Lilliput* 13: 424−426 December.
[About Belisarius.]

1944

C311   *The Door − Death by Drums − Under the Pot − To Lucia at Birth − Through Nightmare. *Wales* 4: 32−33 January.

C312   It Happened in 513 B.C. *Lilliput* 14: 122−134 February.
[About Darius and Herodotus.]

C313   Dog, Lapwing and Roebuck. *Wales* 4: 34−51 Summer.

C314   Bards and Gleemen. *Wales* 4: 95−97 Summer.
[Review of *Other Men's Flowers* by Field-Marshal Viscount Wavell.]

C315   [Letter on Independence Day broadcast.] *The Times* 7 July, p.5.

C316   [Letter on the unicorn's beard.] *The Times*, 7 August, p.5.

C317   [Letters on the teaching of English.] *The Times*, 29 August, p.5, 8 September, p.8; 13 September, p.8; 20 September, p.8.

C318   Dog Lapwing and Roebuck (2). *Wales* 4: 36−50 Autumn.

C319   [Letter about Thomas Atkins.] *The Times*, 23 October, p.5.

C320   [Letter on usage of 'from' and 'to'.] *The Times*, 17 November, p.5.

1945

C321   Dog, Lapwing and Roebuck (3). *Wales* 4: 57−67 Winter.

C322   The Search for Thomas Atkins. *Lilliput* 16: 99−103 February.

C322.1   The Ethics of Quotation. *The Times*, 10 April, p.5.
[Letter.]

C322.2   The Number of the Beast. *Lilliput* 17: 147–151 August.

C323   *The Shot. *Tomorrow* 5: 40 October

C324   *A Stranger at the Party. *Tomorrow* 5: 27 December.

C325   *The Blodeuwedd of Gwion ap Gwreang – Battle of the Trees. *Wales* 5: 22–25 December.

1946

C326   A Conversation at Paphos, A.D. 43. *Windmill* 1: 143–154 [Winter].

C327   *The Persian Version. *Atlantic* 177: 146 March.

C328   The Scholar in the Scullery. *The Times*, 2 March, p.5.
[Letter on manual work necessary for scholars.]

C329   *To Juan at the Winter Solstice. *Nation* 163: 19, 6 July.

C330   It Was a Stable World. *Cornhill* 162: 113–120 Autumn.

C330.1   [Reponse to a questionnaire on 'The Cost of Letters.'] *Horizon* 14: 147–148 September.

C331   'King Jesus.' *Times Literary Supplement* 21 December, p.629.
[Reply to review, 7 December, p.601. See C332.]

1947

C331.1   [Letter in response to a review of *King Jesus*.] *Listener* 37: 69, 9 January.

C331.2   The Crime of Jesus. *John O'London's Weekly* 10 January, p.209.

C331.3   'King Jesus'. *New Statesman* 33: 74, 25 January.
[Reply to E.E. Kellett's review.]

C332   'King Jesus.' *Times Literary Supplement* 25 January, p.51.
[Further reply to review (see C331). Further reply by Graves, 29 March, p.141. Rejoinders, 4 January, p.9; 15 February, p.91; 8 March, p.103.]

C332.1   The History and Logic of 'King Jesus.' *New York Herald Tribune Weekly Book Review*, 2 February, pp.7–8.

C333   [Reply to review of *King Jesus*.] *Tablet* 189: 122, 8 March.

C334   *Gulls and Men. *Tomorrow* 7: 42 May.

C335   'King Jesus.' *Commentary* 4: 84–86 July.
[Reply to review by Mordecai S. Chertoff, 3: 391–393 April.]

C336   The Feud of St. Peter and St. Paul. *Tomorrow* 6: 19–26 August.
        [Reprinted as Ėstá en su casá.]

C337   *The Sirens' Welcome to Red-Faced Cronos. *Tomorrow* 7: 49 September.

C338   Historic Logic of 'King Jesus'. *Cornhill* 162: 433–439 Autumn.

C339   Folk Dance in Majorca. *Dance Index* 6: 149 October.

C340   *Return of the Goddess Artemis – Intercession in Late October. *Poetry*
        71: 22–23 October.

C341   *To Be Named a Bear. *Tomorrow* 7: 31 October

C342   *The Last Day of Leave. *Tomorrow* 7: 16 November.

1948

C343   *Return of the Goddess Artemis – Intercession in Late October. *New
        Statesman* 35: 29, 10 January.

C344   *The Sirens' Welcome to Red-Faced Cronos. *New Statesman* 35: 69, 24
        January.

C345   What Is Asphodel? *Fortnightly Review* 169: 214–215 March
        [Reprinted as 'The Common Asphodel'.]

C346   [Analysis of 'The Return of the Goddess Artemis.']
        Poetry: A Critical Supplement (April), pp.18–21.
        [Reply to John Frederick Nims' analysis, October 1947, pp.14–16.]

C347   The Song the Sirens Sang. *Times Literary Supplement*, 24 April, p.233.
        [Mentions the forthcoming A61.]

C348   'Digested Classics.' *Times Literary Supplement*, 12 June, p.331.
        [About A39. Part of a lengthy correspondence.]

C349   The White Goddess. *Spectator* 180: 767, 25 June.
        [Reply to review by G.E. Daniel, 180: 680, 4 June.]

C349.1 The White Goddess. *Listener* 40: 460, 23 September.
        [Reply to a review of *The White Goddess*, 40: 209, 5 August.]

C350   The White Goddess. *Nation* 167: 634, 4 December.

1949

C351   Wordsworth and Annette. *Times Literary Supplement*, 23 April, p.265.
        [About Wordsworth's guilt: reply to letter by John Eglinton, 19 March,
        p.185.]

C352   *The Chink. *Poetry Review* 40: 172 June–July.

C352.1 *The White Goddess. *Enquiry* 2: 15 August.

C353   *The Chink. *Poetry Review* 40: 298 August–September.
[Corrected text of C352 and letter.]

C354   *Conversation Piece. *Tomorrow* 8: 48 August.

C355   The Future of Western Religion. *Tomorrow* 9: 5–10 September.

C356   Parable of the Talents: A Suggested Emendation. *Listener* 42: 445, 448, 15 September.

C357   'The Common Asphodel.' *Times Literary Supplement*, 4 November, p.715. [Letter in reply to review, 30 September, p.632, and to letter, 14 October, p.665. Rejoinder 11 November, p.733.]

C357.1   A Motley Hero. *Sewanee Review* 57: 698–702 Autumn. [Review of Joseph Campbell's *The Hero With a Thousand Faces*. See C368.]

1950

C358   [Answer to a religious questionnaire.] *Partisan Review* 17: 133–137 February.

C359   *The Jackals' Address to Isis. *Poetry* 75: 257 February.

C360   *The Death Room. *New Yorker* 25: 35, 4 February.

C361   How Mad Are Hatters? *Lilliput* 26: 31–33 March.

C361.1   The First Biography of Skelton. *Now & Then* 80: 20–22 Spring. [Review of H.L.R. Edwards' *John Skelton*.]

C362   *Counting the Beats. *Good Housekeeping* 130: 42 April.

C362.1   Did Jesus Have a Fair Trial? *Leader Magazine* 7: 7–9, 8 April.

C362.2   [Letter about the encouragement of poetry.] *Observer*, 16 April, p.5.

C363   *Conversation Piece. *New Statesman* 39: 518, 6 May.

C363.1   Revolt in the Desert. *Leader Magazine* 7: 31–34, 10 June.

C364   'The Golden Ass.' *The Times Literary Supplement*, 30 June, p.405. [Reply to review, 2 June, p.336.]

C365   My Favorite Forgotten Book. *Tomorrow* 9: 59–60 August. [Reprinted as 'The Age of Obsequiousness'. See C368.]

C366   *Homage to Texas. *New Yorker* 26: 28, 2 September.

C367   *Advice to Lovers. *New Yorker* 26: 28, 16 September.

C368   A Mantelful of Northwind. *Nine* 5: 291–297 Autumn. [The first half is a review of Joseph Campbell's *The Hero with a Thousand Faces*; the second half is C365. See C357.1.]

C369   *'Wellcome to the Caves of Arta.' *New Yorker* 26: 42, 9 December.

1951

C370   *My Name and I. *New Yorker* 26: 38, 6 January.

C371   *For the Rain It Raineth Every Day. *New Yorker* 27: 28, 24 March.

C372   The Language of Myth. *Hudson Review* 4: [5]6–21 Spring.

C373   *The Survivor. *Tomorrow* 10: 41 May.

C374   Bunyan at the Siege of Leicester. *Times Literary Supplement*, 11 May, p.293.
[letter.]

C375   *The Young Cordwainer. *New Statesman* 41: 685, 16 June.

C375.1 *Queen-Mother to New Queen. *Quarto* no. 2: 5 Summer.

C376   *Primrose and Periwinkle – Prometheus – Darien. *Hudson Review* 4: 204–207 Summer.

C377   *The Ghost and the Clock. *Tomorrow* 10: 49 July.

C378   *The Survivor. *New Statesman* 42: 160, 11 August.

C379   *Questions in a Wood. *Listener* 46: 787, 8 November.

C380   *Prometheus. *Listener* 46: 829, 15 November.

C381   *With the Gift of a Ring – Cry Faugh! – The Foreboding – The Straw – Hercules at Nemea. *Poetry* 79: 125–12 December.

C382   *Damocles. *New Yorker* 27: 54, 1 December.

1952

C383   Mother Goose's Lost Goslings. *Hudson Review* 4: 586–597 Winter.

C384   *Lovers in Winter. *New Yorker* 27: 82, 19 January.

C385   *The Foreboding – Cry Faugh! – The Straw – With the Gift of a Ring. *New Statesman* 43: 101, 26 January.

C385.1 The Pharisees and Jesus. [With Joshua Podro.]
History Today 2: 108–122 February.

C386   Mr. Alexander Clifford. *The Times*, 28 March, p.8.
[Obituary.]

C387   *I'm Through with You Forever. *New Yorker* 28: 89, 29 March.

C388   The Future of Western Religion. *Nine* 8: 209–219 Spring [April].

C389   The Shout. *Fantasy and Science Fiction* 3: 75–91.
[See C612.]

C390   *I'm Through with You Forever. *Spectator* 188: 543, 25 April.

C391 *A Pinch of Salt. *Saturday Review of Literature* 35: 8, 3 May.

C392 *Dialogue on the Headland. *New Statesman* 43: 746, 21 June.

C393 Jungian Mythology. *Hudson Review* 5: 245–257 Summer.
    [Discussion of Jungian response to mythology.]

C394 *Rhea. *New Statesman* 44: 109, 26 July.

C395 The Seventh Man: Tributes to Sir Max Beerbohm on His Eightieth
    Birthday. *Listener* 48: 338, 28 August.
    [Part IV is by Graves.]

C396 *The Sacred Mission. *Poetry* 81: 39 October.

C397 *Dethronement. *Atlantic* 190: 75 December.

C398 *Advice to Col. Valentine. *New Yorker* 28: 26, 27 December.

1953

C399 The Devil is a Protestant. *Botteghe Oscure* 12: 114–123.

C400 *The Devil at Berry Pomeroy – Hippopotamus's Address to the
    Freudians – The Portrait – Twin to Twin – Leaving
    the Rest Unsaid. *Hudson Review* 5: 517–520 Winter.

C401 *The Devil at Berry Pomeroy. *New Statesman* 45: 43, 10 January.

C402 The Old Black Cow. *New Statesman* 45: 299, 14 March.

C403 *Cat-Goddesses. *New Yorker* 29: 38, 14 March.

C404 *From the Embassy. *Poetry* 82: 14 April.

C405 *With Her Lips Only. *Times Literary Supplement*, 10 April, p.232.

C406 *Dethronement. *Listener* 49: 726, 30 April.

C406.1 Myths and Matriarchs. *Spectator* 190: 731–732, 5 June.
    [Letter.]

C407 *To the Queen. *Time and Tide* 34: 747, 6 June.

C408 The Marriage of Hercules and Eve. *New Statesman* 45: 781–782, 27 June.
    [Review of Levy's *The Sword from the Rock*.]

C409 *Sirocco at Deyá. *New Statesman* 45: 738, 20 June.

C410 *The Mark. *Listener* 50: 12, 2 July.

C411   *The Blue-Fly. *New Yorker* 29: 28, 11 July.

C412   *Leaving the Rest Unsaid. *Times Literary Supplement*, 31 July, p.490.

C413   *The Sea Horse. *Atlantic* 192: 96 August.

C414   *The Encounter. *New Statesman* 46: 211, 22 August.

C415   The Lower Criticism. *New Statesman* 46: 237–238, 29 August.
        [Review of Rupert Furneaux's *The Other Side of the Story*.]

C416   *Cat-Goddesses. *New Statesman* 46: 291, 12 September.

C417   *Liadan and Curithir. *Time and Tide* 34: 1210, 19 September.

C418   Progressive Puericulture. *Hudson Review* 6: 476–480 Autumn.
        [Review of Meigs, Eaton, Nesbitt and Vigners' *A Critical History of Children's Literature*.]

C419   What Happened to Atlantis? *Atlantic* 192: 71–74 October.

C420   *Considine. *Punch* 225: 57, 14 October.

C421   *Juggler. *Saturday Review of Literature* 36: 12, 17 October.

C422   Dr. Syntax and Mr. Pound. *Punch* 225: 498, 21 October.

C423   *To the Queen. *Atlantic* 192: 47 November.

C424   *The Hippopotamus's Address to the Freudians. *Punch* 225: 568, 11 November.

C424.1 Nazarene Gospel. [With Joshua Podro.] *Observer*, 29 November, p.2.
        [Letter in response to G.H. Cohen concerning A69.]

C425   Juana Inés de la Cruz. *Encounter* 1: 5–13 December.
        [Reprinted as 'Juana de Asbaje'.]

C426   *The Juggler. *Time and Tide* 34: 1575, 5 December.

C427   Gospel Truth. [With Joshua Podro.] *New Statesman* 46: 762, 12 December.
        [Letter in reply to review of A69 by H.L. Short, 46: 692, 694, 28 November; see C431.]

C428   *Esau and Judith. *New Statesman* 46: 765, 12 December.

1954

C429   Paul's Thorn. *Literary Guide* 69: 3–4 January.

C430   School Life in Majorca. *Punch* 226: 56–57, 6 January.
       [Reprinted with the addition of the *Bulletin*.]

C431   Gospel Truth. [With Joshua Podro.] *New Statesman* 47: 70, 16 January.
       [Reply to review of A69; see C427.]

C432   [Letter.] [With Joshua Podro.] *Listener* 51: 142–143, 21 January.
       [Reply to review of A69, 50: 1136, 31 December 1953.]

C433   Royal Victims. *Spectator* 192: 103–104, 22 January.
       [Review of Margaret Alice Murray's *The Divine King in England*.]

C434   *Young Witch. *Atlantic* 193: 49 February.

C435   *Advice to Col. Valentine. *New Statesman* 47: 196, 13 February.

C436   Treacle Tart. *Punch* 226: 236–238, 17 February.

C437   'The Nazarene Gospel Restored.' *Times Literary Supplement*, 5 March,
       p.153.
       [Reply to review, 19 February, p.125. Further reply by Graves and Podro,
       26 March, p.201. Rejoinders 12 March, p.169 and 2 April, p.217. See also
       the editorial apology, 22 July, 1955, p.413.]

C438   Week-End at Cwm-Tatws. *Punch* 226: 404–405, 31 March.

C439   The Language as Spoken. *Hudson Review* 7: 155–160 Spring.
       [Review of *The Oxford Book of English Talk*.]

C440   *Birth of a Great Man. *New Yorker* 30: 30, 10 April.

C441   [Reply to review of A69.] [With Joshua Podro.] *Twentieth Century* 155:
       431–435 May.
       [Reply to review by E.L. Allen, 155: 256–262 March; rejoinder 155:
       435–436 May.]

C442   The Full Length. *Punch* 226: 546–547, 5 May.

C443   *The Spoils of Love. *New Yorker* 30: 36, 22 May.

C444   From 'The Uneconomist.' *Punch* 226: 640–641, 26 May.
       [Reprinted as 'Sappy Blancmange'.]

C445   God Grant Your Honour Many Years. *Punch* 227: 10–11, 31 May.

C446   Books in General. *New Statesman* 47: 761, 12 June.
       [Reprinted as 'The Essential E.E. Cummings'.]

C447   *The Spoils of Love. *New Statesman* 47: 792, 19 June.

C448   Six Valiant Bulls. *Punch* 226: 752–754, 23 June.
       [Reprinted as '6 Valiant Bulls 6'.]

C449   Discoveries in Greek Mythology. *Hudson Review* 7: 167–181 Summer.

C450   Books in General. *New Statesman* 48: 17–18, 3 July.
[Review of John Clare's *Poems*, ed. James Reeves.]

C451   No. 2 Polstead Road. *New Statesman* 48: 105–106, 24 July.
[Reveiw of T.E. Lawrence's *Home Letters*.]

C452   Flesh-Coloured Net Tights. *Punch* 227: 176, 4 August.

C453   Freud and Gotthilf von Schubert. *Times Literary Supplement*, 6 August, p.501.
[Letter suggesting anticipation of Freud in von Schubert (Graves' great-grandfather).]

C454   Thy Servant and God's. *Punch* 227: 232–233, 18 August.

C455   Majorca, the Fortunate Island. *Harper's Bazaar* 88: 184–189, 272–273 September.
[Reprinted as 'Why I Live in Majorca'.]

C456   *Birth of a Great Man. *New Statesman* 48: 269, 4 September.

C457   Varro's Four Hundred and Ninety Books. *Punch* 227: 320–322, 8 September.

C458   How the Gospels Were Written. [With Joshua Podro.] *Literary Guide* 69: 18–22 October.
[Material of A69.]

C459   Working Models for Young Poets? *Times Literary Supplement*, 1 October, p.625.
[Letter in reply to suggestion that he and Empson might serve as such. Further replies by Graves, 29 October, p.689 and 19 November, p.739. Rejoinders, 15 October, p.657 and 12 November, p.721. Initiated by a review of Richard Aldington's *Ezra Pound and T.S. Eliot*, 10 September, p.574.]

C460   'A Man May Not Marry His ...' *New Statesman* 48: 386–387, 2 October.

C461   *The Window Sill. *New Statesman* 48: 476, 16 October.

C462   *Beauty in Trouble. *New Yorker* 30: 34, 16 October.

C463   A Poet and His Public. *Listener* 52: 711–712, 28 October.

C463.1   The Clark Lectures. *Sunday Times*, 7 November, p.2.
[Letter expressing respect and gratitude to Basil Willey.]

C464   The Nativity – I. [With Joshua Podro.] *Literary Guide* 69: 21–23 November.
[Material from A69.]

C465   The Nativity – II. [With Joshua Podro.] *Literary Guide* 69: 17–20 December.
[Material from A69.]

C466   An Appointment for Candlemas. *Punch* 227: 680–682, 1 December.

C467   Kynge Arthur is Nat Dede. *New Statesman* 48: 745–746, 4 December.
            [See C473.]

C468   *Beauty in Trouble. *New Statesman* 48: 746, 4 December.

C469   *The Lost Jewel. *New Yorker* 30: 22, 25 December.

C470   The Five Godfathers. *Punch* 227: 824–826, 29 December.

1955

C471   The Nativity – III. [With Joshua Podro.] *Literary Guide* 70: 17–21
            January.
            [Material from A69.]

C472   The White Horse. *Punch* 228: 95–97, 12 January.

C473   Malory's Arthur. *New Statesman* 49: 107, 22 January.
            [Letter in reply to Hugh Vaudrey, 49: 45, 8 January, which is a reply to
            C467.]

C473.1   The Lawrence I Knew. *News Chronicle*, 31 January, p.4.
            [Review of Richard Aldington's *Lawrence of Arabia*.]

C474   Epics are out of Fashion. *Punch* 228: 234–236, 16 February.

C475   Earth to Earth. *New Statesman* 49: 240–241, 19 February.

C475.1   [Reply to a book review.] [With Joshua Podro.] *Truth Seeker* 82: 43
            March.

C476   'The Greek Myths.' *Times Literary Supplement*, 25 March, p.181.
            [Reply to review, 4 March, p.137. Rejoinder 29 April, p.209.]

C477   The Integrity of the Poet. *Listener* 53: 579–580, 31 March.
            [Letters in reply 53: 623, 7 April and 53: 669, 14 April.]

C478   Peasant Poet. *Hudson Review* 8: 99–105 Spring.
            [Review of John Clare's *Poems*.]

C479   These be Your Gods, O Israel! *Essays in Criticism* 5: 129–150 April.
            [Replies 5: 293–298 July.]

C480   The Terror of History. *Spectator* 194: 399–401, 1 April.
            [Review of Mircea Eliade's *The Myth of the Eternal Return*.]

C481   *The Lost Jewel. *New Statesman* 49: 476, 2 April.

C482   Numismatics for Student Christians. *New Statesman* 49: 546, 16 April.

C483   They Say … They Say. *Punch* 228: 491–493, 20 April.

C484   Gerard Manley Hopkins. *Times Literary Supplement*, 29 April, p.209.
            [Letter of apology for siring the new critical approach to Hopkins.]

C485   *The Clearing. *New Yorker* 31: 33, 30 April.

C486   The Oedipus Myth. *Atlantic* 195: 56–59 May.
         [Version of A72.]

C487   Christ and Caesar. *New Statesman* 49: 650, 7 May.
         [Letter in reply to letter by W.A. Wordsworth 49: 580, 23 April, which is
         reply to C482.]

C488   *(Say) – The Three Pebbles – Penthesilea. *London Magazine* 2: 35–36
         June.

C489   The Abominable Mr. Gunn. *Punch* 228: 782–784, 29 June.

C490   Greek Myths and Pseudo-Myths. *Hudson Review* 8: 212–230 Summer.
         [About the Trojan War and myths surrounding it; material of A72.]

C490.1   [Letter on *Poetry*'s fund raising.] *Poetry* 86: [inside front cover] July.

C491   The Whitaker Negroes. *Encounter* 5: 21–29 July.

C492   *The Clearing. *New Statesman* 50: 19, 2 July.

C493   *Question. *New Yorker* 31: 24, 30 July.

C494   New Light on Dream-Flight. *New Republic* 133: 18–19, 8 August.

C495   Under the Shadow of Yggdrasil. *New Statesman* 50: 219–220, 20 August.
         [Review of Brian Branston's *Gods of the North* and Walter Otto's *Homeric
         Gods.*]

C496   *The Tenants. *New Yorker* 31: 18, 3 September.

C497   *To a Spiteful Critic. *Punch* 229: 327, 21 September.

C498   [Letter about review of A69.] *Shenandoah* 7: [65] –66 Autumn.
         [Review by Hugh Kenner, 6: 44–53 Spring 1955; rejoinder by Kenner 7:
         66–67 Autumn.]

C499   An Appointment for Candelmas. *Fantasy and Science Fiction* 9: 124–128
         October.

C500   Graves, Gods and Psychoanalysts. *New Statesman* 50: 398, 1 October.
         [Reply to Jacquetta Hawkes, 50: 243, 27 August, which is a reply to
         C495.]

C501   Trín-Trín-Trín. *Punch* 229: 394–395, 5 October.

C502   The Spoiled Honeymoon. *Atlantic* 196: 72, 74, 76, 78, 80 December.
         [On George Sand and Chopin. See A77.]

C503   *The Tenants. *New Statesman* 50: 800, 10 December.

1956

C504   The Etruscans. *Art News Annual* 25: 100–120, 180, 183.
[Reprinted as 'The Cultured Romans'.]

C505   English Nursery Rhymes. *Listener* 55: 99–101, 19 January.
[Review of *The Oxford Nursery Rhyme Book*, ed. Peter and Iona Opie.]

C505.1   George Sand. *Sunday Times*, 26 February, p.2.
[Letter about A77.]

C506   These Be Thy Gods, O Israel! *New Republic* 134: 16–18, 27 February; 134: 17–18, 5 March.

C507   *End of the World. *Poetry London-New York* 1: 16 March–April.

C508   Cambridge Upstairs. *Punch* 230: 316–317, 14 March.

C509   'Ha, Ha!' Chort-led Nig-ger. *Punch* 230: 331–333, 21 March.

C510   *The Coral Pool. *Punch* 230: 424, 11 April.

C510.1   Decline of Roman Emperor. *Daily Telegraph*, 27 April, p.8.
[Review of G. Maranon's *Tiberius*.]

C511   Edmund Wilson: A Protestant Abroad. *New Republic* 134: 13–16, 30 April.
[Reprinted as 'Religion: None; Conditioning: Protestant'.]

C512   Culture Creep. *Commentary* 21: 573–577 June.
[Review of Richard Dorson's *The Negro Folktale in Michigan*.]

C513   *Gratitude for a Nightmare. *New Statesman* 51: 631, 2 June.

C514   *Woman and Tree. *New Yorker* 32: 38, 9 June.

C515   *Max Beerbohm at Rapallo. *Punch* 230: 755, 27 June.

C516   *A Bouquet from a Fellow Roseman. *New Yorker* 32: 30, 30 June.

C517   *The Grandfather's Complaint. *Punch* 231: 155, 8 August.

C518   Pandora's Box and Eve's Apple. *New Republic* 135: 16–18, 13 August.

C519   *Song: A Beach in Spain. *Punch* 231: 251, 29 August.

C520   Ditching in a Fishless Sea. *Punch* 231: 276–278, 5 September.

C521   Pandora's Box and Eve's Apple. *Spectator* 197: 324, 7 September.

C522   Soldier's Homer. *New Republic* 135: 17–19, 24 September.
[Reprinted as 'Colonel Lawrence's *Odyssey*'.]

C523   *The Demon. *Poetry London-New York* 1: 13 Winter.

C524   Jewish Jesus, Gentile Christ. *New Republic* 135: 25–27, 15 October.
[Reprinted as 'Don't Fidget, Young Man!']

C525   *To a Caricaturist, Who Got Me Wrong. *New Republic* 135: 27, 17 October.

C526   Robert Graves Demurs. *Commentary* 22: 471–472 November.
[Reply to Arnold Sherman, 'A Talk with Robert Graves', 22: 364–366 October. Rejoinder by Sherman, 22: 472.]

C527   I Hate Poems. *Punch* 231: 612–614, 21 November.

C528   *A Ballad of Alexander and Queen Janet – Destruction of Evidence. *London Magazine* 3: 17–19 December.

C529   *A Plea to Boys and Girls. *Time and Tide* 37: 1460, 1 December.

C530   Roots of Arthurian Mythology. *Times Literary Supplement*, 21 December, p.766.
[Reprinted as 'The Gold Roofs of Sinadon'.]

C531   Criticism of Sir Herbert Read. *New Republic* 135: 17–19, 24 December.
[Reprinted as 'An Eminent Collaborationist'.]

C532   Two Celtic Anthologies. *New Statesman* 52: 848, 29 December.
[Review of *Early Irish Lyrics*, ed. Gerard Murphy and *The Burning Tree*, ed. Gwyn Williams.]

1957

C533   *The Second-Fated. *New Republic* 136: 17, 7 January.

C534   *The Face in the Mirror. *New Yorker* 32: 34, 12 January.

C535   Majorca Xuetas. *Jewish Chronicle*, 18 January, p.17; 25 January, pp.17, 27; 1 February, pp.17, 22.
[Reprinted as 'A Dead Branch on the Tree of Israel'.]

C536   *A Plea to Boys and Girls. *Atlantic* 199: 59 February.

C537   A Dead Branch on the Tree of Israel. *Commentary* 23: 139–146 February.

C538   *The Naked and the Nude. *New Yorker* 32: 105, 16 February.

C539   *Yes. *New Yorker* 3: 82, 23 February.

C540   The Cultured Romans. *Listener* 57: 341–342, 28 February.

C541   Comments on 'Lineal and Non-Lineal Codifications'. *Explorations* 7: [46]47–51 March.

C542   Comments on 'Symbolization and Value'. *Explorations* 7: [67]68–73 March.

C543   *Jorrock's Warehouse. *London Magazine* 4: 13 March.

C544   The Diseases of Scholarship Clinically Considered. *New Republic* 136: 13–15, 6 March; 136: 17–19, 20 May.

C545   The Most Cultured of All Romans. *Listener* 57: 379–380, 7 March.
       [About Nero. See C617.]

C546   Caesar: When Comes Such Another? *New York Times Magazine*, 10
       March, pp.17, 28, 31.

C547   [Letter about C540.] *Listener* 57: 428, 14 March.

C548   *The Naked and the Nude. *New Statesman* 53: 356, 16 March.

C549   An Even More Cultured Roman. *Listener* 57: 471–472, 21 March.
       [About Lucan.]

C550   [Letter about C545.] *Listener* 57: 643, 18 April.

C551   *The Face in the Mirror. *New Statesman* 53: 517, 20 April.

C552   *Fever. *Atlantic* 199: 35 May.

C553   *The Outsider. *Harpers* 241: 72 May.

C554   How to Avoid Mycophobia. *Saturday Review* 40: 21–22, 47, 11 May.
       [Review of the Wassons' *Mushrooms, Russia and History*.]

C555   John Milton Muddles Through. *New Republic* 136: 17–19, 27 May.
       [Reprinted in 'Legitimate Criticism of Poetry'.]

C556   Legends of the Jews. *Commentary* 23: 583–586 June.
       [Reprinted as 'Legends of the Bible'.]

C557   *The Outsider. *New Statesman* 53: 784, 15 June.

C558   *To a Caricaturist Who Got Me Wrong. *Time and Tide* 38: 736, 15 June.

C558.1 A Deciduous Family. *New Statesman* 53: 768, 15 June.
       [Letter in response to Ralph Partridge's review of *They Hanged My
       Saintly Billy* (A82), 53: 680, 25 May.]

C559   A Bicycle in Majorca. *New Yorker* 33: 28–32, 22 June.

C560   The White Goddess. *New Republic* 136: 9–15, 24 June.

C561   *A Fever. *New Statesman* 54: 24, 6 July.

C562   All Child's Children Got Itch. *Times Literary Supplement*, 19 July, p.441.
       [Reply to review of A20b, 5 July, p.414.]

C563   *Bitter Thoughts on Receiving a Slice of Cordelia's Wedding Cake. *New
       Yorker* 33: 34, 27 July.

C564   Mushrooms, Food for the Gods. *Atlantic* 200: 73–77 August.
       [Reprinted as 'What Food the Centaurs Ate' (A86) and 'Centaur's Food'
       (A90).]

C565   Imaginary Museums. *Times Literary Supplement*, 9 August, p.483.
       [Reply to a quotation in a leader of 19 July, p.441. Further reply by
       Graves, 15 November, p.689.]

C566   Jesus in Rome. [With Joshua Podro.] *Times Literary Supplement*, 16 August, p.495.
        [Reply to review, 26 July, p.461. Rejoinder 30 August, p.519. Further letter by Graves and Podro, 20 September, p.561.]

C567   After a Century, Will Anyone Care Whodunit? *New York Times Book Review*, 25 August, pp.5, 24.
        [About detective stories.]

C568   Wordsworth by Cable. *New Republic* 137: 10–13, 9 September.
        [Reprinted in 'Legitimate Criticism of Poetry'.]

C569   *Augeias and I. *New Statesman* 54: 321, 14 September.

C570   [Letter on Thomas Atkins.] *The Times*, 24 September, p.9.

C571   Evidence of Affluence. *New Yorker* 33: 38–42, 12 October.

C572   And the Children's Teeth Are Set on Edge. *New Republic* 137: 15–18, 28 October.

C572.1 Houses in My Life. *House and Gardens* 12: 73–75 November.
        [Reprinted in *House and Gardens Weekend Book*, ed. Elizabeth Brayne, 1969; not recorded in Section B.]

C573   *The Second-Fated. *Encounter* 9: 13 November.

C574   *Friday Night. *Punch* 233: 535, 6 November.

C575   *Bitter Thoughts. *Time and Tide* 38: 1530, 7 December.

C575.1 Mont Blanc Milestone. *Sunday Times*, 22 December, p.7.
        [Review of Graham Brown and Sir Gavin de Beer's *The First Ascent of Mont Blanc*.]

C576   Maenads, Junkies and Others. *New Republic* 137: 16–18, 23 December.
        [Reprinted in A86 and A90.]

C576.1 *Yea or Neigh? *Argosy* 18: 86 December.

C576.2 *Is It Peace? *What's New* 203: 7 Christmas

1958

C577   A Life Bang-Full of Kicks and Shocks. *New York Times Book Review*, 5 January, p.6.
        [Reprinted as 'It Ended with a Bang' (A86, A90). Rejoinders 16 February, p.36 and 9 March, p.36.]

C578   The Glass Castle and the Grail. *Time and Tide* 39: 45–46, 11 January.
        [Review of Geoffrey Ashe's *King Arthur's Avalon*. Reply by Ashe 39: 70, 18 January.]

C579   *Fingers in the Nesting Box. *New Yorker* 34: 104, 29 March.

C580   Sweeney among the Blackbirds. *Texas Quarterly* 1: 83–102 Spring.

C581   *Nothing. *Saturday Review* 41: 69, 12 April.

C582   Archetypal Wise Old Man. *New Statesman* 55: 538, 26 April.
            [Review of C.G. Jung's *The Undiscovered Self*.]

C583   A Toast to Ava Gardner. *New Yorker* 34: 34–38, 26 April.
            [Also published in *Books & Bookmen* 11 (December 1965), pp.6, 8,
            92–94.]

C584   Two Studies of Scientific Atheism. *New Republic* 138: 13–17, 28 April.
            [Review of Bertrand Russell's *Why I Am an Atheist* and Julian Huxley's
            Religion without Revelation. Reprinted in A125.]

C585   *The Stable Door. *New Statesman* 55: 640, 17 May.

C586   New Light on an Old Murder. *Sunday Times*, 18 May, p.9.
            [Letter in reply, 25 May, p.4. Graves' reply, 15 June, p.4.]

C587   *The Enlisted Man. *New Yorker* 34: 115, 24 May.

C588   Caesar and the Pirates. *New Republic* 138: 17–18, 26 May.
            [Reprinted as 'The Pirates Who Captured Caesar' in A90 and A125.]

C588.1   The Historical Novel: II. *The Author* 68: 88 Summer.
            [Contribution to a symposium on the future of the novel.]

C589   *Augeias and I. *Harpers* 216: 35 June.

C590   *Woman and Tree. *Time and Tide* 39: 704, 7 June.

C590.1   Murder of Claudius. *Sunday Times*, 15 June, p.4.
            [Letter about the Pumpkinification of Claudius.]

C591   *Around the Mountain. *New Yorker* 34: 26, 5 July.

C592   Doctor Paccard of Mont Blanc. *New Republic* 139: 21–22, 7 July.
            [Review of Brown and de Beer's *The First Ascent of Mont Blanc*.]

C593   Mostly It's Money That Makes a Writer Go, Go, Go. *New York Times Book
            Review*, 13 July, p.5.

C594   *Flight Report. *Saturday Review* 41: 30, 9 August.

C595   The Wall. *Times Literary Supplement*, 15 August, p.x.
            [About bad books and the difficulties of publishing.]

C596   Praise Me, and I Will Whistle to You. *New Republic* 139: 10–15, 1
            September.
            [Reprinted in A125.]

C597   *The Twin of Sleep. *New Yorker* 34: 107, 27 September.

C598   The American Poet as a Businessman. *Esquire* 50: 47, 51, 56, 58 October.
            [Reprinted as 'The Making and Marketing of Poetry' in A90.]

C599 The Viscountess and the Short-Haired Girl. *Gentleman's Quarterly* 27: 82–83, 124, 126, 128, 130, 132, 138, 140, 141 October.

C600 *Call It a Good Marriage. *New Statesman* 56: 534, 18 October.

C601 *Read Me, Please! *New Yorker* 34: 44, 18 October.

C602 What Was That War Like, Sir? *Observer*, 9 November, pp.3–4.
[About World War I, reprinted in A125. Letters of reply, 16 November, p.6; 23 November, p.6; 30 November, p.20. Reprinted in A125.]

C603 The Sinking of the Sea Venture. *The Times*, 20 November, p.13.

C604 Seven Poets. *New World Writing* 14: 7–10 [December].
[Introduction to a small anthology of poems by T.S. Matthews, James Reeves, Sally Chilver, Alastair Reid, Terence Hards, Martin Seymour-Smith and Marnie Pomeroy.]

1959

C605 How to Pull a Poem Apart. *Harpers* 218: 78–80 January.
[Reprinted as 'Pulling a Poem Apart' in A86 and A90.]

C605.1 [Letter on Ezra Pound.] *Yale Literary Magazine* 127: 10 January.

C606 *Superman on the Riviera. *Spectator* 202: 19, 2 January.

C607 *Old World Dialogue. *Harpers* 218: 58 March.

C608 She Landed Yesterday. *New Yorker* 35: 31–37, 7 March.

C609 *Here Live Your Life Out! *New Yorker* 35: 34, 28 March.

C610 She Landed Yesterday. *Lilliput* 44: 31–35 April.

C611 What It Feels Like to be a Goy. *Commentary* 27: 413–419 May.
[Reprinted as 'To be a Goy' in A90 and as 'A Goy in Israel' in A125.]

C612 The Shout. *Fantasy and Science Fiction* 16: 51–67 May.
[See C389.]

C613 *Picture Nail. *Spectator* 202: 667, 8 May.

C614 *Heroes in Their Prime. *New Yorker* 35: 42, 23 May.

C615 *The Enlisted Man. *Times Literary Supplement*, 5 June, p.338.

C616 *Heroes in Their Prime. *New Statesman* 57: 832, 13 June.

C617 Ignoblest Roman of Them All. *New York Times Magazine*, 14 June, pp.22, 26, 28, 30, 32.
[About Nero. See C545.]

C618 Dour Man. *New Republic* 141: 16–17, 14 July.

C619 Puck, Mab and the Billy Blin. *New Statesman* 58: 83, 18 July.
[Review of *The Anatomy of Puck* by K.N. Briggs.]

C620   *Established Lovers. *Spectator* 203: 107, 24 July.

C621   *Catkind. *Spectator* 203: 115, 24 July.

C622   *Here Live Your Life Out! *New Statesman* 58: 250, 29 August.

C622.1 Graves on Fairies. *New Statesman* 58: 248, 29 August.
        [Letter.]

C623   Dour Man. *Encounter* 13: 66–69 September.

C624   Interview with a Dead Man. *Fantasy and Science Fiction* 17: 87–89
        September.

C625   Enter, the Leaden Age of Bullfighting. *New York Times Magazine*, 13
        September, pp.28–29, 51–52, 54.
        [See C635.]

C626   And What Would We Do without 'Etc.'? *New York Times Magazine*, 20
        September, pp.47, 50.

C627   Would-Be Jews. *New Republic* 141: 24–25, 28 September.
        [Review of *San Nicandro: The Story of a Religious Phenomenon* by Elena
        Cassin. Letter in reply by Solomon H. Green 141: 30–31, 9 November;
        reply by Graves 141: 31, 9 November.]

C628   *Established Lovers. *Atlantic* 204: 44 October.

C629   *Catkind. *Harpers* 219: 77 October.

C630   *The Person from Porlock. *Papeles de son Armadans* 15: 50 October.
        [Issued as a two-leaf offprint in covers; see D21 of first edition of this
        bibliography.]

C631   *The Quiet Glades of Eden. *Spectator* 203: 479, 9 October.

C632   Pen and Gown. *The Times*, 22 October, p.15.
        [Why modern literature should not be in the curriculum.]

C633   Homer's Winks and Nods. *Atlantic* 204: 101–107 November.
        [Reprinted as part of introduction to A89.]

C634   [Quotes from *The Anger of Achilles* as captions to illustrations from the
        book by Ronald Searle.] *Harper's Bazaar* 93: 136–137.

C635   Bullfighting. *Lilliput* 45: 35–37 November. [See C625.]

C636   I Discover Israel. *Holiday* 26: 66–77, 234, 239–243 December.

C637   The Lost Chinese. *Lilliput* 45: 46–52. December. [See C643.]

C638   *Joan and Darby. *New Yorker* 35: 54, 12 December.

C639   *Joan and Darby. *Sepctator* 203: 911, 18 December.

C640   *The Young Goddess. *New Yorker* 35: 58, 26 December.

1960

C641 [Letter in reply to review of A89.] *The Fat Abbot* 1: 54–55 Winter.
[Review by Adam Parry, 1: 52–59 Fall; rejoinder by Parry 1: 55–56 Winter.]

C642 Isle of Tranquillity: Minorca. *Holiday* 27: 50–55, 154–157 January.
[Reprinted as 'To Minorca!' in A90.]

C643 The Case of the Difficult Husband. *Playboy* 7: 51–52, 54, 85–87 January.
[Reprinted as 'The Lost Chinese' in A90 and A106. Also see C637. This and all subsequent references to *Playboy* should be assumed to be U.S.A. printings unless otherwise specified.]

C643.1 *Twice of the Same Fever. *New Yorker* 35: 32, 16 January.

C644 ENTRY CANCELLED.

C644.1 *Surgical Ward: Men. *Spectator* 204: 113, 22 January.

C645 ENTRY CANCELLED.

C646 Hebrew and Greek. *Commentary* 29: 173–175 February.
[Review of Moses Hadas' *Hellenistic Culture*.]

C647 You Win, Houdini! *London Magazine* 7: 28–37 February.

C648 *The Were-Man. *Saturday Review* 43: 20, 6 February.

C648.1 Eccentric. *Observer*, 28 February, p.4.
[A letter about Clark Lectures.]

C648.2 Eccentric. *Observer*, 13 March, p.24.
[Letter in response to John Wain.]

C649 *Twice of the Same Fever. *Spectator* 204: 438, 25 March.

C650 *Surgical Ward: Men. *Atlantic* 205: 50 April.

C651 An Imperial Tale. *Holiday* 27: 74–79, 151–154 April.
[Reprinted as 'The Apartment House' in A106.]

C652 *Song: A Month of Sundays. *London Magazine* 7: 29 April.

C653 *The Mysteries of the Toadstool God. *London Magazine* 7: 11–12 May.

C653.1 *The Young Goddess. *Listener* 63: 838, 12 May.

C653.2 Sealed Lips. *Listener* 63: 939, 26 May.
[Review of Fall's *First World War*.]

C654 November 5th Address, *X* 1: 171–176 June.

C654.1 *The Simpleton. *Listener* 63: 1059, 16 June.

C654.2 *A Piebald's Tail. *Listener* 63, 1135, 30 June.

C655 *The Intruders. *Saturday Review* 43: 31, 2 July.

C656   The Gaudy Games. *Sports Illustrated* 13: 56–64, 1 August.
        [Reprinted as 'The Myconian' in A106.]

C657   *Teiresias. *New Statesman* 60: 191, 6 August.

C658   *The Intruders – Lyceia. *Listener* 63: 299, 25 August.

C659   *Two Rhymes about Fate and Money. *Spectator* 205: 344, 2 September.

C660   *Burn It. *New Statesman* 60: 392, 17 September.

C661   The Case for Xanthippe. *Kenyon Review* 22: 597–605 Fall.
        [Reason and philosophy vs. poetry. Reprinted in A125.]

C662   Party of one. *Holiday* 28: 8, 10–13 October.
        [Reprinted in B60.2.]

C663   *Song: The Smile of Eve. *New Statesman* 60: 532, 8 October.

C664   What Bird for Britain? *The Times*, 28 October, p. 13.
        [About a national bird.]

C665   *Jock o' Binnorie – Robinson Crusoe. *New Statesman* 60: 654, 29 October.

C666   *The Person from Porlock. *Atlantic* 206: 170 November.

C667   *Fate and Money. *Good Housekeeping* 151: 234 November.

C668   *How and Why. *Saturday Review* 43: 34, 5 November.

C669   *Lyceia. *Saturday Review* 43: 108, 12 November.

C670   *Nightfall at Twenty Thousand Feet. *New Yorker* 36: 50, 19 November.

C671   *Conversaciones Poeticas de Formentor. *Papeles de Son Armadans* 57: 14 December.
        [Issued as an offprint in wrappers; see D22 of the first edition of this bibliography.]

C672   *Song: A Month of Sundays. *Saturday Review* 43: 39, 24 December.

C673   *The Quiet Glades of Eden. *Saturday Review* 43: 25, 31 December.

1961

C674   *Symptoms of Love – The Sharp Ridge – Under the Olives – The Visitation – Fragment – Apple Island – The Falcon Woman – Troughs of Sea – The Laugh – The Death Grapple – In Single Syllables – The Starred Coverlet – The Intrusion – Patience – Hag-Ridden – The Cure – Turn of the Moon – Seldom, Yet Now – The Secret Land – To the Muse Goddess – Anchises to Aphrodite. *Observer*, 22 January, p.21.

C674.1 [Letter about Graves' Oxford degrees.] *Daily Telegraph*, 2 February, p.12.

C674.2   Two Poets. *Manchester Guardian,* 11 February, p.6.
           [Letter about James Reeves and Graves.]

C674.3   *The Dangerous Gift. *Listener* 65: 295, 16 February.

C674.4   *[Verses composed over the telephone to William Hickey to mark
           Graves' election as Oxford Professor of Poetry.] *Daily Express,* 17
           February, p.3.

C675   An Uneasy Compromise. *Observer,* 19 March, pp.21–22.
           [Review of the *New English Bible.* Letters of reply 26 March, p.22.
           Reprinted in A125.]

C676   Dead Man's Bottles. *Fantasy and Science Fiction* 20: 52–60 April.

C677   *A Lost World. *New Yorker* 37: 39, 1 April.

C677.1   *Ruby and Amethyst. *Observer,* 30 April, p.30.

C678   *Piebald's Tail. *Ladies Home Journal* 78: 112 May.

C679   Before the Ceiling Falls In. *Daily Express,* 31 May, p.6.
           [Interview, mainly quotations.]

C680   Service to the Muse. *Atlantic* 207: 43–44 June.
           [Introductory comments to C681.]

C681   *Symptoms of Love – The Sharp Ridge – Under the Olives – The
           Visitation – Fragment – Apple Island – The Falcon Woman –
           Troughs of Sea – The Laugh – The Death Grapple – The Starred
           Coverlet – The Intrusion – In Single Syllables – Patience – Hag-
           Ridden – The Cure – To the Muse Goddess – The Secret Land –
           Seldom Yet Now – Turn of the Moon -Anchises to Aphrodite. *Atlantic*
           207: 45–48 June.

C681.1   [Review of Harriette Wilson's *Mistress of Many.*] *Evening Standard,* 27
           June, p.11.

C681.2   *The Two Witches – Song: Gardens Close at Dusk. *Listener* 65: 1127, 29
           June.

C681.3   [Letter objecting to a reference by A. Alvarez to the Clark Lectures.]
           Observer, 9 July, p.18.

C682   *Sullen Moods. *New Yorker* 37: 44, 9 September.

C683   *The Cool Web. *Times Literary Supplement,* 13 October, p.695.
           [A translation into German by Erich Fried.]

C683.1   *Privacy. *New Yorker* 37: 52, 21 October.

C683.2   Accents. *Sunday Telegraph,* 22 October, p.18.
           [In 'Words of the Week about. . . .']

C684   *The Dialecticians. *Atlantic* 208: 157 November.

C685   *Two Witches. *Good Housekeeping* 153: 218 November.

C686	*Matador Gored. *Saturday Evening Post* 234: 53, 4 November.
C687	*Four New Love Poems: Horizon – In Her Praise – Trance – Variables of Green. *Saturday Evening Post* 234: 93, 11 November.
C687.1	*Variables of Green. *Listener* 66: 943, 30 November.
C688	The Dedicated Poet: The Oxford Inaugural Lecture. *Encounter* 17: 11–18 December.
C689	*Burn It! *Harpers* 223: 49 December.

1962

C690	The Word Báraka. *Proceedings of the American Academy of Arts and Letters and the National Institute of Arts and Letters*, Series 2, Number 12, pp. 105–115.
C691	Virgil Cult. *Virginia Quarterly Review* 38: 13–35 Winter. [Reprinted as 'The Anti-Poet' in A97.]
C692	*The Ambrosia of Dionysus and Semele. *New Yorker* 37: 30, 13 January.
C693	*Golden Anchor – In Trance at a Distance – Possessed – A Restless Ghost – Uncalendared Love – Vicissitudes of Love. *New Yorker* 37: 30, 27 January.
C694	*Beware, Madam! *Atlantic* 209: 48 February.
C695	[Answer to a questionnaire about poetry.] *London Magazine* n.s. 1: 27 February.
C696	Criticizing Poetry. *Times Literary Supplement*, 2 February, p.73. [Reply to editorial of same title, 12 January, p.25; further reply by Ken Geering, 9 February, p.89; rejoinder by Graves, 23 February, p.121.]
C697	The Tenement: A Vision of Imperial Rome. *New Strand* 1: 331–336 March. [Reprinted as 'The Apartment House' in A106.]
C698	*Two New Poems: Confiteor Ut Fas – O. *Oxford Magazine* n.s. 2: 255, 15 March.
C699	Ignore the Poet. *The Times*, 30 March, p.15. [Letter advising this attitude.]
C700	*Golden Anchor – Horizon – In Her Praise – Uncalendared Love – The Ambrosia of Dionysus and Semele – Trance. *New Statesman* 63: 644, 4 May.
C701	*Three New Poems: The Lion Lover – The Recognition – Not at Home. *Saturday Evening Post* 235: 66, 5 May.
C702	The Virgil Tradition. *The Times*, 22 May, p.13. [Letter in reply to report of public lecture.]

C703   *Between Moon and Moon – Ibycus in Samos – The Meeting – Name Day – The Wreath. *Encounter* 18: 36–37 June.

C704   The Toughest Battle of All: When a Regiment is Fighting for Its Life. *Daily Express*, 9 June, p.8.
[About maintenance of regiments, regimental names and regimental traditions. Reprinted in A125.]

C705   *Lion Lover. *New Statesman* 63: 914, 22 June.

C705.1 A Journey to Paradise. *Argosy* 23: 61–69 July.
[Reprinted as 'The Poet's Paradise' in A97.]

C705.2 Strawberries. *Sunday Telegraph*, 1 July, p.16.
[In 'Words of the Week About. . . .']

C706   Poetic Gold. *Georgia Review* 16: 122–130 Summer.

C707   Journey to Paradise. *Holiday* 32: 36–37, 110–111 August.

C708   *Not at Home – A Restless Ghost – The Recognition. *New Statesman* 64: 364, 21 September.

C709   *The Cliff Edge. *Atlantic* 201: 86 October.

C710   *Ouzo Unclouded. *Poetry* 101: 43 October.

C711   Nummick. *The Times*, 14 November, p.13.
[Etymological speculation.]

C712   *The Passing of Oisín. *Atlantic* 210: 64 December.

C713   *Judgement of Paris. *Georgia Review* 16: 445 Winter.

C714   Robert Graves Writes... *Poetry Book Society Bulletin*, no. 35, pp.1–2 December.

C715   *The Meeting. *Poetry Book Society Bulletin*, no. 35, p.2, December.

C715.1 Poetry. *Sunday Telegraph*, 2 December, p.18.
[In 'Words of the Week About. . . .']

C716   Wave No Banners. *Saturday Evening Post* 235: 34–35, 38, 41, 15 December.
[Reprinted as 'Christmas Truce' in A106.]

C717   [Blurb for Tucci's *Before My Time*.] *Daily Mail*, 20 December, p.10.

C717.1 Three Writers on the Best of Christmas. *Sunday Telegraph*, 23 December, p.4.
[The other writers are William Sansom and Stephen Spender.]

1963

C718   *After the Flood. *Atlantic* 211: 60 January.

C719   Some Hebrew Myths and Legends. [With Raphael Patai.] *Encounter* 20:
          3–18 February
          [Reprinted in A105 as the introduction and sections 5–7, 9–10.]

C720   The Truest Poet. *Sunday Times*, 3 February, p.26.
          [On the death of Frost.]

C721   The Fight to the Finish in 1914–1918. *Sunday Times*, 24 February, p.25.

C721.1   Robert Frost. *Sunday Times*, 24 February, p.33.
          [Letter.]

C722   Hebrew Myths and Legends. [With Raphael Patai.] *Encounter* 20: 12–18
          March.
          [Reprinted in A105 as sections 11, 13–15.]

C723   The Poet in a Valley of Dry Bones. *Horizon* 5: 84–88 March.

C724   *The Corner Knot. *New Yorker* 39: 44, 23 March.

C725   *The Why of the Weather. *Saturday Review* 46: 36, 13 April.

C726   *After the Flood – Endless Pavement – A Late Arrival – The
          Septuagenarian. *New Statesman* 65: 600, 19 April.

C727   Pretense on Parnassus. *Horizon* 5: 81–85 May.
          [Reprinted as 'Some Instances of Poetic Vulgarity' in A111.]

C727.1   The Sacred Mushroom-Trance. *Story* 140: 6–13 May–June.
          [Reprinted from A97.]

C727.2   *A Blind Arrow. *Listener* 69: 744, 2 May.

C728   T.E. Lawrence and the Riddle of 'S.A.' *Saturday Review* 46: 16–17, 15
          June.

C729   *The Why of the Weather. *New Statesman* 65: 934, 21 June.

C730   Redbook Dialogue. *Redbook* 121: 58–59, 112, 114–115, 117 September.
          [See C737.]

C731   The Golden Age. *Times Literary Supplement*, 6 September, p.677.
          [About Virgil.]

C732   *Herself to Herself. *Saturday Review* 46: 28, 28 September.

C733   *To Beguile and Betray – Vixen Goddess – Dance. *Virginia Quarterly*
          39: 597 Autumn.

C734   *The Apple [i.e., Ample] Garden – At Best, Poets – A Measure of
          Casualness – A Time of Waiting – Expect Nothing – She is No Liar –
          The Pearl – New Moon through Glass. *Atlantic* 212: 66–67 October.

C735   *Between Trains. *Harper's Bazaar* 97: 191 November.

C736   Poetry's False Face. *Horizon* 5: 42–47 November.
        [Reprinted as 'Technique in Poetry' in A111.]

C736.1 [Letter responding to earlier letters about C719 and C722.] *Encounter* 21:
        98 November.

C737   The Trouble with Men. *Weekend*, 6 November, pp.16–18.
        [A duologue with Gina Lollobrigida. See C730.]

C738   *Myrrhina. *Poetry* 103: 182 December.

C739   A Poet's Investigation of Science. *Saturday Review* 46: 82–88, 7
        December.
        [Partial reprint of A103.]

1964

C740   *All I Tell You from My Heart – To Myrto about Herself – In Time –
        Man Does, Woman Is – The Leap – In Disguise. *Kenyon Review* 26:
        80–82 Winter.

C741   Real Women. *Ladies Home Journal* 81: 151–155 January.

C742   *Joseph and Jesus. *Sunday Times*, 5 January, p.28.

C742.1 Innocents Abroad. *Sunday Times*, 19 January, p.19.
        [Letter about C742.]

C743   *St. Valentine's Day. *Atlantic* 213: 94 February.

C744   Why Read Poetry? *Holiday* 35: 10, 16–18 February.

C745   *A Time of Waiting – Expect Nothing – The Pearl. *New Statesman* 672:
        212, 7 February.

C746   Poet and Public School. *Sunday Times*, 29 March, p.38.
        [Review of *Charterhouse: An Open Examination Written by the Boys*.
        Replies 5 April, p.19. Reply by Graves, 12 April, p.19. Reprinted in
        A125.]

C747   *Occasions of Love: The Ample Garden – She is No Liar – A Measure
        of Casualness – At Best, Poets. *Critical Quarterly* 6: 8–9 Spring.

C748   *The Encounter. *Georgia Review* 18: 49 Spring.

C748.1 The Inner World. *Greek Heritage* 1: 46–47 Spring.

C748.2 Gold, In Medals and Poems. *Poetry* 104: 53 April.

C749   Insulation. *Times Literary Supplement*, 9 April, p. 291.
        [Letter about an accusation of insularity. See also the leader of 27
        February, a letter by Christopher Middleton, 5 March, p.195 and letters
        of 19 March, p.235.]

C750   *Non cogunt stellae* – Rain of Brimstone – Song: Sword and Rose. *New
        Republic* 150: 21, 11 April.

C750.1   House Training. *Sunday Times*, 12 April, p.19.
[Letter about C746.]

C751   The Lasting Echoes of the Kaiser's War. *New York Times Magazine*, 17 May, pp.16–17, 86, 88, 90.
[Reprinted in A125.]

C751.1   *Poems: To Myrto About Herself – In Disguise – The Leap. *Listener* 71: 892, 28 May.

C752   Mammon. *Encounter* 22: 21–29 June.

C753   *Bank Account. *McCalls* 91: 151 June.

C754   *A Last Poem. *New Yorker* 40: 39, 6 June.

C755   *Rain of Brimstone. *Times Literary Supplement*, 11 June, p.504.

C756   *Vixen Goddess – New Moon through Glass – Dance. *New Statesman* 67: 914, 12 June.

C757   *In Time. *Sunday Times*, 28 June, p.35.

C758   *All I Tell You from My Heart. *Spectator* 213: 52, 10 July

C759   Witches in 1964. *Virginia Quarterly Review* 40: 550– 559 Autumn.
[Reprinted in A125.]

C760   *The Fire Walker – That Other World. *Harper's Bazaar* 98: 261 October.

C761   *Hearth. *New Republic* 151: 20, 3 October.

C761.1   Graves on 'T.E.' and 'S.A.' *Sunday Telegraph*, 15 November, p.13.
[Interview.]

C762   *The Clipped Stater. *Mt. Adams Review* 1: 26–28 November–December.
[Includes a quotation from A49.]

1965

C763   Making Sound Sense of Shakespeare. *Sunday Times*, 14 February, p.49.
[About emending text of *Much Ado* for Franco Zeffirelli's production at the National Theatre.]

C764   *Dynamite Barbee. *Arena* [Ireland] no. 4: 1 Spring.

C765   Moral Principles in Translation. *Encounter* 24: 47–55 April.

C766   Odysseus. *Weekend Telegraph*, 2 April, pp.18, 20.

C767   Britain's Witches Make a Comeback. *Weekend Telegraph*, 21 May, pp.32, 34–35, 37–38.

C768   Invasion of the Island. *Weekend Telegraph*, 14 May, pp.33, 35–36, 38.

C769   Polite Lie. *Atlantic* 215: 74–80 June.

C770   *Those Who Came Short – True Joy – The Fetter. *New Statesman* 69: 885, 4 June.

C771   *Good Night to the Old Gods. *New Statesman* 70: 128, 23 July.

C772   Richard Hughes, Poet with Frying Pan. *Sunday Telegraph*, 25 July, p.14.
[Quotes part of a letter received in 1922 from Graves in 70th birthday tribute to him.]

C773   *Change. *New Republic* 153: 21, 7 August.

C774   [Letter about interview with Philip Toynbee.] *Observer*, 8 August, p.10.

C775   *The Champion. *Weekend Telegraph*, 13 August, p.4.

C776   *Butxoca. *Weekend Telegraph*, 20 August, p.8.

C777   *Good-night to the Old Gods – Snapcomb-Wilderness – Sweetshop Round the Corner. *Atlantic* 216: 75 September.

C778   Are Women More Romantic than Men? *Life* 15 October, pp.126–128, 131, 133, 135, 136, 138, 141.
[Includes 'Son Altesse'; see A113 and A114.]

C779   *When a Necklace Breaks – The Impossible. *New Republic* 153: 28, 16 October.

C780   Graves 1965. *Times Literary Supplement*, 21 October, p.939.
[Letter about A114.]

C781   *Fortunate Child – The Wedding – Tomorrow's Envy of Today – Iron Palace. *New Republic* 153: 20, 27 November.

1966

C782   *Tangled Thread – Lure of Murder – Loving True, Flying Blind. *Mademoiselle* 62: 14 January.

C783   *The Vow – The Fetter – Nothing Now Astonishes – Those Who Came Short – Son Altesse – What Do We Fear? – Conjunction – Postscript. *New Republic* 154: 30–31, 1 January.

C784   George III. *Times*, 13 January, p.11.
[Letter about George III and madness.]

C785   Undiscovered Spain. *Daily Express*, 22 January, p.13.

C786   Oxford Professor of Poetry. *Times*, 16 February, p.13.

C787   Medieval Windsock. *Times*, 23 April, p.11.
[Letter.]

C788   Language Levels. *Encounter* 26: 49–51 May.
[Reprinted as 'Mr Nabokov's Democratic Eclecticism' in A125.]

C789   Graves Readings at Albert Hall. *Daily Telegraph*, 30 June, p.16.

C790   *If Love Becomes a Game. *Atlantic* 218: 93 August.

C791   *If Love Becomes a Game. *New Statesman* 72: 263, 19 August.

C792   [Comment.] *Modern Language Quarterly* 27: 255–256 September.
        [Comment on James Jensen, "The Construction of *Seven Types of Ambiguity* which immediately precedes (243–255).]

C793   *Necklace. *Atlantic* 218: 106 September.

C794   Tomorrow's Bread. *Times*, 22 September, p.11.
        [Letter about Lord's Prayer.]

C795   *Queen Silver and King Gold – Near Eclipse. *New Statesman* 72: 453, 23 September.

C796   *In Perspective. *Harpers* 233: 20 October.

C797   Robert Graves 'Secret Vice' Pays Off. *New York Times Magazine*, 30 October, pp.36–37, 142, 144–145, 147, 149–150, 156.
        [Interview by Anne Sinclair Mehdevi. Also reprints the following poems: Face in the Mirror – Portrait – Your Private Way – I will write – Like Snow.]

C798   *Gooseflesh Abbey. *Atlantic* 218: 136 November.

C799   *Mist – Sun-Face and Moon-Face. *New Republic* 155: 23, 12 November.

C800   *Utter Rim of Nowhere – Necklace. *New Statesman* 72: 745, 18 November.

C801   *Queen Silver and King Gold – The Near Eclipse – On Giving – The Utter Rim of Nowhere. *New Republic* 155: 19, 26 November.

C802   *Palm Tree. *Opera News* 31: 17, 10 December.

C803   *Twins – Sail and Oar – Gooseflesh Abbey – All Except Hannibal. *Minnesota Review* 6: 267 Fourth Quarter.

1967

C804   No, Mac, It Just Wouldn't Work. *Playboy* 14: 117, 195 January.

C805   *Mist. *New Statesman* 73: 89, 20 January.

C806   *Gooseflesh Abbey. *New Statesman* 73: 300, 3 March.

C807   Poetry Chair at Oxford. *Times*, 6 March, p.11.
        [Letter.]

C808   *Song: The Palm Tree. *New Statesman* 73: 369, 17 March.

C809   ᴬWild Cyclamen. *Ladies Home Journal* 84: 139 April.

C810   Matter of Address. *Times*, 24 April, p.9
        [Letter on epistolary etiquette.]

C811   On Poetry. *Virginia Quarterly Review* 43: 196–219 Spring.

C812   *Wigs and Beards. *Atlantic* 219: 60 June.

C813   *In Perspective. *New Statesman* 73: 767, 2 June.

C814   Robert Graves on John Masefield. *Times Literary Supplement*, 22 June,
        p.568.
        [Extracts from an address by Graves at the memorial service for John
        Masefield in Westminster Abbey on 20 June 1967. See also B67.1 and
        C820.]

C815   Crane Bag. *New York Review of Books* 8: 21–24, 29 June.
        [Review of Anne Ross, *Pagan Celtic Britain*. Reprinted in A125.]

C815.1 *Our Self – Pride of Love – The Beggar Maid and King Cophetua –
        Crown of Stars. *The Journal of Creative Behaviour* 1. 3[poetry
        supplement]: 10–12 July.

C816   *Brief Withdrawal – Perfectionists – Bites and Kisses – Like Owls –
        Word – Blackening Sky. *New Yorker* 43: 32, 8 July.

C817   *Wigs and Beards. *New Statesman* 74: 90, 21 July.

C818   *The Beggar Maid – Work Room – Is Now the Time – To Ogmian
        Hercules – The Narrow Sea – Possibly. *Daily Telegraph Magazine*, 26
        July, p.9.

C819   *Fact of the Act. *Atlantic* 220: 71 August.

C820   Chaucer's Man. *Poetry Review* 57: 241, 243, 245–246 Autumn.
        [An expanded version of the address given at the memorial service for
        John Masefield. See also B67.1 and C814.]

C821   *Twins – Sail and Oar – Sun-Face and Moon-Face. *New Statesman* 74:
        361, 22 September.

C822   Miss Britain's Lady Companion. *Family Circle*, 24 September.

C823   One of the Few. *Listener* 78: 426, 5 October.
        [Remarks on Robert Frost including BBC1's 'Robert Frost — A Lover's
        Quarrel with the World'.]

C824   *Crown of Stars. *New Statesman* 74: 440, 6 October.

C825   Robert Graves Translates the Rubaiyat. *Daily Telegraph Magazine*, 13
        October, pp.40–42, 44.

C826   Dr. Starkie for Oxford. *Guardian*, 28 October, p.8.
        [Letter in support of Starkie's candidacy for the Oxford Professorship of
        Poetry.]

C827   *November 11th, 1918. *Daily Express*, 9 November, p.7.

C828   *All Except Hannibal. *New Statesman*, 74: 643, 10 November.

C829   Omar's Puppet Show. *Listener* 78: 670, 23 November.
[Letter in reply to review by Martin Dodsworth, 9 November, of the Graves/Shah *Rubaiyat*.]

C830   The Rubaiyat. *Times*, 30 November, p.11.
[Letter concerning the Graves/Shah translation.]

C831   Penthouse Interview: Robert Graves. *Penthouse* 3: 67–70 December.

C832   *Song: One in Many. *Atlantic* 220: 66 December.

C833   Reincarnation. *Playboy* 14: 174, 177, 233–239 December.
[Includes poem 'The Castle' (see A33). Reprinted in A125.]

1968

C834   A dusty answer to the Persicologists. *Sunday Times*, 7 April, p.8.
[Letter concerning articles about the Graves/Shah translation of the *Rubaiyat*.]

C835   The shocking case of Miss Sweet. *Sunday Times*, 14 April, pp.1–2.
[Reprinted as 'An Absolute Criminal' in A125.]

C836   *Bracelet. *Atlantic* 221: 59 May.
[reprinted with worksheets in *Malahat Review 25*, p. 156, January 1973.]

C837   What is a Monster. *Horizon* 10: 50, 54, 56 Summer
[Reprinted as 'The Language of Monsters' in A125.]

C838   The Riddle of 'S.A.' of the Seven Pillars. *Sunday Times*, 23 June, p.15.
[Letter about T.E. Lawrence.]

C839   *Song: Cherries or Lilies. *Harpers* 237: 97 July.

C840   Translating the Rubaiyat. *Commentary* 46: 66–71 July.

C841   *Olive Yard. *New Yorker* 44: 30, 13 July.

C842   *World Awoke Me – Bath in Pylos – His Life. *New Hungarian Quarterly* no. 31: 170–171 Autumn.
[Translations of three poems by Gábor Devecseri.]

C843   The Amorous Verse of P. O. Naso. *Queen* 431: 37–41, 11 September.
[Reprinted as 'Ovid and the Libertines' in A133.]

C844   *Spite of Mirrors. *McCalls* 96: 166 October

C845   Robert Graves Guesses About the Resurrection — in Conversation with Robert Kee. *Listener* 80: 443–444, 3 October.

C846   How to Hold the Reader's Attention. *Virginia Quarterly Review* 44: 108–120 Winter.

C847   Greece, Gods and Art. *Vogue* 152: 138–39, 198, 15 November.

C848   Robert Graves on Women. *Guardian*, 18 December, p.9.

1969

C849   Place for the Old Magic. *Sunday Times*, 26 January, p.60.
[Review of Dorsan's *The British Folklorist*.]

C850   *Troublesome Fame. *New Yorker* 45: 150, 26 April.

C851   *Unicorn and the White Doe. *Atlantic* 223: 73 May.

C852   Art of Poetry, XI: Robert Graves. *Paris Review* 12: 118–145 Summer.
[Interview with Peter Buckman and William Fifield. This interview was reprinted, in translation in *Revista de Occidente* 31: 1–25 in 1970.]

C853   *What We Did Next – Semi-Detached – Blanket Charge. *Transatlantic Review* 32: 32–34 Summer.

C854   Fifty Helpful Hints. *Esquire* 72: 54, July.
[Graves was one of fifty figures asked to suggest first words to be spoken by the first man on Moon. Graves' words: 'Forgive the intrusion, Ma'am. Don't smile so bitter / At good Yanks tidying up your Sputnik litter.']

C855   *Death of Love – In the Vestry – Through a Dark Wood – 1999 – When Love is Not. *Daily Telegraph Magazine*, 18 July, p. 25.
[Also includes an interview.]

C856   Una Conversacion con Robert Graves. *La Estafeta Literaria*, 15 September, pp.39–40.
[Conversation (in Spanish) with Juan Bonet.]

C857   Robert Graves: An Interview. *Impact of Science on Society* 19: 319–330 October–December.
[Interview by Bruno Friedman.]

C858   One Foot in the Trenches. *Guardian*, 24 October, p.8.
[Interview with Terry Coleman.]

C859   Goodbye to all what? *Daily Mirror*, 7 November, pp.16–17.

C860   Genius. *Playboy* 16: 127–128, 276, 279–280 December.

C861   *Carols for Christmas, 1969: Shepherds Armed with Staff Sling. *New York Times Magazine*, 21 December, p.5.

1970

C862   Export of MSS. *Times*, 20 January, p.9.
[Letter.]

C863   Divine Rite of Mushrooms. *Atlantic* 225: 109–113 February.
[Review of Gordon Wasson's *Soma: Divine Mushroom of Immortality*.]

C864   *Ambrosia of Dionysus and Semele. *Atlantic* 225: 113 February.

C865   *Robbers Den. *Atlantic* 225: 90 March.

C866   *Uncut Diamond – Poisoned Day. *New Statesman* 79: 370, 13 March.

C867   Alas, What has happened to the Arts? *Boston Sunday Globe*, 19 March.
[A syndicated article appearing with this title in a number of American newpapers.]

C868   *Lily Bed. *New Statesman* 79: 449, 27 March.

C869   *Death of Love. *Harpers* 240: 28 March.

C870   What the Gods Turned on. *Queen*, 18–31 March, pp. 53–55.
[Reprinted in A133 as 'The Two Births of Dionysus.]

C871   *Tolling Bell. *Poetry Review* 61: 3 Spring.

C872   *Brief Reunion. *New Yorker* 46: 40, 11 April.

C873   *Judges. *New Yorker* 46: 38, 25 April.

C874   Jesus as Toadstool. *New Statesman* 79: 694–695, 15 May.
[Review of J.M. Allegro's *The Sacred Mushroom and the Cross*.]

C875   *At the Well – Powers Unconfessed – Child with Veteran – Solomon's Seal. *Listener* 83: 716, 28 May.
[Also includes an interview.]

C876   Where the Crakeberries Grow — Robert Graves Gives an Account of Himself. *Listener* 83: 715–716, 28 May.
[Reprinted in Hungarian translation as 'In Cultura Engleza: Robert Graves despre sine insusi poezie si legatura cu traditia' in *Romania Literara* 31: 21 July.]

C877   *Work Drafts. *New Statesman* 79: 776, 29 May.

C878   *Odysseus in Phaeacia. *New Hungarian Quarterly* no. 38: 81–82 Summer.
[Translation of poem by Gábor Devecseri.]

C879   *Research and Development: Classified. *New Statesman* 79: 811, 5 June.

C880   *Olive Tree. *New Statesman* 79: 880, 19 June.

C881   *Strangling in Merrion Square. *New Statesman* 79: 921, 26 June.

C882   *Strayed Message. *Atlantic* 226: 103 July.

C883   *Love and Night – Pandora. *Listener* 84: 278, 27 August.

C884   *Women and Masks. *Poetry Wales* 6: 23 Autumn.
[Translation of poem by Gábor Devecseri.]

C885   *Angry Gardener. *Mediterranean Review* (Orient, N.Y.) I. i. Fall. p.47.
[Also includes an interview.]

C886   If it Looks Like Zeus, and Sounds Like Zeus, It Must be Robert Graves:
Or else some kind of nut. *Esquire* 74: 144, 180, 182–85 September.
[Primarily article by Jack Skow, but contains an interview with Graves
and quotations from his poems.]

C887   *Song: Once More – Gold Cloud – Compact – Trial of Innocence –
Logic – The Accomplice – H – Invitation to Bristol. *Times Literary
Supplement*, 4 September, p. 966.

C888   *Man of Evil – Angry Gardener – Purification. *Listener* 84: 481, 8
October.

C889   Borges, Banshees and Basilisks. *New Statesman* 80: 716, 718, 27
November.
[Review of J.L. Borges, with Margarita Guerrero, *The Book of Imaginary
Things*, trans. N.T. di Giovanni.]

C890   Playboy Interview: Robert Graves. A Candid Conversation with the
Venerable Poet, Author, Critic and Mythologist. *Playboy* 17: 103–104,
106, 108, 110, 112, 114, 116 December.
[Interview with Jim McKinley.]

C891   Obscenity in Snowdonia. *Western Mail* [Cardiff], 21 December, p.7.
[Letter about industrial encroachment in Wales.]

C892   Entry cancelled.

C893   Deyá. *Arion* 5: 151.
[Translation of poem by Gábor Devesceri.]

1971

C894   *My Ghost. *Atlantic* 227: 85 January.

C895   *Green-Sailed Vessel. *New Yorker* 47: 46, 20 March

C896   *To Put It Simply – Song: Weather – The Garden – Fiery Orchard.
Virginia Quarterly Review 47: 227–228 Spring.

C897   *Jus Primae Noctis. *New Statesman* 81: 600, 30 April.

C898   *Tilth. *New Statesman* 81: 633, 7 May.

C899   *Those Blind from Birth. *New Statesman* 81: 710, 21 May.

C900   *Reduced Sentence. *Times Literary Supplement*, 28 May, p.611.

C901   *Strangeness. *Ladies Home Journal* 88: 111 June.

C902   *Fools. *New Statesman* 81: 775, 4 June.

C903	Great Years of Their Lives — Robert Graves, Brigadier C.E. Lucas Phillips, Henry Williamson and Lord Chandos talk to Leslie Smith about the 1st World War. *Listener* 86: 73–75, 15 July.

C904	*Song: Reconciliation. *Atlantic* 228: 110 September.

C905	Crane and the Horse. *New Hungarian Quarterly* no. 44: 145–147 Winter. [Text of talk given to the members of Hungarian PEN Centre, Budapest, 28 May 1971. Reprinted as 'Address to the Poets of Hungary' in A133.]

C906	*Defeat of Time – Gorgon Mask. *Mademoiselle* 74: 70 November.

C907	[Quotation from letter by Graves to William Marchant about *Goodbye to All That*.] *Daily Telegraph*, 20 November, p.15.

C908	*Age Gap. *New Statesman* 82: 741, 26 November.

C909	Science, Technology and Poetry. *New Scientist* 52: 34–35, 2 December.

C910	*Dream of Frances Speedwell. *New Statesman* 82: 928, 31 December.

1972

C911	My First Amorous Adventure. *Playboy* 18: 91, 246–247 January.

C912	*Six Blankets. *Malahat Review* no. 21: 9 January.

C913	*Hedgepig. *New Statesman* 83: 247, 25 February.

C914	Lilliburlero. *Times*, 26 February, p.13.
[Letter.]

C915	Lilliburlero on the Overseas News. *Times*, 15 February, p.13.
[Letter concerning the introductory air on the BBC Overseas News.]

C916	*Title of Poet. *Esquire* 77: 22 March.

C917	Gábor Devecseri: Record of a Poetic Friendship. *New Hungarian Quarterly* 13: 121–123 Spring.

C918	Where Has Art Gone. *Daily Telegraph Magazine*, 12 May, p.7.

C919	He Looked at a Taxi with the Numberplate EUC 377 J and Said that was Euclid's 377th Theorem. *Guardian*, 17 July, p.8.
[Interview by Terry Coleman.]

C920	*Dilemma. *New Yorker* 48: 30 29 July.

C921	*St. Antony of Padua. *Atlantic* 230: 60 September.

C922	*Three Times in Love. *Esquire* 78: 36 September.

C923	*Traditionalist – Beatrice and Dante – Silent Visit. *Listener* 88: 342, 14 September.

C924	*Records – Always. *Times Literary Supplement*, 15 September, p.1049.

C925   *Wall. *New Statesman* 84: 400, 22 September.

C926   *Prepared Statement. *Atlantic* 230: 119 October.

C927   Absentee Fusilier. *Encounter* 39: 3–5 October.

C928   *Cupboard. *Poetry* 121: 9 October.
        [Reprint of C69.]

C929   *Noose – Her Beauty. *Playboy* 19: 220 December.

C930   *Toast to Death – Pity. *Littack* 1: 107 December.

C931   *No one can understand our habit of love – Love makes poor sense in
        either speech or letters. *Daily Telegraph Magazine*, 8 December, pp.[41],
        [43].

C932   *Strongest Moonlight. *Daily Telegraph Magazine*, 8 December, p.45.

C933   Strongest Moonlight. *Daily Telegraph Magazine*, 8 December, pp.45,
        47–48.
        [Article by Edward Booth-Gibbon on the publication of A132; article
        contains a number of quotations from Graves.]

1973

C934   *As All Must End. *Esquire* 79: 62 January.

C935   *Marmosite's Miscellany. *Malahat Review* no. 25: 31–48 January.

C936   Pickwick Papers Re-Written. *Malahat Review* no. 25: 10–30 January.
        [Prefatory note by A.S.G. Edwards, pp.9–10.]

C937   *Song: From Otherwise or Nowhere – The Moral Law. *Listener* 89: 174,
        8 February.

C938   *With A Gift of Rings – Five. *New Yorker* 48: 42, 10 February.

C939   *Scared Child – Impossible Day – As All Must End – Touch My Shut
        Lips – Timeless Meeting – Should I Care – Unposted Letter –
        Moon's Last Quarter – Poet's Curse. *Daily Telegraph Magazine*, 22 June,
        p.49.

C940   [All Things Must Pass.] *Haaretz*, 10 August, pp.18–19.
        [Translation into Hebrew by Avraham Yavin of Act 3, Scene 2 of Graves'
        play, *All Things to All Men*. This was the first publication of the play in
        any form.]

C941   *Truly to Love You. *Atlantic* 232: 72 October.

C942   *Fast Bound Together. *Mademoiselle* 78: 180 December.

1974

C943   *L.s.d. *Listener* 91: 2, 3 January.

C944   *Curious Love – Seven Years – Discarded Love-Poems – Bodies Entrances. *Listener* 91: 107, 24 January.

C945   *If no Cuckoo Sings – Moon's Tears – Who Must It be? *Listener* 91: 355, 21 March.

C946   *This is the Season. *Listener* 91: 841, 27 June.

C947   *History of the Fall. *Esquire* 82: 190 July.

C948   *Unco. *Listener* 92: 73, 18 July.

C949   *September Landscape. *Atlantic* 234: 85 September.

C950   *Ours is No Wedlock – Song: Seven Fresh Years – Earlier Lovers – Charm for Sound Sleeping – To Come of Age. *Encounter* 43: 38 September.

C951   *Mountain Lovers. *Listener* 92: 541, 24 October.

1975

C952   *Singleness in Love. *Listener* 93: 372, 20 March.

C953   *Unpenned Poem. *New Yorker* 51: 40, 19 May.

C954   *Advent of Summer. *Boston University Journal* 23.2

C955   *Advent of Summer. *New Statesman* 90: 119, 25 July.

C956   *Love Letter. *Listener* 94: 157, 31 July.

C957   PW Interviews Robert Graves. *Publishers' Weekly* 208: 50–51 11 August. [Interview by Robert S. Latona.]

1976

C958   Foreword to 'Teknosis' by John Biram. *Malahat Review* no.38: 73–74 April

1977

C959   All Things to All Men. *Malahat Review* 43: 8–54 July.

Appendix I: Translations of selections of Graves' work

(The discontinuous numbering of the appendices is intentional.)

App. 1   I POETI SONO UOMINI   [1964]

[2 lines set flush right:] Robert | Graves | [4 lines set flush left:] I POETI SONO UOMINI | *con testo a fronte* | *introduzione di Carlo Izzo* | *traduzione di Giovanni Galtieri*] [set flush right:] GUANDA

Collation: [1]⁸ 2–18¹⁸, 144 leaves.

pp.[i]–[ii] blank; p.[iii] [stylized bird, set right] | [remainder set flush left:] COLLANA FENICE 10 | *nuova serie* | *diretta da Giacinto Spagnoletti* | [short rule] | *sezione poeti*; p.[iv] blank; p.[v] title-page; p.[vi] copyright, edition and designer's notices; p.[vii] [set flush right:] INTRODUZIONE; p.[viii] blank; pp.[ix]x–xxi introduction; p. [xxii] blank; pp.xxiii–xxiv NOTA DEL TRADUTTORE; pp.xxv–xxix VITA E OPERE DI ROBERT GRAVES; p.[xxx] blank; pp.[xxxi]–xxxii BIBLIOGRAFIA CRITICA; P. [1] section title; pp.2–245 text, with pp.[153, 215] being section titles and pp.[152– 214] being blank; p.[246] blank; p.[247] [set flush right:] INDICE; p. [248] blank; pp.[249]250–251 indexes; p.[252] blank; p.[253] printer's notice; p.[254] blank; p.[255] publisher's advertisements; p.[256] blank.

22 × 14 cm. Bulk: 1.4/1.8 cm. White wove paper; all edges trimmed. White wove endpapers. Bound in white cloth; back printed in grey silk screen with brown twig and leaf at top, at foot, flush left: introduzione di Carolo Izzo | & cura di Giovanni Galtieri; front printed in black lettering with face and landscape design centre right printed in red, green, brown, black and grey, upper left, 3 lines flush left: Robert Graves | I POETI | SONO UOMINI | [at foot, flush right:] GUANDA; spine printed in black, top to bottom: Graves [remainder upright:] 10 | [publisher's emblem].

Price: 3200 lira. Number of copies undetermined. Published in April 1964.

Contents: Collected Poems 1959: The Haunted House – Reproach – Rocky Acres – Outlaws – Lost Love – Mermaid, Dragon, Fiend – The Witches' Cauldron – Children in Darkness – The Cool Web – The Presence – Return – The Bards – Vanity – Pure Death – The Furious Voyage – Song: Lift-boy – The Succubus – The Legs – Gardener – In Broken Images – Sea Side – Midway – Leda – Recalling War – Time – The Philosopher – To Bring the Dead to Life – Defeat of the Rebels – Certain Mercies – The Laureate – The Foreboding – Lovers in Winter – On Portents – The Terraced Valley – The Climate of Thought – The Suicide in the Copse – Frightened Men – Mid-Winter Waking – The Beach – The Door – She Tells Her Love While Half Asleep – Dream of a Climber – The Weather of Olympus – The White Goddess – Lament for Pasiphaë – Return of the Goddess – The Survivor – Questions in a Wood – Dialogue on the Headland – The Mark – Cat-Goddesses – The Blue-Fly – Spoils – Rhea – The Face in the Mirror – Gratitude for a Nightmare – The Naked and the Nude – Woman and Tree – Nothing – Call it a Good Marriage – The Second-Fated – Around the Mountain – Leaving the Rest Unsaid – *More Poems 1961*: Lyceia – Symptoms of Love – The Sharp Ridge – The Visitation – Apple Island – Troughs of Sea – The Death Grapple – In Single Syllables – The Starred Coverlet – The Intrusion – Patience – The Cure – Turn of the Moon – The Secret Land – Two Children – The Dangerous Gift – Twice of the Same Fever – Surgical Ward: Men – Nightfall at Twenty Thousand Feet – The Simpleton – The Were-Man – The Person from Porlock – Established Lovers – The Quiet Glades of Eden – Here Live Your Life Out! – Burn It! – Song: Come, Enjoy Your Sunday! – *New Poems 1962*: Recognition – The Watch – Uncalendared Love – The Meeting – Not at Home – Possessed – The Winged Heart – A Restless Ghost – Between Moon and Moon – Beware, Madam! – The Cliff Edge – Acrobats – The Ambrosia of Dionysus and Semele.

Notes: This collection is made up of selections from A87, A93 and A101.
   The poems appear in English on versos and in Italian translation on facing rectos.
   The title of 'The Survivor' (p.108) is given as 'The Surviver'.

App. 3   WIERSZE   [1968]

ROBERT GRAVES | wiersze | [publisher's device in green, black and white] | WYBÓR I PRZEKLAD | BOLESL-AW TABORSKI | [green dot] | PAŃSTOWOY INSTYTUT WYDAWNICZY

Collation: [1]⁸ 2–4⁸, 32 leaves.

   p.[1] GRAVES | Wiersze; p.[2] blank; p.[3] title-page; p.[4] series, permission and copyright notices; pp.5–[6] biographical note; pp.7–57 text; p.[58] blank; pp.59–60[61] SPIS RZECZY; pp.[62]–[63] publisher's advertisements; p.[64] printing, publishing and price notices.
   13.2 × 10.5 cm. Bulk: 0.4 cm. White wove paper; all edges trimmed. Bound in white wove wrappers printed in black, red and green.

Price: zl. 10.00. Number of copies undetermined. Published in late 1968.

Contents: Rocky Acres – Warning to Children – The Cool Web – It Was All Very Tidy – The Legs – The Devil's Advice to Story-Tellers – Sea Side – Interruption – The Florist Rose – Lost Acres – Certain Mercies – The Cuirassiers of the Frontier – The Cloak – The Climate of Thought – The Fallen Tower of Siloam – A Love Story – Dawn Bombardment – The Shot – The Persian Version – Spoils – Leaving the Rest Unsaid – The Sharp Ridge – Apple Island – The Death Grapple – Turn of the Moon – The Secret Land – The Meeting – Acrobats – Food of the

Dead – The Metaphor – The Green Castle – Not to Sleep – Good Night to the Old Gods – Iron Palace – Nothing Now Astonishes.

Note: This translation of selections, entirely in Polish, is based on A114.

App. 5 A SZERELEM TÜNETEI [1974]

p.[2] [set left:] ROBERT GRAVES | FORDÍTOTTA | DEVECSERI GÁBOR | GERGELY ÁGNES | KÁLNOKY LÁSZLO' | NEMES NAGY ÁGNES | OBÁN OTTÖ | SOMLYÓ GYÖRGY | TANDORI DEZSÖ | VÉGH GYÖRGY
p.[3] [set left on grey field:] A SZERELEM | TÜNETEI | [publisher's emblem set right at foot, off grey field]

Collation: 80 leaves, glued at the spine.
p.[1] [set lower left:] EURO'PA KÖNYVKIADÓ BUDAPEST 1974; pp.[2]–[3] title-pages; p.[4] [set upper left:] VÁLOGATTA ÉS AZ UTÓSZÓT ÍRTA VAJDA MIKLÓS; pp.5–140 text; pp.141–152 UTO'SZO'; p.153–157 TARTALOM; p.[158] blank; p.[159] copyright, permissions, publisher's, designer's, printer's and ISBN notices.
15 × 15.1 cm. Bulk: 1.2 cm. White laid paper, watermarked with oak leaves and acorns; bottom edge only trimmed. Bound in white paper covers, extended to produce flaps at front and back; front printed in burgundy, gold and white.

Price: 10.50 ft. Number of copies undetermined. Published in 1974.

Contents: The Haunted House – Reproach – One Hard Look – Love Without Hope – Lost Love – Warning to Children – I'd Die for You – Love in Barrenness – The Presence – The Bards – Nobody – Ulysses – The Legs – Front Door Soliloquy – In Broken Images – Flying Crooked – Brothers – The Devil's Advice to Story-Tellers – Time – To Evoke Posterity – Never Such Love – On Portents – The Thieves – To Sleep – Despite and Still – Mid-Winter Waking – The Door – She Tells Her Love While Half Asleep – The Death Room – My Name and I – 1805 – The Persian Version – The White Goddess – The Story of Blodeuwedd – Counting the Beats – The Blue-Fly – Spoils – The Face in the Mirror – Friday Night [1] – The Naked and the Nude – Woman and Tree – The Second-Fated – The Twin of Sleep – Around the Mountain – Symptoms of Love – The Sharp Ridge – Under the Olives – The Visitation – Apple Island – The Two Witches – The Quiet Glades of Eden – Recognition – The Meeting – Ibycus in Samos – The Wreath – Not at Home – Acrobats – Three Songs for the Lute – At Best, Poets – The Three-Faced – I Will Write – The Metaphor – The Septuagenarian – Non Cogunt Astra – A Measure of Casualness – In Time of Absence – Not to Sleep – The Hung Wu Vase – Lamia in Love – All I Tell You from My Heart – After the Flood – Good Night to the Old Gods – A Shift of Scene – A Court of Love – Ambience – The Vow – The Frog with the Golden Ball – The Impossible – What Will Be, Is – Nothing Now Astonishes – All Except Hannibal – On Giving – The Necklace – Spite of Mirrors – Song: Dew-Drop and Diamond – Song: Sullen Moods – Fact of the Act – The Yet Unsayable – The Narrow Sea – Song: Beyond Giving – Trial of Innocence – What Is Love? – Solomon's Seal – To Put It Simply – To Be Poets – Serpent's Tail – Cliff and Wave – Always – Pity – A Toast to Death – The Encounter – Where is the Truth? – Song: The Queen of Time –

Should I Care? – Fast Bound Together – The New Eternity – Friday Night[2] – History of the Fall – Singleness in Love.

Notes: 'Song: Dew-Drop and Diamond' (p.113) is mistitled as 'Song: Beyond Giving Diamond'.

All poems have titles in both English and Hungarian.

This collection of poems translated into Hungarian by various hands is drawn from A114a, A129a, A83d, A134a, A135 and 'Fast Bound Together,' 'The New Eternity,' 'Friday Night[2],' 'History of the Fall,'' Singleness in Love' which had not been collected at this time.

App. 7 POEZJE WYBRANE [1977]

[all within single rules:] ROBERT GRAVES | POEZJE WYBRANE | Wybór, przekl-ad i Sl-owo wste,pne | BOLESL-AW TABORSKI | [AM STWOWY | INSTYTUT WYDAWNICZY

Collation: [1]⁸ 2 – 10⁸, 80 leaves.

p.[1] [publisher's emblem] | GRAVES | POEZJE WYBRANE; p.[2] blank; p.[3] title-page; p.[4] permissions, printer's and publisher's notices; pp.5–9[10] *ROBERT GRAVES*; p.[11] POEZJE WYBRANE; p.[12] blank; pp.13–149 text; p.150 blank; pp. 151–154[155] SPIS REZECZY; pp.[156] – [160] publisher's advertisements.

16.3 × 11.5 cm. Bulk: 0.7/1.2 cm. White wove paper; all edges trimmed. White wove endpapers; outer sides printed in pale orange with flower in oval medallion in white on both free and pastedown endpapers front and back. Bound in pale yellow paper printed in white in boxes filled with floral ornaments and flower in box alternately. Back blank; front printed in brown: GRAVES | POEZJE WYBRANE | [publisher's emblem]; spine printed in brown: GRA- | VES | PIW

Price: zl. 25.00 Number of copies undetermined. Published in late 1977.

Contents: In the Wilderness – Rocky Acres – The Pier-Glass – The Witches' Cauldron – The Cool Web – Lost Acres – Warning to Children – The Castle – It Was All Very Tidy – Front Door Soliloquy – Interruption – The Legs – On Rising Early – Thief – The Bards – Trudge, Body! – Time – Angry Samson – The Devil's Advice to Story-Tellers – Welsh Incident – The Florist Rose – Recalling War – The Philosopher – Single Fare – To Walk on Hills – To Bring the Dead to Life – Defeat of the Rebels – Certain Mercies – The Cuirassiers of the Frontier – The Cloak – The Halls of Bedlam – The Climate of Thought – The Fallen Tower of Siloam – Leaving the Rest Unsaid – A Love Story – Lament for Pasiphaë – Dawn Bombardment – The Worms of History – The Shot – Despite and Still – Language of the Seasons – Through Nightmare – The Persian Version – Apollo of the Physiologists – The Eugenist – The White Goddess – The Last Day of Leave – Sea Side – From the Embassy – Spoils – Call It a Good Marriage – Forbidden Words – The Sharp Ridge – Apple Island – The Death Grapple – Turn of the Moon – The Secret Land – The Meeting – Acrobats – Food of the Dead – The Metaphor – The Green Castle – Not to Sleep – Iron Palace – Nothing Now Astonishes – The Red Shower – Above the Edge of Doom – Gift of Sight – The Vow – Good Night to the Old Gods – Arrears of Moonlight – Fortunate Child –

Fact of the Act – Dancing Flame – The Word – Strangeness – The Olive Yard – Gorgon Mask – To Be Poets – Dreaming Children – Testament – Those Blind from Birth – Advice from a Mother – Work Drafts – The Title of Poet – The Half-Finished Letter – Pity – The Pact – Beatrice and Dante – The Encounter – Nightmare of Senility – At the Gate – Song: From Otherwhere to Nowhere – Name – The Crystal – A Charm for Sound Sleeping – Three Words Only – Elsewhere – September Landscape – Crucibles of Love – Spring 1974 – Advent of Summer.

Notes: All the poems appear in Polish translation only. They are based on A87 and A138 but the list of contents (pp. 151–[155]) records from which of the various volumes of Graves' poetry each poem is taken.

Appendix II: Collections of manuscripts and printed books

App. 10 *The Robert Graves Collection of the University of Otago Library, A Checklist.* Dunedin: University of Otago, 1972.

13 leaves. Photographically reproduced from typescript and printed catalogue entries of books by Graves in this library (136 items). The checklist was compiled by Max Broadbent and Catherine Swift.

App. 12 *The Robert Graves Manuscripts and Letters at Southern Illinois University: an Inventory.* Troy, New York: Whitston Publishing, 1976.

pp.viii + 262. Reproduced from typescript. 1,365 items, with index and introduction. Organized in the following categories: poetry, prose fiction, critical prose, unpublished manuscripts, letters to Graves, letters from Graves, manuscripts by others [Edmund Blunden, Laura Riding, and others; 19 items only], miscellaneous items and ephemra.

Compiled by John W. Presley.

App. 14 The Robert Graves Collection in The Poetry/Rare Books Collection, University Libraries, State University of New York at Buffalo [Lockwood Memorial Library in the first edition of this bibliography].

A catalogue for this collection is currently in preparation. The collection holds a complete first edition collection of all books and pamphlets published from 1913 to the present; 314 letters, 9 linear feet of manuscripts covering the years 1911 to 1980; 52 letters and 1 foot of manuscripts in the Laura Riding Collection; plus four linear feet of Graves materials in the Martin Seymour-Smith archive.

The present curator and chief compiler of the catalogue is Robert J. Bertholf.

App. 16 The Fred H. and Jeannette Higginson Robert Graves Collection, University Libraries, Kansas State University, Manhattan, Kansas.

Several hundred printed books by and about Graves, including many items of ephemera. This collection was acquired by Kansas State in 1983 and is currently in the process of being catalogued.

The present Special Collections Librarian is John J. Vander Velde.

App. 18   The Berg Collection, New York Public Library.

Items in this collection include business and personal letters (many to Sir Edward Marsh), fair copies of poems, corrected typescripts and a notebook of early poems.

App. 20   Humanities Research Center, University of Texas, Austin.

This collection includes business and personal letters and some fair copies of poetry.

App. 22   McFarlin Library, University of Tulsa, Tulsa, Oklahoma.

Aside from their original holdings, this library acquired the Graves Collection of Ellsworth Mason in the 1980s. The collection includes several hundred items of printed books and ephemera and is particularly strong on variant copies.

App. 24   William Reese, William Reese Company, 409 Temple Street, New Haven, Connecticut 06511. Mr Reese is both a dealer and Graves collector, his collection and stock are open to any responsible scholar for use. Aside from rare and scarce printed editions his collection holds significant Graves manuscripts, advance and proof copies, and other material.

In addition to these collections, in *Focus on Robert Graves* January 1972, Ellsworth Mason records the following collections which have special holdings of Robert Graves material:

Lilly Library
University of Indiana, Bloomington, Indiana

University Library
University of Nevada,Reno, Nevada

University Library
Northwestern University, Evanston, Illinois

University Library
University of San Francisco, San Francisco, California

University Library
University of Victoria, Victoria, British Columbia

To my knowledge, none of these libraries has published, or contemplates publishing, a catalogue of their Graves holdings.

Addenda and miscellanea

Items in this section are either publications seen too late to be included in the main section of the bibliography, or which have been noted through secondary sources but which I have not been able to trace, or they are of an ephemeral character (the emphera section from the first edition of this bibliography is not reproduced). This section is organized by year of publication and alphabetically within years.

1929

*In the Sand Hills, *The New Age*, January 1929.
The April issue of this journal lists tables of contents of previous issues and this is recorded for the January issue (not seen).

1963

I DISCOVER ISRAEL

'I Discover Israel' (C636) was first published in book form in *The Mission of Israel*, ed. Jacob Baal-Teshuva, published by Robert Speller & Sons, Inc. in 1963. It was later published in *Israel, A Reader*, ed. Bill Adler (Philadelphia: Chilton Book Co., 1968). I have not seen the former publication.

1966

MUCH ADO ABOUT NOTHING

[printed in white on orange and black horizontally striped background:] [set right:] The National Theatre | Much Ado About Nothing | William Shakespeare | [at centre foot illustration of a stage]

Collation: 1 sheet stiff card, as cover; 2 sheets of slick paper; 1 sheet purple paper; 5 sheets of slip paper. All folded once, quired, and stapled twice at centre. 18 leaves.

p.[1] cover as title-page; p.[2] printed solid black; pp. [3] – [6] advertisements; p.[7]

blank; p.[8] Acknowledgements and typography and printer's notices; p.[9] photograph; pp. [10] – [11] stage history of play; pp.[12] – [16] photographs of performances; p.[17] A Note on Shakespeare's Italy; p.[18] – [20] photographs of this production; pp.[21] – [22] About the Director; p.[23] photos of Zeffirelli; p.[24] photo of Graves at his hom in Mallorca by Tom Blau; pp.[25] – [26] The Textual Changes | A note by Robert Graves; pp.[27] – [28] Bernard Shaw on Beatrice and Benedick; pp.[29] – [30] The National Theatre: a Short History; pp.[31] – [34] advertisements; p.[37] printed solid black; p.38 printed in black, orange, red and magenta as cover.

22.5 × 13.1 cm. Bulk: 0.4 cm. White, yellow and purple wove paper, all edges trimmed.

Price: undetermined. Number of copies undetermined. Published in 1966.

Note: Graves' contribution is 'The Textual Changes' (pp. [25] – [26]).

1970

ADVICE FROM A MOTHER

Broadside, recto contains text, verso blank.

[above and below a box rule:] ADVICE | FROM A | MOTHER | [text of the poem and signature of Graves within the box rule] | [at foot, outside box rule:] Advice from a Mother by Robert Graves | published by Poem-of-the-Month Club Ltd, 27 Brymaer Road, S.W. 11. | Printed by John Roberts Press Ltd. | Copyright (1970) Poem-of-the-Month Club Ltd.

37.4 × 28.0 cm. White laid paper, watermarked: *Arnold* | *Signature*; all edges trimmed.

Price: undetermined. Number of copies undetermined. Published in 1970.

QUEEN-MOTHER TO NEW QUEEN

[Title-page is drawing of Graves printed in red]

Collation: [1]⁴, 4 leaves

p.[1] title-page; p.[4] facsimile reproduction of manuscript of poem; p.[5] text of poem with title and ascription printed in red; p.[8] *Two hundred copies have been designed and printed by Lawton and Alfred Kennedy | for the Richard A. Gleeson Library, University of San Francisco | and presented to the joint meeting of the Roxburghe and Samorano Clubs in Los Angeles | September 26th and 27th, 1970:* with pp.[2] – [3] and [6] – [7] being blank.

35.7 × 26.5 cm. White wove paper, all edges untrimmed, uncut, and unopened.

Price: gratis. Number of copies: 200. Published 26 September 1970

STRAYED MESSAGE

South Bank Poetry (London: Shenval Press, 1970).

The collection is reported to have 'The Strayed Message' in it. If this is correct then it would be the first book publication of this poem. However, I have not seen a copy of this book.

1978

OGHAM

Ogham: a calendar of season bardic lore based on an interpretation by Robert Graves of the Cypheres used in the Book of Ballymore. Burnt Woods Press, 1978. 100 copies printed.

Not seen.

TEKNOSIS

John Briam, *Teknosis* (London: Arlington Books, 1978), 314 pp.

Foreword by Graves (not seen).

1979

IN THE WILDERNESS

Broadside, text and illustration on recto, verso blank.

[illustration in centre printed in blue]; text of poem in handwriting printed on either side:] [open hand, palm outward] | [in centre face of Christ with crown of thorns, in white on blue background. To the left:] Christ of his | gentleness | Thirsting and | hungering | Walked in | the | wilderness | soft words | of grace | [to the right:] He spoke | Unto lost | desart folk | That | listened | wondering | [rule] | ROBERT GRAVES | (IN THE | WILDERNESS) [illustration signed at foot:] Piech 6/15 1979

63.9 × 44.7 cm. White wove paper, all edges trimmed.

Price: undetermiend. Number of copies undetermined. Published in the last half of 1979.

Notes: The text printed is an early version of lines 1–6 of 'In the Widerness'.

The illustrations are by Peter Piech. This broadside was done for Charles Seluzicki, a bookseller in Salem, Oregon.

1981

THE SECRET LAND

Broadside, recto contains text, verso blank.

[within dark blue bled rules:] [water-colour of landscape, 5.5 × 10.4 cm., pasted on] | THE SECRET LAND | [text of poem] | *by Robert Graves* | [within rectangle at foot formed by bled rules:] With the permission of Robert Graves, seventy-five copies of THE SECRET LAND | were designed, handcolored, and printed by Carol J. Blinn at Warwick Press, | Easthampton, Massachusetts for Charles Seluzicki, Bookseller | of Salem, Oregon. All copies have been numbered | and are signed by the printer. | [signature] | [number]

37.8 × 27.8 cm. Cream laid paper, bottom edge untrimmed.

Price: undetermined. Number of copies 75. Published in 1981.

Index

Titles of books are in italics; poems are starred; prose appears in quotation marks; other entries are conventional. Appendices are not indexed.

Titles beginning with the definite or indefinite article have been indexed according to the second word of the title and the article transposed to the end of the title.

Variant titles are preceded by the letter V.